COMPREHENSIVE

*UNITED STATES
HISTORY*

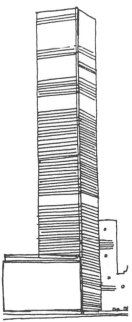

When ordering this book, please specify:
either **R 412 P** or
Comprehensive United States History

AMSCO SCHOOL PUBLICATIONS

315 Hudson Street/New York, N.Y. 10013

COMPREHENSIVE

UNITED STATES HISTORY

Revised

Paul M. Roberts

Paula A. Franklin

Grateful acknowledgment is made to
Joan Daves Literary Agency
for permission to reprint an excerpt from
I Have a Dream *by Martin Luther King, Jr.*
Copyright © 1963 by Martin Luther King, Jr.

ISBN: 978-1-56765-662-6

Printed in the United States of America

4 5 6 7 8 9 10   09 08 07

Preface

YOU KNOW THAT the United States is one of the great nations of the modern world. But you may not know all the reasons for its greatness. To understand our nation, you need to be aware of events that influenced its development 10 years ago . . . 50 years ago . . . 200 years ago. The main purpose of this text is to acquaint you with America's past so that you can better understand the American present and be better equipped to play a part in our nation's future.

In this text you will learn:

- How democratic institutions have developed since colonial times.
- How a nation of only 13 states on the Atlantic coast expanded westward to the Pacific in less than 75 years.
- What contributions were made to American life by immigrant groups from every continent of the world.
- What policies our government has adopted to maintain U.S. leadership in world affairs.
- How new technologies have transformed American society.

There is more. But the above list suggests why knowledge of history is vitally important to all Americans.

This text, *Comprehensive United States History*, tells the story of our nation's past in clear, simple prose organized around a chronological framework. A number of features will make your study easier. Many *maps* are provided to help you locate the events you are reading about. Numerous *tables* and *charts* offer a bird's-eye view of developments that were changing the nation at different times. Short *biographies* of famous Americans tell you about people who played a part in our nation's history, such as Benjamin Banneker (the first black person employed by the federal government) and Amelia Earhart (the first woman to fly the Atlantic).

Brief *quotations* present interesting historical sidelights. *Political cartoons* illustrate some of the key issues that concerned various groups of Americans.

To help you remember what you have read, there are helpful *quizzes* at the end of every chapter. Among them are *map tests* and thought-provoking *essay questions*.

You can also acquire a useful social studies vocabulary by regularly turning to the *glossary* in the back of the book. The items listed and defined here provide an A-to-Z summary of all the important terms you will encounter in your study of American history.

The United States has built its current greatness on a remarkable history of struggle and achievement. As the authors of this text, we feel privileged to present that history to you.

Paul M. Roberts

Paula A. Franklin

Contents

Charts, Graphs, Tables

Notable Americans

UNIT 1

The
First
Americans

CHAPTER 1

From Nomads to City Dwellers

THE YEAR 1776 marks the birth of the United States as an independent nation. But that date does not represent the starting point of America's story. In fact, the American past is rooted in events that took place long before the United States existed.

HUNTERS OF THE ICE AGE

There was a time, many thousands of years ago, when the continents of North and South America had no human inhabitants. The Western Hemisphere was an immense wilderness. It was the home of mammoths, mastodons, saber-toothed tigers, and other animals that are now extinct. People arrived only after a change in the earth's climate caused a change in geography.

Migrations From Asia

In the distant past, during an era known as the Ice Age, a gigantic glacier covered the land we now call Canada. The level of the oceans fell because so much water froze into ice. As ocean waters receded, they exposed a piece of underwater land between eastern Asia and western Alaska. This stretch of dry land formed a kind of bridge linking Asia and North America. Bands of humans from Siberia (northeastern Asia) wandered across this land bridge. They were probably tracking herds of wild animals. Thus, nomadic Asian hunters and their families were the first humans to arrive and settle in North America. Some scholars think that the first nomads may have come as early as 40,000 years ago. Others believe that this event occurred about 20,000 years ago.

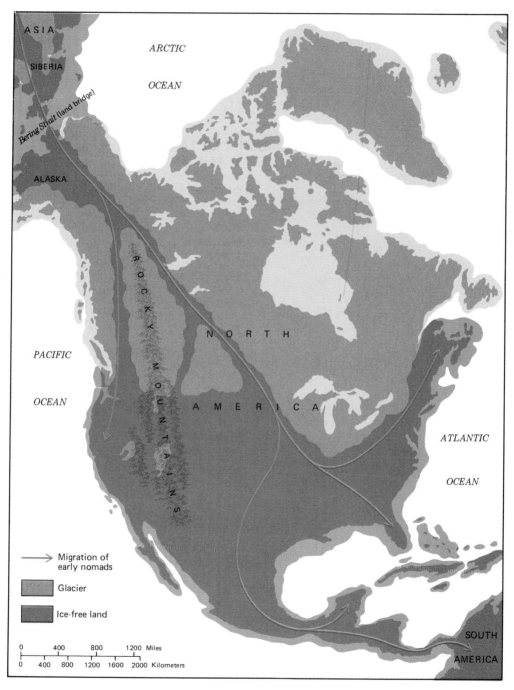

ICE AGE MIGRATIONS

The migration of Asian hunters continued for a long time. It came to an end when another change in climate caused the northern glacier to melt. Rising water submerged the Siberia-Alaska land bridge around 8000 B.C.

Meanwhile, new generations of American-born hunters had migrated southward and eastward until they occupied most of North and South America. By the time the land bridge disappeared, people had settled throughout the two continents of the Western Hemisphere.

IMPORTANT EVIDENCE OF EARLY HUMANS
IN NORTH AMERICA

Location	Date Found	Evidence	Significance
Folsom, New Mexico	1927	Spear point in ribs of type of bison extinct for 10,000 years	First evidence that humans were in America 10,000 years ago
Clovis, New Mexico	1932	Stone points with bones of extinct mammals	May be 13,000 years old; pushed back date of first human arrival
Sandia cave, New Mexico	1936–1941	Stone points with bones of extinct mammals	Perhaps 10,000–12,000 years old (finder claims they are 25,000 years old)
Tepexpán, Mexico	1947	Human skeleton found with mammoth bones	Estimated to be 10,000 or more years old
Midland, Texas	1953	Piece of human skull	Dated from 10,000 to 20,000 years ago
Laguna Beach, California	1933, but not scientifically tested until 1967	Piece of human skull	Possibly 15,000 to 18,000 years old
Old Crow Flats, Yukon Territory, Canada	1973	Scraper made from caribou bone	Dated at about 27,000 years old; thus, oldest evidence of human presence in America
Mohave River, California	1978	Footprints of five humans	About 5000 years old; oldest known footprints in America

Columbus's Mistake

The early people of America lived in many different groups speaking many different languages. Each group had a name for itself—in most cases, one that meant simply "the people."

Later settlers of the Western Hemisphere called the first Americans "Indians"—a name given them by the Italian explorer Christopher Columbus on his arrival in America in 1492. He so named them because he thought he had landed in a part of Asia known as the Indies. The term continued in use even after people realized Columbus's mistake. Today, descendants of America's first settlers are most frequently identified as Native Americans, especially in the United States.

Earliest Culture

In American history, the period of time *before* the voyages of Columbus is called the pre-Columbian period. It covers the huge span of years going back to the first Ice Age hunters. Our knowledge of pre-Columbian times is limited because most Native Americans had no form of writing and thus left no written records.

The first Americans had a very simple culture, or way of life. We know that they used stone-tipped spears to hunt animals, because spear points have been found at various sites. These early peoples may also have domesticated (tamed) dogs to help them in the hunt. They wore clothing made of animal skins, and they probably knew how to make fire.

AGRICULTURE AND OTHER ADVANCES

As time passed, Native Americans slowly developed a more complex culture. They invented the bow and arrow. They learned how to make a wide variety of stone points, scrapers, knives, and other tools. Some groups fished as well as hunted. Most became expert at gathering wild plants, seeds, and fruit for food.

The most important advance of all was the discovery of agriculture. More than 5000 years ago, some Native American peoples discovered that food could be grown and harvested, not simply gathered from wild plants. We do not know where farming began in America. It may have started in Mexico and spread from there to Central America and South America. Perhaps it started in several different places at the same time.

One of the first plants to be grown by Native Americans—and the most important crop in terms of later Native American life—was maize, or corn. This plant, native to the Western Hemisphere, was developed from wild types into several different varieties. Other important Native American crops were beans, potatoes, peppers, pumpkins, cotton, and tobacco.

Changes in Native American Life

Farming brought about fundamental changes in the way Native Americans lived. It led to the following:

1. A more dependable food supply.
2. Settlement in permanent locations instead of movement from place to place in search of food.
3. The banding together of families to form small farming villages.
4. The development of such crafts as pottery, basketry, and weaving.
5. The expansion of some villages into cities.
6. In cities, the organization of formal government, the emergence of different social classes, and the growth of trade and commerce.

Contrasts With Other Cultures

Compared to the peoples of other continents, Native Americans had one serious handicap. In the pre-Columbian era, there were no horses, cattle, oxen, sheep, goats, or pigs in the Americas. This meant that the Indians' supply of food was limited. More important, there were no draft animals—animals such as horses and oxen used to plow fields and carry heavy loads.

The lack of draft animals prevented Native Americans from making certain advances in their technology. They never developed wheeled vehicles, for example, because they had no horses or oxen to pull them.

Mining and metalworking were also slower to develop in pre-Columbian America than in other parts of the world. Several Native American peoples used gold, silver, and copper to make jewelry and small ceremonial objects. But there was no large-scale mining of iron for tools or weapons. Nor did the Indians know how to build large sailing ships.

Population

In pre-Columbian times, North and South America were not densely populated. Scholars disagree on the total population. Many believe that there were only about 20 million people in the Americas when Columbus made his historic voyage in 1492. Of this number, about 10 million lived in South America and 7 million in Central America and Mexico. The area that is now the United States was inhabited by some 2 million people. A smaller number—perhaps 500,000—lived in Canada.

Varied Languages and Cultures

The land forms, resources, and climate of the Western Hemisphere are extremely varied. Native Americans adapted to this variety as they

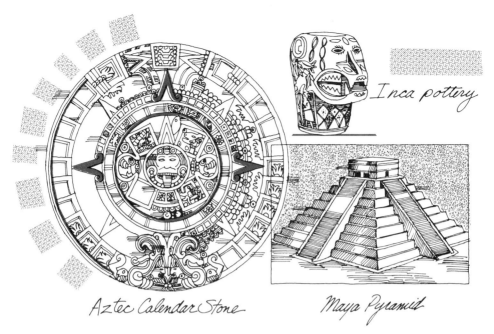

Aztec Calendar Stone   Maya Pyramid

Inca pottery

migrated from region to region. Gradually, they developed different cultures suited to their surroundings.

At the same time, a great number of languages developed as one group separated from another. Altogether, more than 1500 languages were spoken in pre-Columbian America. About 200 of this total were spoken in the region north of Mexico (present-day Canada and the United States).

Scholars classify languages into large groupings called language families. (All the languages within a given family have similar grammar and word origins.) In North America, for example, the Algonquian language family consisted of more than 25 languages. These included Pequot and Narraganset on the Atlantic coast, Shawnee and Ojibwa in the Midwest, and Cheyenne and Blackfoot on the Great Plains. Other important language families were Athapascan (Apache, Navajo) and Iroquoian (Cherokee, Erie, Huron, Iroquois). The culture of these North American peoples will be discussed in Chapter 2.

This chapter presents the history of three Indian peoples who built impressive cities and civilizations in the regions south of the present-day United States. First, about 2000 years ago, the Maya Indians built immense pyramids and temples in the jungles of Central America. Later, the Aztecs established a large empire in the highlands of Mexico. During the same period, shortly before Columbus, Inca Indians ruled over another large empire in the Andes Mountains of South America.

THE MAYAS AND THE AZTECS

A culture area is a large region inhabited by people who share a similar way of life. One culture area, known as Middle America, extended in pre-

Columbian times from central Mexico into Honduras. Among the many Indian cultures that flourished here, the most remarkable were those of the Mayas and the Aztecs.

The Mayas

Maya culture originated about 1500 B.C. in the highlands of Guatemala and gradually spread to the nearby lowlands and river valleys. The first great era of Maya culture, called the Classic period, dates from about A.D. 200 to 800. Important Maya centers that flourished during this period include Tikal, Copán, Palenque, Piedras Negras, and Uaxactún. After A.D. 900, for reasons unknown to us, these sites were abandoned.

The second major flowering of Maya culture took place in northern Yucatán. There, the main urban centers were Chichén Itzá, Mayapán, and Uxmal. Because of strong influences from Mexico, this second era— from about A.D. 925 to 1500—is called the Mexican period. In the late 1400s, this phase of Maya culture also declined. By the early 1500s, when Europeans arrived, Maya greatness was no more.

ECONOMY   The Mayas lived in a hot tropical region of dense forests and wetlands. They had to use slash-and-burn methods to clear away the dense vegetation. With stone axes, they cut down jungle growth and then burned it to make room for crops. When the soil wore out, Maya farmers abandoned the old fields and slashed and burned again to clear new fields.

The basic crop of the Mayas was corn. They also raised beans, squash, chilis, sweet potatoes, cassava, cotton, and tobacco.

POLITICAL AND SOCIAL ORGANIZATION   Maya society was rigidly organized. At the top of the social scale were nobles, who inherited their position, and a very powerful class of priests. In the middle were farmers (the majority), merchants, and crafts workers. At the bottom of the scale were slaves. The slave class comprised prisoners of war and former criminals.

The Mayas lived in small villages grouped around an urban complex such as Tikal or Chichén Itzá. The cities were ceremonial centers rather than places for living and working. On special religious occasions, they were crowded. At other times, they remained empty except for the priests who tended the shrines.

RELIGION   The supreme god of the Mayas was Itzamná. Below him were a number of lesser gods. Among the most important were the four Chacs, or rain gods, who made the crops grow. Each Chac was associated with one of the four directions—east, west, north, and south. Each Chac was also known by one of the four basic colors of corn—red, black, white, and yellow. (This fourfold sacred division existed among many Indians.)

Maya religious celebrations usually involved fasting. People refrained from eating for a period of time so that they could purify their bodies. The celebrations also included elaborate processions and sacrifices. People offered corn and animals to the gods. The supreme sacrifice, however, was the killing of a human being, often a slave. The Mayas thought that human sacrifice won and kept the favor of the gods. This ritual, relatively rare in Classic times, became more common in the Mexican period.

CULTURAL ACHIEVEMENTS   The many achievements of the Mayas made them the most highly advanced of all American Indian peoples. Their civilization is famous for the following:

1. **Architecture and Sculpture.**   The Mayas built stepped pyramids of stone, with small temples on top. Other Maya constructions included hundreds of free-standing pillars. Buildings and pillars, grouped around open courtyards, were richly decorated with carvings and writing.
2. **Writing.**   The Mayas were the only Indians with a highly developed system of writing. They used picture symbols called *glyphs* to represent numbers, periods of time, heavenly bodies, and, probably, speech sounds. Scholars have not yet figured out what all the Maya glyphs mean. The Maya number system was based on a unit of 20 (ours is based on 10) and included the useful concept of zero. Maya writing was used chiefly to record observations of the heavens and predictions of the future.
3. **Astronomy and the Calendar.**   Maya priests had a good knowledge of astronomy. (One of the buildings at Chichén Itzá seems to have been designed for use as an observatory.) Phases of the moon, eclipses of the sun and moon, and planetary movements especially interested the priests. They worked out a series of complex calendars to keep track of such data. One 365-day calendar was more accurate than the one used in Europe at the time of Columbus. There were also a 260-day sacred year and cycles relating to the moon and to the planet Venus. Using all these calendars, the priests made predictions about individual and community matters, and planned appropriate religious ceremonies.

The Aztecs

Another major civilization in Middle America was developed by the Aztecs, an Indian people who were relative newcomers to this culture area. Originally a warlike hunting tribe living either in northern Mexico or the present-day American Southwest, the Aztecs migrated southward to the Valley of Mexico in A.D. 1200. This section of central Mexico, located some 500 miles west of the flourishing Maya cities in the Yucatán, was inhabited by Indians whose culture resembled that of the Mayas in many ways.

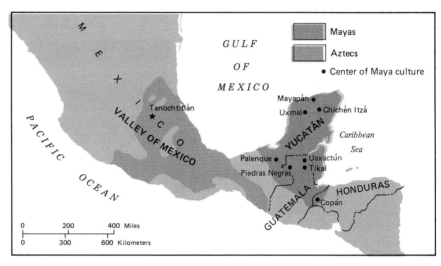

MAYA AND AZTEC CIVILIZATIONS

From the civilized peoples in this valley, the Aztecs learned how to farm, build cities, and conduct complex religious rituals. But because war was still important to them, they fought with their neighbors and conquered them. Eventually, they gained control of a large region stretching from the Pacific coast to the Gulf of Mexico and measuring about 500 miles from north to south.

After learning about agriculture, the Aztecs grew corn as their basic crop, as well as squash, peppers, avocados, tomatoes, and cacao (the source of chocolate). From the maguey plant, they obtained fibers for rope and fabric, leaves for thatching house roofs, and sap for *pulque* (a kind of beer).

CULTURE   The Aztecs imitated and mastered the arts which had been practiced in the Valley of Mexico for centuries. They built large stepped pyramids, erected temples, used complex calendars, kept records, and sculpted images of their gods. Aztec priests carried the practice of human sacrifice to extremes, sometimes killing thousands of victims at one time.

CITY AND EMPIRE   The pride of Aztec builders was the capital city of Tenochtitlán, now Mexico City. This great American city was built on an island in Lake Texcoco. Causeways connected the island city to the mainland, and fresh water flowed to it through aqueducts. The chief means of traveling between city buildings was to paddle boats up and down Tenochtitlán's crisscrossing canals.

From Tenochtitlán, the Aztecs ruled the many provinces they conquered. They required subject peoples to pay them tribute in the form of food, gold, silver, and other goods. But they did not govern the provinces directly. As a result, the conquered peoples felt no loyalty to the Aztec empire.

CONQUEST BY EUROPEANS   The Aztecs were still expanding their territory when Columbus and other explorers arrived in the New World. A small band of Spanish soldiers, led by Hernando Cortés, advanced on Tenochtitlán in 1519. Along the way, they won the support of Indians who hated paying tribute to the Aztecs. Upon reaching Tenochtitlán, the Spaniards were at first welcomed by the Aztec emperor Moctezuma (or Montezuma). The Spaniards later seized and imprisoned him, however, and, in 1521, they destroyed the Aztec capital and took possession of Mexico for Spain.

THE INCAS

The third great civilization of pre-Columbian America—the Inca empire—developed in the Andes Mountains on the western coast of South America. Today, this region includes all of present-day Peru and parts of Ecuador, Bolivia, Chile, and Argentina. For pre-Columbian times, the culture area known as the Central Andes was heavily populated. Early peoples there developed advanced cultures many centuries before the Incas built their remarkable empire.

The Incas came into the region around Cuzco, in present-day Peru, about A.D. 1250. Not until around 1400 did they begin to expand outward, but this expansion was swift and overwhelming. Within a hundred years, the Inca empire stretched nearly 3000 miles along the Pacific—from Quito, Ecuador, to the Rio Maule in Chile. Subject peoples within the empire may have totaled some 7 million.

Economy

The Incas, like the Mayas and Aztecs, grew corn. Another important crop was white potatoes (native to the Western Hemisphere). Potatoes could be grown in the highlands of the Andes Mountains, where the climate was too cold for corn. In the warmer regions east of the mountains, farmers grew corn, manioc, cacao, squash, chilis, peanuts, tomatoes, and cotton. The Incas domesticated the llama as a beast of burden and the alpaca as a source of meat and wool. They also learned to make fine fabrics from the wool of the wild guanaco and vicuña.

Political Organization

Ruling over the Inca empire was a prince or monarch who claimed to be a kind of god. He believed that his royal family was directly descended

VENEZUELA

COLOMBIA

Quito ●
ECUADOR

P
A
C
I
F
I
C

O
C
E
A
N

ANDES MOUNTAINS

P E R U

★ Cuzco

B R A Z I L

BOLIVIA

CHILE

Rio Maule

ARGENTINA

A
T
L
A
N
T
I
C

O
C
E
A
N

N

0   200   400   600 Miles

0   400   800 Kilometers

Inca empire (about 1500)

INCA CIVILIZATION

from the Incas' chief god—the sun. This religious belief caused Inca princes to think that they were especially fitted to rule others.

Unlike the Aztecs, the Incas made conquered peoples a part of the Inca empire. They introduced their language, Quechua, and their sun worship to subject peoples. Lands seized by the Incas were divided into communities called *ayllus.* One third of the produce grown went to the emperor and the Inca nobility. One third supported the religious class. And one third was divided among the people who raised it. Most of the food set aside for the first two groups was stored in royal warehouses. In times of need, it was distributed to soldiers or to the people.

In order to strengthen their hold over newly won territory, the Incas sometimes moved entire villages or tribes to older parts of the empire. The Incas might also resettle a new area with people who had lived a long time under Inca rule. These loyal subjects taught Inca culture—and also served as spies. Another practice was to move the sons of upper-class families from newly conquered regions to Cuzco. Officially, these youths were sent to learn Inca culture, but they were actually hostages. While they remained in Cuzco, it was unlikely that their families would rebel against the Inca rulers.

Major Achievements

While the Mayas excelled at artistic and intellectual skills, such as sculpture and the measurement of time, the Incas are noted for the attention they paid to the practical tasks of ruling an empire. Inca achievements included the following:

1. **Roads.** Inca lands were connected by an elaborate road network. Its foundations had undoubtedly been laid by earlier Andean peoples. The Incas joined separate systems, built bridges, and kept the roadways in good repair. Rest stops with shelters and supplies were located at frequent spots along the way. Government runners could relay messages from one end of the empire to the other—some 3000 miles—in just a few days.
2. **Other Engineering Feats.** To make as much land as possible available for farming, the Incas shaped the hillsides into steplike terraces. They also dug complex irrigation systems to water their crops. They learned to put up strong buildings made of huge, tightly fitted blocks of stone. (The fortress of Sacsahuamán still stands near Cuzco.) The Spaniards destroyed the upper parts of many of Cuzco's buildings, among them the temple of the sun and the emperor's palace. But the foundations of the buildings that remain are so solid that they easily withstand the frequent earthquakes of the area.
3. **Record Keeping.** A messenger on the royal roads often carried a *quipu*. This device was made of knotted strings in different colors. The quipu helped the messenger recall an oral message committed to memory. Quipus were also used for record keeping—for example, to keep track of supplies stored in government warehouses. The exact meaning of the few surviving quipus can only be guessed at.

Conquest by Europeans

The Inca empire had just passed to a new ruler, Atahualpa, when the first Europeans arrived in 1532. Led by Francisco Pizarro, the Spanish adventurers were few in number. Even so, they managed to capture

Atahualpa and hold him for a huge ransom in gold. The ransom was paid, but Pizarro had Atahualpa executed anyway. Without its ruler, the Inca empire quickly fell to the Spanish conquerors.

True-False Test

Write the letter *T* if the statement is true or *F* if it is false.

1. The first settlers came to America in search of game.
2. The first Americans made progress after they domesticated cattle.
3. North America in pre-Columbian times was densely populated.
4. Indian cultures reached their highest levels in Middle America and the Central Andes.
5. The Mayas were the only American Indians to have a highly developed system of writing.
6. The Mayas did not have accurate calendars.
7. The Aztecs migrated northward into the Valley of Mexico.
8. The Aztecs conquered their territories in Mexico during the Classic period of Maya history.
9. It took the Incas five centuries to create their empire.
10. One of the most notable accomplishments of the Incas was an elaborate network of roads.

Multiple-Choice Test

Select the letter before the word or expression that best completes the statement.

1. The first settlers in America came from   (a) Siberia   (b) Europe   (c) the East Indies   (d) India.
2. A land bridge connected Asia and North America until about   (a) 8000 B.C.   (b) 200 B.C.   (c) the time of the birth of Christ   (d) A.D. 1500.
3. One of the most important Indian crops, native to the Western Hemisphere, was   (a) wheat   (b) corn   (c) barley   (d) rye.
4. Indian cultural developments included all of the following *except*   (a) farming   (b) domesticated llamas and alpacas   (c) sailing ships   (d) cities.
5. The total number of languages spoken in pre-Columbian America was   (a) about 200   (b) 650   (c) about 1500   (d) more than 3000.

6. Maya culture flourished in   (a) northern Mexico   (b) the Yucatán peninsula   (c) what is now Peru   (d) the Andes Mountains.
7. The following were all features of Maya culture *except*   (a) pyramid building   (b) writing   (c) belief in only one god   (d) human sacrifice.
8. The Aztecs were conquered by   (a) Francisco Pizarro   (b) Hernando Cortés   (c) Christopher Columbus   (d) Atahualpa.
9. The Inca empire extended along the Pacific coast for nearly   (a) 100 miles   (b) 500 miles   (c) 1500 miles   (d) 3000 miles.
10. The Incas conquered their extensive empire   (a) beginning around A.D. 1250   (b) during the Classic period of Maya culture   (c) in about 100 years   (d) in about three centuries.

Map Test

Answer the following questions by referring to the maps on pages 3, 10, and 12.

1. In what general direction did the nomads travel to reach the region where their descendants became known as the Mayas?
2. In which continent was the Aztec empire located?
3. The distance along the migratory route between the Bering Strait and the Florida peninsula is approximately   (a) 2500 miles   (b) 7500 miles   (c) 5500 miles.
4. In what present-day country is   (a) Tikal   (b) Chichén Itzá   (c) Copán   (d) Quito   (e) Cuzco?
5. What present-day countries, in whole or in part, were included in the Inca empire?

Essay Questions

1. Describe the culture of the earliest inhabitants of America at the time of their arrival in North America.
2. What improvements in living conditions does agriculture make possible?
3. In what ways did pre-Columbian American cultures differ from emerging cultures in other parts of the world?
4. Compare the major achievements of the Mayas, Aztecs, and Incas.
5. Of the achievements listed in answer to question 4, which do you think was the most important? Explain your answer.

CHAPTER 2

Native Cultures of North America

IN THE PART OF the New World that eventually became the United States and Canada, pre-Columbian culture never reached the high levels it did in Middle America and the Central Andes. It was quite varied, however. This book discusses ten culture areas in North America. The Inuit are not considered to be Indians because their ancestors arrived in America long after the Ice Age had ended. Nevertheless, they are discussed in this chapter as one of America's early peoples.

(As used in this chapter, "North America" refers to the part of the continent north of Mexico. Locations of culture areas are given in terms of their present-day names.)

THE SOUTHWEST

The Southwest culture area included most of Arizona and New Mexico, plus parts of neighboring states and northernmost Mexico. The Southwest is a warm, dry, generally flat land. There are also some mountains and valleys, and large, flat-topped rock formations. The area supported a fairly large population of Native Americans from earliest times.

The Pueblos

Pueblo is the Spanish word for "village." This name is applied to one group of Native Americans because they were living in villages when the Spaniards arrived. This group had a long history of settled community life.

MAJOR CULTURE AREAS OF NORTH AMERICA

Ruins of ancient Indian settlements have been found in many parts of the Southwest. Some of the buildings were made of earth and logs, others of stone or adobe (sun-dried brick). Many were constructed at ground level, while some stood on ledges in steep cliffs. Several were like apartment houses, with many levels. In one of these dwellings, five stories high, more than 1000 people lived in some 800 rooms. The earliest "apartment house" ruins date back to A.D. 700. For some unknown reason, the inhabitants abandoned their cliff houses in the late 13th century.

The descendants of these Indians, the Pueblo people, moved elsewhere and built simpler multifamily dwellings, usually at ground level. These complexes were from one to five stories high. About 30 of them still exist, most in northern New Mexico. The pueblo called Zuñi is in western New Mexico, and three Hopi villages are found in Arizona.

The Pueblos were (and still are) excellent crafts workers and peaceful farmers. They developed special methods for growing crops on their dry land, including large irrigation systems in the river valleys. The Pueblos grew mainly corn, beans, and squash. Surpluses were stored, to be used when crops failed. After the Spaniards brought sheep to the New World, the raising of livestock became an important part of Pueblo life. The culture of the Pueblos was also reflected in their handicrafts. They made beautifully decorated pottery, baskets, blankets, and turquoise and silver jewelry.

Pueblo life was regulated by an elaborate series of religious ceremonies. Each season had its own spirits and rituals, and every village formed organizations devoted to carrying out the proper observances. The Pueblos believed in supernatural beings, called *kachinas*, who acted as messengers between gods and humans. These beings were thought to live among the Pueblo people for six months of the year and vanish into the hills for the other six months.

The Navajos and Apaches

Two other groups of Native Americans in the Southwest, the Navajos and Apaches, were latecomers to the region. They arrived sometime after A.D. 1200, probably from the north. (Their languages, closely related to each other, are like some spoken in western Canada.)

The Navajos built *hogans* (eight-sided houses of earth and wood) near Pueblo settlements. From the Pueblos, the Navajos learned how to weave and make pottery. With the introduction of sheep, the Navajos took up sheepherding and blanket weaving. They also became the finest of all Indian silversmiths.

Unlike the Navajos, the Apaches had little interest in settling down in permanent villages. Most of them were nomadic hunters. They also became known as fierce fighters, preying on the farms and livestock of their more peaceable neighbors.

THE SOUTHEAST

The Southeastern culture area extended from the Gulf of Mexico northward to Kentucky and from eastern Texas eastward to the Atlantic Ocean. Like the Southwestern peoples, those of the Southeast had a long history.

Beginning about 700 B.C., large earth mounds were built in many parts of the Mississippi River Valley. (They were located in the East-

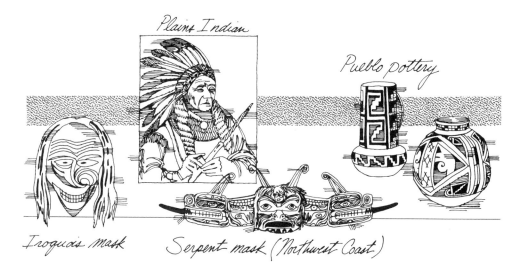

Plains Indian

Pueblo pottery

Iroquois mask   Serpent mask (Northwest Coast)

ern Woodland culture area, as well as the Southeast.) Some of the mounds contained burials. Others had temples on top. The most unusual mounds were built in the shape of animals, such as birds and turtles. The mounds have yielded beautiful carvings and jewelry made of copper, stone, and mica. Many of these arts and crafts are decorated with designs like those on objects found in Mexico. It seems clear that there was trade back and forth across the Gulf of Mexico.

When European settlers arrived, Native Americans in the area knew nothing about the origins of the mounds. For a long time, people thought that a mysterious race of "Mound Builders" had once existed and then died out. We now know that the mounds were built by earlier Native Americans.

At the time Europeans came to the Southeast, the Native Americans were living in simple villages surrounded by log fences. Since the climate was mild, the people preferred light, airy houses—sometimes just a roof supported by poles. Clothing was simple, too. Women wore wraparound skirts; men wore breechcloths. Bare legs and arms were decorated with tattoos, which the Indians made by scratching the skin with a fish tooth and then rubbing soot into the scratch.

Southeastern peoples hunted, fished, and farmed. Their main crop was corn. They also grew potatoes, melons, tobacco, and sunflowers (for their seeds). For travel along the many streams and swamps of the region, Southeasterners used cane rafts and dugouts (boats made from hollowed-out logs).

The tribal groupings of this region included the Creeks, Choctaws, Chickasaws, Cherokees, and Seminoles. It was common for tribes and villages to form alliances. One of the most important of these alliances was the Creek Confederacy, which linked more than 50 settlements in Alabama and Georgia.

THE EASTERN WOODLANDS

A large culture area was that of the Eastern Woodlands. This forest region extended from Kentucky into Canada and from the Atlantic coast to beyond the Mississippi River. Many tribes—from the Penobscots in the east to the Chippewas in the west—spoke languages in the Algonquian language family. Most others spoke Iroquoian languages.

Woodland Culture

The Eastern Woodland peoples were hunters and farmers. They depended for much of their food on deer, bear, and wild fowl, and on fish caught in the region's many lakes and streams. They also raised corn, beans, squash, and tobacco. From the sap of maple trees, Eastern Woodland peoples made syrup and sugar. Those in the upper Great Lakes region harvested wild rice. (Menominee, the name of a tribal group in Wisconsin and Michigan, means "wild rice people.")

Nearly all the Eastern Woodland tribes lived in villages. The commonest kind of dwelling was the cone-shaped or dome-shaped *wigwam,* covered with bark or hides. The Iroquois lived in big rectangular *longhouses.* Each one could house many families. Eastern Woodland clothing, made from animal skins, was simple and practical—breechcloths, leggings, and shirts for the men, and skirts and jackets for the women. Both men and women wore moccasins.

POLITICAL ORGANIZATION   Most Woodland peoples had a simple, democratic political organization. There were no hereditary rulers. People valued the opinion of a good military leader or someone in close touch with the spirit world. Usually a group of such "chiefs" made the major decisions for a tribe.

A notable political achievement was the Iroquois Confederacy, or Five Nations, formed around 1570. Its members were the Mohawks, Oneida, Onondaga, Cayuga, and Seneca tribes of central New York. They were later joined by the Tuscaroras of North Carolina to form the Six Nations. Although each tribe was independent in local affairs, a central governing body of *sachems* decided matters of common interest. Older women chose the sachems to represent their nation. (Iroquois women played an important role, for society was organized around the "fireside"—a woman and her children.) The Iroquois Confederacy dominated much of the Eastern Woodlands region for 200 years.

RELIGION   Throughout the Americas, Native Americans believed in a supernatural force inhabiting all living things, human and nonhuman. The

Algonquians called this power *manitou,* and the Iroquois called it *orenda.* The Native Americans tried to communicate with this power and gain its favor through visions and dreams.

The Eastern Woodland peoples, like Native Americans elsewhere, practiced many rituals and ceremonies. Some had to do with planting, growing, and harvesting crops. Others marked important events in a person's life, such as birth, puberty, marriage, and death. There were also rituals for driving out evil spirits, for victory in war, and for a successful hunt.

THE WOODLAND LEGACY   Inhabitants of the Eastern Woodlands were the first Native Americans the English settlers met. Thus, many Woodland words for distinctively American plants and animals entered the English language. Examples are *catalpa, hickory, tamarack, chipmunk, moose, opossum, raccoon,* and *skunk.* From these Native Americans, English settlers also learned about many customs common to most North American Native Americans. Such traditions included ceremonial smoking (passing the "peace pipe") and burying a hatchet (*tomahawk*) to signal peace, holding councils of elders (*powwows*), and carrying babies (*papooses*) in cradleboards.

THE PLAINS

The best-known Native Americans are those of the plains. Their distinctive feather headdresses, their skill on horseback, and their bravery as fighters made them famous all over the world. Plains peoples inhabited a large territory between the Mississippi River and the Rocky Mountains. This is a dry and treeless region covered with tall grass.

Early Days

Centuries ago, the Plains peoples, like those of the Southeast and Eastern Woodlands, depended on both hunting and farming. Unlike these eastern groups, however, the Plains peoples did not stay in one place. Most of the year, they lived in solid *earth lodges,* built partly underground along riverbanks in the eastern plains. Nearby, the community grew corn, beans, squash, and other crops. But in the summer, they moved westward into the area called the High Plains, there to live as nomads. Wherever they could find buffalo, they set up cone shaped *tepees,* made of animal skins.

Vast herds of buffalo once lived on the plains. (As late as 1850, there were more than 20 million of them.) From buffalo, the Plains peoples obtained not only meat but also fur (for robes), hides (for clothing, tepees, and shields), and bones (for tools). Buffalo sinews were used as bowstrings, their hooves and horns were heated to make glue, and their droppings were burned as fuel.

The Coming of the Horse

Hunting buffalo on foot required special skills. One method Native Americans used was to disguise themselves in buffalo robes and sneak up on a herd. Another was to stampede the animals into pens or over a cliff. But days or weeks might go by before scouts could track down a herd.

Then, about 1700, things changed. By this time, Spaniards had settled in Mexico and the Southwest, bringing horses with them. Some of the horses escaped, and others were traded. Early in the 18th century, Plains peoples started to acquire horses in large numbers. Now buffalo hunting became much easier. Many Native Americans gave up their farming life and stayed permanently on the High Plains as nomadic hunters. Those who did so include the best-known of the Plains tribes: the Cheyenne, Blackfoot, Crow, Comanche, Arapoho, and Kiowa. Other tribes, including the Mandans, Pawnees, and Omahas, kept to the old ways. The Sioux (or Dakota) split up; some lived as part-time farmers in Minnesota, and others moved westward onto the plains.

Life on the Plains

Plains peoples moved about in groups of a few families. For varying periods, these groups would settle here and there within a large tribal territory. (Like most Native Americans, Plains people did not believe in individual land ownership. They did, however, regard certain regions as tribal homelands.) Several bands might assemble once or twice a year for a council or special celebration. As in most other culture areas, chiefs who had proved themselves as hunters, fighters, or spiritual leaders made the important decisions.

Fighting was important to Plains peoples. They often conducted raids to steal horses. But the most important reason for fight was to gain honor. As a measure of honor, individuals "counted *coup*." (Coup—pronounced KOO—is the French word for "blow".) They received credit for certain brave deeds, such as touching an enemy in combat without being hurt, or downing a buffalo with one shot. A man might record his coups by painting distinctive designs on his tepee or his body. He might also wear special feathers or furs.

Like most North American Native Americans, Plains peoples sought spiritual help through personal religious experiences. A person might go alone to a special place and fast for several days, hoping for a vision. If a spirit appeared, it might predict the future. The spirit could also advise the vision-seeker to get help from a special animal or sacred object. Some people with noted for their ability to get in touch with the spirit world. They were called upon to heal illness or cast spells on enemies. The Europeans called such gifted Native Americans "medicine men" (although women might also perform these functions).

THE PLATEAU

The Plateau peoples lived in the rugged region drained by the Columbia River and its branches—Idaho, eastern Oregon and Washington, and southeastern British Columbia. Plateau peoples lived in small fishing villages along the banks of major streams and traveled mostly by canoe. Their winter houses were built partly underground for warmth. Summer shelters were rough wooden frames covered with thick plant stems or bark.

Plateau peoples did not raise any crops. The yearly return of salmon to the Columbia River provided huge catches of fish. These the Indians dried, smoked, and stored for future use. Other sources of food were berries, edible roots, and small game. Lacking pottery, the Plateau peoples wove baskets for use as utensils and food containers.

The culture of neighboring Plains peoples influenced some of the eastern Plateau tribes, such as the Nez Percés and Flatheads. They acquired horses and traveled eastward from time to time to hunt buffalo on the plains. The Cayuses bred a type of small horse that became popular and was named after the tribe.

THE GREAT BASIN

Small nomadic band of Utes, Paiutes, and Shoshones lived in the barren region between the Rockies and the Sierra Nevada. This area, shaped like a giant dish, included Utah, Nevada, and eastern California. Here, large game was scarce, and the land was too dry for farming.

Basin peoples had to work hard to find enough food to eat. They gathered the nuts of the piñon tree and ground them into meal. These Native Americans also caught grasshoppers, hunted rabbits and other small animals, collected wild seeds, and dug for edible roots. (The last activity earned the Great Basin peoples the nickname "Digger Indians.") Shelter was provided by caves or by brush huts called *wickiups*. Among the tribes in the area, basketry developed into a distinctive art form. Women wove reeds and plant fibers so tightly together that their baskets could hold water. They cooked in the baskets by dropping in heated stones until the contents were hot.

CALIFORNIA

Many small tribes—among them the Hupas, Modocs, and Pomos—inhabited the coastal section and interior valleys of California. California tribes lived apart from one another and spoke a variety of related languages. The mild climate, abundant food, and favorable environment enabled these Indians to live simply and peaceably. They made brush huts or tepeelike bark shelters. Men wore loincloths. Women wore short, bark-cloth skirts and cloaks of dried plant stems. Fiber moccasins protected the feet in colder weather.

Native Americans of California made the finest baskets in America. Women wove colored grasses, fibers, and feathers to form artistic containers with intricate designs. The coils of some baskets are so fine that a microscope is needed to count them.

The California Native Americans, who did not farm, relied on acorns as a staple food. These were shelled, ground, and soaked with water to remove the bitter, poisonous tannic acid. After being dried, roasted, and ground again, acorn meal was cooked as porridge or baked as bread. These peoples also hunted deer and other game, fished, and gathered wild berries, seeds, and fruits.

THE NORTHWEST COAST

Along the northern Pacific stretched a narrow region with a very special culture. Here, in western Oregon, Washington, and British Columbia, the natural resources were rich. The forestland was full of game, and the waters teemed with salmon and other fish. The Northwest Coast tribes from the Tlingits in the north to the Chinooks in the south, lived among such abundance that they had no need to grow their own food.

A Land of Plenty

Depending on their location, Northwest Coast peoples relied on various staples. Those living along the rivers could catch enough salmon during the spawning season to last them the rest of the year. (The fish were dried or preserved in oil.) Those close to the ocean caught halibut, cod, herring, and shellfish. Group hunts for sea lions, otters, porpoises, and whales were organized as well. To add to their food supply, Northwest Coast peoples gathered berries and hunted game in the nearby woodlands.

Most Native Americans of the Northwest Coast lived in villages of wooden houses with slanting roofs. Built of posts, beams, and planks, each house was generally large enough for dozens of people. In front of each house stood the family totem pole. This tall wooden post was carved with animal, bird, and human figures sacred to the family.

Skilled woodworkers, the Northwest Coast peoples could make a boat up to 60 feet in length from one tree. They carved handsome, watertight storage boxes and richly ornamented masks. Many of these objects were painted with beautiful black and red designs representing animals. Other Northwest crafts included hammering copper into thin, shield-shaped ornaments and weaving decorative blankets from cedar bark and animal hair.

Ceremonial Life

Most of the gods of the Northwest Coast peoples were associated with animals of the region. In many of their ceremonies, these Native Americans acted out roles as animal spirits. Wearing fantastic costumes and giant masks, dancers flew through the air (suspended by cords) or appeared from the floor (out of trapdoors). By speaking through hidden reeds, some of the actors even made their voices seem to come from flames.

Wealth and social position were extremely important in the culture of the Northwest peoples. Society was divided into noble families, common people, and slaves. (Slaves were taken during raids on other tribes.) The nobles competed keenly to improve their social standing. This competition gave rise to the *potlatch*. At such an event, the host and hostess fed their guests lavishly. But the main purpose of the celebration was to show off wealth by giving away or destroying valuable possessions. The more a family distributed or destroyed, the greater the honor. Guests and rivals would then have to hold even more costly potlatches, or else be publicly disgraced. This unique type of festival has been called "fight with property."

THE SUBARCTIC

The dense forests of interior Canada and Alaska and the treeless region north of the forests were the home of the Subarctic Native Americans. These people—the Crees, Chipewyans, Dogribs, and Tananas, among others—lived by hunting and fishing. Those in the south hunted moose, elk, beaver, and wild fowl, and also fished in the many lakes and streams. Subarctic peoples in the north followed herds of caribou. The game animals provided not only meat for food but also furs and skins for clothing, wigwams, ropes, and thongs. For travel, Subarctic Native Americans used birchbark canoes during the summer and snowshoes and toboggans in the winter.

Life in the Subarctic was very hard. Its nomadic peoples had few comforts. Their way of life was simpler than that of any other culture area in North America and, in fact, resembled the culture of the very first Americans.

THE ARCTIC

The Arctic region of North America (as well as Greenland) was the home of the Inuit, or Eskimos. Their languages and racial characteristics were different from those of the Native Americans. So was Inuit history. The ancestors of both groups were from Asia. But the first Indians to arrive in North America came more than 20,000 years ago, traveling by foot from Siberia. The first Inuit probably arrived about 2000 years ago. Since there was no longer a land bridge connecting Siberia and Alaska, these adventurous people came by boat.

Over the years, the Inuit developed a way of life that enabled them to survive in one of the earth's harshest environments. The Arctic is cold much of the year, and for months the ground is covered with snow and ice. In the open waters of the Pacific, Alaskan Inuit hunted such sea mammals as walruses, seals, and whales. Inuit farther inland tracked caribou and polar bears. In northern Canada, where the seas are frozen, Inuit caught seals and fish through holes in the ice.

From the bones of sea mammals and the ivory tusks of walruses, the Inuit made many objects—harpoons, fishhooks, ice picks, knives, needles,

NATIVE AMERICAN CONTRIBUTIONS TO THE WORLD
(Words in italics come from Native American languages.)

Foods	Drugs
avocados	cascara
beans (lima and kidney)	*coca*
cashews	*curare*
chocolate	*ipecac*
corn	*quinine*
hominy	witch hazel
maple syrup	
peanuts	**Miscellaneous**
pecans	
peppers	canoe
pineapples	*chicle* (for chewing gum)
potatoes (sweet and white)	*hammock*
pumpkins	lacrosse
sassafras	*moccasins*
squash	*poncho*
succotash	rubber
tamales	snowshoes
tapioca	tobacco
tomatoes	*toboggan*
tortillas	
turkey	
vanilla	
wild rice	

SOME NATIVE AMERICAN PLACE NAMES IN THE UNITED STATES
(a sampling of thousands)

	Language	Meaning
States		
Arizona	Papago	Place of small spring
Kentucky	Iroquois	Meadowland
Massachusetts	Natick	Big hills
Nebraska	Omaha or Otoe	Flat water (of Platte River)
Wyoming (originally a valley in Pennsylvania)	Delaware	Big flats
Cities		
Chattanooga	Creek	Rock rising to point (Lookout Mountain)
Chicago	Sauk, Fox, Kickapoo	Onion place
Roanoke	Powhatan	Shell beads
Tallahassee	Creek	Old town
Walla Walla	Cayuse or Nez Percé	Little, swift river
Natural Features		
Allegheny (mountains)	Delaware	Beautiful stream (nearby Ohio River)
Chattahoochee (river)	Creek	Marked rocks
Niagara (river and falls)	Iroquois	Neck of land
Tahoe (lake)	Washo	Lake
Tamalpais (mountain)	Miwok	Western mountain

snow goggles, and ornaments. Animal skins were sewn into warm, weatherproof garments such as trousers, shirts, parkas, boots, and mittens. Hides were stretched over wood frames to make *kayaks* and *umiaks*. (A kayak is a one-person canoe; the larger umiak can carry goods or several people.) During the summer, the Inuit lived in tents made of hides. The traditional winter house was the *igloo*, a domed structure built of snow blocks. Another Inuit contribution was the dog sled, a useful means of travel over ice and snow.

A people related to the Inuit, the Aleuts, inhabited the chain of islands that extends westward from Alaska. The Aleuts, too, used kayaks and took their food supply from the sea. But their tools, clothing, and shelters show that Aleut culture was less developed than that of the Inuit.

True-False Test

1. Native Americans in the region that became the United States tended to have less complex cultures than those of Latin America.
2. The Apaches fought with other tribes of the Southwest.
3. The Iroquois Confederacy was organized in the 17th century.
4. Most North American tribes were governed by chiefs who had distinguished themselves in some way.
5. Most North American Native Americans spoke the same language.
6. Plains peoples became buffalo hunters only after the introduction of the horse.
7. Few Native Americans believed in individual ownership of land.
8. Personal religious experiences were highly valued by most Native Americans of North America.
9. Tribes of the Plateau lived in large, settled communities.
10. Northwest Coast peoples were noted for their skill in carving wood.

Multiple-Choice Test

1. The "apartment house" dwellings of the ancient Southwest were built by (a) ancestors of the Pueblos (b) the Navajos (c) the Apaches (d) the Spaniards.
2. The finest Native American silversmiths were the (a) Navajos (b) Sioux (c) Creeks (d) Menominees.
3. Tribes in the Southeast (a) lived in pueblos (b) caught salmon (c) formed many confederations (d) were nomadic hunters.
4. The culture area that contributed such Native American words as *chipmunk, hickory, moose,* and *raccoon* to the English language was the (a) Eastern Woodlands (b) Southwest (c) Northwest Coast (d) Plains.
5. The buffalo was a mainstay of the tribes of the (a) Great Basin (b) Eastern Woodlands (c) Southwest (d) Plains.
6. Native Americans of the Great Basin were called "Diggers" because they (a) mined precious metals (b) gathered and ate the roots of wild plants (c) lived in underground huts (d) farmed with crude digging tools.
7. California Native Americans made especially fine (a) baskets (b) pottery (c) boats (d) jewelry.
8. Northwest Coast peoples made (a) earth mounds (b) totem poles (c) tepees (d) hogans.
9. Tribes of the Northwest Coast (a) were among the poorest in America (b) grew vast fields of corn (c) competed by giving away property (d) lived in skin tepees.

10. A small boat of the Inuit is called a (a) potlatch (b) kayak
(c) wickiup   (d) kachina.

Map Test

Answer the following questions by referring to the map on page 17 and to
the text.

1. In which culture area did the Nez Percé live?
2. Which Native Americans were more dependent on the sea for their
   food, the Chinooks or the Pawnees?
3. Locate and name a Native American group that inhabited the area that
   is now known as Texas.
4. Which culture area was bounded on the west by the Rocky Mountains?
5. Name an Algonquian tribe that inhabited the region later called New
   England.

Essay Questions

1. Compare any two culture areas described in this chapter.
2. Describe the following shelters, and show how each was related to its
   environment: wigwam, earth lodge, tepee, igloo.
3. Describe some of the ways in which Native Americans made use of
   animal skins and fur.
4. Define the following terms and explain how each was important to the
   culture associated with it: sachem; coup; potlatch.
5. From what you have read of Native American culture in North America,
   which of its features might have made it difficult for Native Americans
   and Europeans to live together in peace? Explain your answer.

UNIT 2

European Exploration and Colonization

CHAPTER *3*

Continental
Europeans
in the New World

THE FIRST EUROPEANS to explore America were probably the daring people known as Vikings, or Norsemen. During the 9th and 10th centuries, these adventurous seafarers from Scandinavia raided much of Europe. Viking families also journeyed across the northern Atlantic to settle the islands of Iceland and Greenland. From there, a few adventurers sailed to the mainland of North America.

Icelandic legends describe the Viking voyages to America, which seem to have taken place around the year 1000. On one of these journeys, Leif Ericson, a Norseman from Greenland, probably visited Newfoundland or Nova Scotia. He may also have reached the coasts of Maine and Massachusetts. Because he saw many wild grapes, he called the area Vinland (land of vines).

The Viking explorations of America had no lasting effects. The settlements in Vinland were short-lived, and news of the Viking discoveries did not reach many people in Europe.

THE BACKGROUND OF EXPANSION

Between A.D. 500 and 1000, much of Europe was a backward region. Travel and trade were limited. Most of the people were very poor, and few could read or write. This situation began to change about the 12th century.

The Crusades

European interest in other lands was aroused by a series of military expeditions known as the Crusades. The crusaders sought to win control of Palestine, at the eastern end of the Mediterranean. Christians called this region the Holy Land because it was the birthplace of Jesus.

In the 11th century, Muslim Turks had occupied Palestine. They persecuted Christians who were making religious pilgrimages to the Holy Land. The Turks also threatened the Byzantine Empire—a Christian state—and its capital, Constantinople.

To end the threat to Christendom, Pope Urban II called on the people of Western Europe for help. At a great meeting held in 1095, he appealed for a march on the Holy Land to drive out the invaders. Thousands responded to his call and set off on the First Crusade (1096–1099). The crusaders seized territory on the eastern shore of the Mediterranean but eventually lost it. Many other expeditions took place during the next 200 years. No lasting territorial changes resulted, but Europe was never the same again.

By taking part in the Crusades, thousands of Europeans had the opportunity to broaden their horizons. They observed different cultures and learned new ways of doing things. For instance, the Europeans became acquainted with the crossbow as a weapon of warfare and the use of carrier pigeons to send written messages. For the first time, people from the West saw paper. They were also impressed by unfamiliar foods and other products. Some things that were new to Europeans—rice, sugar, lemons, apricots, melons, and fine rugs and tapestries—were locally produced in the Middle East. Others, including silk, perfumes, drugs, dyes, and spices, came from the Far East. The crusaders' tales of adventure and travel made other Europeans curious about these foreign places and strange cultures.

Marco Polo

Interest in lands beyond the continent of Europe was stirred up by other travelers, too. One of the most important was Marco Polo, the son of a wealthy Italian merchant from Venice. In the 1270s, Marco went with his father and uncle on a journey to the Far East. Young Polo won the friendship of Kublai Khan, the ruler of China, and served him as a diplomat. For nearly 20 years, Polo traveled to various parts of the Orient on the Khan's business.

In 1295, the Polos returned to Italy loaded with treasures. Marco Polo then wrote an account of his travels. He vividly described the magnificent cities, great riches, and unfamiliar products of the East. (One such "strange" product was coal—black stones that burned.) Polo's book was

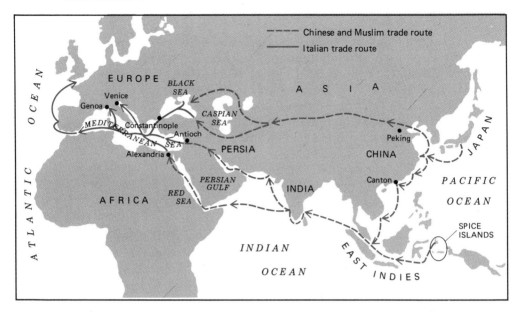

MEDIEVAL TRADE ROUTES

widely read throughout Europe. As a result, Europeans became more curious than ever about the Orient and learned more about the geography of Asia.

Trade With the East

As European demand for Eastern goods rose, a brisk trade developed. It relied on two groups of traders. One group was made up of Chinese and Muslim merchants who carried goods from the East toward Europe. The second group consisted of Italian traders who transported these goods to and throughout Europe.

There were three major trade routes between Asia and Europe. One, the northern route, was mostly overland. Camel caravans traveled across Asia to ports on the Black Sea. From these ports, ships carried the goods west to Constantinople and beyond. The other two routes were mostly by sea. From China and the East Indies, ships sailed to India and then across the Indian Ocean. Traders taking the middle route then voyaged north through the Persian Gulf. Those traveling the southern route took the Red Sea. On both these routes, the last part of the journey was by land to ports on the eastern Mediterranean.

The trade routes connecting Europe and Asia were beset by difficulties. Robbers attacked caravans on land, and pirates looted ships at sea. After the Turks captured Constantinople in 1453, they imposed heavy taxes on goods passing through the city.

Even without the losses to bandits and the Turkish taxes, the cost of Eastern goods to Europeans would have been very high. Each shipment passed through many hands before reaching the marketplaces of Europe. Every trader handling the goods wanted to make a profit. The price of an article in Europe was generally 70 to 100 times what it was in the Orient.

Progress in Technology

Starting about 1350, Europe entered a period of artistic and intellectual activity known as the Renaissance. It was marked by a renewed interest in learning, by great cultural achievements, and by progress in science and invention. Several developments in technology encouraged European expansion:

1. **Ships.** Until the 15th century, most European ships could not make long voyages. The ships were not sturdy enough and could not change direction easily. Many had only a single mast and, thus, few sails. Because the rudder was at the side, steering was difficult. During the 15th and 16th centuries, ship designers added masts and sails, and moved the rudder to the stern (rear).
2. **Aids to Navigation.** Other improvements also made longer voyages possible. The compass helped sailors learn their direction when they were out of sight of land. An instrument called an astrolabe measured latitude (the distance north or south of the equator). Mapmakers, using details reported by sailors and other travelers, prepared more accurate charts of the seas and coastal areas.
3. **Printing.** Until the 1440s, European books were copied by hand and were very expensive. With the invention of movable type and the introduction of the printing press, books became cheaper and more plentiful. The printing press led to the wide distribution of maps, sea charts, and travelers' tales.
4. **Gunpowder.** Late in the 13th century, Europeans learned about gunpowder from the Arabs. (The Arabs had probably brought the invention from China.) Cannons and muskets gave Europeans a military advantage over peoples with less advanced weapons.

EARLY VOYAGES OF EXPLORATION

In the 14th and early 15th centuries, the city-states of Italy—chiefly Venice and Genoa—controlled European trade in Eastern goods. During this period, however, the nations along the Atlantic coast of Europe were changing. They were gaining power under strong and ambitious rulers. These nations resented the Italian control of trade and wanted a share of it for themselves.

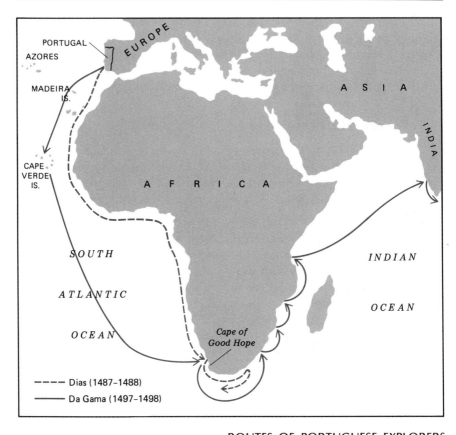

ROUTES OF PORTUGUESE EXPLORERS

The Portuguese

The Italians controlled the Mediterranean Sea. For this reason, anyone else who wanted to trade with the Orient would have to avoid this inland sea. The Portuguese did so by sailing south around Africa and then eastward.

HENRY THE NAVIGATOR   The man behind early Portuguese exploration was Prince Henry, known as Henry the Navigator. He founded a school of navigation at the Portuguese port of Sagres in 1419. There, people interested in sea travel could pool their knowledge. One of Prince Henry's goals was the spread of Christianity in Africa. He also wanted a share of the African slave trade, controlled at that time by Muslims. Commerce with the Orient was his third important goal.

Portuguese sea captains undertook many voyages of discovery. By the time of Prince Henry's death in 1460, these explorers had made

Christopher Columbus 1492

Santa Maria   Niña   Pinta

settlements on the Azores, Madeira, and the Cape Verde islands. Just as important, the Portuguese had traveled 1500 miles south along the west coast of Africa.

DIAS AND DA GAMA   After Prince Henry's death, the Portuguese continued to press southward. They reached a milestone in 1488. In that year, Bartholomeu Dias became the first European to round the Cape of Good Hope, at the southern tip of Africa.

Ten years later, in 1498, Vasco da Gama completed an even more important voyage. After sailing around southern Africa, he pushed on across the Indian Ocean until he reached India. He returned to Portugal with a ship full of spices and jewels, valued at 60 times the cost of his voyage. Da Gama's voyage proved that an all-water route to the East existed. Since this route bypassed the Mediterranean, it enabled merchants to obtain goods directly from the Orient without relying on Italian traders.

Columbus

A sailor from Genoa, Italy, named Christopher Columbus had a different idea for simplifying East-West trade. Instead of sailing eastward to reach the Orient, he wanted to go west. Like most educated people of his day, he knew that the world is round. But he thought it was smaller than it is.

For many years, Columbus tried to raise funds to pay for a westward voyage. Finally, he won the financial support of King Ferdinand and Queen Isabella of Spain. They hoped that such a voyage would bring wealth, power, and prestige to their country.

In August 1492, Columbus left Palos, Spain, with three ships—the

Santa Maria, the *Pinta*, and the *Niña*. For weeks, they sailed westward. At last, on October 12, Columbus sighted land, probably Watlings Island in the Bahamas. He went ashore and took possession of the area in the name of Spain. Believing that he had reached the East Indies, he called the inhabitants Indians. While searching for the Asian mainland, he landed on the Caribbean islands of Cuba and Hispaniola. In the spring of 1493, Columbus returned to Spain, where he was received with great honor.

Columbus made three more voyages across the Atlantic. In the Caribbean Sea, he explored the islands of Jamaica, Puerto Rico, and Trinidad. He also explored part of the coastline of present-day Honduras and Panama in Central America, and the mouth of the Orinoco River in South America. He searched in vain for a westward passage that would lead to the riches of the Indies. Until his death in 1506, Columbus believed that he had reached the Orient. He never realized that he had voyaged to a part of the world that few, if any, Europeans knew about.

Exploration After Columbus

With both Portugal and Spain sending out expeditions, the two nations sometimes claimed the same lands. To prevent disputes, the pope divided the world into two parts. The so-called "Line of Demarcation," drawn in 1493, ran from the North Pole to the South Pole, through a point about 300 miles west of the Azores. (In the following year, the line was moved 1000 miles farther west.) Portugal could claim all newly found lands east of the line, while Spain could claim those west of the line. Thus, Spain gained control over most of the New World. Portugal had a free hand in Africa and Asia. Although Portugal and Spain accepted the Line of Demarcation, other European countries ignored it.

The papal line helped Portugal in eastern South America. In 1500, the Portuguese seaman Pedro Cabral sailed south along the African coast on his way to India. He swung so far west that he sighted the coast of what is now Brazil. After landing, he claimed the area for his country. According to the papal line, this was Portuguese territory, and the Portuguese soon began colonizing it.

VESPUCCI   The Italian navigator Amerigo Vespucci did much to convince Europeans that a New World had been found. He traveled to South America with a Spanish expedition in 1499 and with a Portuguese voyage of exploration two years later. He then wrote letters claiming that he had discovered a new continent. Vespucci's claims impressed a German geographer who published a new map of the world in 1507. He labeled the southern part of the New World "America" in honor of Amerigo (*Americus* in Latin). The name was later applied to the northern part as well.

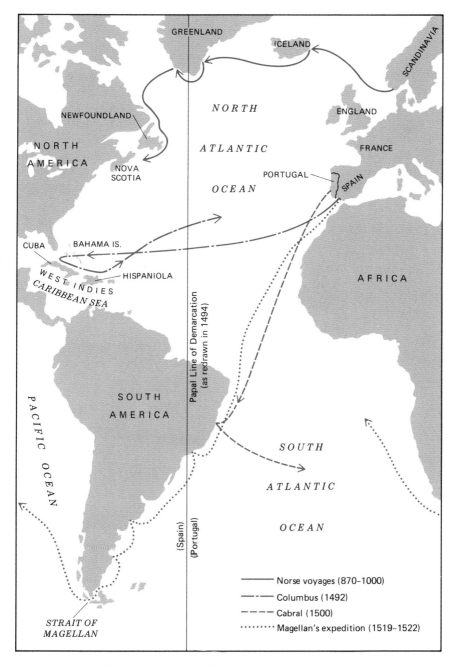

EARLY EUROPEAN VOYAGES TO AMERICA

MAGELLAN   Like Columbus, Ferdinand Magellan wanted to reach the East by sailing west—and he succeeded. A Portuguese in the service of Spain, Magellan left Sanlucar in 1519 with five ships. After crossing the Atlantic, he sailed along the coast of South America to the southern tip. He then passed through the Strait of Magellan (named after him) and entered the Pacific Ocean.

By this time, one ship had sunk, and one had deserted. The three remaining vessels made a very difficult voyage across the Pacific. Many crewmen died of starvation. After three months, the small fleet reached the Mariana Islands. Soon afterward, Magellan was killed by natives in the Philippines. But one of his ships, the *Victoria*, finally made it back to Spain in 1522. The *Victoria* thus became the first ship to circumnavigate (go completely around) the world.

SPANISH COLONIES IN AMERICA

Although Spain's rulers had not been looking for a New World, they quickly realized that it offered them an opportunity to acquire land, wealth, and power. In addition, adventurous and ambitious Spaniards saw a chance to win fame and fortune in the new lands. Others were motivated by the desire to spread Christianity by converting the Indians. These goals of Spanish expansion are sometimes summarized as "glory, God, and gold."

Government of the Empire

Beginning in the late 15th century, the Spaniards created a vast empire in North and South America. In time, Spanish control extended from southern Chile as far north as California. The empire also included most of the islands of the Caribbean. (Brazil, a Portuguese possession, was the only major non-Spanish territory in South America.)

The Spanish colonies were grouped into large districts, each ruled by a viceroy. This representative of the Spanish king exercised almost total power. The viceroy's main responsibility was to carry out the laws made by a governing body in Spain called the *Council of the Indies*. The viceroy also collected taxes and decided how money was to be spent. In addition, he was responsible for the well-being of the Indians. The Spanish settlers had little voice in the government.

Spain strictly supervised the economic life of its colonies in America. It forbade colonists to produce any goods that might compete with Spanish manufactures. It also prohibited the colonists from trading with any country other than Spain. On the other hand, it encouraged agriculture and mining in the colonies. Huge quantities of gold and silver

MAJOR SPANISH EXPLORATIONS IN AMERICA (1513–1542)

Date	Explorer	Achievement
1513	Juan Ponce de León	Searched for legendary Fountain of Youth and explored (and named) Florida
1513	Vasco Núñez de Balboa	Crossed Isthmus of Panama and sighted Pacific Ocean
1519–1521	Hernando Cortés	Defeated Aztecs and claimed Mexico for Spain
1528–1536	Álvar Núñez Cabeza de Vaca	Explored southwest region of United States
1531–1533	Francisco Pizarro	Defeated Incas and added their territories to Spanish empire
1540–1542	Francisco Vásquez de Coronado	In search of legendary "Seven Cities of Cibola," explored southwestern United States; one member of party was first European to see Grand Canyon
1541	Hernando de Soto	Crossed Mississippi River while exploring southern United States
1542	Juan Cabrillo (Portuguese in service of Spain)	Explored coast of California

were shipped to the home country. This wealth made Spain, for a time, the richest and most powerful nation in Europe.

The People

There were four main social classes in Spanish America:

1. The ruling upper class was made up of European-born Spaniards.
2. A second group, called *Creoles*, consisted of colonists born in South America to Spanish parents. Creoles owned or managed the plantations, ranches, and mines. They also worked in commerce and the

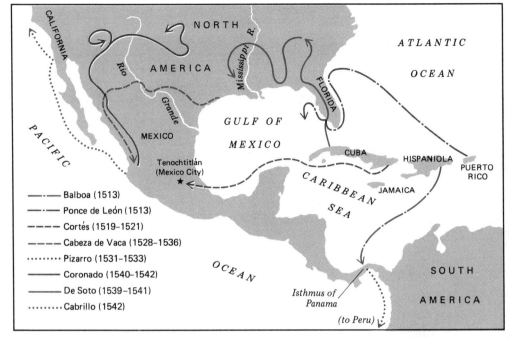

SPANISH EXPLORATIONS IN AMERICA

professions. Although they served as local officials, Creoles were not allowed to fill high government positions.

3. A third class comprised those of mixed Spanish and Indian parentage, the *mestizos*. They worked as laborers, small farmers, artisans, and tradespeople.

4. At the bottom of the social scale were people whom the Spaniards enslaved. First, they forced Indians to work for them. After thousands died, the Spaniards began to rely on black slaves brought from Africa.

The Spanish Legacy

A major contribution of Spain was the introduction of Christianity into the New World. The Spaniards abolished the practice of human sacrifice and converted millions of Indians to Roman Catholicism. In every city and village in Spanish America, the newcomers built churches, including the magnificent cathedrals in Lima (Peru) and Mexico City. The cathedral in Mexico City, begun in 1573, is still the largest church structure in North America.

Catholic missionaries tried to help the Indians by gathering them into mission villages, where they learned trades and better ways to farm. Missionaries also tried to keep the Indians from being forced into slavery.

IMPORTANT SPANISH SETTLEMENTS
IN THE NEW WORLD (1496–1781)

Date	Settlement	Location
1496	Santo Domingo	Dominican Republic
1511	San Juan	Puerto Rico
1514	Santiago	Cuba
1519	Veracruz	Mexico
1524	Granada	Nicaragua
1525	Santa Marta	Colombia
1533	Cartagena	Colombia
1535	Lima	Peru
1535	Guayaquil	Ecuador
1537	Asunción	Paraguay
1538	Bogotá	Colombia
1541	Santiago	Chile
1542	Antigua	Guatemala
1548	La Paz	Bolivia
1565	St. Augustine	Florida
1567	Caracas	Venezuela
1580	Buenos Aires	Argentina
1597	Portobello	Panama
1609	Santa Fe	New Mexico
1706	Albuquerque	New Mexico
1718	San Antonio	Texas
1769	San Diego	California
1770	Monterey	California
1775	Tucson	Arizona
1776	San Francisco	California
1781	Los Angeles	California

Spain introduced to the New World the Spanish language as well as the books and learning of Western Europe. In 1531, the Spaniards set up the first printing press in America, in Mexico City. Twenty years later, Spanish settlers founded the first universities in the Western Hemisphere—in Lima and Mexico City.

To this day, Spanish remains the dominant language of Latin America. Spanish is widely spoken in many parts of the United States as well, particularly in the Southwest. American English has also adopted many words from New World Spanish. Some examples are *bronco*, *desperado*, *bonanza*, *patio*, *canyon*, *mustang*, *rodeo*, and *plaza*. The Spanish influence is equally apparent in many American place-names, from Florida through Colorado and Nevada to California.

Spanish contributions to agriculture were many. The newcomers introduced several animals unknown in the New World, among them horses, cattle, donkeys, pigs, and sheep. The Spaniards also brought in a great variety of plants—wheat, sugarcane, oranges, lemons, and olives.

The coming of the Spaniards had many harmful effects, too. One of the most devastating was the introduction of new diseases such as smallpox, measles, and diphtheria. Because Native Americans had no immunity to these diseases, epidemics swept across America and killed millions. As early as 1510, for example, it was reported that few Indians remained alive in the Bahamas and Hispaniola. According to another estimate, some 90 percent of those in the former Aztec empire died within 50 years of Cortés's arrival.

Spanish rule had other negative aspects, as well. Native Americans, forced to learn Spanish ways, abandoned or forgot much of their own culture. The harsh conditions of slavery destroyed whole communities. And the economy of the Americas lost valuable mineral resources when they were removed to enrich Spain.

OTHER COLONIAL POWERS

Spain and Portugal got a head start in overseas exploration and colonization. But other nations on the Atlantic coast of Europe were not far behind. In America, Spain and Portugal dominated the central and southern regions. So the other powers sent explorers farther north. They wanted to find a northwest passage—a route through or around North America leading directly to the Orient. No one found the shortcut. In time, France, the Netherlands, and England gave up the search and set up colonies to make use of the riches of North America itself.

France

The first explorer sent out by France was Giovanni da Verrazano, an Italian navigator. In 1524, he sailed along the North American coast from North Carolina to Nova Scotia. He was probably the first European to enter New York Bay. Not long afterward, in 1534, Jacques Cartier explored the eastern part of Canada along the Gulf of St. Lawrence. The following year, he made a second voyage, sailing up the St. Lawrence River to the present site of Montreal.

Civil wars in France slowed down further French efforts in the New World. Years later, in 1608, another great French explorer, Samuel de Champlain, founded the settlement of Quebec on a height overlooking the St. Lawrence River. This was the beginning of the first permanent French colony in North America. Champlain also explored parts of New England and New York, and sighted the large lake named after him, Lake Champlain. His exploits earned him the title "father of New France."

FRENCH TERRITORIES The French soon moved out from their bases at Quebec and Montreal to explore the forested lands to the south

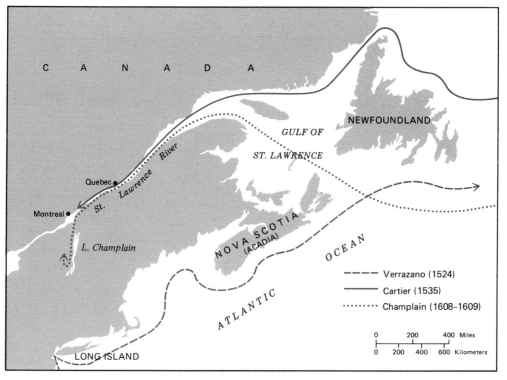

FOUNDING OF FRENCH CANADA

and west. Robert Cavelier de La Salle traveled through the Great Lakes and the Ohio River Valley. Sailing down the Mississippi River to the Gulf of Mexico in 1682, he claimed the entire Mississippi River Valley for France. He called it Louisiana in honor of the French king, Louis XIV.

The French established few large settlements in New France. They wanted mainly to develop a profitable fur trade with the Indians. Thus, the newcomers built trading posts and forts at strategic points. These helped control the waterways and served as centers for the Indian trade. On the whole, the French maintained better relations with the Indians than did other Europeans in the New World. French fur traders lived among the Indians, generally treating them fairly and helping them in many ways. Many Frenchmen married Indian women. Their children, called *métis*, contributed to the spread of white settlement by serving as scouts, guides, and explorers.

FRENCH COLONIAL RULE   New France, the French empire in America, was divided into two provinces, Canada and Louisiana. Each was directed by a royal governor, known as the *intendant*. Intendants were appointed by the king of France and had complete control over the colonists. The people had no voice in the government. Only French

IMPORTANT FRENCH SETTLEMENTS
IN THE NEW WORLD (1608–1764)

Date	Settlement	Location
1608	Quebec	Quebec
1634	Green Bay	Wisconsin
1642	Montreal	Quebec
1673	Fort Frontenac (Kingston)	Ontario
1675	Grand Pré	Nova Scotia
1679	Fort Niagara (Niagara Falls)	New York
1699	Biloxi	Mississippi
1701	Fort Detroit (Detroit)	Michigan
1710	Mobile	Alabama
1716	Fort Rosalie (Natchez)	Mississippi
1718	New Orleans	Louisiana
1719	Baton Rouge	Louisiana
1720	Louisbourg	Nova Scotia
1754	Fort Duquesne (Pittsburgh)	Pennsylvania
1764	St. Louis	Missouri

Catholics could settle in New France. French Protestants (called Huguenots) who wanted to make a fresh start in the New World had to settle elsewhere.

The system of landholding in New France was similar to that in France. Large estates were granted to *seigneurs* (lords). In turn, they rented small farms to *habitants* (settlers). This system tended to discourage the immigration of French families who wanted farms of their own. After 150 years of French control, New France had only 80,000 European settlers.

THE FRENCH LEGACY   French missionaries followed the fur traders into the wilderness to convert the Indians to Christianity. These Catholic priests were called "Black Robes" by the Indians because of their clothing. Many of the missionaries were explorers as well as preachers. Father Louis Hennepin was the first European to see the Falls of St. Anthony on the upper Mississippi River (in present-day Minneapolis). Father Jacques Marquette, along with fur trader Louis Joliet, explored the central Mississippi Valley. Father Isaac Jogues explored Lake George. Killed by the Iroquois, this priest was later declared a saint by the Catholic church. As a result of the work of French missionaries, Catholicism became firmly established in the Mississippi Valley and in eastern Canada.

French culture took hold chiefly in what is now the province of Quebec, in Canada. The lower Mississippi Valley (present-day Louisiana) also developed a distinctly French flavor. In the 18th century, thousands of

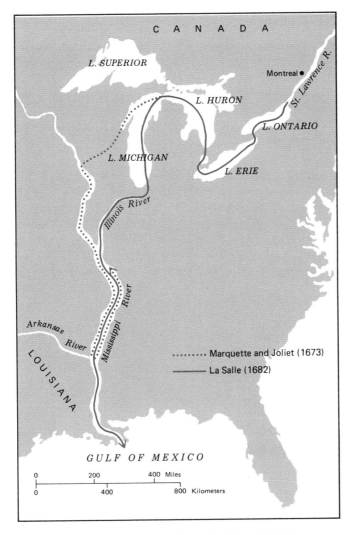

Marquette and Joliet (1673)
La Salle (1682)

EXPLORING THE GREAT LAKES AND THE MISSISSIPPI

French settlers from Acadia (Nova Scotia) were moved to Louisiana. There, they became known as *Cajuns*.

Many place-names in the United States are of French origin. Some well-known examples are Maine, Vermont, Fond du Lac, Eau Claire, and Duluth. The English language has also been enriched by numerous French borrowings. Hundreds of these go back to the 11th century, when barons from France conquered England. But many words are a result of the French experience in the New World. They include *butte, chowder, gopher, lacrosse, portage*, and *rapids*.

The Netherlands

The people of the Netherlands, the Dutch, also set out to obtain a share of the rich trade with Asia. A group of Dutch merchants hired Henry Hudson, an English navigator, to find a new water route to the Indies. In 1609, Hudson sailed his ship the *Half Moon* along the North American coast from Maine to the Carolinas. He entered Delaware Bay and, later, New York Bay. From there, he sailed up the Hudson River as far as present-day Albany.

DUTCH SETTLEMENTS   As a result of Hudson's voyage, the Netherlands claimed the area from the Hudson River Valley south to Delaware Bay. The Dutch called this region New Netherland. In 1613, Dutch merchants established a trading post near Albany. Then, in 1624, a trading company called the Dutch West India Company sent 30 families to be the first European settlers of New Netherland. The Dutch government had granted this company all trading and colonizing rights in the Dutch part of the New World. Most of the settlers went up the Hudson River to the area of the first Dutch trading post. There they founded Fort Orange.

Within the next two years, more colonists arrived. Many of them settled around the area of New York Bay and on the lower Delaware River. A large settlement, New Amsterdam, was made on Manhattan Island. New Amsterdam soon became the seat of government, chief port, and main trading center of New Netherland.

THE PATROON SYSTEM   The Dutch West India Company wanted to encourage settlement in New Netherland. It offered a reward to any company member who transported 50 adults to America and settled them on the land. A member who did this was given the title of *patroon*, along with a large estate on the Hudson River. The patroon supplied the settlers with homes, cattle, and tools. In return, he received part of their produce. A patroon had complete authority over the tenants living on his estate.

Patroonships were granted to a number of rich men from the Netherlands. The Hudson Valley became a region of large estates. But New Netherland failed to attract many settlers. Many of the Dutch who were interested in immigrating did not want to submit to the strict economic and political controls of the patroon system. They could buy land and have more freedom in other colonies.

DUTCH COLONIAL GOVERNMENT   New Netherland was governed by a director general (governor) appointed by the Dutch West India Company. The main purpose of the colony was to earn profits for the company's shareholders by trading with the Indians. Therefore, the company took little interest in the welfare of the settlers and gave them no voice in the government. The company imposed heavy taxes but left education, care of the sick and poor, and other social services to the Dutch Reformed church.

Like the Spanish and French, the Dutch left their mark on North America. Many places in the New York area have Dutch names. Schenectady, Brooklyn, the Bronx, Staten Island, Harlem, and the Bowery are just a few. English words of Dutch origin include *boss*, *bush*, *cookie*, *keelboat*, *scow*, and *sleigh*.

Multiple-Choice Test

1. About how many years before Columbus's voyages did the Vikings explore North America? (a) 100 years (b) 300 years (c) 500 years (d) 1000 years.
2. In the 14th and early 15th centuries, the European trade in goods from the East was dominated by the (a) Dutch (b) Italians (c) Arabs (d) Spanish.
3. Prince Henry's aims included all of the following *except* (a) trading with the Orient (b) winning converts to Christianity (c) finding the New World (d) gaining a share of the slave trade.
4. The first Portuguese explorer to sail around Africa to India was (a) da Gama (b) Dias (c) Vespucci (d) Magellan.
5. Columbus wanted to (a) reach Asia by sailing east (b) prove that the earth is round (c) discover America (d) reach Asia by sailing west.
6. At the top of the social scale in Spanish America were (a) Creoles (b) mestizos (c) métis (d) European-born Spaniards.
7. Spanish settlers introduced to the New World all of the following *except* (a) horses (b) sugarcane (c) wheat (d) corn.
8. Europeans looked for a northwest passage in hopes of (a) escaping Spanish pirates (b) reaching the Orient (c) exploring the Great Lakes (d) trading with the Indians.
9. The French founded all of the following *except* (a) Louisiana (b) Fort Orange (c) Quebec (d) Montreal.
10. The main reason why the Dutch settled in North America was to gain (a) trade (b) political freedom from Spain (c) religious liberty (d) converts for Christianity.

Matching Test

Match the items in column A with those in column B.

COLUMN A
1. Bartholomeu Dias
2. Venice, Genoa
3. astrolabe
4. *Santa Maria, Pinta, Niña*
5. Amerigo Vespucci
6. Pedro Cabral
7. Watlings Island
8. Lima
9. intendant
10. Giovanni da Verrazano

COLUMN B
a. probable site of Columbus's first landing in America
b. first European explorer to land in Brazil
c. site of one of first universities in New World
d. instrument to measure latitude
e. first European explorer to see New York Bay
f. Italian trading cities
g. royal governor in New France
h. navigator for whom New World was named
i. Columbus's ships
j. first European explorer to round Cape of Good Hope

Time-Line Test

On the time line that follows, the letters A–G represent 100-year periods. For each event listed, write the letter that indicates the time period in which the event occurred.

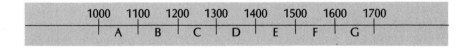

1. Prince Henry founded a school of navigation in Portugal.
2. Marco Polo visited the Orient.
3. Constantinople was captured by the Turks.
4. Magellan's ship the *Victoria* sailed around the world.
5. The printing press came into use.
6. The Renaissance began.
7. The First Crusade was organized.
8. The first Portuguese mariner sailed around Africa to India.
9. Columbus first voyaged to America.
10. The Dutch first settled in the New World.

Map Test

GROUP A

Answer the following questions by studying the map on page 34.

1. On which continent is each of the following places located: (a) Alexandria (b) Antioch (c) Venice?
2. Name the southwest Pacific region now known as Indonesia that was a source of Eastern goods.
3. What countries in northeast Asia produced silk, perfume, and other products greatly valued by Europeans?
4. What was the last body of water that ships carrying Eastern goods had to pass through before they reached (a) Alexandria (b) Constantinople (c) Genoa?
5. What Asian waterway was bypassed by caravans on the overland route to the eastern Mediterranean?

GROUP B

Answer the following questions by referring to the maps on pages 36, 39, 42, 45, and 47, and to the text.

1. What three groups of islands in the eastern Atlantic did the Portuguese discover and settle during the time of Prince Henry?
2. Which Portuguese voyager took possession of land in the Western Hemisphere? Was the area he claimed east or west of the papal Line of Demarcation? What was this region named?
3. Magellan's expedition crossed all of the following waterways *except* the (a) Pacific Ocean (b) Indian Ocean (c) Strait of Magellan (d) Caribbean Sea (e) Atlantic Ocean.
4. From which New World starting point did each of the following Spanish explorers set out: (a) Ponce de León (b) Balboa (c) Cortés (d) Coronado (e) De Soto?
5. Name four large North American lakes sighted by French explorers.

Essay Questions

1. Why was Europe ready to explore and colonize America in 1500 but not in 1000?
2. Describe the voyages of Dias, da Gama, Columbus, and Magellan.
3. Which of these voyages do you think was most important? Why?
4. Describe the main effects of Spanish rule in America.
5. How did the French and Dutch organize their American colonies? Why did their systems fail to attract many settlers?

CHAPTER 4

The English
in North America

Lᴉᴋᴇ ᴏᴛʜᴇʀ ɴᴀᴛɪᴏɴꜱ along the Atlantic coast of Europe, England wanted its share of trade with the East. In 1497 and again in 1498, King Henry VII sent an Italian navigator, John Cabot, to search for a northwest passage to the Orient. Cabot sailed along the east coast of North America from Newfoundland to Chesapeake Bay and claimed the region for England. At this time, however, England lacked the resources and sea power to compete with Spain in the New World.

ENGLAND'S RISE TO POWER

During the reign of Queen Elizabeth I, the granddaughter of King Henry VII, England grew stronger and more adventurous. In the 1560s and 1570s, daring English sailors called "sea dogs" began to challenge Spain's control of the seas. Some sea dogs, such as Sir John Hawkins, smuggled slaves and English goods into Spanish America. Other sea dogs, such as Sir Francis Drake, preyed on Spanish treasure ships and looted Spanish settlements in the New World.

On one of his voyages (1577–1580), Drake retraced Magellan's route around the southern tip of South America and raided Spanish settlements along the Pacific coast of that continent. Continuing northward, he explored the coastline of California and searched for the western end of a northwest passage. Failing to find it, he turned south, landed near present-day San Francisco, and claimed the region for England. Drake then headed west across the Pacific and returned to England via the

RULERS OF ENGLAND (1485–1820)

Ruler	Dates of Rule
Henry VII	1485–1509
Henry VIII	1509–1547
Edward VI	1547–1553
Mary (I)	1553–1558
Elizabeth I	1558–1603
James I	1603–1625
Charles I	1625–1649
(Puritan republic)	(1649–1660)
Charles II	1660–1685
James II	1685–1688
William III and Mary (II)	1688–1702
Anne	1702–1714
George I	1714–1727
George II	1727–1760
George III	1760–1820

Indian Ocean. He thus became the first Englishman to circumnavigate the globe.

The Spanish Armada

The English attacks on Spanish ships and colonies angered King Philip II of Spain. In the summer of 1588, he sent a mighty fleet of 130 ships to conquer England. This Spanish Armada was met by a force of smaller English vessels.

Although the English ships were no match for the armada in size and firepower, they were swift and easy to handle. The English skillfully outmaneuvered their attackers and kept the armada from landing its troops. After several days, the Spanish fleet tried to take refuge in a French port, only to be driven away by exploding English fireboats. The armada retreated north around Scotland, turned south into the Irish Sea, and headed for home. But a terrible storm arose and sank almost half the fleet. The defeat of the Spanish Armada marked the beginning of Spain's decline as a naval power and undisputed ruler of the seas.

Search for a Northwest Passage

Despite Cabot's failure to find a northwest passage, English mariners clung to the belief that there was one. In 1576, Sir Martin Frobisher, in search of such a route, reached Baffin Island and explored Frobisher Bay. Finding traces of gold (or so he thought) on Baffin Island, he made two more trips to the area to develop this resource. But his venture was unsuccessful.

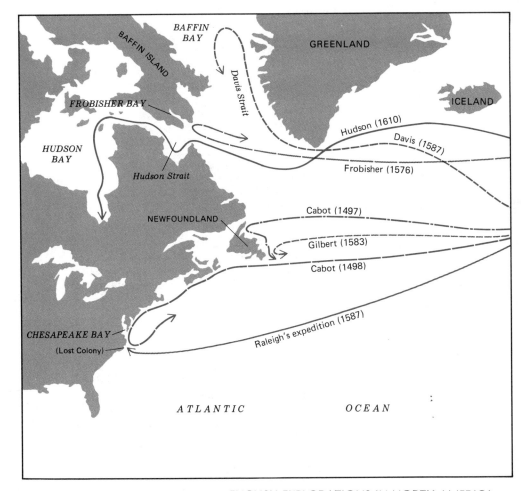

ENGLISH EXPLORATIONS IN NORTH AMERICA

Continuing the search for a northwest passage, John Davis led three expeditions between 1585 and 1587. He discovered the strait that bears his name and explored Baffin Bay. Another effort was made by Henry Hudson in 1610. He sailed through Hudson Strait and entered Hudson Bay. There, mutinous crewmen turned on him and set him adrift in a small boat to die.

Reasons for Colonization

England's rise as a major naval power encouraged merchants to expand foreign commerce and to develop new markets abroad. English sea power also paved the way for the establishment of colonies in the New

World and elsewhere. Since these outposts provided an opportunity to escape from the problems at home, many people were eager to leave England for a fresh start overseas.

ECONOMIC REASONS   Economic need was one reason for the urge to colonize. The population of England was increasing, but the food supply was not. Landlords were finding it more profitable to raise sheep for wool than to grow crops. Landowners turned thousands of their tenant farmers off the land. These laborers had trouble finding work, and many of them wandered about homeless. It was felt that colonies would be useful for resettling the unemployed.

The English also thought that colonies would help the nation's economy in general. A widespread belief at this time was that nations should be self-sufficient and own large stores of gold and silver. A country unable to produce all the raw materials it needed should not buy them from foreigners. Instead, it should own colonies that could supply needed raw materials, provide a market for manufactured goods, and, perhaps, even yield gold and silver. This economic theory about national wealth and the role of colonies is known as mercantilism.

RELIGIOUS REASONS   Religious factors also encouraged colonization. In 1543, the Church of England (the Anglican church) had split from the Roman Catholic church. Instead of the pope, the head of this new church was the English monarch. Everyone was required by law to attend the Anglican church and pay taxes for its support. But there was considerable opposition to the new church. Catholics viewed it as too Protestant; many Protestants considered it too "popish." One group of Protestants—the Puritans—wanted to "purify" the Anglican church by making its rituals simpler. Another Protestant group—the Separatists— broke away completely and worshiped secretly in independent congregations.

There was no religious freedom in England for these opposition groups. People who wanted to worship as they pleased were especially attracted to settling in the colonies.

THE FIRST FOOTHOLDS

The English government did not itself establish colonies abroad, but left the task to private developers. Promoters of a colonizing venture had to seek a grant of land from the monarch, as well as the right to govern the area and to control its trade. Such rights and privileges were granted by the crown in the form of a royal patent, or charter. Those who obtained

Captain John Smith

Jamestown Stockade, 1619

early musket

charters were usually people of wealth, social position, or influence at court.

The first patent authorizing the establishment of a colony in America was granted by Queen Elizabeth to Sir Humphrey Gilbert. In 1578 and again in 1583, Gilbert tried to start a settlement in Newfoundland, but both efforts failed. After Gilbert's death, his colonizing rights passed to his half-brother, Sir Walter Raleigh. In 1587, Raleigh sponsored a settlement on Roanoke Island, off the coast of North Carolina. The settlement disappeared without a trace sometime before 1590 and became known as the "Lost Colony."

It soon became clear that the expense of planting a colony was too great to be borne by a single individual. Therefore, groups of wealthy merchants and investors banded together to sponsor colonial projects. Some formed small companies with only a limited number of members. Others organized larger enterprises called joint-stock companies. Investors who purchased stock in such a company became shareholders and were entitled to a proportionate share of any profits earned.

Jamestown

The first permanent English settlement in America was made at Jamestown, in the region called Virginia. It was sponsored by a group of merchants and investors called the London Company. The company hoped to earn a profit by mining precious metals, exporting New World products to Europe, and trading with the Indians.

EARLY HARDSHIPS   The first group of settlers (about 100 men) landed at the mouth of the James River in the spring of 1607. At the start, everything went wrong with the settlement. The Jamestown colonists, interested chiefly in finding gold, did not concern themselves with planting crops or building shelters. The place the colonists chose for the settlement was swampy and unhealthful. During the first seven months, more than half the settlers died of starvation and disease. Frequent Indian attacks also threatened Jamestown's survival.

Captain John Smith, an adventurer and soldier, did much to save the colony. He took command and put all able-bodied settlers to work building houses and planting crops. Smith also succeeded in obtaining food from the Indians. Because of an injury, Smith returned to England in the fall of 1609. Without his leadership, the colony almost failed. The winter of 1609–1610 was known as the "starving time."

A TURN FOR THE BETTER   Fresh supplies and more settlers kept Jamestown alive. But the colony remained on the edge of failure until several important changes took place:

1. **Land Ownership.**   One of the main reasons for the lack of progress was the system of land ownership. Originally, the Jamestown colonists were merely employees of the London Company, which owned all property, including land. Later, under the governorship of Sir Thomas Dale, individual settlers received their own land. This change encouraged them to work harder.
2. **Family Life.**   The first few women came to Jamestown in 1611. Starting in 1620, many more were encouraged to come. As family life developed, the community became more settled and stable.
3. **Tobacco Cultivation.**   Tobacco was a plant originally grown by the Indians. Its use had become popular in England during the 16th century. One Jamestown colonist, John Rolfe, made a successful business of cultivating and curing tobacco. Soon, the colonists were raising it on a large scale. In 1617, Virginia shipped 20,000 pounds of tobacco to England. Within the next ten years, the figure jumped to 500,000 pounds.
4. **Increased Labor Supply.**   At first, the tobacco fields were worked by indentured servants. These men and women wanted to settle in the New World but did not have enough money to pay for their passage. They agreed to work for a certain period without wages for anyone who paid their way to America. During the time of the indenture agreement—usually from four to seven years—the servants received food and clothing.

In 1619, the first black Africans arrived as prisoners aboard a Dutch ship. They were purchased by the settlers as indentured servants. To meet the ever-growing need for labor, merchants later brought over other Africans and sold them to the colonists as slaves.

5. **Relations With the Native Americans.** Initially, the Indian leader Powhatan tried to drive out the Jamestown colonists. According to legend, John Smith was captured by the Indians and was about to be killed when the chief's daughter, Pocahontas, saved him. In 1614, Pocahontas married John Rolfe, the tobacco planter. For some time thereafter, there was peace between the English and the Indians. In 1622, the Indians broke the peace by killing nearly 350 settlers. The colonists fought back and drove the Indians out of the area.

REPRESENTATIVE GOVERNMENT   At the start, the Virginia colonists had little voice in their own affairs. Laws for the colony were made by a governor and a council—a group of men who advised the governor. All these officials were appointed by the London Company in England. Then, in 1619, the Virginia Company (as the London Company was now called) allowed the colonists to form a representative assembly called the *House of Burgesses*. It was made up of two delegates, or burgesses, from each settlement in Virginia. The House of Burgesses was the first elective legislature in America.

In 1624, King James I canceled the Virginia Company's charter and made Virginia a royal colony. This meant that the king appointed the governor and council. The colonists, however, continued to elect the members of the House of Burgesses.

Plymouth

The second permanent English colony in North America was at Plymouth, Massachusetts, near Cape Cod. (Earlier, John Smith had named this region New England.) The Plymouth colonists had intended to settle in part of the territory granted to the Virginia Company. But their ship was blown off course to the north.

BEGINNINGS   The Plymouth colony was organized by Separatists, many of whom had been living in the Netherlands. The Separatists had gone there to escape religious persecution but were not happy because they wanted to raise their children in an English environment. For this reason, they decided to seek a new home in America.

A group of English merchants agreed to finance the venture. In return, the Separatists promised the merchants all the profits earned by the colony in its first seven years. For the trip to America, some 35 Separatists were joined by about 65 other people from England. The non-Separatists were looking for economic betterment or adventure. Setting sail on the *Mayflower* in September 1620, the group arrived at Plymouth in December and established a settlement.

Before landing, the Pilgrims, as these settlers came to be known, faced the need to form a government of their own. Since they were outside the limits of Virginia, they could not be ruled by the Virginia Company. Pilgrim leaders, therefore, drew up the *Mayflower Compact*. In this document, they agreed to make and obey just and equal laws for the common good. This agreement is one of the earliest expressions of self-government in America.

THE FIRST YEARS   The Pilgrims suffered greatly during the first winter at Plymouth. Shelter was poor, disease widespread, and food scarce. Fortunately, the Indians proved to be friendly. Massasoit, an Indian leader, made a peace treaty with the Pilgrims that lasted for many years. Two other Indians, Squanto and Samoset, showed the Pilgrims how to grow corn and where to hunt and fish.

In the fall of 1621, the Pilgrims set aside a day of thanksgiving for the year's blessings. They invited the Indians to join them in a celebration of peace and plenty—the first Thanksgiving.

John Carver, the first governor of the Plymouth colony, died soon after the Pilgrims landed. His place was filled by William Bradford, who governed wisely for many years. Under Bradford's leadership, two important changes took place: (1) Each adult male acquired land for himself. Earlier, all the land had belonged to the community and was worked in common. (2) The Pilgrims became financially independent by repaying the merchants who had sponsored the new colony.

Massachusetts Bay

In 1628, a small group of Puritans, led by John Endecott, settled in Salem, Massachusetts. Like the Separatists at Plymouth, these people came to the New World in search of religious freedom. The following year, leading Puritans in England formed a joint-stock company called the Massachusetts Bay Company. They acquired the rights to a large piece of land in New England. Under the company's sponsorship, more than 1000 Puritans sailed to the Massachusetts Bay area in 1630, settling in and around Boston. John Winthrop, an able and wealthy Puritan, was the first governor of the Massachusetts Bay Colony.

We must consider that we shall be as a City upon a Hill; the eyes of all people are upon us.

—John Winthrop, addressing Puritan settlers
before their ship landed in Massachusetts

At this time, England was troubled by conflict between its Anglican rulers and religious dissenters. The result was the "Great Migration" of the 1630s. More than 60,000 people, unhappy about conditions in England, came to the New World. Of this number, about 20,000 settled in New England. The Massachusetts Bay Colony grew in strength. It first took over the Maine-New Hampshire region and, later, Plymouth Colony.

Puritanism was the official religion of Massachusetts Bay. Everyone who lived there was forced to support the Puritan church. Only church members were permitted to vote and hold public office. The clergy held great political power as governmental advisers. They also supervised daily life to ensure that people lived according to Puritan values. Anyone who criticized the regime was threatened with banishment from the colony.

OTHER NEW ENGLAND COLONIES

The number of New England settlements grew steadily. Some were established by colonists who moved north and south from Massachusetts. Other colonies were founded by newcomers from England.

Connecticut

Thomas Hooker, a Puritan minister in Massachusetts, disapproved of the harsh rule of the Bay Colony's leaders. In 1636, he led a number of his followers westward to the fertile Connecticut River Valley. They settled in Hartford, which had been founded the previous year by a pioneering group from Hooker's congregation. Other colonists from Massachusetts founded the nearby river towns of Wethersfield and Windsor. Farther south, Puritans from England settled in and around New Haven.

In 1639, Hartford, Wethersfield, and Windsor joined together to form a government. They drew up a constitution with provisions for (1) electing deputies from each town to a legislature, (2) choosing a governor, (3) limiting the terms of office of public officials, and (4) assuring fair taxation. This document, the *Fundamental Orders of Connecticut*, was the first written constitution in America.

Until the 1660s, the settlements in lower Connecticut acted independently as New Haven Colony. In 1662, King Charles II of England united all the towns of Connecticut into a single colony.

Rhode Island

Another clergyman who opposed Puritan rule in Massachusetts was Roger Williams. His outspoken views on religious freedom angered

Massachusetts officials. When they brought Williams to trial and ordered him back to England, he fled and took shelter among the Indians. Other colonists from the Bay Colony soon joined him. Williams then bought land in the Narragansett Bay area from the Indians and, in 1636, founded Providence.

Anne Hutchinson was still another remarkable leader driven out of Massachusetts for religious reasons. With her followers, she moved to Portsmouth. Other Massachusetts colonists founded Newport and Warwick. In time, Providence, Portsmouth, Newport, and Warwick received a charter from England allowing them to set up a government. The four settlements formed a colony known at first as Providence Plantations and later as Rhode Island.

Under Roger Williams, Rhode Island adopted the principle of complete separation of church and state. This meant that the government could not pass laws restricting religious liberty. Nor could the government set religious standards for voting or holding office. Rhode Island was the first American colony to guarantee all its people religious freedom. As a

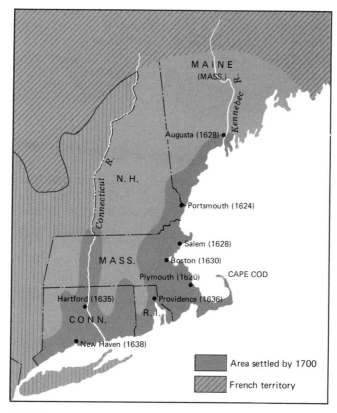

THE NEW ENGLAND COLONIES

result, the colony attracted people of all faiths. Many who were treated badly elsewhere, such as Quakers and Jews, settled in Rhode Island.

New Hampshire and Maine

As early as 1622, two English developers, Captain John Mason and Sir Ferdinando Gorges, acquired the rights to a large area in northern New England. In 1629, they divided their holdings. Mason took New Hampshire, and Gorges took Maine.

The principal towns of New Hampshire were established between 1623 and 1640. Anglicans from England founded Dover and Portsmouth. Exeter was founded by followers of John Wheelwright, a Puritan minister who had been banished from the Bay Colony. In the 1640s, Massachusetts claimed and annexed all these settlements. It retained control of the area until 1679, when New Hampshire received a charter making it a separate royal colony.

In Maine, beginning in the 1620s, a few small towns—Kittery and York, among them—were established along the coast and on rivers. Augusta, the present capital, was founded as a fur trading post on the Kennebec River in 1628. At Casco Bay, settlements that later became the city of Portland were established in 1631. Claiming that Maine, too, was within its boundaries, the Bay Colony took over the region in the 1650s. Massachusetts held Maine until 1820.

THE MIDDLE COLONIES

South of New England lay a region that became known as the Middle Colonies. The first Europeans in this area, the Dutch, had established the colony of New Netherland along the Hudson River. By the 1660s, the colony had 8000 inhabitants.

New York

For many reasons, the Dutch settlement of New Netherland was a great source of irritation for England:

1. The English considered the area rightfully theirs, as a result of Cabot's explorations.
2. New Netherland was a barrier separating the English colonies in New England from those farther south.
3. The Dutch were carrying on extensive trade with the English colonies, in violation of English trade laws.

4. The English were envious of the profitable Dutch fur trade with the Indians.

5. England wanted to control New Amsterdam, with its fine harbor.

OVERTHROW OF THE DUTCH   When Charles II became king of England, he gave New Netherland (which he regarded as English territory) to his brother James, the Duke of York. In 1664, an English fleet sailed to New Amsterdam and called for the surrender of New Netherland. Its governor at this time was Peter Stuyvesant, a haughty, bad-tempered man. He wanted to resist the English, but the people refused to support him. Stuyvesant had to surrender without firing a shot.

In honor of the Duke of York, the English changed the name of the colony and its main town to New York. Beverwyck, the settlement that had grown up around Fort Orange, was renamed Albany.

GOVERNMENT   As proprietor (owner) of the colony, the Duke of York exercised complete control. He ruled through an appointed governor and council, and denied the people representation in the government. After the colonists protested, the Duke of York appointed Thomas Dongan as governor and authorized him to hold elections to a representative assembly. When it met in 1683, it drew up a *Charter of Liberties and Privileges.*

This document provided for an elective assembly, freedom of worship, and trial by jury. Dongan's charter was short-lived, however. When the Duke of York became King James II in 1685, he threw out the charter and did away with the legislature. Representative government was not restored until 1691.

New Jersey

New Netherland had included the region between the Hudson and Delaware rivers. It had a few Dutch and Swedish settlers. When the Duke of York took over New Netherland, he gave the area between the rivers to two of his friends, Sir George Carteret and Lord John Berkeley. The new proprietors named their colony New Jersey. They encouraged colonization by promising settlers large grants of land, representative government, and freedom of religion. English Puritans and Quakers, as well as Scots, Scotch-Irish, and Germans, flocked to New Jersey. The colony grew rapidly.

A group of Quakers purchased Berkeley's rights to the section known as West Jersey. Another group of Quakers and some non-Quakers acquired Carteret's province of East Jersey. In 1702, these new owners surrendered their governmental powers to the king, and the two provinces of New Jersey were united into a single royal colony.

Pennsylvania

Like other English dissenters, members of the Society of Friends (Quakers) lacked religious freedom. They were persecuted not only in England but also in many of the American colonies. The Quakers, believing that war is sinful, refused to serve as soldiers or to pay taxes for military purposes. This stand, in particular, made them unpopular.

WILLIAM PENN'S "HOLY EXPERIMENT" William Penn, the son of a wealthy English admiral, became an ardent Quaker as a young man. His father had long been owed a large debt by King Charles II. After the elder Penn died, his son inherited the claim. To pay it off, the king, in 1681, gave Penn land in the New World. The area was called Pennsylvania ("Penn's woods").

Penn planned a colony where people of all beliefs and nationalities could live together in peace. They would be equal before the law and enjoy freedom of speech and religion. Penn called his plan a "holy experiment." The first settlers arrived early in 1682 and founded Philadelphia (city of "brotherly love"). Before the year ended, Penn arrived to take charge of his colony. He remained in Pennsylvania for two years.

GROWTH AND PROSPERITY Under Penn's direction, Pennsylvania grew quickly. It became one of the largest and most successful of the English colonies, for several reasons:

1. **Many Settlers.** Penn believed in self-government, in making land available on good terms, and in freedom of religion. These ideas attracted many Europeans. Among them were English and Welsh Quakers, Irish Catholics, Scotch-Irish Presbyterians, and German Protestants of various denominations. (The Germans were the ancestors of the Pennsylvania Dutch of today.) Settlement spread northward and westward along the Delaware, Schuylkill, and Susquehanna rivers. Philadelphia became the largest city in the colonies.

2. **Good Government.** Penn wanted to guarantee his colonists a responsible and democratic government. To do this, he drew up a constitution that became known as the first *Frame of Government*. It provided for a deputy governor to be appointed by the proprietor and for a council and an assembly to be elected by the people. At its first meeting, held in 1682, the legislature adopted a code of laws for the colony. Based on Penn's proposals, the code was called the *Great Law*. It declared that all people in Pennsylvania should have the right to worship as they pleased. (Only those who believed in the divinity of Christ could vote or hold office, however.) Provision was also made for the care of the poor and orphans, for protection against unfair trials, and for reasonable punishment and humane treatment for wrongdoers.

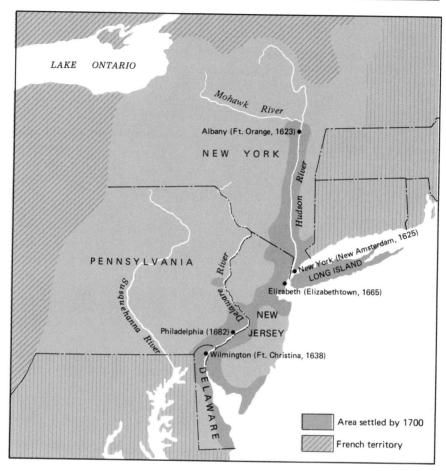

THE MIDDLE COLONIES

3. **Friendly Relations With the Indians.**   Penn dealt fairly and honestly with the Indians. He paid them for their lands and negotiated a treaty that bound whites and Indians in peace "as long as the sun and moon give light." Penn kept his promises to the Indians and remained on friendly terms with them as long as he lived.

Delaware

Among the earliest non-English colonists of North America were Swedes. One group, sponsored by a Swedish trading company, settled Fort Christina (present-day Wilmington) in 1638. Shortly afterward, more settlers arrived. They built forts along the Delaware River and named the region New Sweden.

The idea of sharing the Indian fur trade with the Swedes did not please the Dutch. They also feared that Sweden would expand its colony. The Dutch, therefore, took over New Sweden in 1655. When New Netherland fell to the English in 1664, New Sweden also became English property. The new owner, the Duke of York, renamed it Delaware.

To provide Pennsylvania with access to the sea, the Duke of York gave Delaware to William Penn. It remained "the three lower counties" of Pennsylvania until 1703. At that time, Delaware became a separate colony with a legislature of its own. But Delaware continued to share governors with Pennsylvania until the 1770s.

THE SOUTH

After Jamestown began to do well, the Virginia colony grew steadily. Settlement spread from the banks of the James River to the York and Rappahannock rivers. Restless pioneers began to leave the coast for inland regions. As in other colonies, the frontier (the edge of settlement) moved constantly westward. In 1650, the population of Virginia was 18,500. By 1690, it was 53,000.

Williamsburg, a settlement north of Jamestown, became the colony's capital in 1699. It remained the political, cultural, and social center of Virginia until 1780, when the capital was moved to Richmond.

Maryland

Meanwhile, settlement had begun just north of Virginia. The most important developer in this area was George Calvert, the first Lord Baltimore. He was a prominent Catholic nobleman and a friend of King Charles I. Seeking a haven for Catholics, Lord Baltimore obtained a tract of land from the king but died shortly afterward. The grant then passed to his son, Cecilius Calvert. As proprietor of the colony, the second Lord Baltimore owned all the land and could assign, sell, or rent it as he saw fit. He also had the power to levy taxes, establish courts, and control church matters. But he could not make laws without the advice and consent of the freemen of the colony.

A GOOD START   In 1634, a settlement was started at St. Mary's near the mouth of the Potomac River. Leonard Calvert, the proprietor's brother, became the first governor. The colony did well from the start. Climate and soil were well suited to growing tobacco. This crop soon became an important source of income.

RELIGIOUS FREEDOM FOR CHRISTIANS   Although Maryland was founded as a refuge for Catholics, Christians of all denominations were welcome. People from Virginia and New England, as well as from England, flocked to the colony. Soon Protestants outnumbered Catholics.

Lord Baltimore wanted to prevent religious disputes and protect Catholics against discrimination. Responding to his request, the Maryland assembly passed the *Toleration Act* in 1649. It provided that all Christians were free to worship as they pleased. Although the law did not protect non-Christians, it was an important step toward full religious liberty in America.

The Carolinas

The region south of Virginia was named Carolina for King Charles I (*Carolus* in Latin). The earliest attempt to develop the area was made in

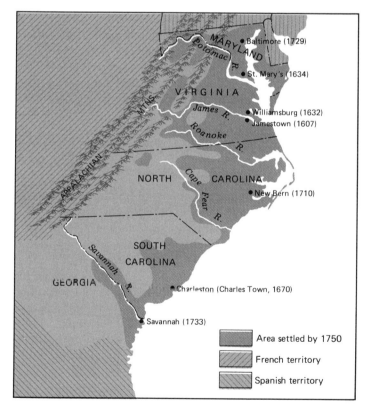

THE SOUTHERN COLONIES

1629, when the king granted Carolina to one of his friends. But this venture produced no results. After Charles II became king, he issued a new charter to eight noblemen in 1663. They received the same proprietary rights as Lord Baltimore had in Maryland.

Ten years earlier, in 1653, pioneers from Virginia had begun to move southward into Carolina, settling along the Chowan River near Albemarle Sound. Their farms became the colony's first settlement. To encourage others to settle, the proprietors offered liberal land terms, freedom of religion, and representation of landowners in an assembly.

The proprietors brought in the first large group of settlers in 1670. They founded Charles Town (Charleston), which soon became a thriving seaport and main center of the colony. Among the immigrants drawn to Carolina were French Huguenots, Scots, Germans, and Scotch-Irish. From England came Anglicans, as well as Quakers and other dissenters.

From the beginning, Carolina seemed to divide itself naturally into a northern and southern section. In the north, the colonists raised tobacco and produced forest products. In the south, the settlers grew rice and indigo. (Indigo is a plant from which a deep blue dye is made.) Carolinians in the north traded mainly with New England merchants, while those in the south dealt directly with England.

The Carolinians grew dissatisfied with proprietary rule. Frequent quarrels broke out between the elective assemblies and the owners' officials. Unable to maintain law and order, the proprietors finally surrendered their charter to the king. In 1729, North Carolina and South Carolina became separate royal colonies.

Georgia

The last of the 13 original colonies to be established was Georgia, named after England's King George II. The colony was founded by James Oglethorpe, an influential member of the English legislative body, *Parliament.* His purpose was to provide a refuge for imprisoned debtors who wanted to make a fresh start in the New World. (At that time, people who could not pay their debts were sent to jail.) The king supported Oglethorpe's plan because a colony in Georgia would serve as a barrier to Spanish expansion northward from Florida. Oglethorpe arrived with a small band of settlers in 1733 and founded Savannah. Few debtors came to Georgia, but the colony did attract settlers from the Carolinas and from Germany, Switzerland, Scotland, and Wales.

The colony was governed by a board of trustees, made up of Oglethorpe and his associates. Aiming to make Georgia a region of small, independent farms, the trustees limited landholding and forbade the use of slaves. These policies, though well-intentioned, were opposed by the colonists and were soon abandoned. In 1752, the trustees surrendered their rights to the king, and Georgia became a royal colony.

THE THIRTEEN ENGLISH COLONIES

Colony	Date of First Settlement	Colony	Date of First Settlement
Virginia	1607	Delaware[†]	1638
Massachusetts	1620	Pennsylvania[†]	1643
New Hampshire	1623	North Carolina	1653
New York*	1624	New Jersey*	1660
Connecticut	1633	South Carolina	1670
Maryland	1634	Georgia	1733
Rhode Island	1636		

*first settled by Dutch   [†]first settled by Swedes

Matching Test

The people listed in column A were important in the founding or early history of the colonies listed in column B. Match the person with the correct colony.

COLUMN A

1. John Smith
2. William Bradford
3. John Winthrop
4. Roger Williams
5. Sir George Carteret
6. William Penn
7. Cecilius Calvert
8. James Oglethorpe
9. Thomas Hooker
10. Thomas Dongan

COLUMN B

a. Pennsylvania
b. Rhode Island
c. Maryland
d. Connecticut
e. Plymouth
f. Georgia
g. New York
h. Jamestown
i. Massachusetts Bay
j. New Jersey

Multiple-Choice Test

1. A major reason for sending the Spanish Armada to England was (a) Spain's desire to take over England's colonies in North America (b) English attacks on Spanish ships (c) Spain's need for northern European ports (d) Spanish dissatisfaction with the papal Line of Demarcation.
2. The first man to explore for the English was (a) Sir Francis Drake (b) Sir Walter Raleigh (c) John Cabot (d) Henry Hudson.
3. John Rolfe aided the Jamestown colony by (a) developing tobacco as a trade item (b) transporting indentured servants (c) granting land to individual settlers (d) forcing the colonists to work harder.

4. Plymouth Colony was organized by (a) Separatists (b) Catholics (c) Quakers (d) Anglicans.
5. The following individuals all left Massachusetts Bay to escape harsh Puritan rule *except* (a) Roger Williams (b) Thomas Hooker (c) Anne Hutchinson (d) William Penn.
6. The first American colony to guarantee all its people religious freedom was (a) Massachusetts Bay (b) Maryland (c) Pennsylvania (d) Rhode Island.
7. The first European settlers in the Middle Colonies were the (a) Swedes (b) Dutch (c) English (d) French.
8. England resented New Netherland for all of the following reasons *except* (a) the Dutch colony divided English colonies in the north from those in the south (b) the Dutch traded with English colonists (c) the Dutch barred English ships from New Amsterdam (d) the Dutch had a profitable fur trade with the Indians.
9. The first governor of Maryland was (a) Leonard Calvert (b) the second Lord Baltimore (c) King Charles I (d) George Calvert.
10. North Carolina and South Carolina (a) were at first part of Georgia (b) were founded as one colony (c) began as a home for jailed debtors (d) attracted few settlers at first.

Time Test

Groups A and B each contain five events in colonial history. The five events in each group are listed in incorrect order. Rearrange each group so that the events are listed in correct order from first to last.

GROUP A

1. first Thanksgiving
2. disappearance of Raleigh's Lost Colony
3. formation of first elective legislature in America
4. founding of Jamestown
5. founding of Plymouth

GROUP B

1. adoption of first written constitution in America
2. founding of Georgia
3. founding of Philadelphia
4. passing of Toleration Act in Maryland
5. surrender of New Netherland to English

Map Test

GROUP A

Answer the following questions by studying the map on page 54.

1. Which explorer seeking a northwest passage was the first to sight and enter Baffin Bay?
2. What landmass did Cabot sight on his 1497 voyage of exploration?
3. Name a strait and a bay discovered by an English explorer in 1610.
4. Who was the first English explorer to reach Baffin Island?
5. What was the farthest point south reached by an English explorer in 1498?

GROUP B

Using maps on pages 61, 65, and 67, answer the following questions.

1. In what present-day state was each of the following settlements located: (a) New Bern (b) Ft. Orange (c) St. Mary's (d) Ft. Christina (e) Elizabethtown?
2. What river served as the boundary between each of the following: (a) Maryland and Virginia (b) South Carolina and Georgia (c) Pennsylvania and New Jersey?
3. Name a settlement on each of the following: (a) Kennebec River (b) Connecticut River (c) James River.
4. Name three settlements that were founded between 1640 and 1685.
5. What settlement was located near the junction of the Hudson and Mohawk rivers?

Essay Questions

1. Why did the English want to colonize the New World in the 1600s?
2. Why was life difficult for the early Jamestown colonists?
3. Describe the system of indentured servitude. Why was it introduced? What system eventually replaced it? Why?
4. What was the role of religion in the founding of Pennsylvania? Massachusetts Bay? Rhode Island? Plymouth? Maryland? Which of these colonies was the most tolerant? the least tolerant?
5. The following documents had to do with government in the English colonies: Mayflower Compact, Fundamental Orders of Connecticut, (New York) Charter of Liberties and Privileges, (Pennsylvania) Frame of Government. Compare the provisions of any two of them.

CHAPTER 5

Colonial Life

THE ENGLISH COLONIES in North America attracted more and more immigrants. At first, the newcomers kept to the customs they had known in their native lands. As the years went by, however, the colonists began to create a distinctly American culture.

THE PEOPLE

Population in colonial America grew steadily. In 1630, there were fewer than 6000 newcomers scattered along the coast. By 1775, the number of settlers and their descendants had risen to 2.5 million. Most of this growth was due to natural population increase—the excess of births over deaths. But immigration also added to the total.

Settlers of English origin made up the largest single group in the colonies. There were also sizable numbers of Africans, Dutch, Irish, and Germans. Other, smaller groups included Belgians, French Huguenots, Scots, Scotch-Irish, Spaniards, Swedes, and Welsh.

Social Classes

Class differences existed in colonial America. But they did not depend entirely on family background, as they did in Europe. A person's ancestry did make a difference, but so did occupation, property, and income. The population was divided into three broad classes:

1. The upper class controlled the economic, political, and social life of the colonies. This group was made up of (*a*) plantation owners in the South

COLONIAL POPULATION GROWTH (1620–1780)

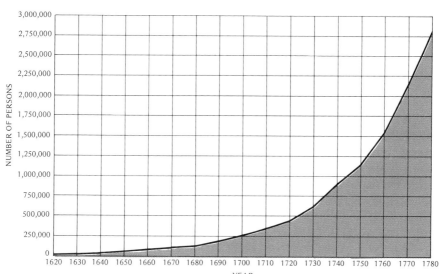

and large landholders in the Middle Colonies, (*b*) wealthy merchants in the cities of New England and the Middle Colonies, (*c*) Puritan clergymen in New England, and (*d*) government officials, lawyers, and doctors.

2. The middle class made up the largest part of the colonial population. This group consisted of (*a*) independent farmers with small plots of land, (*b*) skilled workers, and (*c*) shopkeepers and other tradespeople.

3. The lower class included mainly indentured servants and slaves.

African Americans

A major immigrant group in colonial America consisted of black people from Africa. In the mid-1700s, they and their descendants made up about 20 percent of the population of the English colonies. Almost all blacks were slaves.

Slavery existed in all the colonies but was most widespread in the South. Southern tobacco and rice plantations were large and required much hard work. Most whites, having a choice, were unwilling to do plantation labor. Slaves, bound to their owners for life, provided a constant supply of labor.

The slave trade brought to America thousands of blacks taken on the west coast of Africa. (The trade enriched many "first families" of colonial times, among them the Byrds of Virginia and the Livingstons of New York.) Because of harsh conditions on the slave ships, many of the Africans died on the way to America. Those who survived lost their freedom and much of their culture.

Native Americans

The earliest European settlements could not have survived without Native American help. But friendly feelings between whites and Native Americans soon changed to mistrust. The settlers wanted the Indians' land and took thousands of acres. Although the takeovers were usually arranged through treaties, these were often meaningless. For example, settlers might select one "chief" to speak for hundreds of Native Americans, even though he had no right to do so. Because the idea of land transfer through sale was totally foreign to the Native Americans, the settlers were able to take advantage of their inexperience. They acquired vast tracts of land in exchange for a few trinkets, some iron pots or guns, and several gallons of liquor.

On many occasions, the Native Americans fought back. In the 1670s, for example, King Philip's War destroyed many New England towns. But after "King" Philip (a Wampanoag leader) was killed, the Native Americans were scattered. They were at a disadvantage for several reasons. They were seriously outnumbered. Their bows and arrows were no match for the settlers' guns. They were weakened, too, by diseases (smallpox, measles) brought by the settlers to the New World. Moreover, as the displaced Eastern tribes were pushed westward, they fought among themselves and with tribes into whose territory they moved.

ECONOMIC DEVELOPMENTS

The area of the 13 original colonies contained rich natural resources. There were thick forests, fertile land, broad rivers, and a generally favorable climate. These resources enabled the hard-working colonists to build a good life for themselves. By their efforts, they also helped to create a healthy and growing economy in colonial America.

Farming

About nine-tenths of the colonists made their living by farming. Although farms varied in size and type, most of them were small, family-operated, and self-supporting.

Because farms were widely scattered and travel was slow and difficult, a colonial farm family had to rely on itself for most of its needs. Men and boys cleared the land and raised all the food the family ate. They built the family's house and furniture and made many of the farm tools. Women and girls took care of the vegetable garden and the poultry. They also preserved food, made candles and soap, spun wool and linen yarn, wove cloth (called homespun), and made the family's clothes.

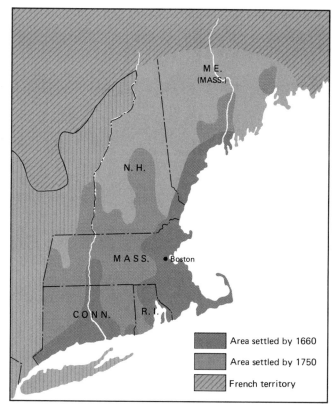

GROWTH OF THE NEW ENGLAND COLONIES (1660-1750)

NEW ENGLAND   New England's soil was rocky, and the land hilly. In addition, the growing seasons were short, and the winters long and severe. Since good farmland was limited, the average farm was small. It produced food primarily for the family, with little left over for sale. The main crop was corn. Other crops included barley, rye, flax (used for making linen), vegetables, and fruits. Farmers raised chickens, pigs, cows, and sometimes a few sheep. A farm family usually owned one or two horses and a pair of oxen.

THE MIDDLE COLONIES   This area had broad, fertile plains and a moderate climate. The Middle Colonies were known as the "breadbasket" because of their large grain crops, especially corn and wheat. Farmers also planted orchards, grew vegetables and flax, and raised livestock. Much of the farm produce was sold. The average farm was of medium size. Only in the Hudson Valley were there large estates.

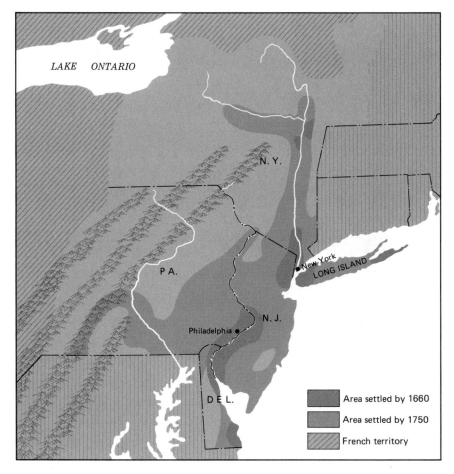

LAKE ONTARIO

N. Y.

P A.

New York
LONG ISLAND

N. J.

Philadelphia ●

D E L.

Area settled by 1660
Area settled by 1750
French territory

GROWTH OF THE MIDDLE COLONIES (1660-1750)

THE SOUTH   The South had good soil, a warm climate, and a long growing season. For their own needs, Southern farmers raised corn, wheat, vegetables, fruits, and livestock. In addition, they produced three major cash crops—crops grown for sale rather than for home use:

1. **Tobacco.**   For a long time, tobacco was the most important crop in the South. Virginia, Maryland, and North Carolina shipped millions of pounds of tobacco to Europe every year. By 1700, Virginia alone was exporting 37 million pounds annually.
2. **Rice.**   The coastal lowlands and marshes of South Carolina and Georgia were ideal for growing rice. It was the chief cash crop of this region.

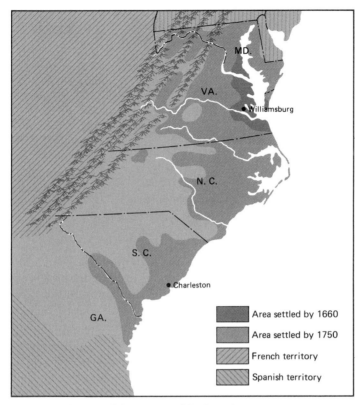

GROWTH OF THE SOUTHERN COLONIES (1660-1750)

3. **Indigo.**   This plant, the source of a blue dye, was second only to rice as a cash crop in South Carolina and Georgia.

Most Southern farms were small, family-operated holdings, similar to those in other colonies. But the South also had large plantations that covered thousands of acres. These big farms produced most of the cash crops. Charles Carroll of Maryland, one of the richest men in the colonies, owned 40,000 acres, worked by 285 slaves.

Industry

In every well-established community, local industries served colonists' needs. Blacksmiths shod horses and produced tools and ironware. Coopers made barrels. Leatherworkers turned out shoes and animal harnesses. Cabinetmakers built furniture. Millers operated gristmills to grind grain into flour.

Local businesses were usually small-scale enterprises, run by the owner and a few boys known as apprentices. Apprentices lived and

Pillory in a New England town

Williamsburg, Virginia

worked with the master craftsman for a number of years, until they learned the trade. (Women were generally excluded from this system, although widows sometimes took over their husbands' businesses.)

Some colonial industries produced goods on a large scale, for sale to other localities and to England. Such businesses had to abide by regulations established by England to prevent violation of its mercantilist policies (see pages 55 and 101).

FISHING AND WHALING The waters off New England teemed with cod, halibut, mackerel, haddock, and herring. Tons of fish were salted, dried, and shipped to Europe and the West Indies. Most of the fishing fleets in New England sailed out of the Massachusetts ports of Gloucester, Marblehead, and Salem. Oyster fishing was a profitable occupation in the Long Island region of New York and in Maryland and Virginia.

Whaling was another important industry. Whaling ships sailed from New Bedford, New London, and Nantucket Island in New England, and from Sag Harbor on Long Island. Whale oil, widely used as fuel for lamps, brought high prices.

SHIPBUILDING To meet the big demand for fishing boats and trading vessels, New England developed a shipbuilding industry. Its main centers were Boston and Salem. Shipbuilders used wood from nearby forests, and they imported iron, canvas, and rope from England. New England vessels became world-famous for their speed and easy handling.

LUMBER AND NAVAL STORES New England's forests also provided lumber for general building purposes. So did the forests in the Hudson Valley, southeastern Pennsylvania, and North Carolina.

The pine trees of North Carolina were the main source of pitch, tar, resin, and turpentine. Because these products were used mainly in shipbuilding, they were called naval stores.

FUR TRADING   Furs and hides were valuable products in all the colonies. In New England and the Middle Colonies, Indians brought pelts (animal skins with the fur on) to such trading centers as Springfield, Massachusetts, and Albany, New York. There, the Indians would exchange their furs for axes, knives, beads, cloth, guns, ammunition, and rum. In the Southern Colonies, fur traders traveled to Indian villages far in the interior to buy pelts and hides (animal skins with the fur removed, used to make leather).

DISTILLING   Molasses imported from the West Indies was used to make rum. By 1750, distilleries in New England were producing several million gallons a year. Rum was sold in the colonies and used as an item of exchange in the fur trade and the African slave trade.

IRONWORKING   The discovery of iron ore in southern New England, the Hudson Valley, and southeastern Pennsylvania led to the establishment of a small but thriving ironworking industry. Colonists in these areas produced unfinished bar and pig iron for export to England. In addition, finished articles were made for local use. They included chains, anchors, barrel hoops, household implements, and tools.

Commerce

Trade and commerce were regulated in accordance with England's mercantilist policies. The American colonies exported raw materials to England and imported finished products mainly from that country. The American colonists also traded with other European countries, with the West Indies, and among themselves.

NEW ENGLAND   Merchants from New England carried on a busy trade with Europe, the West Indies, and other colonies. The colonists exported fish, whale oil, furs, lumber, ships, leather goods, and iron bars. Imports included cloth, glass, china, silverware, tea, and wine. Boston was the region's trading center.

THE MIDDLE COLONIES   Philadelphia and New York were the chief ports of the Middle Colonies. From these cities, ships carried furs, iron, and lumber to England, in exchange for manufactured goods. To the West Indies went wheat, beef, lumber, and horses, in return for sugar, molasses, and wine.

THE SOUTH The South traded mainly with England. Southern exports included tobacco, rice, indigo, naval stores, and hides. In return, the South imported tools, furniture, clothing, tableware, linens, wine, and tea. Charleston, Savannah, and Baltimore were the main trading centers.

TRIANGULAR TRADE Much colonial commerce took the form of triangular trade. One pattern worked like this:

1. Grain, meat, lumber, and fish were taken to the West Indies and exchanged for sugar, molasses, and fruit.
2. These products were transported to England and traded for manufactured goods.
3. The finished articles, such as cloth and glass, were shipped to America and sold to the colonists.

Another pattern of triangular trade operated as follows:

1. Rum made in America was carried to western Africa and traded for slaves.

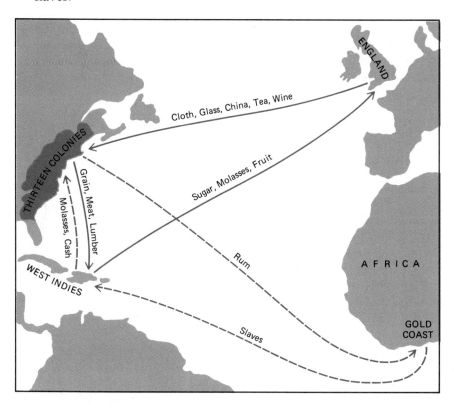

TRIANGULAR TRADE

2. The slaves were transported to the West Indies and exchanged for molasses and cash.
3. The molasses and cash were shipped to New England. The molasses was made into more rum; the cash was used to buy European imports.

RELIGION

In the early days, many colonies set up an established religion—an official church supported by taxes. Anglicanism (the Episcopal church) was the official religion of Virginia, Maryland, Georgia, the Carolinas, and New York. Puritanism (which came to be called Congregationalism) was established in Massachusetts, Connecticut, and New Hampshire.

The power of established religion was made very clear by a witchcraft scare in Salem, Massachusetts. In 17th-century Europe and America, belief in witchcraft was widespread. Respected Puritan clergymen advised church members to be alert for agents of the devil. Early in 1692, several young girls in Salem began accusing villagers of working for the devil. Fear gripped the community. Before the hysteria subsided, 19 people were brought to trial, found guilty of practicing witchcraft, and put to death. Later, many of the accusers and one of the judges asked forgiveness for their part in the tragedy.

The Growth of Toleration

Before long, many other religious denominations took root in America. Most of the Scots and Scotch-Irish were Presbyterians. Americans of Dutch descent belonged to the Dutch Reformed church. Many Germans were Lutherans, while others belonged to smaller groups such as the Mennonites. Quakers were fairly numerous. So were Baptists (of whom Roger Williams is considered the first in America). There were also some Roman Catholics and a few Jews.

Religious toleration increased in America chiefly because people practiced so many different forms of worship. By the 1700s, the strict rules of earlier times had been largely relaxed. Most people found a place where they could worship as they pleased.

But many religious inequalities remained. Roman Catholics were distrusted, mainly because of colonists' fear of the pope. Ironically, Maryland—noted for its early toleration—passed anti-Catholic laws after 1691, when it became a royal colony. Catholics were deprived of their right to vote and to hold public religious services. Although some colonial governments allowed Jews to worship in public, they were barred from voting and holding public office in nearly all the colonies.

The Great Awakening

As time passed, religious enthusiasm tended to weaken. For many colonists, this trend was reversed in the 1730s and 1740s. A new religious movement, the Great Awakening, attracted many followers. Traveling clergymen preached fiery sermons that stirred up crowds. These preachers promised salvation for the repentant and eternal punishment for the wicked. The Great Awakening stimulated church building, the founding of new sects, and the growth of a spirit of concern for the poor and oppressed.

POLITICAL AFFAIRS

England was separated from America by 3000 miles of ocean. The English were busy acquiring territory and expanding trade in other parts of the world. They made little attempt, therefore, to supervise their North American settlements closely during the early years of the colonial period. With colonial governments left pretty much on their own, the settlers learned to rely on themselves and to manage their own political affairs.

Colonial Government

The earliest English colonies were of two types. They were controlled either by trading companies or by individual proprietors. In the 1620s, a third type came into being. This was the royal colony, supervised directly by the English crown.

With the emergence of new colonies and the spread of settlement, many political changes took place. By 1775, there were three kinds of English colonies in America. Rhode Island and Connecticut were self-governing. Maryland, Pennsylvania, and Delaware were proprietary. The remaining eight were royal.

Despite these differences, the structure of government in all the colonies was similar. Each had (1) a governor, (2) a council that served both as adviser to the governor and as the upper house of the legislature, and (3) a representative assembly, or lower house. In the self-governing colonies, qualified voters elected the governor and members of both houses of the legislature. In the proprietary and royal colonies, the proprietor or king appointed the governor. He, in turn, usually selected the council. Voters elected only members of the assembly.

REPRESENTATIVE ASSEMBLIES   Over the centuries, the people of England had fought for, and gained, many important political and civil rights. Some were guaranteed by such documents as *Magna Carta* and the English *Bill of Rights*. Others were part of English common law—law based on court decisions rather than a code of rules.

When the English settlers came to the New World, they brought with them "the rights of Englishmen." These included (1) trial by jury, (2) protection against unreasonable imprisonment, (3) the right to petition the government to correct abuses, and (4) the right to a voice in the government. The latter guarantee was the basis for the establishment of representative assemblies in the colonies.

Like the *House of Commons*—the lower house of the English Parliament—the colonial assemblies had the sole right to levy taxes and decide how public funds should be spent. This "power of the purse" was used as a weapon to curb the authority of the governors and protect the interests of the people represented by the assemblies. By threatening to withhold the money needed to pay salaries, for instance, an assembly could force a governor to approve laws it had passed.

The right to vote was granted only to white male property owners. In some colonies, voters also had to meet certain religious qualifications. Blacks, both slave and free, were denied suffrage (the right to vote). So were women. Despite these restrictions, government, on the whole, was more democratic in the colonies than in England or continental Europe.

TOWN MEETINGS   A special form of local government was the town meeting of New England. People in this region settled close to one another in small villages. The center of village political activity was the town hall, where town meetings were held. In open discussion, the colonists passed laws and levied taxes to support the minister and local schools. Colonists also selected local officials and representatives to the colonial legislature. The town meeting was (and is) a good example of direct democracy. In this form of government, people manage their own affairs rather than relying on elected representatives to govern the community.

THE MILITIA   Every colony had its militia, a local group of armed citizens. Communication and travel were slow in colonial times. As a result, the colonists could not count on the help of regular English troops in emergencies. If an Indian attack or other disorder occurred, militiamen were ready to spring into action together to protect the community.

Serving in the militia gave the colonists valuable public experience. Members learned to work together as an effective fighting unit. Militia officers gained leadership skills. Like the town meeting, the militia provided the colonists with useful training in self-government.

Stresses and Strains

Political life in England's colonies did not always run smoothly. Sometimes, fighting broke out between the people and their government.

BACON'S REBELLION   In the 1670s, there was trouble between colonists and Indians in the frontier areas of Virginia. The royal governor, Sir William Berkeley, followed a cautious policy in order to keep the peace. But backwoods farmers, feeling that more should be done, decided to act on their own. Led by Nathaniel Bacon, they organized a small force and destroyed a band of Indians in 1676. Berkeley proclaimed Bacon a traitor. Many people, however, rallied to his support. Bacon marched to Jamestown, the capital, with 500 men and forced the governor to agree to a campaign against the Indians.

After Bacon's men had left the capital, Berkeley ordered their arrest as rebels. Upon hearing this, Bacon attacked Jamestown, set it on fire, and took control of the government. The governor fled. Shortly afterward, Bacon fell ill and died. Berkeley then returned, put down the revolt, and hanged several of Bacon's followers. King Charles II, angered by the governor's harshness, removed Berkeley from office.

THE DOMINION OF NEW ENGLAND   After James II became king of England, he decided to strengthen English control in the colonies. In 1686, he united New York, New Jersey, and the New England colonies into a single royal province. He called it the Dominion of New England and appointed Sir Edmund Andros as governor. Colonial charters were revoked, and elective assemblies abolished. Town meetings were curbed as well. Aided by a council appointed by the king, Andros made the laws, imposed taxes, and set up his own courts. He also put a stop to colonial trade with countries other than England.

Late in 1688, King James II was overthrown. When the news reached America, a Boston mob attacked Andros, forced him to surrender, and sent him back to England. The new king broke up the Dominion of New England and restored the colonies' charters. But Massachusetts, largely self-governing before 1686, became a royal colony.

LEISLER'S REBELLION   While New York was part of the Dominion of New England, Andros appointed Francis Nicholson as deputy governor there. Nicholson's harsh rule aroused much anger.

When King James II was overthrown and Andros forced out, New Yorkers revolted. They were led by Jacob Leisler, a German-born merchant and a captain in the militia. He took control of the colony, and Nicholson fled to England.

Leisler headed the government for two years, from 1689 to 1691. He was popular with the common people but not with the upper classes, whose influence he tried to curb. Leisler lost power when a new royal governor was appointed to replace him. His enemies convinced the new governor that Leisler was guilty of treason. He was then arrested, sentenced to death, and hanged.

EDUCATION

Educational facilities in the colonies were quite limited. Wealthy families had tutors for their children or sent them to private academies or to school in England. In most towns and cities, schooling of some sort was available to local residents. But in many remote areas, there were no schools at all. And in most colonies, it was forbidden to teach slave children to read or write.

Schools

Massachusetts Puritans set up the first public school system in the colonies. In 1647, the Bay Colony passed a law requiring each town of 50

THE FIRST AMERICAN COLLEGES

Date	Name	Location	Denomination
1636	Harvard	Cambridge, Mass.	Congregationalist
1693	William and Mary	Williamsburg, Va.	Anglican (Episcopal)
1701	Yale	New Haven, Conn.	Congregationalist
1748	College of New Jersey (Princeton)	Princeton, N.J.	Presbyterian
1749	College and Academy of Philadelphia (University of Pennsylvania)	Philadelphia, Pa.	nonsectarian
1754	King's College (Columbia)	New York, N.Y.	Anglican (Episcopal)
1764	College of Rhode Island (Brown)	Providence, R.I.	Baptist
1766	Queen's College (Rutgers)	New Brunswick, N.J.	Dutch Reformed
1769	Dartmouth	Hanover, N.H.	Congregationalist

families to have a primary school. Each town of 100 families also had to have a Latin grammar school (a sort of high school). It prepared qualified boys for college. Similar laws were later enacted in Connecticut and New Hampshire.

Harvard, the first college in the English colonies, was also established by Massachusetts Puritans. It was founded in 1636 to train young men for the ministry. Almost all colonial colleges were started by various religious groups for the same purpose.

In the Middle Colonies, schools were generally church-sponsored or privately owned. The Dutch Reformed church opened the first primary school in New Amsterdam in 1638 and the first Latin school about 20 years later. William Penn established the first private schools in Pennsylvania in 1683. They were supported by the students' families. In the South, private academies were the rule.

Subjects Taught

Most schoolchildren did not advance beyond the "three r's" (reading, 'riting, 'rithmetic). Pupils often learned their letters by using a hornbook. This was a sheet of paper mounted on a board and protected with a thin covering of transparent animal horn. The hornbook displayed the alphabet, the Lord's Prayer, and the Roman numbers.

The most widely used textbook in colonial days was the *New England Primer*. It taught the alphabet, reading, and religion by means of rhymed sayings, such as the following:

> In *Adam's* Fall
> We Sinned all.
>
> Thy Life to Mend
> This *Book* Attend.
>
> The *Cat* doth play
> And after slay.

COLONIAL CULTURE

The writings of the colonial period dealt mainly with religion and history. Roger Williams, Thomas Hooker, Jonathan Edwards, and other New England clergymen wrote sermons and religious tracts. A noted historical work was William Bradford's *History of Plymouth Plantation*, completed in 1651.

An outstanding contributor to the literature of the period was Benjamin Franklin. Under the name Richard Saunders, he published *Poor*

Richard's Almanac every year from 1732 to 1757. It presented useful information, proverbs, and rules of conduct in a witty and interesting style. The almanac was widely read throughout the colonies.

Newspapers

The *Boston News-Letter,* started in 1704, was the first colonial newspaper to last more than a short time. By the middle of the century, weekly newspapers were being published in almost every colony. At a time when communication was limited, newspapers did much to shape American public opinion.

A milestone in colonial life was the Zenger trial. John Peter Zenger, a German immigrant, settled in New York City in the 1720s. He became a printer and publisher. His newspaper, the *Weekly Journal,* carried articles criticizing the royal governor, William Cosby. Angered by these attacks, Cosby ordered Zenger's arrest. At his trial in 1735, Zenger was defended by Andrew Hamilton of Philadelphia, one of the ablest lawyers of the time. He argued that a paper had the right to publish anything that was true.

The jury ruled that Zenger was not guilty, and he was freed. His case strengthened freedom of the press in the colonies. Newspapers could now criticize colonial authorities and their policies openly.

Libraries

During the early colonial period, people had little free time for reading or studying. Moreover, not everyone knew how to read. Books, imported from Europe, were expensive and were bought mainly by ministers, lawyers, and wealthy merchants. The only books in most homes were the Bible and an almanac.

With time, leisure and literacy increased. The first circulating library was founded in Philadelphia in 1731, through the efforts of Benjamin Franklin. Called a subscription library, it was supported by its members, and only they could use it. By the 1770s, there was a subscription library in every large town.

EVERYDAY LIFE

Life for the first settlers was harsh and often cheerless. But by the end of the colonial period, about 170 years later, the standard of living in America had improved greatly. There was also a good deal of variety in everyday customs. Social position made a difference in how Americans lived. So did the region in which they settled.

Homes

The shelters of the earliest settlers were of two main types, either bark-covered huts or log cabins. Later, when more attention could be paid to comfort and beauty, the colonists built better homes.

In New England, the typical colonial house was a low wood cottage with a sloping roof. It was simple, with little outside decoration. (This style is known as a "salt box.") In New York, the Dutch influence could be seen in the brick houses with steeply slanted roofs. Many houses in Pennsylvania were made of local stone.

In the Southern Colonies, wealthy planters built roomy mansions with wide porches, large halls, and graceful stairways. The main house was usually surrounded by a number of separate buildings. These included a kitchen, barn, carriage house, and laundry. Slaves' cabins formed a separate community nearby.

In the average home, furniture was simple and practical. Whether made by the man of the house or by the village carpenter, colonial furniture was built for long life and hard wear. Its beauty and simplicity are admired and copied to this day.

Wealthy merchants and planters imported furnishings from England. Upper-class homes contained fine mahogany furniture and expensive linens, silverware, and china.

A necessary feature in a colonial house was the fireplace. It was used not only for heating but also for cooking. Whale-oil lamps and candles supplied light.

Food

Colonial food was plentiful but plain. Women did most cooking in iron pots hung over a fire in the fireplace. Meat was roasted on rotating spits, and bread and cakes were baked in ovens built into the fireplace.

There was no refrigeration. Meat was salted, dried, or smoked. Vegetables and fruits were pickled, dried, or preserved.

Recreation

The colonists worked hard, but they also found time to have fun. They fished and hunted all year round. In the winter, they enjoyed ice skating and sleigh riding. Dancing, card playing, cricket, and cockfighting contests were other popular pastimes. People also got together at house-raisings, corn huskings, elections, fairs, church services, and weddings. Wealthy Southern planters enjoyed horse racing, fox hunting, and elaborate balls.

The Puritans in New England disapproved of "idle amusements." The sabbath was to be a day of rest and worship. To make sure of this, the

Puritans passed strict "blue laws" banning all forms of entertainment on Sunday.

Travel and Communication

The earliest colonial roads followed narrow Indian trails. By the middle 1700s, the main seacoast cities were connected by post roads— routes for the transport of mail (post). Travelers journeying over these roads on horseback or by stagecoach faced many hazards. They jounced over deep ruts and tree stumps, and got wet crossing streams that had no bridges. They traveled through mud in the spring, dust in the summer, and snow in the winter.

Inland travel was even more difficult because the country was covered with dense forests. Travelers followed Indian trails or paddled boats along one of the many rivers. Because of the lack of good roads, few colonists journeyed far from home.

TEN NOTABLE COLONIAL AMERICANS

ANNE BRADSTREET (1612–1672)   A devout Puritan and mother of eight, she wrote what have been called "the first good poems in America." An early edition of her works (1650) contained much ordinary verse. But a later edition (1678) included poems of great feeling and keen observation.

WILLIAM BYRD (1674–1744)   This wealthy Virginia planter eventually owned almost 180,000 acres. Well educated and widely traveled, he held many offices, including member of the House of Burgesses. His diaries and books (*Journey to the Land of Eden, Progress to the Mines*) give an excellent picture of life in the colonies.

JONATHAN EDWARDS (1703–1758)   After graduating from Yale at 17, this Puritan scholar introduced the Great Awakening to New England. His most important written work is *On the Freedom of the Will*. He was also famous for his emotional sermons, such as those collected in *Sinners in the Hands of an Angry God* (1741).

JOHN ELIOT (1604–1690)   Known as the "Apostle to the Indians," this Puritan clergyman learned the language of the Massachusetts Indians so that he could preach to them. He also helped found 14 protected communities for Indian converts. He translated the Bible into Natick (an Algonquian language) and helped write the *Bay Psalm Book* (1640), one of the first colonial publications.

BENJAMIN FRANKLIN (1706–1790)   Both Americans and Europeans admired this Philadelphian's wisdom and wide range of interests. He turned his talents to many fields, including printing and publishing, invention (the Franklin stove, bifocal glasses), and science (experiments with electricity). During his long public career, he organized the colonial postal system, represented various colonies in Europe, and served the United States during and after its struggle with England.

PETER HARRISON (1716–1775) "America's first architect" was a merchant of Newport and New York. A versatile amateur, he built ships, surveyed land, and designed such classically graceful buildings as King's Chapel in Boston, Christ Church in Cambridge, and the Touro Synagogue in Newport.

COTTON MATHER (1663–1728) This severe Puritan clergyman helped bring on the Salem crisis with his writings on witchcraft. But he also furthered learning. He was a founder of Yale and a respected amateur scientist. Mather was the first native-born American to become a member of the (English) Royal Society.

ELIZA LUCAS PINCKNEY (1722?–1793) Put in charge of three South Carolina plantations at the age of 16, she helped make indigo a commercial crop in the South. She also experimented with flax, hemp, and silkworms. Her example was important to the brilliant careers of her sons Charles and Thomas.

CATHERINE TEKAKWITHA (1656–1680) A New York Indian, she is sometimes called the "Lily of the Mohawks." French missionaries converted her to Christianity. She soon became known for her holiness and charity. In 1980, the Roman Catholic church beatified her (declared her a blessed soul in heaven).

JOHN WOOLMAN (1720–1772) This Pennsylvania Quaker gave up his prosperous business to preach and teach throughout the colonies. He was one of the first Americans to attack slavery. He also worked to help the poor and landless. He gave up wearing dyed clothes because dyes harmed workers, and he refused to eat sugar because it was grown by slave labor. His *Journal* (1774) clearly reveals his simplicity and moral vision.

True-False Test

1. The largest single group of European colonists was of English descent.
2. Slavery existed only in the Southern Colonies.
3. During the colonial period, about 90 percent of the people were farmers.
4. Colonial trade was regulated according to mercantilist policies.
5. King Philip's War was an armed uprising by the colonists against the English army.
6. In most colonies, only white male property owners could vote.
7. The Dominion of New England was organized by colonists in order to overthrow English rule.
8. Most of the colleges founded in colonial times were set up to train young men for the ministry.
9. "Blue laws" were passed to stop the sale of liquor to the Indians.

10. Colonial transportation was aided by an excellent system of paved roads.

Multiple-Choice Test

1. By 1750, the percentage of African Americans in the colonies was **(a)** 5 percent **(b)** 15 percent **(c)** 20 percent **(d)** 30 percent.
2. All of the following were important economic activities in colonial times *except* **(a)** fishing **(b)** coal mining **(c)** shipbuilding **(d)** lumbering.
3. Puritans were the forerunners of today's **(a)** Presbyterians **(b)** Baptists **(c)** Quakers **(d)** Congregationalists.
4. During the colonial period, representative assemblies exercised control over their governors by **(a)** using the power of the purse **(b)** vetoing royal orders **(c)** refusing to meet **(d)** forming alliances with the French.
5. The region noted for town meetings was **(a)** Chesapeake Bay **(b)** the Middle Colonies **(c)** New England **(d)** New Netherland.
6. Bacon's Rebellion was an armed uprising against the royal governor of **(a)** Maryland **(b)** South Carolina **(c)** Virginia **(d)** Pennsylvania.
7. The first public schools in the colonies were organized in **(a)** Massachusetts **(b)** Rhode Island **(c)** Connecticut **(d)** New York.
8. The first college founded in the 13 original colonies was **(a)** Harvard **(b)** Yale **(c)** William and Mary **(d)** Columbia.
9. The Zenger trial was important because it **(a)** increased religious toleration **(b)** led to the founding of the first colonial newspaper **(c)** freed New York from royal control **(d)** strengthened colonial freedom of the press.
10. During the colonial period, food was kept from spoiling by all the following methods *except* **(a)** drying **(b)** refrigerating **(c)** smoking **(d)** salting.

Defining Terms

Give a brief definition for each of the following terms.

apprentice	homespun	pelts
"breadbasket"	hornbook	post road
cooper	miller	rights of Englishmen
Great Awakening	naval stores	"salt box"
hides	*New England Primer*	subscription library

Map Test

Answer the following questions by studying the maps on page 75, 76, 77, and 80.

1. In which of the following colonies had settlement spread farthest west by 1750: (a) Pennsylvania (b) Virginia (c) New York (d) Georgia (e) South Carolina?
2. What was the chief product that colonial merchants shipped to Africa?
3. From what region did colonial merchants obtain molasses?
4. Name five products that were brought to the colonies from England.
5. List three products that the colonists exported to the West Indies.

Essay Questions

1. What were the three main classes in colonial society? Describe the kinds of people in each one.
2. Explain three present-day practices or institutions that we have inherited from the colonial period.
3. What is the meaning of the term "triangular trade"? Describe the operation of one such form of trade.
4. What basic features of government did all 13 colonies have in common in the early 1770s? How did their governmental structures differ?
5. Describe life in either colonial New England or colonial Virginia. Include in your answer the following: economic activities, religion, education, government, amusements.

UNIT 3

An Independent Nation

CHAPTER 6

Difficulties
With
England

FOR MANY YEARS, there was little friction between England and its colonies in North America. Then, in the 1760s, relations began to worsen. A major reason for this change was war between Great Britain* and France.

THE END OF THE FRENCH THREAT

Beginning in the 17th century, England and France were the two main rivals for leadership in Europe. They also competed for control of the seas and for territory and influence in India and North America. Several times during the 17th and 18th centuries, conflicting interests led the two nations into war.

In North America, the underlying causes of Anglo-French rivalry were (1) overlapping territorial claims and (2) competition over the fur trade. Between 1689 and 1748, three wars that started in Europe soon spread to the colonies. In the course of these struggles, the French and their Indian allies raided English frontier settlements. The British, in turn, tried unsuccessfully to seize Canada.

The fourth and final struggle was the French and Indian War

---

*When England and Scotland became one country in 1707, the resulting union was known as *Great Britain*. The people were called *British*. The terms *England* and *English*, however, continued in use.

WARS BETWEEN ENGLAND AND FRANCE (1689–1748)
(Names in parentheses refer to conflicts outside America.)

Dates	War	Main Events
1689–1697	King William's War (War of the League of Augsburg)	French-led Indians raided frontier outposts in New England and destroyed village of Schenectady. English colonials captured Port Royal, Nova Scotia. French later retook this stronghold and forced English out of some Hudson Bay trading posts. Peace treaty provided for return of all seized areas to previous owners.
1702–1713	Queen Anne's War (War of the Spanish Succession)	On northern frontier, French and Indians raided Maine settlements and destroyed Deerfield, Mass. English expedition attacked and seized Port Royal. In the South, colonists from Carolina attacked St. Augustine and Indian missions in Spanish Florida. (Spain was allied with France.) Treaty ceded Newfoundland, Hudson Bay, and all of Acadia (Nova Scotia) except Cape Breton Island to Britain.
1744–1748	King George's War (War of the Austrian Succession)	New Englanders captured French fortress of Louisbourg on Cape Breton Island. Once again, French and their Indian allies raided colonial settlements in Maine and New York, including Saratoga and Albany. Peace treaty restored Louisbourg to France.

(1754–1763). Unlike the other three conflicts, it broke out in North America and then spread to Europe, where it was known as the Seven Years' War (1756–1763).

The French and Indian War: Early Years

The immediate cause of the French and Indian War was a dispute between France and England over land west of the Appalachian Mountains. The French had long claimed the valley of the Ohio River as part of New France. The English also claimed the area, considering it part of Virginia. In the 1740s, American fur traders began to extend their operations into the Ohio Valley. At the same time, other colonists were becoming interested in this fertile region as a place to settle. These trends worried the authorities in New France.

OUTBREAK OF THE WAR   In 1753, the French began to build a chain of forts from Lake Erie south to the Ohio River. Governor Robert Dinwiddie of Virginia then sent George Washington, a 21-year-old surveyor and fellow Virginian, into the area. His mission was to warn the French that they were trespassing on English territory and to demand that they leave. The French rejected the demand and continued to strengthen their position in the Ohio Valley.

In 1754, the French built Fort Duquesne at the point where the Allegheny and Monongahela rivers join to form the Ohio River. This strategic site (present-day Pittsburgh) was the key to the Ohio Valley and a main gateway to the West. This time, Dinwiddie sent a force of militiamen, led by Washington, to take Fort Duquesne. About 40 miles from the fort, the colonials defeated a small group of French soldiers and quickly built an outpost called Fort Necessity. But the French returned with reinforcements and drove out the Virginians. This encounter marked the beginning of the French and Indian War.

THE ALBANY PLAN OF UNION   Meanwhile, the British had set up a meeting to organize the colonies against the French. In 1754, representa-

THE AMERICAN COLONIES
OF ENGLAND AND FRANCE (1750)

	English Colonies	French Colonies
Population	About 1,200,000 concentrated in 13 colonies along Atlantic coast.	About 80,000 widely scattered over area 20 times size of English possessions.
Economy	Mainly agriculture. Also shipbuilding, lumbering, manufacturing, and commerce. Colonists largely self-sufficient.	Fur trading with Indians as main source of income. Heavy dependence on imports from Europe.
Government	Each colony a separate governmental unit. Authority divided between British officials and colonial assemblies. Colonies had great difficulty in uniting, even against common danger.	Highly centralized. King and officials exercised complete authority. Plans of action could be put into effect quickly.
Relations With Indians	Generally poor. Only Iroquois Confederacy sided with English against French.	Generally good. Most Eastern Woodland tribes supported French against English.

This famous cartoon appeared in Benjamin Franklin's newspaper, the *Pennsylvania Gazette*, shortly before the Albany Congress convened in 1754.

tives from seven colonies met at Albany, New York. This *Albany Congress* had two main purposes: (1) to gain the help of the Iroquois Confederacy and (2) to unite the colonies for purposes of defense. To achieve these aims, Benjamin Franklin of Pennsylvania proposed the *Albany Plan of Union*. It provided for a congress of delegates representing all the colonies. This "grand council" would have the power to maintain an army, levy taxes, deal with the Indians, and control westward expansion.

Both Britain and the colonial legislatures rejected Franklin's plan. Britain felt that a union of the colonies would make them too strong. And the individual colonies were unwilling to give up any of their powers to a grand council. Although defeated, the Albany Plan indicated that at least some colonists were thinking about union.

FRENCH VICTORIES   The French did well in the early years of the French and Indian War. They won an important victory in 1755 at Fort Duquesne. Edward Braddock, commander of the British forces in North America, led an army of English soldiers and colonial militiamen against the fort. Unfamiliar with wilderness warfare, Braddock marched into a trap. A few miles from the fort, a combined force of French and Indians, hidden behind trees and rocks, surprised the British and colonials. Braddock was mortally wounded, and his army completely routed. Braddock's aide, Washington, led the survivors back to safety.

In 1757, the French took key British outposts, including Fort Oswego on Lake Ontario and Fort William Henry on Lake George. The French also prevented the British from seizing Ticonderoga in northeastern New York and Louisbourg in Nova Scotia.

The French and Indian War: Later Years

The tide began to turn for the British after William Pitt became prime minister of England in 1757. He sent more soldiers and supplies to America and appointed able officers. Pitt's actions encouraged colonial

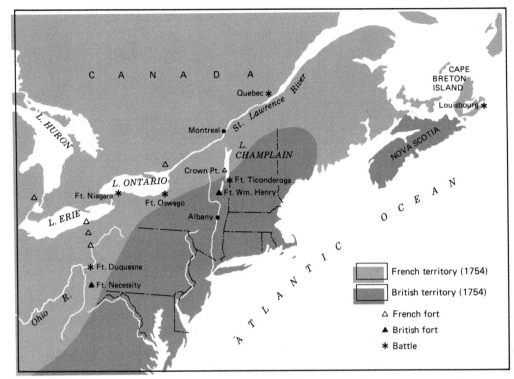

THE FRENCH AND INDIAN WAR: MAJOR BATTLES

legislatures to support the war effort more actively. People in England and in the colonies began to feel that the French could be defeated. Filled with this new spirit, the British and colonials took Louisbourg and drove the French from Fort Duquesne in 1758. The following year, British-led forces captured the French outpost of Fort Niagara in western New York and seized Ticonderoga and Crown Point in northeastern New York.

THE ENGLISH CONQUEST OF CANADA   The most powerful French stronghold in North America was Quebec, situated on a high cliff overlooking the St. Lawrence River. In 1759, a British fleet sailed up the St. Lawrence. The ships carried 9000 British troops under the command of James Wolfe. For four months, Wolfe tried to crack Quebec's defenses. Finally, in the dead of night, he landed his troops at the foot of a cliff near the city. They climbed to the top, something the French had thought could not be done. The next morning, the two forces confronted each other on the Plains of Abraham, a field on the outskirts of Quebec. In the battle that followed, both Wolfe and the Marquis de Montcalm, the French commander, were killed. The British defeated the French and captured the city. This was the decisive battle of the war. The following year, the British took Montreal, and France's power in North America was broken.

THE PEACE TREATY   France and England continued to fight in other parts of the world for another three years. Therefore, the French and Indian War did not end officially until 1763, when the *Treaty of Paris* was signed. Its four provisions relating to America were as follows:

1. France ceded Canada and all the land east of the Mississippi River (except New Orleans) to England.
2. New Orleans and the region that France claimed west of the Mississippi went to Spain, an ally of France.
3. Spain gave Florida to England in exchange for Cuba, which Britain had taken during the war.

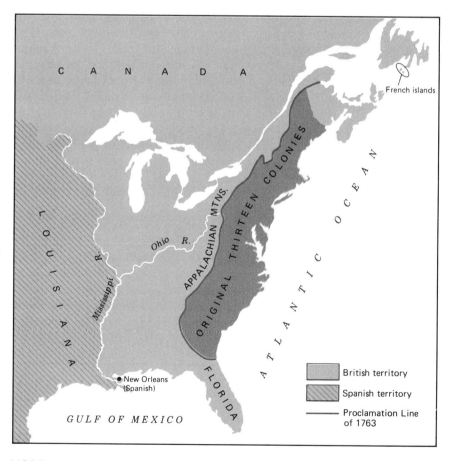

NORTH AMERICA AFTER THE TREATY OF PARIS (1763)

4. France kept two small islands in the Gulf of St. Lawrence for fishing stations. It also retained several islands in the West Indies (Haiti, Martinique, Guadeloupe, St. Lucia).

INCREASED BRITISH CONTROL

At the end of the French and Indian War, Great Britain was the strongest nation in the world and the dominant power in North America. But Britain was also heavily in debt. The war had cost a great deal, and the colonies had not been generous in their financial support.

A Change in Policy

As early as 1650, England had started to pass laws restricting colonial trade and manufacturing. These actions were in line with England's mercantilist aims. In general, the laws had two goals: (1) to expand English shipping and manufacturing, and (2) to encourage colonial production of raw materials needed by the home country.

For many years, the English regulations were not taken seriously. Colonial merchants dealt in forbidden goods and traded with foreign ports that were supposed to be off limits. In addition, the English made little effort to enforce the laws strictly. (When Andros tried to do so in the 1680s, he stirred up violent opposition.) The attitude of the English was known as "salutary neglect"—a helpful policy of letting well enough alone.

After the French and Indian War, Britain decided that it was time for a change. The British empire in North America, which had grown huge, now had to be defended, not neglected. To British leaders, it seemed reasonable to ask the colonists to help pay for the war and share the cost of maintaining troops to protect colonial frontiers.

To carry out its program, the British government decided to enforce the existing trade laws and to introduce new revenue measures as well. Steps were also taken to increase the authority of British officials in America and to send them more help. Unfortunately for Britain, the colonists had become accustomed to salutary neglect. Having acquired the habit of self-rule, they did not welcome increased British regulation. The result was resistance rather than acceptance.

Writs of Assistance

Even before the French and Indian War ended, the colonists showed that they would oppose stricter British control of trade. In 1761, officials began to use writs of assistance to stop colonial merchants from

BRITISH REGULATION OF COLONIAL
TRADE AND MANUFACTURE (1650–1750)

Date	Name	Provisions
1650	Navigation Act	Foreign vessels were banned from trading with colonies without England's approval.
1651	Navigation Act	Goods could be imported into colonies only in ships owned and staffed by English (including colonials).
1660	Navigation Act	"Enumerated articles" from colonies (including sugar, tobacco, and indigo) could be shipped only to England or its colonies.
1663	Staple Act	Most European goods for colonies had to go to England first and be taxed. From there, goods had to be reshipped on English vessels.
1673	Navigation Act	Duties had to be paid on enumerated articles in intercolonial trade.
1696	Navigation Act	To enforce trade regulations, authority of customs and naval officers in colonies was increased.
1699	Wool Act	No colonial wool or wool products could be shipped overseas or from one colony to another.
1705	Enumerated Articles Act	Rice, ship timber, naval stores, and hemp were added to list of enumerated articles.
1721	Enumerated Articles Act	Beaver skins and furs were added to list of enumerated articles.
1732	Hat Act	Intercolonial sale of hats was prohibited.
1733	Molasses Act	High duties were placed on molasses imported by colonists from French West Indies.
1750	Iron Act	Manufacture in colonies of finished iron products was restricted.

illegally trading with foreign nations. The writs were general search warrants. They allowed customs officers to enter any ship, home, or warehouse and search for smuggled goods.

James Otis, a Boston lawyer representing a group of Massachusetts merchants, challenged the use of writs of assistance. He argued that they violated a fundamental English right: to be free from unreasonable

Samuel Adams

The Boston Massacre, 1770

George III

searches and seizures. The courts ruled that the use of writs was legal, but the colonists continued their protest.

The Proclamation of 1763

Another British action that irritated the Americans concerned the Ohio Valley. After the French were defeated, colonists began to pour into this desirable region. The Indians there became alarmed. In the spring of 1763, they rose up under a leader named Pontiac. The Indians destroyed most of the British frontier forts in the area and killed many white settlers before Pontiac's Rebellion was put down in the fall. To avoid further trouble, Britain issued the *Proclamation of 1763*. Among other things, this act (1) ordered all settlers in the Ohio Valley to move back east, (2) forbade the establishment of new settlements west of the Appalachians, and (3) prohibited traders from entering the region without government approval.

American colonists, especially those on the frontier, resented the Proclamation of 1763. They had helped win the Ohio Valley from the French. Now, England was trying to keep them from developing the region. Many pioneers ignored the proclamation and moved into the forbidden area.

The Sugar Act

Another British law of the 1760s was designed to raise more money from the American colonies. This law was the *Sugar Act* of 1764. It increased duties on refined sugar, textiles, and other goods imported from non-British sources. (Duties are taxes on imports.) To discourage smuggling, the act *lowered* the duty on colonial imports of foreign molasses. The Sugar Act also expanded British control by adding more products to the list of enumerated articles—those that could be sold only to Britain or its colonies.

The merchants of New England and the Middle Colonies complained that the higher import duties and the stricter enforcement of old trade laws would ruin the colonial economy. Defying the British authorities, these merchants continued to smuggle goods into the country and to carry on trade with foreign nations.

The Quartering Act

Still another source of colonial irritation was the *Quartering Act* of 1765. This British law was passed in response to a request by Thomas Gage, commander of British forces in America. The act required colonial legislatures to provide funds, living quarters, and supplies to help meet the cost of keeping British troops in America.

The colonists objected to England's policy of maintaining a large peacetime army in America, and they did not want to pay for the army's support. When New York's assembly refused to provide all the supplies Gage requested, Parliament suspended the lawmaking powers of the assembly until it agreed to do so.

The Stamp Act

No other British law of the 1760s stirred up such a storm of protest as the *Stamp Act* of 1765. It taxed newspapers, almanacs, pamphlets, playing cards, and legal documents (wills, licenses, deeds, and so on). A government stamp had to be placed on each of these articles to show that the tax had been paid.

COLONIAL PROTEST   Unlike the trade laws, the Stamp Act affected all the colonists, and they showed their opposition in many different ways. Some formed secret patriotic groups, known as the Sons of Liberty, to resist the tax. Mobs attacked stamp-tax collectors and drove them from their homes. Merchants canceled imports from Britain. People vowed to boycott (stop buying) English products until the tax was repealed. At the urging of Patrick Henry, the Virginia House of Burgesses passed a resolution asserting that it had the sole power to tax Virginians. "No taxation without representation" was the slogan of the day.

In the fall of 1765, delegates from nine colonies met in New York City as the *Stamp Act Congress*. Demanding repeal of the tax, the delegates drew up a declaration that summarized the main arguments of the colonists:

1. The colonists were entitled to the rights of Englishmen.
2. Taxation without the consent of representatives elected by the people violated these rights.
3. Since the colonists were not represented in the English Parliament, it could not tax them.

BRITISH REACTION   England was disturbed by the strong colonial reaction to the stamp tax. Some officials, including William Pitt, protested against the tax. More important, English merchants suffered badly from the colonial boycott. Parliament, therefore, repealed the Stamp Act in 1766. At the same time, however, it passed the *Declaratory Act*, which reaffirmed Parliament's authority over the colonies "in all cases whatsoever."

The Townshend Acts

Britain was still looking for additional revenues from the colonies. In 1767, Parliament passed a group of measures known as the *Townshend Acts*. They levied duties on colonial imports of glass, lead, paint, paper, and tea. The income from these duties was to be used to pay the salaries of such colonial officials as governors and judges. (Previously, their salaries had been controlled by the colonial legislatures.) The Townshend Acts also restated the right of officials to use writs of assistance in the search for smugglers.

The Massachusetts legislature, led by Samuel Adams, urged the colonies to cooperate in resisting English taxation. The colonists responded with a boycott of many English products. It was so effective that it led to the repeal, in 1770, of all the Townshend taxes except the one on tea. This duty, though slight, was kept to show that Parliament still had the right to tax the colonies.

The Boston Massacre

The troubles of the 1760s turned into violence in 1770. The place was Boston. There, as elsewhere, relations between the colonists and British troops were tense. One March evening, a crowd of Bostonians shouted insults and threw snowballs at some British soldiers. The soldiers fired into the crowd, killing five people and wounding six others. Angry citizens called the event the Boston Massacre.

Prominent Bostonians urged the British to remove their troops from the city. When the British did so, further violence was avoided. The captain and a group of the soldiers involved in the shooting were tried for murder. Most of them, including the captain, were found not guilty. Only two were convicted of manslaughter, and they were later released.

A WORSENING CRISIS

For a time after the Boston Massacre, tensions lessened. British officials lived peaceably among the colonists and went about their normal business. But it was the calm before the storm.

Committees of Correspondence

Men like Samuel Adams were determined to keep anti-British feeling alive. In 1772, he and other Sons of Liberty in Boston formed a local Committee of Correspondence to publicize complaints against the British. Adams urged other communities in Massachusetts to form similar committees, and the idea soon spread throughout most of colonial America. This communications network enabled the various towns and colonies to keep one another informed of new developments. The committees not only helped shape public opinion but also encouraged a feeling of unity among the colonies.

Trouble Over Tea

Anger and opposition erupted once again when Parliament passed the *Tea Act* of 1773. This law was designed to aid the financially troubled British East India Company. The Tea Act allowed the company to ship tea directly to America without paying the heavy duty required in England. A small import tax still had to be paid in America, but the company could easily undersell colonial importers of English tea, as well as smugglers of foreign tea.

Even though the Tea Act would actually lower the cost of tea in America, colonists objected to it for several reasons:

1. Colonial tea merchants would be unable to match the company's low prices, and many merchants would be ruined.
2. The move would enable the British East India Company to gain exclusive control of the American tea trade.
3. If Parliament granted similar rights to other English companies, all colonial merchants would be put out of business.

In New York and Philadelphia, public anger forced the East India Company to take its tea back to England. In Charleston, the tea was

Bostonians pay the tax collector—not with money but with tar and feathers and steaming hot tea. This lithograph was published in London in 1774. (The Bettmann Archive)

locked up in a warehouse. In Boston, citizens refused to allow the unloading of three tea ships. During the night of December 16, 1773, Sons of Liberty, dressed as Indians, boarded the ships and quickly dumped 342 chests of tea (worth $75,000) into the harbor. This Boston Tea Party inspired similar "parties" elsewhere in the colonies.

Punishing the Colonies

Determined to make the colonies respect its authority, the British government moved quickly to punish Massachusetts for the Boston Tea Party. In 1774, Parliament passed four *Coercive Acts*, with the following provisions:

1. The port of Boston was closed to all commerce until the colonists paid for the destroyed tea.
2. The people of Massachusetts were deprived of the right to elect certain officials, select jurors, and hold town meetings, except by permission. Thomas Gage was appointed military governor of the colony.
3. British soldiers and officials accused of certain crimes in Massachusetts were to be tried in England, not in the colony.

4. People in all the colonies were required to feed and house British soldiers.

A fifth law enacted at this time was the *Quebec Act*. It extended the boundary of the Canadian province of Quebec southward to the Ohio River. This law was not passed to punish the colonists. But Americans regarded it as a punishment, because it gave the Ohio Valley—claimed by several colonies—to Canada. The act would also subject the area to French-Canadian law (with its emphasis on centralized, royal authority) and to settlement by Roman Catholics. The colonists called this entire group of five laws the "Intolerable Acts."

The First Continental Congress

With Boston Harbor closed to commerce, the people of the city faced economic ruin. The other colonies rallied to Boston's support by sending food and supplies. Some colonial leaders warned that the British punishment of Massachusetts endangered the liberties of all the colonies. Others declared that Massachusetts was "suffering in the common cause of America." There was widespread agreement that united action was necessary. A call went out to convene an intercolonial congress.

Delegates from all the colonies except Georgia met in Philadelphia in September 1774. This *First Continental Congress* took the following three major steps:

1. The Congress issued a *Declaration of Rights*. It stated that the colonists were entitled to all the rights of Englishmen. The colonial legislatures alone had the right to tax the colonists (subject only to veto by the king). The declaration called the Coercive Acts unconstitutional and asked the people not to obey these laws.
2. The delegates organized themselves into the Continental Association. As members, they agreed not to trade with Britain or to use English goods until the Coercive Acts were repealed.
3. The delegates decided to meet again the following spring if their grievances were not settled by then.

Is life so dear, or peace so sweet, as to be purchased at the price of chains and slavery? Forbid it, Almighty God! I know not what course others may take; but as for me, give me liberty or give me death!

—*Patrick Henry, urging the Virginia legislature to prepare for war, March 1775*

Matching Test

CoLumn A

1. Navigation Act of 1651
2. Proclamation of 1763
3. Sugar Act
4. Quartering Act
5. Stamp Act
6. Declaratory Act
7. Townshend Acts
8. Tea Act
9. Coercive Acts
10. Quebec Act

CoLumn B

a. restated right to use writs of assistance
b. punished Boston and Massachusetts
c. extended boundary of Canada southward
d. limited colonial expansion westward
e. confined colonial imports to British ships
f. required colonies to help pay for British troops in America
g. lowered tax on molasses
h. granted favors to British East India Company
i. taxed printed matter and legal documents
j. stated Parliament's authority over colonies

Multiple-Choice Test

1. The causes of the French and Indian War included all of the following *except* (a) conflicting territorial claims by England and France (b) competition over the fur trade (c) the discovery of gold in the Appalachian Mountains (d) the movement of Americans into the Ohio Valley.
2. The Albany Plan of Union was proposed by (a) Samuel Adams (b) Benjamin Franklin (c) George Washington (d) Edward Braddock.
3. The decisive event of the French and Indian War was (a) the French capture of Fort Oswego (b) the British seizure of Fort Niagara (c) the capture of Quebec (d) the fall of Montreal.
4. As a result of the French and Indian War, the western boundary of British territory in North America was fixed at (a) the Appalachian Mountains (b) the Mississippi River (c) the Allegheny and Monongahela rivers (d) Lake Erie.
5. After the French and Indian War, Britain (a) became a second-rate power in Europe (b) began a policy of salutary neglect (c) loosened its hold on its American colonies (d) decided to enforce its trade laws more strictly.

6. The Stamp Act aroused heated opposition because it   **(a)** taxed articles that most colonists used   **(b)** slowed down mail deliveries   **(c)** was passed by the colonial assemblies   **(d)** provided that British soldiers were to be quartered in American towns in peacetime.
7. The British responded to the Stamp Act crisis by   **(a)** sending more troops to America   **(b)** closing the port of Boston   **(c)** stopping colonial exports   **(d)** repealing the law.
8. The colonists forced the British to repeal most of the Townshend taxes by   **(a)** killing troops in Boston   **(b)** boycotting English goods   **(c)** destroying English imports   **(d)** refusing to unload British ships.
9. Colonists objected to the Tea Act of 1773 because it   **(a)** raised the price of tea   **(b)** gave colonial merchants an unfair advantage   **(c)** cut off colonial supplies of tea   **(d)** threatened to put colonial tea merchants out of business.
10. The main reason for calling the First Continental Congress was to   **(a)** protect colonial liberties   **(b)** declare independence from Britain   **(c)** plan an attack on Quebec   **(d)** organize the Boston Tea Party.

Map Test

Locate the following places on the maps on pages 98 and 99. Then, referring to the text, as necessary, explain why each place was important during the time of the French and Indian War.

1. Louisbourg
2. Fort Duquesne
3. Albany
4. New Orleans
5. Quebec

6. St. Lawrence River
7. Ticonderoga
8. Fort Oswego
9. Montreal
10. Mississippi River

Essay Questions

1. Compare the English and French colonies in North America at the beginning of the French and Indian War in terms of population, economy, government, and Indian relations.
2. What effect did the French and Indian War have on the size of Britain's empire in North America? on Britain's relations with its 13 American colonies?
3. Why did Britain change its policy toward the American colonies after 1763?
4. How did American colonists fight the Stamp Act?
5. Why did the First Continental Congress meet? What actions did it take?

CHAPTER 7

The Revolutionary War

ABOUT SIX MONTHS after the First Continental Congress adjourned, war broke out between the American colonies and England. The conflict was to last from 1775 to 1783 and result in American independence. But independence was not the colonists' goal at first—and, indeed, never the goal for some of them.

ATTITUDES OF THE PEOPLE

At the time of the Revolutionary War, about 2.5 million people lived in the 13 American colonies. Approximately a third of the colonists, known as Patriots, actively opposed British rule. Another third, called Loyalists or Tories, remained loyal to Britain. The rest of the people were neutral, favoring neither side. As the war went on, most of the neutral colonists became Patriots.

The Patriot cause had the support of several educated leaders who wrote and spoke well. One of the first to gain public attention was James Otis. He was a Massachusetts lawyer whose pamphlets reached a large audience. His sister, Mercy Otis Warren, wrote political plays and poetry. A Philadelphia lawyer named John Dickinson wrote a series of essays, *Letters From a Farmer in Pennsylvania* (1768), which attracted many readers in both America and England. Another skilled propagandist was Boston's Samuel Adams. He used incidents such as the Boston Massacre to fan public anger. Engraver (and silversmith) Paul Revere produced anti-British cartoons that were circulated throughout the colonies.

The main argument of the Patriots rested on the belief that the colonists were entitled to the "rights of Englishmen." One of these was the right not to be taxed without the people's consent: "no taxation without representation." The Patriots regarded the colonial assemblies as their representative bodies. Only these assemblies, the Patriots insisted, had the authority to levy taxes on the colonists.

The English point of view was that Parliament represented the interests of the entire British empire. No Irish representatives sat in Parliament—and yet Ireland had long been taxed as part of the British empire. Most English political leaders supported the official position that Americans, like the Irish, were indirectly represented by Parliament and should therefore pay the taxes required of them. But some prominent leaders—including William Pitt and Edmund Burke—urged compromise instead of war.

THE EARLY MONTHS

Expecting armed conflict, the men of Massachusetts began to organize into a militia in the fall of 1774. They called themselves Minutemen because they stood ready for action at a minute's notice. They drilled regularly and provided themselves with weapons and ammunition.

Lexington and Concord

In defiance of Thomas Gage, the British military governor, the Massachusetts assembly met secretly and prepared for war. Gage found out about these preparations, however. In April 1775, he sent a detachment of soldiers from Boston to Lexington to capture the "rebel" ringleaders John Hancock and Samuel Adams. The British soldiers were also ordered to seize gunpowder stored at nearby Concord. But the colonists learned of Gage's plans in advance. On the night of April 18, Paul Revere and another Patriot, William Dawes, rode through the countryside, spreading news of the oncoming British.

When the British troops arrived at Lexington on April 19, they were met by 70 local Minutemen. In an exchange of shots, 18 colonists were killed or wounded. The British then went to Concord, where another fight took place. As Gage's troops marched back to Boston, the aroused colonists, hiding behind houses, trees, and stone walls, poured a steady stream of gunfire into the ranks of the "redcoats." (The British soldiers were so nicknamed because of the color of their uniforms.) About 1600 British troops and 4000 American militiamen took part in the action that day. The British suffered 273 casualties (killed and wounded), and the colonists 93.

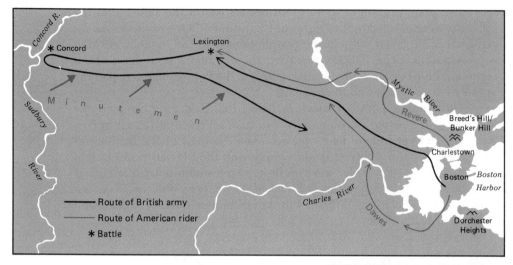

LEXINGTON AND CONCORD

The Second Continental Congress

Three weeks after Lexington and Concord, in May 1775, the *Second Continental Congress* assembled. It met at the State House (later called Independence Hall) in Philadelphia. John Hancock of Massachusetts was elected president. The delegates faced the choice of giving in to the home country or continuing to resist until colonial grievances were satisfied. They decided to resist, by force if necessary.

To provide for the defense of the colonies, Congress (1) established a Continental army, which included the Minutemen in the Boston area; (2) appointed George Washington commander in chief of the Continental army; and (3) issued a call to the colonies to raise troops and help pay for the war effort. At the same time, however, the delegates reaffirmed their loyalty to the crown. They appealed to King George III to prevent further hostile action by Great Britain, so that peaceful relations might be restored.

Disperse, ye rebels; lay down your arms!

—British officer to Minutemen at Lexington

Stand your ground. Don't fire unless fired upon; but if they mean to have a war, let it begin here!

—John Parker's order to Minutemen at Lexington

THE COLONIES VS. GREAT BRITAIN: RELATIVE STRENGTHS AND WEAKNESSES

	Strengths	Weaknesses
Colonies	A great leader, George Washington	Continuous turnover because of short-term enlistments; soldiers unused to military discipline
	Fighting for freedom on familiar ground	Practically no navy
	Soldiers skilled in Indian-style, hit-and-run warfare	Unity hindered by local jealousies
	Foreign military and financial aid	Chronic shortage of money and supplies
Britain	Experienced generals	Fighting in hostile territory
	Well-equipped and disciplined troops	Hampered by traditional strategies
	Good navy	Long supply lines

Ticonderoga and Crown Point

Years before the war started, Ethan Allen had organized a militia in the region of Vermont. Allen's men called themselves the Green Mountain Boys. In May 1775, as the Second Continental Congress was meeting, a small force of Allen's militia secretly crossed Lake Champlain and attacked the British forts at Ticonderoga and Crown Point in northeastern New York. The Americans captured the forts, seized badly needed cannon and ammunition, and sent these supplies to the aid of the Americans in the Boston area.

Fighting Around Boston

After the fighting at Lexington and Concord, about 10,000 militiamen set up camps around Boston. As more and more colonials came to their aid, the American forces decided to drive the British from the city.

BUNKER HILL   To obtain a commanding position over Boston and its harbor, the Americans secretly occupied Breed's Hill, near Bunker Hill, and began to fortify it. On June 17, the British attacked the Americans. The redcoats were pushed back with heavy losses in their first two attempts. But they captured the hill on their third charge, when

Mary Ludwig Hayes ("Molly Pitcher")

the colonists' supply of ammunition ran out. In this Battle of Bunker Hill (actually fought on Breed's Hill), the Americans inflicted far more casualties than they suffered. They also proved their courage and fighting ability.

Don't fire until you see the whites of their eyes.

—William Prescott's instructions to Continental soldiers
at the Battle of Bunker Hill

BOSTON FREED Soon after the Battle of Bunker Hill, George Washington arrived in the Boston area to assume command of the Continental army. The following spring (March 1776), troops under Washington's command seized Dorchester Heights, overlooking Boston Harbor. The American troops fortified the position with the artillery captured at Fort Ticonderoga. Now they had the British at their mercy. William Howe (who had succeeded Gage) was forced to withdraw his troops from Boston by sea. The Americans had freed Boston from British occupation.

Invasion of Canada

Meanwhile, the colonists launched a campaign to gain the support of French-Canadians in the province of Quebec. In the fall of 1775, the Americans began a two-pronged invasion of Canada. One column, led by Richard Montgomery, pushed up along Lake Champlain, captured Montreal, and went on to Quebec. Here, Montgomery's men were joined by a second force under Benedict Arnold. His troops had made a difficult march across the interior of Maine. But the combined attack on Quebec ended in failure. Montgomery was killed, Arnold was wounded, and many Americans were taken prisoner. The colonials then tried to besiege

Quebec. British reinforcements broke the siege, however, and the Americans retreated to Ticonderoga in the spring of 1776.

Fighting in the South

Americans had better luck in the South. Early in 1776, militiamen crushed a 1500-man Loyalist force at Moore's Creek Bridge, in North Carolina. Later that year, the British tried to attack Charleston, South Carolina, but were driven off by American troops.

Moving Toward Independence

Even after fighting had grown bitter, many colonists still hoped to patch up their differences with Britain. But such an outcome became less likely as the months passed. King George III was determined to force the colonists to bow to British authority. He proclaimed them to be in a state of rebellion. He also approved an act of Parliament closing the colonies to all trade and commerce. In addition, the king increased the strength of the British army in America by hiring thousands of foreign soldiers from Germany. (Since many of these mercenaries were from the German state of Hesse-Cassel, they are known as Hessians.)

More and more Americans began to feel that the colonies had to break away from England. The spirit of independence was sparked by a pamphlet called *Common Sense*, published in January 1776 by Thomas Paine, a recent immigrant from England. Paine blamed the king for the colonists' troubles. He argued that it was foolish for a whole continent to be controlled by a small island 3000 miles away. In stirring words, Paine called upon America to break its ties with Britain.

Meanwhile, the Second Continental Congress began to carry out the functions of a central government. It established an intercolonial postal service, with Benjamin Franklin as postmaster general. It sent delegates abroad to seek foreign aid. The Congress also organized a navy, authorized American ships to attack English ships, and proclaimed the opening of colonial ports to trade with all countries except Britain.

Declaring Independence

In June 1776, Richard Henry Lee of Virginia introduced a resolution in Congress declaring that "these United Colonies are, and of right ought to be, free and independent states." Congress then chose a committee to draw up a *Declaration of Independence* (see page 561), which was written chiefly by Thomas Jefferson.

The Declaration first stated that "all men are created equal." They are endowed by God with the rights to "life, liberty, and the pursuit of happiness." If a government threatens these rights, the people are entitled "to alter or to abolish it, and to institute new government." The document then listed 27 "injuries and usurpations"—acts that King George III and Parliament had committed against the colonists. It pointed out that the colonists had repeatedly petitioned the king to correct these injustices but that he had ignored the appeals. For these reasons, the 13 colonies were dissolving their connection with Britain and establishing themselves as free and independent states.

Congress adopted the Declaration of Independence on July 4, 1776. All ties with Great Britain were now cut, and a new nation, the United States of America, was born. The rebellion that had started as an attempt by the colonists to protect their rights as Englishmen had become a struggle for independence.

THE MIDDLE YEARS

After the British left Boston in the spring of 1776, the war shifted from New England to the Middle Colonies. In the two years that followed, both sides won important victories.

Retreat From New York

Recognizing the strategic value of New York City, Washington moved his army south to defend the area. At the same time, Howe made plans to capture it. In July 1776, supported by a strong fleet, the British occupied Staten Island. During the next four months, they drove the Continental army out of Brooklyn Heights on Long Island, Harlem Heights in Manhattan, and White Plains in Westchester County. Washington's skillful handling of his army kept it from being completely destroyed by the more powerful enemy. The Americans finally managed to withdraw across the Hudson River to New Jersey, leaving New York City in the hands of the British.

Trenton and Princeton

Pursued by the British, the battered Continental army retreated south across New Jersey. As the Americans crossed the Delaware River into

I only regret that I have but one life to lose for my country.

—*American spy Nathan Hale before his execution
by the British, 1776*

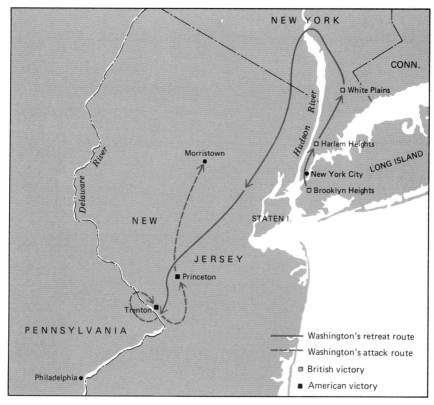

WASHINGTON'S MOVEMENTS (JULY 1776–JANUARY 1777)

Pennsylvania, they seized all the boats on the river to prevent the British from following them. On Christmas night in 1776, during a blinding storm, Washington led his troops back across the ice-choked Delaware. He surprised a force of Hessians camped at Trenton, New Jersey, and completely overwhelmed them. The Americans took some 900 prisoners and a large store of supplies.

Howe sent a force under Lord Cornwallis to catch "the old fox," as Washington was called. Outmaneuvering the redcoats, Washington defeated two British regiments at Princeton. He then set up winter quarters near Morristown, New Jersey. The bold strokes at Trenton and Princeton gave the Continentals new hope.

Failure of the British Plan

The main British objective in 1777 was to divide the colonies by splitting off New England. To do so, the British planned to occupy New York State in a three-pronged drive:

1. Barry St. Leger was to march one force east from Lake Ontario through the Mohawk Valley.
2. Howe was to lead another army northward up the Hudson Valley from New York City.
3. John Burgoyne was to lead a third army south from Canada along Lake Champlain. The three forces were to meet at Albany.

The British strategy was unsuccessful. St. Leger encountered fierce resistance in the Mohawk Valley and was forced to retreat to Canada. Howe and Burgoyne also failed to carry out their parts of the plan.

THE PHILADELPHIA CAMPAIGN Instead of proceeding up the Hudson, Howe sailed from New York City to Chesapeake Bay. He then marched on the American capital, Philadelphia. Washington tried to stop the British but was beaten at Brandywine on September 11, 1777.

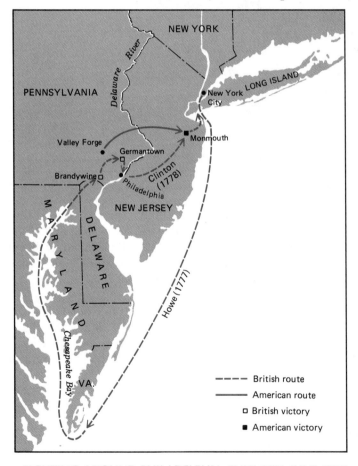

FIGHTING AROUND PHILADELPHIA (JULY 1777–JUNE 1778)

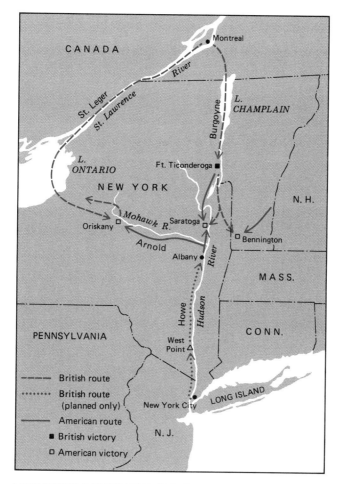

NEW YORK CAMPAIGNS (JUNE 1777–OCTOBER 1777)

Howe occupied Philadelphia later that month. When the Americans tried to drive him out, they were turned back at Germantown.

Washington then withdrew and set up winter quarters at nearby Valley Forge. That winter (1777–1778) was a bitter one for the American army. Shelter and clothing were inadequate, food was scarce, and pay was irregular. The disheartened troops endured almost unbearable hardships. With courage and steadiness, Washington managed to keep his army together as a fighting force during this very trying period.

THE BATTLE OF SARATOGA   Burgoyne, meanwhile, did march south from Canada, according to plan. He captured Fort Ticonderoga in July 1777 but then ran into trouble. His soldiers became exhausted, supplies

These are the times that try men's souls. The summer soldier and the sunshine patriot will, in this crisis, shrink from the service of his country; but he that stands it *now*, deserves the love and thanks of man and woman.

—*Thomas Paine*, Crisis, *1776*

ran short, and the aroused settlers fought him every step of the way. To capture American supplies, Burgoyne sent an expedition to Bennington, in present-day Vermont. But a force of New England militia met the expedition and defeated it. Finally, Burgoyne and his men were surrounded near Saratoga, New York, by a Continental army commanded by Horatio Gates. Two fierce battles followed. Decisively defeated, Burgoyne surrendered on October 17, 1777.

The American victory at Saratoga was the turning point of the war. It wrecked the British plan to divide the colonies. It boosted Patriot morale. And it convinced France to aid the American cause openly.

Foreign Aid

Hoping to weaken England, other European powers—France, Spain, and the Netherlands—had been secretly helping the Americans with supplies, weapons, and credit ever since 1776. After Saratoga, which showed that American victory was possible, France agreed to enter into an open alliance with the United States. Benjamin Franklin, a congressional representative in France, played a key role in the successful negotiations. Early in 1778, France and the United States signed military and trade agreements. Under their terms, France sent money, supplies, a small army, and a fleet of ships to aid the Americans. The Netherlands also signed a treaty of alliance.

In addition, the Americans benefited from the direct assistance of a number of foreign volunteers who served with the Continental army. The Marquis de Lafayette, a wealthy French noble, gave invaluable help as an aide to Washington. Baron de Kalb, a German-born officer in the French army, fought bravely for the Americans until he was killed in the Battle of Camden, in South Carolina. Another German, Baron von Steuben, reorganized and trained the Continentals at Valley Forge. (He is often called the "drillmaster of the Revolution.") Two Poles also aided the American cause. Thaddeus Kosciusko planned the fortifications of West Point, in New York. Casimir Pulaski, leader of a cavalry corps, was killed at the siege of Savannah, Georgia.

THE END OF THE WAR

In the spring of 1778, Sir Henry Clinton replaced Howe as British commander in chief. Fearing a French attack now that a Franco-American alliance had been formed, Clinton decided to abandon Philadelphia and concentrate British strength in New York City. As Clinton's forces marched across New Jersey, Washington left Valley Forge and began to pursue them. In a battle at Monmouth on June 28, Washington's Continentals nearly defeated the retreating English, but the redcoats escaped and reached New York. Washington took up a position north of the city. He kept the British confined within the New York area until almost the end of the war.

Clark in the Midwest

Fighting also took place on the western frontier, in the region called the Northwest Territory. Here, the British were stirring up the Indians to attack American settlements. To end these raids, George Rogers Clark led a band of frontier fighters into the area in the summer of 1778. He captured the British forts at Kaskaskia and Cahokia (in present-day Illinois) and at Vincennes (in what is now Indiana). In December, however, British reinforcements from Detroit retook Vincennes. Clark and his troops then undertook a rugged march of more than 150 miles through the wilderness in the dead of winter (February 1779), surprised the garrison at Vincennes, and forced it to surrender. The Americans thus gained control of the Northwest Territory.

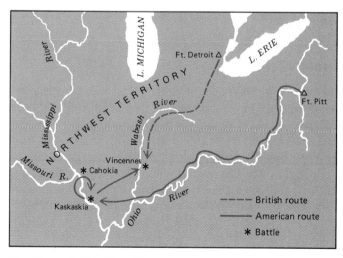

CLARK IN THE MIDWEST (MAY 1778–FEBRUARY 1779)

I have not yet begun to fight.

—*John Paul Jones's reply to the British commander after the latter had demanded the surrender of the* Bonhomme Richard

The War at Sea

Before the French fleet came to the aid of the Continentals, American sea power was very limited. There were a few small warships and a number of privateers. (Privateers are privately owned merchant vessels and fishing boats that are fitted with guns and authorized to attack enemy ships.) These naval units transported supplies and munitions from Europe. They also seized military equipment that was on its way to the British forces fighting in America. In addition, the American vessels attacked British ships on the high seas and raided English coastal towns. By the end of the war, the Americans serving at sea had captured or destroyed nearly 800 enemy vessels.

An outstanding American naval hero was John Paul Jones. This Scottish-born sea captain seized many British merchant ships and raided the coast of England. Commanding the *Bonhomme Richard*, Jones attacked the English warship *Serapis* on September 23, 1779. In the most dramatic naval battle of the Revolution, Jones forced the *Serapis* to surrender and sailed it back to America. Another naval hero was John Barry. A native of Ireland, he won fame for his skill in capturing British fighting ships.

Arnold's Treason

Benedict Arnold had fought valiantly for the American cause in the early part of the war. He had played an important role in the Continental victory at Saratoga. In 1780, he was given command of West Point, a fort controlling the Hudson River. Soon afterward, he entered into a plot to surrender West Point to the British.

Arnold's plan was discovered when John André, an English officer with whom Arnold was negotiating, was captured and found to have plans of the fort in his possession. Learning of André's capture, Arnold escaped to a British warship on the Hudson River. He was subsequently made an officer in the British army and fought against the Patriots for the rest of the war. In America, the name Benedict Arnold became a synonym for traitor.

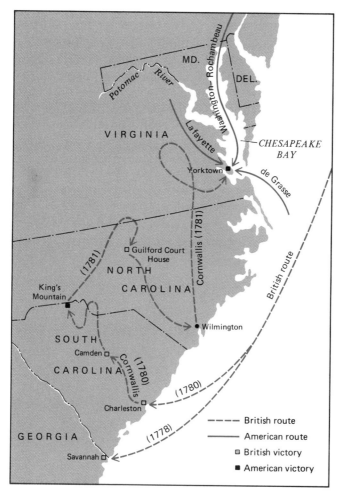

BRITISH CAMPAIGN AND SURRENDER
IN THE SOUTH (1778–1781)

The British Attempt to Win the South

Failing to make headway in New England and the Middle Colonies, the British turned their attention to the South. They captured Savannah in December 1778 and Charleston in May 1780. In August of that year, British forces defeated an American army under Gates at Camden, South Carolina. A British attempt to invade North Carolina, however, was beaten back when sharpshooting frontiersmen defeated a Loyalist force at King's Mountain in October.

AMERICAN COUNTERATTACKS Late in 1780, Washington sent Nathanael Greene, one of his ablest generals, to take charge of the Continental troops in the South. Greene skillfully drew the British army under Cornwallis into the interior of North Carolina, far from British supply bases on the coast. Though Greene lost nearly every battle, he so weakened the British that they were forced to withdraw to the coastal city of Wilmington, North Carolina. Greene then turned south and recaptured most of the inland positions held by the British in South Carolina and Georgia. By the summer of 1781, the British in the South occupied only the seacoast cities of Savannah, Charleston, and Wilmington.

SURRENDER AT YORKTOWN   In May 1781, Cornwallis led his army north from Wilmington and invaded Virginia. He tried to destroy the American forces defending the area. But the outnumbered Continentals,

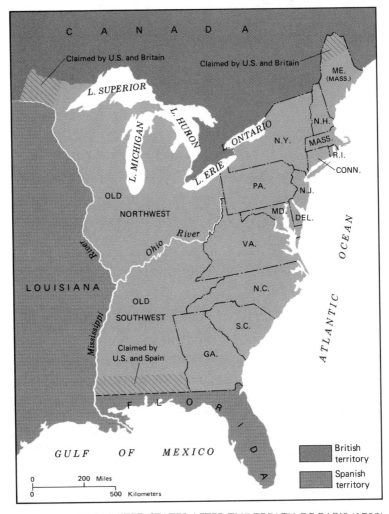

THE UNITED STATES AFTER THE TREATY OF PARIS (1783)

led by Lafayette, eluded the British general. Returning to the coast late in the summer, Cornwallis established a base at Yorktown, near the mouth of Chesapeake Bay. Here, he hoped to obtain supplies and reinforcements by sea. He also wanted to prepare for a more successful campaign the following spring. But he never got the chance.

Washington, working with the French, now decided to strike a surprise blow at the British in the South. A French fleet under Count de Grasse sailed to the Yorktown area from the West Indies and sealed off the entrance to Chesapeake Bay. Washington, reinforced by 5000 French soldiers under Count Rochambeau, marched his forces from New York to Virginia. The combined army then laid siege to Yorktown.

Cornwallis was now trapped by the American and French troops on land and by de Grasse's fleet offshore. After several weeks of desperate fighting, Cornwallis realized that his position was hopeless. On October 19, 1781, he surrendered his entire army of 8000. This was the last major battle of the war.

The Peace Treaty

Although the British still occupied New York City and the Southern seaports, their hopes for victory were shattered. The English people were tired of the war and wanted peace. Early in 1782, Parliament voted to end hostilities and begin peace talks.

In the *Treaty of Paris*, signed in September 1783, Britain acknowledged the independence of the 13 colonies. The boundaries of the new nation were to be the Atlantic Ocean on the east, the Mississippi River on the west, Canada on the north, and Florida on the south. Britain granted Americans full fishing rights in the Newfoundland area. It also returned Florida to Spain.

TEN NOTABLE AMERICANS OF THE REVOLUTIONARY ERA

WILLIAM BILLINGS (1746–1800) The first important American composer was a Boston tanner with no musical training. But his enthusiasm and inventiveness inspired him to write hundreds of lively and charming hymn tunes, which were eagerly performed by the church choirs of his day. He was an ardent Patriot, and his song "Chester" was a favorite among both civilians and Continental troops.

MICHEL-GUILLAUME JEAN DE CRÈVECOEUR (1735–1813) Born in France, he came to America as a young man, married a colonial woman, and settled on a farm in Chester, New York. In *Letters From an American Farmer* (1782), a widely read collection of essays, he was one of the first to ask "What is an American?" and to answer with praise for his adopted country's toleration and republican spirit. A Loyalist during the Revolution, he returned to his native country and later served as French consul to the United States.

PAUL CUFFE (1759–1817)   He was the first black American to become wealthy, starting out as a seaman and gradually acquiring his own fleet of ships. During the Revolutionary War, he and his brother went to court in their native Massachusetts. They charged that, denied the vote, they were suffering from the same taxation without representation that agitated white Patriots. (Their suit was unsuccessful at the time, but did help the state's blacks in the long run.) A devout Quaker, Cuffe built the first schoolhouse in Westport, Massachusetts, and arranged for several black families to settle in Africa's Sierra Leone.

FRANCIS MARION (1732–1795)   After the Continentals were defeated at Camden, South Carolina, Marion and his men carried on guerrilla warfare against the British in the South. He harassed them with surprise attacks, disrupted their lines of communication, and evaded capture by disappearing into the swamps when chased by superior forces. His exploits earned him the title of "the Swamp Fox."

ROBERT MORRIS (1734–1806)   English-born, he came to America as a youth and lived most of his life in Philadelphia, amassing a great fortune as a shipper and banker. His energy and talent as a financier saved the colonists from bankruptcy during the Revolutionary War, and he continued to aid the government after independence was won. But, having overinvested in land, he lost his fortune and served a term in debtors' prison before dying poor and forgotten.

DAVID RITTENHOUSE (1732–1796)   This Pennsylvania astronomer and mathematician made the first telescope in America. His wide-ranging accomplishments included state boundary surveys and extremely accurate planetary observations. He was also the first director of the U.S. Mint. During the Revolution, he supervised arms manufacture, requisitioning, among other things, all the lead from Philadelphia's clock-weights.

BENJAMIN RUSH (1745–1813)   The best-known American physician of his day, he trained in Europe and practiced in Philadelphia, where his teaching drew hundreds of students. Critics charged that he relied too much on bleeding (a standard treatment of the time), but he performed valuable work among the mentally ill. He also helped establish the first free medical clinic in the United States.

HAYM SALOMON (1740–1785)   A Polish Jew, he settled in New York City in the early 1770s and soon took up the Patriot cause. With his knowledge of German, he was effective in persuading Hessians to desert the British side, and was twice arrested for anti-British activity. After escaping to Philadelphia, he was an important financial figure, especially in raising money from the French and Dutch to help supply the Continental army.

DEBORAH SAMPSON (1760–1827)   After several years as a servant girl, she marched off to Boston at the age of 22 and enlisted in the Continental army. Tall and strong, she disguised herself as "Robert Shurtleff" and fought in several Revolutionary engagements. Only when she was hospitalized with fever did the army discover that she was a woman. She later married a Massachusetts farmer and was awarded veteran's pensions by both the state and federal governments.

MERCY OTIS WARREN (1728–1814) She was the equal of her father, husband, and brother (James Otis) in her fervent support of the Patriot cause. Her wartime political satires (featuring such characters as Sir Spendall and Hum Humbug) were followed by a three-volume *History of the Rise, Progress and Termination of the American Revolution* (1805). John Adams, irritated by her attacks on him, declared that "History is not the Province of the Ladies," but her work was as careful and balanced as any of the period.

Matching Test

COLUMN A

1. William Dawes
2. John Hancock
3. Ethan Allen
4. Thomas Jefferson
5. William Howe
6. John Burgoyne
7. Baron von Steuben
8. John Paul Jones
9. John André
10. Nathanael Greene

COLUMN B

a. president of Second Continental Congress
b. organizer of Green Mountain Boys of Vermont
c. general who took Philadelphia in 1777
d. drillmaster of Continental army at Valley Forge
e. British spy whose capture led to discovery of Arnold's treason
f. chief author of Declaration of Independence
g. leader of Continental troops in South
h. loser to Gates at Saratoga
i. commander of naval raids against English ships
j. colonist who warned Minutemen of a British attack

True-False Test

1. At the outbreak of the Revolutionary War, about two-thirds of the American colonists were neutral.
2. The first battle of the war was fought at Saratoga, New York.
3. The Battle of Bunker Hill was a costly victory for the British.
4. An important American victory in 1776 was the capture of Quebec.
5. In 1776, British troops in the New York City area caused serious damage to Continental forces under Washington.
6. Aid from France played an important part in the American victory at Yorktown.

7. A campaign led by George Rogers Clark secured the Northwest Territory for the Americans.
8. Because of its small navy, the American side was not able to win any battles at sea.
9. Benedict Arnold planned to turn West Point over to the British.
10. Most fighting in the final years of the Revolutionary War took place in New England.

Map Test

Locate the following places on the maps on pages 112, 117, 118, 119, 121, and 123. Then, referring to the text, as necessary, state where each place is located, and indicate what important event occurred there during the Revolutionary War.

GROUP A

1. Breed's Hill	6. Harlem Heights
2. Bennington	7. Morristown
3. Valley Forge	8. West Point
4. Vincennes	9. Lexington
5. Trenton	10. Saratoga

GROUP B

1. King's Mountain	6. Brooklyn Heights
2. Yorktown	7. Camden
3. Cahokia	8. Ticonderoga
4. Oriskany	9. Germantown
5. Concord	10. Dorchester Heights

Essay Questions

1. What were the major strengths and weaknesses of the American and British in fighting the Revolutionary War?
2. What was the meaning of the Patriot slogan "no taxation without representation"?
3. Name three of the speakers and writers for the Patriot cause, and identify their contributions.
4. Name three Europeans who volunteered their services to the Continental army. How did these volunteers help?
5. Give two reasons why the battle fought at Saratoga was the turning point of the American Revolution.

CHAPTER 8

Forming a New Government

THE NEWLY INDEPENDENT United States faced a number of difficulties. One of the most troublesome was the creation of an acceptable form of government. The first type of government the Americans set up proved unsatisfactory and had to be abandoned. The second one was far more effective. It not only met the needs of the times but has survived to the present day.

THE CONFEDERATION PERIOD

During the Revolution, the Continental Congress had drawn up a written constitution called the *Articles of Confederation*. Adopted in 1781, the Articles provided a central government for the new nation for eight years—a time often called the Confederation period.

The Articles of Confederation gave to Congress a limited number of powers for governing the nation. All other powers and functions of government were exercised by the separate states. As a result, the central government was unable to deal effectively with many of the problems it faced.

Postwar Problems

One difficulty faced by the new United States was that it was not a truly unified country. People generally felt a greater loyalty to their state than to the nation as a whole.

GOVERNMENT UNDER THE ARTICLES OF CONFEDERATION

Provision	Weakness
States were organized into loose confederation, with single branch of government: Congress.	There was no executive to enforce laws, and no judiciary to settle disputes.
Congress could request funds from states.	Congress lacked power to tax.
Congress could request troops from states.	Congress had no power to raise army.
Congress could issue money and regulate weights and measures.	States could also issue money; their domestic and foreign trade could not be regulated by Congress.
Each state had one vote in Congress.	Heavily populated states were not represented proportionately.
Any measure required 9 of 13 votes for passage; amending Articles required unanimous vote.	Legislation was difficult to pass; amendment was virtually impossible.

There were economic problems, too. The United States after independence was not well off. The old British trade regulations had been bothersome in many ways. But they had provided guaranteed markets in the British empire for colonial goods. Now, the Americans had lost this protection and had to compete with everyone else. Other nations refused to make trade agreements with the United States because Congress, under the Articles, lacked the power to enforce such agreements.

In addition, the government was unable to pay its debts. These were sizable. To carry on the war, Congress had borrowed money from Americans. So much paper money (called "Continentals") had been issued that it was almost worthless. The United States also owed a great deal of money to other countries. Since Congress could not levy taxes, it had to depend on state contributions for funds. But the states refused to give much—barely a sixth of what Congress requested. The result was more borrowing and a bigger debt. Foreigners had little faith that this weak new nation could pay what it owed.

At the same time, there were political disputes over control of the American frontier. Britain had kept its military posts in the Northwest Territory, contrary to the terms of the 1783 peace treaty. Spain claimed land in what the United States considered its own territory west of Georgia. Spain also refused to allow American boats to use the lower Mississippi River.

As for the individual states, they tended to quarrel rather than cooperate with one another. Many states claimed that their western boundaries extended to the Mississippi River or even the Pacific Ocean. The land claims of some states overlapped one another. There was also disagreement over navigation rights on rivers that served as boundaries between states. The states taxed one another's products and set up their own systems of duties on foreign imports.

In the new Code of Laws which I suppose it will be necessary for you to make I desire you would Remember the Ladies, and be more generous and favourable to them than your ancestors. Do not put such unlimited power into the hands of the Husbands. Remember all Men would be tyrants if they could.

—Abigail Adams in a letter to her husband John
(written in 1776, when the Second Continental Congress
began drafting the Articles of Confederation)

Accomplishments of the Confederation

In spite of its limitations and weaknesses, the government of the Confederation achieved notable successes. It led the American people through the last years of the Revolution. It negotiated the Treaty of Paris that ended the war. It also kept the 13 states together until they were able to work out a stronger government.

Probably the most important accomplishment of the Confederation Congress was to lay the foundation for America's later expansion. This was accomplished by two laws. One, the *Ordinance of 1785*, provided for the sale of public land to settlers. The other, the *Ordinance of 1787*, drew up a plan for governing the Northwest Territory. (Both of these measures are discussed at greater length in Chapter 11, page 175.)

Growing Dissatisfaction

Many Americans liked the weak type of government set up by the Articles. After all, they had just fought a revolution to be rid of strong central authority (the British king and Parliament). But other Americans, especially merchants and property owners, wanted a stronger national government. People with this view began to hold meetings and work for change.

In 1785, delegates from Maryland and Virginia met at Mount Vernon, Washington's home. They succeeded in settling some problems concern-

We the People of the United States...

Article 1

James Madison

Benjamin Franklin

Alexander Hamilton

ing shipping on the Potomac River. The success of this *Mount Vernon Conference* prompted Virginia to ask all the states to attend a meeting in 1786 at Annapolis, Maryland. The aim was to discuss common problems of commerce and navigation.

Only five states sent representatives to the *Annapolis Convention*. Because there were so few delegates, commercial problems were not discussed. At the urging of Alexander Hamilton of New York, however, the convention adopted a resolution requesting Congress to convene another conference the following year. The 1787 convention would not only discuss commercial issues but also consider ways of improving the national government.

Response at first was cautious, but then an event in Massachusetts made the situation more urgent. Times were bad, and many farmers had trouble making their mortgage payments to banks. When the farmers fell behind, the result was foreclosure—bank seizure of their property. In western Massachusetts, debt-ridden farmers who feared foreclosure were organized by Daniel Shays, a former captain in the Revolutionary army. In the fall of 1786, the farmers forced the closing of a number of state courts that were prosecuting debtors. In addition, a march on Springfield was organized to seize federal arms stored there. To meet this emergency, Massachusetts raised a large force of state militia, which succeeded in ending the disturbance in February 1787.

Shays's Rebellion was a minor uprising, but it shocked many people. Prominent citizens like George Washington feared the spread of mob rule. Support for a stronger national government increased.

THE CONSTITUTIONAL CONVENTION

Early in 1787, Congress called on the states to send delegates to a meeting to revise the Articles of Confederation. This conference, which later became known as the *Constitutional Convention,* met at Independence Hall in Philadelphia in May 1787.

The Delegates

All the states except Rhode Island sent delegates to the Constitutional Convention. Its 55 members—often called the Founding Fathers, or Founders—were politically experienced, realistic, and well qualified for the task ahead. Most shared a conservative outlook. About half of them were lawyers. Many of the others were planters and merchants.

Of the delegates who met in Philadelphia, the most admired was George Washington, who was elected president of the convention. Other important members included Benjamin Franklin, James Madison, and Alexander Hamilton. Absent from the convention were many outstanding Revolutionary Patriots. Samuel Adams and John Hancock were not chosen as delegates. Patrick Henry refused to attend because he disapproved of the conference. Both John Adams and Thomas Jefferson had diplomatic posts abroad—Adams in England, Jefferson in France.

Constitutional Compromises

Although the original purpose of the 1787 conference was to revise the Articles of Confederation, the delegates soon abandoned this idea. Instead, they turned to the task of working out a new plan of government and spelling out its specific provisions in a new constitution. In doing so, serious differences arose, but compromises resolved them.

STATE REPRESENTATION   One compromise dealt with the question of how the various states should be represented in the national legislature. Should all states be represented equally, or should states with larger populations have more representatives? Large states favored the Virginia Plan, which called for representation based on population. Small states, afraid of being outvoted, supported the New Jersey Plan. It proposed that each state have equal representation.

This problem was solved by what has come to be called the *Great Compromise*—a Congress consisting of two houses. In the upper house, the *Senate*, each state would have two senators. In the lower house, the *House of Representatives*, each state would be represented on the basis of population.

DETERMINING POPULATION   The Great Compromise led to another issue. In counting the people in a state, what about slaves? The Southern states wanted the number of their representatives in the House of Representatives to be based on their total populations, including slaves.

PARTICIPATION IN THE CONSTITUTIONAL CONVENTION

State*	Number of Delegates	Outstanding Delegates	Contribution
Delaware	5		
Pennsylvania	8	James Wilson	Learned and energetic debater
		Gouverneur Morris	Prepared final draft of Constitution
		Benjamin Franklin	Fostered spirit of goodwill and compromise
New Jersey	5		
Georgia	4		
Connecticut	3	Roger Sherman	Introduced Great Compromise (also known as Connecticut Compromise)
Massachusetts	4	Rufus King	Eloquent and persuasive speaker; effectively supported creation of strong central government
Maryland	5		
South Carolina	4	John Rutledge	Hard worker and energetic speaker
		Charles Pinckney	Offered many proposals that became part of Constitution
New Hampshire	2		
Virginia	7	George Washington	Presided over convention with tact and dignity
		James Madison	Led in presenting and arguing for proposals; kept best record of proceedings; known as "father of the Constitution"
New York	3	Alexander Hamilton	Vigorous advocate of strong central government
North Carolina	5		
(Rhode Island)	—		

*listed in order of ratification of the Constitution

But these states did not want slaves to be counted for the purpose of direct taxation by the national government. The Northern states took the opposite position. They did not want to count slaves for representation, but they did want to include them for taxation.

This difficulty was resolved by the *Three-Fifths Compromise.* It stated that three-fifths of the slave population would be counted for both representation and taxation.

REGULATING COMMERCE   Manufacturers and shippers in the North wanted Congress to have the power to regulate interstate and foreign commerce. But farmers in the South were worried that Congress might use this power to tax agricultural exports. Southerners were also afraid that Congress might ban the importation of slaves.

Compromises were worked out on these issues, too. Congress received the power to regulate both interstate and foreign commerce. It could levy tariffs on imports, but it could not tax exports. And the Constitution forbade Congress to restrict the importing of slaves for 20 years (that is, until 1808).

FEATURES OF THE CONSTITUTION

The introduction to the *Constitution of the United States* (see page 565) is known as the Preamble. It begins with these words: "We the people of the United States . . . ." This phrase makes it clear that the document establishes a government of the people. The purposes of the new government are "to form a more perfect union, establish justice, insure domestic tranquility, provide for the common defense, promote the general welfare, and secure the blessings of liberty."

Separation of Powers

The Founders set up three branches of government: legislative, executive, and judicial. This division of governmental authority and duties is called separation of powers.

The chief duty of the legislative branch is to make laws. The legislature, Congress, has two houses. The upper one, the Senate, consists of two members from each state. The present membership is 100, since there are now 50 states. In the lower house, the House of Representatives, each state is represented according to population. The present membership is fixed by law at 435.

The executive branch enforces the laws. The president, as chief executive, is aided by a vice president and numerous executive assistants. At present, there are 14 executive departments and many administrative agencies. The heads of the executive departments serve as the president's cabinet.

The judicial branch interprets the laws. Federal laws are interpreted by judges who preside over various federal courts. The federal court system consists of a Supreme Court and lower federal courts. At present, the Supreme Court has nine justices, one of whom serves as chief justice. The lower courts consist of 13 circuit courts of appeals, 94 district courts, and several special courts.

Checks and Balances

The framers of the Constitution did not want any of the three branches of government to become too powerful. Ways were therefore worked out for each branch to exercise some control over the others. The plan the framers devised is the system of checks and balances.

LEGISLATIVE CHECKS Congress can check the president by refusing to allot money to the executive branch. The legislature can also block the creation of new administrative agencies and do away with existing ones. The Senate can reject a treaty made by the president. (A two-thirds vote of the Senate is required to ratify a treaty.) It can reject presidential appointments by a majority vote. The House of Representatives has the power to impeach the president—that is, to bring charges of wrongdoing. If it does so, the Senate tries the chief executive.

Congress can check the judiciary by creating or abolishing lower federal courts. The legislature can also impeach federal judges. In addition, the Senate must approve the appointment of all federal judges.

The Senate and House can check each other. A bill must be passed by both houses before it becomes law.

EXECUTIVE CHECKS The president can check Congress through the veto, by refusing to sign a bill into law. (But Congress can override a veto by a two-thirds vote of both houses.) The president can check the courts by the power to appoint federal judges and the power to pardon convicted persons.

JUDICIAL CHECKS The judiciary can check the other two branches. It can declare acts of Congress and actions of the president unconstitutional (contrary to the Constitution), and therefore void. The Court's power to make this kind of judgment is called judicial review. (For further discussion of judicial review, see Chapter 10, page 157.)

CHECKS ON THE PEOPLE The delegates to the Constitutional Convention had little confidence in people's ability to choose officials wisely. Therefore, they provided that the president was to be elected indirectly by an electoral college. Judges were to be appointed, instead of elected. Until the passage of the Seventeenth Amendment in 1913, senators were chosen by the legislatures of their states, rather than being elected directly by the people.

The delegates also wanted to keep the people from totally upsetting the machinery of government at any one election. To avoid this, the terms of officeholders were varied. Representatives serve for two years, presidents for four, and senators for six. Members of the federal judiciary hold office for life.

Federalism

Although the delegates aimed to create a strong central government, they also wanted to give the states adequate authority. The solution was federalism. Under a federal system, power is shared by a national government and regional governments, such as states or provinces. In the United States, powers assigned to the national government are known as delegated powers. Those retained by the states are reserved powers. Powers shared by both levels of government are concurrent powers.

The Constitution also granted the national government the right to make all laws that are "necessary and proper" for carrying out its delegated powers. This statement is known as the "elastic clause" because it enables the central government to stretch its powers beyond those specified. Powers derived from the elastic clause are called implied powers. They are not specifically mentioned in the Constitution but are implied from those that are stated.

Amending the Constitution

One of the basic weaknesses of the Articles of Confederation was the extreme difficulty of changing its provisions. Amending the Articles required the consent of every state. The delegates overcame this weakness and made the Constitution a far more flexible instrument of government.

The Constitution can be amended in four ways. The most common method is to have an amendment proposed by a two-thirds vote of both houses of Congress. The amendment must then be ratified by the legislatures of three-fourths of the states. Twenty-seven amendments have been added to the Constitution, and all but the Twenty-first were ratified this way. The Twenty-first Amendment was proposed by Congress and then ratified by state constitutional conventions, instead of state legislatures. (The other two methods, described in Article V of the Constitution, have never been used.)

THE FEDERAL SYSTEM

Division of Powers		
National Government (Delegated Powers)	**National and State Governments (Concurrent Powers)**	**State Governments (Reserved Powers)**
Coin money and regulate its value	Levy and collect taxes	Provide system of education
Establish postal system	Borrow money	Regulate marriage and divorce
Regulate interstate and foreign commerce	Set up courts	Establish voting qualifications (but states may not deny suffrage on basis of race, color, or sex, or withhold voting rights from 18-year-old citizens)
Declare war		
Make treaties with foreign nations		
Create and maintain armed forces		Provide local governments
Regulate naturalization of aliens		Regulate commerce within boundaries of state (intrastate)
Protect federal property throughout country		Build intrastate roads and other public works
Powers Denied		
National Government May Not—	**National and State Governments May Not—**	**State Governments May Not—**
Levy taxes on exports	Grant titles of nobility	Make treaties with foreign governments
Favor trade of one state over trade of another	Pass bills of attainder (legislative acts declaring persons guilty of crime without trial)	Coin money
Suspend, except in emergency, writ of habeas corpus (which requires officials to state reason for holding prisoner; if no legal cause is shown, court will order prisoner's release)	Pass ex post facto laws (laws punishing persons for actions not illegal when committed)	Engage in war unless invaded

RATIFYING THE CONSTITUTION

The members of the Constitutional Convention finished their work in four months. Only then could the public see what had been done, for the meetings of the convention had been held in secret, behind closed doors.

The Struggle for Adoption

Before the new plan of government could be put into effect, at least 9 of the 13 states had to ratify the Constitution. This was to be done by a special convention in each state, not by the people directly. The issue of ratification touched off a great debate, which divided the nation into two groups. The Federalists favored the Constitution, while the Anti-Federalists opposed it.

The Federalists drew their main support from merchants, manufacturers, large landowners, professionals, and holders of government bonds. These people were likely to benefit from a strong central government that could regulate commerce, maintain law and order, and improve the nation's finances. Anti-Federalists were mainly small farmers, city laborers, debtors, and others who believed that the states should retain maximum power and independence. The Anti-Federalists argued that the Constitution gave the federal government too much power and failed to protect fundamental rights of the people. Anti-Federalist opposition lessened after key political leaders promised that a bill of rights would be added to the Constitution after its adoption.

Each side argued its case in a flood of articles and pamphlets. The most important arguments were put forth in a series of Federalist essays that appeared in New York City newspapers in 1788. Written by Alexander Hamilton, James Madison, and John Jay (but signed "Publius"), the articles were soon collected in a book called *The Federalist*. They were persuasive arguments at the time and have served ever since as guides in interpreting the Constitution.

If men were angels, no government would be necessary. If angels were to govern men, neither external nor internal controls on government would be necessary.

—*James Madison in* The Federalist, *No. 47*

Delaware was the first state to ratify. It was soon followed by Pennsylvania, New Jersey, Georgia, and Connecticut. When New Hampshire became the ninth state to ratify, in June 1788, the adoption of the Constitution was certain. But without the support of the two vital states of

Virginia and New York, the new government would be powerless. After heated debates, both states ratified. North Carolina and Rhode Island were the last states to approve, doing so only after the new government had gone into operation.

The Bill of Rights

When the first Congress met, in 1789, it prepared the proposals that were to become the *Bill of Rights*. These first ten amendments were added to the Constitution in 1791. Together, they serve to restrict the central government and assure individual freedoms.

The First Amendment guarantees a number of basic personal rights, including freedom of religion, speech, and press. The First Amendment also guarantees people the right to hold peaceful meetings and to ask the government to correct wrongs. Unhappy memories of British rule led to Amendments Two, Three, and Four. They guarantee citizens the right to bear arms, prohibit the quartering of troops in private homes, and protect people against unreasonable searches of their property. The next four amendments provide legal safeguards (to trial by jury, for example). Amendments Nine and Ten are general guarantees of individual rights and state powers.

Multiple-Choice Test

1. The United States was governed by the Articles of Confederation from   (a) 1776 to 1783   (b) 1776 to 1789   (c) 1781 to 1789   (d) 1775 to 1781.
2. Under the Articles of Confederation, Congress   (a) had the power to tax   (b) could raise an army   (c) had one representative from each state   (d) could amend the Articles by a 9-to-4 vote.
3. All of the following were problems for the United States after the Revolutionary War *except*   (a) failure to negotiate a peace treaty with Britain   (b) lack of unity among Americans   (c) a large debt   (d) British forts in the Northwest Territory.
4. The only state *not* represented at the Constitutional Convention was   (a) Georgia   (b) North Carolina   (c) Virginia   (d) Rhode Island.
5. The Virginia Plan and New Jersey Plan offered different methods of   (a) counting slaves   (b) allotting representation in the national legislature   (c) regulating foreign trade   (d) taxing imports.
6. Under the Constitution, enforcing laws is the main task of   (a) the legislative branch   (b) the executive branch   (c) the judicial branch   (d) all of the above.

7. The power of the courts to declare an act of Congress unconstitutional is called   (a) judicial review   (b) separation of powers   (c) impeachment   (d) federalism.

8. In order to limit the power of the people, the Founders provided for all of the following *except*   (a) the appointment of judges   (b) indirect election of the president   (c) indirect election of senators   (d) election of members of the House of Representatives by state legislatures.

9. The Constitution gives the power to declare war to   (a) the states only   (b) both the federal government and the states   (c) the people only   (d) the federal government only.

10. Anti-Federalists opposed the Constitution because they felt that it   (a) did not give the president enough power   (b) did not safeguard the people's fundamental rights   (c) gave the states too much authority   (d) contained no provisions for regulating commerce.

Matching Test

COLUMN A

1. Daniel Shays
2. Great Compromise
3. Three-Fifths Compromise
4. James Madison
5. Gouverneur Morris
6. George Washington
7. delegated powers
8. reserved powers
9. implied powers
10. federalism

COLUMN B

a. delegate who kept most complete record of Constitutional Convention proceedings

b. proposal for determining how slaves should be included in a state's population

c. system of dividing powers between national and state governments

d. leader of rebellion of Massachusetts farmers

e. proposal for two-house Congress

f. delegate responsible for final draft of Constitution

g. powers assumed under elastic clause

h. president of Constitutional Convention

i. powers given to federal government alone by Constitution

j. powers to be used by states

Essay Questions

1. What were three weaknesses of the Articles of Confederation? How were these weaknesses corrected by the Constitution?
2. Describe two important compromises worked out by the delegates during the Constitutional Convention.
3. Explain the operation of the system of checks and balances, using examples from each branch of government.
4. Why did the Founders set up a federal system? Give examples to show how the system divides governmental power.
5. Why was the Bill of Rights added to the Constitution? List three rights that it guarantees, and tell why you think each is important.

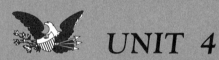

UNIT 4

Growth of
the Republic

CHAPTER 9

The Federalist Period

BY THE EARLY MONTHS of 1789, it was time to elect a president to head the new government. All attention turned to George Washington. He was admired as a national hero. As head of the army, he had shown sound judgment, courage, determination, and leadership. Americans believed that he would bring these qualities to the presidency. Washington agreed to serve, although he would have preferred to remain a private citizen. When the ballots of the electoral college were counted by the first Congress in April, Washington was the unanimous choice for president. John Adams, with the second highest number of votes, became vice president.

DOMESTIC DEVELOPMENTS UNDER WASHINGTON

New York City was chosen as the first capital of the United States under the Constitution. At Federal Hall, on April 30, 1789, Washington took the oath of office and was inaugurated as the nation's first president.

Organizing the Government

To help the president carry out his duties, the first Congress created three executive departments: State, Treasury, and War. Washington appointed as department heads (called secretaries) men whose judgment and opinions he valued. For the most important post at the time—secretary of the treasury—he selected a brilliant young lawyer, Alexander Hamilton. Thomas Jefferson was named secretary of state. One of Washington's generals in the Revolution, Henry Knox, became secretary of war.

Washington met with his department heads to discuss problems of government and important issues of the day. The three secretaries—together with Edmund Randolph, the attorney general—formed the nation's first cabinet.

A major task of Congress was to set up a court system. The *Judiciary Act of 1789* provided that the Supreme Court would have six judges: a chief justice and five associate justices. Washington appointed John Jay as the first chief justice. An experienced lawyer from New York, Jay had actively supported the ratification of the Constitution. To complete the first federal court system, Congress established 13 district courts and 3 circuit courts.

Hamilton's Financial Program

The most serious domestic problem facing the new government was finances. The Second Continental Congress and the Confederation had borrowed money from foreign sources and from American citizens. Most of these loans had not been repaid. The individual states had large debts, too. The federal treasury was empty, and money was needed to operate the government. Secretary of the Treasury Hamilton proposed a number of measures to resolve these problems and to place the nation on a solid financial footing. Congress passed most of the bills he recommended.

RESTORING CREDIT   Hamilton believed that the United States had to establish itself as a responsible government. It had to pay its debts, both abroad and at home. He recommended funding—paying off these debts—in full. There were few objections to funding the $12 million owed to foreign investors. But his proposal to fully repay the debts owed to people at home met with resistance.

The federal government owed about $44 million to American citizens. During the war, the Continental Congress had raised money by selling bonds, and had paid soldiers with IOU's called pay certificates. Many of those who held bonds and certificates doubted that the government would ever redeem them. So these people sold their holdings, for considerably less than their face value, to speculators. (Speculators are people who make risky investments in the hope of big profits.) Funding the national debt at full value would enrich speculators, and there was much objection to the idea. But Congress finally passed the required legislation.

There was even greater resistance to a proposal of Hamilton's called assumption. Under this plan, the federal government would assume, or take over, the debts owed by the states. These debts amounted to some $22 million. Northern states owed more money than Southern states, and Southerners objected to paying off Northern debts. Hamilton overcame the Southerners' opposition by agreeing to support their demand that the nation's permanent capital be located in the South, along the Potomac River. (While Washington, D.C., was being built, Philadelphia served as the temporary capital.)

ESTABLISHING A NATIONAL BANK Since funding and assumption would involve the government in many financial dealings, Hamilton proposed that a national bank be organized. (There were only a few local banks at this time.) He gave three main arguments for a national bank:

1. It would provide a safe place for federal funds.
2. It would make borrowing by the government and private individuals easier.
3. It would create a uniform and dependable currency by issuing sound paper money.

The bank would be chartered for 20 years. Its headquarters were to be in Philadelphia, with branches elsewhere. The bank would be privately owned and managed, but the government would own a fifth of the stock.

Hamilton's bank proposal stirred up controversy. Many people were afraid of a bank with so much power. It would dominate the banking business, they said. Jefferson and others thought that the plan was unconstitutional because the Constitution did not specifically grant Congress the power to create banks. (This view, called strict construction, maintains that the government cannot do anything that is not clearly specified in the Constitution.)

Hamilton held that the bank bill was constitutional because Congress had the right to coin money, collect taxes, and borrow money. And the elastic clause of the Constitution enabled Congress to do what is "necessary and proper" to carry out its specified functions. In this case, a bank was necessary to handle finances. (Hamilton's view, called loose construction, argues that the government has powers that are implied in the Constitution, even if they are not spelled out there.) Hamilton's approach won favor, and, in 1791, Congress established the first Bank of the United States.

CREATING A COINAGE SYSTEM The many different foreign coins in circulation had to be replaced with a uniform metal currency. Hamilton

Abigail Adams

"remember the ladies..."

George Washington

John Adams

proposed a decimal system of coinage. Congress approved the creation of a new series of gold, silver, and copper coins, and the establishment of a mint to produce them. The first U.S. coins became available in 1793.

RAISING MONEY A tariff act of 1789 had placed duties on certain imports. But the levies did not bring in enough money to run the government. Therefore, in 1791, Congress approved Hamilton's recommendation for a tax on the manufacture of whiskey. Frontier farmers strongly resented this tax because they distilled whiskey from their surplus grain. Whiskey was easier to transport than grain and also brought a higher price. The whiskey tax cut seriously into the farmers' profits.

Opposition to the whiskey tax was especially strong in western Pennsylvania. Farmers there refused to pay the tax and threatened federal tax collectors with violence. President Washington raised a force of 13,000 troops and sent it to put down the Whiskey Rebellion of 1794. Several ringleaders were arrested, and order was quickly restored. By taking quick, strong action, the government showed that it was able to enforce the laws.

ENCOURAGING INDUSTRY Hamilton believed that the United States should encourage manufacturing. One way to do so was to adopt a protective tariff. (This kind of tariff places high taxes on imported goods in order to protect domestic manufacturers from foreign competition.) Congress did not approve this measure, mainly because of Southern opposition. The South had fewer factories and imported more foreign goods than the North.

The First Political Parties

Hamilton's financial program created a strong financial foundation for the United States. But it helped the well-to-do more than average

Americans. For this reason, it aroused opposition as well as support. This division of opinion led to the formation of the nation's first political parties. One group called themselves *Federalists*. The other group was known as *Democratic-Republicans*, or simply *Republicans*. (The Democratic-Republican party was a forerunner of the present-day Democratic party. The Republican party of today, however, was not founded until 1854.)

The Federalist party, which backed Hamilton's policies, was especially strong in the Northeast. The party's members were mainly merchants, bankers, and manufacturers. They favored a strong national government and loose construction of the Constitution. They wanted to encourage commerce and industry, as well as farming. Finally, the Federalists distrusted democracy, preferring government to be in the hands of the educated and wealthy.

The Democratic-Republicans united under the leadership of Thomas Jefferson and James Madison. The party's chief strength was in the South and West, and many of its members were small farmers and laborers. Fearing that a strong federal government might hamper individual freedom, these people supported strict construction of the Constitution as a way of limiting the government's power. They agreed with Jefferson that the small farm was the backbone of the United States. In their view, industry and big cities represented a threat to republican principles.

Washington is usually considered to be a Federalist, but he did not side with either party officially. In fact, he even warned against the "spirit of party." Shortly before the end of his second term, in his Farewell Address to the nation, he pointed out that political parties would lead to jealousy, hatred, and "riot and insurrection." The Federalists, however, controlled the government during the presidencies of Washington and his successor, John Adams. Their administrations are therefore generally known as the Federalist period.

FOREIGN AFFAIRS

During Washington's eight years in office, relations with Europe were complicated by the French Revolution. This uprising, which broke out in 1789, greatly changed life and government in France. The revolution also led to a series of wars that eventually involved almost every European nation. (The wars ended only with the final defeat of Napoleon, the French emperor, in 1815.) In the conflicts between France and Britain, Americans took sides. The Democratic-Republicans generally favored France, while the Federalists usually supported Britain.

France and the Genêt Affair

Early in 1793, the French king was overthrown and executed. France then found itself at war with Britain, Spain, and the Netherlands. The French expected the United States to come to their aid because the two nations had signed a treaty of alliance during the American Revolution. But Washington, along with Jefferson and Hamilton, felt that the young nation would be harmed by joining the conflict. Washington issued a *Proclamation of Neutrality* in April 1793. He declared that the United States would remain at peace with both sides and warned American citizens to avoid unfriendly acts against any nation at war.

Meanwhile, the French government had sent a diplomat, "Citizen" Edmond Genêt, to obtain help from the United States. (The French Revolution had abolished titles and replaced them with "Citizen" and "Citizeness.") In the spring of 1793, Genêt created a stir by organizing military expeditions against Spanish-held Florida and Louisiana. He also provided Americans with commissions in the French army. In addition, Genêt arranged for privateers to sail from American ports and attack British merchant ships.

Genêt ignored several warnings to stop these activities. Washington then asked the French government to recall its representative. As it turned out, a new regime had come to power in France, and it wanted Genêt brought home under arrest. Fearing for his life, Genêt requested permission to remain in the United States. He later became an American citizen.

Britain and the Jay Treaty

The new United States government was also having trouble with Britain. In violation of the Treaty of Paris, the British continued to occupy many forts and trading posts in the Northwest Territory. From these bases, they carried on a far-reaching fur trade. They also sold guns to the Indians and stirred up Indian attacks on American frontier settlements.

Britain justified its occupation of American territory by claiming that certain provisions of the peace treaty had not been honored by the United States. These included (1) failure to settle pre-Revolutionary debts owed by Americans to British merchants and (2) failure to pay Loyalists for property taken over by the states.

Another sore point had to do with shipping. American foreign trade increased sharply after the outbreak of war in Europe. As a neutral nation, the United States traded with both sides. To keep supplies from reaching the French, the British navy, in 1793, began seizing neutral ships bound for France or its colonies. In less than a year, the British seized 250

U.S. ships. On many occasions, the British removed American seamen from U.S. ships and forced them to serve in the British navy. This practice was known as impressment. The United States complained bitterly about such violations of freedom of the seas, but Britain ignored the protests.

Washington sent John Jay to Britain to negotiate a settlement of the differences between the two countries. A treaty signed in 1794 provided for (1) withdrawal of British troops from the Northwest Territory, (2) payment of debts owed to British creditors by Americans, and (3) compensation to American shippers for ships and cargoes seized by the British.

The *Jay Treaty* was widely criticized because of things it did *not* say. Britain made no promises to stop seizing U.S. ships bound for French territory. Nor did it agree to halt the impressment of American seamen. Washington himself did not like the treaty. But he felt that it would help keep peace at a time when the United States was not prepared to fight a major war. He urged the Senate to ratify the Jay Treaty, and it finally did so. This agreement succeeded in postponing a showdown with Britain until 1812.

Spain and the Pinckney Treaty

The United States made a better bargain with Spain. One problem concerned navigation rights on the lower Mississippi River. A related issue involved certain privileges in New Orleans, at the mouth of the river. Americans wanted to ship goods down the Mississippi. They also wanted to deposit the goods in New Orleans and then transfer them to ocean-going vessels without paying duties to Spain. This so-called "right of deposit" was important to Western farmers because New Orleans was their only outlet to Eastern and European markets. A third problem concerned the disputed boundary between Georgia and Spanish Florida.

Thomas Pinckney negotiated a settlement of all these issues. The *Pinckney Treaty,* signed in 1795, guaranteed Americans navigation rights on the lower Mississippi River and the right of deposit at New Orleans. The treaty also fixed the boundary between Spanish and U.S. territories east of the Mississippi at the 31st parallel.

It is our true policy to steer clear of permanent alliances with any portion of the foreign world.

—*Washington's Farewell Address, 1796*

ADAMS AS PRESIDENT

When Washington decided not to run for a third term in 1796, the Federalists chose John Adams as their presidential candidate. He won by a narrow margin over his Republican opponent, Thomas Jefferson. Jefferson, with the second highest number of electoral votes, became vice president.

More Trouble With France

Relations with France, already strained, grew worse after the signing of the Jay Treaty. As the French saw it, the Americans were ignoring their mutual-aid agreement with France and moving closer to Britain. Armed French vessels began to seize American merchant ships bound for British ports. In addition, the French government refused to receive the U.S. minister, Charles Pinckney.

In 1797, Adams sent a delegation to France to try to settle the difficulties. The Americans met with three French agents, who demanded the payment of a large bribe and the promise of an American loan to France before negotiations could begin. These demands were rejected.

Early the next year, American newspapers reported the demands made by the French agents, who were identified simply as X, Y, and Z. Americans were outraged by the agents' demands for a bribe. The XYZ Affair, as it was called, aroused a storm of anti-French protest in the United States. A popular slogan was "Millions for defense but not one cent for tribute." In preparation for war, Congress passed a number of defense measures and created the Department of the Navy.

From 1798 through 1800, the United States and France fought a kind of undeclared naval war. The tiny American navy did well. It captured more than 80 French ships, while losing only one of its own vessels. Faced with the prospect of a full-scale war with the United States, the French government agreed to receive another American delegation. The two countries reached a satisfactory agreement, and the undeclared war came to an end.

The Alien and Sedition Acts

At the height of the French crisis, the Federalist-dominated Congress passed four harsh laws, known as the *Alien and Sedition Acts*. (An alien is a resident noncitizen; sedition means treason.) One act raised the residence requirement for citizenship from 5 to 14 years. Another gave the president power to deport any alien considered dangerous to the nation's peace and safety. The third act gave the president authority to arrest or deport enemy aliens in time of war. And the fourth made it a crime to publish "false, scandalous, and malicious writing" about the government or its officials.

The Federalists defended the Alien and Sedition Acts as necessary war measures. The real purpose of the acts, however, was to check the growing power of the Democratic-Republicans. Most immigrants, for example, tended to be anti-Federalist in their outlook. Delaying citizenship for these newcomers would prevent them from voting for Democratic-Republican candidates. And the only people to be arrested for "seditious" writings were Democratic-Republican editors and printers.

The Kentucky and Virginia Resolutions

Two state legislatures, those of Kentucky and Virginia, passed resolutions declaring the Alien and Sedition Acts to be unconstitutional. The *Kentucky Resolutions* were written by Thomas Jefferson and adopted in 1798 and 1799. The *Virginia Resolutions,* written by James Madison, were adopted in 1798. Both sets of statements made essentially the same point. Having created the national government, the states could, therefore, ignore acts of Congress that they regarded as illegal. The resolutions formed the basis of the nullification doctrine. This is the belief that states have the power to nullify (declare invalid) any federal action that they consider unconstitutional.

Virginia and Kentucky sent the resolutions to other states for comment but received little support. The issue of nullification died down for the time being.

THE ELECTION OF 1800

In the presidential election of 1800, the Federalists nominated Adams for a second term. Opposing him was Jefferson as the Democratic-Republican candidate.

Jefferson Chosen

The Democratic-Republicans won a sweeping victory in 1800. But an unusual problem then arose. According to the Constitution, members of the electoral college were to vote for two candidates, without indicating which office each one was to fill. The person receiving the most votes was to become president. The runner-up was to be vice president. The Democratic-Republicans had nominated Jefferson for president and Aaron Burr for vice president. Since each elector cast two votes for his party's candidates, the result was a tie between Jefferson and Burr.

The Constitution provides that when two candidates are tied in the electoral college, the House of Representatives must choose between them. Jefferson was the Democratic-Republicans' choice for president. But Federalist congressmen tried to swing the election to Burr because his political views were closer to those of the Federalists. The deadlock was finally broken by Hamilton. Although a Federalist, he declared himself in favor of Jefferson. Hamilton felt that Burr was dangerous and not to be trusted. (He was certainly right from a personal point of view, for Burr killed him in a duel three years later.) Hamilton's support influenced the House to choose Jefferson.

To prevent such a mixup in the future, the Twelfth Amendment was adopted in 1804. It provided that electors were to cast separate ballots for president and vice president.

Decline of the Federalists

The Federalists' defeat in 1800 marked the beginning of their decline from power. They never won a presidential election again, and they disappeared from the political scene some 15 years later. The Federalists had done much to get the United States off to a good start. Their policies, however, served the interests of commercial and manufacturing groups better than the interests of farmers and laborers, who made up the bulk of the population. And Federalist sponsorship of the Alien and Sedition Acts aroused people's fears that a Federalist administration would destroy civil liberties.

True-False Test

1. When Washington was inaugurated, the capital of the United States was New York City.
2. Alexander Hamilton believed in strict construction of the Constitution.
3. The Whiskey Rebellion was a protest by farmers against a law banning the manufacture of whiskey.
4. The Democratic-Republicans of Jefferson's time were the forerunners of today's Democrats.
5. Citizen Genêt was a problem for the American government because his actions endangered U.S. neutrality.
6. The Jay Treaty kept the peace with Britain for 50 years.

7. One result of the XYZ Affair was the establishment of the Department of the Navy.
8. The main purpose of the Alien and Sedition Acts was to weaken the Democratic-Republican party.
9. The Kentucky and Virginia Resolutions declared that the states must always obey the federal government.
10. Alexander Hamilton was influential in bringing about the election of Thomas Jefferson.

Multiple-Choice Test

1. The first chief justice of the United States was a lawyer named (a) Alexander Hamilton (b) George Clinton (c) John Jay (d) Henry Knox.
2. During Washington's administration, the federal government agreed to pay debts amounting to a total of (a) $12 million (b) $22 million (c) $44 million (d) $78 million.
3. The site of Washington, D.C., was chosen for the nation's capital as a result of a controversy over (a) assumption (b) a national bank (c) a protective tariff (d) the Florida boundary.
4. Foreign affairs during the Federalist period were complicated by (a) a civil war in England (b) wars between Britain and France (c) a revolution in Spain (d) the overthrow of the British king.
5. U.S. grievances against the British in the 1790s included all of the following *except* (a) British trading posts in the Northwest Territory (b) Indian attacks on frontier settlements (c) impressment of American seamen (d) debts owed by the British to American creditors.
6. One accomplishment of the Pinckney Treaty was to (a) settle U.S. claims against Spanish smugglers (b) fix the boundary between the Northwest Territory and Louisiana (c) secure the right of deposit for Americans at New Orleans (d) buy Florida from Spain.
7. The XYZ Affair involved the United States and (a) France (b) Spain (c) Britain (d) the Netherlands.
8. The Kentucky and Virginia Resolutions were a reaction against (a) the XYZ Affair (b) the Jay Treaty (c) an undeclared naval war with France (d) the Alien and Sedition Acts.
9. The Federalist candidate for president in 1800 was (a) Washington (b) Adams (c) Burr (d) Hamilton.
10. The election of 1800 was settled by the (a) Senate (b) Supreme Court (c) House of Representatives (d) electoral college.

Essay Questions

1. Describe the major provisions of Hamilton's financial program. Explain what happened to each provision in Congress.
2. Why did America's first two political parties take shape? What was Washington's attitude toward them?
3. Explain how the power of the federal government was challenged by the Whiskey Rebellion and the Kentucky and Virginia Resolutions.
4. Identify two problems with Britain during Washington's administration, and tell how they were resolved.
5. Why was the election of 1800 unusual? How did it change the Constitution?

CHAPTER 10

The Republicans in Power

T HE ELECTION OF Thomas Jefferson as president in 1800 ended 12 years of Federalist domination of the government. It also marked a shift in political power from wealthy merchants and landowners to small farmers and property holders. For these reasons, Jefferson's election is often called "the revolution of 1800." Such a description is somewhat of an exaggeration, however. Although his administration did reverse some Federalist policies, the changes were fewer than many people expected.

JEFFERSON AS PRESIDENT

Jefferson was one of the best educated and most versatile men ever to be president. As a public servant, he had written the Declaration of Independence and served as governor of Virginia, foreign diplomat, secretary of state, and vice president. In addition, he was an inventor, a musician, a scientific farmer, and an architect. He designed both the University of Virginia and his home, Monticello.

Jefferson's inauguration was the first to be held in Washington, D.C. The capital was then a village of unpaved streets and unfinished public buildings. The new president, who liked simplicity, did away with much of the formality introduced by the Federalists. For instance, he put an end to stately balls and weekly receptions of the kind held by Washington and Adams.

Undoing Federalist Measures

When the Democratic-Republicans assumed control of the government, they repealed some of the Alien and Sedition Acts and allowed others to expire. Jefferson pardoned the people who had been imprisoned under the acts. Congress lowered the residence requirement for citizenship from 14 to 5 years.

The Democratic-Republicans also repealed the tax on whiskey. At the same time, they cut federal expenses. The army was reduced from 4000 to 2500 men, and the navy from 25 ships to a mere 7.

Marshall and the Judiciary

Jefferson had less success in limiting Federalist influence on the judicial branch of government. Shortly before the Federalists left office, Congress passed the *Judiciary Act of 1801*, which authorized an increase in the number of federal judges. By filling these positions with their supporters, the Federalists hoped to keep control of the judiciary. In his last hours as president, Adams worked far into the night signing appointments to the new positions. The newly appointed officials thus became known as "midnight judges."

When the Democratic-Republicans came into office, they quickly repealed the Judiciary Act and removed most of the last-minute appointees. But the episode led to another judicial development that was quite contrary to Jefferson's principles. This was the Supreme Court decision in a case called *Marbury* v. *Madison* (1803).

One of the "midnight judges," William Marbury, had not received his judicial appointment. He asked the Supreme Court to issue an order forcing Jefferson's secretary of state, James Madison, to deliver it. An earlier Judiciary Act, passed in 1789, had given the Supreme Court jurisdiction (the right to judge) in certain cases involving federal officials. In *Marbury* v. *Madison*, decided in 1803, the Supreme Court ruled against Marbury. The Court held that it did *not* have jurisdiction in this kind of case. The Constitution had specified the types of cases that could go directly to the Supreme Court, and this was not one of them. Therefore, part of the Judiciary Act of 1789 was unconstitutional. This decision helped establish the principle of judicial review—the idea that the Supreme Court has the power to rule on the constitutionality of acts of Congress and other government actions.

The decision in *Marbury* v. *Madison* was a brilliant move on the part of Chief Justice John Marshall—himself a Federalist appointed by Adams. On the surface, the decision gave the Democratic-Republicans the power to deny a job to a Federalist judge. It also limited the kinds of cases that the Supreme Court could hear. But the underlying idea—that the Supreme

IMPORTANT SUPREME COURT DECISIONS UNDER MARSHALL

Case	Background	Decision	Significance
Marbury v. Madison (1803)	Marbury, "midnight judge" who did not receive his judicial appointment, asked Supreme Court to force secretary of state to issue the appointment.	Court ruled that it did not have power to act in case because law granting it jurisdiction was illegal.	First decision to hold act of Congress unconstitutional; helped establish principle of judicial review.
Fletcher v. Peck (1810)	Georgia legislature, claiming fraud, canceled grant of land awarded by preceding legislature.	Court held that Georgia annulment was illegal because it interfered with right of contract.	First decision to judge a state law unconstitutional.
Dartmouth College v. Woodward (1819)	After New Hampshire annulled charter of Dartmouth College (granted by King George III), college had sued to recover it.	Court ruled in favor of Dartmouth, holding that charter was contract protected by Constitution.	Established Court's right to guarantee contracts between private groups or individuals.
McCulloch v. Maryland (1819)	When Maryland taxed branch of Bank of the United States located there, branch refused to pay.	Court upheld bank, ruling that a state could not hinder operation of federal laws.	Emphasized supremacy of national government over state governments.
Gibbons v. Ogden (1824)	Gibbons held that New York State had acted wrongly in granting Ogden exclusive right to operate steamboats between New York and New Jersey.	Court decided in favor of Gibbons, ruling that a state cannot interfere with interstate commerce.	Broadened commerce clause of Constitution (Art. I, Sect. 8), thus reinforcing loose construction.

Court could judge constitutionality—conflicted with the Democratic-Republican belief in strict construction. Supporters of this view felt that the Supreme Court was taking on powers that the Constitution had not granted.

Marshall dominated the Supreme Court from 1801 to 1835. His views angered Jefferson and his followers. But the force of Marshall's opinions helped make the Court a strong arm of the government.

Defeating the Barbary Pirates

In foreign affairs, Jefferson scored a victory in North Africa. This region included the four Barbary States of Morocco, Algiers, Tunis, and Tripoli. Pirates from these states had made it a practice to seize foreign ships passing through the Mediterranean, loot their cargoes, and hold the crews for ransom. To prevent the seizure of their ships, the United States and several European nations had been paying large sums as tribute to the Barbary States for many years.

In 1801, the ruler of Tripoli demanded a higher tribute from the United States. When Jefferson refused, Tripoli declared war. Jefferson then sent a few ships to blockade that country's coastline. A young naval lieutenant named Stephen Decatur performed the most daring deed of the war. One night, he sneaked into the harbor of Tripoli and destroyed an American vessel that had been captured and converted into a war-ship. The American blockade finally forced Tripoli to ask for peace. In a treaty signed in 1805, Tripoli promised to leave American ships alone. (Tribute continued to be paid to the other Barbary States until 1816.)

THE LOUISIANA PURCHASE

The most significant event of Jefferson's presidency was the purchase of Louisiana. At this time, the term referred to a vast territory lying between the Mississippi River and the Rocky Mountains.

Background

France, which had originally claimed Louisiana, ceded the region to Spain at the end of the French and Indian War. But when Napoleon rose to power in France in the 1790s, he wanted to restore the French empire in America. In 1800, he forced Spain to return Louisiana to France. Two years later, the French canceled the American right of deposit at New Orleans.

Western farmers were worried about shipping their goods. And the American public did not like the idea of having Napoleon's troops at the nation's back door. Therefore, Jefferson decided to buy New Orleans from the French. Early in 1803, he sent James Monroe to Paris. Monroe and Robert Livingston (who was already there, representing the United States) were prepared to offer $10 million for New Orleans.

A Surprise Package

By this time, Napoleon's situation had changed. The French ruler had given up his dream of an empire in America. He had lost thousands of French troops in trying to crush a slave rebellion led by Toussaint L'Ouverture on the Caribbean island of Hispaniola. In addition, France was again on the verge of war with England and needed money. Napoleon surprised Livingston and Monroe by offering to sell all of Louisiana, including New Orleans, for $15 million. Seizing the chance to buy this vast territory at so low a price, the Americans accepted Napoleon's offer.

Jefferson was pleased with his amazing bargain. It doubled the size of the United States. But it also raised a constitutional problem that troubled the president. A believer in strict construction, Jefferson knew that the Constitution did not clearly authorize the government to buy foreign territory. But he was convinced that Louisiana was essential to the future development of the United States. Aware that he was recommend-

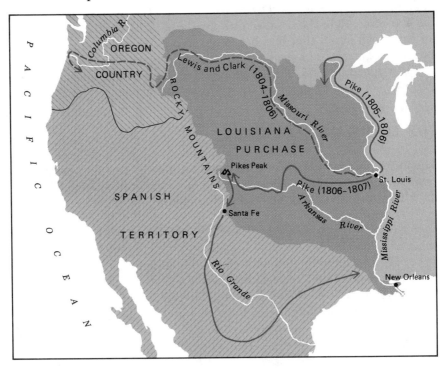

EXPLORING THE LOUISIANA PURCHASE

Thomas Jefferson

Monticello

Lewis and Clark

Sacajawea

ing a loose interpretation of the Constitution, Jefferson persuaded the Senate to ratify the treaty. Later, he admitted that he had "stretched the Constitution until it cracked."

Explorations of the Territory

Few Americans of Jefferson's time knew anything about the region that was now called the Louisiana Purchase. But hardy explorers soon began to bring back reports.

LEWIS AND CLARK   In 1804, Jefferson sent Meriwether Lewis and William Clark to explore the northern part of the Louisiana Purchase. Their expedition started from St. Louis and followed the Missouri River to its source. The group crossed the Rocky Mountains into the area known as the Oregon Country and then followed the Columbia River to the Pacific Ocean. The explorers were aided during their two-year journey by an Indian woman, Sacajawea.

The reports of Lewis and Clark informed Americans about the climate, geography, animals, and Indians of the West. The exploration of the Oregon Country also laid the basis for America's claim to that area.

PIKE   Jefferson sent out another expedition to find the source of the Mississippi River. Led by a young army lieutenant, Zebulon Pike, this group explored the northeastern part of the Louisiana Purchase in 1805 and 1806. Later in 1806, Pike made a second trip of exploration, this time to the southwestern region of the territory. First, he headed west across the plains to the Arkansas River. Then, he followed the river to the Rockies, where he sighted the mountain later called Pikes Peak. Turning south, Pike reached the Rio Grande in Spanish territory. The authorities at Santa Fe seized him and took him into what is now Mexico, but later released him. He returned home by way of Texas. Pike's published account of his travels was widely read and aroused much interest in America's new territory.

APPROACHING CONFLICT

Jefferson was re-elected president in 1804. His second term, from 1805 to 1809, was beset with problems that arose from the outbreak of another war in Europe. Although American interests were seriously threatened, Jefferson managed to avoid armed conflict and to keep the nation at peace.

Interference With American Shipping

Britain and France, briefly at peace, renewed their war in 1803. Their conflict again endangered the neutrality of the United States. Neither warring nation recognized the right of neutral countries to trade with its enemy. Both of them interfered with U.S. shipping, but Britain caused more trouble because it had a larger navy. The British seized hundreds of American ships, confiscated their cargoes, and impressed thousands of American sailors.

Americans were especially outraged by an event that took place off the Virginia coast in June 1807. The *Leopard*, a British man-of-war, demanded to search the American warship *Chesapeake*. The British claimed that deserters from their navy were aboard. When the American commander denied the claim and refused to permit the search, the *Leopard* opened fire, killing or wounding 21 sailors. The British then boarded the *Chesapeake* and removed four men.

Economic Pressure

Jefferson believed that American goods were so important to Britain and France that cutting off the supply would force them to respect U.S. rights. At the president's urging, Congress passed the *Embargo Act of 1807*. It stopped all U.S. trade with foreign countries.

The embargo failed to bring about any change in British or French policy. Worse, it was a disaster for the American economy. Merchants and shippers were faced with ruin, and many turned to smuggling. Shipbuilding came to a halt. Unemployment spread throughout the Northeast, as sailors, longshoremen, clerks, and carpenters were idled. The loss of foreign markets for crops hurt farmers, too.

Opposition to the measure was so great that it was repealed. A substitute, the *Non-Intercourse Act of 1809*, reopened trade with all nations except Britain and France. But the new law failed to change British and French war policies and was allowed to lapse after a year.

The "War Hawks"

Congress at this time was dominated by the so-called "War Hawks," a group of young legislators from the West and South. Strongly nationalistic, the War Hawks were eager for the United States to expand. Their leaders included Henry Clay of Kentucky and John C. Calhoun of South Carolina, both elected in 1810. The War Hawks called for war with Britain. Their aim was to take over British-held Canada and Spanish-held Florida. (Spain was Britain's ally at the time.)

Native Americans and the Frontier

Adding to the mood of tension during this period were troubles on the western frontier. American migration to the West had increased after 1794. In that year, troops under Anthony Wayne had defeated a Native American force at the Battle of Fallen Timbers (near present-day Toledo, Ohio). Wayne's victory ended Native American resistance to settlement in Ohio.

The tide of Western migration then spilled over into Indiana and Illinois, causing the tribes in these areas to become increasingly hostile. Leading the opposition to the spread of settlement were two Shawnee chiefs, Tecumseh and his brother, "the Prophet." They aimed to unite all the tribes east of the Mississippi into a powerful confederacy against settlers from the East.

During the summer of 1811, Native Americans attacked many pioneer settlements. Frontier people blamed the British for stirring up the Native Americans. Spurred by the pioneers' fears, William Henry Harrison, governor of the Indiana Territory, marched on Tecumseh's village. (Tecumseh was away seeking the help of southern tribes.) American troops defeated the Native Americans in the Battle of Tippecanoe (in northwestern Indiana) on November 7, 1811. British arms were found on the Native Americans. Using this evidence, the War Hawks called for an invasion of Canada. Their aim was to stop the British from supplying the tribes.

THE WAR OF 1812

James Madison succeeded Jefferson as president in 1809. For the next three years, he tried to protect American neutrality by using economic pressure against Britain, but to no avail. The British continued to interfere with U.S. ships, impress American seamen, and violate the nation's neutral rights and coastal waters. By the middle of 1812, anti-British feeling in the United States was so strong that Madison asked Congress to declare war against Britain. It did so in June. Though the war lasted for two years, it is known as the War of 1812.

Failure in Canada

The War of 1812 began with an American invasion of the British territory of Canada. American forces attacked from Lake Champlain, from across the Niagara River, and from Detroit. Each of the three attacks failed. The following year, a U.S. force invaded and burned York (Toronto) and then withdrew. The Americans were unsuccessful in a later attempt to take Montreal.

In 1814, a U.S. army crossed the Niagara River into Canada, seized Fort Erie, and defeated the British near the Chippewa River. The two sides next clashed at Lundy's Lane, but neither side won. The Americans then withdrew to Fort Erie and successfully withstood a British siege. Later, the Americans moved back across the border into New York State.

The War at Sea

The U.S. Navy, numbering 16 vessels, was hopelessly outclassed by the British fleet of more than 1000 warships—the largest navy in the world. Even so, the Americans scored several outstanding victories against the British. (Britain was once again at war with France, which helped the United States.) The warship *Constitution*, commanded by Isaac Hull, destroyed the British warship *Guerrière* in a furious battle off Nova Scotia. Later, under William Bainbridge, the *Constitution* also defeated the *Java* off Brazil. These victories made the American ship famous; because of the punishment it could take, it was nicknamed "Old Ironsides." The *United States*, commanded by Stephen Decatur, captured the *Macedonian*. Altogether, U.S. naval vessels and privateers seized or destroyed about 1500 British merchant vessels during the war.

In time, however, the numerically superior British navy drove the Americans from the sea. Beginning in 1813, a British blockade of the Atlantic coast brought U.S. foreign commerce to a halt.

Don't give up the ship!

—*James Lawrence, dying captain of the American warship*
Chesapeake *before its capture by the British*

Success in the Northwest Territory

Early in the war, the British, aided by Tecumseh, captured Detroit. Their Indian allies also seized Fort Dearborn (Chicago), killed or captured everyone in the fort, and burned it down. These victories gave the British control of Lake Erie and the northern Northwest Territory, but only temporarily.

With great difficulty, the Americans built a small fleet of ships at Erie, Pennsylvania, on Lake Erie. Commanded by Oliver Hazard Perry, the ships engaged the British in September 1813. The U.S. sailors decisively defeated the enemy in the Battle of Lake Erie.

Perry's victory forced the British to abandon Detroit. A force of American frontiersmen under William Henry Harrison followed the retreating British and Indians into Canada, overtook them at the Thames River, and defeated them in October 1813. Tecumseh's death during the fighting caused the Indians to desert the British. This battle ended the British hold on the Northwest Territory.

Indians had also been raiding frontier settlements in the territory south of the Ohio River. In the spring of 1814, Andrew Jackson and an army of Tennessee militia subdued a Creek Indian force at the Battle of Horseshoe Bend in Alabama. Indian resistance was now broken in the entire region between the Appalachian Mountains and the Mississippi River.

We have met the enemy, and they are ours.

—Oliver Hazard Perry reporting his victory
at the Battle of Lake Erie

The British Offensive

After a crucial defeat of Napoleon in 1814, the British turned their full attention to the war in America. They sent a large force of experienced troops across the Atlantic. The British planned attacks at three strategic points: Lake Champlain, Chesapeake Bay, and New Orleans.

THE BATTLE OF LAKE CHAMPLAIN   In September 1814, about 11,000 British troops, moving south from Canada, invaded New York along the western shore of Lake Champlain. Both the British and the Americans had ships on the lake. The two fleets met in the Battle of Lake Champlain. The American fleet, commanded by Thomas Macdonough, skillfully outmaneuvered the British and defeated them completely. With its naval support gone, the British army retreated to Canada and gave up its invasion of New York.

CHESAPEAKE BAY   Meanwhile, a British squadron had entered Chesapeake Bay and landed troops in Maryland. They marched into Washington, D.C., almost unopposed. Retaliating for the destruction of York by American raiders the year before, the British set fire to many government buildings. Among them were the Capitol and the White House. Shortly thereafter, the British withdrew from the city.

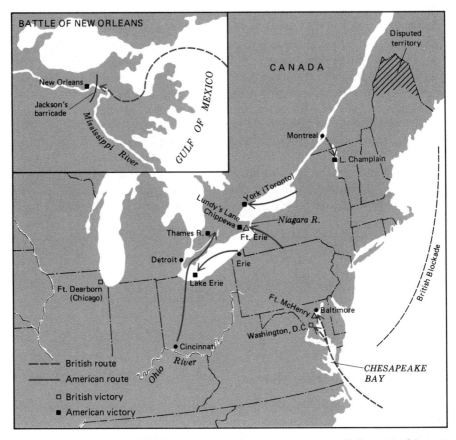

THE WAR OF 1812

The British then sailed north to attack Baltimore but found it better prepared to resist invasion. Their landing party encountered strong opposition and was stopped at the city's outskirts. British ships tried to destroy Fort McHenry, which protected the entrance to Baltimore's harbor. Despite an all-night bombardment, they failed. This unsuccessful attack ended the British offensive in Chesapeake Bay.

One American who watched the attack was Francis Scott Key. The sight of the American flag still flying the next morning inspired him to write the words to "The Star-Spangled Banner." (See page 557.)

THE BATTLE OF NEW ORLEANS   Blocked at Lake Champlain and in Chesapeake Bay, the British next moved against New Orleans. From bases in the Caribbean, they transported some 7500 troops to Louisiana late in 1814. Led by Andrew Jackson, the American frontiersmen defending New Orleans put up a barricade and awaited the enemy. On

January 8, 1815, the British attacked. In the battle that followed, they were thoroughly beaten. They suffered more than 2000 casualties at the hands of the sharpshooting Westerners. U.S. losses numbered 71 killed and wounded.

The victory at New Orleans restored the nation's pride and made a national hero of Andrew Jackson. This encounter had nothing to do with the outcome of the war, though. Unknown to either fighting force, a treaty of peace had been signed in Europe two weeks earlier.

End of the War

By the end of 1814, both sides were eager for peace. Many Americans had never supported the war in the first place. Opposition was particularly strong in the Northeast, where shipping had been hurt badly. In 1814, Federalist delegates from New England met at Hartford, Connecticut, to condemn "Mr. Madison's war." This *Hartford Convention* even talked of secession (withdrawal from the Union), but the coming of peace ended the discussion.

Representatives from Britain and the United States signed a treaty of peace in Ghent, Belgium, late in 1814. The treaty ended the state of war and restored the boundaries as they had been before. Strangely, the *Treaty of Ghent* did not mention two major causes of the war: the impressment of U.S. sailors and the violation of American rights at sea. But the wars with Napoleon were over, so these issues had no meaning anymore.

The War of 1812 did not end in victory for either side, but it did have important effects on the United States:

1. It inspired a feeling of nationalism among Americans.
2. It encouraged the growth of industry in the United States. Americans were unable to buy manufactured goods from abroad during the war. As a result, American factories had expanded their facilities and increased their output.
3. It stimulated westward expansion by ending Indian resistance in a huge area west of the Appalachians.
4. It demonstrated to the world that the United States was capable of defending its rights. As a result, the United States earned the respect of Britain and other foreign nations.

Relations with Britain improved greatly after the war, and several problems were solved by friendly discussion and negotitation. The *Rush-Bagot Agreement* of 1817 provided that neither nation would keep war-ships on the Great Lakes. The *Convention of 1818* fixed the disputed boundary between Canada and the United States, from Minnesota to the Rockies, along the 49th parallel. This agreement also reaffirmed American fishing rights off the coasts of Labrador and Newfoundland, and opened the Oregon Country to settlers from both nations.

TWO IMPORTANT MOVES UNDER MONROE

In the presidential election of 1816, the Federalists ran their last national candidate, Rufus King. The party, already weakened, had been further damaged by its opposition to the War of 1812. King was soundly defeated by James Monroe, the last member of the so-called "Virginia dynasty." Monroe served two terms as president, from 1817 to 1825. The period of his presidency is sometimes called the Era of Good Feelings. It seemed to be a time of political harmony, since there was now only one party, that of the Democratic-Republicans. The period is noted for two developments in foreign relations—the acquisition of Florida and the proclamation of the Monroe Doctrine.

Adding Florida

In the early 19th century, Spain controlled an important area south of the United States. One part of it, known as East Florida, was the long peninsula jutting into the Atlantic. The other part, called West Florida, was a narrow stretch of land extending west along the Gulf of Mexico to the Mississippi River. The United States claimed that a large portion of West Florida was included in the Louisiana Purchase. When American colonists north of New Orleans declared their independence from Spanish rule in 1810, the United States annexed this section. Three years later, during the War of 1812, American troops captured the Spanish fort at Mobile. The

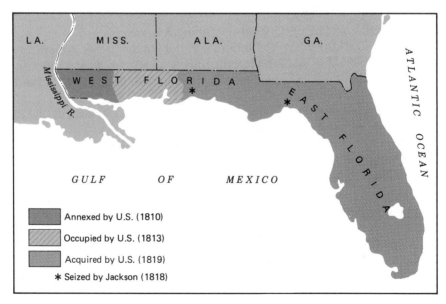

ACQUISITION OF FLORIDA

United States kept this part of West Florida, too, despite Spain's protests.

Americans had long complained about Spanish control of East Florida. Indians escaped to the area after attacking Southern settlements. Runaway slaves fled there, too. And pirates and smugglers used it as a base of operations.

In 1818, Andrew Jackson was sent to subdue some Seminole Indians who had been raiding settlements in Alabama and Georgia. He pursued the Indians into East Florida, defeated them, and also captured several Spanish forts. His expedition made it clear that the United States could take all of East Florida by force if it wanted to. In 1819, Spain agreed to give up the region. In exchange, the United States agreed to cancel Spain's $5 million debt to American citizens. The Spaniards also surrendered their rights to West Florida. The United States, in turn, gave up its claim to Texas (which Americans had argued was also part of the Louisiana Purchase).

The Monroe Doctrine

One reason why Spain could do little about Florida was that Spanish colonies in Latin America were in rebellion. The revolts, which began in Venezuela in 1810, soon spread. One country after another declared independence. In 1824, a Spanish army was decisively beaten in Peru. This defeat signaled the end of Spanish control of Latin America. Only the islands of Cuba and Puerto Rico remained under Spanish rule.

The United States quickly recognized the newly independent nations of Latin America, but Europe lagged behind. In fact, it seemed that Spain, aided by France, might try to recover its colonies.

Meanwhile, another development threatened the Pacific coast. Russia, starting from its base in Alaska, began to expand southward. In 1821, the Russians claimed the Pacific coast as far south as the 51st parallel, within the Oregon Country.

Americans did not like the idea of European intervention in the Western Hemisphere. In 1823, President Monroe issued a strong warning to Europe to keep out. This proclamation, later called the *Monroe Doctrine*, became a cornerstone of U.S. foreign policy. It made three major points:

1. The American continents were closed to further colonization by European nations.
2. Any attempt by European powers to interfere with existing governments in America would be regarded as an unfriendly act against the United States.
3. The United States would not interfere in European affairs or with existing European colonies in the Western Hemisphere.

The British supported Monroe. They feared that Spanish or French occupation of Latin America would cut off British trade with the newly independent countries. Britain also opposed Russian expansion in the Oregon Country, where it had claims of its own.

Faced with the opposition of the United States and Britain, the European powers dropped their plans to retake Spain's former colonies. Russia, too, decided to pull back. In 1824, it agreed to establish the boundary between the Oregon Country and Alaska at 54° 40′ north latitude.

Matching Test

COLUMN A	COLUMN B
1. John Marshall	a. congressman who urged war with Britain in early 19th century
2. Stephen Decatur	
3. Sacajawea	
4. Zebulon Pike	b. victor over Indians at Battle of Tippecanoe
5. Henry Clay	
6. Tecumseh	c. leader of daring raid against Barbary pirates
7. William Henry Harrison	
8. Oliver Hazard Perry	d. leader of U.S. forces invading Florida in 1818
9. Francis Scott Key	
10. Andrew Jackson	e. author of "The Star-Spangled Banner"
	f. guide to Lewis and Clark in their explorations
	g. explorer who had mountain in Rockies named after him
	h. chief justice of United States for over 30 years
	i. victor at Battle of Lake Erie
	j. Indian leader who tried to unite Mississippi Valley tribes

True-False Test

1. One of Jefferson's aims as president was to increase federal spending on U.S. military forces.
2. The case of *Marbury* v. *Madison* grew out of a judicial appointment by President John Adams.
3. The purchase of Louisiana tripled the size of the United States.

4. The explorations of Lewis and Clark laid the basis for later American claims to the Oregon Country.
5. Jefferson tried to end British interference with American shipping by blockading English ports.
6. In the War of 1812, Americans were unsuccessful in their efforts to take Canada.
7. The Battle of New Orleans took place after the War of 1812 had officially ended.
8. A key provision of the Treaty of Ghent was that impressment of U.S. sailors by the British would stop.
9. The United States acquired East and West Florida from Spain.
10. One aim of the Monroe Doctrine was to prevent further European colonization of the Western Hemisphere.

Map Test

GROUP A

Answer the following questions by studying the map on page 160.

1. Name the American settlement that was the point of departure for three separate explorations of the Louisiana Purchase.
2. What natural features made this place a strategic location?
3. Name the river that Lewis and Clark followed on their journey through the new territory.
4. What major river system did they come upon in the Far Northwest?
5. On Pike's 1806–1807 trip, which river did he follow westward?
6. What foreign center did Pike reach in the Southwest?
7. To whom did this place belong?
8. What constituted the eastern boundary of the Louisiana Purchase?
9. What mountain peak was named for one of the explorers of the Louisiana Purchase?
10. In what mountain range is it located?

GROUP B

Locate each of the following places on the map on page 166. Then, referring to the text, as necessary, indicate what important event occurred there during the War of 1812.

1. Fort McHenry
2. New Orleans
3. Lake Erie
4. Washington, D.C.
5. Lake Champlain
6. Detroit
7. Thames River
8. York

Essay Questions

1. Explain the background and importance of the case of *Marbury* v. *Madison*.
2. How did the sale of Louisiana come about? Why was Jefferson troubled by its purchase?
3. Give two main causes of the War of 1812. Why did they convince Americans to go to war?
4. Describe two changes that the War of 1812 helped bring about in the United States.
5. What circumstances led to the issuing of the Monroe Doctrine? What effects did the proclamation have?

CHAPTER *11*

Expansion and Progress

Dᴜʀɪɴɢ ᴛʜᴇ ᴇᴀʀʟʏ 19th century, the United States changed a great deal. Its size doubled, and its population quadrupled. Industrialization began to reshape the nation's economy. A French visitor in the 1830s described the United States as "a land of wonders" where "everything is in constant motion and every change seems an improvement."

THE WESTWARD MOVEMENT

One area of "constant motion" was the region called the West. In the 18th and 19th centuries, "the West" was generally the frontier of settlement at any given time. In the 1770s, it was the land just beyond the Appalachian Mountains. By the 1840s, it had become the region west of the Mississippi River. Wherever it was, the West always attracted people looking for a better life. They included restless adventurers, Eastern farmers whose lands had worn out, unemployed workers, and new immigrants. When the first census was taken in 1790, only about 3 percent of the population lived west of the Appalachians. In 1840, the sixth census showed that more than 37 percent of the American people lived in the West.

The Old Southwest

One of the first trans-Appalachian regions to be settled was the Old Southwest, the area south of the Ohio River. (It is called the Old Southwest to differentiate it from the "newer" Southwest beyond the Mississippi.)

173

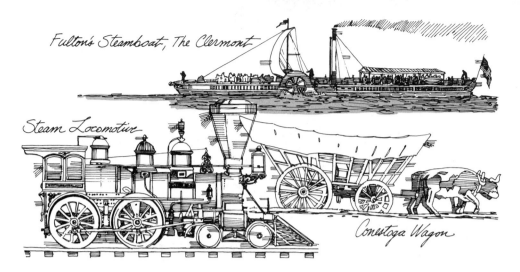

Fulton's Steamboat, The Clermont

Steam Locomotive

Conestoga Wagon

KENTUCKY AND TENNESSEE   Some years before the Revolution, pioneers from North Carolina and Virginia settled near the Watauga River in northeastern Tennessee. Because the region had fertile soil and abundant game, other Americans soon followed. They settled in the rich valleys of the Cumberland, Tennessee, and Kentucky rivers and their tributaries.

The most famous pioneer in this region was Daniel Boone. One of the first to explore Kentucky, he found a pathway across the Appalachians through the Cumberland Gap. This was the Wilderness Road, which became a main route for migration into the territory.

James Harrod established the first pioneer settlement in Kentucky at Harrodsburg in 1774. Boonesborough was founded the following year by settlers led in by Boone. James Robertson, an early settler of the Watauga Valley in Tennessee, founded Nashville in 1780. By 1790, there were some 109,000 people in Kentucky and Tennessee. The settler population grew to nearly 327,000 by 1800 and to more than 1.6 million by 1840.

MISSISSIPPI AND ALABAMA   Farther south, the Old Southwest was organized as the Mississippi Territory. It was opened to settlement in 1798. Southern planters moved there with their slaves and developed large cotton plantations in the fertile lowlands. Indians, however, hindered settlement in the region until Andrew Jackson's victory at Horseshoe Bend in 1814. Thousands of Southerners then gave up their worn-out farms in the Carolinas and Georgia, and headed southwest. The population of the region was about 41,000 in 1810, more than 200,000 ten years later, and almost 1 million by 1840.

The Northwest Territory

The region north of the Old Southwest was known as the Old Northwest, or the Northwest Territory. It, too, began attracting settlers before the Revolution. During the Confederation period, Congress

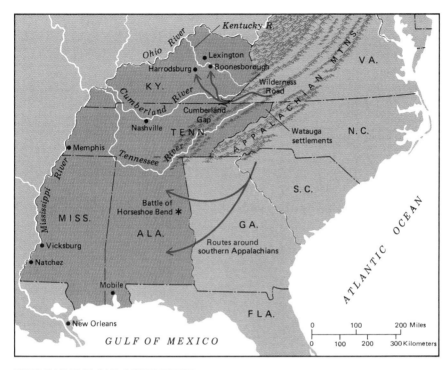

SETTLING THE OLD SOUTHWEST

passed two laws that affected not only the Northwest Territory but other regions of the West as well.

THE ORDINANCE OF 1785   This law provided that the land was to be surveyed and divided into townships six miles square. Each township was to contain 36 sections one mile square (640 acres). One section in each township was set aside for the support of public schools. The rest of the land was then offered for sale at public auction at a minimum price of $1 an acre. A purchaser had to buy a full section of land. Since most settlers could not afford to do this, land companies bought up much of the region. They subdivided the sections and sold the smaller lots to settlers at a profit.

THE ORDINANCE OF 1787   This law is often called the *Northwest Ordinance*. It organized the Old Northwest into the Northwest Territory and provided a plan for governing it. The law included six important provisions:

1. Congress would set up a temporary government by appointing a governor and three judges.

TOWNSHIP PLAN (ORDINANCE OF 1785)

TOWNSHIP
6 MILES

6	5	4	3	2	1
7	8	9	10	11	12
18	17	16	15	14	13
19	20	21	22	23	24
30	29	28	27	26	25
31	32	33	34	35	36

6 MILES

SET ASIDE FOR SUPPORT OF PUBLIC SCHOOLS

EACH SECTION = 640 ACRES

SECTION

1 MILE

HALF SECTION
320 ACRES

QUARTER SECTION

(160 ACRES)

HALF-QUARTER SECTION

QUARTER-QUARTER SECTION

1 MILE

2. When the territory had 5000 free adult males, a representative legislature was to be established.

3. When a part of the territory had a population of 60,000 free settlers, that region would be eligible for admission into the Union as a state. New states would be equal to the original states "in all respects whatsoever." (No fewer than three, and no more than five, states were to be created from the Northwest Territory.)

4. Personal rights, such as freedom of religion, freedom of speech, and trial by jury, were guaranteed.

5. Slavery was prohibited.

6. Public schools were encouraged.

The Northwest Ordinance is generally considered to be the outstanding achievement of Congress under the Articles of Confederation. This law set a pattern for dealing with America's public lands from the Appalachians to the Pacific. It made sure that new states would be added to the Union as equals of the original 13, rather than as colonies. And it guaranteed to Americans in new territories civil liberties, democratic government, and public education.

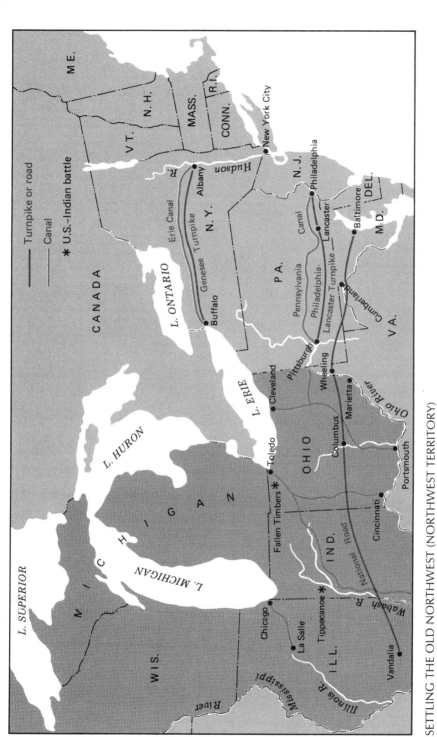

SETTLING THE OLD NORTHWEST (NORTHWEST TERRITORY)

SETTLEMENT   The rich, level land of the Northwest Territory drew many New Englanders away from their rocky hillside farms. It also attracted pioneers from New York and Pennsylvania. The first pioneer settlement in the area was made in 1788 at Marietta, Ohio. Cincinnati was founded later the same year. In 1796, Moses Cleaveland laid out the city that bears his name (in a slightly different spelling).

After their defeats at Fallen Timbers in 1794 and Tippecanoe in 1811, most Indian tribes in the eastern Northwest Territory were moved out. With the Indian threat removed, settlers flocked to the area. Its population rose to about 51,000 in 1800, nearly 272,000 in 1810, and almost 3 million in 1840.

Conditions on the Frontier

Like Europeans who came to the New World, Americans who moved west hoped for a better life. At first, existence was hard, but as the years passed, conditions improved.

POPULATION PATTERNS   Usually, the first people into a new region were scouts and fur traders. They were single men—"loners" who liked independence. Next came speculators. They bought large tracts of land to subdivide and sell to pioneer farmers.

The first farm families in the West lived much as the earliest settlers had along the Atlantic coast. The men hacked clearings out of the wilderness, built simple log cabins, and raised food for their families. Pioneer women were skilled at preserving food, making clothes, and using home remedies to cure sicknesses.

With the arrival of more settlers, small communities arose. Churches, schools, general stores, and local industries were established. A few professionals also settled in the towns to provide medical, legal, financial, and other community services.

NEW STATES (1791-1819)

State	Admitted to Union
Vermont	1791
Kentucky	1792
Tennessee	1796
Ohio	1803
Louisiana	1812
Indiana	1816
Mississippi	1817
Illinois	1818
Alabama	1819

OUTLOOK OF THE WESTERNERS Frontier people respected one another for their courage, skill, and hard work, rather than for their wealth or social position. They accepted one another as social and political equals. Common problems and dangers drew pioneer families together in a spirit of neighborliness and cooperation. Living in a land of opportunity, Westerners were filled with hope for the future. They had a strong sense of loyalty toward the national government and vigorously supported greater political democracy.

NATIVE AMERICANS From the settler's point of view, the Native Americans were holding back the march of civilization by their resistance to the spread of farms and towns. From the Native Americans' point of view, the settlers were destroying their way of life and source of food by cutting down forests and killing off wild game.

The federal government thought of itself as protector of settlers and Native Americans alike. It arranged treaties for the purchase of Native land, setting up smaller tracts for the Native Americans to live on. But many of the sales were fraudulent, taking from the Native Americans territories that had been promised to them for "as long as the grass shall grow." When the Native Americans resisted signing such agreements, government troops used force.

Thousands of Native Americans chose to move west of the Mississippi, where few settlers lived. Others were forcibly moved. This happened in the Southeast during the 1830s. The Native American inhabitants of the area—the Cherokees, Chickasaws, Choctaws, Creeks, and Seminoles—were known as the "Five Civilized Tribes." They had taken up farming and were making a serious effort to adapt to the culture of their white neighbors, but to no avail. Against their will, they were driven from their lands and marched to what is now Oklahoma. So many died on the way that the journey is still called the "Trail of Tears."

It appeared impossible to avoid bitterness and violence between settlers and Native Americans. Two such different cultures seemed bound to clash when they came into contact. In conflict after conflict, the weaker was forced to give way to the stronger (see page 180).

THE BEGINNINGS OF INDUSTRIALIZATION

Around the mid-1700s, England began to experience a great change known as the Industrial Revolution. It had two main elements: (1) hand methods of production gave way to machine methods, and (2) manufacturing shifted from homes to factories.

The Industrial Revolution started in England's textile industry. The invention of spinning and weaving machines, operated by water-

CONFLICTS WITH NATIVE AMERICANS (1790–1842)

Date	Event	Outcome
1790	Defeat of Harmar (Indiana)	Shawnees forced troops under Josiah Harmar to retreat.
1791	Defeat of St. Clair (Indiana)	Miamis and other Native Americans under Little Turtle defeated army detachment under Arthur St. Clair.
1794	Battle of Fallen Timbers (Ohio)	Avenging Harmar and St. Clair, Anthony Wayne defeated Native American army. In subsequent Treaty of Greenville, Native Americans gave up thousands of acres in Ohio and eastern Indiana.
1811	Battle of Tippecanoe (Indiana)	William Henry Harrison's victory dealt blow to confederacy organized by Tecumseh.
1812	Fort Dearborn Massacre (Illinois)	Native Americans killed or captured entire garrison and burned fort.
1813	Fort Mims Massacre (Alabama)	Creeks killed about 500 Americans and their Native American allies.
1814	Battle of Horseshoe Bend (Alabama)	In retaliation for Fort Mims, Andrew Jackson defeated Creeks. Subsequent treaty forced them to give up lands in Mississippi Territory.
1818	First Seminole War (Florida)	Andrew Jackson, invading Florida, broke up Seminole force and seized two Spanish towns. Incident convinced Spain to sell Florida to the United States.
1832	Black Hawk War (Illinois, Wisconsin)	Sauks and Foxes under Black Hawk refused to leave Illinois, were chased into southern Wisconsin, and were massacred at Bad Axe River by U.S. forces.
1835–1842	Second Seminole War (Florida)	Seminoles, led by Osceola, fought against U.S. troops seeking to transfer them to Oklahoma. Osceola was imprisoned, and thousands of his followers were removed. Others fled to the swamps and remained in Florida.

power, made possible the large-scale manufacture of thread and cloth. (Steam replaced water as a source of power later in the century.) Use of machinery and the factory system spread to other industries, and Britain soon became the leading manufacturing country in the world.

Factors Favoring New England

Americans were slow to industrialize at first, because British manufactured goods were readily available to them. But then, during the Napoleonic Wars and the War of 1812, U.S. trade with England almost stopped. To make up for the loss of imported products, enterprising New Englanders began to build factories and turn out manufactured goods for the American market.

Several conditions favored New England as a manufacturing region:

1. Its many swift rivers and streams provided sources of waterpower to run factories.
2. It had an adequate supply of local and, later, immigrant laborers.
3. New Englanders had a tradition of craftsmanship.
4. The interruption of trade with Europe left merchants and shippers with idle capital to invest in factories.

The Textile Business

The English tried to keep their industrial methods secret. They forbade skilled workers to leave the country and prohibited the export of machines, models, or sketches. But one experienced textile worker named Samuel Slater did move to the United States. From memory, he put together the machinery necessary to spin cotton yarn. In 1790, Slater built the first successful cotton mill in America, at Pawtucket, Rhode Island. He is regarded as the father of the American factory system.

One of the first New England merchants to invest in textiles was Francis Lowell. In 1813, he set up a factory at Waltham, Massachusetts. There, for the first time, all the processes for turning raw cotton into woven cloth took place under one roof.

Similar factories were built throughout New England. By 1840, more than 1300 cotton mills there employed 75,000 people. The mills produced $46 million worth of cotton goods a year. The prices of cotton cloth indicate the importance of the factory system and machine production. In 1815, a yard cost 40 cents. By 1830, the cost was only $4\frac{1}{2}$ cents. Machines in factories were able to manufacture more cloth at a lower cost than individuals could produce by hand at home.

Stimulating Industry

The industrial growth of the United States was aided by several factors. One was the ingenuity of the American people. Another was the attitude of the federal government.

INTERCHANGEABLE PARTS   In the early 1800s, several inventors experimented with new methods for manufacturing firearms. Most

TECHNOLOGICAL DEVELOPMENTS (1787–1846)

Date	Inventor	Invention or Discovery
1787	John Fitch	Launched first American steamboat
1787	Oliver Evans	Built first high-pressure steam engine in United States
1793	Eli Whitney	Made first cotton gin; later, one of pioneers in the development of system of interchangeable parts
1797	Charles Newbold	Patented first cast-iron plow
1807	Robert Fulton	Launched first commercially successful steamboat
1819	Jethro Wood	Patented cast-iron plow using three interchangeable parts
1827	John Hall	Demonstrated workable system of interchangeable parts in manufacture of firearms
1829	Joseph Henry	Improved electromagnet, which made telegraph possible
1830	Peter Cooper	Built first U.S. steam locomotive
1834	Cyrus McCormick	Patented mechanical reaper
1835	Samuel Colt	Patented revolver
1837	John Deere	Made plow from steel, which kept soil from sticking
1839	Charles Goodyear	Discovered process of vulcanizing rubber, which made it practical to use
1844	Samuel F. B. Morse	Patented first telegraph and sent first message over wires: "What hath God wrought!"
1846	William T. G. Morton	Introduced use of ether as anesthetic in surgery
1846	Richard M. Hoe	Invented rotary printing press
1846	Elias Howe	Patented first sewing machine

prominent among them were three New Englanders: Eli Whitney, inventor of the cotton gin; Simeon North, a Connecticut gunsmith; and John Hall, a skilled armorer employed at the government armory in Harpers Ferry, Virginia. Their efforts finally led to the development of a workable system for making guns and other finished products out of interchangeable parts.

Whitney started experimenting with interchangeable parts in the late 1790s. Earlier, it had been customary for a single skilled worker to produce all the parts of a gun and then assemble them. Whitney and others thought it might be more efficient to assign each part to a different worker, who would produce large quantities of that unit on a machine especially designed for its manufacture. These standard parts—triggers, barrels, stocks, and so on—could then be assembled into finished products. Whitney's original experiments with the new method fell short of success. It was John Hall who, in the 1820s, demonstrated that firearms made entirely of interchangeable parts could be produced quickly and cheaply.

The system of interchangeable parts soon spread to the production of pistols, clocks, and watches. Later, farm machinery, sewing machines, stoves, and other goods were also made this way. In time, this "American system of manufacturing" was used in all industrial production—both in the United States and abroad.

GOVERNMENT HELP   After the War of 1812, English manufacturers wanted to win back their lost American markets. So they flooded the United States with cheap goods. To prevent the ruin of the nation's "infant" industries, Congress passed the first U.S. protective tariff in 1816. Duties on imports were raised so that American manufacturers could undersell foreign competitors. The tariff thus encouraged the growth of industry.

That same year, Congress chartered the second Bank of the United States. This move also helped American manufacturers because it not only enlarged the banking system but also provided better credit facilities.

The Growth of Cities

Before the Industrial Revolution came to America, almost everyone lived in rural areas. The spread of industrialization changed this. Factories were usually built in or near cities, or cities grew up around new factories. As more and more Americans gained employment as factory workers, they also became city dwellers. Between 1800 and 1840, the number of American cities that could boast a population of 10,000 or more rose from 6 to 37.

Improvements in Agriculture

Machinery also began to aid American farmers in the early 1800s. For a long time, farming methods had been crude and unscientific. In 1800, most farmers were still using simple tools to work their land. Every step in farming, from planting to harvesting, was done by hand.

The most important invention in this period was probably Eli Whitney's cotton gin (short for "engine"), which was introduced in 1793. It was a simple machine that separated seeds from cotton fibers 50 times faster than the process could be done by hand. Because of the cotton gin, the South increased its cotton production tremendously—from 73,000 bales in 1800 to 732,000 bales in 1830. Thus, there was a steady supply of raw cotton for the North's growing textile industry.

Other new or improved implements for farming were introduced early in the 19th century. The cradle and then the reaper replaced the sickle for cutting grain. The thresher replaced the flail for separating grain or seeds from stalks. Metal plows took the place of wooden ones. Mowing and haying machines, seed drills, and cultivators were additional aids that enabled farmers to increase their productivity and meet the nation's rising demand for food.

PROGRESS IN TRANSPORTATION

As the United States increased in size, it needed improved networks of transportation. Industries wanted better and faster ways to get raw materials and to ship finished products to market.

Vehicles and Roads

Land vehicles of the early 19th century, pulled by horses, were slow and hard to handle. The chief means of carrying passengers and mail was the stagecoach. For transporting freight, Americans developed the Conestoga wagon. It was canvas-covered, with a high body, broad-rimmed wheels, and a watertight bottom for crossing streams.

Horse-drawn vehicles were still in wide use in the late 19th century. But there were more roads by then, and they had been considerably improved.

TURNPIKES The first development in land transportation after the Revolutionary War was the building of turnpikes. These were toll roads constructed by private companies for profit. Turnpikes got their name from a pike (pole) across the road that was turned aside after a traveler had paid the toll.

The first turnpike was opened in Pennsylvania in the 1790s. It was called the Philadelphia-Lancaster Turnpike. Thousands of miles of toll roads were built during the next 25 years, especially in New England and the Middle Atlantic states. One of the best known was the Genesee Turnpike in New York, connecting Albany and Buffalo.

The network of turnpikes linking the East with frontier settlements helped farmers carry their produce to market. Turnpikes also stimulated the flow of manufactured goods to the West and South. But toll charges made the cost of traveling and of shipping freight quite high. And private companies lacked the resources to build roads in difficult areas, such as mountain terrain.

THE NATIONAL ROAD   In 1811, the federal government began the National Road, or Cumberland Road, to link the East with the Northwest Territory. The first section, opened in 1818, led from Cumberland, Maryland, to Wheeling, Virginia (now West Virginia). Later extensions reached to Columbus, Ohio, and finally to Vandalia, Illinois. The National Road, one of the chief arteries of western migration and east-west trade, eventually became part of U.S. Route 40.

Canals

Roads helped in transporting goods, but overland hauling was still expensive. Since water travel was cheaper, rivers and lakes were widely used wherever such inland waterways existed. The Ohio River, for instance, was the major route for settlers moving into the Northwest Territory. To connect bodies of water, Americans built a network of canals.

A major achievement was the Erie Canal, started in 1817 under the leadership of De Witt Clinton, governor of New York. This 363-mile waterway linked Lake Erie at Buffalo with the Hudson River at Albany. Goods could now be shipped all the way from the Great Lakes to New York City. Dug by manual labor, the canal took eight years to complete and cost over $7 million. A series of locks raised or lowered boats from one level to another. Building the canal was the greatest engineering project of its time in the United States.

The Erie Canal reduced freight costs between the East and the West to a tenth of their former level. It stimulated the settlement and economic development of upstate New York. The canal also helped make New York City the greatest shipping and trading center in the country. The success of this waterway touched off an era of canal building that lasted for 20 years. By 1837, Americans had dug some 3000 miles of canals.

Another engineering marvel was the Pennsylvania Canal, connecting

Philadelphia and Pittsburgh. This could not be a continuous waterway because of the Allegheny Mountains, which rise between the two cities. To cross the 35-mile stretch of mountains, engineers designed a portage railway. Loaded canal boats, placed on rails, were hauled across the mountains by engines and ropes.

Better Ships

After the War of 1812, the United States developed a merchant navy second in size only to that of Britain. A number of swift and sturdy packet boats were produced in American shipyards. These vessels carried passengers, mail, and cargo on a regular sailing schedule across the Atlantic to European ports.

In the 1840s, American shipbuilders introduced a new type of sailing craft that was capable of outdistancing anything afloat. It was called the "clipper ship" because of its ability to "clip off" the miles. Long and graceful, with high masts and a great spread of sails, American clipper ships dominated the world's sea-lanes for 20 years. Two famous clippers were the *Flying Cloud* and the *Great Republic*, both built by America's leading naval designer, Donald McKay.

Meanwhile, inventors were looking for ways to use steam power in ships. In the late 18th century, John Fitch had succeeded in propelling boats with steam engines. But the credit for building the first commercially successful steamboat goes to Robert Fulton. In 1807, his *Clermont* steamed up the Hudson River from New York to Albany. Within a few years, steamboats were carrying passengers and freight on every navigable waterway. Now, goods could be shipped upstream as well as downstream. The steamboat thus shortened travel time and lowered shipping costs.

Steamboats were especially useful on the broad rivers of the West, where roads were few. The first steamboat to sail Western waters was the *New Orleans*, built at Pittsburgh in 1811. By 1820, there were 60 steamboats in service on the Mississippi and its tributaries. The number rose to nearly 300 in 1837. Many thriving ports sprang up along these rivers. On the Ohio were Pittsburgh, Cincinnati, and Louisville. St. Louis, Vicksburg, and Natchez were important stops on the Mississippi.

Railroads

As in many other aspects of the Industrial Revolution, the British pioneered in developing a practical steam locomotive. They also built the world's first railroad in the 1820s.

Americans were not far behind. The first railroads in the United States were opened to traffic in the 1830s. Among the earliest lines were the

Baltimore and Ohio and the Mohawk and Hudson (operating between Albany and Schenectady, New York). By 1840, nearly 3000 miles of track were in use.

One invention that aided railroad growth was the telegraph, perfected by Samuel F. B. Morse in the 1840s. This instrument sent electrical sounds over wires. Morse also devised a code of dots and dashes (short and long sounds) to represent letters. Using the Morse code, a telegraph operator could tap out messages and transmit them almost instantly to distant points. In addition to speeding communication generally, the telegraph proved to be a valuable tool for routing railroad traffic. By 1860, a network of telegraph lines crisscrossed the United States east of the Mississippi.

INCREASED IMMIGRATION

Another facet of American expansion in the early 1800s was population growth. By 1840, the United States had four times as many people as in 1790. Natural increase accounted for much of this growth, but immigration played a big role, too. The number of newcomers increased almost every year. The average number admitted annually in the 1820s was about 13,000. In the 1840s, the annual average jumped to nearly 143,000.

More Germans and Irish

Two events in Europe stimulated immigration in the 1840s. One was the failure of the potato crop in Ireland. Deprived of their main source of food, thousands of Irish starved to death. Thousands more fled to the

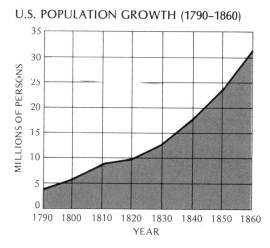

U.S. POPULATION GROWTH (1790–1860)

United States as their only hope for survival. The second event was a series of unsuccessful uprisings by Germans against their rulers in 1848. Fearing imprisonment or other punishment, many Germans left their homeland and came to the United States.

Nativist Reaction

Immigrants did not always get a warm welcome from "native-born" Americans—that is, whites who were descended from earlier European immigrants. The Germans were generally treated better than the Irish. Many Germans had money and could buy a farm or go into business.

Most of the Irish were poor. They tended to cluster in slums in the cities where their ships docked (Boston, especially). They took whatever manual labor they could find, often at lower wages than Americans would accept. Another problem for the Irish was their Roman Catholic religion. In the mainly Protestant United States, distrust of Catholicism had been strong since the 1600s.

Anti-immigrant feeling gave rise to nativism—a movement to "protect" citizens from foreign newcomers. In the 1840s, nativists formed organizations to pass stricter naturalization laws and to keep Catholics out of public office. In 1849, several of these groups formed a secret organization, the Order of the Star-Spangled Banner. Members were also called *Know-Nothings* because they answered "I know nothing" when asked about the organization. The Know-Nothings did not last long as a political party, but nativism remained a strong force in American life.

True-False Test

1. The first settlements in the trans-Appalachian West were made in Kentucky and Tennessee.
2. The Northwest Ordinance set the pattern for the admission of new states into the Union.
3. The Industrial Revolution began in England in the 1700s.
4. America's early industries had trouble surviving because of government opposition.
5. The cotton gin helped both the farmers of the South and the factory owners of the North.
6. The era of canal building was followed by the era of turnpike building.
7. The Erie Canal connected the St. Lawrence River with Lake Erie.
8. Clipper ships were the world's first successful steamboats.
9. The first railroads in America were constructed in the 1830s.
10. Immigration from Europe increased during the 1840s.

Matching Test

Column A	Column B
1. Samuel Slater	a. mechanical reaper
2. Eli Whitney	b. first steam locomotive in America
3. Cyrus McCormick	c. first successful U.S. cotton mill
4. Donald McKay	d. interchangeable parts
5. Robert Fulton	e. sewing machine
6. Peter Cooper	f. telegraph
7. Samuel F. B. Morse	g. vulcanized rubber
8. John Deere	h. clipper ships
9. Charles Goodyear	i. steel plow
10. Elias Howe	j. first commercially successful steamboat

Map Test

Locate the following places or facilities on the maps on pages 175 and 177. Then, referring to the text, as necessary, explain what part each one played in the growth and expansion of the United States.

1. Cumberland Gap
2. Fallen Timbers
3. National Road
4. Harrodsburg
5. Horseshoe Bend
6. Marietta
7. Tippecanoe
8. Erie Canal
9. Ohio River
10. Pennsylvania Canal

Essay Questions

1. What were the chief provisions of the Ordinance of 1787? For what region was it intended? Why was it important there and elsewhere?
2. How did conditions on the frontier affect the outlook of settlers there?
3. Describe three improvements in transportation in early 19th-century America. How did they benefit farms and factories?
4. Why was New England a good location for industry in the early 19th century? How did Francis Lowell contribute to New England's industrial development?
5. Describe immigration in the 1840s. Why did nativists oppose some groups of immigrants?

CHAPTER 12

The Age of Jackson

ANDREW JACKSON WAS A dominant figure of the early 19th century. His military record during the War of 1812 made him a national hero. He added to his reputation with his campaign against the Seminoles and the Spaniards in Florida. Later, he served as governor of the newly acquired territory of Florida and then as a U.S. senator. Aiming for the presidency, he tried for it unsuccessfully in 1824 but won in 1828 and again in 1832. He also chose his successor in 1836. Jackson had a strong character, a colorful personality, and firm beliefs. The period of his influence in American history is often called the Age of Jackson, or the Jacksonian era.

CHANGES IN POLITICAL LIFE

The Age of Jackson is noted for a number of changes that affected American political life. By the end of the era, the United States was a more democratic nation than it had been before.

Reforms at the State Level

In the original 13 states, only a minority of citizens were permitted to vote. All the states had some sort of property qualification for voting. An adult male could vote or hold office only if he owned land or paid taxes. Women and slaves could not vote, nor could free blacks in most states.

The new states that joined the Union after 1789 were more democratic. Most of them allowed all adult white males to vote and hold office. The older states in the East, seeking to keep discontented residents from moving west, gradually did away with property qualifications for voting and officeholding.

There were other changes, too. A number of state officials who had previously been appointed were now elected by the voters. And the terms of elected officials were shortened so that voters could replace unpopular officeholders sooner.

One state reform that affected national politics was the method of electing the president and vice president. At first, each state legislature had selected members of the electoral college. Electors, in turn, cast their ballots in presidential contests. By 1828, nearly all the 24 states allowed the voters at large to choose the electors.

National Parties

As the number of voters and elective offices increased, political parties became more important. They also grew more democratic. Before the Jacksonian era, congressional leaders from each party held a caucus (political meeting) to choose candidates for president and vice president. In the late 1820s, each party began to hold a national nominating convention. Here, party delegates representing the entire membership selected the presidential and vice presidential nominees.

FROM ADAMS TO JACKSON

In the election of 1824, there were four candidates, all of them Democratic-Republicans. The West was represented by Henry Clay of Kentucky and Andrew Jackson of Tennessee. New England supported John Quincy Adams of Massachusetts, and the South favored William H. Crawford of Georgia. Jackson led the other candidates in electoral votes, but no one had a majority. The choice of president was thus decided in the House of Representatives. Clay had a good deal of influence in Congress, and he threw his support to Adams. Adams won.

A "Corrupt Bargain"?

The outcome upset Jackson's supporters because their candidate's electoral vote total had exceeded Adams's. And they were enraged when Adams appointed Clay as secretary of state. In the past, this office had often been a stepping-stone to the presidency. Jacksonians charged that the two men had made a deal. Clay, they said, had entered into a "corrupt bargain" to support Adams, in exchange for a high cabinet post.

Bitterness over the election of 1824 had two chief results. One was that Adams accomplished very little during his administration. The son of John Adams, he had been an outstanding diplomat. But as president, he was blocked at every turn by Jackson's supporters. The other result was a split in the Democratic-Republican party. The group supporting Adams and Clay took the name *National Republicans*. The Jacksonians called themselves *Democrats*.

Jackson Elected

In the election of 1828, the National Republicans nominated Adams for a second term. The Democrats chose Jackson as their candidate. He was backed almost solidly by the West and South. He also received the support of small farmers and factory workers in the Middle Atlantic states. As a result, Jackson was elected by a large majority.

A STRONG PRESIDENT

Jackson was the first Westerner to become president. He had earlier earned the nickname "Old Hickory" for his toughness and endurance.

Opponents of Jackson accused him of trampling on the U.S. Constitution and wielding the power of a monarch. This caricature appeared in an 1832 anti-Jackson pamphlet. (The Bettmann Archive)

These qualities, coupled with his courage, honesty, and independence of character, won him many admirers. But his quick temper and strong will aroused the hostility of others. His opponents called him "King Andrew the First."

The Spoils System

Jackson's motto was "Let the people rule." He believed that every (male) citizen had an equal right to hold a government job. Such jobs, he said, should be simple enough to be handled by "men of intelligence." He also felt that federal positions should be in the hands of friends and supporters of the winning candidate.

Because of Jackson's beliefs, two practices came into wide use during his administration. One was the spoils system, which rewarded loyal party members with government jobs. The other was rotation in office. This meant regularly replacing government employees so that no one held the same job for very long. Actually, Jackson replaced no more federal workers than had some earlier presidents, Jefferson among them. But Jackson's support of the spoils system and rotation in office made these policies more acceptable.

The Nullification Issue

One important conflict of Jackson's administration had its roots in Adams's presidency. In 1828, Congress passed a tariff act that imposed very high duties on imports. Southerners protested because the tariff increased the cost of the manufactured goods they bought. The *Tariff Act of 1828*, they argued, was passed not to raise money but to protect the interests of Northern manufacturers at the expense of Southern farmers. The bill's opponents called it the "tariff of abominations."

CALHOUN'S PROTEST   John C. Calhoun of South Carolina took the lead in opposing the tariff of 1828. He wrote, but did not sign, a pamphlet called *The South Carolina Exposition and Protest*. In it, he argued that the tariff law was unconstitutional and, therefore, could be nullified at the state level. Jefferson and Madison had made the same argument for states' rights in the Kentucky and Virginia Resolutions. Calhoun, however, went further. He described the steps that a dissatisfied state should take.

Meanwhile, Jackson had been elected president, with Calhoun as his vice president. The new president's views on states' rights were unclear. In 1830, two senators, Daniel Webster of Massachusetts and Robert Hayne of South Carolina, made long speeches on the issue. Webster argued that the federal government was supreme. Hayne said that the states could

Andrew Jackson

John C. Calhoun

Henry Clay

overrule it. The Webster-Hayne Debate, as it was called, aroused national attention. The public wondered how Jackson and Calhoun would react. At a public dinner shortly afterward, Jackson offered a toast— "Our Union: It must be preserved." These words indicated his support of Webster's position. Calhoun responded with a toast of his own—"The Union, next to our liberty, most dear." He, of course, favored Hayne.

THE CRISIS OF 1832   In 1831, Calhoun came out into the open with his nullification views. He split with Jackson over this issue, as well as others. A new tariff of 1832 lowered some duties but kept the principle of protection. The South Carolina legislature then called for a state convention. At this meeting, an *Ordinance of Nullification* was adopted. It declared the tariffs of 1828 and 1832 null and void, and prohibited federal officials from collecting duties in the state.

Jackson was furious and persuaded Congress to pass the *Force Bill* in 1833. It authorized the use of the military, if necessary, to enforce the tariff laws. At the same time, however, a revision of the tariff was being worked out. This compromise, proposed by Henry Clay, provided for a gradual reduction of import duties over the next ten years. As a result, South Carolina repealed its Ordinance of Nullification, and the crisis died down.

Jackson's Indian Policy

As a Westerner, Jackson had always been for the settlers and against the Indians. During his presidency, several states in the South forced the Indians to move off tribal lands and go farther west. Jackson approved of these actions. In 1832, the Supreme Court, in *Worcester* v. *Georgia*, handed down a decision about Indian removals in Georgia. Chief Justice Marshall ruled that Georgia had no constitutional right to control the Indians in the state. Only the federal government had this authority. In other words, the federal government could step in to prevent the seizure of Indian lands.

Georgia did not obey the Court's ruling, but Jackson did nothing to enforce it. His refusal to protect Native Americans led to the wholesale removal of Indians in Georgia (and elsewhere) to what is now the state of Oklahoma.

The Bank War

The second Bank of the United States, authorized in 1816, was due to have its charter renewed in 1836. Jackson was strongly opposed to this bank. He felt that it aided merchants, manufacturers, and bankers, at the expense of ordinary people. By concentrating power in the hands of a few, Jackson said, the bank was undemocratic. He also believed that it exerted too much political and economic influence. In 1832, four years before the bank's charter was due to run out, Congress voted to renew it. Jackson vetoed the bill.

The second Bank of the United States became the main issue in the election of 1832. Henry Clay, who ran against Jackson, favored the bank. Jackson spoke out forcefully against the bank, which he called "the monster." He won the election by a landslide. He then proceeded to destroy the bank by withdrawing government funds from it. He deposited the money in several dozen state banks. His enemies charged that these "pet banks" were selected because they supported Jackson.

AFTER JACKSON

In the early 1830s, the National Republicans joined with other anti-Jackson groups to form a new party, the *Whigs*. Led by Henry Clay and Daniel Webster, the Whigs were supported mainly by commercial and manufacturing people in the Northeast. Most Whigs favored such measures as rechartering a national bank, high protective tariffs, and a strong federal government. Some, however, were simply against Jackson.

John Marshall has made his decision; now let him enforce it.

—*Andrew Jackson commenting on the Supreme Court decision in* Worcester v. Georgia

Van Buren as President

As Jackson neared the end of his second term, he persuaded the Democrats to nominate his personal choice for the presidency. The candidate he selected was his long-time adviser, Martin Van Buren of New York. Van Buren had been vice president in Jackson's second administration. He ran against three Whigs and easily won the election of 1836.

PANIC AND DEPRESSION   No sooner had Van Buren taken office than the United States suffered a financial upset, the Panic of 1837. Its causes went back to Jackson's administration. The "pet banks" had carried on risky business practices. For example, they had granted loans too freely and issued paper money that was not backed by gold and silver. The result was a flood of paper money and widespread speculation in public lands. These practices alarmed President Jackson. In 1836, he issued the *Specie Circular*. It provided that government land had to be paid for in specie (gold or silver), not paper money.

By early 1837, the country was in a financial panic. Land prices fell sharply because money was hard to borrow and land purchases had to be made in gold or silver. Speculators were ruined. People rushed to their banks to exchange paper money for specie. Lacking enough gold and silver to satisfy the demand, hundreds of banks failed.

As is often the case, the panic led to a depression (a period of slow business activity and high unemployment). Factories and mills closed down, canal and railroad building all but stopped, and unemployment spread. Wage earners in the Northeast were especially hard hit. The depression was severe and lasted for about five years.

THE INDEPENDENT TREASURY SYSTEM   The federal government was unable to do much about the depression. But Van Buren made one important change in the nation's finances. In 1840, he succeeded in establishing the Independent Treasury System. (The act creating the system was repealed in 1841 but was passed again in 1846.) The new system set up so-called "subtreasuries" in several key cities. There, federal funds were deposited and kept safe. By taking charge of its own funds, the government became independent of the nation's private banks. The Independent Treasury System lasted until the early 20th century, when it was replaced by the Federal Reserve System.

A Whig Victory

The Democrats nominated Van Buren for a second term in 1840. But many blamed him for the country's hard times. Van Buren had other problems as well. The Whigs staged a colorful campaign to promote their candidate, William Henry Harrison. This military hero had defeated the Indians at the Battle of Tippecanoe in 1811. He ran with John Tyler of Virginia. "Tippecanoe and Tyler too" became the Whigs' catchy slogan.

The campaign of 1840 was the first to use the techniques of mass appeal and showmanship that became common in later American elections. Huge meetings and torchlight parades attracted thousands. Harrison had no clear political program. But he was portrayed as a man of the people, happily drinking hard cider in his log cabin. (In reality, he came from a distinguished Virginia family and lived in a fine house.) The "log cabin and hard cider" campaign resulted in a Whig victory.

But the triumph was short-lived. A month after the inauguration, Harrison died of pneumonia. He was the first president to die in office. Tyler, who succeeded him, was a former Democrat who had broken with Jackson over the nullification issue. As a believer in states' rights, he did not agree with the Whig policy of a strong central government. Tyler vetoed many bills passed by the Whig-controlled Congress. He finally broke with the Whigs completely.

One of the few positive results of Tyler's administration was the settlement of a dispute with Britain. The two countries disagreed about the boundary between Maine and Canada. In the *Webster-Ashburton Treaty* of 1842, the United States received a large part of the disputed area. It included the fertile Aroostook Valley in northern Maine. The British also agreed to adjust the U.S.-Canada boundary between Lake Superior and Lake of the Woods. The section of northeastern Minnesota acquired by the United States included the Mesabi Range, which later proved to be a major source of iron ore.

TEN NOTABLE AMERICANS
OF THE EARLY NATIONAL PERIOD

JOHN JAMES AUDUBON (1785–1851)   Born in Haiti to French parents and educated in France, he settled near Philadelphia as a young man. Hunting spurred his interest in painting birds, as did several years spent on the Kentucky frontier. His great collection, *Birds of America*, began to appear in 1827. His dramatic color representations of birds and animals united the two worlds of art and science.

BENJAMIN BANNEKER (1731–1806)   This black, born free in Baltimore, was probably the first of his race to be employed by the federal government. In 1790, he served on a team of surveyors laying out the new District of Columbia. An astronomer, he also published a popular annual almanac for several years. He was an ardent pacifist, and urged that the first cabinet include a secretary for peace as well as a secretary of war.

DANIEL BOONE (1734–1820)   America's most famous woodsman was born in Pennsylvania, spent much of his life in Kentucky, and was at home in the wilderness anywhere. He led parties of pioneers into the unsettled

West and gained a reputation as an excellent hunter and fearless Indian fighter. His own investments in land left him in debt, and he spent years squaring his accounts in order to satisfy his high standards of honesty and responsibility.

JOHN CHAPMAN (1775?–1847) We know him as "Johnny Appleseed" because of the apple trees he planted all over the Ohio frontier. This gentle wanderer was also a deeply religious Christian, who preached a message of love and of fair dealing toward the Indians. His arrival in a pioneer clearing, dressed in ragged trousers and a shirt made from a coffee sack, was always welcomed by lonely settlers.

PETER COOPER (1791–1883) One of America's most successful business-men, this New Yorker's varied concerns included glue factories, iron works, and blast furnaces. He not only built the first American steam locomotive—the "Tom Thumb" (1830)—but also sponsored Cyrus Field's work on the first transatlantic cable. Although (or perhaps because) he had no formal education, he endowed the Cooper Union of New York City, a free school that still teaches art, architecture, and engineering.

FRANCIS LOWELL (1775–1817) This member of an illustrious Massachu-setts family did much to introduce the factory system into the United States. While traveling in England, he visited a textile factory and took elaborate mental notes on how the machinery worked. Back home, aided by an expert mechanic, he reproduced the machines in a new, centralized mill at Waltham. Lowell's "Waltham System" was noted for its employment of young, unmarried women in a strictly supervised setting.

SACAJAWEA (1786–1812) Born in central Idaho, this Shoshone woman was captured by an enemy tribe and sold into slavery farther east. By 1804, she was married to a Canadian guide and fur trapper, Toussaint Charbonneau, and living in North Dakota. When Lewis and Clark passed through on their expedition west, they hired Charbonneau, who took along his wife and infant son. Sacajawea's services were invaluable, for she not only found food in inhospitable surroundings but also acted as a translator and diplomat when the expedition reached the Shoshone country.

SEQUOYA (1770?–1843) Born to an Indian mother and white father, this Tennesseean grew up illiterate. He became intensely curious about the "talking leaves" (books and papers) through which whites communi-cated. After learning to read and write, he spent years working out a Cherokee alphabet of 85 characters. This made it possible for thou-sands of Indians to become literate. Americans honored this innovator by naming California's giant redwood tree (sequoia) after him.

JEDEDIAH SMITH (1798–1831) The Far West attracted this New Yorker at an early age. During several years as a "mountain man," he was a fur trapper in the Rockies. Later, he led several exploring expeditions in the Great Basin area and from California into the Oregon Country. He was a pious man who never traveled without his Bible. In the last year of his life, he took up the Santa Fe trade, and was killed by Comanche Indians in New Mexico.

NOAH WEBSTER (1758-1843)   America's most famous maker of dictionaries was a patriotic Federalist. The spellers, grammars, and readers he developed for schoolchildren included examples from American history and geography, and sold millions of copies. His monumental *American Dictionary of the English Language* (1828) was one of the first such works to use examples from nonliterary sources. Webster's books helped establish uniform standards in American education.

Multiple-Choice Test

1. John Quincy Adams was unable to do much as president because of (a) war with France (b) a border dispute with England (c) bitterness over his appointment of Clay (d) opposition from National Republicans.
2. All the following trends characterized the Age of Jackson *except* (a) broadening of voting rights (b) an increase in the number of elective offices (c) a shift toward popular election of presidential electors (d) replacement of national nominating conventions by caucuses.
3. Andrew Jackson was the first president who (a) came from the West (b) was a military hero (c) favored the rights of Indians (d) was inaugurated in Washington.
4. The practice of rewarding loyal party members with government jobs is known as (a) the specie system (b) the spoils system (c) rotation in office (d) speculation.
5. Southerners called the 1828 tariff the tariff of abominations because they felt that it (a) would not raise enough revenue (b) should have been adopted sooner (c) was harmful to manufacturers (d) increased the cost of goods they had to buy.
6. One of the most important critics of the tariff of 1828 was (a) Henry Clay (b) Martin Van Buren (c) John C. Calhoun (d) Daniel Webster.
7. The major issue in the presidential campaign of 1832 was (a) nullification (b) the second Bank of the United States (c) Indian policy (d) the Force Bill.
8. A new political party formed in the 1830s was the (a) Whigs (b) Democrats (c) National Republicans (d) Know-Nothings.
9. The Panic of 1837 led to (a) the election of Van Buren to the presidency (b) the establishment of pet banks (c) a severe depression (d) increased land speculation.

10. The presidential campaign of 1840 was the first to **(a)** pit Democrats against National Republicans **(b)** be decided in the House of Representatives **(c)** result in a tie **(d)** feature mass campaign techniques.

Time Test

Following are five groups of three related items. In each group, rearrange the items in the order in which they happened.

1. "corrupt bargain"
   election of 1824
   choice of J. Q. Adams by House of Representatives
2. *The South Carolina Exposition and Protest*
   Tariff Act of 1828
   South Carolina Ordinance of Nullification
3. founding of second Bank of the United States
   establishment of pet banks
   campaign of 1832
4. Panic of 1837
   Specie Circular
   Independent Treasury System
5. presidency of Tyler
   presidency of Van Buren
   presidency of Harrison

Essay Questions

1. In what ways did political life become more democratic in the Age of Jackson?
2. In your opinion, which of the changes that you noted in answering question 1 was the most important? Why?
3. Explain the causes and outcome of the nullification crisis of 1832.
4. What brought on the Panic of 1837? What was one important change made in the nation's financial system soon afterward?
5. When and why did the Whig party come into existence? How did the Whig victory in 1840 turn out to be a disappointment for the party's supporters?

CHAPTER 13

An Era
of Reform

THE DEMOCRATIC SPIRIT of the Age of Jackson was reflected not only in political reforms but also in efforts to correct social abuses and improve American society. Many of these movements actually began before the 1820s and continued after the 1840s. But they were greatly influenced by the reformist trends of the Jacksonian era and are, therefore, linked with that period in American history.

MAKING LIFE BETTER

Since colonial times, Americans had believed that their country offered special opportunities to all its citizens. There was much pride in what had already been accomplished. But many people also realized that much remained to be done.

Humanitarian Movements

Several reforms of the early 1800s were humanitarian in nature—that is, concerned with easing human distress. One such movement related to the mentally ill. At this time, people judged to be insane were treated like animals, unworthy of humane care. Few Americans were aware of the problem until Dorothea Dix brought it to public attention. A Boston schoolteacher, Dix visited a Massachusetts jail in 1841. She was shocked to see mentally ill persons living in chains. In 1843, she made a strong appeal to the Massachusetts legislature to provide better facilities and

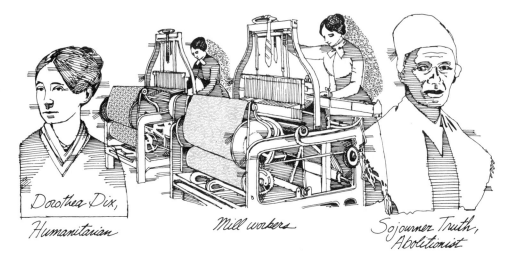

Dorothea Dix,
Humanitarian

Mill workers

Sojourner Truth,
Abolitionist

treatment for the insane. She later carried her message to other states. During the next few years, 15 states built mental hospitals where patients could be properly treated.

Dix was also interested in the treatment of criminals. The common practice for centuries had been to punish wrongdoers with long jail terms, flogging, mutilation, or public execution. Reformers urged a different approach. They believed that wrongdoers should not merely be imprisoned but should also be taught how to lead useful lives after they were freed. One new technique was to isolate prisoners in solitary confinement so that they could examine their consciences, free from harmful influences. The change in emphasis was reflected in the names of prisons. They came to be called penitentiaries (places for penitence) and reformatories (places for reform).

A third area of humanitarian concern was treatment of the handicapped. Reformers wanted to teach them basic skills, train them to care for themselves, and make them independent. Thomas H. Gallaudet founded the first school for the deaf at Hartford, Connecticut, in 1817. In 1832, Samuel Gridley Howe started what is now the Perkins School for the Blind in Boston. He became world famous for his success in teaching the sightless.

Temperance

Many people of the early 1800s felt that excessive drinking was a basic cause of misfortune in society. The amount of alcohol consumed in the United States was indeed very great. Drunkenness was common at almost every public and private celebration.

The first antidrinking organization in the United States was formed in 1808. Along with several other groups, it urged temperance (drinking in moderation). Temperance groups were opposed to the drinking of distilled liquor, although some were less strict about beer or wine. By the

1830s, however, anti-alcohol societies were proposing abstinence (no alcohol at all). From then on, temperance reformers formed lobbies at the local and national levels of government. (Lobbies are special-interest groups that try to influence government to act in their favor.) Temperance lobbyists wanted prohibition—a ban against the manufacture and sale of all alcoholic beverages. Maine was the first state to adopt prohibition, in 1846. In the next ten years, several other states followed the example set by Maine.

Religion

Several new or expanding religious groups attracted members in the early 1800s. One new denomination was the Disciples of Christ (known today as the Christian Church), which split from the Presbyterians. Another new group was to play a prominent role in American history. It was called the Church of Jesus Christ of Latter-Day Saints, or Mormons. Joseph Smith founded the denomination in upstate New York in 1830. He reported that an angel had guided him to a set of golden plates, which Smith translated as the *Book of Mormon.* The new religion gained thousands of followers but also made many enemies (see Chapter 14, page 225).

A group with roots in Europe, the Unitarians, appealed to many New England intellectuals, including Ralph Waldo Emerson. The name of the

Women were ardent crusaders in the temperance cause from its beginnings. They achieved a milestone with the founding of the Woman's Christian Temperance Union in 1874, the year in which this Currier and Ives print was published. (The Bettmann Archive)

sect was derived from the belief that God exists as a single Being, not as a Trinity. Unitarians stressed that people are basically good, and that moral living and good works are the road to salvation.

Two churches that dated from the colonial period grew rapidly in the early 1800s. One, that of the Baptists, traced its beginnings to Roger Williams in the 1630s. Another group, the Methodists, had broken away from the Anglican church in the 1760s. Both denominations attracted new members in the South and West. Black people, drawn to these churches in large numbers, formed separate Baptist and Methodist congregations of their own. One reason for the success of the Methodists was their use of "circuit riders." These traveling preachers carried the faith to widely scattered communities in rural areas.

Traveling preachers were also the backbone of the religious revival movement that flourished in the late 1700s and early 1800s. Although it influenced city people, its impact on farm and frontier families was far greater. In outlying regions, hundreds of people would gather at camp meetings to sing, pray, and listen to sermons.

With the surge of Irish immigration in the 1840s and 1850s, the Roman Catholic church grew rapidly. Much of the gain was concentrated in such large cities as Boston, New York, and Philadelphia. At first, immigrant Catholics ran into strong opposition from "native" Americans, who viewed them as members of a "foreign" church. In time, however, anti-Catholic feeling died down.

Planned Communities

Some reformers believed that society had to be changed completely in order to wipe out crime, poverty, and other ills. Such reformers set up ideal communities in which people were expected to cooperate with one another. Few of these planned communities lasted very long, however.

In 1815, a German named George Rapp founded a religious settlement, called Harmony, in Indiana. Ten years later, it was taken over by a Scottish manufacturer, Robert Owen, and renamed New Harmony. Its inhabitants, who numbered about a thousand, promised to live in equality and freedom. Without a central authority, however, there were many conflicts, and the community broke up in a few years. Even so, New Harmony made its mark. It pioneered in the teaching of science in America. It also set up the first trade school and one of the first public libraries in the country.

Another planned community, Brook Farm, was founded by Massachusetts intellectuals in 1841. Its members included the writer Nathaniel Hawthorne. Other New England thinkers were frequent guests. Poor harvests, as well as a bad fire, forced the community to close in 1847.

A longer-lasting cooperative group, also founded in the 1840s, was the Oneida Community of Oneida, New York. Its members believed in economic sharing and owned all property in common. They also practiced "complex marriage," in which couples paired off in temporary relationships. Women had equal rights, and all members shared child-rearing tasks. The community manufactured steel traps and chains, silver-plated tableware, and silk thread. It also devoted itself to farming, fruit growing, and canning. For more than 30 years, the community prospered. But public pressure finally forced it to abandon its social and economic innovations. In 1881, the Oneida Community put an end to its communal way of life and became a business, with its members as shareholders.

Another group that lasted for a considerable time was the Shakers. This religious sect, an offshoot of the Quakers, originated in England in the early 1700s. Its leader, Mother Ann Lee, led a band of followers to America in 1774, where they set up a community at Watervliet, New York. The Shakers owned all property in common, lived simply, and kept themselves apart from the world. Since they did not marry, they acquired new members only by conversion. Several communities were founded in Kentucky, Ohio, and New England. At its peak in the 1840s, the sect had a membership of more than 6000.

Excellent farmers and artisans, the Shakers made many useful contributions to American life. They were the first to grow and package seed for sale to gardeners. They invented the circular saw, a mechanical washing machine, metal pen points, and flat brooms. They also designed furniture for their own use that is admired and copied to this day.

Early Unions

The planned communities of the early 19th century affected few Americans. But many found their lives changed by the growth of manufacturing. The factory system was giving rise to an American laboring class—people who depended on wages for a living. Their working conditions were grim. Men, women, and children usually worked from dawn to dusk, six days a week, in buildings that were often uncomfortable, unsanitary, and even dangerous. The average pay for men was about $5 a week. Women earned less than half as much, and children received as little as $1 a week.

Obviously, no individual wage earner could change conditions. Only by organizing into groups could laborers offset the power of owners. The first workers to do so were skilled artisans in the late 1700s. Printers and shoemakers formed societies for mutual aid that were the nation's first labor unions. The democratic spirit of the Age of Jackson helped this movement grow. In the early 1830s, city-wide unions appeared in Philadelphia, New York, Boston, and other industrial centers. The *National Trades Union*, formed in 1834, was the first American labor organization to represent workers in more than one city. An important gain won by organized labor in this period was the ten-hour workday.

These early unions, however, faced serious problems. Union organization was challenged in the courts. And the depression of the late 1830s threw many people out of work. As a result, most early unions disappeared. Organized labor did not recover from its setback until after the Civil War.

IMPROVEMENTS IN EDUCATION

Before the 1830s, opportunities for schooling in the United States were few. Many people learned to read and write, but they did so at religious or other private schools. During the Jacksonian era, Americans began to feel the need for better education. The growth of political democracy was partly responsible. People realized that they needed to be well informed in order to participate intelligently in government.

Public Schooling

One of the most outstanding figures in American education was Horace Mann. A Massachusetts lawyer, he supervised the state's public education system from 1837 to 1848. He persuaded Massachusetts to set aside more money for schools and teachers' salaries and to increase the number of subjects taught. The school year was extended from a few weeks to six months. Fifty new high schools were opened.

Under Mann's guidance, the first American school for the training of teachers was established at Lexington, Massachusetts, in 1839. Several other states, particularly in the Northeast, followed the example of Massachusetts.

Private Institutions

Public education was spreading, but most secondary schools and colleges were still private. By 1860, there were some 6000 private academies and only 300 public high schools.

Secondary schools and colleges were generally open to boys only. One exception was the Troy (New York) Female Seminary, founded in 1821 by Emma Willard. The Emma Willard School, as it was later known, taught girls philosophy, mathematics, and other subjects that many educators had considered too difficult for women. Another good school for young women was the Mount Holyoke Female Seminary, established by Mary Lyon in 1837. (It later became Mount Holyoke College.) Lyon believed in physical, as well as intellectual, training. She also introduced music and the sciences as courses of study.

Most colleges of this period were associated with churches. There was no coeducational college until 1837, when Oberlin (in Ohio) admitted four young women.

WOMEN'S RIGHTS

In the early 19th century, the position of women in American society was far inferior to that of men. Female slaves, of course, had no rights at all, and free black women had few. But the rights of white women, too, were very limited. They could not vote, nor could they, in most cases, own or hand down property. Even if women earned money, it usually belonged to their fathers or husbands. In case of divorce, the father almost always won custody of the children. Women were discouraged from acquiring an advanced education, learning a profession, or speaking in public. (Reformers such as Dorothea Dix and Mary Lyon had to present their ideas through men.)

A number of women became increasingly concerned about their situation. In a changing United States, women's roles were changing, too. Women worked in the new factories. (But only in light industries considered appropriate for "women's work," such as textile mills.) More and more women taught in public schools. Wherever women worked, they were always paid less than men doing the same job. A few brave women—and men—felt that the time had come to press for greater equality for women. This was the goal of feminism, as the movement came to be called.

I ask no favors for my sex. . . . All I ask our brethren is, that they will take their feet from off our necks, and permit us to stand upright on that ground which God designed us to occupy.

—*Sarah Grimké in*
Letters on the Equality of the Sexes, 1838

Individual Achievements

Against great odds, a small number of women managed to win respect for their work outside the home. Dorothea Dix, as mentioned earlier, greatly improved the lot of the mentally ill. Emma Willard and Mary Lyon founded schools where young women could obtain some advanced education.

Two women who made names for themselves in fields dominated by men were Maria Mitchell and Elizabeth Blackwell. Mitchell learned astronomy from her father. In 1847, she discovered a comet. She later taught astronomy at Vassar College, which opened in 1861. Blackwell was born in England and came to the United States at the age of 11. In 1849, she became the first woman in the world to receive a medical degree. When Blackwell tried to practice medicine in New York City, she ran into strong opposition. To have a place where she could work, she opened a hospital staffed entirely by women. (In 1869, she returned to England to teach at a medical school.)

The Beginnings of Organized Efforts

The active campaign for women's rights did not begin until the 1840s. Its start was linked to women's participation in another reform movement—abolition. (Abolition means doing away with something; in the early 1800s, the term meant doing away with slavery.)

Many women, especially in the Northeast, were strongly opposed to slavery. They wrote against it, signed petitions against it, and pressured politicians to take a stand against it. When these women spoke out in public, however, they were often ridiculed for being "unfeminine." This denial of their rights outraged women like the Grimké sisters, Angelina

During the women's rights convention held in 1859, the speaker of the day defies an unruly gallery of men by denouncing the "*Lords* of Creation." (The Bettmann Archive)

and Sarah. Said Sarah: "Whatsoever it is morally right for a man to do, is morally right for a woman to do."

In 1840, Lucretia Mott and Elizabeth Cady Stanton were forbidden to take their places as delegates to an international meeting against slavery, held in London. Mott and Stanton were struck by the injustice of their situation. While working to free blacks, they themselves were denied freedom because they were women. Over the next few years, Mott and Stanton talked and wrote about the issue of equality for women. In 1848, they organized a meeting at Seneca Falls, New York, where Stanton lived. This first *Women's Rights Convention* was attended by about 300 delegates (some 40 of them men). It adopted a number of resolutions. The convention also issued a *Declaration of Sentiments*, written by Stanton and based on the Declaration of Independence. The declaration first stated that "all men and women are created equal." Then, it proclaimed that "the history of mankind is a history of repeated injuries and usurpations on the part of man toward woman." The declaration also demanded that women must "have immediate admission to all the rights and privileges which belong to them as citizens of the United States."

The Seneca Falls meeting was the beginning of an organized feminist movement in the United States. But the struggle for women's rights made little progress until the post–Civil War period.

THE CRUSADE AGAINST SLAVERY

Of all the reform movements of the early 19th century, none stirred up such strong feelings as the crusade against slavery. This cause united people of different aims and backgrounds, black and white, young and old. Many of the reformers in other fields—the Grimkés and Lucretia Mott, for example—also took a strong stand against slavery. Antislavery crusaders often disagreed about how to end slavery. But their common belief that slavery was evil and had to end helped to shape public opinion on the issue. The movement played an important role in the events that led to the Civil War.

Early Opposition

For a long time, the issue of slavery had troubled many Americans. Men like George Washington and Thomas Jefferson, who owned slaves, were aware that human slavery was contrary to the principles of freedom and equality in which they believed. The Northwest Ordinance banned slavery in the Northwest Territory. Although the Constitution did not mention slavery by name, it did give Congress the right to end the "importation of such persons" (meaning slaves) after 1808, which Congress did. By that date, too, every Northern state had taken steps to abolish slavery within its borders.

But what of the other states? Their population included about 900,000 slaves in 1800 (and more than 3 million in 1850). Most early opponents of slavery believed that the institution should be ended gradually. Individual slave owners, these reformers hoped, would emancipate (free) their slaves voluntarily. But there were doubts about what would happen afterward. Could freed slaves find a place in American society?

One group thought that the best solution would be to send freed slaves to Africa. The American Colonization Society, founded in 1817, sponsored the colony of Liberia on the west coast of Africa. But the society was not very successful, mainly because the nation's blacks felt themselves to be Americans, not Africans. "Here we are born," a New York City convention of free black people declared, "and here we will die."

The Abolition Movement

Beginning about 1830, antislavery forces put less emphasis on the gradual emancipation of slaves, and more on a quick end to slavery. The term "abolition" is usually applied to the movement that grew out of these efforts.

One of the most famous fighters in the cause of abolition was William Lloyd Garrison. A New Englander, he began publishing an antislavery paper, *The Liberator*, in 1831. Two years later, he helped found the American Antislavery Society. It was the parent of many organizations that sprang up all over the North.

Garrison urged immediate abolition. He refused to work within the existing political system because he regarded it as corrupt. Those who agreed with him included the Grimké sisters and former slaves Sojourner Truth and Frederick Douglass. All of them wrote at length and lectured widely, trying to inform Americans of the moral evil of slavery.

Moderate abolitionists formed the *Liberty party*, which ran presidential candidates in 1840 and again in 1844. The party's main aim was to keep slavery out of new territories, rather than to abolish it entirely.

The Underground Railroad

One of the best-known abolition activities was helping slaves escape. Abolitionists organized a network, the "underground railroad," that guided blacks from one house ("station") to another. Local men and women acted as "conductors." The "end of the line" was usually Canada, where slavery was illegal and blacks could live in peace. Two leaders of this operation were Levi Coffin, a Quaker, and Harriet Tubman, a former slave.

A DEVELOPING AMERICAN CULTURE

Until the 19th century, American writers and artists created few works of lasting interest or wide appeal. As American society matured, however, so did its culture. People had more leisure time. Education improved. And the nationalism of the early 1800s inspired pride in the American scene, as well as self-confidence in expressing that pride.

Literature

Most colonial literature consisted of religious works and moral tales. But by 1860, Americans had proved that they could write first-rate novels, short stories, poems, and essays.

TWO EARLY FIGURES   The first American writer to gain widespread attention at home and abroad was Washington Irving of New York. In *Diedrich Knickerbocker's History of New York* (1809), he poked good-natured fun at Dutch manners and customs. (The word "Knickerbocker" has been used ever since as a nickname for New Yorker.) Irving's most famous stories about the early Hudson Valley are "Rip Van Winkle" and "The Legend of Sleepy Hollow."

Another writer who popularized the American scene was James Fenimore Cooper. His Leatherstocking Tales are dramatic stories of the adventures of frontier heroes and noble Indians. The best known of this series of five novels is *The Last of the Mohicans* (1826).

NOTED WORKS OF THE 1850S   A very different kind of writer was Herman Melville. His early years at sea gave him the background for many of his novels. Although his works can be read as adventure stories, they also deal with deep human fears and desires. *Moby Dick* (1851), the most famous of Melville's novels, is about a crazed sea captain and his hunt for a great white whale.

New England was a fertile field for writers. Many of them were influenced by the essayist and critic Ralph Waldo Emerson. He urged Americans to use their own experiences in their writings. One of his disciples was Henry David Thoreau, a very independent thinker. Thoreau once went to jail rather than pay a tax that, in his opinion, supported the evil of slavery. His *Walden* (1854) describes the two years that he spent living alone in a cabin on the shore of Walden Pond.

I went to the woods because I wished to live deliberately, to front only
the essential facts of life, and see if I could learn what it had to teach, and
not, when I came to die, discover that I had not lived.

—*Henry David Thoreau,* Walden

A New Englander noted for his brooding short stories and novels was
Nathaniel Hawthorne. He was fascinated by the Puritan past. (One of his
ancestors was a judge in the Salem witch trials.) His best novel, *The Scarlet
Letter* (1850), is set in this period.

The strict conscience of New England also helped to form the
character of Harriet Beecher Stowe. In *Uncle Tom's Cabin* (1852), she not
only described slave life in the South but also told a dramatic story of
escape and sacrifice. The book became an instant best-seller. It was
praised by abolitionists and condemned by advocates of slavery.

POETRY   Several American poets became widely known. One was
Edgar Allan Poe, most of whose poems—"The Raven" and "Annabel Lee,"
among others—date from the 1840s. He also wrote eerie tales of suspense
and is credited with inventing the detective story.

Walt Whitman, in a bold poetic style unusual for its day, praised the
individual and democracy. He first published his best-known work,
Leaves of Grass, in 1855 but later revised and expanded it many times.
The poetry of Henry Wadsworth Longfellow was less inventive, but
more popular, than Whitman's. Generations of Americans learned history
from such Longfellow poems as *The Song of Hiawatha* (1855), *The Court-
ship of Miles Standish* (1858), and "Paul Revere's Ride" (1861).

Painting

American painting began to come of age in the late 1700s. Most of the
best artists of the time, however, were strongly influenced by European
styles and spent much time in Europe.

Benjamin West, who lived most of his life in England, is noted for his
elaborate historical paintings. His *Death of General Wolfe* (1771) was the
first large work to show figures dressed realistically, rather than in Greek
or Roman clothing. Several of West's students did outstanding work. John
Singleton Copley painted portraits of important New Englanders, including Samuel Adams and Paul Revere. Gilbert Stuart is famous for his
portraits of George Washington. John Trumbull produced many works
illustrating events in American history. Among them are four large

Revolutionary War scenes that decorate the Capitol in Washington, D.C.

The so-called "Hudson River school" developed a more truly American kind of painting in the 1820s. Its most famous member, Thomas Cole, painted landscapes of the Hudson Valley, the Catskill Mountains, and New England. Another painter of American scenes, especially of frontier life, was George Caleb Bingham. His most famous work is *Daniel Boone Coming Through Cumberland Gap* (1851).

Popular Culture

Although more Americans were learning to read, not all of them spent their time on Cooper or Emerson. In the 1830s, a new trend arose in newspaper publishing—the "penny press." To attract readers, newspapers reported the happenings of the day in a lively style and charged only 1 cent a copy. The first successful penny daily was the *New York Sun*, founded in 1833 by Benjamin H. Day. Two years later, James Gordon Bennett started the *New York Morning Herald*. The paper was the first to print financial news, report crimes and social events, and discuss the theater. In 1841, Horace Greeley founded the *New York Tribune*, which opposed slavery and campaigned for temperance, women's rights, and American expansion. Ten years later, *The New York Times*, one of America's most influential papers, began publication.

A number of other city dailies date from this period. They include the *Detroit Free Press* (1835), the *New Orleans Picayune* (1836), the *Philadelphia Public Ledger* (1836), the *Boston Daily Times* (1836), the *Plain Dealer* of Cleveland (1845), and the *Chicago Daily Tribune* (1847).

Magazines also attracted many readers. *Godey's Lady's Book*, started in 1830, brought news of the latest Paris fashions to American women. It published serious fiction as well. Two other journals that began publishing in the 1850s were *Harper's New Monthly Magazine* (later called *Harper's Magazine*) and the *Atlantic Monthly*.

Live entertainment was well attended. Whether acting in the plays of Shakespeare or in sentimental dramas, traveling performers usually drew large audiences. Minstrel shows were very popular. They featured white performers in blackface. Minstrel humor was crude, but some of the music is still sung. Many of Stephen Foster's best-loved songs, such as "My Old Kentucky Home," "Oh! Susanna," and "Old Black Joe," were written for minstrel shows.

True-False Test

1. Beginning in the 1830s, temperance reformers lobbied mainly for prohibition.

2. The religious revival movement of the early 19th century was strongest in and near cities.
3. Public education became more widespread in the 19th century because Americans felt that citizens of a democracy should be well informed.
4. Mount Holyoke was the first coeducational college.
5. The organized movement to extend women's rights began in the 1840s.
6. The aim of the American Colonization Society was to send freed slaves to Latin America to live.
7. The Liberty party was organized to oppose the abolitionists.
8. James Fenimore Cooper was the first American writer to gain widespread attention outside the United States.
9. Edgar Allan Poe is given credit for inventing the detective story.
10. The first successful penny newspaper in the United States was *The New York Times*.

Matching Test

Column A	Column B
1. Dorothea Dix	a. reformer who worked for better public education
2. Joseph Smith	b. author of Seneca Falls declaration
3. Horace Mann	c. reformer who helped improve treatment of mentally ill
4. Mary Lyon	d. author of *Uncle Tom's Cabin*
5. Elizabeth Blackwell	e. former slave who called for immediate abolition
6. Elizabeth Cady Stanton	f. New England writer who lived at Brook Farm
7. William Lloyd Garrison	g. organizer of Mormon church
8. Frederick Douglass	h. founder of Mount Holyoke Female Seminary
9. Nathaniel Hawthorne	i. publisher of *The Liberator*
10. Harriet Beecher Stowe	j. first woman to receive medical degree

Essay Questions

1. Describe four ways in which social reformers tried to improve American society in the Age of Jackson.

2. How was women's freedom limited in the early 19th century? Why did feminists become active in the 1840s?
3. What was Garrison's position on abolition and how it should be achieved? In what way did moderate abolitionists disagree with him? What did they do?
4. Describe three changes in education that took place in the early 1800s.
5. Identify and discuss two major developments in American literature *or* American painting in the early 19th century.

CHAPTER 14

Expansion
to the Pacific

THE AMERICAN MOVEMENT WESTWARD, which had settled the Old Southwest and the Northwest Territory, did not stop at the Mississippi. In the 1830s and 1840s, restless pioneers pushed farther west. By 1853, the United States had expanded all the way to the Pacific Ocean.

SETTLING THE FAR WEST AND SOUTHWEST

Pioneers did not settle the trans–Mississippi West in a step-by-step movement from east to west. Americans of the early 19th century regarded the Great Plains as a desert unfit for civilized life, so most people bypassed this region. (It was not settled until after the Civil War, as you will see in Chapter 18.) Instead, those who moved westward traveled either to the Rockies and beyond (the Far West) or to the area south and west of the Red River (the Southwest). In doing so, many of them settled in areas claimed by foreign nations. When conflicts arose, some were resolved peaceably. Others, however, led to war.

Trappers and Traders

The first non-Indians to live in the Rocky Mountain region were fur trappers. Beginning about 1820, hardy "mountain men" explored much of this area. Among the best known were Jim Bridger and Jedediah Smith.

Mountain men spent months setting traps, collecting furs, and trading with the Indians. (Many of them married Indian women and adopted Indian customs.) Every summer, they met at a designated location to sell their pelts to buyers from fur companies. Most of the trappers then squandered their earnings on a few days of high living.

Some frontier adventurers headed toward the Southwest and into Mexican territory. Mexico, which had won its independence from Spain in 1821, was eager to increase its contacts with Americans. The Mexican town of Santa Fe attracted many traders. To get there, caravans started at Independence, Missouri, and traveled more than 700 miles along the Santa Fe Trail. Traders carried manufactured goods to exchange for silver, wool, and mules. Kit Carson was a famous Western scout who traveled this route and made the Southwest his headquarters.

The Republic of Texas

In the province known as Texas, the Mexican government encouraged American immigration by offering liberal land grants. The earliest American settlements there were founded in the 1820s under the leadership of Stephen Austin. The area was well suited to cotton growing on a large scale. Many Southern planters moved there and took their slaves

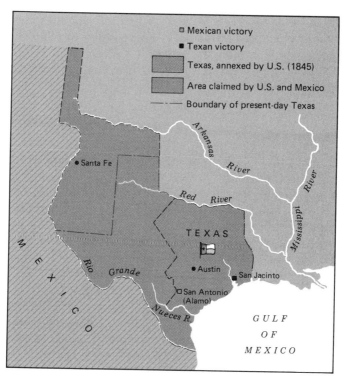

THE REPUBLIC OF TEXAS (1836-1845)

with them. By 1835, there were about 30,000 Americans in Texas.

Before long, trouble developed between the Americans and the Mexicans. It was caused partly by differences in language and customs, partly by quarrels over taxation and political representation. When the Mexican government tried to stop the importation of slaves and to halt further immigration, the Texans rebelled. Early in 1836, they declared their independence.

Antonio de Santa Anna, the Mexican president, was determined to win Texas back. He led a large force of Mexican troops northward. In February, Santa Anna's forces surrounded a small band of Americans stationed in the Alamo, an old Spanish mission in San Antonio. The Americans, commanded by William Travis, included frontiersmen Davy Crockett and Jim Bowie. They fought to the last man but were finally overwhelmed after 12 days.

"Remember the Alamo!" became the rallying cry of the Americans in Texas. Led by Sam Houston, they defeated the Mexicans at the Battle of San Jacinto in April and captured Santa Anna. Mexico then agreed to recognize the independence of the Republic of Texas. (Texas was also called the Lone Star Republic because of the single star on its flag.) Sam Houston became its first president.

Texas soon asked to be admitted to the Union as a new state. Its request was rejected. Northerners opposed the extension of slavery and the increase of Southern strength in Congress. And many Americans feared that annexing Texas would involve the United States in a war with Mexico.

Settling Oregon

Another region attracting Americans at this time was the Oregon Country, bounded by the Rocky Mountains on the east and the Pacific Ocean on the west. To the south of it was Mexican territory, and to the north, lands belonging to Russia and Britain. The northern boundary had been set at 54° 40 ' north latitude in 1824, when Russia withdrew its claim to territory south of that line. Both the United States and Britain claimed Oregon, but they had agreed to a joint occupation of the region in 1818.

Among the first Americans in the region were missionaries, who arrived in the 1830s to convert the Indians. Jason Lee was sent by the Methodists, and Marcus and Narcissa Whitman by the Presbyterians. The Catholics sent Father Pierre Jean de Smet. The early settlers wrote to families and friends about the fertile soil and pleasant climate beyond the Rockies. Many Easterners decided to see for themselves.

A "Great Migration" to Oregon began in 1843. Caravans left from Independence, Missouri, and crossed the Great Plains. Then, they went through the Rockies at South Pass and followed the winding Snake River

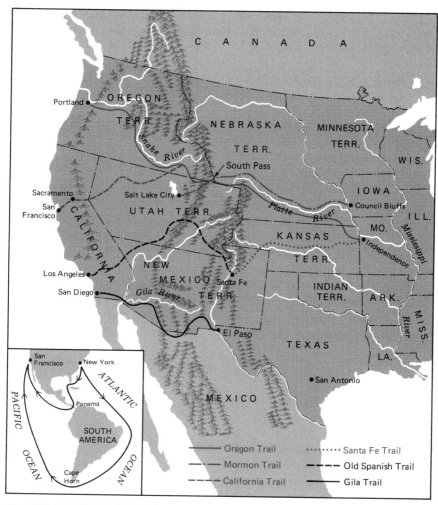

ROUTES TO THE FAR WEST

to the Columbia River. Mountain men often guided travelers along this route of 2000 miles, known as the Oregon Trail. By 1845, about 5000 Americans had moved to Oregon, founded settlements, and introduced self-government.

COMPROMISE AND CONFLICT

In the 1840s, American expansion westward came to be thought of as the "manifest destiny" of the nation. This phrase caught the public's fancy after it was used in a magazine article in 1845. The writer stated that it was the "manifest destiny" of the nation to "overspread the continent allotted by Providence for the free development of our yearly multiplying millions." The feeling was widespread that American expansion was not only right but also inevitable.

The Election of 1844

Expansionism was the major issue in the election campaign of 1844. The Whigs nominated Henry Clay. The Democrats ran a little-known Tennessee politician, James K. Polk. He has been called the first "dark horse" in American presidential politics. (A dark horse is a candidate who is not known nationally and whose nomination is, therefore, unexpected.)

Clay argued that the United States should not annex Texas without the consent of Mexico (which was unlikely). Polk came out strongly in favor of what the Democratic platform called the "re-occupation of Oregon" and the "re-annexation of Texas." (These terms suggested that the two regions had once belonged to the United States.) Antislavery forces still opposed adding Texas to the Union as a slave state, so the Democrats focused on the Oregon issue instead. Their catchy slogan was "Fifty-four forty or fight!" It meant that the United States had a right to the entire Oregon Country and would use force if Britain objected. A majority of Americans voted for Polk and expansionism.

The Annexation of Texas

Even before Polk took office, the Democrats, who had a majority in Congress, acted to acquire Texas. In December 1844, President Tyler recommended that Congress pass a joint resolution authorizing annexation. (A resolution, requiring only a simple majority in both houses, is easier to pass than a treaty, which needs a two-thirds majority in the Senate.) The resolution was soon adopted, and Tyler signed it just before leaving office. Texans later voted in favor of annexation, and the new state joined the Union in December 1845.

Meanwhile, Mexico had broken off diplomatic relations with the United States. The break resulted not only from the annexation but also from a dispute over the size of the Lone Star Republic. The United States claimed that the southern and western boundaries of Texas lay along the Rio Grande. Mexico contended that Texas comprised the area north and east of the Nueces River, a region about half as big as the U.S. claim.

Dividing Oregon

As trouble with Mexico became more of a threat, Polk's new administration backed down on its Oregon claim. The British suggested that the territory be divided along the 49th parallel. The northern part

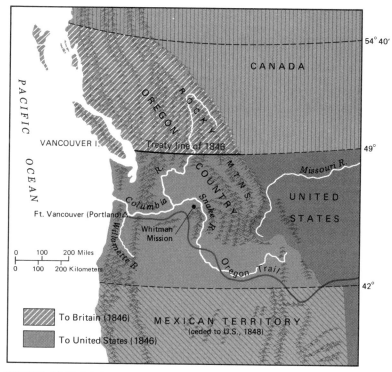

SETTLEMENT OF THE OREGON DISPUTE (1846)

(including Vancouver Island) would go to Canada, and the southern part to the United States. Polk passed the suggestion on to the Senate. It approved the British proposal and ratified the resulting treaty in 1846.

In 1848, a territorial government was set up in the Oregon Territory. Eleven years later, the southern part of the area was admitted to the Union as the state of Oregon. Toward the end of the century, the states of Washington and Idaho and parts of Montana and Wyoming were formed from the balance of the territory.

Troubles in California

Although Spain owned California, the territory's main inhabitants until the 18th century were a relatively small number of Native Americans. In the 1760s, however, settlers from Mexico established military outposts, trading centers, and large ranches. Franciscan priests (notably Father Junípero Serra) also founded a chain of Roman Catholic missions, from San Diego in the south to Sonoma in the north. Here they gathered Indian converts and taught them farming and other skills.

When Mexico became independent in 1821, the new nation included

The Oregon Trail

California Forty-Niner

Texans defending the Alamo

California and the intevening territory in the Southwest. Mexican control meant few changes for the *Californios*, as Spanish-speaking Californians were called. But for Native Americans it was a disaster. Mexico transferred the Catholic missions to private owners. The Indians, no longer protected, were widely victimized by white settlers.

Americans began to travel to California in the early 1840s. The explorer John C. Frémont was especially interested in the area. With Kit Carson as guide, he traveled throughout the region and wrote glowing reports about it. By 1846, about 500 Americans had settled there.

At various times, the U.S. government tried to buy California from Mexico, but without success. Then, in June 1846, dissatisfied American settlers at Sonoma declared the independence of California. The flag they raised was decorated with a picture of a grizzly bear, so this event came to be known as the Bear Flag Revolt. The California revolt soon became part of a larger struggle between Mexico and the United States.

The Mexican War

President Polk, an ardent expansionist, wanted not only southern and western Texas, but also the rest of the Southwest and California, as well. The president sent John Slidell to Mexico City to negotiate, but the Mexican government refused to see him. An angry Polk then ordered troops under Zachary Taylor into the disputed area of Texas and moved warships into the Gulf of Mexico and along the Pacific coast. In April 1846, a skirmish between Mexican and U.S. troops near the Rio Grande provided the needed spark. Polk asked Congress for a declaration of war, which it passed on May 13.

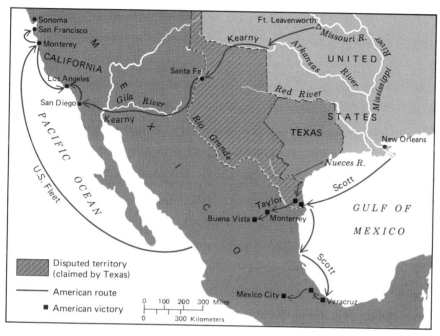

THE MEXICAN WAR (1846–1848)

ATTACKS ON MANY FRONTS   Hoping for a quick victory, the United States planned to attack Mexico on several fronts. In the spring of 1846, Taylor defeated Mexican forces in brief battles along the eastern Rio Grande and pursued the retreating enemy across the river. In the fall, he marched farther into Mexico. He captured Monterrey in September and won the Battle of Buena Vista in February 1847.

In the meantime, U.S. forces had gained control of New Mexico and California. Stephen Kearny marched his troops from Fort Leavenworth on the Missouri River and occupied Santa Fe in July 1846. He then continued on to California, which was in the midst of the Bear Flag Revolt. The rebelling settlers had been supported by a U.S. naval force, which took possession of the ports of Monterey, Los Angeles, and San Francisco. When Kearny reached California late in 1846, he helped end Mexican resistance and complete U.S. occupation of the region.

Taylor's offensive in northern Mexico had bogged down in mountainous terrain. In March 1847, another U.S. invasion force, under Winfield Scott, landed farther south at Veracruz. After a short siege, Scott captured the fortress there. He then marched on the capital, Mexico City, 250 miles inland. Along the route, the U.S. troops defeated the Mexicans in a series of battles. The last barrier to the capital was the fortified hill of Chapultepec, held by the Mexicans. In September, Scott's force took the hill and occupied Mexico City. These victories brought the war to an end.

THE PEACE TREATY   The *Treaty of Guadalupe Hidalgo* was signed in 1848. Mexico recognized the Rio Grande as the boundary of Texas. It also ceded New Mexico and California to the United States. In exchange, the United States paid Mexico $15 million in cash and agreed to pay all claims made by U.S. citizens against Mexico. The vast territory known as the *Mexican Cession* was eventually carved into many states: California, Nevada, Utah, and parts of Arizona, New Mexico, Colorado, and Wyoming.

A MILITARY HERO AS PRESIDENT   Another result of the Mexican War was the election of Zachary Taylor as president. In 1848, "Old Rough and Ready," as he was nicknamed, ran as the Whig candidate. His opponents were Democrat Lewis Cass and various minor-party candidates. Taylor's victories at Monterrey and Buena Vista, which had made him a national hero, helped him win the election. But he died in the summer of 1850, after serving as president for only 16 months. Vice President Millard Fillmore of New York succeeded him.

SURGES OF SETTLEMENT

Even as war with Mexico was bringing new lands under U.S. control, waves of new settlers were moving into them.

The Gold Rush

Early in 1848, shortly before the Treaty of Guadalupe Hidalgo was signed, gold was discovered in California. The find occurred at the sawmill of John Sutter, in the Sacramento Valley. The news traveled quickly, not only to the eastern United States but also to Europe and Asia. "Gold fever" spread like wildfire. Miners, soldiers, laborers, farmers, clerks, and professionals raced to California. The "forty-niners," so named after the first year of the gold rush, used every available means of transportation. Overland travelers on the California, Old Spanish, or Gila trails went by horseback or wagon. Some of those who made the long trip by water sailed all the way around Cape Horn. Others sailed to the Isthmus of Panama, crossed it by muleback, and then boarded another ship bound for California.

An estimated 100,000 people flocked to California in 1849. Many more arrived during the next few years. The value of the gold being mined

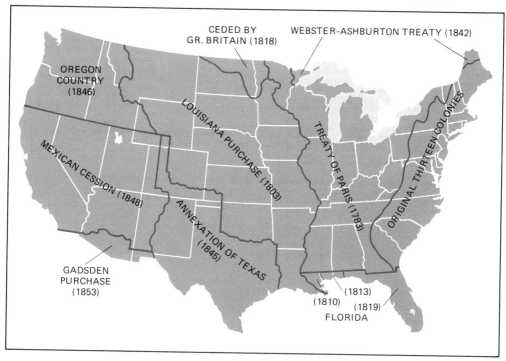

CEDED BY
GR. BRITAIN (1818)

WEBSTER-ASHBURTON TREATY (1842)

OREGON
COUNTRY
(1846)

LOUISIANA PURCHASE (1803)

TREATY OF PARIS (1783)

ORIGINAL THIRTEEN COLONIES

MEXICAN CESSION (1848)

ANNEXATION OF TEXAS (1845)

GADSDEN
PURCHASE
(1853)

(1810) (1813) (1819)
FLORIDA

TERRITORIAL GROWTH TO 1853
(INCLUDING PRESENT-DAY STATE BOUNDARIES)

rose from $5 million in 1848 to $40 million in 1849 and $55 million in 1851. A few forty-niners struck it rich in the goldfields almost overnight. Other newcomers made fortunes by selling the miners food, supplies, and services at high prices. Those who failed to get rich quickly turned to cattle raising and fruit growing, or moved elsewhere.

The Mormons in Utah

The Mormon church gained many new members in the 1830s and 1840s. Led by Joseph Smith, the Mormons left New York and migrated first to Ohio and then to Missouri and Illinois. In each place, their attempts to settle failed because of the hostility of non-Mormon neighbors. Some disapproved of the Mormon system of owning property in common. After 1843, when Smith announced that Mormon men could have more than one wife, opposition to the sect increased sharply.

In 1844, Smith was killed by a mob in Illinois. Brigham Young then became the leader of the Mormons. He led them west in search of a place where they would be free from persecution. In 1847, Young and a pioneer band of Mormons reached the valley of the Great Salt Lake in Utah. There, they founded Salt Lake City. Other Mormons soon followed. With cooperative effort and religious zeal, the settlers transformed the barren wasteland into a land of plenty. In 1850, Utah was organized as a territory, with Young as its governor.

The Gadsden Purchase

The southwestern United States was enlarged in 1853 with the addition of land along the southern boundary of New Mexico and Arizona. The United States needed the area for a proposed railroad to the Pacific, and Mexico agreed to sell it for $10 million. James Gadsden, the U.S. representative to Mexico, arranged the agreement. The acquisition thus became known as the *Gadsden Purchase*.

Multiple-Choice Test

1. The first non-Indians to live in the Rocky Mountain region were **(a)** fur trappers **(b)** Spanish missionaries **(c)** miners **(d)** Mormons.
2. Americans who traveled on the Santa Fe Trail were chiefly **(a)** traders **(b)** farmers **(c)** missionaries to the Indians **(d)** rebels against Mexican rule.
3. The southwestern state that was first an independent republic for nine years is **(a)** Colorado **(b)** Texas **(c)** Utah **(d)** Nevada.
4. Opposition to the annexation of Texas came mainly from **(a)** Americans in Texas who did not want to be part of the United States **(b)** Congress, which felt that the region was too big to be governed well **(c)** Northerners who disapproved of adding another slave state to the Union **(d)** Southerners who refused to recognize the independence of Texas.
5. The first dark horse to be elected to the presidency was **(a)** Lewis Cass **(b)** James K. Polk **(c)** Zachary Taylor **(d)** Millard Fillmore.
6. U.S. claims to the Oregon Country were settled by **(a)** an agreement with Spain **(b)** a war with Russia **(c)** a purchase from Mexico **(d)** a treaty with Britain.
7. The Bear Flag Revolt occurred in **(a)** Oregon **(b)** Texas **(c)** California **(d)** New Mexico.
8. All of the following were American military leaders in the Mexican War *except* **(a)** Zachary Taylor **(b)** Stephen Kearny **(c)** Joseph Smith **(d)** Winfield Scott.
9. The Mexican War was ended by the **(a)** Treaty of Guadalupe Hidalgo **(b)** Great Migration **(c)** Battle of Buena Vista **(d)** Gadsden Purchase.

10. The discovery of gold in California   **(a)** was one of the causes of the Mexican War   **(b)** helped bring about the Bear Flag Revolt   **(c)** helped Zachary Taylor in his campaign for the presidency   **(d)** drew 100,000 people to the region in the following year.

Matching Test

COLUMN A

1. Jim Bridger
2. Stephen Austin
3. "Remember the Alamo!"
4. Sam Houston
5. Marcus Whitman
6. "Fifty-four forty or fight!"
7. James K. Polk
8. John C. Frémont
9. Millard Fillmore
10. Brigham Young

COLUMN B

a. first president of Texas
b. president of United States during Mexican War
c. president who succeeded Zachary Taylor
d. famous mountain man
e. founder of first American settlements in Texas
f. American settlers' slogan during
   war for Texan independence
g. American missionary in Oregon
   Country
h. Mormon leader after Joseph
   Smith
i. Democrats' slogan during presidential campaign of 1844
j. American explorer of California

Map Test

GROUP A

Answer the following questions by studying the maps on pages 217 and 219, and the text.

1. The section of Texas claimed by both Mexico and the United States in 1845 represented about what percentage of the state's present-day size?
2. Locate and identify **(a)** the settlement that was named for an early American pioneer in Texas and **(b)** the settlement that was the site of a Spanish mission where a band of Americans was wiped out by the Mexicans.
3. Locate and name the access route through the mountains that was used by emigrants heading for California and Oregon.
4. **(a)** What was the point of departure for American traders seeking to

do business with the Mexicans in the Southwest?   (b) What was the name of the trail these traders followed?

5. Study the route used by Brigham Young and his followers.   (a) Where did it start?   (b) Where did these pioneers finally settle?   (c) What is the present-day name of the state they established?

GROUP B

Locate the following places on the map on page 223. Then, referring to the text, as necessary, explain why each place was important either before or during the Mexican War.

1. Nueces River
2. Veracruz
3. Sonoma
4. Santa Fe
5. Mexico City

6. Buena Vista
7. Fort Leavenworth
8. San Diego
9. Rio Grande
10. Monterrey

GROUP C

Answer the following questions by referring to the maps on pages 221 and 225, and to the text.

1. According to American expansionists in the early 1840s, what parallel of latitude constituted the U.S. boundary in the Pacific Northwest?
2. At what parallel of latitude did the United States and Great Britain agree to divide the Oregon Country?
3. How many states were ultimately created, in whole or in part, from the Oregon Country? Can you name them?
4. Of the territories that were to become the 48 adjoining states, which territory did the United States acquire last?
5. From which territorial acquisition, after 1783, was the largest number of states formed? How many states, in whole or in part, were created from this acquisition?

Essay Questions

1. Why did Texas break away from Mexico in 1836? Why did it not become a state at that time?
2. What does the phrase "manifest destiny" mean?
3. How did the United States put the idea of manifest destiny into action in the 1840s?
4. Describe the major military campaigns of the Mexican War.
5. What were the chief results of the conflict with Mexico?

UNIT 5

Division
and
Reunion

CHAPTER *15*

Slavery and Sectionalism

Since colonial times, Americans have viewed their country as comprising different sections, or regions. These areas differed in their geography, economic interests, and social structure.

The earliest regional division of the United States grouped the 13 original colonies into New England, the Middle Colonies, and the South. In the early 1800s, westward expansion and industrialization led to the emergence of three different sections: the Northeast, the West, and the South. And by the middle 1800s, still another sectional regrouping took place—a division of the nation into North and South.

The North stretched across the country north of the Ohio River from the Atlantic Ocean to the Mississippi River and beyond. Below it lay the South. The two sections were divided by the Mason-Dixon line. The original line, drawn by two surveyors in the 1760s to settle a boundary dispute, divided Pennsylvania from Maryland. In time, the Mason-Dixon line was thought of as extending west to the Mississippi.

The North and South differed in their geography and climate. There were other differences, too. The North had many cities and industries, and a large working class. Northerners came from many different ethnic and religious backgrounds. The South, mainly rural, depended heavily on farming. Most of its white inhabitants were Protestants whose ancestors had come from the British Isles. But the chief difference between North and South was slavery.

THE SYSTEM OF SLAVERY

The practice of slavery goes back to ancient times. As it developed in the United States, it differed from other slave systems in at least two ways. First, slaves in the United States had no legal rights. (In various African kingdoms, slaves could own property and were protected from abuse.) Second, American slaves, being black, were racially distinct. (In ancient Greece and Rome, most slaves were white, like their owners.)

Slave Ownership

The first Africans came to the North American colonies early in the 17th century. Their numbers increased steadily, and by 1800, there were about a million black people in the United States. Sixty years later, there were about 4.5 million. Nearly 90 percent of them were slaves.

Slavery existed at one time or another in all the colonies. After the Revolutionary War, however, slavery was gradually eliminated in the North. Even in the South, slaves were not found in every area. There were few in the Appalachian Mountains region. Many slaves lived in the fertile flatlands of the Deep South (the band of states stretching from South Carolina to Texas). In the mid-19th century, three states—South Carolina, Louisiana, and Mississippi—had more blacks than whites.

In 1860, only about a fourth of all Southern white families owned slaves. Of these families, fewer than 1 percent owned 100 or more slaves. Thus, the huge plantation, worked by an army of blacks, was quite rare. But the planter class—the wealthy plantation owners with many slaves—dominated Southern life.

On the whole, the slave system was a source of profit for owners. They had to feed, clothe, and house their black workers. But they could count on a steady supply of labor, which grew with the birth of slaves' children. After the overseas slave trade ended in 1808 (except for smuggling), the price of slaves rose steadily. By 1860, a strong young male cost more than $1500.

How Slaves Lived

The majority of slaves worked as field hands, growing and harvesting such crops as cotton, rice, sugar, and tobacco. A smaller number were servants in their masters' houses. Slaves also performed skilled labor as masons, carpenters, blacksmiths, seamstresses, and so on.

Owners and overseers (white field bosses) varied widely in their treatment of slaves. The labor of field hands in particular, however, was backbreaking. Slaves generally lived in family groups in simple, dirt-floor

"A house divided against itself cannot stand" Abraham Lincoln

Slave family in the cotton fields

cabins, but their marriages were not recognized and their family could be split up by sale at any time. It was illegal to teach slaves to read, but a rich cultural life centered around music, religion, and story telling developed.

Under the best conditions, however, slavery was harmful to both owners and owned. Having total control over other human beings tended to make whites callous. And lack of freedom threatened the very identity of blacks.

THE POLITICS OF SLAVERY

For a time during the late 18th century, slavery seemed to be dying out. Tobacco production had declined, thus reducing the need for large numbers of field-workers. Then, in the 1790s, Eli Whitney invented the cotton gin. By speeding up cotton processing, this device encouraged Southern planters to expand their acreage and raise larger crops. The planters had a good market for their output in the textile factories of England and, later, New England. Since cotton growing required many laborers, it helped make slavery a basic feature of Southern life.

There was one drawback to increasing cotton production. The crop wore out the soil. Therefore, cotton planters in the original Southern colonies along the Atlantic coast welcomed the opening of the Old Southwest. When that region began to fill up, Southerners looked to the territories beyond the Mississippi for further expansion. The annexation of Texas and the Mexican Cession in the 1840s seemed to offer new possibilities.

But while slavery had been expanding, so had opposition to it. The goal of abolitionists, both moderate and radical, was to end the system. There were abolitionists even in the South, at least in the early days. Some were people who did not own slaves. Others lived in border states—slave states, such as Kentucky and Maryland, that bordered on the North. These abolitionists favored gradual emancipation.

After 1831, however, the antislavery crusade was almost entirely a Northern effort. This was the year of the Nat Turner uprising. Turner, a slave preacher in Virginia, led some 70 followers in a bloody attack on whites, killing nearly 60 men, women, and children. The rebellion was easily put down, but it frightened whites all over the South, whether or not they owned slaves. Abolitionists were blamed for stirring up the attack. Soon, abolitionist literature was no longer allowed to go through the mail in the South.

Southerners had first defended slavery as a necessary evil. Now, they began to look on it as a positive good. They declared that it was the economic mainstay of a whole region. They also argued that it offered protection for a race that could not provide for itself. One advocate of slavery wrote: "What a glorious thing to man is slavery, when want, misfortune, old age, debility [weakness], and sickness overtake him."

As the years passed, positions hardened. Many Northerners believed that there was a "slave power conspiracy" aimed at extending slavery to the whole United States. Many Southerners feared that their property would be seized by wild-eyed radicals who had no understanding of the Southern way of life.

A SHAKY BALANCE

By the early 19th century, Northern states had either abolished slavery or provided for its gradual elimination. States south of the Mason-Dixon line allowed slavery. Of the original 13 states, 7 were free and 6 were slave.

FREE AND SLAVE STATES (1776–1819)
(in order of ratification or admission to Union)

	Free States	Slave States
Original Colonies	Pennsylvania	Delaware
	New Jersey	Georgia
	Connecticut	Maryland
	Massachusetts	South Carolina
	New Hampshire	Virginia
	New York	North Carolina
	Rhode Island	
New States (1791–1819)	Vermont	Kentucky
	Ohio	Tennessee
	Indiana	Louisiana
	Illinois	Alabama
		Mississippi

(Free states prohibited slavery, while slave states did not.) Between 1791 and 1819, 9 new states were admitted to the Union. Of these, 4 were free and 5 slave, thus equalizing the number of free and slave states at 11 each.

Keeping this balance became a key issue for both North and South. Neither section wanted the other to gain control of the Senate. Equality in the Senate was especially important to the South. It was losing voting strength in the House of Representatives because its population was not growing as fast as that of the North.

The Missouri Compromise

In 1819, Missouri, a slaveholding area, applied for statehood. Northern politicians opposed this request for two reasons. It would upset the balance between free and slave states. And it would officially establish slavery in the northern part of the Louisiana Purchase. If slavery were allowed there, what would happen when additional states were made from Louisiana territory to the west and north?

The problem was resolved when Maine requested admission as a free state. Congress could then enact the *Missouri Compromise* of 1820. It provided that (1) Maine be admitted as a free state, (2) Missouri be admitted as a slave state, and (3) slavery be prohibited in the rest of the Louisiana Purchase north of latitude 36° 30 '. (This line of latitude formed the southern boundary of Missouri.)

The Compromise of 1850

In the 1830s and 1840s, the North and South continued to have equal representation in the Senate. Between 1836 and 1848, six more states were added to the Union—Michigan, Iowa, Wisconsin, Arkansas, Florida, and Texas. The first three were free states, and the other three, slave states. The balance was thus kept at 15 states each.

The Mexican Cession caused the problem of slavery in new states to flare up again. Southerners demanded that slavery be permitted in the region. Northerners insisted that it be kept out. The issue came to a head in 1850 when California, a part of the Mexican Cession, asked for admission as a free state. Bitter sectional quarreling broke out.

Henry Clay offered one solution. California would be admitted as a free state, but there would be no restrictions against slavery in the rest of the Mexican Cession. Intense debate followed. Calhoun argued against any compromise. Both Clay and Webster pleaded for a spirit of moderation.

POPULATION OF SLAVEHOLDING STATES (1850)

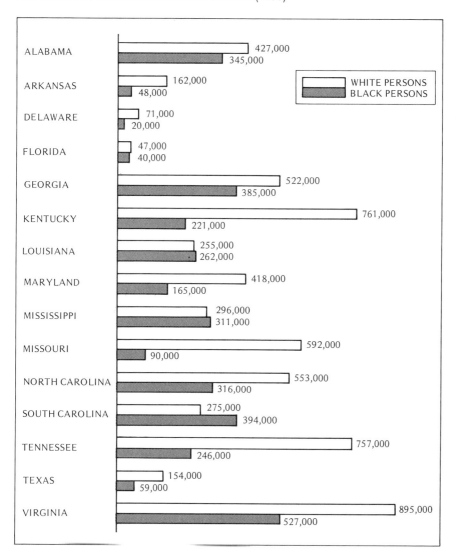

Finally, what came to be called the *Compromise of 1850* was passed as five separate bills:

1. California was admitted as a free state.
2. Texas gave up its claim to eastern New Mexico in return for $10 million.
3. The territories of New Mexico and Utah were organized on the principle of popular sovereignty (squatter sovereignty). That is, the people of each region would decide whether they wanted slavery.

4. A new, more severe *Fugitive Slave Law* imposed heavy fines on people who helped slaves to escape. (An earlier law, passed in 1793, had not been strictly enforced.)

5. The slave trade (but not slavery) was abolished in the District of Columbia.

SECTIONAL STRAINS

The Compromise of 1850 eased relations between North and South for a short while. But tensions remained. Abolitionists continued to attack slavery. The publication in 1852 of *Uncle Tom's Cabin,* an antislavery novel, aroused strong feelings. So did the new Fugitive Slave Law, which was widely disobeyed.

The Kansas-Nebraska Act

Sectional conflict erupted again in 1854 with passage of the *Kansas-Nebraska Act.* It was sponsored by Senator Stephen A. Douglas, a Democrat of Illinois.

The Kansas-Nebraska Act came about because the growing population of the West needed a railroad. Some Americans wanted a southern route. It would start at New Orleans and cross Texas and the part of New Mexico recently acquired by the Gadsden Purchase. Others wanted a northern route, starting at Chicago, in Douglas's home state.

The trouble with the northern route was that, unlike the proposed southern one, it would cross territory that was politically unorganized. Douglas, therefore, proposed a bill to organize this region into two territories: Nebraska in the north and Kansas in the south. To gain Southern support, the Kansas-Nebraska Bill provided that popular sovereignty would decide the slavery question in each territory. This meant that the Missouri Compromise, banning slavery north of 36° 30', was being repealed.

The Kansas-Nebraska Act, passed in May 1854, had two important results. One was the formation of a new political party. The other was an outbreak of violence in Kansas.

THE REPUBLICAN PARTY Many antislavery Northerners were angered by the Kansas-Nebraska Act. They were also unhappy with the Democratic and Whig parties, which had not taken a strong stand against the law. The discontented Northerners deserted these older parties and formed a new one, the *Republican party.* (One Northern Whig who did so was Abraham Lincoln, a young congressman from Illinois.)

The Republican party began to take shape early in 1854. It called for

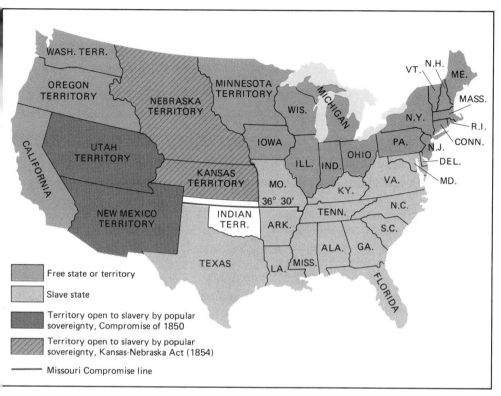

THE FREE-SLAVE BALANCE (1854)

repeal of the Kansas-Nebraska Act and the Fugitive Slave Law, and the abolition of slavery in the District of Columbia. The party soon added other aims, including a high protective tariff, construction of a railroad across the continent, and free land for Western settlers.

In 1856, the Republicans nominated John C. Frémont of California for president. He ran against James Buchanan, a Democrat from Pennsylvania, and former President Millard Fillmore of New York, the Whig candidate. Buchanan won the election, but the Republicans showed surprising strength. Frémont received a large popular vote and won the electoral votes of about two-thirds of the free states. After this election, the Whigs ceased to be a force in American political life. (Most Southern Whigs joined the Democratic party.) There were now two sectional parties: the Republicans in the North and the Democrats in the South.

"BLEEDING KANSAS"   Meanwhile, popular sovereignty in Kansas, as provided by the Kansas-Nebraska Act, was turning the region into a battleground. Both proslavery and antislavery forces tried to gain control of the territorial legislature, which was to vote on whether Kansas would allow slavery. Violence broke out in 1855, and some 200 people were killed. "Bleeding Kansas" became a symbol of the sectionalism that threatened the whole nation. (Kansas eventually joined the Union as a free state in 1861.)

The Dred Scott Decision

Early in 1857, sectional feeling was further aroused. This time, the cause was a Supreme Court decision about a slave named Dred Scott.

Scott's master had taken him from the slave state of Missouri into free territory. After a few years, Scott was taken back to Missouri. He then sued for his freedom, arguing that he had lived in free territory and was no longer a slave.

In *Dred Scott* v. *Sanford*, the Supreme Court ruled that Scott was a slave, not a citizen. Therefore, he had no right to sue in a federal court. The Court further declared that the Missouri Compromise was unconstitutional because it prohibited slavery in the northern part of the Louisiana Purchase. Slaves were property, said the Court, and Congress had no right to deprive citizens of their property. In other words, owners could take their slaves anywhere they pleased.

Northerners were enraged. The Dred Scott decision, in effect, made it legal to extend slavery into all U.S. territories.

The Lincoln-Douglas Debates

In 1858, the slavery question remained in the forefront, partly because of a senatorial campaign in Illinois. Democrat Stephen A. Douglas was opposed by Republican Abraham Lincoln. Douglas was a powerful speaker and a nationally known U.S. senator. Lincoln challenged him to a series of debates on the vital questions of the day.

These public debates attracted national attention. The candidates discussed every aspect of the slavery issue. In one debate, held at Freeport, Illinois, Lincoln presented Douglas with a problem. The principle of popular sovereignty permitted a territory to exclude slavery. The Dred Scott decision held that slavery could *not* be excluded from a territory. Which of these two positions, Lincoln asked, did Douglas favor? Douglas answered that a territorial legislature could keep out slavery by not passing laws to protect it.

Douglas won election to the Senate, but his "Freeport Doctrine" turned Southern Democrats against him. The debates, as a whole, made Lincoln nationally famous as a spokesman for the principles of Republicanism.

John Brown's Raid

In the fall of 1859, an event occurred that made North-South relations even worse. The man who brought it about was a fanatical abolitionist named John Brown.

Brown, who had killed slavery supporters in Kansas, conceived a plan to stir up a slave uprising in the South. In October, with 18 men, he attacked and seized the government arsenal at Harpers Ferry, Virginia (now West Virginia). His purpose was to obtain weapons for the slaves he hoped would join his force. But no mass uprising took place, and Brown and his men were soon killed or captured. Brown was tried for treason and found guilty. He was hanged in December, 1859.

Abolitionists regarded Brown as a hero who gave his life for the antislavery cause. They mourned his death with rallies and speeches. (He also became the subject of a marching song, "John Brown's Body.") Many Southerners already believed that Northerners were plotting to destroy their way of life. John Brown's raid confirmed these fears.

THE ELECTION OF 1860

Democrats held their presidential nominating convention in the spring of 1860. They could not agree on a candidate or a platform that everyone in the party could support. So they split into two groups. The Northern delegates chose Douglas as their presidential candidate, and the Southerners selected John C. Breckinridge of Kentucky.

The Republicans nominated Lincoln. Aided by the split in the Democratic party, Lincoln won the election. His victory was clearly sectional. He won the electoral votes of every free state but failed to carry a single slave state.

NEW STATES (1820–1859)

State	Admitted to Union
Maine	1820
Missouri	1821
Arkansas	1836
Michigan	1837
Florida	1845
Texas	1845
Iowa	1846
Wisconsin	1848
California	1850
Minnesota	1858
Oregon	1859

Secession and the Confederacy

Early in 1860, Southern leaders had begun to warn that the election of a Republican president would cause the South to secede. Lincoln had not threatened to abolish slavery everywhere. But Southerners regarded him as an enemy because he opposed the extension of slavery in the territories.

After Lincoln's victory, South Carolina took a fateful step. Delegates to a state convention on December 20, 1860, declared that "the union now subsisting between South Carolina and the other states, under the name of the 'United States of America,' is hereby dissolved." The process of secession had begun.

By February 1861, six other states had joined South Carolina: Mississippi, Florida, Alabama, Georgia, Louisiana, and Texas. On February 4, delegates from the seceding states met at Montgomery, Alabama, and formed the *Confederate States of America*. The constitution the delegates drew up was like the U.S. Constitution in many ways. But it had four important differences:

1. It emphasized "the sovereign and independent character" of each state.
2. It recognized and protected slavery.
3. It forbade protective tariffs.
4. It prohibited the use of government funds for internal improvements.

The delegates chose Jefferson Davis of Mississippi as president of the Confederacy. Alexander H. Stephens of Georgia became vice president.

In this anti-Buchanan cartoon, the eagle, symbol of the United States, is thriving when Buchanan takes office in 1857 and a sorry specimen four years later. (Courtesy of the New-York Historical Society, New York City)

Buchanan's Position

While these events were taking place, President Buchanan stood by helplessly. (Lincoln had not yet been inaugurated.) Buchanan hoped to see the Union preserved. In his view, however, neither the president nor Congress had the power to prevent a state from seceding. During the last months of his administration, secessionist forces seized most of the federal property in their states—including forts, arsenals, customhouses, and post offices. The New Orleans Mint, which contained $500,000 in gold and silver, was also taken. Buchanan, determined to keep the peace until his term was over, did not interfere.

The Inauguration of Lincoln

On March 4, 1861, Abraham Lincoln took the oath of office as the 16th president of the United States. In his inaugural address he made a strong appeal to the South to preserve the Union. He said that he would not interfere with slavery in the states where it existed. But he added that no state could lawfully secede from the Union. Federal laws would be carried out in all the states.

In your hands, my dissatisfied fellow-countrymen, and not in mine, is the momentous issue of civil war. The government will not assail you. You can have no conflict without being yourselves the aggressors. You have no oath registered in heaven to destroy the government, while I shall have the most solemn one to "preserve, protect, and defend" it.

—Abraham Lincoln's
First Inaugural Address, March 4, 1861

Multiple-Choice Test

1. The major issue separating North and South in the 1850s was **(a)** the tariff **(b)** immigration policy **(c)** slavery **(d)** competition for cotton markets.

2. The proportion of white Southern families owning slaves in 1860 was about **(a)** 15 percent **(b)** 25 percent **(c)** 40 percent **(d)** 75 percent.

3. Slavery might have died a natural death if it had not been for **(a)** the invention of the cotton gin **(b)** the constitutional provision protecting the slave trade **(c)** the Missouri Compromise **(d)** the importing of additional slaves after 1808.

4. Beginning in the 1830s, the abolition movement (a) gained new members in the South (b) lost members in the North (c) drew strength from the death of John Brown (d) became mainly a Northern effort.

5. Southerners defended slavery by arguing that (a) it was guaranteed by the First Amendment of the Constitution (b) slaves were skilled farmers (c) it was the mainstay of their economy (d) 90 percent of Southern families depended on slave labor.

6. The Compromise of 1850 dealt with all of the following *except* (a) the eastern boundary of New Mexico (b) the territory of Utah (c) the slave trade in Washington, D.C. (d) the status of Missouri.

7. The Kansas-Nebraska Act was passed in order to (a) help build a western railroad (b) guarantee more free states (c) aid Stephen A. Douglas in his debates with Lincoln (d) provide a home for eastern Indians.

8. In the Dred Scott decision, the Supreme Court ruled that (a) Congress had the power to abolish slavery (b) Congress could not prohibit slavery in the territories (c) slavery was illegal north of 36° 30′ (d) the issue of slavery should be settled by popular sovereignty.

9. All of the following were presidential candidates in the election of 1860 *except* (a) Abraham Lincoln (b) John C. Breckinridge (c) Jefferson Davis (d) Stephen A. Douglas.

10. The secession of the first Southern states took place during the administration of President (a) Franklin Pierce (b) James Buchanan (c) Abraham Lincoln (d) Millard Fillmore.

Map Test

The following statements identify states and territories on the map of the United States in the 1850s. For each statement, choose the letter that indicates the location of the area on the map. (A letter may be used more than once, or not at all.)

1. The Mason-Dixon line was drawn along the southern boundary of this state.

2. As a result of the Compromise of 1820, this state was admitted to the Union as a slave state.

3. This state was admitted as a free state by the Compromise of 1820.

4. According to the Compromise of 1850, this state entered the Union as a free state.

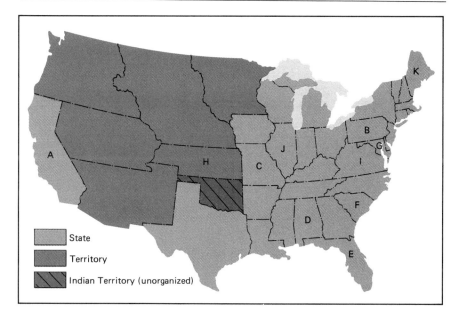

5. Violence in this territory came about over the issue of popular sovereignty.
6. This state was Dred Scott's original home.
7. This state was the scene of the Lincoln-Douglas debates.
8. This state was the scene of John Brown's raid.
9. This state was the first to secede from the Union.
10. In this state, delegates from the seceding states organized the Confederacy.

Essay Questions

1. Why was a balance of free states and slave states important in the period before the 1860s? How did this balance affect the admission to the Union of Missouri? of California?
2. How and why was sectional tension between North and South affected by each of the following: (a) the Kansas-Nebraska Act? (b) the Dred Scott decision? (c) John Brown's raid?
3. Why did South Carolina and other Southern states secede from the Union after Lincoln's election?
4. How did the constitution of the Confederacy differ from the U.S. Constitution?
5. What was Buchanan's response to Southern secession? What attitude did Lincoln show in his inaugural address?

CHAPTER 16

The Civil War

E VEN AS LINCOLN was giving his inaugural address in March 1861, the United States was moving toward a civil war. Seven states had seceded from the Union. They had formed the Confederate States of America and seized federal property within their borders.

It was on this last issue that Lincoln soon took a stand. One federal post that had not been seized was Fort Sumter, located on an island in the harbor of Charleston, South Carolina. Late in March, the troops at the fort ran short of supplies. If the government did not send help, the federal force would have to abandon the fort and, thus, give in to the South. But if the president sent provisions, the Confederates would probably regard the shipment as a hostile act. Lincoln chose the second option and ordered supply ships sent in. When they neared their destination, on April 12, Confederate guns along the shore opened fire on the fort and forced it to surrender. The war had begun.

EARLY YEARS

The fall of Fort Sumter stirred strong feeling on both sides. In the North, Lincoln called for volunteers, and thousands flocked to join the Union army. In the South, four more states—Virginia, Arkansas, North Carolina, and Tennessee—seceded and joined the Confederacy. Richmond, Virginia, became the Confederate capital.

Eleven states had now left the Union. But whether the four remaining slave states of Maryland, Kentucky, Missouri, and Delaware would follow was still in doubt. Their decision would have an important impact on the course of the war. If Maryland joined the Confederacy, Washington, D.C., the Union capital, would be completely cut off from the North. The other three states were also important from a military standpoint because of their location between the North and South.

After much political maneuvering, all four border states rejected secession. Thousands of men from Kentucky and Missouri, however, enlisted in the Confederate army. The people of Virginia were also divided in their loyalties. The state joined the Confederacy, but its western part remained loyal to the Union. (This region eventually split off from the east and became the separate state of West Virginia.)

War Leadership and Aims

The Civil War pitted two very different commanders in chief against each other. Abraham Lincoln was a self-educated lawyer from the Midwest. He had practically no military experience. But his wisdom, understanding, and humor won him wide support. He played an active role in making military decisions and proved to be an excellent strategist.

Jefferson Davis had graduated from West Point (the United States Military Academy) and served in the Mexican War. His intelligence and dignity were admired. But his aloof manner turned people away. And military leaders criticized him for being overly cautious and stubborn.

The two sides had different war aims. The North's objective (at least at the start of the war) was not to free the slaves but to preserve the Union.

RESOURCES OF THE NORTH AND SOUTH

	North (Union)	South (Confederacy)
Population	23 states, with population of 22 million	11 states, with population of 9 million (including 3.5 million slaves)
Industry	85% of nation's factories; 90% of its skilled workers	15% of nation's factories; 10% of its skilled workers
Transportation	22,000 miles of railroads; large merchant marine; naval supremacy	9000 miles of railroads; few merchant ships and naval vessels
Finances	Control of 70% of nation's wealth	Control of 30% of nation's wealth
Military Forces	Few experienced officers; soldiers poorly prepared for army life (many of them former city dwellers and factory workers)	Superior military leadership; good soldiers

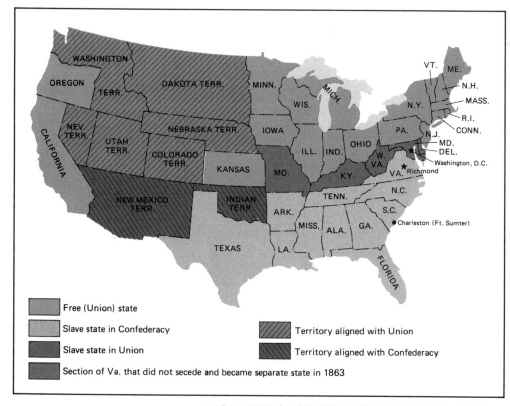

Free (Union) state

Slave state in Confederacy

Slave state in Union

Section of Va. that did not secede and became separate state in 1863

Territory aligned with Union

Territory aligned with Confederacy

ALIGNMENT OF STATES AND TERRITORIES (1861)

This goal required the Union forces to take the offensive and strike at the South. The South had an easier task—to withstand enemy attack. Like the colonists during the Revolutionary War, Confederate soldiers would be fighting a defensive war on their own territory.

First Campaigns

Many Northerners believed that the war would be over in 90 days. Army leaders decided that the best way to end the conflict quickly would be to capture the Confederate capital, Richmond. In July 1861, a Union force under Irvin McDowell advanced into northern Virginia and attacked a Confederate army at a creek called Bull Run. The Union troops were badly defeated by the Confederates. (At this battle, the Southern general Thomas J. Jackson stood his ground and earned the nickname "Stonewall.") The defeat at Bull Run made Northerners realize that victory would not be won quickly.

THE WAR AT SEA   At the outbreak of the war, Lincoln ordered Union ships to blockade the Southern coast, from Virginia to Texas. The blockade was so effective that the export of cotton from the South dwindled to 2 percent of its prewar volume. With its main source of income cut off, the South had difficulty buying the supplies it needed.

Southerners tried to counteract the blockade by building a number of fast ships that could evade the Northern patrols. These blockade-runners often succeeded in bringing in supplies from abroad. But as the war progressed, the Union tightened its control and captured many Southern ships.

In another attempt to break the Northern blockade, the Confederates produced one of the first armored warships. They covered the sides of a standard wooden vessel, the *Merrimac*, with metal plates. On March 8, 1862, off the coast of Virginia, the *Merrimac* destroyed two Northern ships made of wood. The next day, however, it met its match in the North's *Monitor*, an odd-looking warship designed by John Ericsson. The *Monitor* was described as "a cheese box on a raft." It had a flat iron hull topped by a revolving turret, from which powerful guns could be fired in any direction. The *Monitor* engaged the *Merrimac* in a fierce sea battle and forced the Confederate warship to withdraw. This historic naval battle not only saved the Northern blockade but also demonstrated the superiority of such ironclad vessels over wooden ones.

THE WAR IN THE WEST   One of the main aims of Union forces in the West was to gain control of the Mississippi River and, thus, divide the Confederacy. In time, the Union plan succeeded.

In February 1862, Union troops under Ulysses S. Grant, aided by river gunboats, moved against two Confederate forts in northern Tennessee. Grant's army first captured Fort Henry on the Tennessee River. Then, it took Fort Donelson on the Cumberland River. The Confederates retreated southward but then attacked Grant at Shiloh, in southwestern Tennessee. They were again defeated after a hard-fought battle. These victories gave the Union control of western Tennessee and the upper Mississippi River.

Meanwhile, another Northern force was moving on New Orleans. In April, David G. Farragut led a fleet of Union warships from the Gulf of Mexico into the mouth of the Mississippi. His ships fought their way past the Confederate forts on the river. They then defeated the gunboats sent to stop them and took New Orleans on May 1. Except for a 200-mile stretch between Port Hudson and Vicksburg, all of the Mississippi was in Union hands by the end of 1862 (see the map on page 248).

FURTHER DRIVES ON RICHMOND   In the East, the Union was still trying to capture Richmond. During the spring of 1862, George B. McClellan

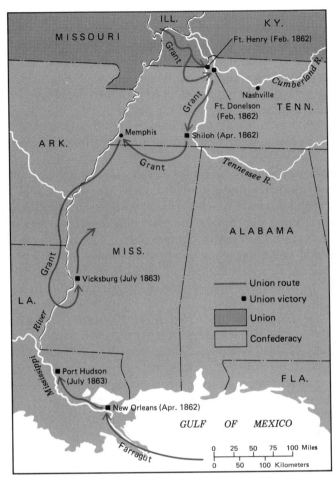

THE UNION GAINS CONTROL OF THE
MISSISSIPPI RIVER (1862–1863)

began a drive on the Southern capital through the peninsula formed by the York and James rivers. In his Peninsular Campaign, McClellan got to within a few miles of Richmond but then stopped to await reinforcements.

Meanwhile, in the Shenandoah Valley of western Virginia, Confederate troops under Stonewall Jackson launched a series of hit-and-run attacks on Union forces encamped there. His moves in this Valley Campaign were so rapid and unexpected that they kept the Northern troops in the area too busy to help McClellan. On the peninsula itself, Robert E. Lee, in charge of Confederate forces in northern Virginia, engaged McClellan in a series of encounters called the Seven Days' Battles. He forced the Union general to retreat to the James River and then northward.

A CONFEDERATE OFFENSIVE   As McClellan moved north, Lee decided to attack another Union force in northern Virginia. At the second Battle of Bull Run (August 1862), the Confederates were the victors. They then invaded Maryland, where Lee met McClellan at Antietam. This battle, in September 1862, is usually considered the bloodiest of the war. More than 20,000 men were killed or wounded. Although neither side really won, Antietam is counted as a Union victory because Confederate troops

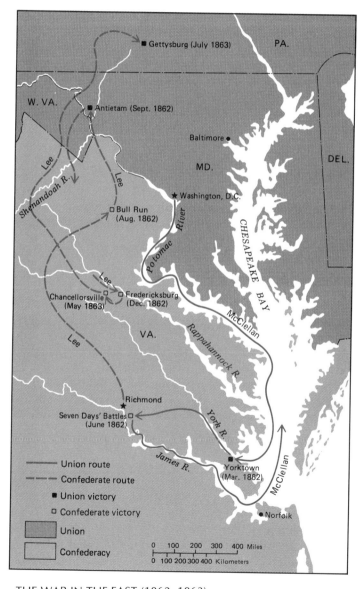

THE WAR IN THE EAST (1862–1863)

Clara Barton, Civil War Nurse   Union Artillery   Robert E. Lee

withdrew across the Potomac to Virginia.

The final Union campaign of 1862 was another fruitless attempt to take Richmond. Ambrose Burnside opposed Lee at Fredericksburg, Virginia, in December. The battle ended in a crushing defeat for the Union.

BEHIND THE LINES

The Civil War demanded more sacrifice and intensity of effort from Americans than they had ever made in a conflict. Resources were strained to the limit, especially in the South.

Foreign Diplomacy

Both the Union and the Confederacy sought the support of Great Britain. But the British were divided in their attitude. The upper classes sided with Southern planters, while workers and reformers, opposed to slavery, favored the North. The Confederacy believed that the English textile industry was so dependent on Southern cotton that it would persuade the British government to aid the South. But the mill owners had a surplus of raw cotton at the start of the war and later obtained new supplies from India and Egypt. Britain remained neutral throughout the conflict.

THE *TRENT* AFFAIR   One wartime incident led to much ill feeling between Great Britain and the Union. In 1861, the British ship *Trent* sailed from Cuba for Europe with two Confederate representatives on board. (The Southerners had evaded the blockade to reach the Caribbean.) A Union warship stopped the *Trent* at sea. The Northern commander, Charles Wilkes, boarded the *Trent,* searched it, and seized the two Confederates, James Mason and John Slidell. Britain strongly protested this interference with its shipping and demanded that the two men be freed. To back up its demand, Britain sent military reinforcements to

Canada. To avoid war with England, Lincoln ordered the release of Mason and Slidell.

THE *ALABAMA* CLAIMS   Although Britain was neutral, it allowed Confederate ships to be built in British shipyards. One of these ships, the *Alabama*, did a great deal of damage to Northern shipping. The Union held Britain responsible for the damages and demanded repayment. (In 1872, a special court awarded the United States $15.5 million to settle these claims).

MAXIMILIAN IN MEXICO   France was also officially neutral during the Civil War but tended to favor the South. French leaders believed that a divided United States would be less resistant to French expansion in the Western Hemisphere. France granted loans to the Confederacy and permitted French shipyards to build ships for the Southerners.

In 1863, the French ruler, Emperor Napoleon III, attacked Mexico. He occupied Mexico City and made an Austrian archduke, Maximilian, the emperor of Mexico. At the time, the United States was too involved in the Civil War to do anything about this violation of the Monroe Doctrine. When the war was over, however, the United States sent an army to the Mexican border, and France withdrew its troops. The Mexicans then overthrew the unprotected Maximilian, executed him, and regained control of their country.

The Home Front

The people of the Confederacy experienced great hardship during the Civil War. Most of the fighting took place on Southern soil, causing destruction to homes, businesses, and farms, and disrupting vital public services. The breakdown of the region's system of railroads created serious supply problems after 1863. Shortages of basic necessities forced some Southerners to eat weeds and wear rags. Prices late in the war reached absurd heights. A barrel of flour cost $300 and a pair of men's boots $125.

Another problem for the Confederacy was effective political leadership. Many Southerners resisted central authority. Strong believers in states' rights, they objected to wartime controls and, in some cases, refused to pay taxes to the Richmond government.

Conditions in the North were quite different. The economy boomed, as farmers and manufacturers stepped up production for both military and civilian needs. Growth and expansion were stimulated by a number of measures passed by the Republican Congress:

• The *Morrill Tariff Act* (1861) protected domestic manufacturers against foreign competition. Later revisions increased the tariff rate.

- The *Homestead Act* (1862) offered settlers 160-acre farms in the West. Settlers were required to occupy the land for five years and pay a small registration fee.
- The *Morrill Act* (1862) granted states large tracts of public land. Income derived from the sale of this land was to be used to establish in each state at least one college for the teaching of "agricultural and mechanical arts."
- The *Pacific Railroad Act* (1862) authorized the building of a railroad to the Pacific coast. For its construction, the act provided grants of land and federal loans.
- The *Legal Tender Act* (1862) authorized the issuance of treasury notes (greenbacks) as a substitute for gold and silver (specie). This move increased the amount of money in circulation and facilitated financial transactions. To help finance the war, the government imposed an income tax for the first time and levied heavy taxes on manufactured goods and consumer products. Large sums of money were also raised at home and abroad through the sale of bonds.

The Northern economy was also bolstered by a continuous stream of European immigrants. More than 800,000 newcomers arrived during the wartime years. The new arrivals provided labor for factories and farms, and swelled the ranks of people moving westward.

Peace Democrats in the guise of Copperheads threaten the Union cause. (*Harper's Weekly,* 1863)

Like the South, the North was not completely united behind the war. One group of Northerners, the Peace Democrats, wanted peace on almost any terms. (Their enemies called them "Copperheads," after a kind of poisonous snake.) The Democratic platform in the presidential election of 1864 called the war a failure. Lincoln, running against George McClellan, won a huge electoral victory. But his popular majority was quite small.

The Draft

The fighting forces suffered huge casualties in the long and bloody war. Both sides, therefore, resorted to something new in American history—the draft. (In a draft, or conscription, people are legally forced to register for military service. In earlier wars, troops had been either career soldiers or volunteers.) The South adopted the draft in 1862, the North in 1863.

No one liked the idea much. Antidraft protests in some Northern cities touched off violence. In New York City, a large-scale riot broke out in July 1863. Mobs of white laborers, protesting against being drafted into a war to free the slaves, burned the draft office, sacked the homes of prominent Republicans, and roamed the streets in search of blacks. The riots, the worst in American history, resulted in the lynching of more than a dozen black people, the destruction of an orphan asylum for black children, and the death of some 120 rioters.

The Role of Blacks

In the South, most able-bodied white men went off to fight, while slaves remained at home to tend the farms and work the factories. Many blacks refused to cooperate in the war effort, however, and thousands deserted when Union forces approached. Some Southerners wanted blacks to serve in the Confederate army. But fear of what armed slaves might do delayed this move until early 1865. By then it was too late.

At first, Northerners were also unwilling to arm blacks. Only in the summer of 1862 were blacks allowed to enlist in the army. They were restricted to all-black regiments, were paid less than whites, and were issued inferior supplies and weapons. Even so, they served with distinction. About 180,000 blacks served in the Union army, and some 20,000 did duty as sailors in the Union navy.

The issue of whether to emancipate (free) the slaves posed a difficult problem for Lincoln. During the early months of the war, he refrained from promising to free the slaves, partly because he wanted to keep the support of the border states. But there was also mounting pressure to do something about slavery. Such demands came not only from abolitionists and black leaders in the North but also from the so-called "radical" wing of the

Republican party. In the second year of the war, Lincoln decided to act, but he waited for a Northern victory in order to do so from a position of strength. The Battle of Antietam served his purpose. A few days later, on September 22, 1862, the president announced that he would proclaim emancipation at the start of the new year.

The Emancipation Proclamation was issued on January 1, 1863. It declared free those slaves living in states and districts then "in rebellion against the United States." Its immediate effect was limited. The Proclamation did not apply to slaves in border states and in Confederate areas already under Union control. Slaves in the Confederacy were not affected either, because Southern slave owners ignored Lincoln's order.

Although the Emancipation Proclamation freed few slaves immediately, it did help the Northern cause by giving it a moral force it had lacked earlier. It also paved the way for the total abolition of slavery after the war.

The Role of Women

Women played an important part in the war. They ran farms and businesses, and raised money for medical care. In both North and South, thousands served as professional and volunteer nurses in army hospitals. Dorothea Dix was appointed superintendent of female nurses in the Union army. Mary Edwards Walker, a Northern physician, was commissioned as an army surgeon. Clara Barton, who served as a Union field nurse, later founded the American Red Cross. Harriet Tubman, a former slave, acted as a Union spy behind Confederate lines.

LATER CAMPAIGNS

The Civil War has been called the first "modern" war because of its new weapons and military techniques. Most of these changes were introduced during the last two years of the conflict. They included ironclad ships, mines, trenches, balloon observation, telegraphy, and rifles (which were more accurate than muskets). The conflict was the first American war to be photographed and the first in which railroads played a key role in transporting military personnel and supplies.

In the West

In the spring of 1863, Grant launched a fierce attack on the fortified city of Vicksburg—the last key Southern stronghold on the Mississippi. The town surrendered on July 4, after a long siege. Port Hudson fell a few days later. These victories gave the North complete control of the Mississippi. The states west of the river were now cut off from the rest of the Confederacy.

In the fall of 1863, William S. Rosecrans led Union forces against Southern armies in eastern Tennessee. He occupied Chattanooga without resistance. A few days later, however, the two sides clashed at the Battle of Chickamauga, in northwestern Georgia. The Union army was saved from total defeat by the heroic stand of George H. Thomas. (His bravery won him the title "the Rock of Chickamauga.") The Northern forces pulled back into Chattanooga, and the Confederates surrounded the city. Grant was then put in charge of operations around Chattanooga. He quickly took the offensive and defeated the Southerners. By the end of 1863, almost all of Tennessee was in Union hands.

Sherman's March

The Northern successes in eastern Tennessee made possible a Union advance into the Deep South. The attack was led by William T. Sherman. His army invaded Georgia in May 1864 and pushed relentlessly toward Atlanta, a rail center that supplied much of the South. After capturing the

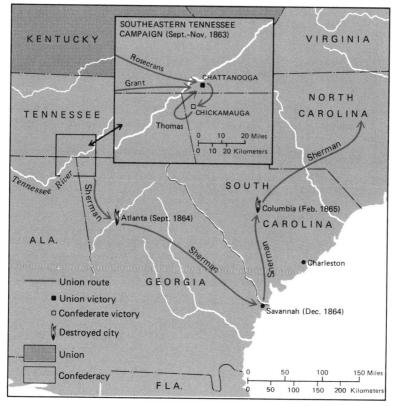

THE UNION STRIKES AT THE
CONFEDFRATE CENTER (1863–1865)

city in September 1864, he began a march from Atlanta to Savannah. Sherman's army swept through central Georgia, leaving a path of destruction 60 miles wide. The Union troops burned crops, killed cattle, wrecked railroads, and destroyed dams. They reached Savannah in December 1864, further dividing the Confederacy.

In the East

Early in 1863, Lee resumed the offensive begun at Antietam the previous fall. In May, he defeated a Union army under "Fighting Joe" Hooker at Chancellorsville, in northern Virginia. The Southern victory was marred by the loss of Stonewall Jackson, who was accidentally killed by his own men.

GETTYSBURG   In a second invasion of the North, Lee led his army into southern Pennsylvania. He was met by George G. Meade, in command of the Union army, at Gettysburg. The clash between the two forces began on July 1 and lasted three days. It was climaxed by a Confederate charge led by George E. Pickett. Fierce Union fire mowed down the Southerners by the thousands. The Confederate army was decisively beaten.

The Battle of Gettysburg proved to be the turning point of the war.

Fourscore and seven years ago our fathers brought forth on this continent a new nation, conceived in liberty, and dedicated to the proposition that all men are created equal.

Now we are engaged in a great civil war, testing whether that nation, or any nation so conceived and so dedicated, can long endure. We are met on a great battle-field of that war. We have come to dedicate a portion of that field as a final resting-place for those who here gave their lives that that nation might live. It is altogether fitting and proper that we should do this.

But, in a larger sense, we cannot dedicate—we cannot consecrate—we cannot hallow—this ground. The brave men, living and dead, who struggled here, have consecrated it far above our poor power to add or detract. The world will little note nor long remember what we say here, but it can never forget what they did here. It is for us, the living, rather, to be dedicated here to the unfinished work which they who fought here have thus far so nobly advanced. It is rather for us to be here dedicated to the great task remaining before us—that from these honored dead we take increased devotion to that cause for which they gave the last full measure of devotion; that we here highly resolve that these dead shall not have died in vain; that this nation, under God, shall have a new birth of freedom; and that government of the people, by the people, for the people, shall not perish from the earth.

—Abraham Lincoln, Gettysburg Address, November 19, 1863

The Confederacy never again undertook a major offensive. Gettysburg is also linked with one of the most famous speeches in American history. When a national cemetery was dedicated at the site in November 1863, Lincoln delivered his famous Gettysburg Address.

THE RICHMOND CAMPAIGN   Early in 1864, Grant was given command of all the Union armies and brought east. He set out to destroy Lee's army and capture Richmond. Taking the offensive, the Union forces fought their way south, forming a half-circle around the city. The opposing armies met in a region called the Wilderness. In this densely wooded area, soldiers fought blindly, and neither side could claim victory. Other indecisive battles followed—at Spotsylvania in May and Cold Harbor in June. Union losses were staggering, but Grant pressed on.

I propose to fight it out on this line if it takes all summer.
—*Ulysses S. Grant, message to army headquarters in Washington, D.C., before the Battle of Spotsylvania*

Moving his army across the James River, Grant planned to attack Richmond from the south. To guard the southern approach to the Confederate capital, Lee massed his forces at Petersburg, which Grant besieged for nine months.

To relieve the pressure on Richmond, Lee sent Jubal Early north through the Shenandoah Valley to attack Washington, D.C. Early was stopped near the capital and driven back to Virginia. Philip H. Sheridan then pursued the retreating Confederates. To make sure that the Southerners could never again use the Shenandoah Valley as a route into Northern territory, he ordered his troops to devastate the region. Sheridan declared that "a crow flying over the country would need to carry his rations."

COSTS OF THE CIVIL WAR

	Union	Confederacy
Troops Killed in Battle	110,000	95,000
Troops Dead From Illness	250,000	165,000
Troops Wounded	275,000	100,000
Estimated Wartime Expenditures	$3 billion	$2 billion (plus cost of freed slaves)

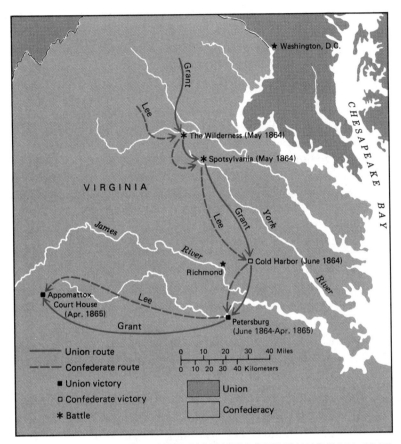

THE LAST MAJOR CAMPAIGN OF THE WAR (1864–1865)

END OF THE WAR   By 1865, the South was beginning to crumble under the furious attacks of the Union armies. The destruction in Georgia, the exhaustion of Confederate manpower, and the failure to obtain foreign recognition—all contributed to the decline of Southern morale.

Lee (now commander in chief of all Confederate forces) saw that he could no longer hold Petersburg or protect Richmond. He left the area and tried to unite with the forces of Joseph E. Johnston in North Carolina. A Union army set out to catch Lee. Some 80 miles from Richmond, Grant and Sheridan surrounded the Confederate army. Realizing that further resistance was useless, Lee surrendered his army to Grant at Appomattox Court House on April 9. A few weeks later, Johnston surrendered to Sherman. The long war was over.

With malice toward none, with charity for all, with firmness in the right as God gives us to see the right, let us strive on to finish the work we are in, to bind up the nation's wounds, to care for him who shall have borne the battle and for his widow and his orphan, to do all which may achieve and cherish a just and a lasting peace among ourselves and with all nations.

—Abraham Lincoln's
Second Inaugural Address, March 4, 1865

Matching Test

COLUMN A

1. Fort Sumter
2. Bull Run
3. *Monitor*
4. Stonewall Jackson
5. Fort Donelson
6. Shiloh
7. Antietam
8. *Trent*
9. Homestead Act
10. Copperhead
11. Harriet Tubman
12. William T. Sherman
13. Chickamauga
14. George G. Meade
15. Appomattox Court House

COLUMN B

a. fort seized by Grant in February 1862
b. fort whose fall touched off Civil War
c. British ship captured by Union in 1861
d. spy for Union side
e. commander of Union forces at Gettysburg
f. 1863 Confederate victory in northwestern Georgia
g. scene of two Confederate victories
h. one of first ironclad warships
i. location of Lee's surrender to Grant
j. legislation that provided free land in West
k. general who led Valley Campaign in western Virginia
l. 1862 Northern victory in southwestern Tennessee
m. bloodiest battle of war
n. Northerner who opposed Civil War
o. victor at Atlanta in September 1864

True-False Test

1. Maryland's decision to join the Confederacy isolated Washington, D.C., from the rest of the Union.
2. The initial war aim of the North was to free the slaves.
3. A major military objective of Union forces in the East was the capture of Richmond.
4. England became an ally of the Confederacy during the Civil War.
5. The Northern economy did very well during the war.
6. Blacks were kept out of the Union army until the last year of the war.
7. Because of strong opposition, neither the Confederacy nor the Union adopted a draft.
8. After the Northern victory at Vicksburg, the Confederacy was split in two along the Mississippi River.
9. Sherman's march led first south and then north through the state of Alabama.
10. The Confederate defeat at Gettysburg is usually regarded as the turning point of the war.

Map Test

Locate the following places or groups of places on the maps on pages 246, 248, 249, 255, and 258. Then, referring to the text, as necessary, explain why each place or group was important in the indicated year of the Civil War.

GROUP A

1. Delaware, Maryland, Kentucky, Missouri (1861)
2. Bull Run (1862)
3. Antietam (1862)
4. Western Virginia (1861)
5. Forts Henry and Donelson (1862)
6. New Orleans (1862)
7. Vicksburg (1863)
8. Chickamauga (1863)
9. Fort Sumter (1861)
10. Richmond (1861)

GROUP B

1. Gettysburg (1863)
2. Savannah (1864)
3. Columbia (1865)
4. Chattanooga (1863)
5. Appomattox Court House (1865)
6. Petersburg (1865)
7. Spotsylvania, the Wilderness, Cold Harbor (1864)
8. Atlanta (1864)
9. Fredericksburg (1862)
10. Port Hudson (1863)

Essay Questions

1. Compare the North and South at the beginning of the Civil War in terms of population, industry, transportation, and military and civilian leadership.
2. Why is the Civil War considered to be the first modern war? Include in your answer both technological developments and means of recruitment.
3. Describe the background of the Emancipation Proclamation. What did it accomplish?
4. Summarize the roles played in the Civil War by (a) England (b) France.
5. Describe the opposition to wartime government policies in the North and in the South.

CHAPTER 17

Reconstruction

In AMERICAN HISTORY, the term "reconstruction" refers to the restoration of the South to the Union after the Civil War. The Reconstruction era lasted from 1865 to 1877. It was a time of bitter political quarrels and disappointed hopes.

FIRST ATTEMPTS AT RECONSTRUCTION

Even before the end of the Civil War, political leaders had begun to think about the problems of reconstruction. There were three major questions to be faced:

1. What was the relationship between the 11 seceded states and the Union?
2. How should Southern whites be treated?
3. What would become of the freed slaves?

An additional question emerged during the Reconstruction era itself: Who should decide on the details of reconstruction, the president or Congress?

Lincoln's Plan

In Lincoln's view, the seceding states had not left the Union but had rebelled against it. Late in 1863, he announced his plan of reconstruction, to be put into effect in Confederate areas occupied by Union troops:

1. Southerners who had taken part in the war would be pardoned if they took an oath of allegiance to the United States. (The chief Confederate military and political leaders were excluded from this offer.)
2. The president would recognize the political restoration of a secessionist state that met the following conditions: (*a*) At least 10 percent of the men who had voted in the 1860 presidential election took the oath of allegiance. (*b*) These qualified voters established a new state government that guaranteed the abolition of slavery.

Under Lincoln's so-called "10-percent plan," new governments were set up in Louisiana, Arkansas, and Tennessee in 1864. But Congress refused to recognize them, and, by mid-April 1865, the situation had reached a deadlock.

A New President

Less than a week after Lee's surrender at Appomattox, Lincoln and his wife, in a relaxed mood, went to the theater. During the performance, John Wilkes Booth, a Southern actor, shot the president, leaped onto the stage, and escaped (but was later killed). Lincoln died the next morning, on April 15, 1865.

Andrew Johnson became the new president. Like Lincoln, he was a man of humble background. But he lacked Lincoln's popularity and political skill. A Democrat and former governor of Tennessee, Johnson had remained loyal to the Union when his state seceded. He had been nominated as Lincoln's running mate in 1864 to attract Democratic support for the Republican president's re-election.

Johnson's Reconstruction Policy

Congress was not in session during Johnson's first months in office, so the new president had a free hand in governing. Adopting Lincoln's plan of reconstruction, Johnson recognized the state governments already restored—those in Louisiana, Arkansas, and Tennessee. He also recognized a pro-Union faction in Virginia as the official government of the state. In the other seven Confederate states, he appointed temporary governors and gave them power to hold elections and form state governments. Johnson pardoned almost all Southerners who took the oath of allegiance. The only exceptions were a few important ex-Confederates. They had to request special pardons, which Johnson was liberal in granting.

By the end of 1865, all the Confederate states except Texas had set up new state governments. They had also elected representatives to Congress. As required, these states had ratified the Thirteenth Amendment to the Constitution, which abolished slavery. (This amendment

Ruins of Richmond

Freedmen registering to vote

became law in December 1865.) Since ten states had fulfilled his conditions, Johnson announced that they were restored to the Union.

The Black Codes

Although the slaves were now free, few Southerners regarded them as equal. The slave system had been based on a racist assumption—that one race (in the United States, the white race) was superior to all others. This outlook did not disappear in 1865.

The newly elected state legislatures in the South quickly passed a series of "black codes." These laws aimed to restore much of the old order by regulating the status of freedmen, as freed slaves were known. (The term also referred to black women and children.) The codes granted freedmen the right to own property, make contracts, and bring suit in court. But the laws prohibited blacks from serving on juries, testifying in court against whites, and bearing arms. Many of the codes restricted the kinds of work that blacks could do and threatened arrest of the unemployed. No state gave blacks the right to vote.

Attitude of Congress

When Congress reconvened in December 1865, it refused to admit the newly elected congressmen from the former Confederate states. (One of them was Alexander H. Stephens, vice president of the Confederacy.) It also declared that the Southern states had not been restored and that their newly formed state governments were invalid. Among the reasons why Congress rejected Johnson's reconstruction program were the following:

1. Congress was dominated by the "radical" Republicans, a group led by Representative Thaddeus Stevens of Pennsylvania and Senator Charles Sumner of Massachusetts. They regarded the former Confederate states as "conquered provinces" and favored a harsh policy that would punish Southerners for their disloyalty.
2. Congress wished to curb the powers of the president, which had expanded greatly during the war. Only the legislative branch, it was claimed, had the authority to readmit the states that had seceded.

3. Moderate and conservative Republicans in Congress, as well as radicals, viewed the enactment of the black codes as proof that Southern whites were seeking to re-enslave the blacks. All three groups were determined to postpone the readmission of the South until steps could be taken to protect the freedmen.

4. Under Johnson's plan, Southern whites had the right to vote, but little had been done to give the vote to blacks. Since the whites were overwhelmingly Democratic, the congressmen they elected were all members of that party. The Republicans feared that their control of the legislative branch would be endangered if they permitted the admission of the Southern congressmen.

CONGRESSIONAL RECONSTRUCTION

Early in 1866, Congress began to put into action its own plan of reconstruction. It did so through a Joint Committee on Reconstruction, made up of six senators and nine representatives. One of the first steps taken by Congress was to broaden the scope of the Freedmen's Bureau. This agency had been set up in 1865 to provide former slaves with food,

Johnson, by his veto, administers a kick to the Freedmen's Bureau (depicted as a piece of furniture) and dislodges the blacks it had sheltered. (Republican cartoon by Thomas Nast, *Harper's Weekly,* 1866)

clothing, and shelter. It also organized schools for blacks and found jobs for them. Congress now proposed to give the Freedmen's Bureau more duties. For instance, it would have the power to hold trials to protect the rights of blacks. President Johnson thought that the expanded Freedmen's Bureau violated states' rights and was, thus, unconstitutional. He vetoed the *Freedmen's Bureau Bill*, but Congress overruled him.

Civil Rights

Another bill that Congress passed over Johnson's veto was the *Civil Rights Act of 1866*. It granted black Americans all the legal rights of citizens. As a further guarantee, Congress enacted the Fourteenth Amendment, which granted citizenship to blacks. The amendment also provided that no state should "deprive any person of life, liberty, or property, without due process of law; nor deny to any person within its jurisdiction the equal protection of the laws." In addition, the amendment contained these provisions:

1. Confederate officials who had held government positions before the war were barred from holding public office again.
2. The Confederate war debt was canceled, thus punishing those who had lent money to the Confederacy.
3. Southern states were forbidden to compensate slave owners for the loss of their slaves.

Congress pledged to restore to the Union any Southern state that ratified the Fourteenth Amendment. President Johnson encouraged the states not to ratify, however, and all but one followed his advice. Only Tennessee ratified the amendment. It was readmitted to the Union in the summer of 1866.

Elections and the Reconstruction Acts

Congressional elections held in the fall of 1866 were a test of how voters felt about reconstruction. Johnson campaigned against the Republicans running for re-election. His attacks, especially on the radicals, were so extreme that he lost much public support and increased Republican opposition to him. The Republicans swept the elections, winning enough seats to override any future vetoes by Johnson.

Congress stepped up its program with a series of bills known as the *Reconstruction Acts*. All of them were passed over Johnson's veto. They provided for the following:

1. The ten unreconstructed states were divided into five military districts. Each was policed by federal troops under the command of a military governor.

STATES OF THE CONFEDERACY

State	Seceded	Readmitted Under Lincoln/ Johnson	Readmitted Under Congress	End of Congressional Reconstruction
Alabama	1861	1865	1868	1874
Arkansas	1861	1865	1868	1874
Florida	1861	1865	1868	1877
Georgia	1861	1865	1868*	1871
Louisiana	1861	1865	1868	1877
Mississippi	1861	1865	1870	1876
North Carolina	1861	1865	1868	1876
South Carolina	1860	1865	1868	1877
Tennessee	1861	1865	1866	1869
Texas	1861	1866	1870	1874
Virginia	1861	1865	1870	1869

*Georgia was readmitted in 1868. When it expelled blacks from the state legislature, it was placed under federal military control. It then ratified the Fifteenth Amendment and allowed the blacks to return to office. Georgia's readmission was restored in 1870.

2. Southerners who had voluntarily fought in the Confederate forces were deprived of the right to vote or hold office.
3. To qualify for readmission, a state had to hold a convention and frame a new constitution guaranteeing black suffrage. Delegates to this convention were to be chosen by all citizens eligible to vote, including blacks.
4. After a state had organized a new government and ratified the Fourteenth Amendment, it would be restored to the Union.

Seven Southern states met these requirements. They were readmitted to the Union in 1868. To further protect black suffrage, Congress passed the Fifteenth Amendment in 1869. It granted former slaves the right to vote. The three unreconstructed states now had to ratify both the Fourteenth and Fifteenth amendments as a condition for readmission. They did so, and in 1870, Congress approved their restoration to the Union.

The Impeachment of Johnson

Relations between the president and Congress were very strained. Johnson regarded Republican reconstruction as too extreme and too harsh. For their part, Republican congressmen distrusted Johnson as a Southerner and a Democrat. His vetoes of the Reconstruction Acts convinced them that he had no interest in real changes for the South.

To weaken the president's power, Congress passed the *Tenure of*

Office Act early in 1867. It prohibited the president from dismissing, without the Senate's consent, any high official whose original appointment had been confirmed by that body. Johnson believed that this law was unconstitutional. In August, he dismissed his secretary of war, Edwin Stanton, without consulting the Senate.

Early in 1868, radical Republicans decided to remove Johnson from office. As a first step, the House of Representatives impeached the president—that is, it charged him with wrongdoing. The charges against him included violation of the Tenure of Office Act and attempts to disgrace and belittle Congress.

The Senate, sitting as a court, tried Johnson on the impeachment charges in the spring of 1868. By a margin of one vote, the radicals failed to get the two-thirds vote necessary to remove Johnson. He was judged not guilty and remained in office until the end of his term.

THE RECONSTRUCTED SOUTH

After the war, the South faced enormous problems. Farms, cities, railroads, and factories lay in ruins. Thousands of soldiers had lost their lives, and thousands more suffered from wounds or illness. The whole social and economic system that had depended on slave labor had been destroyed.

Republican Rule

After Congress assumed control, the former Confederate states were subjected to congressional reconstruction. For some of them, it lasted only a short time—three years in Tennessee, for example. For others, such as Florida, it lasted more than ten years. In all these states, reconstruction was in the hands of Republicans, not only at the national level but also in the states themselves. (Thousands of Democrats had been deprived of the vote by the Reconstruction Acts.)

The new black voters were, of course, Republicans. They were joined by two groups of whites. One was made up of Southerners who wanted to cooperate with the new governments. Some sincerely believed that cooperation was best for the South; others hoped for political or economic gain. (Their critics called them "scalawags.") The other group consisted of Northerners who had moved south to aid the freedmen or to fill their own pockets. (Their critics called them "carpetbaggers.")

Blacks served in the legislatures of all the Southern states. But only in one house of the South Carolina legislature did they form a majority. Two black men from Mississippi—Hiram R. Revels and Blanche K. Bruce—

were elected to the U.S. Senate. Fourteen Southern blacks served in the House of Representatives.

Charges of Corruption

At the time and for many years afterward, Southern reconstruction governments were accused of waste and corruption. They did spend more than prewar governments. But large sums were required to pay for war damage, to rebuild public facilities, and to provide badly needed services. For example, there was little public education in the South before the war. After the war, it was made available to black, as well as white, children.

Corruption certainly existed. (One Southern state legislature voted a bonus of $1000 to an important member after he had reportedly lost that amount at a horse race.) But graft and swindles were widespread in the North as well as the South, and among Democrats as well as Republicans. During the administration of Ulysses S. Grant, corruption spread almost to the presidency itself. Grant had been a great Civil War hero. But his two terms as president—from 1869 to 1877—showed his lack of political experience. He chose advisers and appointed officials unwisely. As a result, his administration was marred by political and financial scandals.

Regaining Democratic Control

In a fairly short time, Southern Democrats were again in control of the South. Adult white males who had not been in the war still had the right to vote. And more and more boys who had been too young to fight reached voting age each year. Southerners were also helped by a law passed by Congress in 1872. It restored the right to vote and hold office to all but about 500 former Confederates.

Reconstruction could not end quickly enough for Southern whites. They wanted to regain the political control that they had enjoyed before the war. To achieve this goal, they resorted to racist appeals, urging whites to vote Democratic, the "white man's party." Economic pressure and terrorism were also used to keep people—especially blacks—from voting or to force them to vote Democratic. The best-known terrorist organization was the Ku Klux Klan. To prevent cooperation with the Republicans, Klan members destroyed the property of blacks and whites, beat them, and even resorted to lynchings. After the end of reconstruction in 1877, Southern states gradually deprived most black people of the vote (see Chapter 21, page 319).

The attitude of Northerners helped put an end to Republican rule in the South. The strong emotions of the immediate postwar period had cooled. In Congress, moderate and conservative Republicans were tired of "the Negro question," and even radicals had lost some of their zeal. Racism, widespread in the North as well as in the South, contributed to Northerners' loss of interest. Few cared about protecting the rights of people they considered inferior.

THE END OF RECONSTRUCTION

In the presidential election of 1876, Republican Rutherford B. Hayes of Ohio ran against Democrat Samuel J. Tilden of New York. Both candidates promised to end reconstruction. Tilden won a larger popular vote than Hayes but was one electoral vote short of a majority. Twenty electoral votes from four states remained uncounted because of election disputes. Both parties claimed the votes. In January 1877, Congress appointed an electoral commission to settle the dispute. It consisted of eight Republicans and seven Democrats. Voting strictly along party lines, the Republican-dominated commission gave every disputed vote to Hayes, thereby assuring his election.

Congress still had to ratify this decision, however. Fearing that Democrats might start a filibuster in the Senate (a tactic to delay legislative action), the Hayes forces appealed for Southern Democratic support by making several informal pledges: to appoint a Southerner to the cabinet, grant federal aid to Southern railroads, and withdraw the last federal troops from the South. The Southerners voted with the majority, and Hayes took office. Shortly after his inauguration, he recalled the soldiers. Military occupation of the South and reconstruction were at an end.

The Republican-controlled governments remaining in the South were soon voted out of office. Southerners, however, continued to resent the Republican party. For the next 75 years, they voted overwhelmingly Democratic, thus earning their region the nickname of the "solid South."

True-False Test

1. Andrew Johnson tried to carry out a much harsher reconstruction plan than that of Lincoln.
2. The Thirteenth Amendment abolished slavery in the United States.
3. Radical Republicans in Congress were led by Thaddeus Stevens of Pennsylvania.
4. The black codes of the Southern states guaranteed freed slaves all the rights of white citizens.
5. The Freedmen's Bureau was established to pay former slave owners for their slaves.

6. Under congressional reconstruction, former volunteers in the Confederate army were forbidden to hold public office.
7. The aim of the Fifteenth Amendment was to guarantee former slaves the right to vote.
8. Congress accused President Johnson of treason.
9. The Ku Klux Klan wanted to restore Southern Democrats to political power in the South.
10. The phrase "solid South" referred to the importance of cotton in the Southern economy.

Multiple-Choice Test

1. The reconstruction period lasted from   (a) 1861 to 1865   (b) 1865 to 1870   (c) 1865 to 1877   (d) 1860 to 1876.
2. Under Lincoln's plan for reconstruction, the Confederate states were to be   (a) treated as territories   (b) readmitted to the Union only by Congress   (c) regarded as still within the Union   (d) occupied by military troops for 20 years.
3. Radical Republicans in Congress   (a) regarded the former Confederate states as conquered territory   (b) passed the black codes   (c) favored Lincoln's ideas on reconstruction   (d) introduced legislation to pardon Jefferson Davis.
4. The Fourteenth Amendment provided for all of the following except   (a) citizenship for blacks   (b) equal protection of the laws for all Americans   (c) cancellation of the Confederate war debt   (d) military districts for the South.
5. The first state to be readmitted to the Union under congressional reconstruction was   (a) Arkansas   (b) Louisiana   (c) South Carolina   (d) Tennessee.
6. Andrew Johnson was impeached by the   (a) House of Representatives   (b) Senate   (c) Joint Committee on Reconstruction   (d) Supreme Court.
7. Southern state governments during reconstruction were controlled by   (a) black voters   (b) groups of black and white Republicans   (c) Northern Democrats   (d) former Confederate army officers.
8. A major criticism of reconstruction governments in the Southern states was that they   (a) were corrupt   (b) did not allow blacks to participate   (c) excluded women from voting   (d) did not allow whites to serve in the legislatures.
9. Andrew Johnson was succeeded in office by   (a) Ulysses S. Grant   (b) Charles Sumner   (c) Abraham Lincoln   (d) Samuel J. Tilden.

10. A major factor in the election of Rutherford B. Hayes was (a) his popular majority (b) charges of fraud against his opponent (c) an agreement between Republicans and Southern Democrats (d) his promise to retain military rule in the South.

Essay Questions

1. What were the major questions facing government leaders in the reconstruction period? What positions on these major questions were taken by (a) Lincoln (b) Johnson (c) radical Republicans?
2. List and explain the chief steps in congressional reconstruction.
3. Summarize the background and outcome of Johnson's impeachment.
4. What was the main criticism of Republican reconstruction governments in the South? Do you think it was justified? Explain.
5. When and how did reconstruction come to an end?

 **UNIT 6**

The
Nation
Transformed

CHAPTER 18

The Last Frontier

A T THE END OF the Civil War, one large part of the United States still had relatively few settlers. This was the area between the Missouri River and the settlements in California, the Northwest, and the Southwest. Stretching more than 1500 miles from east to west, the territory comprised two main regions. One, the Great Plains, lay between the Missouri and the Rockies. It was a dry, treeless expanse of land, covered with fields of high grass. The other region, west of the plains, included the Rocky Mountains and the arid plateaus beyond them.

In the 1860s, this huge territory was inhabited chiefly by Native Americans. But by 1900, many thousands of newcomers had settled there. Settlement of the "last frontier" was one of several developments that transformed the United States in the late 1800s.

MINES, TRAILS, AND RAILS

Lewis and Clark and other explorers had visited the region of the last frontier in the early 1800s. They were followed by fur traders and pioneers on their way to the Pacific coast. To all of these visitors, the area appeared to be a wasteland, incapable of supporting civilized settlement. Beginning in the 1850s, however, attitudes changed.

The Lure of Wealth

The California gold rush of 1849 was the first of many mineral strikes that brought riches to some and hope to many others. In the 1850s, gold was discovered near Pikes Peak, Colorado, and gold and silver in Nevada. In the 1860s, gold was also found in Idaho and Montana. Later, rich strikes were made in the Black Hills of South Dakota and in Arizona.

These discoveries led to a new mining boom, similar to the earlier one in California. Miners and prospectors rushed to the mining sites. In hundreds of remote places, makeshift towns of tents and shanties sprang up overnight. Eager fortune hunters staked out their claims and dug for the precious metals. Many of the ore deposits were very valuable. At Virginia City, Nevada, the Comstock Lode alone yielded $300 million in gold and silver in 20 years. (The Nevada gold deposits, never abundant, became impractical to mine, but the rich silver finds continued to be profitable for many years.) By 1890, the Rocky Mountain area had produced precious metals worth $2 billion.

Life in the mining camps was rough and lawless at first, as it had been in the early days of the California gold rush. Law-abiding citizens, seeking to protect themselves, formed local governments and organized groups of vigilantes to track down and punish lawbreakers.

Some of the prospectors who failed to strike it rich settled down to ranching and farming. Others drifted away after surface deposits gave out. Still others took jobs with mining companies. These companies replaced individual prospectors because mining below the surface required large sums of money to sink shafts, dig tunnels, and buy expensive machinery. In addition to gold and silver, the companies found copper, lead, zinc, and other minerals. Mining became a permanent industry of the last frontier.

Early Transportation and Communication

One of the first regularly scheduled means of reaching the West was a stagecoach line called the Butterfield Overland Mail. Beginning in 1858, it carried mail and passengers from St. Louis, Missouri, through Texas and the New Mexico Territory to Los Angeles and San Francisco. (The starting point was St. Louis because, at that time, railroad service from the East ended there.) Each Butterfield coach carried about ten passengers, their baggage, and several bulky sacks of mail. The trip west took at least three weeks.

To speed up mail delivery, a group of investors founded the Pony Express in 1860. Relays of riders traveled a central route from St. Joseph, Missouri to Sacramento, California. Mounted on swift horses (not ponies) and riding day and night, Pony Expressmen could carry mail from Missouri to California in ten days.

The Pony Express was a daring experiment, and only one of its deliveries failed to get through. But the service lasted a mere 18 months. A new form of communication, the telegraph, was rapidly taking over.

Lines to carry telegraph messages already linked most cities in the East. With the completion, in October 1861, of the first telegraph line to the Far West, the Pony Express ceased operations.

Railroad Links

The need for western railroads was clear by the 1850s (see Chapter 15, page 236). During the Civil War, the government licensed two railroad companies to build the first transcontinental line jointly. (The line was not actually to cross the entire continent, but would link the Pacific coast with the Missouri River. There, a connection would be made with eastern lines already in place.) The government offered good terms to the companies. They received a free right-of-way across public land, financial assistance in the form of loans, and large grants of land for every mile of completed track.

One of the companies was the Union Pacific. It began construction at Omaha and built westward across the Nebraska prairie into Wyoming and Utah. The other company was the Central Pacific. Starting at

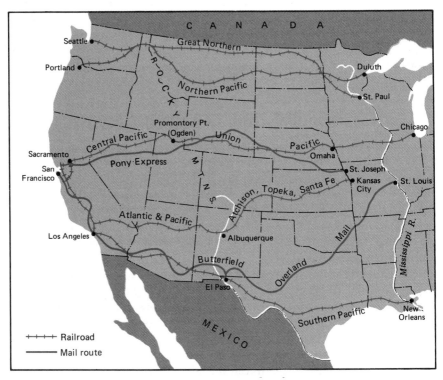

ROUTES ACROSS THE LAST FRONTIER

Sacramento, its tracks advanced eastward across the mountains into Nevada and Utah. Hoping for a bigger share of loans and land grants, each company tried to build faster than the other. Both hired huge gangs of hard workers. The Union Pacific employed thousands of Irish-Americans, many of them Civil War veterans. The Central Pacific signed on some 10,000 Chinese. The two railroads met at Promontory Point, near Ogden, Utah, in May 1869.

The completion of the first transcontinental railroad was a milestone in American history. Finished goods could now be shipped by rail to Western markets, and Western raw materials and farm products could be sent eastward. The mineral and forest resources of the West were opened to development, and Western settlement was made easier.

Several other railroads also built lines west. By the 1890s, they included the Great Northern; the Northern Pacific; the Atchison, Topeka and Santa Fe; and the Southern Pacific. The government encouraged the building of these important transcontinental links by granting the companies some $60 million in loans and more than 125 million acres of public land.

THE CATTLE FRONTIER

Western railroads not only aided mining and forestry but also made large-scale cattle ranching practical. When Americans first settled in Texas, they found huge herds of half-wild long-horned cattle. These sturdy animals had developed from cattle originally brought to America by the Spaniards. The longhorns grazed freely over the open range— unfenced, unpopulated grassland owned by the federal government. Texans established ranches and raised the longhorns for beef, hides, and tallow. But the industry was a local one because of the difficulty of transporting cattle to Eastern markets.

Then, in the 1860s, railroads were extended into Kansas, Nebraska, and Colorado. Texas cattle raisers now had an opportunity to sell to a larger market. They drove their animals north to rail centers and loaded them onto railroad cars for shipment to Eastern cities. The introduction of the refrigerator car in the 1870s made the process even easier. It was no longer necessary to send live cattle halfway across the country. Instead, they could be slaughtered in Midwestern meat-packing centers such as Kansas City and Chicago. From there, butchered beef could be shipped by rail to distant markets without spoiling.

The 1870s and early 1880s were the great era of the "cattle kingdom." Ranchers owned enormous herds of cattle, which were branded with a ranch's identifying mark. The animals were allowed to roam on the open range. Each spring, cowboys rounded up the owner's

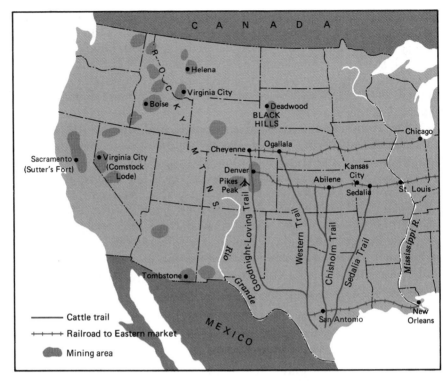

WESTERN MINES AND CATTLE TRAILS

cattle, branded the new calves, and chose the animals to be sold. These were then herded on the "long drive" north to "cow towns" along the rail lines. One favorite route was the Chisholm Trail, from San Antonio, Texas, to Abilene, Kansas. Another, the Western Trail, ended at Ogallala, Nebraska. Along the drive, the cattle fed on the rich prairie grass of the open range. Cowboys accompanying the herds were responsible for preventing stampedes and fighting off rustlers (cattle thieves).

Ranching was hugely profitable, and it soon spread from Texas to other parts of the Great Plains. But the era of the cattle kingdom did not last long. Many areas of grassland became overgrazed, and some animals went hungry. The introduction of sheep into the plains made matters worse. The sheep nibbled the grass so low that the cattle had nothing left to feed on. Conflicts between cattle ranchers and sheep owners led to a number of "range wars." The open range itself grew smaller as thousands of acres were sold to farmers. Worst of all, two terrible winters in the mid-1880s brought blizzards that killed thousands of cattle.

By 1890, the era of the open range was over. Cattle raising continued to be a big industry in the West, but it was generally confined to fenced ranches in dry areas unsuited to farming.

FARMERS ON THE PLAINS

The largest group of newcomers to the last frontier were farmers. They settled chiefly on the Great Plains. Many of them were Easterners and Midwesterners looking for a new start. Former slaves and their families headed west, too, as did numerous Civil War veterans. And a large number of the new settlers were immigrants, especially Scandinavians.

The Homestead Act of 1862 provided that settlers could receive 160 acres of public land. In return, the settlers paid a small fee and promised to live on the land and work it for five years. Only about 20 percent of the farm families, however, were actually homesteaders. Most of the new settlers bought land from railroads or from speculators who had obtained large tracts of homestead land illegally.

Farming on the Great Plains was very hard. Winters were bitter cold, and summers extremely hot. The area had little rainfall. As a result, few trees grew there, and underground water supplies were far below the surface.

But the pioneers coped with these problems. They built homes out of chunks of sod (earth), or they dug caves into hillsides. They burned dried cornstalks, corncobs, and animal dung for fuel. And they dug wells to a depth of 200 feet or more to obtain water.

Several techniques aided plains farmers. One was dry farming—plowing and planting in ways that conserved precious moisture. Another was using windmills to pump water from far below the earth's surface. A

NEW STATES (1861–1959)

State	Admitted to Union
Kansas	1861
West Virginia	1863
Nevada	1864
Nebraska	1867
Colorado	1876
Montana	1889
North Dakota	1889
South Dakota	1889
Washington	1889
Idaho	1890
Wyoming	1890
Utah	1896
Oklahoma	1907
New Mexico	1912
Arizona	1912
Alaska	1959
Hawaii	1959

Go West, young man, and grow up with the country.

—*Horace Greeley, editor of the*
New York Tribune, in 1865

third was fencing in the land with barbed wire to keep out stray cattle and sheep. Barbed wire was first marketed in 1874.

But no one could do much about such hazards of plains life as dust storms, blizzards, and swarms of grasshoppers. Nor did anyone know when drought would make plains farming riskier than ever. (A series of dry years in the late 1880s forced many farm families off the land.) No matter how hard they worked, plains farmers also needed luck to make a living.

TRAGEDY FOR NATIVE AMERICANS

Every since the arrival of Europeans along the Atlantic coast of North America, Native Americans had been pushed westward. The *Indian Removal Act* of 1830 forced Eastern tribes to move west of the Mississippi. Most of present-day Oklahoma then became Indian Territory, reserved for the Five Civilized Tribes. Because these tribes had sided with the Confederacy during the Civil War, the western half of the region was taken away from them and reserved for other Eastern tribes. In addition, huge tracts in the Dakotas, Wyoming, Montana, and elsewhere were set aside for Plains and other western tribes. As long as the last frontier was more or less uninhabited, Indian-settler relations were fairly peaceful. But with the coming of miners, ranchers, and farmers in the 1860s and 1870s, trouble arose.

The federal government tried to ease tensions by reducing the size of the Native Americans' land and setting aside reservations for them to live on. Many Native American groups agreed to move to reservations. They had little choice because they could no longer support themselves by buffalo hunting.

The vast buffalo herds that had long served as the main source of food, clothing, and shelter for the Plains tribes were dwindling rapidly. With the extension of railroads westward, Americans from the East organized hunting parties and headed for the Great Plains to shoot buffalo. They killed thousands of these animals for their fur, leaving the carcasses to rot. In 1850, there had been some 20 million buffalo on the plains. by 1889, there were fewer than a thousand left.

prairie windmill

Texas longhorns

Resistance to the Newcomers

Not all Native Americans moved to reservations without a struggle or stayed there peacefully. In the 1860s and 1870s, there were a number of clashes. One in 1877 gained nationwide attention.

In the summer of that year, a group of Nez Percés under Chief Joseph refused to move from their home in Oregon to a reservation in Idaho. Pursued by army troops, they fled hundreds of miles toward safety in Canada. By late September, the Nez Percés had almost reached their goal. But many were hungry and sick, and the early plains winter had begun. After a pitched battle early in October, Chief Joseph and his people surrendered. He and his band were then confined to a reservation far from their homeland.

Nor did the Sioux give up without a fight. One group had been promised the Black Hills of South Dakota as a permanent hunting ground. But gold was discovered there in the 1870s, and the promise was forgotten. When miners and others moved in, two Sioux leaders, "medicine man" Sitting Bull and war chief Crazy Horse, led armed resistance against the newcomers. Army troops then set out after the Sioux. In 1876, at the Little Bighorn River in Montana, the Sioux and Cheyenne completely destroyed

---

I am tired of fighting. Our chiefs are killed. The old men are all dead. . . . I want to have time to look for my children and see how many of them I can find. Maybe I shall find them among the dead. Hear me, my chiefs, I am tired. My heart is sad and sick. From where the sun now stands I will fight no more forever.

—*Chief Joseph at the time of his surrender*

an army force under George A. Custer. In the long run, however, the Native Americans were no match for the U.S. Army. Band by band, they gave up and moved to smaller reservations.

In the 1880s, many Sioux, bitter and disappointed, turned to a new religion called the "Ghost Dance." It promised to end the rule of their enemies and to restore their freedom and way of life. Believers gathered to perform a special dance that they thought put them in touch with their ancestors. As the the new faith spread, federal authorities feared that it would stir up the Sioux and lead to an uprising. The government blamed Sitting Bull for the rapid spread of the Ghost Dance and sent an army unit to his reservation to arrest him in December 1890. In the confusion that followed, Sitting Bull was killed.

Fearing more violence, several hundred Sioux fled the reservation to seek safety in the Badlands area of South Dakota. The U.S. Cavalry went after them. The opposing forces met at Wounded Knee Creek on December 28. The next day, fighting broke out. At least 150 Sioux— many of them women and children—were killed, as were 25 of the

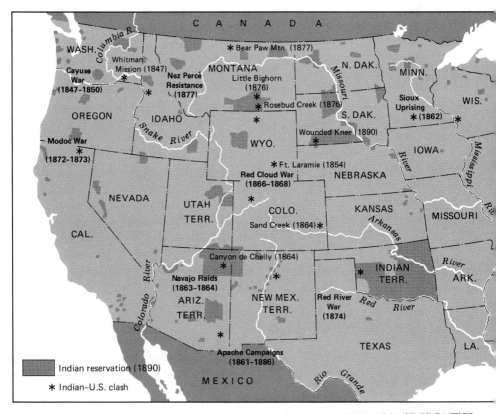

NATIVE AMERICANS AND THE LAST FRONTIER

CONFLICTS WITH NATIVE AMERICANS (1847–1890)

Date	Event	Outcome
1847	Whitman massacre, Washington	Cayuses, fearful of settlers and disease, killed missionaries Marcus and Narcissa Whitman, and 12 others.
1847–1850	Cayuse War, Oregon	In retaliation for Whitman massacre, settlers waged war against Cayuses. Five of their leaders finally surrendered and were hanged.
1861–1886	Apache campaigns, Arizona, New Mexico, Texas, Mexico	Warriors conducted numerous hit-and-run raids; campaigns ended with Geronimo's surrender.
1862	Sioux uprising, Minnesota	Threatened by starvation, Sioux under Little Crow conducted campaign of murder and looting. Some 450 on both sides were killed, and 39 Indian leaders executed.
1863–1864	Navajo defeat, Arizona and New Mexico	Kit Carson trapped raiding Navajos in Canyon de Chelly, Arizona. They were forced to march 300 miles to eastern New Mexico, imprisoned for four years, then allowed to return to Arizona.
1864	Sand Creek Massacre, Colorado	Colorado militia led by J. M. Chivington ambushed peaceful Cheyenne village, killing more than 100 men, women, and children.
1866–1868	Red Cloud War, Wyoming	Sioux under Red Cloud fought to keep settlers from using forts and Bozeman Trail to new mine fields. In Treaty of Fort Laramie, government gave up forts and trail.
1872–1873	Modoc War, Oregon and California	Small force of Modocs resisted move to reservation. They held out in lava beds of Tule Lake for six months. Their leader, "Captain Jack," surrendered and, with three others, was hanged.
1874	Red River War, Texas Panhandle	Several Plains groups, unhappy with reservation life, escaped and raided settlements. They surrendered after 14 battles with U.S. army forces.

CONFLICTS WITH NATIVE AMERICANS (cont.)

Date	Event	Outcome
1876	Battle of the Rosebud, Montana	Sioux, led by Crazy Horse, defeated army troops under George Crook.
1876	Battle of the Little Bighorn, Montana	Sioux and Cheyennes trapped troops led by George Custer. His entire force of about 230 men was wiped out in "Custer's Last Stand."
1877	Nez Percé resistance, Oregon, Idaho, Montana	Under Chief Joseph, the Nez Percés retreated 1500 miles toward Canada. They were forced to surrender just 30 miles from border.
1890	"Battle" of Wounded Knee, South Dakota	While moving camp, Sioux were killed by army detachment.

cavalry. Wounded Knee was part battle, part massacre. It was also the last significant armed Native American resistance in the United States.

Reservation Life

Life for Native Americans on reservations was at best boring, at worst disastrous. Most had little to live for and little to live on, except government handouts of beef and flour. Reservations were run by Indian agents, non-Indian officials of the federal government. Many of them were dishonest and pocketed funds meant for the Native Americans.

A book published in 1881, *A Century of Dishonor*, brought the hardships of the Native Americans to public attention. Its author, Helen Hunt Jackson, recounted with indignation how Native Americans had suffered for a hundred years from broken promises, cheating, and ill treatment. Public criticism of the government's Indian policy led to the passage of the *Dawes Act* in 1887.

The Dawes Act granted 160 acres of land to the head of each Native American family. This land came out of former tribal holdings. What was left over was to be sold to non-Indians. The aim was to encourage Native Americans to give up tribal culture and live like other Americans. The government hoped the Native Americans would learn to support themselves by farming or ranching.

Unfortunately, much of the land granted to the Native Americans was not suitable for such purposes. In any case, many Native Americans regarded farming and ranching as "women's work," unworthy of warriors. Thousands of them rented or sold their land to settlers for cash. When the money was gone, the Native Americans were worse off than before. Poverty, disease, alcoholism, and suicide became a familiar part of reservation life.

THE END OF THE FRONTIER

In 1890, the Census Bureau announced that unsettled areas of the United States had been "so broken into by isolated bodies of settlement that there can hardly be said to be a frontier line." In other words, the frontier no longer existed, at least officially. Of course, there were still many areas of "wide open spaces" (as there are to this day), but an era had come to an end.

Multiple-Choice Test

1. The last frontier was (a) east of the Missouri River (b) south of the Northwest Territory (c) east of California and the Northwest (d) north of the Old Southwest.
2. The Pony Express became unnecessary after (a) the establishment of the Butterfield Overland Mail (b) the construction of the Union Pacific Railroad (c) the opening of the Chisholm Trail (d) the completion of a transcontinental telegraph.
3. All of the following were Western mining areas during the post–Civil War period *except* (a) Pikes Peak (b) Promontory Point (c) the Black Hills (d) Virginia City.
4. The first railroad line to cross the last frontier connected (a) Omaha and Sacramento (b) Promontory Point and San Francisco (c) Kansas City and Santa Fe (d) New Orleans and Los Angeles.
5. Large-scale cattle ranching began in (a) Kansas (b) Texas (c) Arkansas (d) Nebraska.
6. The percentage of plains farmers who were homesteaders was about (a) 10 percent (b) 20 percent (c) 40 percent (d) 75 percent.
7. After the Civil War, the goal of the federal government was to (a) move all the Native Americans to Indian Territory (b) force the Indians to migrate to Canada (c) reduce the land holdings of Western tribes (d) prevent settlers from taking Indian land.
8. A major reason why the Native Americans were willing to resettle on reservations was (a) their desire to learn farming (b) their wish to become ranchers (c) the invention of barbed wire (d) the great reduction of buffalo herds.
9. All of the following were Sioux leaders *except* (a) Red Cloud (b) "Captain Jack" (c) Crazy Horse (d) Sitting Bull.
10. The frontier came to an end officially in (a) 1890 (b) 1860 (c) 1900 (d) 1875.

Matching Test

COLUMN A	COLUMN B
1. Great Plains	a. area originally reserved for Five Civilized Tribes
2. St. Joseph, Missouri	b. site of last significant armed Indian resistance in United States
3. Comstock Lode	
4. long drive	
5. Abilene, Kansas	c. northern end of Chisholm Trail
6. Indian Territory	d. grassy, treeless region west of Missouri River
7. Chief Joseph	
8. Little Bighorn	e. eastern end of Pony Express route
9. Geronimo	
10. Wounded Knee	f. site of Custer's Last Stand
	g. Apache warrior
	h. rich deposit of gold and silver
	i. leader of Nez Percé retreat
	j. movement of cattle herds to railroad lines

Map Test

Answer the following questions by referring to the maps on pages 276, 278, and 282, and to the text.

1. What were the western terminals of the Butterfield Overland Mail stagecoach line?
2. Name the eastern and western terminals of the Pony Express.
3. Locate and name the present-day city where the Central Pacific and Union Pacific railroads were linked in 1869.
4. What western railroads were built to serve the band of states extending from Wisconsin to the Northwest?
5. Name the railroad that originated in Louisiana and serviced the southernmost section of the United States.
6. Name the route followed by cowboys on their long drive to a cow town in (a) Kansas (b) Nebraska (c) Missouri (d) Wyoming.
7. Where was the Comstock Lode located?
8. What railroad served (a) Albuquerque (b) Portland (c) El Paso?
9. Locate and name a place in the Black Hills where gold was found.
10. Locate and name the site of (a) the last major Indian–U.S. clash (b) Custer's Last Stand (c) an Indian uprising in Texas.

Essay Questions

1. What attracted settlers to the last frontier?
2. What developments in transportation and communication helped open the last frontier to settlement?
3. What were the main factors that led to large-scale cattle raising on the last frontier? Why was it less profitable after the mid-1880s?
4. Why was farming difficult on the Great Plains? Describe some techniques that helped plains farmers.
5. Why did the government pass the Dawes Act? What happened to Indians after its passage?

CHAPTER 19

An Expanding Economy

T HE UNITED STATES, in 1860, was still mainly a land of farms, villages, and small businesses. Fewer than 2 million people worked in mills and factories, and the nation's total output of manufactured goods amounted to less than $2 billion. Manufacturing was concentrated in the Northeast. The typical factory was a small plant, owned and operated by a single proprietor or a few partners. It produced a limited amount of goods for a local market.

Between the Civil War and 1900, a period often called the age of industrialization, the United States experienced tremendous economic growth. Established companies expanded their operations, and new industrial plants sprang up in the Midwest, the South, and the Far West.

By 1900, manufacturing provided employment to more than 6 million people, and the annual output of manufactured goods exceeded $7 billion in value. As the 20th century began, the United States was the world's leading industrial nation.

INDUSTRIAL GROWTH

The Civil War stimulated industrial expansion by creating a huge demand for weapons, war supplies, farm equipment, and machinery of all kinds. Growth continued after the war for five main reasons:

1. The national government maintained high tariffs to protect American industry from foreign competition.

2. An ever-increasing population offered an expanding market for manufactured goods.
3. A continuous flow of immigrants (see Chapter 20, page 301) provided an ample labor force.
4. Abundant natural resources supplied industry with raw materials.
5. A network of railroads opened up national markets to manufacturers.

Railroad Improvements

Beginning in the 1860s (as discussed in Chapter 18), rail lines were extended across the entire United States. Track mileage expanded from about 30,000 miles in 1860 to almost 260,000 miles in 1900. For 50 years after the Civil War, railroad construction and operation was the nation's biggest nonagricultural business.

A number of improvements aided rail transport. In the 1860s, George Pullman developed the sleeping car and the dining car, which made rail travel more comfortable. The invention of automatic couplers, block signals, and air brakes made rail travel safer. The adoption of a standard gauge (the distance between rails) enabled all trains to use tracks anywhere in the country.

Railroads helped bring about the adoption of standard time zones in the United States. Until the 1880s, each locality across the country set its own time, fixing as noon the moment when the sun was directly overhead. The resulting time differences made it difficult for railroads to work out schedules. To overcome the problem, the railway companies, in 1883, agreed to divide the country into four standard time zones. The arrangement was so practical that everyone quickly adjusted to it, and the division has remained in effect to the present day.

Better Communications

The telegraph, in wide use by the 1850s, was followed by several other inventions that also speeded up communication. One was the cable, an underwater telegraph line. Cyrus Field succeeded in laying the first permanently successful cable across the Atlantic in 1866. The line, from Newfoundland to Ireland, made possible telegraphic communication between North America and Europe. (An earlier cable, installed by Field in 1858, broke down after a few weeks of operation.) Cables were later laid across the other oceans, too. Soon, all the continents were linked by the telegraph.

Another communications breakthrough, the telephone, came in the 1870s. It was patented early in 1876 by a Scottish-American teacher of the deaf, Alexander Graham Bell. Later that year, the telephone was exhibited at the Philadelphia Centennial Exposition. The invention met with great acclaim. A visiting celebrity, Emperor Dom Pedro of Brazil, listened to it and exclaimed in awe, "It talks!" The first commercial telephone system was installed in New Haven, Connecticut, in 1878. Two years later, 148 telephone companies were in operation. By 1900, more than a million telephones were in use.

Still another advance in communications was the wireless telegraph. It was developed by Guglielmo Marconi, an Italian scientist, in 1895. This invention made possible ship-to-ship, ship-to-shore, and transoceanic communication without the use of cables. Marconi's work paved the way for the development of radio.

Other inventions in the field of communications changed everyday business operations. The typewriter was first sold in quantity in the 1870s. Adding machines and cash registers were also introduced in this decade.

New Industries

Although railroads offered the prime example of industrial growth in the late 1800s, other industries were also expanding. They included meat packing, flour milling, and the manufacture of clothing and shoes. Another striking feature of this period was the development of entirely new industries.

STEEL   Although the early Industrial Revolution was an age of iron, steel dominated industry's later growth. This metal, stronger and more flexible than iron, can be shaped into a great variety of useful products. It had been known and prized for centuries but was too expensive to produce in quantity.

In the 1850s, William Kelly, a Kentucky blacksmith, discovered a new, cheaper method of making steel. Henry Bessemer, an Englishman, independently developed a similar technique. In the Kelly-Bessemer process (or the Bessemer process, as it is commonly known), cold air is forced through molten iron to remove its impurities. Then, carbon is added to create a tough and elastic steel. The first Bessemer converter in the United States went into operation in 1864. A few years later, a second inexpensive method of making steel, the open-hearth process, was introduced.

These methods made possible the mass production of steel at low cost. Steel replaced iron in trains, railroad track, bridges, ships, and many kinds of machinery. Steel production rose from 222,000 tons in 1873 to more than 11 million tons in 1900. At first, the steel industry was centered in the Pittsburgh area. Steel production then spread to Birmingham, Alabama; to the Great Lakes region, especially Buffalo, Cleveland, Gary, and Chicago; to eastern Pennsylvania; and to Colorado, Utah, and California. The Mesabi Range in Minnesota became the main source of iron ore.

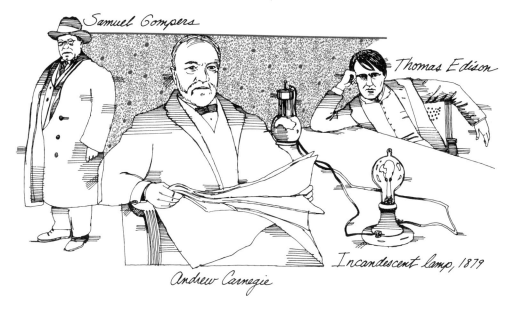

Samuel Gompers

Thomas Edison

Andrew Carnegie

Incandescent lamp, 1879

PETROLEUM   In western Pennsylvania, southwestern New York, and elsewhere, petroleum (crude oil) had long coated the surface of certain streams. It also oozed from cracks in rocks to form small pools on the ground. Indians had used the thick, dark liquid for medicinal purposes, and early settlers had greased their wagon axles with it. Later, quack doctors bottled petroleum and sold it as a cure for all kinds of illness.

In the early 1850s, chemists discovered that petroleum could be made into kerosene, a cheaper and better lamp fuel than whale oil. The available supply of petroleum was limited, however, and little kerosene could be produced. This situation changed dramatically in 1859. In that year, Edwin L. Drake drilled the world's first successful oil well near Titusville, Pennsylvania. Oil prospectors rushed to the area and drilled other wells. Special railroad cars and pipelines were built to transport the petroleum to refineries, where it was processed into kerosene to fuel lamps and into oil and grease to lubricate machinery.

These were the main uses of petroleum until the invention of the gasoline engine, which led to the rise of the automobile industry in the early 20th century. Even before then, however, the production of crude oil increased dramatically—from 2000 barrels in 1859 to more than 5 million in 1870, and more than 63 million in 1900.

ELECTRICAL POWER   Scientists had studied electricity for centuries, but it was not put to use as an energy source until the 1870s. At that time, three important developments took place. Charles F. Brush designed a practical dynamo that could produce a sustained flow of electric current. Thomas A. Edison invented the electric light bulb. And the electric motor

TECHNOLOGICAL DEVELOPMENTS (1851–1893)

Date	Inventor	Invention
1851	William Kelly	Developed new process for making steel
1852	Elisha Otis	Invented practical passenger elevator, making skyscraper possible
1862	Richard Gatling	Perfected machine gun
1864	George Pullman	Built first sleeping car ("Pullman")
1866	Oliver Winchester	Introduced repeating rifle
1868	George Westinghouse	Patented air brake
1868	Christopher Sholes	Developed first practical typewriter
1874	Joseph Glidden	Patented barbed wire
1876	Alexander Graham Bell	Developed telephone
1877	Thomas A. Edison	Invented phonograph
1879	Thomas A. Edison	Invented first practical incandescent electric light bulb
1884	Ottmar Mergenthaler	Invented linotype machine, which set type automatically
1888	George Eastman	Invented Kodak, first hand-held camera
1893	Thomas A. Edison	Patented motion picture projector
1893	Charles E. and J. Frank Duryea	Built and operated first American automobile powered by gasoline engine

came into use. Before long, power plants were built to generate electricity in commercial quantities. The first electric power plant in the United States opened in New York City in 1882.

Within a short time, factories started to switch from steam power to electric power. Electric lights began to replace kerosene and gas lamps, and electrically operated home appliances came into use. By 1900, patents had been granted for an electric iron, an electric stove, and an electric sewing machine.

CHANGES IN BUSINESS METHODS

Post-Civil War industrial growth in the United States was greatly influenced by a group of strong business leaders. They were known to their admirers as "captains of industry" and to their critics as "robber barons." They not only gained control of the nation's leading industries but also changed the structure of American business.

Vertical Integration

One of the most famous of all industrialists was Andrew Carnegie. He came to the United States from Scotland as a poor boy of 13. By his early thirties, he was a millionaire. In 1873, Carnegie founded his own steel company, using the Bessemer process to produce the metal in large quantities.

The Carnegie Steel Company was very profitable. But Carnegie did not like to depend on other companies for raw materials and transportation. He bought mining companies, ore ships, and railroad lines, thereby gaining control of every phase of steelmaking. The process of bringing together the various stages of production, from raw materials to finished products, is called vertical integration. Petroleum refiners followed Carnegie's lead by acquiring oil fields, pipelines, and distribution facilities.

The Corporation

The Carnegie Steel Company was a partnership, meaning that there were just a few co-owners. But many of the new industrial companies were corporations. This type of business is owned not by one individual or by several partners, but by all the people who buy shares in it. There may be thousands of these shareholders (stockholders). They elect a board of directors to manage the business. Each shareholder receives a share of the profits in the form of dividends. The amount of the dividend is based on the number of shares a person owns.

An important advantage of the corporation is its ability to raise a large amount of capital by selling stock to investors. This enables the corporation to build huge factories, buy expensive machinery, and expand nationally and internationally. The corporation soon replaced the single proprietorship and the partnership as the dominant form of business organization in the United States. By 1900, corporations controlled more than two-thirds of all manufacturing.

Combinations

The age of industrialization witnessed the rise of big business in the United States. Individual companies not only grew in size and wealth but also formed combinations—business alliances that increased their assets and power.

THE MERGER   In one form of combination, the merger, two or more companies were consolidated (joined) to form a larger one. A pioneer in this form of combination was Cornelius Vanderbilt. In 1869, he merged a number of short railroad lines between New York City and Buffalo. The result was the country's first great railroad system, the New York Central. It was later extended westward to the Great Lakes region and northeastward to Boston.

Many business leaders arranged mergers to reduce or eliminate their competition. If they could gain control over a product or service—that is, create a monopoly—they could then demand and get high prices. In addition to the merger, several other forms of combination arose in the late 1800s.

THE POOL   A pool was an informal arrangement arrived at by competing companies. They agreed to fix prices, share profits, or divide the market for their products. Rival railroads serving the Midwest set up the first pool in 1870. Pooling soon became a common practice among competing railroads and spread to other industries. But pools were not legally binding and were often broken. The pool was replaced by the trust.

THE TRUST   A trust was a giant business combination consisting of a number of corporations in the same field or in related fields. A small board of trustees managed the combination. Stockholders in the individual companies signed over their stock to the trustees. In exchange, the stockholders received trust certificates that entitled them to a proportionate share of the trust's profits.

The first successful trust was organized by John D. Rockefeller. After starting an oil refining business in the 1860s, he bought out competitors or ruined them by sharply lowering his own prices. In 1879, he formed the Standard Oil Trust, which controlled 90 percent of the oil refining business. During the next decade, trusts were formed in many other industries, including sugar, lead, whiskey, and meat packing. One of the biggest trusts was the American Tobacco Company, formed in 1890 by James B. Duke and his brother Benjamin.

THE HOLDING COMPANY   Another form of business combination was the holding company. It did not produce or distribute goods or services. Instead, the holding company held a controlling interest in the stock of several related companies, called subsidiaries, and concerned itself with directing their operations. A pioneer in this form of combination was the Bell Telephone Company. By the end of the century, 185 industrial holding companies controlled a third of all the capital invested in American manufacturing.

Investment Banking

Big business was aided by a group of bankers who specialized in raising capital for corporations. Investment bankers supervised the issue and sale of securities (stocks and bonds). They often sat on a corporation's board of directors.

In the age of industrialization, the giant of American investment bankers was J. Pierpont Morgan. He headed the largest private bank in the United States. When hundreds of railroads faced ruin after a business panic in 1893, Morgan took the lead in reorganizing and restoring them. In 1901, he and his associates bought the Carnegie Steel Company, merged it with other companies, and formed the huge United States Steel Corporation. It was the nation's first billion-dollar corporation.

New Retailing Practices

Before the rise of big business, people had few choices about where to buy their everyday supplies. Consumers could purchase from small shops where the products were made. Or they could go to general stores, which sold groceries, utensils, tools, fabrics, and other goods. Isolated farm families were served by peddlers, whose wagons were stocked with small wares. The availability of mass-produced goods during the age of industrialization brought changes. Merchants developed new types of stores and new techniques of merchandising.

One innovation was the chain store, a group of retail outlets owned by one company. Chains could sell goods at lower prices because of centralized management and large-scale purchasing. The first grocery-store chain was founded in 1859. It later became known as the Great Atlantic and Pacific Tea Company (A&P). F. W. Woolworth opened the first unit in his chain of five-and-ten-cent stores in 1879.

Another retailing novelty was the department store, which sold goods of almost every description. Each product category—women's clothing, toys, kitchenware, and so on—was carried in a separate department. The first American department stores were founded in the 1860s and 1870s. They included Macy's in New York City, Wanamaker's in Philadelphia, and Marshall Field in Chicago.

Mail-order companies were also founded in this period. They published catalogs offering a wide variety of goods. Customers ordered and received merchandise by mail. Pioneers in this field were Montgomery Ward, founded in 1872, and Sears Roebuck, founded in 1895.

Selling techniques improved in the late 1800s. Foodstuffs, once sold in bulk, were now packaged and labeled. Brand names came into wide use. The number of trademarks registered at the U.S. Patent Office jumped from 121 in 1870 to 10,568 in 1906. Advertising appeared not only in magazines and newspapers but also on big electric signs. Another shopping innovation of this period was installment buying (paying over a period of time).

THE FREE ENTERPRISE SYSTEM

The age of industrialization in the United States took place within the framework of the free enterprise system, or capitalism. This form of economic organization is based on the following principles:

1. A nation's resources should be owned and controlled by private individuals.
2. Producers should be able to compete freely among themselves for a share of the market. Consumers should have the opportunity to make their own choices among the available products. Such competition would establish a firm foundation for a healthy economy and would benefit society as a whole.
3. Government should not interfere with the operation of the economic system. This hands-off attitude is known as a policy of *laissez faire* (French for "let do").

The principles of capitalism dated back to the late 1700s. The system as it existed in the United States during the age of industrialization differed in many ways from the ideal. For instance, trusts and other business combinations severely limited free competition in many fields. But the economy was booming. Many Americans believed that a laissez-faire policy was the best way to sustain economic growth.

THE PROBLEMS OF LABOR

As the United States industrialized, the number of wage earners grew. Employees generally worked long hours for low pay. Working conditions were often poor, and sometimes dangerous. Unemployment was an ever-present threat, too. Acting alone, a worker could do nothing about a bad situation except quit and look for another job.

Organizing Unions

American workers began to realize that the only way they could overcome their weakness was to band together into labor unions. A union's first objective was to win recognition by an employer as the official representative of the employees. Then, it could engage in collective bargaining—negotiations between labor and management officials to settle such issues as wages, hours, work rules, and working conditions.

THE KNIGHTS OF LABOR   The craft unions of the early 19th century were generally small and short-lived. The first important national union was formed in 1869 by garment workers in Philadelphia. Known as the *Knights of Labor*, it aimed to unite all workers, skilled and unskilled, into one large union. Members included blacks and women. The Knights hoped not only to better the worker's lot but also to reform society in general.

The Knights were active in the nation's first major strike, which took place in 1877. Workers on the Baltimore and Ohio and other eastern railroads walked off their jobs to protest a wage cut. The railroads then hired other workers as replacements. When angry strikers tried to keep the trains from running, riots broke out. The militia was called in and pitched battles resulted. Much property was destroyed in several railroad centers, especially Pittsburgh. Order was finally restored when President Hayes sent in federal troops. Unable to stop the trains and afraid of losing their jobs, the strikers grimly accepted the wage cut.

In spite of this setback, the Knights continued to grow, and by 1886, the union's membership totaled more than 700,000. In that year, however, a serious labor disturbance occurred in Chicago. Thousands of workers had gone on strike, seeking an eight-hour workday. Violence broke out between strikers and police at the McCormick Harvester Company, and two men were killed. A protest meeting was then called at Haymarket Square. When police arrived to break up the crowd, someone threw a bomb, which killed or injured a number of people, including some policemen. In the rioting that followed, many others were hurt. Eight radical agitators among the strikers were convicted of conspiracy to commit murder. Although the evidence against them was flimsy, four of them were hanged. Three others were sentenced to long prison terms. (They were later freed by the governor of Illinois on the grounds that they had not received a fair trial.)

Although the Knights of Labor had not been involved in the Haymarket affair and had actually condemned it, the public blamed the union for the incident. As a result, its membership fell off sharply, and it soon declined in importance. Other factors that contributed to the downfall of the Knights were unsuccessful strikes, internal disputes over political activity, and the conflicting interests of skilled and unskilled workers within the organization.

THE AMERICAN FEDERATION OF LABOR   Many of those who left the Knights of Labor joined a new union, the *American Federation of Labor*

(AFL). It had been founded (under a different name) in 1881. The AFL was a craft union in which skilled workers were grouped according to their trades. The emphasis on crafts meant that most blacks and women, who were largely unskilled, were excluded. Each trade formed its own national union, with many locals throughout the country. The AFL served as the parent body of these self-governing national unions. In other words, it was a union of unions rather than a union of individual workers.

Samuel Gompers, a cigarmaker by trade and one of the founders of the AFL, was the union's president from 1886 to 1924. He believed that unions should not aim to reform society, but rather seek to win immediate benefits for their members. Under Gompers's leadership, the AFL's membership grew to about 550,000 in 1900.

A Time of Struggle

Although more successful than the Knights of Labor, the AFL represented less than 10 percent of American nonfarm workers in 1900. One reason why the AFL was unable to attract a larger membership was that the times did not favor organized labor. Big business violently opposed workers' efforts to better their condition. Corporations not only refused to recognize unions but also fired employees who tried to organize other workers. And strikebreakers were hired to work in place of strikers. When labor and management were at odds, government at all levels almost always sided with business. The courts, for example, often issued injunctions (court orders) against strikers. The public and the press supported business, too.

In 1892, a particularly bitter dispute erupted at the Carnegie Steel Company's plant in Homestead, Pennsylvania. Union workers refused to accept a wage cut and went on strike. To protect its property and break the strike, the company tried to bring in 300 armed guards from the Pinkerton detective agency. In a fight between strikers and guards, seven Pinkertons were killed, and the rest driven off. The state militia then stepped in to protect the company, which hired strikebreakers and resumed steel production. The strike collapsed after five months. Many union members were fired, and the power of their union was broken.

Even more discouraging to organized labor was the Pullman strike. The Pullman Company, near Chicago, manufactured sleeping cars for trains. When its workers were threatened with a wage cut, they went on strike in 1894. They were supported by railroad employees—members of the independent *American Railway Union,* headed by Eugene V. Debs. The railway workers refused to handle any trains hauling Pullman cars. Violence flared up when the railroads tried to keep the trains running.

President Grover Cleveland sent in federal troops to restore order so that mail service would not be halted. Meanwhile, the railroads obtained an injunction forbidding strikers to interfere with the mails and interstate commerce. When Debs refused to call off the strike, he was arrested and jailed. Under the protection of federal troops, train service was restored, and the strike was broken.

Matching Test

COLUMN A	COLUMN B
1. George Westinghouse	**a.** invented electric light bulb
2. Cyrus Field	**b.** made millions as steel manufacturer
3. Edwin Drake	**c.** formed Standard Oil Trust
4. Thomas A. Edison	**d.** patented air brake
5. Andrew Carnegie	**e.** formed first great railway system in United States
6. Cornelius Vanderbilt	**f.** led American Railway Workers in Pullman Strike
7. John D. Rockefeller	**g.** drilled world's first successful oil well
8. J. Pierpont Morgan	**h.** laid first successful cable across Atlantic
9. Samuel Gompers	**i.** organized United States Steel Corporation
10. Eugene V. Debs	**j.** was president of AFL for almost 40 years

True-False Test

1. Between 1860 and 1900, the number of Americans engaged in manufacturing more than doubled.
2. Railroad construction was the biggest business in the United States between 1865 and 1915.
3. Steel was manufactured for the first time in the 1860s.
4. Until the early 20th century, the petroleum industry produced mainly kerosene and lubricants for machinery.
5. In 1900, the United States was the world's leading industrial nation.
6. Vertical integration means hiring workers without regard to their race or religion.
7. The first successful trust in the United States was organized by James and Benjamin Duke.

8. Industrialization in the late 19th century led to new retailing techniques, including chain stores and department stores.
9. Capitalism is based on the principle of free competition.
10. The first important nationwide labor union was the American Federation of Labor.

Essay Questions

1. Why did industrial growth occur during and after the Civil War?
2. What is a corporation, and how does it work? Why did corporations have an advantage in an age of industrial expansion?
3. What obstacles did American unions face in the late 19th century?
4. What new industries developed during the age of industrialization? Name a person who was important in the development of each industry listed. Describe each person's contribution.
5. Compare the Knights of Labor and the American Federation of Labor as to organization, membership, and aims.

CHAPTER 20

The Growth of Cities

IN THE PERIOD from the Civil War to 1900, there was a strong trend toward urbanization—the growth of cities. In 1860, less than 15 percent of all Americans lived in cities having a population of 10,000 or more. By 1900, more than 30 percent did.

Cities grew mainly because of industrialization. Urban factories and businesses encouraged many Americans to move from rural areas. Cities also attracted most of the immigrants who arrived in the United States during this period.

THE "NEW" IMMIGRATION

In 1886, the largest statue ever made, the Statue of Liberty, was unveiled in New York Harbor. This gift of the people of France honored the

POPULATION GROWTH (1860–1900)

Year	Total	Urban*		Rural	
		Number	Percent	Number	Percent
1860	31,443,000	6,217,000	20%	25,227,000	80%
1870	38,558,000	9,902,000	25%	28,656,000	75%
1880	50,156,000	14,130,000	28%	36,026,000	72%
1890	62,947,000	22,106,000	35%	40,841,000	65%
1900	75,995,000	30,160,000	39%	45,835,000	61%

*Urban population is defined as all persons living in places of 2500 inhabitants or more.

United States on its 100th birthday in 1876. The statue's location at the entrance to the biggest American port made it a symbol of the nation's welcome and promise to immigrants. And those who sailed past it were numerous indeed. The trend in immigration was almost continuously upward during the age of industrialization. Between 1860 and 1900, the number of newcomers averaged more than 200,000 a year. In some peak years in the 1880s, there were three times as many.

Until the 1880s, most immigrants to the United States came from northern and western Europe. Except for the Irish, most were Protestants. Except for the Germans and Scandinavians, their native language was English. Then, this so-called "old" immigration began to give way to a "new" immigration. More and more people came from eastern and southern Europe—Poland, Russia, the Austro-Hungarian Empire, the Balkan states, and Italy. There were not only thousands of Catholics but

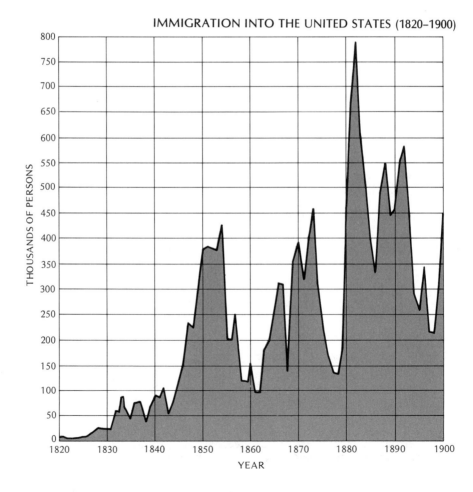

IMMIGRATION INTO THE UNITED STATES (1820–1900)

also large numbers of Jews. Few of the newcomers spoke English, and many could not read or write at all. By 1900, immigrants from eastern and southern Europe outnumbered those from northwestern Europe.

Patterns of Work and Settlement

Because many of the new immigrants were poor and unskilled, they tended to settle in large cities, where they could find factory or construction jobs. Italians worked on subways and bridges in New York City and Boston. Poles and other Slavs mined coal, poured steel, and worked in the stockyards. Jews went into the garment industry or ran small stores. Chinese immigrants—who settled mainly on the West Coast—operated laundries and restaurants.

Like those who came before them, the new immigrants felt more secure among their own people and often formed ethnic neighborhoods within cities. There was "Little Italy" in New York City. Hamtramck was a Polish community in Detroit. Several cities had Chinatowns. In such neighborhoods, the immigrants set up businesses and organizations to help them in their new life. Among these were welfare societies, newspapers, theaters, and sports clubs.

Response to the Newcomers

As in the past, American reaction to the newcomers was mixed. Business leaders welcomed the supply of cheap labor. But American wage earners were less happy. Desperately poor immigrants were often willing to work for less than the normal wage and to take jobs as strikebreakers. In general, people were somewhat suspicious of the "different" customs and "clannish" ways of foreigners. The strongest nativist opposition was directed against Roman Catholics. Members of the American Protective Association, founded in 1887, pledged not to vote for Catholics or employ them.

Some Americans wanted the government to limit immigration. Little was done during this period, however. Congress did rule, in 1882, to keep out criminals, paupers, the insane, and those with certain diseases. But the law was not strictly enforced. Inspectors at Ellis Island in New York—the nation's main immigration station—had only two minutes to ask each new arrival 32 questions and complete a medical examination.

The main exception to free immigration involved the Chinese. Feeling against them was so strong, particularly in California, that Congress passed the *Chinese Exclusion Act* in 1882. It banned all Chinese immigration for 10 years, and was later renewed.

In spite of difficulties, the new immigrants did well in the United

States. While adjusting to their new home, they, in turn, exerted an influence on the American way of life, contributing ethnic variety in food, music, literature, and art. Some of the immigrants became famous and wealthy. Many remained poor. But most found for themselves and for their children a better way of life than they had known in their home countries.

America is God's Crucible, the great Melting-pot where all the races of Europe are melting and re-forming!

playwright Israel Zangwill, in The Melting Pot, *1908*

CITY LIFE

Between 1860 and 1900, the number of American cities with 100,000 or more people jumped from 14 to 38. Urban centers offered not only jobs but also excitement, entertainment, educational opportunities, and such conveniences as electric lights and running water.

How Cities Grew

Most American cities were not planned. They just grew, as more and more houses and factories were needed and built. Since there was no

CITY GROWTH (1860–1900)
(ten largest U.S. cities in 1900)

	1860	1900
New York (including Brooklyn)	1,174,779	3,437,202
Chicago	109,260	1,698,575
Philadelphia	565,529	1,293,697
St. Louis	160,773	575,238
Boston	177,840	560,892
Baltimore	212,418	508,957
Cleveland	43,417	381,768
Buffalo	81,129	352,387
San Francisco	56,802	342,782
Pittsburgh	77,923	321,616

Immigrants arriving in New York Harbor

zoning, builders might place houses next to a packing plant or a chemical factory. And since there were few building regulations, many structures were ugly, unhealthy, and even dangerous.

CONSTRUCTION Because city real estate was expensive, builders tried to cram as many people as possible into the space available. The result was the tenement. Originally, a tenement was any rental dwelling for many families. But it soon came to mean only the kind that was crowded and run-down. Usually, several tenement apartments had to share toilet facilities, which might consist of one privy in a courtyard. Tenements had little light or air. In many cases, inside rooms were lit only by a "window" into an outside room. Tenement neighborhoods, with their narrow, treeless streets, quickly turned into slums. As one observer put it: "Slum, semi-slum, and super-slum—to this has come the evolution of cities."

Overcrowding meant that commercial buildings had to make the most of limited space, too. After the invention of the passenger elevator in the 1850s, buildings began to expand upward. At first, the outside walls had to be thick enough to support the floors. This restricted a building's height to a few stories. A true skyscraper was possible only when builders started using iron frameworks to support both walls and floors. (Steel later replaced iron.) William LeBaron Jenney is generally credited with the first skyscraper. He designed the ten-story Home Insurance Building in Chicago in 1884. Other skyscrapers soon rose in Chicago, New York City, and Boston. The greatest of the early skyscraper architects was Louis H. Sullivan. His motto, "form follows function," pointed the way toward a more modern, less cluttered style.

TRANSPORTATION City transportation was unable to keep up with the increase in city dwellers. Streets were too narrow to handle the traffic. Many of them were unpaved. In Chicago as late as 1890, more than two-thirds of the street mileage consisted of rutted dirt roads—dusty, icy, or muddy, depending on the weather.

Public transportation took the form of streetcars. Horse-drawn at first, they were later powered by electricity. Traffic snarls became so bad that several cities tried other ways of moving people. Chicago and New York raised trains above the ground to make "elevateds" (els). Railroad lines underground were another solution. Boston opened the first subway, a mile and a half long, in 1897.

SERVICES Like transportation facilities, urban services in the age of industrialization were often inadequate. Wooden buildings were common, and fires could do great damage. In Chicago, where even the sidewalks were made of wood, a huge area of the city was burned to the ground in a great fire in 1871. Volunteer fire companies were the rule until the mid-19th century. Only in the 1860s and 1870s did big cities like New York begin to set up professional fire-fighting units.

Sanitation was a problem, too. Sewers often emptied into the same rivers that supplied drinking water. Many cities had no regular garbage pickup. Although several states and localities had established public health departments by 1900, conditions were still far from ideal.

Coping With City Problems

Most city governments had their hands full keeping order and providing minimum services. They could not offer welfare and similar benefits that are taken for granted today. But city dwellers in need of help had other resources to turn to.

POLITICAL MACHINES Strong political organizations first arose in the United States early in the 19th century. In the 1870s, critics began to call these groups "machines" because of their efficiency. Both Republicans and Democrats operated powerful political machines in urban centers. These organizations could be counted on to deliver votes in any district they controlled.

Political machines were usually run by bosses—men who supplied city jobs and city contracts, in exchange for bribes. They rarely held major political office. For business leaders, bosses offered a way of avoiding competitive bidding and other such procedures. For ordinary citizens, bosses provided jobs, legal advice, and loans when times were hard. Poor immigrants, in particular, benefited from political machines—and voted for machine candidates in return.

Almost every big city had its machine and its bosses. The most notorious of all big-city bosses was William M. Tweed. He headed

Tammany Hall, the Democratic machine of New York City. Tweed and his associates, known as the Tweed Ring, are believed to have swindled the city out of $50 million or more. Convicted of fraud, Tweed was sent to prison.

REFORMERS AND SETTLEMENT HOUSES A number of reformers helped bring about changes in city living conditions. One was a Danish immigrant, Jacob Riis. As a police reporter in New York City, be became familiar with slums, vice, and crime. He publicized his findings in such books as *How the Other Half Lives* (1890). Aroused by his writings and public reaction to them, the city took action. It cleaned up its water supply, built playgrounds, improved schools, and tore down some of its worst tenements.

Settlement houses were another response to city problems. These community centers in poor neighborhoods were usually supported by private contributors and run by volunteers. The movement began in the United States when Stanton Coit and Charles B. Stover founded the Neighborhood Guild (later called the University Settlement) in New York City in 1886. Other notable settlement houses were Hull House, founded in Chicago in 1889 by Jane Addams, and New York's Henry Street Settlement, founded by Lillian Wald four years later. A settlement house usually provided free classes in English, cooking, and child care. It also offered medical help and provided recreation in the form of clubs, sports teams, and theaters.

The problems of city living gave rise to a new professional field, social work. Dedicated amateurs and private charities were no longer able to handle the pressing needs of city populations. "Private beneficence," wrote Jane Addams, "is totally inadequate to deal with the vast numbers of the city's disinherited."

AN URBAN CULTURE

As cities grew, so did their influence on life in the United States. More and more, urban people and institutions introduced or popularized new trends in American society. Cities played a key role in the expansion of education, the rise of professional sports, the spread of popular newspapers, and the growth of literature and the visual arts.

Education

During the age of industrialization, Americans became increasingly aware of the importance of education. States passed laws requiring attendance at school. The first one to do so was Massachusetts, in 1852.

> Surplus wealth is a sacred trust which its possessor is bound to administer in his lifetime for the good of the community. . . . The man who dies . . . rich dies disgraced.
>
> —*Andrew Carnegie on the obligations of money, 1889*

Between 1870 and 1900, the number of pupils between ages 5 and 17 who attended public schools more than doubled, from fewer than 7 million to more than 15 million. In the same period, the number of high schools increased from 160 to 6000.

Most of the new schools were in towns or cities. And many of the students were first-generation Americans. Public school was the main place where most of them learned what it meant to be an American. In fact, an important goal of public education in the age of industrialization was "Americanization"—teaching the immigrants English, American history, and the values and traditions of their new homeland.

Education branched out to reach both younger and older students. The first public kindergarten was opened in St. Louis in 1873. Soon, many other cities started classes for preschool children. For high school graduates, there were more colleges available. The 1862 Morrill Act helped states found colleges and universities. The original purpose of this law had been to improve agricultural education. But its main result was the creation of the modern system of state universities.

Adult education was stimulated by the Chautauqua Institution. It was organized in 1874 by John II. Vincent, a Methodist clergyman. Each summer, thousands flocked to Chautauqua, New York, to attend concerts, operas, literary readings, and educational lectures presented by famous people. The idea spread, and so-called "chautauquas" were organized in other parts of the country.

All these educational developments were aided by the growth of public libraries. The nation's first public libraries had been founded before the Civil War, but they became widespread only later in the century. The interest of Andrew Carnegie was an important factor in this development. He donated more than $40 million for the building of libraries.

Newspapers

As more Americans learned to read, newspapers became a vital means of keeping people informed and influencing their outlook. About 575 daily newspapers were published in 1870. By 1900, there were more than 2000. Publishers expanded their coverage of local and national news, and sent correspondents abroad to report on foreign affairs. Wire services gathered news and circulated it to hundreds of papers via telegraph and telephone. Two of the most important news services were Associated Press and United Press (now United Press International). Columnists and political cartoonists did much to mold public opinion. The most famous political cartoonist of the late 1800s, Thomas Nast, helped expose the Tweed Ring.

To attract readers, newspapers added such features as comic strips, sports columns, and women's pages. Some papers tried to increase circulation by "yellow journalism." They featured stories of crime and scandal, and they overdramatized news events with scare headlines and shocking illustrations. Joseph Pulitzer, publisher of the *New York World*, first introduced this technique. It was taken up by William Randolph Hearst, who built a powerful coast-to-coast chain of newspapers in the early 1900s.

Sports

City dwellers had few opportunities for games and exercise. Instead of playing themselves, fans crowded into big arenas and stadiums to watch other people play. The age of industrialization ushered in the era of organized spectator sports.

The most popular American spectator sport of the period was baseball, which may have originated in England (as "rounders") during the 16th century. The rules of the game were standardized in the mid-1800s, and local teams began to draw loyal rooters. The first professional team, the Cincinnati Red Stockings, was organized in 1869. Similar groups were organized elsewhere, and in 1876, eight teams founded the National League.

Another American game with English origins, football, became popular in colleges and universities in the mid-1800s. The early game was like soccer. There were 25 players on a side, and no one was allowed to carry the ball. Walter Camp created the modern game with changes he introduced in the 1880s and 1890s.

One brand new game, basketball, was invented in the United States in 1891. James Naismith, a college instructor in Massachusetts, decided that "there should be a game that could be played indoors in the evening and during the winter seasons." The first game was played with a soccer ball; the hoops were peach baskets nailed to the walls of a gym.

Literature

In the age of industrialization, the United States was a far more complex society than it had been before the Civil War. Writers dealt with the variety of American life in many ways.

REGIONALISTS   One trend in the late 19th century was regionalism, which stressed the customs and characters of particular areas of the country. Bret Harte described the days of the California gold rush in short stories like "The Luck of Roaring Camp" (1868). George W. Cable wrote about Louisiana in such novels as *Old Creole Days* (1879). Another Southern writer, Joel Chandler Harris, retold black folktales in numerous stories about Uncle Remus. New England was the background for *The Country of the Pointed Firs* (1896) by Sarah Orne Jewett.

One of the greatest of all American writers first became famous as a regionalist. His name was Samuel L. Clemens, but he is better known as Mark Twain. His books about the Midwest include *The Adventures of Tom Sawyer* (1876), *Life on the Mississippi* (1883), and *The Adventures of Huckleberry Finn* (1884). Twain also dealt with many other subjects. His writings include humorous adventure yarns, satires, and travel narratives.

REALISTS   Another literary school of the period was realism, an attempt to show life as it was. William Dean Howells depicted the self-made businessman in *The Rise of Silas Lapham* (1885). Hamlin Garland portrayed the bleakness of Midwest farm life in *Main-Travelled Roads* (1891). Stephen Crane gave a vivid account of the horrors of the Civil War in his famous novel *The Red Badge of Courage* (1895).

Henry James was interested in a different kind of realism, the portrayal of people's thoughts and feelings. His best-known novels include *Daisy Miller* (1879), *The Portrait of a Lady* (1881), and *The Wings of the Dove* (1902).

OTHER WRITERS   Few novelists of the 19th century sold as many books as Louisa May Alcott. *Little Women* (1868–1869) was based on her own family experiences. Almost as popular were the stories of O. Henry (William Sydney Porter). He often used a New York City setting and liked coincidental plot twists and surprise endings.

Much less well known was the poet Emily Dickinson. Hardly anyone had ever heard of her when she died in 1886. But volumes published after her death revealed her wit and insight. She has been called "the one authentic poetic genius of the age."

Painting

As in the past, many noted American artists studied in Europe. One of them was the popular landscape artist George Inness. At one time, copies of his painting *Peace and Plenty* (1865) hung in school classrooms all over America. Inness returned to the United States after his studies.

Others, however, remained abroad. Among them was Mary Cassatt, known for her tender paintings of mothers and children. Another, John Singer Sargent, specialized in portraits of the rich and famous. A third, James Abbott McNeill Whistler, is probably most famous for a painting of his mother, done in 1871. He called it *Arrangement in Gray and Black No. 1: The Artist's Mother.* The title indicates his interest in art as an organization of color and form.

Two great painters who concentrated on the American scene were Winslow Homer and Thomas Eakins. Homer excelled at dramatic seascapes. Eakins was more interested in people. He used paint and canvas to study the personalities of those who posed for him. Unlike Sargent and other "society" painters, Eakins did not flatter his subjects. "Respectability in art," he said, "is appalling."

TEN NOTABLE AMERICANS
OF THE MIDDLE AND LATE 1800S

HENRY ADAMS (1838–1918)   This member of a famous family was the grandson of John Quincy Adams and the great-grandson of John Adams. He taught history at Harvard and wrote a nine-volume history of the United States during the administrations of Jefferson and Madison. But he is best known for *The Education of Henry Adams* (1907). It was not a standard autobiography, but rather an account of his pessimistic views on the spread of industrialization.

SUSAN B. ANTHONY (1820–1906)   Denied full participation in the temperance and abolition movements because of her sex, she became a single-minded crusader for women's rights. In 1872, she voted in a local (Rochester, New York) election as a test of the Fourteenth Amendment. Brought to trial, she was fined $100 (by a judge who had written his opinion before the trial began). She vowed never to pay the fine— and kept her promise. Her last words were "Failure is impossible."

FREDERICK DOUGLASS (1817?–1895)   Born a slave in Maryland, he escaped and settled in New York City. His commanding presence and skill as a speaker made him the outstanding black abolitionist. From 1847 to 1864, he edited an abolitionist newspaper in Rochester, New York. He also championed woman suffrage, and raised black troops for the Union army in the Civil War. After the war, he served as a marshal and recorder of deeds in Washington, D.C., and then as U.S. minister to Haiti.

MARY BAKER EDDY (1821–1910)   A lifetime of poor health did not curb this religious leader's strong will. In 1875, she published the first edition of *Science and Health.* It outlined her doctrine that disease is caused by the mind alone, and can be overcome by it. She organized her followers into the Christian Science movement and established the Church of Christ, Scientist. She also wrote widely and founded the newspaper *The Christian Science Monitor.*

CHARLES G. FINNEY (1792–1875)   After a personal religious experience when he was in his twenties, he became a powerful revival preacher. The sermons he delivered throughout the Northeast, and in England, influenced thousands of hearers to repent and change their lives. He also had a strong impact on Oberlin College, with which he was associated for almost 40 years.

SARAH JOSEPHA HALE (1788–1879)   Widowed when still in her thirties, she was left with five young children to support. She soon became editor of a new periodical, the *Ladies' Magazine* (later *Godey's Lady's Book*). Unlike its competitors, which plagiarized shamelessly, it printed only original material, much of which she wrote. *Godey's* growing circulation gave her enormous influence, which she used to promote her view that a woman's place was in the home, where she had a duty to exercise gentle but firm guidance over her family.

LOUIS MOREAU GOTTSCHALK (1829–1869)   The first American piano virtuoso to be acclaimed in Europe, he was born in New Orleans and studied in Paris, where he knew Berlioz and Chopin. His performances in Europe, the United States, and Latin America always featured some of his own compositions, which were spirited and tuneful, if not profound. He died in Brazil after becoming ill while performing his own favorite composition, "Morte" (Death).

THOMAS NAST (1840–1902)   This German-born artist became one of the most influential political cartoonists in American history. His favorite target was the corrupt Tweed Ring of New York City's Tammany Hall. His slashing attacks on the Democratic political machine not only forced "Boss" Tweed to flee the country but also helped bring him back to justice. (He was recognized in Spain by someone familiar with Nast's drawings.) To Nast we owe the political symbols of Democratic donkey and Republican elephant. He also transformed the thin, long-robed Santa Claus of his time into the jolly, chubby figure we know today.

JOHN A. ROEBLING (1806–1869)   After training as an engineer in his native Germany, he came to America at the age of 25. His earliest achievement was to make the first wire rope in America, used to haul boats along the Pennsylvania Canal. But he was most noted for his suspension bridges. Two are located in Pittsburgh and Niagara Falls, but the most important one is the Brooklyn Bridge in New York City. He died when work on the Brooklyn Bridge was about to begin, and its construction was supervised by his son, Washington Augustus Roebling.

CARL SCHURZ (1829–1906)   He was among the best known of those Germans who fled their country after the unsuccessful revolutions of 1848. In the United States, he took up the antislavery cause and actively supported Lincoln and the Republicans. He commanded a division in the Civil War, was elected to the Senate, and later served as secretary of the interior under Hayes. Never abandoning the liberal attitudes of his youth, he favored civil service reform, humane treatment of the Indians, and an anti-imperialist policy in foreign affairs.

Matching Test

Column A	Column B
1. Ellis Island	a. center for adult education
2. tenement	b. Democratic political machine in New York City
3. Tammany Hall	c. crowded, run-down residence for many families
4. Jacob Riis	d. founder of Hull House
5. Jane Addams	e. creator of modern game of football
6. Chautauqua	f. painter of dramatic seascapes
7. wire service	g. main U.S. immigration center
8. Walter Camp	h. author of *The Adventures of Huckleberry Finn*
9. Mark Twain	i. organization for gathering news and circulating it to many newspapers
10. Winslow Homer	j. reporter who publicized big-city problems

Multiple-Choice Test

1. Between 1860 and 1900, the percentage of Americans living in cities   (a) decreased   (b) rose from a third to a half   (c) doubled   (d) tripled.
2. Most "new" immigrants in the late 1800s   (a) settled on farms   (b) were skilled workers and professionals   (c) took factory and construction jobs in cities   (d) moved to the West.
3. The American Protective Association was an organization opposed to   (a) Roman Catholics   (b) Jewish immigrants   (c) foreign imports   (d) Chinese settlers.
4. A major factor in the development of the skyscraper was   (a) strictly enforced zoning   (b) the invention of the passenger elevator   (c) regulations against tenements   (d) the construction of elevated trains.
5. The first subway in the United States was located in   (a) New York City   (b) Chicago   (c) San Francisco   (d) Boston.
6. A notorious political boss was   (a) William LeBaron Jenney   (b) Louis H. Sullivan   (c) Charles B. Stover   (d) William M. Tweed.

7. The settlement house movement began (a) before the Civil War (b) during the reconstruction period (c) in the 1880s (d) in the 1900s.

8. Andrew Carnegie gave more than $40 million to build (a) agricultural colleges (b) kindergartens (c) adult education centers (d) public libraries.

9. The most famous political cartoonist of the late 19th century was (a) Joseph Pulitzer (b) Thomas Nast (c) William Randolph Hearst (d) John H. Vincent.

10. An American college instructor, James Naismith, originated the game of (a) soccer (b) baseball (c) football (d) basketball.

Essay Questions

1. How did the "new" immigrants differ from the "old"? For what reasons did nativists react negatively to the new immigrants?

2. What were some of the advantages of city living in the late 1800s?

3. What were some of the major problems of city living in the late 1800s?

4. Name two well-known private agencies that helped poor people and immigrants in the cities of the late 19th century. What services did such organizations provide?

5. What were two major schools of literature during the age of industrialization? Give examples of writers in each category.

CHAPTER 21

Politics and Protest

W ESTERN SETTLEMENT, industrialization, and the growth of cities transformed the United States after the Civil War. These developments created a number of new problems, too, but politicians demonstrated little interest in solving them. Congress, for example, largely ignored such issues as the growing power of corporations or big-city political corruption. Protest movements did arise, however, and their demands for reform led to some improvements in the 1880s and early 1890s.

THE NATIONAL SCENE

The presidents during the last third of the 19th century were generally earnest administrators, rather than dynamic leaders. But even if they had wanted to introduce broad new programs, they would undoubtedly have run into trouble. Ever since reconstruction, when Congress succeeded in limiting the power of the president, the executive branch of the government had been overshadowed by the legislative branch.

Although Congress was powerful, it was neither distinguished nor respected. The Senate was known as a "rich man's club." The House of Representatives was noisy and disorderly. While a few members devoted themselves to the business of the House, many more ignored the proceedings and spent their time reading newspapers and answering letters.

Many legislators were downright dishonest. Some accepted bribes in return for their support of bills favored by business groups. Others were in the pay of various trusts.

The Role of Government

Passive presidents and incompetent legislators were not criticized as much in the late 19th century as they would be today. Most Americans felt that the government should not concern itself with such matters as regulating the economy or providing financial help to people in need. Grover Cleveland, the only Democratic president of this period, once vetoed a bill that would have extended financial help to farmers hurt by drought. His comment at the time summed up a common attitude: "Though the people support the government, the government should not support the people."

In the Hall of the Presidents, Uncle Sam weighs Benjamin Harrison's record as president and observes: "I'm afraid, Benjamin, that the best we can do for you will be a mighty small statuette." (The Bettmann Archive)

Party Politics

During the late 1800s, Republicans and Democrats differed little on most issues. Both parties were very conservative. Both of them were devoted to the theory of laissez-faire economics, and both employed the spoils system—rewarding loyal party workers with government jobs. Despite these similarities, Americans generally felt a strong loyalty to their own party and supported the party's candidates vigorously. Voter turnout in national elections was high. The percentage of eligible voters that went to the polls was always more than 70 percent, and sometimes higher than 80 percent. (In the 20th century, by comparison, the average was to fall to below 60 percent.)

On a national basis, the two parties had about equal strength. But each was stronger in certain regions than in others. In the solid South, where Republicans were associated with reconstruction, almost all white voters were Democrats. African Americans in the South were largely pro-Republican but were discouraged from voting (see page 319). In New England and some of the plains states, most voters were Republicans. Party strength was more evenly divided in the Middle Atlantic and Midwestern states. Campaigners therefore made their major appeals in these "swing" states. And almost all presidential candidates between 1868 and 1896 came from these key areas.

The two parties also appealed to different groups of voters. Most native-born white Protestants (except in the South) tended to identify themselves as Republicans. Most "new" immigrants, especially Jews and Roman Catholics, joined the Democratic party.

A SPECIAL CASE: THE SOUTH

When studying politics in the late 1800s, it is helpful to consider the South as a special region. As earlier in the century, its economy and its racial makeup made it different from the rest of the country.

Economic Development

After the Civil War, many Southerners felt strongly that their economy should be more varied. Farmers relied too heavily on cotton. In addition, the region needed to industrialize, like the rest of the country.

Southerners made some progress along these lines. Farmers planted more corn, wheat, peanuts, vegetables, and fruits. There was industrial growth in lumbering, mining, tobacco processing, and steel production. Cotton textiles became a big business, too. For this industry, the South, of course, had the raw materials. It also offered cheap labor, low taxes, and abundant waterpower. To take advantage of these features, many New England textile mills moved to the South.

Southern leaders felt that these agricultural and industrial developments had created a "New South." Henry Grady, a prominent newspaper editor in Georgia, praised his region as "thrilling with new life." But the South still lagged behind other regions of the country economically and industrially. In fact, the South actually had a smaller percentage of the nation's factories in 1900 than it had had in 1860.

One nagging problem for the South was its agricultural system. After the Civil War, most big plantations were divided into small farms, which were, in turn, rented to landless farmers. The majority of tenants who worked these farms lacked the cash to rent the land, housing, and barns, or to buy seeds and tools. They therefore paid for these things with a share of the crop. (This practice earned them the name sharecroppers.)

Landowners wanted crops that would bring them the highest profit. Since cotton met this need, dependence on a single crop persisted in the South. But cotton soon wore out the soil unless it was rotated with other crops. In the rush for profits, crop rotation was not practiced. As a result, the land yielded less and less. Sharecroppers could rarely pay off their debts and have enough left to live on. They depended on loans to survive. But since they always owed money to someone, they were not free to leave the land and try something else.

Racial Discrimination

During reconstruction, the federal government had taken steps to protect the rights of Southern black people, especially their right to vote. With the end of reconstruction in 1877, there had been an unspoken agreement that the federal government would interfere less in Southern affairs. President Hayes spoke of the benefits that would result if Southern whites were "let alone by the general [national] government."

These benefits did not apply equally to whites and blacks. Economically, black people—most of them poor sharecroppers—were at the bottom of the scale. They were also second-class citizens socially and politically.

JIM CROW LAWS Measures such as the 1866 Civil Rights Act and the Fourteenth Amendment did little to alter racism in the South (and North). After reconstruction, Southern states were determined to keep African Americans "in their place"—subordinate to whites. They passed laws to maintain segregation, or separation of the races. These were called "Jim Crow" laws after a character in a popular minstrel song.

The first Jim Crow laws were passed in the 1870s. They eventually

W.J. BRYAN

Populist and Democratic
candidate, 1896

Western Farm

imposed segregation in almost every social situation. Marriage between blacks and whites was forbidden. Laws required separate schools, hospital facilities, and railroad accommodations for each race. Segregation was also the rule in hotels, restaurants, parks, theaters, and cemeteries. Courtroom officials even had to use separate Bibles to swear in witnesses.

African Americans protested this discrimination, but the courts ruled against them. In 1883, in the five so-called "Civil Rights cases," the Supreme Court ruled that the Fourteenth Amendment protected people against discrimination by states, but not by individuals. This meant that the federal government could not intervene if a theater owner, for instance, made black patrons sit in the balcony. A landmark decision of 1896, *Plessy* v. *Ferguson*, went even further. At issue was a state law that required separate accommodations for blacks on railroads. The Supreme Court ruled that segregated facilities were legal if they were equal in quality. This ruling became known as the "separate but equal" doctrine. In reality, facilities for blacks were almost always inferior to those for whites. But there was to be no effective legal challenge to the Jim Crow laws for a long time.

DISFRANCHISEMENT   Just as Jim Crow laws deprived black people of social equality, other steps were taken to limit their political rights. This limitation had not seemed necessary when reconstruction first came to an end. Most white Southerners were willing to allow blacks to vote, as long as they voted in support of white interests. The black vote was controlled mainly through the economic power of white landlords over their sharecroppers. Force was also used at times.

By the 1890s, Southern whites felt less confident. There was a good deal of rural discontent at this time (see page 324). Discontented black men threatened to vote in their own interests, thus posing a challenge to white supremacy. So the South set out to disfranchise blacks altogether—that is, to strip them of the franchise (vote).

States used a number of methods to bypass the Fifteenth Amendment, which guaranteed all citizens the right to vote. Some localities imposed heavy poll taxes or set high property qualifications. Others required difficult literacy tests—memorizing or explaining the state constitution, for instance.

Such measures, however, did not always work, because they kept many whites from voting, too. A number of states, therefore, resorted to the so-called "grandfather clause." This provision canceled other voting restrictions if the voter, his father, or his grandfather had been eligible to vote in 1867. Since Southern blacks did not have the franchise then, only whites could make use of this clause.

Statistics from Louisiana show how effective these policies were. Before the state adopted a grandfather clause, 130,344 blacks had been registered to vote. Two years later, the number had been reduced to 5320.

REFORMS AND CONTROVERSIAL ISSUES

Political leaders in the late 1800s were not very interested in reform. But some changes did occur, mostly because of pressure from the public.

Civil Service Reform

The spoils system of rewarding faithful party members had been in effect since the early 19th century. After the Civil War, it came under heavy attack. Government had become increasingly complex, requiring more and more workers with special skills. Reformers argued that government jobs should be awarded on the basis of merit, rather than political connections. They wanted a civil service—a system of hiring government employees by means of competitive examinations.

HAYES   President Hayes had pledged his support for a civil service when he was inaugurated. He appointed a leading reformer, Carl Schurz, as his secretary of the interior. Schurz filled jobs in his department on a merit basis, and so did some other cabinet officers. The Hayes administration also began a reform of the New York City customhouse. This agency, which collected import duties, was controlled by machine politicians and was a hotbed of political corruption. In addition, Hayes issued an executive order—widely ignored—forbidding federal officeholders from taking part in political activities.

GARFIELD AND ARTHUR   In the election of 1880, the Republican winners represented two factions of the party. President James A. Garfield was a so-called "Half-Breed," while Vice President Chester A. Arthur belonged to the "Stalwart" wing. There was little difference between the two groups, although the Half-Breeds claimed to be interested in reform.

Garfield was in favor of a civil service, but he was fatally shot after four months in office. His assassin, Charles Guiteau, was a mentally deranged Stalwart who had failed to obtain a government job in the new administration.

None of the reformers expected much from Arthur. As a New York custom official, he had been fired during the Hayes administration cleanup. But Arthur was outraged by the attack on Garfield and responded to public outcry by pushing for change. In 1883, Congress passed the *Pendleton Act*. It had three main provisions:

1. Competitive examinations were to be used to hire workers for certain government jobs that were placed on a classified civil service list.
2. A Civil Service Commission was created to draw up and give the examinations.
3. Dismissal of federal employees for political reasons was forbidden.

Only about 10 percent of the existing federal jobs were covered by the Pendleton Act, but more were added in the years that followed. By 1900, about 40 percent of federal jobs were filled on the basis of competitive tests.

Tariffs

The tariff had been an emotional issue since the Age of Jackson. Northern manufacturers favored high tariffs to protect American industry from foreign competition. Southerners, who imported many goods from abroad, wanted lower tariffs. During the Civil War, when the Southern states were not represented in Congress, the legislature adopted the highest tariff up to that time.

For the next 40 years, the government followed a policy of protectionism—maintaining high protective tariffs. The policy suited American business interests, which were very powerful at the time. Protectionism was also favored by both political parties, although Republicans supported it more vigorously than the Democrats did. Protective tariffs meant that ordinary citizens had to pay higher prices for both domestic and imported goods. But workers were persuaded that a ban on cheap foreign imports kept their wages up.

President Grover Cleveland, the Democratic winner of the election of 1884, wanted a more moderate tariff. His main reason was a surplus in the federal treasury. This not only kept money out of circulation but also tempted congressmen to appropriate funds for pet projects. Cleveland was a stubborn man of principle, but he could not get a tariff reform bill through Congress. The tariff issue became the deciding factor in the next presidential election.

In 1888, Cleveland ran against Republican Benjamin Harrison, the grandson of the ninth president, William Henry Harrison. Harrison, a high-tariff supporter, won the election. Two years later, Congress passed the *McKinley Tariff*, which raised import duties to a new high. These rates drove up the cost of manufactured goods, and consumers protested. In the 1892 election, Cleveland defeated Harrison, largely because of the unpopular tariff. (Cleveland became the only president to serve two interrupted terms.) Again, he tried to lower tariffs. But the bill that Congress passed—the *Wilson-Gorman Tariff* of 1894—reduced rates only slightly. Protectionism continued to prevail.

Business Regulation

Meanwhile, the government turned its attention to the massive power of big business. This issue had been troubling some Americans for years. Unhappy farmers spurred the government to action.

THE GRANGE AND THE RAILROADS   Because farm output expanded greatly after 1865, prices of farm produce fell. At the same time, the cost of manufactured goods and machinery remained high. Farmers also had to pay high fees to the owners of grain-storage elevators, to the dealers who marketed their crops, and to the railroads that shipped them. Lacking cash, farmers borrowed heavily and mortgaged their farms. When they failed to meet high interest payments, many lost their land.

Farmers who wanted to make their voices heard joined a national farmers' organization. It was known officially as the Patrons of Husbandry but was usually called the Grange, and its members were known as Grangers. The society, founded in 1867 by Oliver H. Kelley, spread rapidly, particularly in the upper Mississippi Valley. By 1875, there were more than 20,000 local lodges, and the total membership exceeded 800,000.

The original aim of the Grange was to bring farm families together for social and cultural activities. But it soon became concerned with other matters. To help its members economically, the Grange founded cooperatives. (A cooperative, or co-op, is a business owned and operated by those who benefit from its services.) These groups marketed produce, stored grain, bought supplies and equipment, and manufactured machinery. The cooperatives failed because big business opposed them and the farmers lacked management skills and adequate capital.

The Grange attempts to alert an indifferent public to the threat of railroad monopolies.

The Grangers also involved themselves in politics. They did so in order to fight abuses by the railroads. In the late 19th century, farmers and other small shippers of freight endured great hardship because railroads charged very high rates. In most cases, the rates were higher for short hauls in areas not served by other lines than for long hauls in competitive territory. The railroads also commonly granted rebates (refunds) to large shippers.

In Illinois and several other Midwestern states, the Grangers influenced legislatures to pass laws regulating railroad freight rates. The constitutionality of the so-called "Granger Laws" was then questioned. The Supreme Court upheld the laws in 1877 (*Munn* v. *Illinois*) and then reversed itself in 1886 (the Wabash Railroad case). In the later decision, the Court held that only the federal government, not the states, could regulate interstate commerce.

Farm groups then turned to the federal government for help.

Congress responded in 1887 by passing the *Interstate Commerce Act*. It provided that railroad rates should be "reasonable and just." It prohibited such practices as rebates and differing rates for short and long hauls. It also created the Interstate Commerce Commission, the nation's first regulatory agency, to carry out the provisions of the law. The Interstate Commerce Act had little effect at the time because the railroads found several ways to get around it. But it was on the books and would in time become more effective.

AN ANTITRUST LAW   The trusts that controlled many industries worried a growing number of Americans. How could competition, the lifeblood of free enterprise, continue to exist in the face of monopolies?

Both political parties officially favored some regulation of trusts. As in the case of railroad reform, individual states tried to act, but without much success. Since monopolies operated interstate, it became apparent that only the federal government had the power to restrain them.

In 1890, Congress passed the *Sherman Antitrust Act*. It made illegal every "combination in the form of trust . . . in restraint of trade or commerce." But the Sherman Act, like the Interstate Commerce Act, had little effect at first. Presidents at that time were not interested in enforcing the act. And businesses easily found loopholes in it because its wording was so vague. (In the last decade of the 19th century, the act was used mainly as a weapon against labor unions.)

THE POPULIST MOVEMENT

In the late 1870s, the Grange lost members and influence. One reason was the failure of its co-ops. Another was a rise in farm prices, which made farmers less eager to take joint action. But their troubles were not over.

Early Success

In the 1880s, farm prices fell once again. By the end of the decade, corn sold for so little that farmers used it for fuel instead of marketing it. Seeking ways to help themselves, they began to form large regional organizations. The National Farmers' Alliance consisted of farmers in the Midwest and the Great Plains. The Southern Alliance served the South's white farmers, and the Colored Farmers' Alliance, its black farmers. By 1890, the three groups claimed a combined membership of about 2 million.

Like the Grange, the Farmers' Alliances started out by providing social and educational programs for their members, but soon began to call for political and economic reforms. In 1890, the alliances succeeded in electing a number of their supporters to state legislatures and to Congress. Thus encouraged, the alliances decided to combine with various labor groups and form a new political party.

In 1892, representatives met at Omaha, Nebraska, and organized the *People's party*, more commonly known as the *Populist party*. (*Populus* is the Latin word for "people.") The party had a number of colorful leaders. They included Ignatius Donnelly of Minnesota, Tom Watson of Georgia, and "Sockless" Jerry Simpson of Kansas, who was also known as the "Socrates of the Prairies." Another prominent Populist was Mary Elizabeth Lease. Her fiery speeches against the "moneyed interests" led her critics to nickname her "the Kansas Pythoness."

The Populist platform called for (1) free coinage of silver; (2) an increase in the amount of money in circulation; (3) a graduated income tax—that is, an income tax that would tax large incomes at progressively higher rates; (4) savings bank facilities at post offices; (5) public ownership and operation of transportation and communication services; (6) election of U.S. senators by popular vote; (7) a one-term limit for presidents; (8) such political reforms as the secret ballot; (9) restrictions on immigration; and (10) a shorter working day.

In the election of 1892, the Populist candidate for president was James B. Weaver. Although he came in third, he received the impressive total of more than 1 million popular votes and 22 electoral votes. A severe business decline the following year increased people's discontent and, thus, strengthened the Populist movement.

The Money Question

The first two Populist demands—free coinage of silver and more money in circulation—concerned money issues that were of great concern in the late 1800s. The United States was undergoing a period of deflation (constantly falling prices). This was particularly hard on farmers and other people with debts, because they had to pay back their loans with money that was worth more than the money they had borrowed earlier. Debtors urged a policy that would bring about inflation (constantly rising prices). If the value of money fell, they would find it easier to repay what they owed.

One way inflation comes about is by an increase in the money supply. So farmers wanted the government to issue more money, and they wanted it backed by silver. For a long time, the government had bought both silver and gold to back its paper currency. But in 1873, the buying of silver stopped. Then, new finds in Western mines led to a surplus of the precious metal. In response to pressure from farmers and mine owners, Congress passed the *Bland-Allison Act* (1878) and the *Sherman Silver Purchase Act* (1890). These laws required the government to buy and coin a limited amount of silver each month. Proponents of silver were still not satisfied, however. They complained that the money supply had not increased enough to spur inflation, and they called for a further expansion of silver coinage. In the phrase of the time, they demanded free silver.

At first, free silver was only one of many planks in the Populist platform. But it quickly became one of the most important because it attracted members of other political parties.

THE ELECTION OF 1896

The early 1890s were a troubled period in American history. Soon after Cleveland began his second term, the financial panic of 1893 shook the country. It was followed by a depression. Hundreds of businesses and banks failed, and thousands of people lost their jobs.

There were many signs of unrest. Early in 1894, an Ohio businessman named Jacob S. Coxey led an "army" of some 500 unemployed men to Washington. They demanded that the government help the jobless by sponsoring public works projects—roads, bridges, and other facilities to benefit the public. But the protesters won no support, and Coxey was arrested (for walking on the grass). Also in that year, the Pullman strike pitted union labor against management and government.

The money issue was pressing, too. Like other conservatives of the day, Cleveland was a firm believer in the gold standard (gold as the only backing for paper money). He believed that the panic of 1893 had been caused by the Sherman Silver Purchase Act, and he persuaded Congress to repeal it. But the depression continued, and the treasury's supply of gold decreased. In 1895, the government had to turn to J. P. Morgan and other private bankers for help. When they bought gold abroad to add to the government's supply, Populists and others accused Cleveland of selling out to Wall Street.

Many Americans now viewed the nation's economic health almost entirely in terms of its currency. People were sharply divided. For the "cheap money" supporters, free silver was the only answer. The "sound money" people were equally certain that the gold standard had to prevail.

The Conventions

The election of 1896 aroused much interest. The Republicans met in June and nominated William McKinley, governor of Ohio, for president. Their platform strongly supported business interests and the gold standard.

The Democrats met in July. They were divided into free-silver and "goldbug" factions. On the second day of the convention, delegates were electrified by a former congressman from Nebraska named William Jennings Bryan. His rousing speech in support of free silver brought his audience to its feet. The next day, the convention nominated him for president. Several goldbugs stormed out.

We will answer their demand for a gold standard by saying to them: You shall not press down upon the brow of labor this crown of thorns, you shall not crucify mankind upon a cross of gold.

—*William Jennings Bryan at the Democratic national convention, July 1896*

The Populists were faced with a difficult choice. Should they support the Democratic candidates or nominate their own? The Democratic platform advocated free silver, but it ignored many other reforms that the Populists wanted. Finally, they decided to support Bryan, but they put him on their own ticket with a Populist vice presidential candidate.

The Campaign

The election campaign of 1896 was the first in a long time to offer a choice between two quite different points of view. McKinley stood for respectability and laissez-faire capitalism. His campaign manager, Ohio businessman-politician Mark Hanna, successfully organized the support of business leaders and industrialists. McKinley himself conducted a quiet "front-porch" campaign, addressing groups of visitors from his home in Canton, Ohio.

Bryan was the first presidential candidate to tour the whole United States. In ringing phrases, he championed the cause of the "toiling masses" against big business. He promised that a free-silver policy would bring back good times. To many Americans, Bryan—allied as he was with the Populists—seemed to represent disorder and upheaval. His opponents denounced him as a revolutionist. They predicted that economic chaos would result if he were elected.

McKinley won by a sizable margin, the biggest in 20 years. Although Bryan carried the South and most of the West, he failed to gain the support of the industrialized Midwest and Northeast. In these states, many Democrats crossed party lines to vote for McKinley. Bryan's defeat marked the virtual end of the free-silver issue and Populism.

True-False Test

1. Congress was widely respected in the late 19th century.
2. All but one of the presidents in the last three decades of the 19th century were Republicans.
3. National elections after the Civil War brought out less than half of the eligible voters.
4. The purpose of Jim Crow laws was to introduce and maintain segregation.
5. Grandfather clauses were used to disfranchise Southern white voters.
6. Civil service reformers wanted to abolish the spoils system.
7. The aim of protectionism was to encourage the growth of American industry.
8. The Patrons of Husbandry was the official name of the Populist party.
9. William McKinley believed that free silver would bring back prosperity.
10. The election of 1896 resulted in a Republican victory.

Multiple-Choice Test

1. In the late 19th century, the executive branch of the government was (a) stronger than the legislative (b) about equal to Congress in power (c) weaker than Congress (d) constantly trying to regain its earlier authority.
2. The swing states to which political parties appealed after the Civil War were in the (a) Northeast (b) South (c) plains (d) Midwest and Middle Atlantic regions.
3. All of the following were aims of white Southerners after the Civil War *except* (a) protecting the civil rights of blacks (b) industrializing (c) growing more kinds of crops (d) becoming less dependent on cotton.
4. The Pendleton Act was passed during the administration of (a) Ulysses S. Grant (b) Rutherford B. Hayes (c) James A. Garfield (d) Chester A. Arthur.
5. The main issue in the presidential campaign of 1888 was (a) civil service (b) the tariff (c) regulating the railroads (d) restricting immigration.
6. Farmers in the late 19th century were disturbed by all of the following *except* (a) inflation (b) railroad freight charges (c) high interest rates (d) loss of their farms.
7. The Grange was strongest in the (a) South (b) Northeast (c) Rocky Mountain states (d) Midwest.

8. The desire to regulate railroads led to the   (a) McKinley Tariff
   (b) Sherman Antitrust Act   (c) Interstate Commerce Act   (d)
   Bland-Allison Act.
9. All of the following were planks in the 1892 Populist platform
   except   (a)   more money in circulation   (b) a gold standard   (c)
   public ownership of railroads   (d) a four-year limit on presidential
   terms.
10. The main campaign issue in the presidential election of 1896 was
    (a) free silver   (b) the Interstate Commerce Act   (c) the Pullman
    strike   (d) Coxey's army.

Essay Questions

1. What is a laissez-faire policy? What attempts were made to modify it in
   the United States late in the 19th century?
2. Describe the sharecropping system. How did it affect the South?
3. How and why did the Southern states restrict the rights of blacks after
   the Civil War?
4. Who wanted high tariffs in the period after the Civil War? Why?
5. Who wanted inflation in the period after the Civil War? Why? How
   did they try to achieve it?

UNIT 7

Emergence as
a World
Power

CHAPTER 22

Overseas Expansion

Eᴠᴇʀ sɪɴᴄᴇ ᴇᴀʀʟʏ colonial times, Americans had been pushing westward into new territories. After crossing the Allegheny Mountains and the Mississippi Valley, they reached the Pacific in the 1840s. Then, they filled in the last frontier—the Great Plains and the Rocky Mountain region. By the late 19th century, Americans began to show interest in lands beyond their borders.

ACQUIRING NEW TERRITORIES

The first new land acquired after the Civil War was Alaska. It had belonged to the Russians since 1741. They had developed a busy fur trade there but had not colonized the territory to any great extent. Since the Russians found Alaska of little value and feared that Great Britain might seize it in case of war, they offered to sell it to the United States. The purchase was arranged in 1867 for $7.2 million by Secretary of State William H. Seward.

Alaska was huge—one-fifth the size of the rest of the United States. And it had few inhabitants. Many Americans considered the region worthless, calling it "Seward's Folly" and "Seward's Icebox." As an expansionist, Seward was ahead of his time. The majority of Americans in the late 1860s were not interested in gaining faraway territories.

Increased Interest in Expansion

Toward the close of the 19th century, American views on overseas expansion underwent a change. Some of the reasons were economic. As the output of American factories increased, industrialists wanted to export their products to new markets abroad. They also needed to import such raw materials as rubber and tin, which were unavailable at home. Business people wished to take advantage of investment opportunities overseas. And farmers sought foreign markets as outlets for their surplus crops. An Indiana senator, Albert J. Beveridge, put it this way: "American factories are making more than the American people can use; American soil is producing more than they can consume. Fate has written our policy for us; the trade of the world must and shall be ours."

There were also emotional reasons for expansion. To many Americans, an overseas empire provided proof that a nation was a world power. In the 1870s, Britain, France, and other European nations had begun to scramble for territory and influence in Africa and Asia. Why, these Americans asked, shouldn't the United States become an empire-builder, too? (The practice of acquiring foreign territories, or of gaining political or economic control over such areas, is called imperialism.)

One of the most influential advocates of American imperialism was Alfred Thayer Mahan, a naval officer and historian. His book *The Influence of Sea Power Upon History, 1660–1783* was published in 1890 and attracted a wide audience. Mahan said that sea power was the key to the rise of all great nations. In his view, the mark of a great nation was not only a powerful navy but also colonial possessions, overseas bases, and coaling stations, where steamships could refuel.

Hawaii

An overseas area that attracted American attention in the early 19th century was Hawaii. Starting in 1820, missionaries began to arrive there to teach Christianity, establish schools, and train native teachers. In addition, American merchant ships en route to China stopped at the islands for supplies. Fishing vessels used Hawaii as headquarters for whaling operations as well. Later, other Americans—many of them descendants of the missionaries—developed sugar and pineapple plantations there. And in 1887, the United States obtained the right to establish a naval base at Pearl Harbor.

By the late 1800s, two-thirds of Hawaii was under American control. In 1891, a new ruler, Queen Liliuokalani, assumed power and began to take steps to reduce American influence in the islands. In response, American planters, led by Sanford Dole, staged a revolt, overthrew the queen, and set up a new government in 1893. Their request for annexation by the United States encountered resistance at first. But annexation was finally approved by Congress in 1898.

Other Pacific Outposts

During this period, Americans also gained control over other Pacific islands, some 50 in all. Midway, 1100 miles west of Hawaii, was occupied by U.S. troops in 1867.

In the 1870s, the United States firmly established its interest in Samoa, an island group southwest of Hawaii. An 1878 treaty granted U.S. ships the right to use the harbor of Pago Pago, on the island of Tutuila, as a coaling station. At the same time, Britain and Germany were also seeking footholds in these islands. After several years of tension, the three nations reached an agreement in 1899. Britain withdrew its claims, in exchange for concessions elsewhere. The United States and Germany then divided the islands between them.

THE SPANISH-AMERICAN WAR

A turning point in the expansionism of the United States was a war with Spain in 1898. The conflict began over Cuba but soon involved other territories as well.

Trouble in Cuba

By the 1890s, Spain had only two possessions in America—Puerto Rico and Cuba. The people of Cuba had been dissatisfied for a long time with Spanish rule, which was corrupt and harsh. In 1895, the Cubans revolted, and the struggle between them and the Spaniards became bitter and violent.

The Cubans had rebelled earlier in the 19th century, too. At that time, the United States had shown little interest. Now, the situation was different, for at least two reasons. One was the fact that the United States was eager to show its strength as a world power. Another reason was the publicity given the rebellion by newspaper giants such as Joseph Pulitzer and William Randolph Hearst. To boost circulation, they filled their pages with tales of Spanish atrocities in Cuba. Some of these accounts were accurate, but many others were exaggerated or untrue.

At first, American sentiment favored action short of war. President Cleveland strongly supported neutrality. But two events during McKinley's administration made Americans fighting mad. Both occurred in February 1898. First, a secret letter was published in Hearst's *New York Journal*. It had been written by a Spanish diplomat in Washington and described McKinley as a weak president and a "would-be politician."

Commodore Dewey

Then, about a week later, the U.S. battleship *Maine* was sunk in the harbor of Havana, Cuba, after a mysterious explosion. The ship had sailed to Cuba to protect American lives and property there. The American public was quick to blame Spain for the disaster. (To this day, no one knows who sank the *Maine*.)

"Remember the *Maine!*" became the slogan of the day, as Congress and the public clamored for war. Although McKinley personally opposed such a move, he responded to the outcry by asking Congress to approve American intervention in Cuba. On April 20, Congress adopted a resolution recognizing the independence of Cuba, and authorizing the president to use force to drive the Spaniards from the island. A few days later, both Spain and the United States issued formal declarations of war against each other.

Conflict in Two Hemispheres

The Spanish-American War was brief and decisive. Although both sides were equally unprepared to fight a land war, the United States had a distinct advantage at sea. Its navy was modern, well equipped, and staffed by highly trained crews. Since the key battles of the war were naval engagements, and the Spaniards were unable to match the Americans in sea power, Spain was easily defeated.

THE PACIFIC   The first fighting took place halfway around the world from Cuba. George Dewey, commander of the American navy in the Pacific, had been ordered to attack Spain's naval forces in the Philippines in case of war. Immediately after war was declared, he headed for Manila Bay, where a Spanish fleet was stationed. On May 1, Dewey's squadron destroyed or captured all the Spanish ships and blockaded the city of Manila. After the arrival of American troops in the summer, Manila fell and the Spanish land forces in the Philippines surrendered.

You may fire when you are ready, Gridley.

—*Commodore Dewey to the captain of his flagship*
at Manila Bay, May 1898

THE CARIBBEAN Meanwhile, the action had shifted closer to the United States. In mid-May, a Spanish fleet, eluding the American navy, anchored in the Cuban harbor of Santiago. It was immediately blockaded by a U.S. naval squadron.

U.S. troops landed in Cuba in June and marched on the city of Santiago. By early July, they had captured the village of El Caney and San Juan Hill, two strategic heights overlooking the city. The Battle of San Juan Hill was noted for the exploits of a young New Yorker named Theodore Roosevelt. The Rough Riders—a volunteer cavalry regiment that he had organized and led—distinguished themselves in the engagement and won national publicity.

During the American siege of Santiago, the Spanish fleet tried to break the blockade and escape from the harbor. In the sea battle that followed, the entire Spanish fleet was destroyed. Santiago surrendered, and Spanish resistance in Cuba collapsed.

At about the same time, another U.S. force invaded Puerto Rico. The troops met with little opposition and soon occupied the island. The conflict ended in August, when Spain asked for peace.

Don't cheer, men; the poor fellows are dying.

—*naval officer John W. Philip, rebuking sailors as a*
Spanish ship went down off Cuba, July 1898

Results of the War

The Spanish-American War cost the United States some $250 million and about 5000 lives. (More than 90 percent of American fatalities were due to disease and food poisoning.) But in return, the United States gained a colonial empire of 120,000 square miles, with more than 8 million inhabitants. No wonder one American politician called the conflict "a splendid little war."

The peace treaty, signed in December 1898, provided for the independence of Cuba. The United States gained Puerto Rico and the

U.S. TERRITORIAL ACQUISITIONS (1867–1917)

Date	Area	How Acquired
1867	Alaska	Purchase from Russia
1867	Midway	Annexation
1898	Hawaii	Annexation after backing revolution of 1893
1898	Puerto Rico	Treaty ending Spanish-American War
1898	Philippines	Treaty ending Spanish-American War
1898	Guam	Treaty ending Spanish-American War
1899	American Samoa	Treaty with Germany and Britain
1899	Wake Island	Annexation
1917	(American) Virgin Islands	Purchase from Denmark

small Pacific island of Guam. Spain was reluctant to cede the Philippines but agreed to do so when the United States offered $20 million in payment.

EXTENDING AMERICAN POWER

American expansionists were pleased with their growing colonial empire. But it led to problems. The nation had to increase its military spending and become more involved in foreign affairs. It also had to find ways of dealing justly with colonial peoples, many of them with very different cultures.

The Philippines

An immediate difficulty was the Philippines. When the war ended, some Americans opposed the idea of taking possession of the islands. The Senate debated the peace treaty for several weeks. Opponents of imperialism argued that American rule over others was not in the nation's democratic tradition. They also pointed out that it would be foolish to assume responsibility for a foreign people living 7000 miles from San Francisco. Expansionists stressed the economic and strategic importance of the Philippines to the United States. McKinley supported the expansionist position by declaring that Americans had a duty to "educate the Filipinos, and uplift and civilize and Christianize them." The expansionists won, and the Senate ratified the treaty.

Many Filipinos resented U.S. occupation of their country. They had expected to be independent after Spain was defeated. Now, they were to be ruled by another foreign power. Early in 1899, Filipinos led by Emilio Aguinaldo began a campaign of guerrilla warfare, with small bands of fighters making surprise raids. American forces fought the guerrillas for three years before suppressing the rebellion. More than 7000 U.S. troops and 20,000 Filipinos were killed in the fighting.

The Philippines were ruled by the United States until the 1940s. William Howard Taft served as the first governor, from 1901 to 1904.

China

After acquiring the Philippines, the United States became much more involved in Asian affairs than it had been earlier. The new problems the United States encountered also brought it into closer contact with European nations, since many of them had interests in Asia, too.

SPHERES OF INFLUENCE   The ancient country of China had long tried to keep foreign influence at a minimum. China resisted modernization and industrialization. By the late 19th century, however, the country had little military power to back up its policy of isolation. China was helpless to resist the inroads of the great powers—among them Britain, France, Germany, Russia, and Japan. All these countries were carving out their own spheres of influence—areas where they could dominate trade and economic resources. It seemed likely that China would soon be completely overrun by foreign imperialists.

OPEN DOOR POLICY   The United States had interests in China, too. Since colonial times, American merchants had carried on a brisk trade with the Chinese. American business leaders now hoped to expand their profitable activities in the Far East. But they were at a disadvantage in areas where foreigners had special commercial privileges.

To protect American interests, Secretary of State John Hay made a proposal in 1899 to six of the great powers. He asked them to agree to an *Open Door Policy* in China. What he meant was that all nations should have equal trading rights in the various spheres of influence. The replies to Hay were evasive, but he decided to treat the great powers' lack of opposition as support. In 1900, Hay announced that all the leading powers had accepted the Open Door Policy.

BOXER REBELLION   China did not remain as passive as the foreign powers would have liked. In 1900, a group of Chinese patriots called the Boxers organized a revolt. Their purpose was to drive out the "foreign devils" who were overrunning China. The Boxers killed more than 200 foreigners, destroyed foreign property, and laid siege to foreign settlements in the capital city of Peking (Beijing). The great powers then raised an international army to rescue their people and put down the Boxer Rebellion. The army included some 2500 Americans.

The United States feared that the other powers would use the rebellion as an excuse to seize more Chinese territory. Hay stated that the United States opposed the creation of further spheres of influence in China. Instead, he said, the Open Door Policy should be extended to cover the whole country. The other powers agreed. But first, they forced China to pay a large indemnity (fine) for foreign losses during the rebellion. The United States returned a large part of its share of the indemnity to China, which used the money to aid Chinese students at American colleges.

Japan

Like the Chinese, the Japanese had kept foreigners out of their country for centuries. The United States succeeded in opening Japan to Western trade by sending a naval expedition, led by Matthew C. Perry, to Tokyo. Perry arranged a treaty of friendship with the Japanese emperor in 1854.

Unlike the Chinese, the Japanese decided to modernize their country. They carried out a program of industrialization and built a strong army and navy. Japan displayed its importance as a world power by defeating China in the Sino-Japanese war of 1894–1895. With this victory, Japan gained the island of Formosa (Taiwan) and a sphere of influence in Korea. Japan annexed Korea in 1910.

Japan's defeat of China was impressive enough. Even more so was its victory over Russia—a Western power—in the Russo-Japanese War of 1904–1905. Japan then asked the American president, Theodore Roosevelt, to help negotiate a peace treaty. (Roosevelt had been elected as McKinley's vice president in 1900. He became president the following year, when McKinley was assassinated.)

Roosevelt won a Nobel Peace Prize for his work in arranging the *Treaty of Portsmouth* (New Hampshire). But the United States gained only the ill will of both sides. The Japanese thought that Roosevelt had kept them from getting some of their demands; the Russians accused him of favoring the Japanese.

Intervention in Latin America

After the Spanish-American War, the United States had greater responsibilities in Latin America, especially in the Caribbean area. At the beginning of the war, the United States had stated officially that

U.S. INVOLVEMENT IN THE CARIBBEAN REGION

(actions initiated 1902–1917)

Map Code	Date	Location	U.S. Action
①	1902	Venezuela	Warning to European powers to stop interference
②	1903	Panama	Support of revolution to gain independence from Colombia
③	1904	Canal Zone	Beginning of U.S. control over region
④	1905–1941	Dominican Republic	Supervision of finances
⑤	1905–1941	Haiti	Supervision of finances
⑥	1906–1909	Cuba	Military occupation to supervise voting reforms and election
⑦	1911–1914	Nicaragua	Supervision of finances
⑧	1912–1933	Nicaragua	Military occupation to maintain order
⑨	1913	Honduras	Landing of marines to protect U.S. property
⑩	1914	Mexico	Occupation of Veracruz to prevent unloading of foreign arms
⑪	1915–1934	Haiti	Military occupation to support U.S. protectorate
⑫	1916–1917	Mexico	Dispatch of troops to pursue Pancho Villa
⑬	1916–1924	Dominican Republic	Military occupation to maintain peace
⑭	1917–1922	Cuba	Military occupation to end revolt and maintain peace

it would withdraw from Cuba when independence was won. U.S. military forces, however, occupied the island until 1902. Cuba then became a republic, but its independence was limited by the Platt Amendment to the new Cuban constitution. This amendment authorized the United States to establish naval bases in Cuba. It also gave the United States the right to take action if Cuban law and order or independence were threatened. In the next 20 years, the United States intervened in Cuban affairs twice.

When Puerto Rico was ceded to the United States, the island was at first placed under military rule. It became an unorganized U.S. ter-

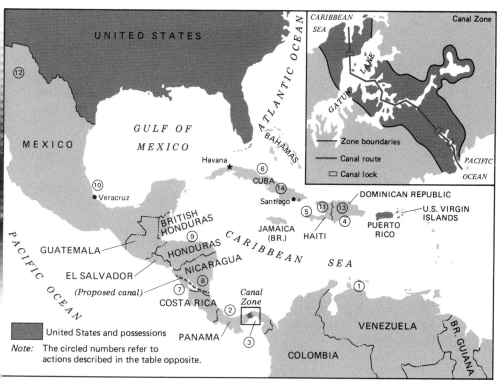

U.S. INVOLVEMENT IN THE CARIBBEAN REGION

ritory by the terms of the *Foraker Act* of 1900. This law authorized the president to appoint a civilian governor and an upper legislative house. The law also created a lower house, elected by the people of Puerto Rico.

Seventeen years later, the *Jones Act* (1) granted Puerto Ricans U.S. citizenship, (2) made the upper house of the legislature an elective body, and (3) changed the island's status to that of an organized territory of the United States.

Events in Venezuela and the Dominican Republic led to further United States involvement in the Caribbean area. Venezuela, heavily in debt to European investors, was unable to meet its financial obligations. Seeking repayment, Britain, Germany, and Italy blockaded Venezuela in 1902, bombarded several of its ports, and sank some of its naval vessels. President Theodore Roosevelt took a strong stand against this European show of power. The matter was then settled by peaceful arbitration.

The possibility of further European interference still worried Roosevelt. In 1904 it seemed likely that the Dominican Republic, like

Venezuela, would be unable to pay its foreign debts. Roosevelt drew attention to the situation in his annual message to Congress. The United States, he said, might have to intervene in the Western Hemisphere "in flagrant cases of . . . wrongdoing or impotence" and exercise "an international police power." This announcement became known as the *Roosevelt Corollary* to the Monroe Doctrine. The United States did take over the management of Dominican finances in 1905. During the next three decades, the United States was closely involved in the internal affairs of several other Caribbean countries as well.

THE PANAMA CANAL

For a long time, there had been great interest in digging a canal across Central America to connect the Atlantic and Pacific oceans. In the 1870s, a private French company acquired the rights to build such a canal across Panama, a province of Colombia. Construction started in 1882, under the direction of Ferdinand de Lesseps. (He had already built the Suez Canal in Egypt.) After seven years, however, lack of funds and problems with tropical diseases brought work to a halt and failure to the company.

The United States stood to benefit greatly from a canal between the two oceans. It would shorten the water route from New York to San Francisco by 8000 miles. The usefulness of such a waterway was even more apparent after the United States became deeply involved overseas. During the Spanish-American War, one U.S. battleship, stationed in California, had to sail all the way around South America to reach the fighting in Cuba. This long voyage did much to convince the public of the need for a shortcut through Central America.

Acquiring the Canal Zone

In 1902, another French company, which had acquired the property and canal rights of the de Lesseps group, offered to sell these assets to the United States for $40 million. Congress authorized President Roosevelt to accept the offer, with one condition. Colombia had to agree to U.S. control of the region through which the canal passed. Such a treaty was negotiated in 1903. The United States agreed to pay Colombia $10 million in cash and $250,000 in yearly rent for a strip of land six miles wide across Panama. But then, the Colombian senate, hoping for better terms, refused to ratify the treaty. Angry at the delay, Roosevelt called the Colombians "inefficient bandits." The Panamanians were also annoyed. They wanted the canal to be built in Panama, and feared that the

United States might switch to another route across Nicaragua.

A group of Panamanians decided to revolt. They first obtained, off the record, an assurance that Roosevelt supported their plan. Then, they proclaimed their independence from Colombia. The revolution was successful largely because U.S. warships and marines, dispatched to the area by Roosevelt, prevented the entry of Colombian military forces into Panama.

The United States quickly recognized the new republic and drew up the *Hay-Bunau-Varilla Treaty*. It granted the United States full and permanent control over a strip of land 10 miles wide, through which a canal would be built. In return, the United States guaranteed the independence of Panama and agreed to pay $10 million for the Canal Zone and an annual rent of $250,000. (This rent went up in later years.) In 1921, the United States also paid Colombia $25 million for the loss of its Panama province.

Building the Canal

The canal project was undertaken by army engineers under George W. Goethals. First, the area had to be rid of malaria and yellow fever. This task was assigned to William C. Gorgas, an army surgeon who had worked with Walter Reed in Cuba. (Reed had proved that yellow fever was carried by mosquitoes, and had supervised measures to eliminate their breeding places in Cuba.) Using Reed's methods, Gorgas was highly successful in fighting the tropical diseases of Panama.

Engineers then turned their attention to constructing a waterway across difficult terrain. They dammed the Chagres River to create Gatun Lake and blasted a channel through eight miles of volcanic rock. Then, they built three sets of locks. These "steps of water" raised and lowered ships sailing between the sea and Gatun Lake, which is 85 feet above sea level. It took more than 40,000 workers to complete the entire project, at a cost of some $335 million.

The 50-mile canal opened to traffic in 1914. The United States took charge of operating and defending the waterway and of administering the Canal Zone. Before long, the Panama Canal became one of the great crossroads of the world.

I took the canal zone and let Congress debate, and while the debate goes on, the canal does also.

—*Theodore Roosevelt after work started on the Panama Canal*

TEN NOTABLE TURN-OF-THE-CENTURY AMERICANS

LOUIS BRANDEIS (1856–1941) The first Jewish justice of the Supreme Court grew up in Louisville, Kentucky. As a Boston lawyer, he became noted for the "Brandeis brief"—an argument based on the expert testimony of sociologists and other nonlawyers. He was a judicial activist and generally supported antitrust legislation, the rights of organized labor, and New Deal economic reforms.

SAINT FRANCES XAVIER CABRINI (1850–1917) Mother Cabrini, born in Italy, was the first American citizen to be declared a saint by the Roman Catholic church. The pope sent her to the United States in 1880 to help Italian immigrants in the slums of New York. (She became a naturalized citizen some 30 years later.) The order she had founded, the Missionary Sisters of the Sacred Heart, eventually set up some 65 convents, orphanages, schools, and hospitals in North America, South America, and Europe.

GEORGE WASHINGTON CARVER (1861?–1943) Born a slave, he overcame many obstacles to gain science degrees from Iowa State University. From there, he went to Booker T. Washington's Tuskegee Institute, where he taught generations of students and directed experimental programs in agriculture. His programs, aimed at helping black farmers, made use of an innovative "school on wheels" that traveled through the countryside. He did much to make sweet potatoes and peanuts leading Southern crops, and is credited with developing some 325 uses for the peanut—as an ingredient in ink and synthetic rubber, for example.

MARY CASSATT (1844?–1926) America's first great woman painter, she was born to wealthy parents in Allegheny City, Pennsylvania. After moving to Paris in 1874, she developed her own distinctive style. She always painted the contemporary world she knew, specializing in unsentimental portraits of women and children. By advising American collectors, she helped introduce the work of the French impressionists to the United States.

CLARENCE DARROW (1857–1938) This Chicago trial lawyer began his career trying to gain amnesty for the defendants in the Haymarket bombing. He also defended numerous labor leaders, including Eugene Debs after the Pullman strike. A witty and outspoken debater, he was especially noted for introducing psychiatric evidence in murder cases, and for his confrontation with William Jennings Bryan in the Scopes trial of 1925.

JOHN DEWEY (1859–1952) One of the most important of American philosophers, he taught that ideas should be examined in terms of their practical consequences. He had an idealistic vision of the future, in which reason would liberate humankind from poverty and oppression. His belief in "learning by doing" had a strong influence on education, especially the schooling of young children.

WILLIAM DEAN HOWELLS (1837–1920) The man who dominated the American literary scene in the 1870s and 1880s attended neither college nor high school, but loved books. As an editor and author, he was said to have taken the nation's literary capital with him when he moved from Boston to New York City. His insistence on a realistic approach to literature—"that is the right American stuff"—encouraged younger writers, among them Stephen Crane and Hamlin Garland.

MARY HARRIS JONES (1830–1930)   Born in Ireland, she was living in Memphis with her husband and four children when her entire family died in a yellow fever epidemic. She then became interested in the Knights of Labor (her husband had been an ironworker), and soon turned to labor organizing. For decades, the courageous presence and fiery speeches of "Mother Jones" encouraged strikers from New York to Arizona. Although she was famous for mobilizing workers' wives in labor struggles, she opposed woman suffrage.

HENRIETTA SZOLD (1860–1945)   This rabbi's daughter, born in Baltimore, set up one of the nation's first schools to teach adult immigrant Jews about their new homeland. At an early age, she became interested in Zionism—the movement to re-establish a Jewish state in Palestine. In 1912, she helped found Hadassah, a women's Zionist group dedicated to medical work in Palestine. During the 1930s, she was active in bringing Jewish youths out of Nazi Germany to safety.

FREDERICK JACKSON TURNER (1861–1932)   Although he wrote little, this historian did a great deal to shape Americans' ideas about themselves. His most important work was an essay, "The Significance of the Frontier in American History" (1893). This work advanced the idea that many distinctively American qualities—democracy, individualism, nationalism—grew out of the presence of open land to the west. At the University of Wisconsin, and later at Harvard, Turner taught his many students to pursue history as a disciplined, scientific investigation of the past.

True-False Test

1. Alaska was the first new territory acquired by the United States after the Civil War.
2. In the 1890s, Americans led a revolt against the ruler of Hawaii and set up a new government.
3. A major cause of the Spanish-American War was an uprising on the island of Puerto Rico.
4. An investigation after the Spanish-American War revealed that Spanish patriots had blown up the battleship *Maine*.
5. After the Spanish-American War, Filipinos waged a guerrilla war against the United States.
6. The Open Door Policy provided that the United States would have its own sphere of influence in China.
7. Theodore Roosevelt won a Nobel Peace Prize for arranging the treaty that ended the Sino-Japanese War.
8. The Platt Amendment gave the United States the right to intervene in Cuba to protect Cuban independence.

9. The French had to stop work on a canal across Panama because they ran short of money.
10. The Panama Canal was constructed on land originally owned by Nicaragua.

Matching Test

Column A	Column B
1. William H. Seward	a. proposed Open Door Policy
2. Matthew C. Perry	b. argued that sea power was key to national greatness
3. Alfred T. Mahan	c. defeated Spanish fleet at Manila
4. Sanford Dole	d. negotiated purchase of Alaska
5. William McKinley	e. arranged treaty of friendship with Japan in 1854
6. George Dewey	f. served as first U.S. governor of Philippines
7. William Howard Taft	g. was president during Spanish-American War
8. John Hay	h. acquired land for building Panama Canal
9. Theodore Roosevelt	i. helped rid Panama of yellow fever
10. William C. Gorgas	j. led revolt of American planters in Hawaii

Essay Questions

1. Why did the United States become interested in expanding beyond its borders late in the 19th century?
2. Summarize the arguments for and against American acquisition of the Philippines after the Spanish-American War. Which side do you think was right? Why?
3. What was the Roosevelt Corollary? How did it come about?
4. What was the Open Door Policy? Why did the United States favor such a policy?
5. Why was the construction of a canal linking the Atlantic and Pacific oceans in the interests of the United States? What were some of the problems of building such a canal?

CHAPTER 23

The Progressive Era

POLITICAL LEADERSHIP from reconstruction until the turn of the century had been uninspired. But Theodore Roosevelt, who became president in 1901, brought new zest to the American scene. A strong and popular leader, he helped introduce many changes during his administration. From his time until the entry of the United States into World War I in 1917, a spirit of active reform dominated national politics. Other phases of American life, social and economic as well as political, were also affected. Those who sought change, and who were often successful in bringing it about, came to be known as Progressives. The years from 1901 to 1917 are frequently called the Progressive era.

VOICES OF PROTEST

Progressives did not form one single group. Like the reformers of the Jacksonian era, they were interested in a wide range of issues. Some of their concerns had to do with making politics more democratic. In this respect, they were like the Populists. But there were important differences. Most of the Populists had been rural Americans from Southern and Western states. They were chiefly concerned with the problems of farmers. The majority of Progressives were middle-class city dwellers from the Midwest and Northeast. And their interests were broader than those of the Populists.

The Muckrakers

Many of the conditions that the Progressives wanted to correct were brought to public attention by skillful reporters. Their findings were published in newspapers, magazines, and books. These reporters came to be called "muckrakers," a term coined by Roosevelt. He compared writers who made sensational attacks to "the Man with the Muckrake" in the book *Pilgrim's Progress*. This character was so busy cleaning up filth that he failed to see the heavenly crown suspended above him. Roosevelt meant the term to be critical, but crusading writers welcomed it.

One of the best-known muckrakers was Lincoln Steffens. He was editor of *McClure's Magazine*, which published many articles exposing public dishonesty and social evils. Steffens's descriptions of corruption in several cities were collected in *The Shame of the Cities* (1904). *McClure's* also printed the results of a full investigation of the Rockefeller oil trust and its cutthroat practices. Written by Ida Tarbell, these articles later appeared in book form as *The History of the Standard Oil Company* (1904). David Graham Phillips was another muckraker. In *The Treason of the Senate* (1906), he charged that most U.S. senators represented railroads and trusts, rather than the American people. John Spargo, in *The Bitter Cry of the Children* (1906), described the dreadful working conditions of child laborers.

Muckrakers also attacked living conditions in the slums, discrimination against black Americans, unsanitary practices in the meat-packing industry, and the excessive power of big business.

Feminists

By the turn of the century, the position of women had improved somewhat, compared to what it had been at the time of the Civil War. Laws to protect the property and earnings of married women were in effect in a number of states. About 20 percent of American women were in the labor force (although some earned as little as $6 a week). There were almost 130 women's colleges in the United States, and a fourth of the nation's college students were women.

Despite some progress, women were still second-class citizens in the critical area of suffrage (the right to vote). From the 1860s on, the main aim of feminists was to get the vote for women. The most prominent suffragists were Susan B. Anthony, Carrie Chapman Catt, and Anna Howard Shaw. In 1890, these leaders and others joined to form the National American Woman Suffrage Association. In the same year, Wyoming became the first state to provide for women's suffrage in its constitution. During the next three decades, similar steps were taken by several other states, most of them in the West. But these were local gains,

Woodrow Wilson   *"Teddy" Roosevelt*   *"Fighting Bob" La Follette*

and Progressives continued to press for the adoption of a constitutional amendment that would guarantee voting rights to women everywhere in the country.

African American Reformers

Several black American leaders rose to prominence during the Progressive era. One was Booker T. Washington, a former slave. He founded and headed Tuskegee Institute in Alabama. Washington advised black people to be patient and responsible laborers, even though their position in American society was humble. "No race can prosper," he said, "till it learns that there is as much dignity in tilling a field as in writing a poem."

Washington's approach was too conservative for another black leader, William E. B. Du Bois. Educated at Harvard University, he was a professor of economics and history at Atlanta University. Du Bois argued that black Americans should be neither content with menial jobs nor silent about unjust treatment. In 1905, he founded the Niagara Movement, the first organization of black Americans to protest racial discrimination. (The founding members met on the Canadian side of Niagara Falls because American hotels would not provide rooms for them.)

In all things that are purely social we can be as separate as the fingers, yet one as the hand in all things essential to mutual progress.

—*Booker T. Washington, Up From Slavery, 1901*

Three years later, a race riot broke out in Springfield, Illinois. Two blacks were lynched and four whites killed, but the ringleaders of the mob were never punished. This riot led to the formation, in 1909, of the *National Association for the Advancement of Colored People (NAACP)*. This group aimed to put an end to discrimination by means of legislation and court decisions. Another organization concerned with the rights of black people was the *National Urban League*. It was founded in 1910 to help black Americans get better jobs and housing, particularly in cities.

REFORMS AT CITY AND STATE LEVELS

One major goal of the Progressives was to eliminate corruption in local and state governments. Reformers introduced a number of changes that aimed to reduce the power of political machines and make elected leaders more responsible to the people. Very often, a reform adopted by one city or state quickly spread to other localities.

Cities

One of the best-known Progressive politicians was Samuel ("Golden Rule") Jones, mayor of Toledo, Ohio, from 1897 to 1904. He introduced civil service into the police department, set a minimum wage for city employees, built public parks and playgrounds in the city's poorer sections, and established kindergartens. Another outstanding local leader was Tom Johnson, mayor of Cleveland, Ohio, from 1901 to 1909. He conducted citizen meetings in a movable tent that held 5000 people. One of his aims was greater home rule—that is, independence from outside (in this case, state) control. As a result of his efforts, the state passed a law guaranteeing home rule to all Ohio towns.

Progressives backed two new types of city government. One was the commission plan. Under this plan, voters elect a small group of nonpartisan (politically unaffiliated) commissioners. Each one heads a government department. Together, they carry out both the executive and legislative duties of the city. In 1901, Galveston, Texas, became the first city to adopt this plan of government.

The other new form of city government was the city-manager plan. Under this system, the voters elect commissioners, who, in turn, hire a professional manager to run the city. The first city to introduce this plan was Staunton, Virginia, in 1908. By the end of the Progressive era, some 400 cities had adopted the commission plan, and about 50, the city-manager plan.

States

At the state level, Progressives were especially concerned about curbing the power of state legislatures. In many cases, these bodies did not defend citizens' interests. Their members, being poorly paid, were frequently bribed by big business and public utilities. Several Progressive reforms increased citizen participation. One was the direct primary, which allowed voters to select a party's candidates for office. (Formerly, candidates had been chosen by politicians at party conventions.) Minnesota became the first state to require a statewide direct primary, in 1901. In the next few years, most other states adopted it as well.

Another reform was the secret ballot. By voting in private, citizens could avoid being pressured by observers who wanted to influence them or buy their votes. The secret ballot had appeared as early as 1888. But only during the Progressive era did it gain widespread acceptance.

Three other political reforms also came into use at this time. One, the initiative, provides that the legislature must consider a proposed law if a certain percentage of voters sign a petition in favor of it. Another, the referendum, requires that a law or constitutional amendment passed by a legislature be submitted to voters for their approval. The first state to adopt the initiative and referendum was South Dakota, in 1898. A third reform, recall, permits voters to petition for, and vote upon, the removal of elected officials before their terms expire. In 1908, Oregon became the first state to adopt the recall.

In the early 20th century, Progressives helped elect many reformers as state governors. One of them was Wisconsin's Robert ("Battling Bob") La Follette. He brought in experts to draft laws that lowered railroad rates, regulated public utilities, established workers' compensation, and reformed the tax system. His reform program became known as the Wisconsin Idea. Another reformer, Charles Evans Hughes of New York, succeeded in regulating public utilities in his state. Hiram Johnson of California was elected on the slogan "Kick the Southern Pacific out of politics," and he did so. (This powerful railroad had dominated the state's political life for four decades.)

THEODORE ROOSEVELT: PROGRESSIVE PRESIDENT

Some reforms associated with Progressivism were adopted in the late 19th century. As noted earlier, however, the movement is usually dated from the beginning of Theodore Roosevelt's term as president. This energetic New Yorker, who came from a wealthy and conservative family, was the strongest president since Lincoln. Roosevelt brought Progressivism to the White House.

After replacing the assassinated McKinley in 1901, Roosevelt was elected in his own right in 1904. "Teddy" Roosevelt (or "T. R.") was fond of saying that every American deserved a square deal. His term in office is, therefore, often labeled the Square Deal.

Some of Roosevelt's most noted accomplishments were in the field of foreign affairs. As discussed in Chapter 22, he acquired the Canal Zone and began construction of the Panama Canal, issued the Roosevelt Corollary, and arranged the Treaty of Portsmouth. One of his favorite slogans was "Speak softly and carry a big stick." (By "big stick," he meant a powerful military force.) Eager to impress the world with U.S. naval might, he sent a force of 16 battleships and 4 destroyers on a round-the-world cruise in 1907. This "Great White Fleet" was the first fleet of warships to circumnavigate the globe.

Regulating Business

Ever since the 1870s, business combinations had been gaining greater and greater control over American industry, trade, and transportation. Despite this trend, the government had made little effort to enforce the Sherman Antitrust Act. Progressives worried that big business seemed to be running the country. Although Roosevelt shared this concern, he made a distinction between good and bad trusts. (At this time, the word "trust" was generally used to refer to any business monopoly.) And he

TR, trust buster—a 1906 cartoon in the *New York Globe*. (The Bettmann Archive)

vowed to bring the bad trusts under control.

Under Roosevelt's direction, the Department of Justice succeeded in breaking up the Northern Securities Company, a powerful railroad holding company. Successful lawsuits were also brought against beef, oil, chemical, and tobacco trusts. Roosevelt became known as a "trust buster," although his approach was actually quite moderate. In fact, several big business leaders made large contributions to his 1904 election campaign.

The Roosevelt administration also took action against railroad abuses. The Interstate Commerce Commission (ICC), set up by the Interstate Commerce Act of 1887, had been unable to prevent such practices as rebates and unfair freight charges. The *Elkins Act* of 1903 made rebates illegal. And the *Hepburn Act* of 1906 went much further. For the first time, the ICC was given the power to set railroad rates.

Public Health

In the field of public health, the Roosevelt administration focused on unsafe food. It became a special target after the publication of Upton Sinclair's *The Jungle,* in 1906. This muckraking novel was set in and around the Chicago stockyards. Among the book's vivid details was a description of sausage ingredients, including moldy meat, dirt, and dead rats.

Horrified public reaction spurred passage of the *Meat Inspection Act* of 1906. It gave the federal government power to enforce sanitary regulations in meatpacking plants. The act also provided for federal inspection of meat shipped in interstate commerce. The *Pure Food and Drug Act*, another law of 1906, banned the sale of harmful and impure foods and medicines. It also required truthful labels on foods and drugs. Sinclair, who had wanted to arouse interest in the idea of reforming the entire American political system, found the response to his book disappointing. "I aimed at the public's heart," he said, "and hit it in the stomach."

Conservation

Some of Roosevelt's most important and lasting contributions were in the field of conservation. An ardent naturalist and sportsman, he was the first president to take an active interest in preserving the environment. He worked for passage of the *Newlands Act* (1902), which provided that money from the sale of Western lands be used for irrigation projects. He stopped the public sale of about 80 million acres of mineral land and 1.5 million acres of land suitable for waterpower sites. During his administration, nearly 150 million acres of public land were set aside as national forest reserves.

In 1908, Roosevelt called the state governors to a national conference on conservation. They discussed how to preserve and develop the nation's natural resources. As a result of this meeting, Roosevelt appointed a National Conservation Commission, headed by Gifford Pinchot. It conducted the first scientific study of the country's water, forest, soil, and mineral resources.

Other Actions

In general, Roosevelt was a Progressive in his social policy. He invited Booker T. Washington to the White House for dinner, which pleased the black community (and angered Southern whites). He also acted in a 1902 Pennsylvania coal miners' strike. When mine owners refused to negotiate with the strikers, Roosevelt took the unusual step of appointing an impartial committee to try to settle the dispute. The miners won some of their demands and went back to work. For the first time, a president had intervened in a labor dispute without taking sides against labor.

In immigration policy, Roosevelt tried to steer a middle course. The number of Japanese immigrants had begun to increase in the 1890s. Most of them settled in the Western states, where many people became concerned about the competition for jobs. Nativists launched an emotional campaign against the "Yellow Peril," demanding that the government stop all Japanese immigration. In 1906, San Francisco announced plans to set up a segregated school for Japanese and other Oriental students. When Japan protested against this discrimination, Roosevelt persuaded the city to cancel its plan. He then negotiated a so-called "Gentlemen's Agreement" with Japan, by which that country agreed to restrict the migration of laborers to the United States.

TAFT IN THE WHITE HOUSE

After the election of 1904, Roosevelt announced that he would not seek another term. Four years later, he persuaded the Republicans to nominate his friend, Secretary of War William Howard Taft. The genial, placid Taft ran against William Jennings Bryan and won a sweeping victory in the 1908 election.

Progressive Accomplishments

As president, Taft was much less dynamic than Roosevelt, but he did manage to achieve a number of Progressive reforms. He continued the fight against monopolies, initiating many lawsuits against trusts. In two important cases, the Supreme Court ordered the breakup of the Standard Oil Trust and the reorganization of the American Tobacco Company. In all, 90 antitrust suits were started during Taft's term in office, compared with 44 in Roosevelt's time.

Progressive reforms also affected other areas. Government-operated savings bank facilities were set up in post offices, and a parcel post service was begun. The *Publicity Act* required that contributions to campaigns for federal election be made public. The *Mann-Elkins Act* of 1910 placed telephone, cable, and wireless companies under the supervision of the ICC. (Supervision was later transferred to the Federal Communications Commission.) Taft also supported the Sixteenth Amendment, ratified in 1913, which authorized Congress to impose an income tax.

Foreign Policy

In foreign affairs, Taft favored what he called "dollar diplomacy," or "substituting dollars for bullets." This meant encouraging American loans, investments, and trade in areas of strategic importance to the United States. Dollar diplomacy had little effect in Asia because American investments there were not large enough to affect the balance of power. It had more impact in Latin America. There, the United States increased its investments and also actively intervened in the financial affairs of several countries. These moves angered many Latin Americans.

Political Blunders

Along with his accomplishments, Taft made many mistakes. They turned Progressives against him and led to a split between him and Roosevelt.

A major cause of discontent was the tariff. Progressives wanted to lower tariff rates in order to stimulate competition and reduce prices for consumers. Taft had promised to work toward this goal. The *Payne-Aldrich Tariff*, passed by Congress in 1909, lowered rates somewhat, but less than Progressives had hoped for. They were upset when Taft not only signed the measure but also called it "the best bill that the Republican party ever passed."

Taft made no attempt to patch up the rift with the Progressives. Worse, he became involved in a quarrel over conservation. It involved Gifford Pinchot, a Roosevelt appointee in the Department of Agriculture, and Richard Ballinger, Taft's secretary of the interior. Pinchot criticized Ballinger for reopening federal waterpower sites to private developers and accused the secretary of mishandling Alaskan coal reserves. Amidst noisy controversy, Taft supported Ballinger and fired Pinchot. Progressives then attacked Taft as an enemy of conservation.

The arithmetic of Democratic victory. (*Puck,* 1912)

The Election of 1912

Roosevelt had turned against Taft early in 1910. Later that year, he launched a speaking tour to proclaim what he called the New Nationalism. This far-reaching program called for stricter regulation of corporations and such welfare proposals as workers' compensation.

Roosevelt hoped to be nominated for president on the Republican ticket in 1912. But the convention, dominated by party regulars rather than Progressives, chose Taft instead. Roosevelt's supporters then broke away, formed the *Progressive party,* and nominated him as their candidate. Because Roosevelt liked to say that he felt "as fit as a bull moose," the new party was popularly called the "Bull Moose party." Its platform included a host of Progressive objectives: women's suffrage; initiative, referendum, and recall; workers' compensation; and strict business regulation.

The Democratic party nominated Woodrow Wilson, the Progressive governor of New Jersey and the former president of Princeton University.

The election campaign turned into a contest between Roosevelt and Wilson. Both of them advocated reform. But Wilson's program—which he called the New Freedom—differed from Roosevelt's. Roosevelt wanted to regulate trusts, not destroy them. Wilson believed that monopolies were a threat to the survival of free enterprise and should be abolished.

The Bull Moose party attracted many Republicans, thus splitting the party vote between Taft and Roosevelt. As a result, Wilson carried 40 states and won the election. His popular vote, however, was less than the combined total of his two rivals.

WILSON'S ADMINISTRATION

Woodrow Wilson, the son of a Presbyterian minister, was born and raised in Virginia. He was the first Southerner to occupy the White House since Andrew Johnson. A man of high moral purpose, he was able to inspire the public. But he was also rigid in his beliefs. On a personal level, people found him formal and reserved.

The New Freedom

Wilson had promised to provide Americans with greater freedom of opportunity than ever before. During his two terms (he was re-elected in 1916), he proposed, and Congress enacted, a broad program of Progressive legislation. In achieving his program, Wilson stressed the importance of presidential leadership. One indication of his approach was the fact that he delivered his key messages to Congress in person—a practice discontinued by Jefferson in 1801.

Wilson, determined to end high tariffs, persuaded Congress to pass the *Underwood Tariff* in 1913. It reduced import duties to the lowest level since 1860. To make up for the expected loss of revenue, Congress levied an income tax. This action was made possible by the Sixteenth Amendment.

Another important financial measure was the *Federal Reserve Act* of 1913. It was designed to regulate credit and improve banking services. The law divided the country into 12 districts, each of which was assigned its own Federal Reserve Bank. The Federal Reserve Board was to supervise the entire system. It had power to control credit by increasing or decreasing the amount of money in circulation and by setting the interest rate on loans.

Although Wilson had campaigned on a platform of breaking up trusts, he took few steps to do so once elected. But he did favor two regulatory laws that Congress passed in 1914. One set up the Federal Trade Commission to investigate and stop unfair business practices. The other was the *Clayton Antitrust Act*. It broadened the Sherman Act by clearly defining unfair business practices and gave the federal government more power to deal with business combinations. The act also exempted labor organizations from its antitrust provisions, a step that encouraged unionization.

Other measures also helped labor. The *La Follette Seamen's Act* (1915) regulated working conditions of sailors on American ships. The *Adamson Act* (1916) established a shorter working day for railroad employees. Two laws were passed to end child labor, but the Supreme Court declared both of them unconstitutional.

Three New Amendments

During Wilson's administration, three new amendments were added to the Constitution. Each one advanced Progressive principles in a different area. The Seventeenth Amendment, ratified in 1913, changed the procedure for electing senators. The Constitution had specified that they be elected by state legislatures, but this method had played into the hands of political machines and encouraged bribery. The new amendment, providing that senators be elected by the people, made Congress more democratic.

The Eighteenth Amendment established nationwide prohibition. Since the early 1800s, reformers had campaigned to end the manufacture and sale of alcoholic beverages. By 1917, 26 states had adopted prohibition. In the same year, the United States entered World War I. Temperance advocates then gained additional support by arguing that the grain used to make alcohol would be better used to feed the nation and its allies. The Eighteenth Amendment was ratified in 1919.

A year later, in 1920, the Nineteenth Amendment granted women throughout the nation the right to vote. By this time, 29 states already allowed women to vote in some elections. And President Wilson, who had earlier taken the position that voting rights should depend on state law, had come to favor such an amendment. Ratification marked the end of a long struggle and, for the time being, removed the issue of women's rights from the national agenda.

Foreign Affairs

Wilson did not approve of dollar diplomacy. Instead, he wanted to encourage "the development of constitutional liberty in the world." As it turned out, his policy led to just as much American involvement overseas as had the policies of his predecessors.

Like the three presidents before him, Wilson played an active role in the Caribbean area. He strengthened the U.S. occupation of Nicaragua with the *Bryan-Chamorro Treaty* of 1916. This agreement granted the United States a canal route across Nicaragua. It also guaranteed long-term U.S. leases to a naval base on Nicaragua's Pacific coast and to the Corn Islands off its Caribbean coast. In return, Nicaragua received a payment of $3 million. When trouble broke out in Haiti and the Dominican Republic, Wilson sent troops into both countries and took over management of their finances. U.S. marines remained in the Dominican Republic until 1924, and in Haiti until 1934.

Wilson's major foreign involvement (before the United States entered World War I) was with Mexico. Early in 1913—at the end of Taft's administration—Victoriano Huerta led a successful revolution against Mexico's reform government. The Mexican president, Francisco Madero, was murdered. When Wilson became president, he refused to recognize the new regime, calling it a "government of butchers." In addition, he placed an embargo on American arms shipments to Mexico and stationed U.S. ships off the Mexican port of Veracruz to keep European military equipment from reaching Huerta.

Relations grew worse in 1914. First, Huerta's troops arrested a group of American sailors in Tampico. Then, when a German ship carrying a cargo of arms approached Veracruz, U.S. ships bombarded and captured the city. Only the combined peace efforts of Argentina, Brazil, and Chile prevented war between Mexico and the United States. Huerta resigned, and a more acceptable president, Venustiano Carranza, took office. The United States then withdrew its troops.

But troubles continued. In 1916, one of Carranza's former generals, Pancho Villa, tried unsuccessfully to overthrow him. Villa then tried to start a war between the United States and Mexico by invading the American Southwest. His band raided border towns in Arizona and New Mexico and killed at least 17 Americans. Wilson sent an army force under John J. Pershing into Mexico to punish Villa. Tension between the two countries mounted. Pershing's pursuit was unsuccessful, and in 1917, the troops were recalled. They were soon to be needed elsewhere.

Multiple-Choice Test

1. The Progressive era lasted from   (a) 1865 to 1900   (b) 1890 to 1917   (c) 1900 to 1950   (d) 1901 to 1917.
2. From the 1860s to 1920, the major feminist effort was to   (a) increase the number of jobs open to women   (b) broaden women's educational opportunities   (c) gain the vote for women   (d) elect more women to Congress.
3. An important aim of the Federal Reserve Act of 1913 was to   (a) guarantee the safety of depositors' money   (b) regulate credit by increasing or decreasing the amount of money in circulation   (c) make state banks illegal   (d) make private banks unprofitable.
4. All of the following political reforms were widely adopted during the Progressive era *except*   (a) election of U.S. senators by state legislatures   (b) initiative and referendum   (c) recall   (d) the direct primary.
5. Theodore Roosevelt's presidential administration is known as the   (a) Square Deal   (b) New Deal   (c) New Freedom   (d) New Nationalism.
6. Upton Sinclair's *The Jungle* led to the adoption of the   (a) Interstate Commerce Act   (b) Newlands Act   (c) Meat Inspection Act   (d) Hepburn Act.
7. Theodore Roosevelt was the first president to intervene in a labor dispute   (a) on the side of labor   (b) on the side of management   (c) as an enemy of both labor and management   (d) in a neutral capacity.
8. The Sixteenth Amendment to the Constitution   (a) provided for prohibition   (b) allowed Congress to impose an income tax   (c) created the Federal Reserve Board   (d) set aside millions of acres of land for national parks.

9. Taft lost the support of many Progressives when he **(a)** spoke out in favor of the Payne-Aldrich Tariff **(b)** persuaded Congress to pass the Underwood Tariff **(c)** fired Secretary of the Interior Richard Ballinger **(d)** advocated dollar diplomacy.
10. The election of Woodrow Wilson to the presidency in 1912 came about mainly because of **(a)** Taft's refusal to run **(b)** the death of Theodore Roosevelt **(c)** a split in the Republican party **(d)** the U.S. entry into World War I.

Matching Test

COLUMN A

1. Lincoln Steffens
2. Ida Tarbell
3. Susan B. Anthony
4. Urban League
5. Samuel Jones
6. Robert La Follette
7. Gentlemen's Agreement
8. dollar diplomacy
9. Bull Moose party
10. Pancho Villa

COLUMN B

a. Mexican who led raids into southwestern United States
b. leader in struggle to gain women's suffrage
c. Progressive governor of Wisconsin
d. arrangement to limit Japanese immigration into United States
e. author of *The Shame of the Cities*
f. Progressive mayor of Toledo, Ohio
g. policy for increasing U.S. investment in strategic regions overseas
h. group that chose Theodore Roosevelt as its presidential candidate in 1912
i. author of *The History of the Standard Oil Company*
j. organization formed to increase jobs and improve housing conditions for blacks in cities

Essay Questions

1. Who were the muckrakers? Where did their name come from? What goal did they have in common?

2. How did Booker T. Washington and William E. B. Du Bois differ in their approach to opposing discrimination against blacks?
3. Briefly explain initiative, referendum, and recall. How did these three reforms help promote democracy?
4. Why did big business favor high tariffs? Why were the Progressives opposed to them?
5. Compare and contrast Theodore Roosevelt and Woodrow Wilson as Progressives.

CHAPTER 24

World War I

In the presidential election of 1916, Woodrow Wilson's campaign was organized around one theme: "He kept us out of war." A terrible conflict had broken out in Europe two years earlier, and Americans wanted no part of it. But the United States was unable to avoid involvement for long.

THE EUROPEAN CONFLICT

Since the time of Napoleon in the early 1800s, there had been no general war in Europe. The continent had experienced limited conflicts, including one between France and the German state of Prussia (the Franco-Prussian War) in 1870–1871. But these clashes did not slow down economic or social progress, especially in the industrializing nations.

Causes of Tension

Although Europe appeared peaceful and prosperous on the surface, underlying tensions were building up. One cause was imperialism. Since the late 1800s, many European powers had been competing with one another for trade, raw materials, and colonies in other parts of the world. The most dramatic takeover occurred in Africa. Between 1870 and 1914, the whole continent, except Liberia and Ethiopia, came under European control. During this period, the imperialist nations narrowly avoided war several times over conflicting claims to territory and influence.

Another cause of tension was nationalism. Some countries wanted to annex foreign areas inhabited by people of their own nationality. France, for example, longed to regain Alsace and Lorraine. After the Franco-Prussian War, both areas, with French majorities, had become part of the newly created German Empire. Elsewhere, minorities living in larger political units wanted to be independent. This was true, for instance, of Czechs and Slovaks in the huge Austro-Hungarian Empire.

Imperialism and nationalism fostered a spirit of distrust. This, in turn, led to the buildup of armed strength. Between 1900 and 1914, Germany tripled its spending on naval construction, and Russia almost doubled expenditures on its army. With the military buildup came a general feeling that war was unavoidable.

Perhaps the greatest danger to the peace of Europe was the alliance system. Over the years, two opposing groups had taken shape. One was the *Triple Entente*. (*Entente* means "understanding" in French.) It consisted of Britain, France, and Russia. The other was the *Triple Alliance*, made up of Germany, Austria-Hungary, and Italy. If fighting were to break out between any two nations in opposing alliances, it might easily involve all the others.

The Outbreak of War

The immediate cause of war was an assassination. It took place in the town of Sarajevo, in the southern part of the Austro-Hungarian Empire. On June 28, 1914, the heir to the throne of Austria-Hungary, Archduke Franz Ferdinand, was visiting there. Suddenly, a man stepped out of the crowd, drew a revolver, and killed both the archduke and his wife. The assassin, a visitor from the neighboring country of Serbia, belonged to a secret terrorist organization. Its aim was to bring under Serbian rule the southern Slavs in Austria-Hungary.

Blaming Serbia for the assassination, Austria sent the Serbian government a list of harsh demands. Dissatisfied with Serbia's response, Austria declared war.

In earlier times, Austria-Hungary and Serbia probably could have settled such an incident by themselves. But now, the alliance system came into play. Russia, a Slavic country, felt close to Serbia and competitive toward Austria-Hungary. The Russians came to the defense of Serbia. Soon, most of the members of the Triple Entente and Triple Alliance were drawn in. Other European nations became involved as well. By August 1914, the war was general. One side, the *Central Powers*, consisted of Germany and Austria-Hungary. They were eventually joined by the Ottoman Empire (Turkey) and Bulgaria. The other side, the *Allies*, included Britain, France, Russia, and a number of smaller countries.

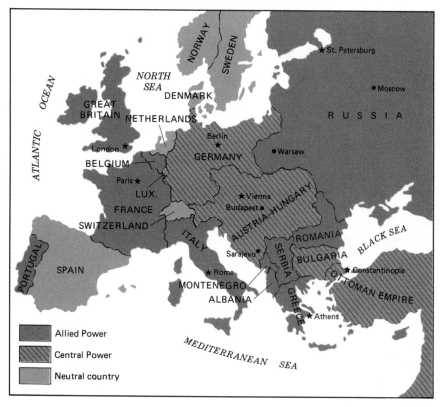

ALLIES AND CENTRAL POWERS IN WORLD WAR I

(Italy, a member of the Triple Alliance, remained neutral at first, but later joined the Allies.)

The conflict was fought on a huge scale and involved millions of people. At the time, it was called the "Great War." (It became known as World War I only after a second worldwide conflict broke out in 1939.) The Central Powers fought the Allies on three main fronts. One was in the east, along the Russian border. Another was in the south, along the Italian border. The third front was in the west, in Belgium and northern France.

World War I introduced horrors that no one was prepared for. New techniques of warfare—machine guns, poison gas, and tanks—caused unbelievable destruction. The result was stalemate, particularly on the western front. Here, the opposing armies, occupying huge networks of foul-smelling, rat-infested trenches, faced each other across "no man's land." Time after time, one side or the other would try to take an enemy position. Thousands of lives were lost, as soldiers fought to gain a few hundred feet of pitted, muddy ground.

American Neutrality

Soon after the war began, Wilson issued a proclamation urging Americans to be "impartial in thought as well as in action." But few were truly neutral. Some Americans favored the Central Powers. Many more sympathized with the Allies. Like the president, these Americans felt ties of friendship to Britain and France.

SUBMARINE WARFARE   The United States showed its sympathy for the Allies by supplying them with needed goods and equipment. It also loaned the Allies millions of dollars to buy American arms and foodstuffs. In response, the Germans launched submarine attacks on U.S. and Allied supply ships, as they crossed the Atlantic.

The submarine was another new weapon of war. Its torpedo attacks—without warning and from underwater—were contrary to what people of the time considered to be "civilized" warfare. German submarines (U-boats) sank not only merchant ships but also passenger vessels. One such attack, on the British liner *Lusitania*, resulted in the deaths of almost 1200 people, including more than 100 Americans. After Wilson protested sharply, Germany promised to restrict submarine warfare. It would not, it said, attack passenger liners, and it would give warnings before attacking other ships.

Relations between the United States and Germany were relatively calm until early 1917. Germany then announced a return to unrestricted submarine warfare. The Germans knew that their move might bring the United States into the war. But they believed that they could defeat Britain and France before the Americans were fully ready to help the Allies.

OTHER FACTORS   Two other events helped bring the United States closer to war. One was the release of a secret message from the German foreign secretary, Alfred Zimmermann, to the German representative in Mexico. (The message was intercepted by the British and turned over to the United States in February 1917.) The "Zimmermann Note," as it was called, proposed that Mexico attack the United States if the Americans entered the war. The Germans promised to reward the Mexicans by returning to them their "lost territories" in the American Southwest. News of this proposal enraged Americans.

The other event concerned Russia. Its government, headed by the all-powerful czar, was repressive, and neither Wilson nor other democratic leaders sympathized with it. In March 1917, Russian moderates overthrew the czar and began to establish a constitutional regime. For the time being, Russia had become an ally with whom democratic nations could feel comfortable. (This Russian government, however, lasted only until the fall. At that time, the Bolsheviks under Lenin staged a second revolution and took Russia out of the war.)

THE UNITED STATES AT WAR

In mid-March 1917, German U-boats sank four U.S. ships on the high seas. Wilson and his cabinet then agreed that it was time to act. The president sent a message to Congress early in April, condemning the German submarine policy and asking for a declaration of war. Congress passed a war resolution on April 6.

Efforts at Home

The United States, poorly prepared for war, immediately geared up to produce more arms, munitions, and food. By mid-June, a draft was in effect, and almost 10 million men had registered for service in the armed forces.

The Allies needed more supplies and troops immediately. France, in particular, was being bled white. But it took months to train new draftees. In the meantime, massive shipments of food and other supplies were sent overseas. To ward off attacks by German submarines, the Americans and British adopted a convoy system, with warships providing protection for merchant vessels.

The government set up a number of agencies to coordinate war production. Farmers grew more crops. Workers kept strikes to a minimum. The government helped in this effort by encouraging unionization, fair working hours, and ample pay.

Many blacks and women found jobs in industry. Some 500,000 black Americans moved from the rural South to the industrial North. Women's

---

We are glad . . . to fight . . . for the ultimate peace of the world and for the liberation of its peoples, the German peoples included: for the rights of nations great and small and the privilege of men everywhere to choose their way of life . . . . The world must be made safe for democracy . . . . We have no selfish ends to serve. We desire no conquest, no dominion . . . . We are but one of the champions of the rights of mankind.

—*Woodrow Wilson's war message to Congress, April 2, 1917*

I WANT YOU FOR U.S. ARMY
NEAREST RECRUITING STATION

American soldier in France

INVEST IN THE VICTORY LIBERTY LOAN

THEY KEPT THE SEA LANES OPEN

World War I poster

participation in the war effort made ratification of the Nineteenth Amendment easier.

The United States raised $33 billion to fight the war. About a third of it came from taxes. The other two-thirds was borrowed from the public through the sale of government war bonds. Patriotic rallies and appeals stimulated millions of citizens to contribute to the war effort. Americans not only gave money to the cause. They also conserved fuel and food by observing "gasless Sundays," "heatless Mondays," "meatless Tuesdays," and so on.

Americans were exposed to an outpouring of anti-German propaganda—posters, news stories, and speeches. The Germans were pictured as savage "Huns" who murdered helpless civilians, looted their homes, and committed other atrocities. In response, a wave of hatred for anything German swept the country. The teaching of German in schools was forbidden. German music was banned from concert halls. People with German names were fired from their jobs. Even common German foods were renamed. Sauerkraut became "liberty cabbage"; wieners, "liberty sausage"; and hamburgers, "liberty steak."

On the Western Front

When the United States declared war, John J. Pershing was named commander of its army, the American Expeditionary Force (AEF). His goal was to land a million U.S. troops in France by the summer of 1918—and he achieved it.

The first American troops, in small numbers, went into action in the

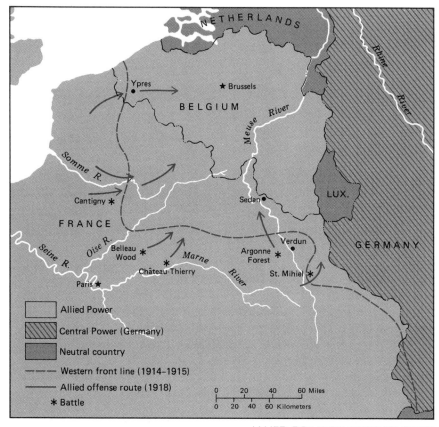

ALLIED DRIVE TO VICTORY (1918)

fall of 1917 on the western front. This blood-soaked region had been the scene of a major German attack in 1914 that had come within 15 miles of Paris before being pushed back. Two years later, brutal assaults along the Somme River took more than a million lives.

In the spring of 1918, Germany launched another all-out offensive on the western front. Again, its army approached Paris. This time, however, U.S. troops were present in force. Their courageous fighting at Château-Thierry, Belleau Wood, and Cantigny stopped the German advance. The Allies then united under a French commander, Ferdinand Foch. In July, they began a counteroffensive in which the Americans played a major role. They defeated the Germans at St.-Mihiel and drove them from the Argonne Forest. Then, the Americans advanced along the Meuse River Valley toward the German-held city of Sedan, a key position.

By the end of October, the German army was retreating all along the western front. And the Central Powers were in even greater trouble in southern and eastern Europe. There, the Ottoman army had been destroyed, Bulgaria had surrendered, and Austria-Hungary was suing for peace. In addition, threats of revolution had begun to surface within Germany itself. Realizing that the war was lost, the Germans asked for an armistice (an end to the fighting). The German emperor, Kaiser Wilhelm II, abdicated and fled the country. On November 11, 1918, the armistice was signed, and World War I was over.

Here and now in the presence of the illustrious dead we pledge our hearts and our honor in carrying this war to a successful issue. Lafayette, we are here.

—*Charles F. Stanton, a member of Pershing's staff, at the tomb of Lafayette in Paris, July 4, 1917*

AFTERMATH OF THE WAR

Both sides suffered enormous casualties in World War I—a total of 10 million killed and twice as many wounded. Among the major participants, France, Russia, and Germany each lost about 1.5 million men, the British Empire and Austria-Hungary nearly 1 million each, and Italy 500,000. U.S. casualties were about 116,000 dead (more than half from disease) and 206,000 wounded. Some Americans boasted that the United States had won the war. Although this was an exaggeration, America's participation did tip the scale in favor of the Allies. The United States also played an important part in drafting the peace settlements.

The Peace Conference

In December 1918, Wilson went to the peace conference, held in Paris. He was the first president to travel to Europe while in office. All the Allies (who had eventually totaled 23) were represented. But the major leaders were Wilson, Prime Minister David Lloyd George of Great Britain, Premier Georges Clemenceau of France, and Premier Vittorio Orlando of Italy.

WILSON'S FOURTEEN POINTS   From the beginning, Wilson had viewed the war, especially America's role in it, in idealistic terms. The aim of the Allies, he said, should be "peace without victory," a "peace between equals." In January 1918, he presented Congress with his *Fourteen Points*. This was a program for working out a just and lasting peace. Among other things, it called for the following:

1. Abolition of secret treaties
2. Freedom of the seas in peace and in war
3. Removal of all trade barriers between nations
4. Reduction in arms
5. Fair settlement of colonial claims
6. Recognition of the right of national groups to self-government
7. Formation of "a general association of nations" to protect the territory and guarantee the independence of "great and small states alike"

AIMS OF THE ALLIES   On the surface, the Allies seemed to agree on Wilson's Fourteen Points as the basis for their negotiations at Paris. But they did not really have the same aims. The United States had no territorial claims and no desire for revenge. The other Allies felt differently. France had suffered enormous casualties and considerable destruction of property. Britain, too, had been severely hurt. Both of them wanted Germany to make substantial reparations (payments for war damages).

Territories were also at stake. Italy had agreed to fight on the Allied side, in exchange for land in southern Austria where Italians lived. Japan had joined the Allies in hopes of gaining Germany's Pacific possessions. Everywhere in Europe, national groups—Finns, Poles, Czechs, Hungarians—wanted to govern themselves.

THE TREATIES   A fair solution to all the national goals and claims after World War I would have been difficult, if not impossible. The treaties that were finally drawn up at Paris granted some wishes and denied others. What resulted was not a peace between equals, but a harsh settlement imposed by the winners on the losers.

There were five treaties in all. The most important one was the *Treaty of Versailles*, between the Allies and Germany. German representatives signed it under protest in June 1919.

The Versailles Treaty forced the Germans to accept responsibility for causing the war. They were to pay at least $5 billion in reparations to the Allies, with additional sums to be decided on later. (The eventual total was about $33 billion.) Germany returned Alsace and Lorraine to France and lost eastern territories to an enlarged, newly independent Poland. Germany gave up all its colonial possessions in Africa and Asia. And the Germans were disarmed and forbidden to rebuild a strong military force. The Versailles Treaty, like the other Paris settlements, also included the covenant (constitution) of a new international organization, the *League of Nations*.

EUROPE AFTER WORLD WAR I

The Paris treaties drastically changed national boundaries in Europe. Poland, which had disappeared from the map in the 18th century, was re-created. Austria and Hungary were split. And a number of new nations came into being.

Wilson was able to soften some of the Allies' more extreme demands. For instance, he blocked French efforts to set aside part of western Germany as a buffer state (neutral territory between rival powers). He was also successful in resisting Italian demands for the city of Fiume (later Rijeka, Yugoslavia), a key seaport on the Adriatic. But he gave way on German reparations and on the "war guilt" clause that placed all blame on Germany.

Rejection of the League

Wilson knew that the Versailles Treaty was far from perfect. But he believed strongly in the League of Nations. He hoped that it would prevent future alliances of the kind that had helped cause World War I. American public opinion seemed to favor the League of Nations, too. But the Treaty of Versailles, containing the covenant of the League, had to be approved by the Senate.

At this point, Wilson ran into trouble. Some senators were totally opposed to the League. They feared that American democracy would suffer if the nation joined an international organization. Leaders of this group included Robert La Follette of Wisconsin, Hiram Johnson of California, and William Borah of Idaho. Other senators, notably Henry Cabot Lodge of Massachusetts, favored the League, but only with changes designed to guarantee American independence.

Wilson's tactics were unsound. His first mistake had been not to take any prominent Republicans to Paris with him. This oversight cost him the support of the Republican party, which he needed. Wilson also showed poor judgment by refusing to make any compromises in dealing with the Senate. Faced with continued Senate opposition, Wilson set out on a nationwide tour to appeal to the people. Partway through the trip, in September 1919, he collapsed and was forced to return to Washington, D.C. Early in October, he suffered a stroke from which he never fully recovered.

In the months that followed, the Senate held votes on the Versailles Treaty, both with and without changes. On each occasion, the treaty was defeated. By this time, the American people had lost interest in international issues and were turning to their own affairs. Thus, the United States did not become a member of the League of Nations. (In 1921, a joint congressional resolution ended the state of war between the United States and Germany, Austria, and Hungary.) Wilson left office in March 1921, a sick and disappointed man.

THE LEAGUE OF NATIONS

Although the United States never joined the League, more than 50 other countries did. They pledged to submit disputes to the League for settlement and to abide by its decisions. They also agreed that any member resorting to war would become the target of economic sanctions (such as a halt in trade) and, if necessary, military force.

The League, headquartered in Geneva, Switzerland, had three main bodies. One was the Assembly, in which all member nations were represented. Another was the Council, made up of delegates from four permanent members—Great Britain, France, Italy, and Japan—and four (later nine) temporary members. The temporary members of the Council were chosen by the Assembly. The third League body was the Secretariat, which handled administrative and clerical work. A fourth group, associated with the League but not part of it, was the Permanent Court of International Justice, or World Court. League members could bring disputes to the Court for settlement.

Work of the League

The League lasted for a quarter century and performed many useful services. It carried on relief work in war-torn countries and aided war refugees. Its Mandates Commission supervised the former colonies of the Central Powers. The World Court settled a number of international disputes. The League also gathered statistics, published reports, and held international conferences to improve labor conditions, public health, education, communication, and transportation throughout the world. The United States took part in many of the League's nonpolitical activities.

Weakness of the League

In spite of its accomplishments, the League was unable to succeed at its major task—preventing aggression and war. There were four main reasons for this failure:

1. The League lost prestige at the very start, when the United States, a leading world power, refused to join.
2. The League lacked the means to punish an aggressor nation. It could suggest that its members take action but could not force them to do so.
3. Member nations accused of aggression chose to withdraw from the League, rather than give in to its demands.
4. Leading members did not pool their strength to prevent aggression, unless their own interests were directly involved.

True-False Test

1. Between 1815 and 1914, Europe was at war almost continually.
2. Before the United States entered World War I, most of its people were sympathetic to the Allies.
3. The convoy system is a method of protecting merchant ships at sea.
4. A major goal of the United States in World War I was to gain control of German colonies in Africa.
5. The U.S. Senate never ratified the Treaty of Versailles.

Multiple-Choice Test

1. Before World War II, the war from 1914 to 1918 was called   (a) World War I   (b) the Franco-Prussian War   (c) the War Between the States   (d) the Great War.
2. All of the following were new techniques of warfare in World War I *except*   (a) machine guns   (b) tanks   (c) battleships   (d) poison gas.
3. U.S. participation in World War I lasted   (a) about a year   (b) about 20 months   (c) two years   (d) three years.
4. The Treaty of Versailles included provisions for all of the following *except*   (a) creation of a buffer state in western Germany   (b) the return of Lorraine to France   (c) the surrender of all German colonial possessions   (d) the League of Nations.
5. When Wilson encountered Senate opposition to the League of Nations, he   (a) compromised on several points   (b) gave up the struggle for ratification   (c) went on a nationwide speaking tour   (d) made it an issue in his third presidential campaign.

Matching Test

Column A	Column B
1. Triple Entente	a. alliance of Germany, Austria-Hungary, and Ottoman Empire
2. Sarajevo	b. site of American victory over Germans
3. Central Powers	c. alliance of Britain, France, and Russia
4. Alfred Zimmermann	d. commander of AEF
5. John J. Pershing	e. leader of united Allied forces in 1918
6. Ferdinand Foch	f. French representative at Paris peace conference
7. St.-Mihiel	g. region awarded to France by Versailles Treaty
8. Fourteen Points	h. town where Archduke Franz Ferdinand was assassinated
9. Georges Clemenceau	i. German foreign secretary during World War I
10. Alsace	j. Wilson's program for peace settlement after World War I

Map Test

Answer the following questions by referring to the maps on pages 364, 368, and 371, and to the text.

1. Name the capital cities of the countries that were members of the Triple Entente.
2. Name the capital cities of the countries that were members of the Triple Alliance. Which of these countries did not join up with the Central Powers?
3. Describe the location of the country that was given an ultimatum after the assassination of Archduke Franz Ferdinand.
4. What German-occupied French city on the Meuse River was a major objective in the American offensive that helped end the war in 1918?
5. Locate and list five new nations that emerged in Europe after World War I.

Essay Questions

1. What factors contributed to tension among European nations in the late 19th and early 20th centuries? How did war come about?
2. What developments led to the U.S. declaration of war on Germany in 1917?
3. How did the United States contribute to the Allied war effort after April 1917?
4. How did the aims of the United States at the Paris Peace Conference differ from those of its allies?
5. Why did the United States fail to join the League of Nations?

UNIT 8

Trial
and
Hope

CHAPTER 25

The Twenties

W ITH THE END OF World War I in 1918, a new era in American history began. Although it lasted for more than a decade, it is commonly known as the Twenties. It was characterized by political conservatism, economic prosperity (for most), great social change, and notable artistic creativity.

THREE REPUBLICAN PRESIDENTS

During the transition from war to peace, the United States experienced a period of economic and social unrest. With the lifting of wartime controls, prices rose sharply. Unionized workers, seeking to keep pace with the rising cost of living, struck for higher wages. Many factories closed down to retool for peacetime production. As a result, unemployment spread. The return of thousands of war veterans seeking jobs also helped swell the ranks of the unemployed. This was the situation as the presidential election of 1920 neared.

Harding in the White House

The party in power is blamed for most national problems, and the Democrats in 1920 were no exception. To make matters worse, they were still bickering over Senate ratification of the Versailles Treaty. The Republicans were so sure they would win the election that they made no effort to put forward a strong presidential candidate. Instead, they chose an amiable but otherwise undistinguished party regular, Senator Warren

G. Harding of Ohio. The Democrats nominated another Ohioan, Governor James M. Cox.

Cox centered his campaign on the issue of joining the League of Nations, which he favored. But most Americans had lost interest. They were more impressed with Harding's pledge to return the country to "normalcy." (This was a reference to "the good old days," a mythical past without problems.) Harding won by a landslide.

America's present need is not heroics but healing; not nostrums [cure-alls] but normalcy; not revolution but restoration.

—*Warren G. Harding at Boston, June 1920*

TURNING BACK THE CLOCK   One of the first steps of the new Republican administration was to reverse the Democratic policy of low tariffs. First, Congress passed an emergency tariff to raise rates on imported agricultural products. Then, in September 1922, it passed the *Fordney-McCumber Tariff*, which set high duties on manufactured imports. Without effective foreign competition, most American-made products rose in price. They still sold well abroad, however, because Europeans were able to borrow heavily from American investors.

The United States acted to keep out foreign people, as well as foreign goods. In 1921, Congress passed the *Emergency Quota Act*, the first law to set quotas. It limited the total number of immigrants in any year to 357,000. It also limited the number of people from any one country who could enter the United States annually. The total was set at 3 percent of that country's nationals who were living in the United States in 1910. A second law, the *Immigration Act of 1924*, lowered each country's quota from 3 to 2 percent, based on the census of 1890 instead of 1910. Far fewer people from eastern and southern Europe had lived in the United States at the earlier date. Thus, this law reduced immigration from those areas of Europe by nearly 85 percent, which was its intent. The 1924 law also put an end to all immigration by Asians.

SHADY DEALS   Harding's chief qualification for high office was that—in the words of his campaign manager—"he looked like a president." He did choose some able advisers. Charles Evans Hughes became secretary of state; Herbert Hoover, secretary of commerce; and Andrew Mellon, secretary of the treasury. But Harding also put a number of old cronies into important jobs.

Although Harding was an honest man, many of his "Ohio gang" of friends were not. Two of them, the head of the Veterans' Bureau and

Babe Ruth

Jazz Singer, Bessie Smith

1928 Packard

the Custodian of Alien Property, were jailed for stealing huge sums of money from the government. Another friend, Attorney General Harry Daugherty, was charged with the illegal sale of pardons and liquor permits, and forced to resign. The most sensational incident was the Teapot Dome scandal (named after a Wyoming oil reserve). It involved Secretary of the Interior Albert B. Fall, who accepted bribes from oilmen, in exchange for leasing them government oil reserves on good terms. Fall was tried, convicted, and sent to jail.

Harding never knew the full extent of his friends' betrayals. In August 1923, while traveling in the West, he suffered a heart attack and died. Vice President Calvin Coolidge was sworn in as his successor. (The full story of corruption in the Harding administration became public knowledge after the president's death.)

Coolidge as President

Coolidge was a New Englander—a native of Vermont and a resident of Massachusetts. Personally very different from the genial Harding, he was severe, reserved, and frugal. People called him "Silent Cal." But he was like Harding in his conservatism. People liked Coolidge's homespun ways. When he ran for president in his own right in 1924, voters elected him by a wide margin.

Coolidge was a firm believer in laissez faire and followed a "hands-off" policy toward business and agriculture. He also took steps to lower the cost of government and to reduce the national debt. His tax policy was based on the advice of Secretary of the Treasury Andrew Mellon. Mellon believed that the rich should pay low taxes. They would then invest more in industry, thus helping the nation's economy to expand. "The prosperity of the middle classes," he said, "depends on the good fortune and light taxes of the rich." This point of view led to a series of tax laws that reduced the taxes of the wealthiest Americans by two-thirds.

The Election of Hoover

When Coolidge let it be known that he would not be a candidate for re-election in 1928 ("I do not choose to run"), the Republicans nominated Herbert Hoover for the presidency. An Iowa-born mining engineer, Hoover had served as secretary of commerce in the Harding-Coolidge administrations. The Democractic candidate was the governor of New York, Alfred E. Smith.

From the point of view of rural and small-town Americans, who still played a big role in politics, Smith had several disadvantages. For one thing, he was a Roman Catholic. For another, he opposed prohibition. If elected, he said, he would do everything he could to have the Eighteenth Amendment repealed. In addition, Smith was a "city slicker" with ties to Tammany Hall, New York City's political machine. All these factors worked to Hoover's advantage, and he won by a landslide. The Republicans even carried four of the Democratic states of the "solid South."

During his campaign, Hoover announced: "We in America today are nearer to the final triumph over poverty than ever before in the history of any land." His supporters promised "a chicken in every pot, a car in every garage," if Hoover won the election.

THE ECONOMY IN THE "NEW ERA"

Although there was a brief recession after World War I, the Twenties was a time of business expansion. Industrial activity rose to a new high level. So did the Gross National Product (GNP)—the total value of goods and services produced by the nation. Jobs were plentiful, and the average city family had a larger income than ever before. Most Americans felt optimistic. They believed that the nation had entered a New Era—a time of ever-increasing prosperity.

Expanding Industries

Probably the best symbol of industrial growth in the 1920s was the automobile. Europeans had pioneered in its development, but Americans soon began to design their own cars. The first Americans to build and market a commercially successful automobile were Charles and Frank Duryea, in the 1890s. Henry Ford introduced his first car in the same decade.

Early automobiles were so expensive that only a few people could buy them. In 1900, there were only 8000 motor vehicles registered in the United States. Henry Ford changed all that. In 1908, he developed a simple car, the "Model T," and set up a factory to mass-produce it. His factory combined the use of interchangeable parts with the assembly line—a system made up of workers, tools, and a conveyor belt. As a car moved along the belt, each worker performed one or more operations on it. By 1916, a Ford could be made in 90 minutes and cost only $345. The average family was now able to afford an automobile. Car ownership rose to more than 450,000 in 1910, and by 1918 exceeded 5.5 million.

During the 1920s, the yearly output of passenger cars rose from 1.9 million to nearly 4.8 million. The automotive industry also turned out hundreds of thousands of trucks, buses, and tractors. The automobile became one of the most important factors in the national economy, providing employment for millions of people. Some made cars. Others had jobs in related industries, including tires, glass, steel, and oil refining. Still others worked in gas stations and garages, attending to the needs of motorists. Thousands more built and maintained the network of new and improved roads that crisscrossed the country.

A new means of transportation, the airplane, was also beginning to

TECHNOLOGICAL DEVELOPMENTS (1901–1928)

Date	Inventor	Invention or Discovery
1901	Otis Elevator Company	Installed first escalator in U.S.
1901	Peter C. Hewitt	Patented mercury vapor lamp
1902	Willis H. Carrier	Designed first scientific air-conditioning system
1903	Orville and Wilbur Wright	Designed, built, and flew heavier-than-air craft
1907	Lee De Forest	Developed triode, a three-element vacuum tube
1908	Henry Ford	Introduced Model T car
1909	Leo H. Baekeland	Patented thermosetting plastic (Bakelite)
1916	John T. Thompson	Patented submachine gun
1923	Vladimir Zworykin	Invented television camera
1925	Clarence Birdseye	Marketed first frozen food
1926	Robert H. Goddard	Built first liquid-fuel rocket
1927	John D. and Mack D. Rust	Invented mechanical cotton picker
1927	Warner Brothers	Produced first full-length motion picture with spoken dialogue
1928	Philip Drinker and Louis A. Shaw	Developed iron lung

take hold. It had been developed by the Wright brothers early in the 20th century. Planes had played a limited role in World War I. After the war, they began to be used commercially. By the end of the 1920s, about 50 private airlines were in operation. They carried mail and some passengers.

Other industries that thrived during the Twenties were construction and home appliances. New houses were built throughout the country, and big cities were transformed by skyscrapers. Among the many tall structures that altered skylines in the 1920s were New York City's Chrysler Building and Chicago's Tribune Tower. The average middle-class American family not only parked a car in its garage but also owned a refrigerator, a vacuum cleaner, and an electric iron. Most people bought these items "on time," using the installment plan.

Business Growth

Just as the automobile symbolized industrial growth, the stock market typified business growth. An increasing number of Americans were making quick profits by buying and selling corporate shares. Financial success stories encouraged speculation. There was a steady increase in the number of shares traded, from 236 million in 1923 to more than a billion in 1928.

The trend toward business consolidation, which had begun after the Civil War, continued in the 20th century. During the 1920s, about 8000 manufacturing and mining companies were absorbed by larger concerns. Some 5000 public utilities were swallowed up by holding companies. By 1929, roughly half the corporate wealth of the country was controlled by the 200 largest nonfinancial business enterprises.

The growth of big industry and the concentration of wealth in a few hands were encouraged by the federal government's high tariffs and its tax policies. The Progressives had been suspicious of big business, but government leaders of the 1920s admired it. "This is a business country," said Coolidge, "and it wants a business government." Herbert Hoover, a self-made millionaire, was also a strong supporter of the laissez-faire capitalism of the New Era. If there were abuses, he thought, the best remedy was for business to correct them voluntarily. In Hoover's view, such self-policing would benefit the American economy more than any amount of government regulation.

Agriculture and Labor

Farmers were one group of Americans who did not share in the prosperity of the Twenties. They had made good money during the war and had expanded their acreage. But when European farm production returned to normal after the war, the American supply exceeded demand,

The Twenties were "boom" times for some—but not for the farmers. (Fitzpatrick in the *St. Louis Post-Dispatch*)

and prices fell sharply. Throughout the decade, while other sections of the economy were booming, farmers had to cope with surplus crops, heavy debts, and declining income. Thousands went bankrupt and either moved to cities or became tenants on other people's land.

Unions did not do well in the 1920s, either. Most individual workers earned a decent living. But they made little progress in the struggle for shorter hours, higher wages, and other benefits. Business, government, and much of the public strongly opposed unions. Some companies, Ford among them, voluntarily raised wages. But the corporate attitude toward workers tended to be high-handed and arbitrary. Union membership declined from more than 5 million in 1920 to fewer than 3.5 million in 1929.

CHANGE AND TENSION

The "normalcy" that Americans yearned for after World War I was an idealized version of small-town life. It was an existence based on the traditional values of home, family, community, and hard work. These values were still very much alive in the United States. But they were being challenged by new trends that were reshaping society.

Fewer and fewer Americans actually lived in small towns. The census of 1920 was the first to show that more people were living in urban areas than in rural ones. Society was being changed by the automobile, too. By making people more mobile, it fostered a sense of personal freedom, encouraged an exodus from central cities to suburban areas, stimulated travel, and afforded new ways of using leisure time. The automobile also reduced the isolation of rural dwellers. It even changed relations between the sexes by providing young people with freedom and privacy unknown to earlier generations.

For some, the new ways were exciting. For others, they produced uncertainty and fear. Despite its prosperity, the Twenties was a time of conflict and violence.

Attacks on Radicals

American society had long had its moderate critics. Among them were the Populists and Progressives of the late 19th and early 20th centuries. But other critics in this period had more extreme points of view.

One group, the Socialists, opposed the capitalist economic system of free enterprise. They called for public rather than private ownership of factories, mines, utilities, and transportation systems. These changes, they believed, could be achieved through the democratic process. A leader in this movement was Eugene V. Debs, who helped form the *Socialist party of America* in 1901. Several crusading figures of the Progressive era, including Upton Sinclair, were Socialists.

The anarchists were another, more radical, group. They believed in doing away with government altogether. Many of them resorted to terrorism. It was an anarchist who assassinated President McKinley in 1901.

Some members of the political left belonged to the *Industrial Workers of the World (IWW)*, a labor union founded in 1905. These so-called "Wobblies"—whether Socialists, anarchists, or others—believed that the AFL was too timid to achieve real reform.

All the various radical groups included sizable numbers of immigrants from Europe. Many came from countries where political dissent was more common, and regarded as more respectable, than in the United States.

WARTIME DEVELOPMENTS   Americans had always been suspicious of radicals, and World War I increased this distrust. During the war, German-Americans were not the only targets of hate campaigns. Pacifists—people opposed to war—were branded as "slackers" and even traitors. (Most radicals in Europe and the United States opposed the war, arguing that it would make capitalists rich at the workers' expense.) Congress passed laws that provided severe penalties for spying, obstructing the war effort, refusing to serve in the armed forces, and making disrespectful remarks about the U.S. government, Constitution, or flag. Under these laws, the government arrested more than 1500 persons.

William Haywood, leader of the IWW, was sentenced to 20 years in prison, and Debs to 10. (Haywood jumped bail and fled to Russia; Debs was pardoned by Harding in 1921.)

World War I also saw the rise of a new and threatening power in Europe, when the Russian government was taken over by Bolsheviks. They were Communists—dedicated to achieving socialist aims by violence. They aimed to do this not only in the Soviet Union (as they renamed Russia) but all over the world. The *American Communist party* was organized in 1919.

THE RED SCARE   The so-called "Red Scare" in the United States began in the spring of 1919 and lasted about a year and a half. It was a time of violent clashes among Americans of differing views, and of extreme steps taken by the authorities to end the unrest. Most of the violence was blamed on "reds." (Although this term is generally used to describe avowed Communists, people also applied it to union organizers, activist clergy, and other dissidents.)

Bitter strikes convinced many Americans that radical agitators wanted to destroy the country. In February 1919, one strike nearly shut down the city of Seattle, Washington. The following fall, Boston police went on strike. Coolidge, then governor of Massachusetts, gained nationwide fame when he spoke out firmly against the strike (after the mayor of Boston had already restored order). Several unexplained bombings also contributed to the Red Scare. One, in the nation's capital, destroyed the home of the attorney general, A. Mitchell Palmer. Another, on Wall Street in New York City, killed 38 people and injured many others. Postal inspectors also discovered bombs in a number of packages addressed to government officials.

Palmer set up a new division of the Justice Department to combat radicalism. (This division later became the FBI.) In November 1919 and in January 1920, Palmer ordered raids on the headquarters of radical organizations. Several thousand aliens were arrested. Some 800 of them were eventually deported.

The "Palmer raids" ended when the attorney general was curbed by more moderate leaders. But suspicion and fear of radicals continued. The case of Nicola Sacco and Bartolomeo Vanzetti symbolized the unrest of the period. These Italian immigrants were both anarchists. They were accused of murdering the paymaster of a Massachusetts shoe factory and his guard. Tried and found guilty, Sacco and Vanzetti were sentenced to death in July 1921. Their case touched off widespread protests, both in America and abroad. Many people felt that the evidence against the two men was flimsy, and that they had been convicted only because of their radicalism. In spite of repeated appeals and worldwide protests, Sacco and Vanzetti were executed in 1927.

In this 1919 cartoon, a torch-bearing "red" sneaks onto the American scene. (*The Philadelphia Inquirer*)

Troubles for African Americans

Wartime and the postwar years were a crucial period for black Americans. Almost 400,000 of them served in the armed forces. Thousands of others moved north to take jobs in factories. The black community hoped that its members would benefit from greater freedom and opportunity. But this was not to be.

Black Americans still faced discrimination in jobs, housing, and civil rights. They also encountered racial antagonism and threats of violence. For the slightest of reasons, mobs lynched black people—many of them soldiers in uniform. Race riots broke out in more than 25 cities. The worst of them, in Chicago, left 38 dead.

Much of this brutality was the work of the newly revived Ku Klux Klan. The KKK, which had come into being during the Reconstruction era, had died out in the late 1800s. During the war, however, a new KKK became active. Its targets included Catholics, Jews, "reds," and foreigners. But its most intense hatred was reserved for blacks. The KKK worked secretly, and usually at night. White-robed and hooded members beat, tortured, and sometimes killed their chosen victims.

The organization was at its peak in the mid-1920s, with 5 million dues-paying members. In some states, Klansmen won election to high office. In others, the KKK had such political power that people were afraid to oppose it. But then the tide turned. Investigative reporters began to publicize the Klan's terrorist activities. Charges of corruption and graft within the movement finally led to its collapse. The KKK lost most of its membership and influence in the late 1920s. The racial hatred it preached, however, continued to trouble American society.

The "Noble Experiment"

Early in 1919, the United States began what Hoover later called a "noble experiment"—national prohibition. The Eighteenth Amendment called for a ban on the manufacture, importation, and sale of all alcoholic beverages.

Most Americans who drank alcoholic beverages were determined to continue doing so. Some of them made liquor, wine, and beer at home. Many others bought from bootleggers (illegal sellers of alcohol). They, in turn, obtained their stock from American or foreign suppliers. Illegal bars, called "speakeasies," opened in almost every town. The federal bureau set up to enforce prohibition had fewer than 3500 agents. They could not begin to track down all the sources of illegal liquor.

Prohibition did not put an end to drinking in the United States. It did drive it underground, turning millions of otherwise law-abiding citizens into lawbreakers. Prohibition also spurred the growth of organized crime. Most of the illegal alcohol business was in the hands of criminal gangs. As they grew in wealth and power, they extended their operations into a number of legitimate businesses.

Despite the obvious failure of the "noble experiment," the Hoover administration was unwilling to see it brought to an end. The next administration, however, acted quickly. In February 1933, Congress passed the Twenty-first Amendment, ending prohibition. It became part of the Constitution by the end of the year.

Women's New Freedom

One of the features that set the Twenties apart from earlier years of the century was the way women—especially young women—looked and acted. Bulky, ankle-length dresses gave way to close-fitting, knee-length shifts. According to one estimate, the amount of fabric in a woman's complete outfit decreased from 19 to 7 yards. Long hair that had been worn in elaborate buns was cut short. Women began to use lipstick and rouge, and to smoke cigarettes. They went with their husbands and friends to speakeasies for drinking and dancing. The stylish young woman of the period became known as a "flapper."

Women's lives were also changing in more fundamental ways. More of them than ever were going to college and working at salaried jobs. (Middle-class people, however, still regarded work as something that a woman did only until she married. She might hold a job, but she did not aim for a career.) Women's housekeeping chores became easier as electrical appliances, packaged foods, and other labor-saving improvements became available. And women had fewer children to raise. The birthrate declined about 25 percent between 1915 and 1929.

THE ROARING TWENTIES

The tempo of life in the 1920s seemed so much faster than it had been earlier that the period came to be called the "Roaring Twenties." In their search for novelty and excitement, Americans created (and discarded) celebrities overnight. They idolized sports heroes: Babe Ruth of baseball; prizefighters Jack Dempsey and Gene Tunney; and Gertrude Ederle, the first woman to swim the English Channel. They admired the feats of polar explorers and the stunts of publicity seekers who perched for days on flagpoles. The most famous figure of the decade was Charles Lindbergh. In 1927, he became the first person to make a solo flight nonstop across the Atlantic. When he returned from France, he was decorated by President Coolidge and honored with huge parades.

Popular Culture

Overnight sensations owed much to radio, which came into its own in the 1920s. The first commercial stations in the United States were WWJ of Detroit and KDKA of Pittsburgh. They began broadcasting in 1920. Soon, Americans were listening to election returns, sports events, and variety shows. By 1930, one home in three owned a radio.

Another mass medium of the 1920s was the motion picture. Several inventions of the late 19th century—in both the United States and Europe—made motion pictures possible. Public showing of short films began to draw audiences in the early 1900s. By 1920, Hollywood, California, had become the world's movie capital. It turned out hundreds of full-length films. These early motion pictures were silent, black-and-white productions, shown to the accompaniment of piano music. One of the greatest American movie directors of this period was D. W. Griffith. His famous epics on film include *The Birth of a Nation* (1915) and *Way Down East* (1920).

With movies came movie stars, whose glamorous lives became front-page news. Rudolf Valentino's portrayal of exotic lovers in *The Sheik* (1921) and *Blood and Sand* (1922) made him the idol of millions. Mary Pickford specialized in plucky young girls, while Theda Bara played sultry charmers. Comedy ranged from the slapstick antics of the Keystone Kops to the subtle humor of Buster Keaton and Harold Lloyd. Charlie Chaplin, in his role as a lovable tramp, charmed moviegoers in such films as *The Kid* (1921) and *The Gold Rush* (1925).

In addition to making most of the world's movies, Americans

created the era's most distinctive music, jazz. This rhythmic style was developed by black musicians in the South. But its origins—and its very name—may have been African. Jazz came north with such early greats as Louis Armstrong, Joe "King" Oliver, and "Jelly Roll" Morton. By the late 1920s, white jazz players such as Bix Beiderbecke and Benny Goodman were also becoming known. Jazz influenced several classical composers, notably George Gershwin. His *Rhapsody in Blue* (1924) and *An American in Paris* (1928) gave concert-hall respectability to the new music.

The Arts

In the early decades of the 1900s, the arts flourished in the United States as never before, and rarely since. The works produced were often critical of American society, but they were also widely admired.

FICTION   In literature, the realism of the late 1800s continued to find expression. Edith Wharton's *Ethan Frome* (1911) is a tragedy set in rural New England. Most of her other novels, such as *The Age of Innocence* (1920), deal with worldly, upper-class New Yorkers. Willa Cather grew up in Nebraska. Her most famous novel, *My Ántonia* (1918), is the story of an immigrant girl living on the plains. Theodore Dreiser was a powerfully realistic writer, best known for *An American Tragedy* (1925). Middle-class conformity and shallowness were brilliantly ridiculed by Sinclair Lewis in his 1922 masterpiece, *Babbitt*.

One group of Americans, who disliked the materialism they saw in the United States, spent years abroad. Gertrude Stein, an experimental writer who lived most of her life in France, called these expatriates a "lost generation." One of the best known, Ernest Hemingway, wrote of Americans living in Europe in *The Sun Also Rises* (1926). His novel *A Farewell to Arms* (1929) is a tragic love story set in Italy and Switzerland during World War I.

The novelist who probably best captured the spirit of the times was F. Scott Fitzgerald. His book *The Great Gatsby* (1925) is a story of love, materialism, and murder during the "boom" years of the 1920s.

THE HARLEM RENAISSANCE   An important development of the Twenties was a flowering of creativity among black Americans. It was known as the Harlem Renaissance. One of its best writers was Claude McKay. His poem "If We Must Die" is a passionate outcry against the racism that led to the postwar riots. Countee Cullen, another poet, wrote lyrical verses in the style of John Keats. The poems, novels, and plays of Langston Hughes display jazzlike verbal rhythms and a dry wit.

OTHER POETRY AND DRAMA   Other American poets of the 1920s produced outstanding works, too. Edwin Arlington Robinson dramatized the lives of eccentric New Englanders. Robert Frost also dealt with New England in such lyrics as "Stopping by Woods on a Snowy Evening" (1923). The Midwest, especially Chicago, was the locale of many of the poems of Carl Sandburg. His energetic language, forceful rhythms, and praise of ordinary people recall the earlier works of Walt Whitman. In contrast to Sandburg's optimism, the poems of T. S. Eliot are expressions of despair. Like Sandburg, Eliot was a Midwesterner, but he became a British subject. His long poem *The Waste Land* (1922) sums up the pessimism that many intellectuals felt after the horrors of World War I.

In a class by himself was Eugene O'Neill, the first important American playwright. Some of his works, such as *Desire Under the Elms* (1924), were realistic dramas. In others, he experimented with unusual techniques. The characters in *Strange Interlude* (1928), for example, speak their most secret thoughts as if they were alone.

THE VISUAL ARTS   In the early 20th century, a group of American painters banded together for mutual encouragement. They became known as the "ashcan school" because many of them liked to paint homely, if not downright ugly, urban sights. John Sloan and Robert Henri were among the most important of these painters.

One of the ashcan group's most impressive achievements was to organize the 1913 Armory Show in New York City. It introduced to Americans such new European trends as cubism and surrealism. Most viewers reacted with dismay, and the public continued to prefer realism. This tradition was seen at its best in the work of a pupil of Henri's, George Bellows, noted for his scenes of prizefights.

Frank Lloyd Wright was an outstanding American architect of the period. He first became known for his "prairie houses" in Illinois and Wisconsin. These low dwellings introduced a new idea—open interior spaces unbroken by walls and doors. In his long career, Wright also designed an earthquake-proof hotel in Tokyo, a house over a waterfall in Pennsylvania, and the circular Guggenheim Museum in New York City.

True-False Test

1. The first law setting up quotas for immigrants was passed during Harding's administration.
2. The Teapot Dome scandal involved the secretary of the interior under Coolidge.
3. Some people opposed Democratic presidential candidate Alfred E. Smith because he was a Roman Catholic.
4. During the 1920s, the American GNP rose higher than ever before.
5. Farm income fell during the 1920s mainly because of crop failures caused by bad weather.

6. Carpetbaggers were the chief target of the revived Ku Klux Klan in the 1920s.
7. One result of prohibition was an increase in organized crime.
8. The first commercial radio stations in the United States started broadcasting during World War I.
9. Jazz originated among black musicians in the southern United States.
10. The Harlem Renaissance was an attempt to rebuild slum neighborhoods in New York City.

Matching Test

COLUMN A	COLUMN B
1. Andrew Mellon	a. developers of first airplane
2. Charles and Frank Duryea	b. author of *Ethan Frome*
3. Orville and Wilbur Wright	c. first Americans to produce commercially successful automobile
4. Nicola Sacco and Bartolomeo Vanzetti	d. first important American playwright
5. Charles Lindbergh	e. secretary of treasury under Harding and Coolidge
6. D. W. Griffith	f. radicals whose trial and execution drew worldwide attention
7. George Gershwin	g. designer of "prairie houses" in Midwest
8. Edith Wharton	h. composer of classical music influenced by jazz
9. Eugene O'Neill	i. early motion picture director
10. Frank Lloyd Wright	j. first aviator to make solo nonstop flight across Atlantic Ocean

Essay Questions

1. What was the government's attitude toward business in the 1920s? What specific policies and actions resulted from this attitude?
2. Why was Ford's Model T an important breakthrough? What effects did automobiles have on the American economy? on society in general?
3. How did farmers fare in the 1920s? Explain your answer.
4. What was the Red Scare? What events helped bring it about?
5. How did women's lives change in the 1920s?

CHAPTER 26

Depression and the New Deal

A s the decade of the 1920s neared its end, the United States was struck by a sudden business panic. It was followed by the worst depression the country had ever experienced. The resulting economic and social problems, persisting throughout the 1930s, presented the American people with their severest challenge since the Civil War. Under the leadership of a strong president, the nation managed to overcome the threat to its stability. It also emerged from this troubled period transformed in many ways.

THE CRASH AND ITS AFTERMATH

Greed for big profits from the stock market seemed to infect the whole country by the late 1920s. Only about 1.5 million Americans invested in stocks and bonds. But market trading was important as a gauge of the nation's economy. By 1929, some danger signals were apparent. One was the fact that stock prices were unrealistically high. They did not reflect what corporations were actually earning. Another unhealthy trend was the practice of buying stocks "on margin." This meant that a buyer paid only a small amount of cash to cover a stock purchase. Brokers lent the buyer the rest, with the stock as security. Buying on margin drove stock prices up and led to a risky credit situation.

Panic on Wall Street

The constant rise of stock prices ended abruptly on October 24, 1929—a day that became known as "Black Thursday." Without warning,

Migratory worker

Breadlines

Rural hardship

wave after wave of selling hit the market, and prices began to fall sharply. In less than three weeks, the average price of stocks dropped by 40 percent. Some popular stocks fell even more. Before the crash, for example, General Electric stock sold at $396\frac{1}{4}$. By November 13, its price was $168\frac{1}{8}$—a loss in value of 58 percent. Speculators who had bought on margin were asked to put up more cash to secure their loans. Those who could not do so lost everything.

Like the earlier get-rich-quick fever, panic spread like wildfire. A person might wake up a millionaire and go to bed penniless. Billions of dollars in paper profits were wiped out.

Beginning of the Depression

The stock market crash of 1929 marked the beginning of the Great Depression. This economic disaster affected not only the United States but, eventually, most other countries, too.

CAUSES The crash did not cause the depression. It simply brought into the open several problems that had been hidden up to that time.

One problem was that the 1920s were not prosperous years for everyone. Farmers had been in trouble since the end of World War I. Most minority groups were poor: black sharecroppers, black city dwellers, Mexican-Americans in the Southwest, and Indians in the West. According to one estimate, a third of the American population was living in or near poverty in the 1920s.

Another problem was unsound financial practices. Selling stocks on margin encouraged speculation. Banks granted risky personal and business loans, and sought quick profits in stock market trading. Such practices threatened the financial stability of the banks and the safety of their depositors' funds. (Over 300 banks failed in 1929 *before* the crash.)

Many consumers went deeply into debt by buying expensive goods on the installment plan. When they could not meet their payments, their purchases were repossessed.

The most serious problem was a lack of balance in the economy itself. Industrial production kept rising, but wage earners' incomes did not. People could not buy all the automobiles, appliances, and other goods being manufactured. Foreign demand for American products was limited, too. Europe was still recovering from the effects of World War I and had serious economic problems of its own. High protective tariffs added to the slowdown in international trade.

EFFECTS   The Great Depression showed dramatically how all the parts of an industrial society depend on one another. After the crash, funds for investment dried up. Many businesses then cut production or closed down. Thousands of workers lost their jobs. Unable to meet mortgage payments, many people were forced to give up their homes. Those with savings tried to withdraw them from banks. But many banks did not have ready cash because they had invested it. Hundreds of them simply closed their doors.

The worst year of the depression was 1933. By that time, 100,000 businesses had gone bankrupt, and some 5000 banks had failed. Farmers could no longer support their families. The price of wheat, for example, had dropped to an all-time low of 38 cents a bushel the previous year (compared to $2.16 in 1919, and 92 cents in 1923). About 13 million people—25 percent of the work force—were jobless. Thousands of those who still had jobs were forced to take pay cuts.

Homeless people jammed the country's roads, drifting from place to place looking for work. Makeshift villages of tar-paper shacks arose on the outskirts of cities. With bitter humor, Americans called them "Hoover-villes." Local governments and private charities set up soup kitchens and tried to provide some money to the destitute.

Hoover's Administration

In the beginning, President Hoover was optimistic. The country had gone through depressions before. Each time, it had recovered in a year or two without government interference. The economy, he said, was "fundamentally sound."

GOVERNMENT MEASURES   Hoover's administration did make several attempts to deal with the economy. Before the crash, it took steps to solve the persistent problem of falling farm prices by urging Congress to pass the *Agricultural Marketing Act*. This law aimed to stabilize farm prices by

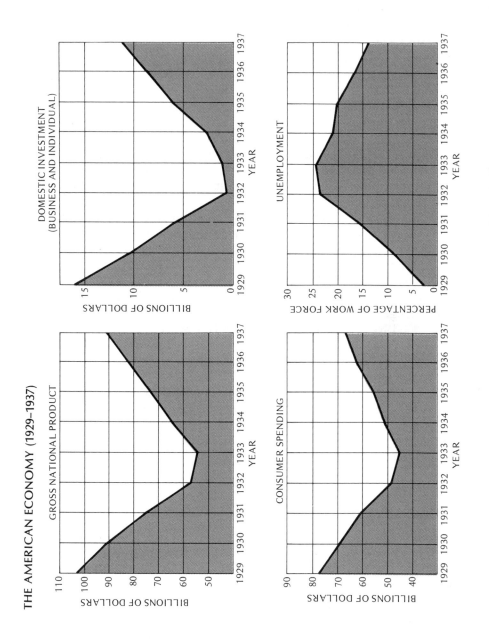

THE AMERICAN ECONOMY (1929–1937)

GROSS NATIONAL PRODUCT

BILLIONS OF DOLLARS

YEAR

CONSUMER SPENDING

BILLIONS OF DOLLARS

YEAR

DOMESTIC INVESTMENT
(BUSINESS AND INDIVIDUAL)

BILLIONS OF DOLLARS

YEAR

UNEMPLOYMENT

PERCENTAGE OF WORK FORCE

YEAR

creating a central fund and setting up a federal farm board to buy and store crop surpluses. After three years, however, warehouses were full, the fund was used up, and farm prices were lower than ever.

After the crash, in 1930, Congress passed and Hoover signed the *Hawley-Smoot Tariff*. It set rates at the highest level in U.S. history. The tariff was supposed to help manufacturers, but it harmed them. Europeans reacted by raising their tariffs, and foreign trade almost stopped. At the same time, Americans cut back on their investments overseas. In 1931, one of the biggest European banks failed. This led to panic and bank "runs." (A run occurs when depositors lose confidence in a bank and rush to withdraw their money.) The European depression that followed was as bad as the one in the United States.

As the depression dragged on, the Hoover administration took a bold step. On its recommendation, Congress in 1932 created the Reconstruction Finance Corporation (RFC), which lent money to banks, insurance companies, farm groups, and railroads. It also helped states in their relief efforts. But Hoover vetoed a proposal for large-scale federal public works. He thought that the plan would strike "at the roots of self-government" by interfering with state control over such matters.

THE BONUS ARMY   In the summer of 1932, thousands of unemployed veterans traveled to Washington, D.C. They wanted Congress to authorize early payment of their bonuses. (The bonuses were not due to be paid until 1945.) When Congress failed to act, several thousand members of the "bonus army" stayed on in shanties they had built near the Potomac River. The administration finally used an army unit under Douglas MacArthur to evict the veterans. The sight of soldiers attacking veterans shocked Americans all over the country.

THE ELECTION OF 1932   The Republicans renominated Hoover for the presidency in the summer of 1932, but with little hope of winning. The president had become linked to the depression in the mind of the public, and he himself conveyed an image of pessimism and gloom. The Democrats, on the other hand, had high hopes of regaining control of the White House. Their nominee was Franklin Delano Roosevelt, governor of New York. Roosevelt, a distant relative of Theodore Roosevelt, came from a wealthy old Dutch family. He had served as assistant secretary of the navy under Wilson and had run unsuccessfully for vice president in 1920. Though crippled by polio in 1921, Roosevelt returned to politics and had served as governor of New York since 1928.

The Democratic platform called for repeal of prohibition, banking and financial reforms, aid to the unemployed, and help for the farmers. Roosevelt became the first nominee to appear before a convention and make an acceptance speech. He declared: "I pledge you, I pledge myself, to a new deal for the American people."

The two candidates provided a great contrast as they campaigned. Hoover was grim and tired. "FDR" (as Roosevelt was often called) was the picture of self-confidence. Hoover warned that the depression would get even worse under the Democrats. Roosevelt promised to help the "forgotten man at the bottom of the economic pyramid." Roosevelt won by a landslide. He carried 42 states to Hoover's 6, and the Democrats gained control of both houses of Congress.

THE EARLY NEW DEAL

Hoover was the last president to remain in office for four months after his defeat. The Twentieth Amendment, ratified in February 1933, provided that future presidents would take over on January 20, instead of March 4.

In the interval between the election and Roosevelt's inauguration, economic conditions continued to worsen. Industrial production kept declining to new lows, the nation's banking system was approaching total collapse, and more and more people were finding it impossible to support themselves and their families.

The only thing we have to fear is fear itself—nameless, unreasoning, unjustified terror which paralyzes needed efforts to convert retreat into advance.

—Franklin D. Roosevelt's First Inaugural Address,
March 4, 1933

Advisers and Aims

Roosevelt gathered around him a number of energetic and committed public servants. His cabinet included Secretary of State Cordell Hull, a Southern supporter; Secretary of Labor Frances Perkins, the first woman to serve in a presidential cabinet; and two Republicans, Henry A. Wallace as secretary of agriculture and Harold L. Ickes as secretary of the interior. Roosevelt also sought advice from many respected scholars and other professionals—a group that came to be known as the "brain trust."

Another important influence on Roosevelt was his wife, Eleanor, Franklin's cousin and Theodore's niece. She worked hard on behalf of the poor, minorities, and women. Although she lacked FDR's easy manner, her deep concern for others helped shape the administration's actions and image.

Roosevelt and his advisers put forward a series of programs and set up a number of agencies that, together, made up the New Deal. Its aims are often summarized as relief, recovery, and reform—relief for the needy, recovery from the depression, and economic reform to prevent future depressions.

Many New Deal measures had their roots in Progressivism. Roosevelt greatly admired his Progressive forerunners in office, Theodore Roosevelt and Woodrow Wilson. Other New Deal programs had precedents in the increased government activity of the World War I period. Certainly, Roosevelt had no intention of overturning the American free-enterprise system. But, because of his willingness to experiment with new ideas, the government played a more active role in American life than it ever had before.

Roosevelt's great personal charm won him the support of all sorts of people—conservatives as well as liberals in Congress, journalists, and much of the public. He changed the presidential press conference from a formal question-and-answer session to a relaxed, good-natured exchange of views with reporters. From time to time, he made speeches over the radio. These "fireside chats" made Americans feel that they had a friend in the White House.

The Hundred Days

Roosevelt's first three months as president—a period that became known as the "hundred days"—was a time of hectic government activity. Within days of his inauguration, FDR summoned the new Congress to convene in special session, and issued a proclamation ordering all banks in the country to close. The four-day "bank holiday" stopped the rising tide of bank runs. Sound banks were then permitted to reopen. In his first fireside chat, the president told his listeners that the reopened banks were backed by the resources of the federal government. They were "safe." His statement reassured the nation and helped ease the banking crisis. A few months later, the *Glass-Steagall Act* created the Federal Deposit Insurance Corporation (FDIC) to insure depositors' accounts against loss in case of bank failure.

RELIEF Some measures of the hundred days provided help to people without jobs. The Federal Emergency Relief Administration (FERA) distributed federal funds to state and local agencies for direct relief to the unemployed. Millions of families received cash for food, clothing, and shelter. The Civilian Conservation Corps (CCC) hired young men for such conservation projects as replanting forests, controlling floods, and improving national parks.

RECOVERY More controversial were two recovery measures passed during the hundred days. Both of them aimed to raise prices by cutting production. The *Agricultural Adjustment Act (AAA) of 1933* was designed to help farmers. It paid growers to reduce their output of basic farm commodities such as wheat, corn, and cotton. Because the law was passed after the start of the growing season, thousands of acres had to be plowed under—a distressing practice when people were hungry. In 1936, the Supreme Court declared the AAA unconstitutional because of the way it was funded. (A revised farm bill was passed two years later.)

The second recovery bill, the *National Industrial Recovery Act*, was supposed to help industry. It suspended antitrust laws and encouraged manufacturers to cooperate in setting up codes of fair competition. These included industry-wide schedules of production and prices, as well as agreements on workers' wages and hours. The act also recognized the right of labor to form unions. The National Recovery Administration (NRA), created to administer the act, soon ran into criticism. Its many regulations helped big businesses rather than small ones. And it did little to help the average consumer. In 1935, the Supreme Court declared the act unconstitutional because it granted too much legislative power to the NRA, an executive agency.

REFORM   One of the most successful reforms of the hundred days was the Tennessee Valley Authority (TVA). This was a giant public power project in the valley of the Tennessee River. Designed to control floods, it also improved the region's standard of living by providing cheaper electricity, producing fertilizers, halting soil erosion, and improving river navigation. Opponents criticized the TVA as socialistic, but it did help the people in the Tennessee River basin.

After the Hundred Days

The early months of the New Deal did not bring the quick recovery everyone had hoped for. Roosevelt then tried additional measures. Some of them were responses to the growing criticism of his administration.

NEW DEAL CRITICS   The New Deal was criticized from two different points of view. Some people argued that it had gone too far. Among those who felt this way were wealthy Republicans and conservative Democrats, including 1928 presidential candidate Al Smith. A group of these anti-New Dealers formed the Liberty League to defend the free enterprise system from what they regarded as Roosevelt's attacks on it.

Other Americans believed that the New Deal had not gone far enough. One such critic was Father Charles Coughlin (the "radio priest"). He advocated the Populist cure-all of silver inflation. Another critic was Dr. Francis E. Townsend, who proposed government-funded pensions for the elderly. The critic with the biggest following was Senator Huey P. Long of Louisiana. His "Share Our Wealth" program won millions of supporters. It promised to tax the rich and use the money to provide an annual income to the poor. (Long's career ended when he was assassinated early in 1935. Leadership of his movement was then taken over by Gerald L. K. Smith.)

THE SECOND NEW DEAL   Roosevelt launched the so-called "second New Deal" in 1935. He did so partly in response to criticisms and partly because the Democrats did well in the 1934 congressional elections. A major relief and recovery measure was a huge public works program, to be supervised by the Works Progress Administration (WPA). The WPA built and repaired highways, bridges, sewers, hospitals, schools, and parks. It also employed people in the arts. Writers produced state histories, painters created murals in public buildings, and entertainers toured the country in plays and musicals.

Two reform bills went even further. One was the *Wagner Act* (or *National Labor Relations Act*). It was designed to protect workers' rights after the failure of the NRA. It banned "unfair practices" by management, such as firing workers who joined unions. The bill also set up the National Labor Relations Board (NLRB) to enforce the act by supervising collective bargaining and union elections.

The other major reform of the second New Deal was the creation of a social security system. Secretary of Labor Perkins had joined Roosevelt's cabinet on the condition that such a program be enacted. The *Social Security Act* provided for (1) pensions to retired workers or their survivors, (2) aid to states so that they could offer unemployment compensation, and (3) aid to states so that they could help support dependent and handicapped children.

LATER YEARS

In the presidential election of 1936, Roosevelt ran against Alf Landon, the governor of Kansas and a former Bull Moose Progressive. FDR won 62 percent of the popular vote and the electoral votes of all but two states. Even so, Roosevelt's domestic policies met with greater resistance during his second term.

Trouble Over the Supreme Court

Roosevelt regarded the Supreme Court as the one government institution that stood in the way of progress. It had ruled against the NRA and the AAA. Would it do the same with the Wagner Act and social security? Were the justices rejecting New Deal measures because of old-fashioned notions of laissez-faire economics? Roosevelt thought so.

Early in 1937, Roosevelt sent a proposal to Congress that came to be

FDR's "court-packing" scheme runs into trouble from a resistant Congress. (Copyright © 1953 by the New York Times Company. Reprinted by permission)

called his "court-packing" plan. He suggested that one new justice be added to the Supreme Court for every justice over the age of 70 who refused to retire. (Six of them were over 70 at the time.) Roosevelt presented his plan as a way to ease the Court's work load. But his critics viewed it as an attempt to destroy the independence of the judiciary.

There was nothing unconstitutional about changing the number of Supreme Court justices; it had been done before. But few Americans liked Roosevelt's way of going about it. His plan was widely opposed, not only by the public at large but in the Democratic-controlled Congress as well. After five months of debate, the proposal was rejected.

Shortly afterward, the Supreme Court upheld both the Social Security Act and the Wagner Act. Then, a conservative justice resigned, and Roosevelt nominated a more liberal one. (By 1941, he was to fill seven vacancies.) Thus, on the Supreme Court issue, Roosevelt lost the battle but won the war.

Labor Problems

The Wagner Act encouraged labor unions to recruit new members. Union membership grew from fewer than 3 million in 1933 to almost 9 million in 1939. But not all union leaders favored the AFL type of craft organization. Its member unions were made up of skilled workers only.

Several people wanted to organize workers into industrial unions that would include all the workers (skilled and unskilled) in a given industry.

John L. Lewis, head of the *United Mine Workers (UMW)*, had such a goal. In 1935, his supporters formed a committee for industrial organization within the AFL. Three years later, they broke away and formed the independent *Congress of Industrial Organizations (CIO)*.

Industrial organizers faced opposition both from corporations and from the AFL. One crucial struggle involved workers in the auto industry. They could not gain recognition for their industrial union, the *United Auto Workers (UAW)*. So, in the winter of 1936–1937, they staged a series of sit-down strikes, staying in the auto plants but refusing to work. Afraid of property damage, management would not use force against the workers. Eventually, the strikers won recognition. So did steelworkers, after a number of pitched battles with the police.

Farm Problems

Despite New Deal efforts to help farmers, many of them were still very poor in the late 1930s. For those who lived in the southern plains, conditions were especially bad. Several years of serious drought, beginning in 1933, led to severe dust storms. They swept up tons of topsoil and whirled it as far away as the Atlantic Ocean.

Millions of acres in the Oklahoma Panhandle, western Kansas, and northwestern Texas were particularly hard hit. This region became known as the Dust Bowl. Thousands of families, unable to survive there, piled into their old cars and moved west, looking for seasonal work as migrant farm laborers. (John Steinbeck told the story of several of these "Okies" in his novel *The Grapes of Wrath*.) The emergency ended with the return of normal rainfall in the late 1930s.

To prevent such disasters from happening again, Roosevelt introduced a series of conservation measures. Millions of trees were planted on the Great Plains. They protected open fields from the force of the wind and held the topsoil down. Farmers were taught new techniques of plowing and crop rotation to improve their land.

To cope with the continuing problem of farm surpluses, Congress passed a second *Agricultural Adjustment Act* in 1938. Like the first one, it paid farmers to limit production. If there were still surpluses, the government stored them for future use. Meanwhile, it made loans to farmers at rates that were below parity (a figure based on prices between 1909 and 1914). If the market price rose to parity or higher, farmers were allowed to sell their crops and repay the loans. If not, farmers kept the money and the government kept the crops. This method of keeping agricultural income fairly stable through farm subsidies has been used, with slight changes, ever since.

Final New Deal Legislation

The last New Deal measure was the *Fair Labor Standards Act* (or *Wages and Hours Act*), passed in June 1938. Its purpose was to help nonunion workers. The act set maximum hours and minimum wages in industries that engaged in interstate commerce. It also banned the employment of children under 16, except on farms. In order to get the bill passed, Congress had to exempt several categories of workers. These included farm laborers, domestic servants, and professionals.

By this time, the early enthusiasm for the New Deal had waned. And events abroad were so threatening that Americans were more and more concerned with national defense.

THE NEW DEAL LEGACY

Roosevelt was a controversial president. He was feared, and even hated, by some people. They felt that he had endangered the American way of life by undercutting "rugged individualism." Business leaders and the wealthy denounced him as a "traitor to his class." But millions of other Americans admired, even idolized, FDR. They felt that he had saved the country from disaster. Postal authorities knew exactly where to deliver letters addressed to "Benedict Arnold 2nd"—or to "God's Gift to the U.S.A."

People are still arguing about the achievements and shortcomings of the New Deal. It did not end the Great Depression. In 1939, the Gross National Product totaled about $90 billion, compared to $103 billion ten years earlier. There were still 9.5 million people out of work. (Only the increased spending of the World War II era finally ended the depression.) But the New Deal had a number of important consequences. Perhaps the most fundamental was the restoration of national confidence. Other lasting results may be summed up in four main areas.

Minority Participation

The New Deal did not end discrimination against black Americans. Segregation continued, even in such New Deal programs as the CCC. Black people continued to be the "last hired and first fired." But there were improvements. The Roosevelts, especially Eleanor, established closer contact with the black community than did earlier presidents or their wives. The government hired more blacks. And black Americans, in particular, benefited from relief and recovery programs because there were so many poor among them.

American Indians likewise benefited from relief measures. They were also helped by a new bill aimed at correcting the abuses caused by the Dawes Act. The *Wheeler-Howard Act* of 1934 put an end to individual land sales and restored surplus reservation land to tribal ownership. It also encouraged Indians to form tribal cooperatives and to maintain their ethnic traditions.

Until the 1930s, the most influential members of American society were white, Anglo-Saxon Protestants (so-called WASPs). More than previous administrations, the New Deal brought into government Americans of other ethnic and religious backgrounds. Only 3 percent of all the judges appointed by Harding, Coolidge, and Hoover were Catholics. Under Roosevelt, the proportion rose to 26 percent. Minority opportunities in education and the professions also began to improve. "On a very wide front and in the truest possible sense," wrote one journalist, "Franklin Delano Roosevelt included the excluded."

The New Deal Coalition

Roosevelt was a master politician, and he served longer than any other president in history. (He was re-elected in 1940 and again in 1944.) During his years in office, the Democratic party became a majority party for the first time since the Civil War. FDR built a coalition that was to last nearly 50 years. (A coalition is an alliance of people or groups with different views.)

The "old guard" of the New Deal coalition was made up of politicians from the solid South and from big-city machines, such as that of Chicago. New Democrats included most blacks. They deserted the Republican party that they had been supporting since reconstruction. Organized labor, benefiting from the Wagner Act, also voted Democratic. Most Catholics and Jews regarded themselves as Democrats as well. So did a large number of intellectuals.

A Welfare State

One of the most important results of the New Deal was the creation of a welfare state—one in which the government assumes prime responsibility for the well-being of its citizens. Before the 1930s, the victims of economic hardship were helped by private or local charities, if they were helped at all. The New Deal convinced most Americans that the government had a duty to provide economic security for all its people. The federal government was no longer a remote organization. It became a real presence in the lives of almost all Americans.

Big Government

A welfare state requires more personnel and more money than does a simpler type of government. Just as the late 1800s saw the rise of big

IMPORTANT NEW DEAL MEASURES (1933–1938)

Act	Purpose	Results
Emergency Banking Relief Act, March 1933	To save failing banks	Lent money to sound banks; closed unsafe banks; did away with gold standard
Civilian Conservation Corps Reforestation Relief Act, March 1933	To relieve unemployment and conserve natural resources	Established Civilian Conservation Corps (CCC), which eventually employed more than 2 million young men in forestry and related projects
Federal Emergency Relief Act, May 1933	To provide money for jobless	Through Federal Emergency Relief Administration (FERA), gave funds to states for relief to unemployed
Agricultural Adjustment Act, May 1933	To restore farmers' purchasing power	Set up Agricultural Adjustment Administration (AAA), which paid farmers to reduce production; lent them money to refinance mortgages
Tennessee Valley Authority Act, May 1933	To develop region's resources	Set up Tennessee Valley Authority (TVA), which built more than 20 dams; supplied electricity and fertilizer
Federal Securities Act, May 1933	To regulate sale of securities (stocks and bonds)	Required most corporations to register new securities issues with Federal Trade Commission (FTC); control later transferred to Securities and Exchange Commission (SEC)
Home Owners Refinancing Act, June 1933	To help nonfarm families keep their homes	Created Home Owners Loan Corporation (HOLC); eventually refinanced mortgages on a million homes
Glass-Steagall Act (Banking Act), June 1933	To protect bank depositors	Through Federal Deposit Insurance Corporation (FDIC), insured individual deposits in case of bank failures
National Industrial Recovery Act, June 1933	To revive industry and reduce unemployment	Set up National Recovery Administration (NRA), which supervised industrial codes; created Public Works Administration (PWA), which directed the building of more than 30,000 public projects
Civil Works Administration (established by president), November 1933	To relieve unemployment	Employed millions of people; became Works Progress Administration (WPA) in May 1935

Securities Exchange Act, June 1934	To regulate stock exchanges	Created Securities and Exchange Commission (SEC)
Frazier-Lemke Farm Bankruptcy Act, June 1934	To prevent farm foreclosures	Enabled farmers to extend their credit
National Housing Act, June 1934	To stimulate new construction	Established Federal Housing Administration (FHA), which insured loans for private and commercial buildings
Emergency Relief Appropriation Act, April 1935	To provide work for unemployed	Established Works Progress Administration (WPA), which gave jobs to 8.5 million people; spent $11 billion on the building of public works projects over period of 8 years
Rural Electrification Administration (established by president), May 1935	To bring electricity to remote areas	Made loans to utilities to improve electric service in rural areas
National Youth Administration (established by president), June 1935	To help needy students continue their education	Provided part-time employment for more than 2 million high school and college students
Wagner Act (National Labor Relations Act), July 1935	To guarantee labor rights (after NRA was declared unconstitutional)	Created National Labor Relations Board (NLRB); upheld collective bargaining and closed (all-union) shops
Social Security Act, July 1935	To provide for old-age and other insurance	Set up pension system; provided for unemployment compensation and aid to dependent children
Public Utility Holding Company Act, August 1935	To break up monopolies	Restricted public utilities from forming holding companies
National Housing Act, September 1937	To improve housing for low-income Americans	Established United States Housing Authority (USHA), which lent funds for slum clearance and housing projects
Agricultural Adjustment Act, February 1938	To replace first AAA (after it was declared unconstitutional)	Set quotas for various farm products; restored principle of parity
Fair Labor Standards Act, June 1938	To help workers	Set minimum wages and maximum hours for some workers; banned employment of children under 16

407

business, the 1930s saw the rise of big government.

The number of civilian employees grew from under 600,000 in 1929 to almost a million ten years later. Government expenses mounted, too. In 1932—Hoover's last year as president—the government spent about $4.5 billion for all purposes. In 1939, it spent about $9 billion. The government was spending more than it took in, a situation that Roosevelt himself disapproved of. (Even earlier, Hoover had unhappily resorted to this practice, known as deficit spending.) The national debt rose higher than ever during the Roosevelt administration. Most of this increase, however, was the result of wartime spending, rather than the cost of peacetime programs.

Multiple-Choice Test

1. The Great Depression began with the stock market crash of (a) April 1929 (b) October 1929 (c) January 1932 (d) March 1933.
2. A major agency created during the Hoover administration to combat the depression was the (a) Reconstruction Finance Corporation (b) Civilian Conservation Corps (c) Civil Works Administration (d) Securities and Exchange Commission.
3. The Glass-Steagall Act set up the (a) FTC (b) FHA (c) FDIC (d) WPA.
4. Both the AAA and the NRA were designed to (a) aid industry (b) help farmers (c) raise prices by limiting production (d) encourage the growth of labor unions.
5. The second New Deal brought about all the following *except* (a) the Works Progress Administration (b) the Wagner Act (c) social security (d) the Tennessee Valley Authority.
6. Roosevelt's court-packing plan for the Supreme Court was aimed at (a) increasing the justices' work load (b) decreasing the total number of justices (c) ensuring a more favorable attitude toward New Deal legislation (d) creating a more conservative Court.
7. Between 1933 and 1939, union membership (a) increased by 6 million (b) increased by 50 percent (c) decreased by 3 million (d) decreased by 50 percent.
8. The purpose of the second AAA was to (a) increase agricultural production (b) keep farm income up (c) aid migrant farm workers (d) help farmers with their mortgages.
9. The Great Depression ended (a) in 1935 (b) in 1938 (c) during World War II (d) in 1945.
10. The New Deal coalition included all of the following *except* (a) the solid South (b) blacks (c) organized labor (d) wealthy business leaders.

Matching Test

CoLUMN A

1. Hawley-Smoot Tariff
2. bonus army
3. Henry A. Wallace
4. Glass-Steagall Act
5. Liberty League
6. Huey Long
7. Alf Landon
8. John L. Lewis
9. Fair Labor Standards Act
10. Wheeler-Howard Act

CoLUMN B

a. advocate of guaranteed annual income
b. union leader who helped organize CIO
c. law that raised prices on imports to highest level in U.S. history
d. organization that opposed New Deal programs
e. World War I veterans who met in Washington in 1932
f. candidate who ran against Roosevelt in presidential election of 1936
g. secretary of agriculture under FDR
h. law that set new policies for American Indians
i. law that insured bank deposits
j. law that set maximum hours and minimum wages for many workers

Essay Questions

1. In what ways was the American economy unsound during the 1920s?
2. What were the three main aims of the New Deal during the hundred days? Give an example of a measure in each category.
3. In what ways did the New Deal help labor?
4. Why did some Americans dislike FDR and oppose the New Deal?
5. What were the most important consequences of the New Deal?

 **UNIT 9**

War
and
Peace

CHAPTER 27

World War II

A SECOND WORLD WAR engulfed the globe in 1939, less than 21 years after the end of the Great War. The United States played a much larger role in World War II than it had in World War I, but it again escaped the devastation that left much of Europe and Asia in ruins.

U.S. FOREIGN POLICY BETWEEN WARS

Part of the American wish for "normalcy" after World War I was a desire to retreat from foreign entanglements. Many ordinary Americans favored a policy of isolationism—remaining aloof from involvement overseas. Most of the nation's political leaders, however, saw things differently. They realized that the United States, as a nation of power and influence, could not be a mere onlooker in world affairs.

Republican Diplomacy

Although the United States did not join the League of Nations after World War I, it did take part in international conferences and agreements. The Harding administration organized the *Washington Naval Conference* of 1921-1922. Delegates from nine nations discussed Asian affairs and a reduction in naval strength. The five leading naval powers—the United States, Britain, Japan, France, and Italy—agreed to limit the number of their battleships, aircraft carriers, and heavy cruisers for ten years. (The United States, Britain, and Japan renewed this agreement at the *London*

Naval Conference of 1930.) Conference delegates also pledged to guarantee the independence of China and to continue an Open Door Policy there.

The United States also played a role in European affairs. In the early 1920s, Germany had trouble making reparations payments to France. President Coolidge appointed a commission headed by Charles Dawes to work out a settlement. The *Dawes Plan* provided for foreign loans to Germany so that it could resume the payments.

A high point of international cooperation in the 1920s was the *Kellogg-Briand Pact* of 1928. Its sponsors were Coolidge's secretary of state, Frank Kellogg, and the French foreign minister, Aristide Briand. Most nations signed this agreement to outlaw war as a way of settling international disputes. The Kellogg-Briand Pact, however, was little more than a gesture. There was no way to enforce it.

Under Harding and Coolidge, U.S. policy toward Latin America continued to be one of intervention, as in the Progressive era. U.S. troops, in Nicaragua since 1912, were withdrawn in 1925 but were sent back a year later. Haiti remained an American protectorate throughout the 1920s. Only in the Dominican Republic did the situation ease. American marines, stationed there since 1916, were withdrawn in 1924.

Hoover opposed interventionism. As president-elect, he toured 11 Latin American countries, urging that the nations of the Western Hemisphere treat each other "as good neighbors." Backing up his words with deeds, he later refrained from interfering when troubles broke out in Cuba, Panama, and El Salvador. He also ordered the withdrawal of U.S. troops from Nicaragua before he left office in 1933.

Changes Under Roosevelt

In 1933, when Roosevelt became president, the world was in the depths of the Great Depression. Many people felt that high American tariffs (such as the Hawley-Smoot Tariff of 1930) had contributed to the problem. Two actions taken by the Roosevelt administration in 1934 were designed to improve the situation. One was the establishment of the Export-Import Bank, which made loans to stimulate foreign trade. The other was the *Trade Agreements Act.* It allowed the president to lower tariffs on specific items by as much as 50 percent, without congressional approval. By 1939, tariffs had been reduced by about 30 percent.

Another step to stimulate trade was diplomatic recognition of the Soviet Union. Ever since the Bolshevik revolution of 1917, Americans had been suspicious of, if not hostile toward, the new state. Between 1918 and 1920, U.S. troops (and other Allied forces) had even aided anti-Soviet Russians in their attempt to overthrow the Bolsheviks. Over the years, however, fear of a Communist-inspired revolution in the United States had lessened. At the urging of farmers and business leaders, Roosevelt established diplomatic relations with the Soviet Union in 1933.

In Latin American relations, Roosevelt reaffirmed and expanded the Good Neighbor Policy that his predecessor had begun. In 1934, he pulled U.S. troops out of Haiti. That same year, the United States also revoked the Platt Amendment, thereby surrendering its right to intervene in Cuba.

The Good Neighbor Policy was put to a serious test in 1938, when Mexico took over foreign oil properties there. Although the U.S. companies in Mexico valued their oil holdings at more than $200 million, the Mexican government agreed to pay them only about $34 million. The oil companies protested, but the U.S. government advised them to accept the offer, and the affair was settled peacefully.

THE COMING OF WAR

In spite of its problems during the 1930s, the United States maintained its basic political system and a stable government. Many other nations were not so lucky. Upheavals in Japan, Italy, and Germany were a primary cause of war in 1939.

Militarism in Japan

After World War I, the Japanese were in a strong economic position. Politically, they took steps to make their country more democratic. The Diet (parliament) gained greater power, and all men over 25 were granted the vote.

But the Great Depression hit Japan hard. Its silk trade was all but wiped out. Japan's leaders seemed unable to restore prosperity, and people grew impatient with parliamentary government. To make matters worse, many Japanese viewed their country's agreement to limit its warships—undertaken at the naval conferences in Washington and London—as a national insult.

In 1931, Japanese military units, without government authorization, seized the Chinese province of Manchuria. (When the League of Nations condemned this aggression, Japan withdrew from membership.) From then on, Japan's military leaders gained greater and greater control over the country. The military did not actually take over civilian institutions such as the Diet, but they made such institutions powerless.

At home, military leaders called for strict obedience to Japan's emperor and other authorities. Abroad, militarism led to an aggressive foreign policy, especially toward the Chinese. China had been in a state of unrest ever since a revolution in 1911. Japan lacked both raw materials and room for its growing population. A weakened China seemed

The Japanese invasion of Manchuria in 1931 signaled a new policy of militarism that would bring Japan and the United States into direct conflict within ten years. (Jerry Doyle, *Philadelphia Record*)

the obvious place for the Japanese to expand. They moved south from their base in Manchuria in 1937. When the United States protested against this violation of the Open Door, Japan declared that it no longer accepted that policy. For the next eight years, it waged an undeclared war against the Chinese.

Fascism in Europe

Japan was not the only country to turn to an aggressive foreign policy. This approach was also a key element in dictatorships that rose to power in Europe during the 1920s and 1930s.

ITALY'S MUSSOLINI   After World War I, Italy was disrupted by labor unrest and fear of a Communist revolution. A political leader named Benito Mussolini had little difficulty winning support when he promised order and a return to the glories of the ancient Roman Empire. In 1922, he led a march of his own private soldiers on Rome, and was soon made prime minister.

Roosevelt and Churchill
U.S. 5th Army, 1944
British Tanks, 1945
U.S.S. Missouri

Mussolini preached a doctrine called fascism. (He took the name from a Roman symbol, the *fasces*—a bundle of rods wrapped around an ax. Mussolini said that it stood for the many groups of Italians, unified into one state.) Fascism glorified the nation at the expense of the individual. Citizens had few, if any, rights. They were expected to fight and die for the state. Police and spies kept the people in line and answered only to the dictator, Mussolini. Dictatorship was not new. What made fascism different was its control over almost every aspect of people's lives.

Fascist Italy was one of the first modern police states. Regimes of this type have more than armed force on their side. They keep a close watch over people's activities, often through spies and hidden microphones and cameras. Their mass media subject citizens to constant streams of propaganda. A police state may be based on various political ideas, usually fascism or communism. All such states are described as totalitarian, because their rulers seek total control over the people they rule.

GERMANY'S HITLER   Like Italy, Germany had troubles after the war. Its parliamentary government lasted until the 1930s, but it was greatly weakened by the depression. Many Germans were bitter as well as poor. They deeply resented the Versailles Treaty. It had branded Germany as the sole power responsible for World War I, and it had burdened the Germans with heavy reparations.

An Austrian-born veteran, Adolf Hitler, found a ready audience when he promised that better times were in store for Germany. The German people, he argued, had been sold out by their political leaders, by foreigners, and by Jews. (Hitler played on the anti-Semitism—hatred of Jews—that was widespread in Germany.) Hitler's new party, called the *National Socialists*, or *Nazis*, aimed to revive the German Empire. During the early 1930s, the Nazis became a powerful force in the Reichstag (parliament), and in 1933, Hitler was made chancellor. Within a year, he ruled Germany as dictator.

Nazism, a form of fascism, was particularly vicious because of its racial policies. According to Hitler, the Germans were a master race. He viewed Slavs, Jews, and blacks as "inferior peoples" and claimed that Germans were destined to control them. Hitler soon began to carry out a policy of depriving Jews of their rights and property. Before long, this policy was to reach monstrous proportions.

A String of Aggressions

In five short years, from 1935 through 1939, Mussolini and Hitler made a series of aggressive moves that brought on World War II. Britain and France were so anxious to avoid armed conflict that they let the dictators seize territory with little opposition. This policy of making concessions to aggressors to keep the peace became known as appeasement.

INITIAL MOVES   In 1935, Hitler and Mussolini made their expansionist intentions clear. Ignoring the Versailles Treaty, Hitler announced that he would rearm Germany. (He had already taken his country out of the League of Nations.) In the fall of that year, Mussolini attacked the African state of Ethiopia. He used a clash along its border with Italian Somaliland as his excuse. Italy's advanced weapons enabled it to defeat the Ethiopians in a few months. The League took little action.

The following spring, Hitler marched troops into the Rhineland. This German area along the French border was supposed to be free from military installations. But Hitler built fortifications there.

THE SPANISH CIVIL WAR   Spain was the scene of further Fascist aggression. The country was already troubled by conflict between pro- and antigovernment elements. A civil war broke out in the summer of 1936. Francisco Franco led the Nationalists in an uprising against the forces of the government, known as Loyalists or Republicans. Both Italy and Germany sent troops and planes to help Franco. The people of the United States, Britain, and France tended to sympathize with the Loyalists. But the three democracies declared themselves neutral, and none sent aid. The only country to supply substantial arms to the Loyalist cause was the Soviet Union. It also helped organize an International Brigade of volunteer soldiers from several countries, including the United States.

Franco's forces defeated the Loyalists in 1939. He then set up a Fascist dictatorship. He imprisoned thousands of Spaniards and ruthlessly suppressed all opposition to the government.

FINAL MARCH TO WAR   In 1936, Mussolini and Hitler signed an alliance called the *Rome-Berlin Axis.* The name was meant to suggest that the

AXIS AGGRESSIONS IN EUROPE (1935–1939)

world turned around Italy and Germany. Japan joined the alliance in 1940, and it then became known as the *Rome-Berlin-Tokyo Axis*.

Early in 1938, Hitler annexed Austria. Nazis in Austria had paved the way for this union, which had been forbidden by the Versailles Treaty. The annexation gave Germany a better position from which to control central Europe.

Hitler then turned to another strategic country, Czechoslovakia. First, he demanded that Germany be allowed to annex border areas of the country, where many Germans lived. Representatives of France, Britain, and Italy met with Hitler at Munich, Germany, in the fall of 1938. Without consulting Czechoslovakia, they let Hitler have his way. The German dictator promised that this would be his last territorial demand. Six months later, he took over the rest of Czechoslovakia.

By early 1939, it was obvious that appeasement was not working. The policy had been based on the assumption that the dictators could be trusted. Clearly, this was not the case. The only choice left, it seemed, was to stop them by force.

In the spring of 1939, Mussolini invaded Albania and soon annexed it. Hitler's next target was Poland. In August, he signed a nonaggression pact with Josef Stalin, dictator of the Soviet Union. The two countries agreed not to attack each other. The Hitler-Stalin pact left the German dictator free to act against Poland, the Soviet Union's western neighbor. Hitler began by making impossible demands on the Poles. This time, Poland's allies, Britain and France, stood firm. On September 1, 1939, Germany launched an all-out attack on Poland. Two days later, Britain and France declared war on Germany. World War II had begun.

Peace is not the absence of war. Peace is a positive condition—the rule of law.

—journalist Dorothy Thompson, 1938

EARLY YEARS OF THE CONFLICT

Poland was no match for the armed might of Germany. The Poles were battered by dive bombers, artillery, and tanks. This combined assault was what the Germans called *blitzkrieg* ("lightning war"). While the Germans tore at Poland from the west, Soviet troops attacked the country from the east. Poland surrendered late in September. The two invaders then divided the helpless nation between them.

Western Europe

Germany was inactive for several months. Then, in the spring of 1940, it suddenly launched another blitzkrieg toward the north and west. By the end of May, the Germans had overrun Denmark, Norway, Luxembourg, the Netherlands, and Belgium. Next, German forces pushed into France, which fell in 17 days.

Britain now stood alone. The new prime minister, Winston Churchill, helped his people keep their spirits up. "We shall defend our island, whatever the cost may be," he declared. "We shall never surrender." His bravery and firmness inspired the British to withstand punishing attacks. In the fall, the German *Luftwaffe* (air force) began a series of massive air raids on London and other British industrial centers and ports. According to the German plan, this "Battle of Britain" was designed to knock out the country's defenses and soften British resistance to an invasion. But the Royal Air Force (RAF) put up such a valiant defense that the Germans abandoned their invasion plans.

Fighting Elsewhere

Halted in the west, the Axis leaders turned to the Balkans. German forces occupied Romania, and Italy invaded Greece. When the Greeks held off the Italians, Germany sent in troops. By the spring of 1941, both Greece and Yugoslavia had fallen. At the same time, the Axis began an attack on British possessions in North Africa. The Axis goal was to gain control of the Suez Canal and the oil fields of the Middle East. For months, the advantage swung back and forth from one side to another.

Hitler, meanwhile, turned his attention eastward. Ignoring his treaty with Stalin, he invaded the Soviet Union in June 1941. German armored divisions quickly overran the Ukraine and reached the outskirts of Moscow. The Soviet Union, now an ally of Britain, fought the Germans to a standstill by the winter of 1941. But the Axis could look back on two years of warfare and see little but success.

United States Neutrality

Events in Europe in the early 1930s made Americans more determined than ever not to become involved overseas. Between 1935 and 1937, Congress passed several *Neutrality Acts*. Among other things, they (1) prohibited the export of arms to countries at war, (2) authorized the president to require warring powers to pay cash for American goods and to transport the cargoes in their own ships, and (3) banned loans to nations at war.

Then, World War II broke out, and one country after another fell before the Axis. Americans began to fear for their own safety. In 1939, Congress revised the neutrality laws. The sale of arms and munitions on a cash-and-carry basis to warring nations was now allowed, a change that benefited the Allies. In 1941, Congress passed the *Lend-Lease Act*. It authorized the president to sell, exchange, lease, or lend articles of defense to any nation whose defense he considered vital to U.S. security. The United States became, in Roosevelt's words, the "arsenal of democracy." It extended to the Allies lend-lease aid valued at more than $50 billion.

The United States also prepared for its own defense. Congress set aside money to strengthen the armed forces. In 1940, it passed the *Selective Service Act*. This was the first peacetime program of compulsory military service in American history. In the same year, the United

Praise the Lord and pass the ammunition.

—naval chaplain Howell M. Forgy,
on board a ship counterattacking the Japanese
at Pearl Harbor, December 7, 1941

States traded 50 old destroyers to Britain, in return for the lease of naval and air bases on British possessions in the Western Hemisphere.

Pearl Harbor

A shocking event in the Pacific brought American neutrality to an abrupt end in December 1941. For some time, relations between the United States and Japan had been deteriorating. In 1940, after the fall of France, the Japanese had started moving into French Indochina, an area made up of Vietnam, Laos, and Cambodia. Soon afterward, Japan joined the Axis alliance. In response, the United States banned the export of steel and scrap iron to Japan. Later, the U.S. embargo was extended to include oil and airplane fuel as well. The United States also stepped up its aid program to China.

In the fall of 1941, Japanese diplomats traveled to Washington, D.C., to discuss how Japanese-American relations might be improved. On December 7, while the diplomats were still in the U.S. capital, Japanese planes launched a surprise attack on Pearl Harbor, the U.S. naval base in Hawaii. They killed more than 2000 Americans and destroyed 15 ships and 150 planes. "Remember Pearl Harbor!" became the rallying cry of a shocked and angry nation. The next day, President Roosevelt asked Congress to declare war on Japan. He called December 7 "a date which will live in infamy." On December 11, Germany and Italy declared war on the United States. For the first time in history, the United States was involved in a life-or-death struggle across both the Atlantic and the Pacific.

The American Home Front

Americans mobilized for war even more completely in World War II than they had in World War I. The draft age was changed so that all men between 18 and 45 were subject to military service. By 1945, more than 12 million Americans were serving in the armed forces, most of them overseas. A total of about 285,000 women joined the military, performing noncombat duties. In addition, some 75,000 women served as army and navy nurses.

WAR PRODUCTION   American industry tooled up to produce essential war materials, especially airplanes, guns, tanks, and ships. War plants operated 24 hours a day, 7 days a week. More than 20 million people worked in key war industries. This total included millions of women. They took over many jobs that had previously been open only to men. The GNP rose to more than $200 billion, and the national debt to some $260 billion.

To finance the war, Americans invested billions of dollars in war bonds. Taxes were increased, and income taxes were collected on a pay-as-you-go plan. A part of each worker's earnings was deducted in the form of withholding taxes. This system replaced the older method of paying income taxes in one lump sum.

The government rationed food and other scarce items, such as shoes, gasoline, and fuel oil. Millions of Americans joined in drives to collect paper and scrap metal for the war effort.

RELOCATION OF JAPANESE-AMERICANS   Americans of the World War II era showed little prejudice toward citizens of German or Italian descent. But this tolerance did not extend to Japanese-Americans. Early in 1942, government authorities decided that people of Japanese ancestry living near the Pacific coast might aid Japan if it invaded the U.S. mainland. Orders were issued to move them to relocation camps inland. Feelings against Asians had always been strong in the West, and most people approved of the government order.

More than 110,000 Japanese-Americans were uprooted. Given short notice of the transfer, many of them had to sell their homes and businesses at rock-bottom prices. Two-thirds of them were American-born citizens. None of them—or any other Japanese-Americans elsewhere in the country—was ever found guilty of working for the enemy. In fact, thousands of Japanese-Americans enlisted in the armed forces and fought with distinction and bravery.

After the war, when the relocation camps were closed, Japanese-Americans received some money to compensate for their sufferings. It amounted to roughly 10 percent of the value of their claims. In 1983, a congressional commission held that relocation had been a "grave injustice." In its report, the commission blamed "racial prejudice, war hysteria, and failure of political leadership" for the internment. Five years later, the government granted $20,000 tax-free to each living former internee.

ALLIED VICTORY IN EUROPE AND AFRICA

Allied war planners agreed that their first aim was to defeat the Axis in Europe and North Africa. When the United States entered the war in

December 1941, Britain and the Soviet Union had their backs to the wall. German bombs were battering London and other English cities. German planes, submarines, and mines menaced the sea-lanes to Britain, threatening to halt the flow of vitally needed supplies. Axis forces had pushed deep into the Soviet Union and were besieging many of its major cities.

Soon, however, thousands of U.S. merchant ships were steaming across the Atlantic in navy-protected convoys. They carried planes, tanks, jeeps, guns, and other supplies. And millions of "GI's" (U.S. soldiers) were arriving at camps and bases in the British Isles.

In the spring and summer of 1942, the Allies began massive bombing raids of their own. Their targets were enemy industrial centers and military installations. This was the first step in the Allied counteroffensive. In the fall of 1942, the Allies began to fight their way toward victory on several fronts.

Sighted sub. Sank same.

—*pilot David F. Mason, flying a routine patrol over the Atlantic, 1942*

The Soviet Union

By the fall of 1942, a huge Axis army had driven 1000 miles into the Soviet Union and was encamped on the outskirts of Stalingrad (now Volgograd). There, the Red (Soviet) army made its stand. In bloody house-to-house fighting, the Russians finally defeated their German attackers in February 1943. The Germans alone lost more than 200,000 men. After this decisive victory, the Soviet forces began to push the enemy back.

North Africa

Another Allied offensive was aimed at North Africa. Early in 1942, Axis forces there, commanded by Erwin Rommel, were threatening Britain's hold on Egypt. In the fall, the British, led by Bernard L. Montgomery, defeated Rommel at El Alamein, in northern Egypt. They then pursued the retreating Germans westward across Libya. Meanwhile, in November 1942, British and U.S. troops under Dwight D. Eisenhower landed at Casablanca, Oran, and Algiers. (These cities were in French colonies that had become enemy territory because of the German occupation of France.)

Axis forces in Africa were caught between Eisenhower's troops in

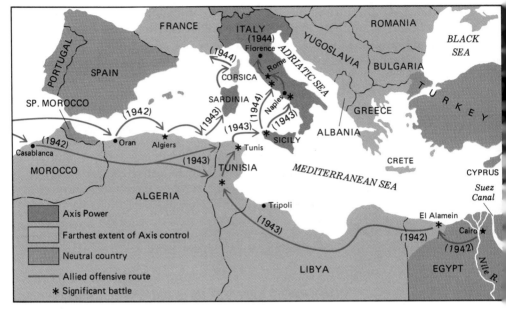

ALLIED CAMPAIGN IN NORTH AFRICA AND
THE MEDITERRANEAN (1942–1944)

the west and Montgomery's in the east. Rommel's army was finally
trapped in Tunisia in May 1943 and forced to surrender. All of North
Africa was now in Allied hands.

Italy

For months, Stalin had been urging the Allies to open a second
front—that is, to attack the Axis elsewhere in Europe. Such a move
would force Germany to pull some of its troops out of the Soviet Union
and, thus, ease pressure on the Russians. The Allies made the decision
to invade Italy.

In July 1943, a combined force of U.S., British, and Canadian troops
landed on the Italian island of Sicily, which soon fell. The attack brought
on a political crisis in Italy, and Mussolini was forced to resign. In
September, the Allies invaded the Italian mainland.

The Italian government surrendered, but German troops continued
to defend the Italian peninsula fiercely. The Allies struggled northward
for many months. They took Naples in October 1943, Rome in June 1944,
and Florence in August 1944. At the very end of the war, in April 1945,
Mussolini was captured and executed by Italian resistance fighters (pro-
Allied partisans).

COLLAPSE OF NAZI GERMANY (1943–1945)

The Invasion of France

The Allies had long planned to cross the English Channel for a full-scale attack on the Germans in France. In 1944, they were ready. A combined Allied force stormed ashore onto the beaches of Normandy, France, on D-Day (June 6). Eisenhower directed this invasion, the largest land-air-sea operation in history. The initial force of 175,000 men included airborne parachute troops and fully equipped tank divisions.

After a beachhead was established along the coast, reinforcements poured in, and the Allies smashed ahead in several directions. Paris was freed in August. Next came Brussels and Antwerp, in Belgium. In September, the Allies invaded the Netherlands. More than 2 million Allied troops took part in the final push toward Germany.

German Surrender

In December 1944, the Germans launched a counterattack on the Allies in Belgium. This action threatened to wipe out a large U.S. force at Bastogne, but the Allies finally won this Battle of the Bulge. Resuming their offensive, the Allies pressed forward into Germany. At the Elbe River, in April 1945, they joined forces with the Red army. It had fought its way across Poland and occupied most of eastern Germany.

On May 1, the German radio made the startling announcement that Hitler had committed suicide in an underground bunker (fortified shelter) in Berlin. The following day, the Russians entered Berlin. Germany's armies were now destroyed, its territory overrun, and its major cities in ruins. It surrendered unconditionally on May 8. The war in Europe was at an end.

The Holocaust

After the defeat of Germany, the world became fully aware of the true horror of nazism. As the Germans overran Europe, they had put their racial policies into effect. They had forced hundreds of thousands of Europeans into slave labor. This was a common fate for Slavs and other peoples that the Germans regarded as "inferior." Slave laborers were treated as if they were merely human machines, to be used until they fell apart.

But it was the Jews whom the Germans singled out for the most barbaric treatment. Jews were deprived of their property and citizenship, and isolated in ghettos. Many were sent to concentration camps, such as Dachau and Buchenwald in Germany. They died by the thousands in the early years of the war, but Hitler was still not satisfied. In January 1942, he adopted what he called the "final solution of the Jewish question." This was a program of mass murder, and its aim was to destroy every European Jew.

In some areas, all the Jewish residents were gathered together and shot. More commonly, Jews were sent by train to camps built for the purpose of extermination. The most notorious camps were Auschwitz, Majdanek, and Treblinka, all in Poland. Here, the Germans killed their victims with poison gas and then burned their bodies. This organized murder of Europe's Jews came to be called the "Holocaust." It took 6 million lives. An equal number of other victims also died in the camps. They included Poles, Gypsies, resistance workers, political prisoners, and the handicapped.

A long tradition of anti-Semitism in Europe helped make the Holocaust possible. Even in France, which had always been proud of its civilization, local authorities cooperated with the Germans by seizing Jews and sending them off to die. Countries beyond Hitler's control, such as Britain and the United States, were slow to act when they heard about the extermination policy. For instance, Allied planes, in their raids on German-held territory, did not bomb the concentration camps (which might have put them out of operation). Many historians believe, however, that little could have been accomplished in the face of Hitler's insane determination.

ALLIED VICTORY IN THE PACIFIC

By the time the Allies defeated the Axis in Europe, they were well on their way to victory in the Pacific region, too. But it had been a long and costly struggle.

Japanese Successes

The Japanese attack on Pearl Harbor in December 1941 temporarily crippled U.S. naval and air power in the Pacific. The other Allies were likewise unable to withstand Japanese military strength.

A few weeks after Pearl Harbor, the Japanese seized Guam, Wake Island, and Hong Kong. They also invaded the Philippines. The city of Manila fell in January 1942. Led by Douglas MacArthur, the outnumbered U.S. and Filipino troops withdrew to Bataan Peninsula across Manila Bay. There, they resisted the enemy for more than three months. On Roosevelt's order, MacArthur was taken out by boat and then flown to Australia, where he was given command of the Allied forces in the southwest Pacific. When he arrived in Australia, he defiantly declared, "I shall return" (to retake the Philippines). The Japanese overran all the Philippine Islands by May.

By the middle of 1942, Japan had won control of a vast empire, rich in oil, rubber, tin, and other vital natural resources. In addition to its other conquests, it held French Indochina, Thailand, Burma, the Dutch East Indies (Indonesia), and Singapore. From footholds on New Guinea and the Solomon Islands, the Japanese were menacing Australia. They had also seized Attu and Kiska, the westernmost of the Aleutian Islands. These positions gave them a base of operations against Alaska.

Stopping the Advance

Two important U.S. victories began to turn the tide for the Allies in the Pacific. One was the Battle of the Coral Sea, in May 1942. It took place off the eastern coast of Australia. A Japanese fleet was on its way to invade Port Moresby, in southern New Guinea, when American ships intercepted it. Both sides suffered heavy losses in the four day battle. The U.S. force finally turned back the Japanese, removing a threat to Australia. This engagement was the first naval battle in history in which surface vessels did not fire a single shot. Planes based on aircraft carriers did all the fighting.

The other turning point was the Battle of Midway, a month later. A large enemy fleet steamed out to seize Midway Island—the first step in a planned Japanese invasion of Hawaii. The United States, however, had recently broken the Japanese naval code and, therefore, knew of the enemy's attack plan in advance. American ships defeated the Japanese naval force decisively.

Taking the Offensive

By the late summer of 1942, the Allies were no longer merely reacting to enemy moves in the Pacific. They were taking the offensive. They had three major objectives: (1) to cut Japan's lines of communication with its possessions, (2) to retake the Philippines, and (3) to attack Japan.

The first Allied offensive was a U.S. attack on the enemy-occupied island of Guadalcanal, in the Solomon Islands. The marines landed in August 1942. After six months of sea, air, and land battles, they drove off the Japanese.

ISLAND HOPPING   Allied planners decided that a campaign to win back every Japanese-held island would be too costly. Instead, they adopted a tactic of "island hopping." This meant that the Allies would make the most of their strength by taking only certain strategic islands that would move them ever closer to Japan. At some point, they could gain bases within bombing range of the enemy homeland. And the less important islands, bypassed in the fighting, would eventually surrender for lack of supplies.

One of the first targets in this campaign was heavily fortified Tarawa, in the Gilbert Islands. It fell in November 1943, after a bloody three-day battle. The next leap was to Kwajalein and Eniwetok, in the Marshall Islands (February 1944), and then to Saipan and Guam, in the Marianas (July and August 1944). From Saipan, American long-range planes began to bomb industrial centers in Japan.

THE PHILIPPINES   MacArthur opened a drive to retake the Philippines by landing troops on the island of Leyte in October 1944. In a desperate effort to stop the Americans, the Japanese hurled their main fleet at the invasion forces. The result was the Battle of Leyte Gulf, the largest naval-air engagement in history. The U.S. force destroyed much of the enemy fleet, won a decisive victory, and gained control of Philippine waters. MacArthur then continued the land offensive, captured Manila in February 1945, and regained the entire Philippines by July.

The Final Assault

The Americans were getting closer and closer to Japan. In February 1945, marines stormed the island of Iwo Jima, 750 miles from the

Japanese city of Yokohama. They completed their conquest of the island in mid-March.

In April, U.S. troops landed on Okinawa, just 360 miles from Japan. Enemy forces resisted fiercely, and the United States lost over 10,000 men before defeating the Japanese. During the three-month campaign, the U.S. fleet suffered severe damage from *kamikaze* attacks. These were suicide missions in which Japanese pilots crashed their bomb-laden planes into enemy warships.

TRUMAN IN CHARGE   In April 1945, shortly before the end of the war in Europe, President Roosevelt died suddenly of a brain hemorrhage.

WORLD WAR II IN THE PACIFIC (1942–1945)

Harry S. Truman of Missouri became the new president. He had served in the Senate for ten years before being chosen as FDR's running mate in 1944. Since his election as vice president, Truman had taken no part in high-level planning or decision making.

After he was sworn in as president, Truman learned that American and foreign scientists had been working together for several years to develop the world's first atomic bomb. Their research, called the Manhattan Project, had been carried on in total secrecy. Now, their weapons were ready. In July 1945, the first successful atomic bomb test took place at a remote desert site near Alamogordo, New Mexico.

HIROSHIMA AND NAGASAKI   Should Truman use the atomic bomb, now that it was available? The alternative, as he saw it, was a full-scale invasion of Japan. He and his military advisers believed that such a campaign would cost the United States dearly. The Japanese, although now suffering from heavy bombing raids, seemed determined never to surrender. Truman chose atomic attack.

On July 26, Allied leaders, meeting in Potsdam, Germany, issued an ultimatum to Japan: surrender unconditionally or suffer total destruction. The Japanese did not reply. On August 6, a single U.S. plane dropped one atomic bomb on the city of Hiroshima. A blinding explosion killed at least 80,000 people immediately and injured many more. It destroyed every structure within a four-square-mile area of the city. Still, Japan would not surrender. A second A-bomb was dropped on Nagasaki three days later.

Japan now gave up. The formal surrender took place on September 2, 1945, aboard the U.S. battleship *Missouri* in Tokyo Bay. World War II was over.

True-False Test

1. After World War I, many Americans were eager to keep out of European affairs.
2. The United States established diplomatic relations with the Soviet Union two years after the Bolshevik revolution.
3. During the 1930s, the Japanese government gradually lost power to the country's military leaders.
4. The Rome-Berlin Axis was formed the same year that the Spanish Civil War broke out.
5. World War II began when Germany launched a blitzkrieg attack on Czechoslovakia.

6. The Selective Service Act of 1940 provided for the first peacetime draft in American history.
7. The Axis powers wanted to seize Egypt in order to control the Suez Canal and gain access to Middle Eastern oil fields.
8. Hitler's invasion of the Soviet Union resulted in the occupation of Moscow by the Germans.
9. In the closing days of World War II in Europe, Hitler escaped to South America.
10. The Allies adopted a plan of island hopping in the Pacific in order to conserve their armed strength.

Multiple-Choice Test

1. At the Washington Naval Conference, all of the following nations agreed to limit the size of their navies *except* (a) the United States (b) Great Britain (c) Germany (d) France.
2. The Kellogg-Briand Pact was not very effective because (a) few nations signed it (b) it could not be enforced (c) the United States refused to take part in the agreement (d) it went into effect after Hitler had begun to rearm Germany.
3. A Good Neighbor Policy was first advocated by (a) Warren Harding (b) Calvin Coolidge (c) Herbert Hoover (d) Theodore Roosevelt.
4. Hitler's rise to power in Germany was aided by all of the following *except* (a) widespread prosperity (b) the Great Depression (c) bitterness toward the Versailles Treaty (d) anti-Semitism.
5. In their relations toward Hitler and Mussolini in the 1930s, the European democracies followed a policy of (a) isolationism (b) intervention (c) appeasement (d) aggression.
6. The United States was brought into World War II when Japan struck suddenly at (a) Guam (b) Hawaii (c) Midway (d) the Philippines.
7. The Allied troops invading Italy met heavy resistance from (a) the Italian army (b) Italian resistance fighters (c) Mussolini's private troops (d) German forces.
8. By mid-1942, Japan controlled all of the following *except* (a) Indochina (b) Australia (c) Burma (d) Singapore.
9. The Allies went on the offensive against Japan (a) early in 1941 (b) in January 1942 (c) in August 1942 (d) late in 1943.
10. A new kind of warfare used by the Japanese in the final months of the war was (a) poison gas (b) guided missiles (c) atomic warheads (d) suicide attacks by pilots.

Map Test

Locate the following places on the maps on pages 418, 424, 425, and 429. Then, referring to the text, as necessary, explain why each place was important either before or during World War II.

GROUP A

1. Manchuria	6. Auschwitz
2. Rhineland	7. Coral Sea
3. Stalingrad	8. Guadalcanal
4. El Alamein	9. Leyte Gulf
5. Normandy	10. Hiroshima

GROUP B

1. Munich	6. Saipan
2. Casablanca	7. Okinawa
3. Bastogne	8. Bataan
4. Tunisia	9. Attu
5. Suez Canal	10. Midway Island

Essay Questions

1. What is fascism? Who originated the term? Name three countries that had Fascist governments during the 1930s.
2. In the early 1930s, what were Roosevelt's policies toward each of the following: (a) the Soviet Union?   (b) Latin America?
3. Describe how the United States mobilized to fight World War II.
4. What was the Holocaust? When did Hitler begin carrying it out? How many victims did it claim?
5. Explain why President Truman decided to use atomic bombs against Japan.

CHAPTER *28*

The Cold War

W ORLD WAR II WAS the most destructive war in history. It took the lives of 14 million soldiers and more than 20 million civilians. Millions more were wounded. There was widespread suffering from disease and starvation, and many people were left homeless. At the war's end, thousands of cities, villages, factories, and farms lay in ruins.

The war had other consequences as well, not all of them immediately apparent. One was a change in the balance of power. European nations such as Britain and France were too weak to play a decisive role in the postwar world. Two superpowers, the United States and the Soviet Union, now dominated international affairs. Another consequence was a surge of nationalism, especially in colonial regions. North Africa and Southeast Asia, for example, had been freed from French control during the war. The people of these regions soon made it clear that they were unwilling to be dependent colonists again. Between 1945 and 1960, more than 30 former colonies became independent countries.

Among the damaging effects of World War II were alarming changes in attitude. Senseless destruction came to be accepted almost as a matter of course. During the Spanish Civil War, the world had been horrified by the German bombing of Guernica, a little town of no strategic value. In 1945, far less outrage greeted the Allied leveling of Dresden, a beautiful German city that was crowded with refugees and had no industrial importance.

A world accustomed to destruction found it more and more difficult to believe in progress or to look to the future with hope. Who could understand how a nation that had produced the music of Bach and the poetry of Goethe came to support the barbarism of Hitler's "final solution"? What would the future hold, now that the United States had unleashed the awesome power of atomic energy?

PLANNING THE POSTWAR WORLD

The scope of World War II was so vast, and the pace of change so swift, that arranging for the future was extremely difficult. But the Allies did try to work out some postwar strategies. In this planning, the United States played a key role. Unlike Americans after World War I, who had wanted to concentrate on their own affairs, the World War II generation was more willing to commit the nation to foreign alliances, foreign aid, and other forms of international involvement.

Wartime Conferences

Allied leaders met from time to time during the war, not only to devise military strategy but also to discuss the future. In 1941, four months before Pearl Harbor, Roosevelt and Churchill met at sea and issued a statement known as the *Atlantic Charter*. Though not a binding document, it set forth a number of aims later agreed to by other anti-Axis countries. These included the right of people to choose their own form of government, freer trade, and the disarmament of aggressor nations.

After the United States entered World War II, there were several important meetings of the leaders of the "Big Three"—the United States,

---

In the future days, which we seek to make secure, we look forward to a world founded upon four essential human freedoms.

The first is freedom of speech and expression—everywhere in the world.

The second is freedom of every person to worship God in his own way—everywhere in the world.

The third is freedom from want—which, translated into world terms, means economic understandings which will secure to every nation a healthy peacetime life for its inhabitants—everywhere in the world.

The fourth is freedom from fear—which, translated into world terms, means a world-wide reduction of armaments to such a point and in such a thorough manner that no nation will be in a position to commit an act of physical aggression against any neighbor—anywhere in the world.

—*Franklin D. Roosevelt's annual message to Congress, January 1941*

U.S. Troops in Korea, 1950

Great Britain, and the Soviet Union. At Teheran, Iran, in November 1943, Roosevelt, Churchill, and Stalin not only discussed the Normandy invasion but also talked about reducing the power of Germany after the war.

The three leaders met again at Yalta, a Soviet resort on the Black Sea, in February 1945. Now, with the war in Europe nearly over, postwar planning could be more specific. The Big Three agreed on a joint military occupation of Germany after the war. They promised to support free elections and the establishment of "broadly representative" governments in liberated countries. Roosevelt and Churchill also made a secret agreement with Stalin. They promised the Russian leader territory in Asia if the Soviet Union would enter the war against Japan. In addition, Roosevelt and Churchill approved the Soviet annexation of eastern Poland and the transfer of a part of eastern Germany to Poland.

A final Big Three meeting took place at Potsdam, Germany, in July 1945. (Roosevelt had died in April, and the United States was now represented by Truman. Near the end of the conference, Churchill was replaced by Clement Attlee, Britain's new prime minister.) At this meeting, the Allied leaders made plans for the occupation and control of recently defeated Germany, and set up a council of foreign ministers to draw up peace treaties. (They also issued the "unconditional surrender" ultimatum to Japan that was followed by the atomic bombing of Hiroshima.)

The Question of Germany

By the time the war in Europe ended, Soviet troops had advanced far into eastern Germany. The area they had taken became the Soviet zone of occupation. Western Germany was divided into three zones—British, U.S., and French. Berlin, located in the Soviet zone, was subdivided into four sectors. (The occupation of Austria and its capital, Vienna, was arranged in a similar fashion.)

RESETTLEMENT AND REPARATIONS   During the war, the Allies had agreed to give to Poland the German territory east of the Oder and Neisse rivers. Millions of Germans living in this region, as well as others in Czechoslovakia and Hungary, were forced to resettle in Germany.

The Allies had more trouble agreeing on German reparations. The original plan was to take payment in goods, rather than money. The Soviet Union wanted its share to be in the form of German industrial capacity. The Russians dismantled most of the heavy machinery in their zone and shipped entire factories to the Soviet Union. The other Allies took steps to carry out a similar program in their zones. Realizing, however, that a permanently weakened Germany would create future problems for western Europe, they soon discontinued the plan. Reversing its previous position, the United States adopted a new policy of supporting the economic recovery of Germany.

PUNISHING THE NAZIS   In their wartime meetings, the Allies had also made plans to root out nazism in Germany. One goal was "denazification"—the removal of all former Nazis from positions of authority in Germany. Courts were set up to judge individual cases. But the program was soon abandoned because it required huge amounts of time and money, and reliable evidence was hard to uncover. (One problem was that many Germans accused their fellow citizens of Nazi sympathies simply to settle personal grudges.)

Another way of discrediting nazism was to hold public trials of major German leaders. These took place in Nuremberg, Germany, in 1945-1946. The main trial involved 22 officials charged with waging aggressive war and committing "crimes against humanity." A panel of judges represented the Soviet Union, Britain, France, and the United States. They sentenced 12 of the accused to death and 7 to prison. (The others were acquitted.) The Nuremberg trials publicized some of the worst deeds of the Nazi regime.

The United Nations

As early as 1941, Roosevelt and Churchill had declared their interest in "the establishment of a wider and permanent system of general security." In 1944, representatives of the United States, Great Britain, the Soviet Union, and China met at Dumbarton Oaks, an estate in Washington, D.C. There, they drew up plans for a postwar international organization to replace the League of Nations. It was to be called the *United Nations (UN)*.

THE UNITED NATIONS

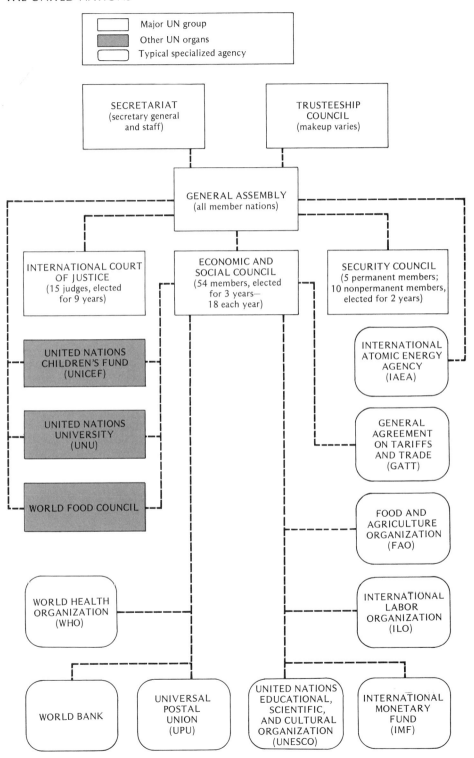

Major UN group
Other UN organs
Typical specialized agency

SECRETARIAT
(secretary general
and staff)

TRUSTEESHIP
COUNCIL
(makeup varies)

GENERAL ASSEMBLY
(all member nations)

INTERNATIONAL COURT
OF JUSTICE
(15 judges, elected
for 9 years)

ECONOMIC AND
SOCIAL COUNCIL
(54 members, elected
for 3 years—
18 each year)

SECURITY COUNCIL
(5 permanent members;
10 nonpermanent members,
elected for 2 years)

UNITED NATIONS
CHILDREN'S FUND
(UNICEF)

INTERNATIONAL
ATOMIC ENERGY
AGENCY
(IAEA)

UNITED NATIONS
UNIVERSITY
(UNU)

GENERAL
AGREEMENT
ON TARIFFS
AND TRADE
(GATT)

WORLD FOOD COUNCIL

FOOD AND
AGRICULTURE
ORGANIZATION
(FAO)

WORLD HEALTH
ORGANIZATION
(WHO)

INTERNATIONAL
LABOR
ORGANIZATION
(ILO)

WORLD BANK

UNIVERSAL
POSTAL
UNION
(UPU)

UNITED NATIONS
EDUCATIONAL,
SCIENTIFIC,
AND CULTURAL
ORGANIZATION
(UNESCO)

INTERNATIONAL
MONETARY
FUND
(IMF)

The founding nations of the UN sent delegates to San Francisco in the spring of 1945 to work out a charter. The organization formally came into being in October, with 51 members. UN headquarters were established in New York City.

Although the United States had refused to join the League of Nations after World War I, it became a charter member of the UN with little protest. This change in attitude was due partly to experience during the prewar years. Many Americans felt that their isolationism had helped bring on the war. Another reason was that the UN had bipartisan support—that is, support from both political parties. Unlike Wilson, Roosevelt sought the advice of Republicans as well as Democrats in planning for the international body. And he chose both Republicans and Democrats to represent the United States at the San Francisco conference. After Roosevelt's death, Truman continued to follow his predecessor's bipartisan approach.

STRUCTURE OF THE UN   The General Assembly of the United Nations is the organization's democratic forum. Each member nation is represented in it and has an equal vote. The Security Council has a more active role. This is especially true of its five permanent members—the United States, Russia, the United Kingdom, France, and China. Unlike any group within the League of Nations, the UN Security Council can take military action against aggressors. Decisions on important matters, however, require the support of all the "Big Five" members. Each one can veto any action being considered.

Other parts of the UN and their duties are as follows:

1. The Secretariat does the administrative and clerical work of the organization.
2. The Economic and Social Council makes recommendations and coordinates activities in a wide variety of fields, from trade and development to population and human rights. It does so through specialized agencies (such as the FAO) and other UN organs (such as UNICEF).
3. The International Court of Justice settles legal disputes between nations.
4. The Trusteeship Council was set up to supervise colonial possessions. Over the years, as former colonies became independent, its field of responsibility steadily diminished.

THE UN IN ACTION   The UN, from the beginning, was a meeting place where nations could bring their problems, state their opinions on issues of the day, and register complaints. It was less successful in maintaining peace and ending world tensions. Nevertheless, it had many accomplishments to its credit. In 1948, it issued a *Declaration of Human Rights.*

The small society. (Brickman in the *Washington Star*. Reprinted with special permission of King Features Syndicate, Inc.)

Members were urged to guarantee their people the right to life, liberty, and safety. The UN also outlawed genocide—the mass killing of national, racial, or religious groups. It helped to formulate an international agreement banning nuclear weapons in outer space and the establishment of military bases on the moon or the planets. And it sent peacekeeping forces to maintain order in a number of trouble spots, including Egypt, the Congo, Lebanon, Somalia, and the Balkans.

Various specialized agencies have worked to aid refugees, care for child victims of war or poverty, and fight epidemics in disease-ridden areas. Technical advice and aid have been extended to developing countries. The UN has also made loans to member nations for constructing public works; improved worldwide weather forecasting; and set international standards and regulations for civil aviation, shipping, and postal services.

BEGINNING OF THE COLD WAR

When World War II ended, the Russians occupied not only eastern Germany but also Poland, Hungary, Romania, Bulgaria, and eastern Czechoslovakia. During the war, the Soviet Union had taken over Estonia, Latvia, and Lithuania, and these nations lost their independence.

The Iron Curtain

Within a short time after the end of the war, the governments of all the countries of Eastern Europe were controlled by Communists. In some cases, Communists came to power through elections. These were usually one-sided affairs in which non-Communists were not allowed to run or vote. In other cases, the Communists seized power by force and imprisoned or murdered members of opposition parties. As early as March

1946, Britain's former prime minister, Winston Churchill, spoke of an "iron curtain" descending across Europe and separating Communist from non-Communist countries. The last Eastern European country to fall under Communist domination was Czechoslovakia, in 1948.

Poland, eastern Germany, Czechoslovakia, Hungary, Bulgaria, and Romania were closely linked to the Soviet Union, both politically and economically. These nations became known as satellites, since they depended on Russia as the planets in our solar system depend on the sun. Two other Eastern European countries, Albania and Yugoslavia, also set up Communist governments but broke away from Soviet domination.

Events in Eastern Europe dismayed the non-Communist world. Serious tension developed between the two superpowers, the United States and the Soviet Union. The result was the Cold War—a conflict fought mainly with economic, political, and diplomatic weapons, rather than guns. It pitted the non-Communist (Western) bloc against the Communist (Eastern or Soviet) bloc.

The Cold War had a number of causes. One had to do with basic political and economic systems. Ever since the Bolshevik Revolution, Soviet leaders had been calling for world revolution to overthrow capitalism, the economic system of the West. Another factor was the wartime experience of the Soviet Union. The Russians had suffered more casualties than any other nation. They were determined to protect themselves from future attack by setting up a ring of satellite states around their borders. Neither superpower trusted the other, and a climate of suspicion prevailed.

Containment

During this time of confusion, American leaders were impressed by advice from a State Department expert, George Kennan. In an influential article, he wrote that the Soviet Union would attempt to expand wherever it could. Therefore, he urged, the United States should be on its guard and take firm action to contain (restrict) such Soviet moves. Americans who favored this policy of containment felt that the United States should commit itself to combat communism almost everywhere in the world.

THE TRUMAN DOCTRINE Containment was first put into action in Greece and Turkey. Greek revolutionists, aided by neighboring Communist countries, were waging war against the government. Britain had been helping the Greek government but, early in 1947, announced that it could no longer do so. At the same time, the Soviets were demanding that Turkey allow them to share control of the straits between the Black Sea and the Mediterranean.

The United States was afraid that both Greece and Turkey would fall under Communist control. To keep this from happening, President Truman declared that "it must be the policy of the United States to support free peoples who are resisting attempted subjugation by armed minorities or by outside pressures." This principle became known as the *Truman Doctrine*. To reinforce it, the United States sent military equipment, supplies, and advisers to Greece and Turkey. The Greek government put down the rebellion, and Turkey successfully resisted Soviet demands.

THE MARSHALL PLAN   The policy of containment was also behind a plan proposed by Secretary of State George C. Marshall in 1947. Concerned about the widespread devastation caused by the war, he offered American financial aid to Europe. He also asked the Europeans to draw up a blueprint of their needs. Without "normal economic health in the world," Marshall said, "there can be no political stability."

In response, 16 European nations met in Paris and adopted a four-year, multibillion-dollar plan. Its aim was to provide the participating nations with food, fuel, raw materials, and machinery. In 1948, Congress approved the *Marshall Plan* (also known as the *European Recovery Program*) and set aside $5 billion for its first year of operation. The Soviet Union and its satellites were eligible to take part in the plan but rejected it as a form of "American imperialism." In fact, they did everything they could to oppose it. They organized strikes in Marshall Plan countries and sabotaged U.S. foreign aid shipments.

The United States spent more than $15 billion on the Marshall Plan during its four-year life span. This economic aid helped the participating nations raise their industrial and agricultural production above prewar levels. It also greatly stimulated their international trade. The Marshall Plan helped the United States, too, by reviving the European market for American goods. And the plan held communism in check by reducing the conditions it thrives on—unemployment, poverty, and political instability.

Foreign aid was scheduled to end in 1952. But the Cold War continued, and so did American economic assistance. As time went on, the United States placed less emphasis on Europe and more on developing countries—the so-called "Third World." To these nations in Asia, Africa, and Latin America, the United States provided not only food, raw materials, and machinery but also scientific and industrial know-how.

Crisis in Germany

By 1948, it was clear that the Western powers and the Soviet Union could not agree on a peace treaty for Germany or on the establishment of a unified German government. To end the stalemate, the United States, Britain, and France announced that they would combine their zones of

MILITARY ALLIANCES IN POSTWAR EUROPE

occupation in western Germany to create a single republic. In retaliation, the Soviet Union refused to allow trucks and trains from the West to travel through its zone in eastern Germany to Berlin. Cut off from their main source of supplies, two million West Berliners faced starvation.

The Western Allies responded to the blockade with a gigantic airlift. For 11 months, starting in June 1948, huge cargo planes flew tons of food, coal, and other supplies into Berlin. The Soviets finally lifted the blockade in May 1949. In that same month, the new Federal Republic of Germany (West Germany) came into being. Its capital was at Bonn. West Germany received Marshall Plan aid and was slowly brought into the ranks of the Western powers. In 1955, the Western Allies ended their ten-year occupation of West Germany and granted the country full independence. They also allowed West Germany to rearm. It was authorized to establish an army of up to 500,000 troops. In addition, it was permitted to manufacture its own military equipment (except atomic weapons, guided missiles, and large warships).

Meanwhile, in 1949, the Communist sector of Germany became the German Democratic Republic (East Germany), with East Berlin as its capital. East Germany became a major Soviet satellite.

Military Alliances

The Cold War was reflected in two opposing military alliances. The first to be formed was the *North Atlantic Treaty Organization (NATO)*,

IMPORTANT POSTWAR ALLIANCES*

Organization of American States (OAS), 1948–Present

Antigua-Barbuda	Colombia	Guyana	St. Kitts-Nevis
Argentina	Costa Rica	Haiti	St. Lucia
Bahamas	Cuba (inactive)	Honduras	St. Vincent-the
Barbados	Dominica	Jamaica	Grenadines
Belize	Dominican Republic	Mexico	Suriname
Bolivia	Ecuador	Nicaragua	Trinidad-Tobago
Brazil	El Salvador	Panama	United States
Canada	Grenada	Paraguay	Uruguay
Chile	Guatemala	Peru	Venezuela

North Atlantic Treaty Organization (NATO), 1949–Present

Belgium	Germany	Italy	Portugal
Canada	Great Britain	Luxembourg	Spain
Denmark	Greece	Netherlands	Turkey
France	Iceland	Norway	United States

Southeast Asia Treaty Organization (SEATO), 1954–1977

Australia	Great Britain	Pakistan	Thailand
France	New Zealand	(until 1973)	United States
		Philippines	

Central Treaty Organization (CENTO), 1955–1979

Great Britain	Iraq (until 1959)	Turkey	United States
Iran	Pakistan		(participating
			nonmember)

Warsaw Treaty Organization (Warsaw Pact), 1953–1991

Albania (until 1968)	Czechoslovakia	Hungary	Romania
Bulgaria	East Germany	Poland	USSR

*For alliances now in existence, membership is given as of 1992.

in 1949. Its original members were the United States, Canada, and ten countries of Western Europe—Belgium, Denmark, France, Iceland, Italy, Luxembourg, the Netherlands, Norway, Portugal, and Britain. By joining NATO, the United States gave up its traditional policy of neutrality in time of peace. The NATO nations agreed to treat an armed attack on one member as an attack on all. They set up a unified military force, to which each member contributed funds and personnel. Greece and Turkey became members in 1952, West Germany in 1955, and Spain in 1982.

After West Germany joined NATO, the Communist bloc announced the formation of its own military alliance, the *Warsaw Pact*. When organized in 1955, it had eight members—the Soviet Union, Poland, Czechoslovakia, Bulgaria, Hungary, Romania, Albania, and East Germany. The armed forces of these nations were placed under a unified command, with headquarters in Moscow. (Albania withdrew from the pact in 1968.)

FOCUS ON ASIA

The Cold War was not confined to Europe. At one point, events in the Far East threatened to plunge both superpowers into a "hot" war again.

Japan

At the end of World War II, Japan was occupied by U.S. troops, with Douglas MacArthur in charge. Under his direction, Japan was disarmed, its war industries dismantled, its war criminals tried, and its government made more democratic. (The emperor, however, was allowed to keep his throne.) Japan was forced to withdraw from territories it had seized during the war. It also had to surrender all of its prewar acquisitions. Among these were Manchuria, Korea, and many islands throughout the Pacific, including Taiwan (formerly Formosa).

For five years, the Western Allies and the Soviet Union tried and failed to agree on a peace treaty for Japan. Finally, the United States drew up a treaty without Soviet cooperation. It was signed in 1951 by the United States and 48 other countries. The agreement provided that occupation forces would be withdrawn from Japan and that the country would regain its independence. Japan promised to abide by the principles of the UN charter, and became a UN member in 1956. In the same year, the Soviet Union concluded a separate peace treaty with Japan.

China

Ever since the 1920s, a civil war had pitted Chinese Communists, led by Mao Zedong, against the Nationalist government of Chiang Kai-shek.

When the Japanese invaded China in 1937, both political factions in China fought the common enemy. But they resumed their internal struggle after Japan's defeat in 1945.

At the end of the war, the Chinese Communists were strengthened by huge quantities of captured Japanese weapons turned over to them by the Russians. Although the Nationalists were aided by the United States, they were unable to withstand the stepped-up Communist attacks. In 1949, Mao's forces overran the country and set up the People's Republic of China. Chiang and his Nationalist followers withdrew to Taiwan. The United States refused to recognize the new Communist government on the mainland. It regarded the Taiwan regime as the legitimate government of China. So did the United Nations.

The Korean War

Korea, annexed by Japan in 1910, was surrendered to the Allies in 1945. The Soviet Union occupied the northern part of the country, and the United States, the southern part. The dividing line was set at the 38th parallel. A single government was supposed to be set up after national elections. Instead, two rival nations emerged. One was North Korea, backed by the Soviet Union. The other was South Korea, with ties to the United States.

BEGINNING OF THE CONFLICT   Suddenly, in June 1950, North Korea invaded South Korea. The UN Security Council ordered the invaders to withdraw, but they refused. The council then called on all UN members to help enforce its demands. (It was able to act promptly because the Soviet Union, boycotting UN meetings at the time, could not veto the resolution.)

President Truman (who had been elected in his own right in 1948) immediately ordered U.S. armed forces to support South Korea. Other UN members also pledged aid. But the war was fought mainly by South Korean and U.S. troops. Douglas MacArthur commanded the UN forces in Korea.

The North Koreans quickly captured the capital city of Seoul. They then pushed the outnumbered UN forces southward. By September 1950, only a small area around the southeastern city of Pusan remained in UN hands. In that month, however, MacArthur launched a daring counterattack. He landed 50,000 U.S. troops at Inchon, 150 miles north of the enemy lines. At the same time, UN troops in the Pusan area began to drive northward. MacArthur forced the invaders back across the 38th parallel and captured the North Korean capital of Pyongyang. Then, he moved toward the Yalu River, the boundary between North Korea and the Chinese province of Manchuria.

CHINESE INTERVENTION   The fighting in Korea entered a new phase in November 1950, when more than 200,000 Chinese soldiers from the People's Republic entered North Korea from Manchuria. They drove the UN armies from North Korea, crossed the 38th parallel, and advanced 70 miles into South Korea. In the spring of 1951, UN troops counterattacked and forced the enemy back into North Korea. The opposing lines continued to face each other about 25 miles north of the 38th parallel.

To force the withdrawal of Chinese troops from Korea, MacArthur wanted to bomb military targets in China. Truman opposed this plan

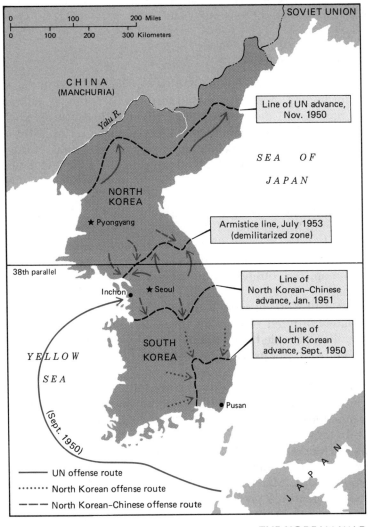

THE KOREAN WAR

because it might involve the United States in a large-scale war with China and its ally, the Soviet Union. MacArthur persisted, arguing that "there is no substitute for victory." Then, he made the disagreement public, in an attempt to gain the support of Congress. Truman, who felt that he had to uphold his authority as commander in chief of the nation's armed forces, responded by removing MacArthur from his command.

NEGOTIATING PEACE   In July 1951, the two sides in the Korean War began to discuss a cease-fire. But they soon came to a deadlock over the question of exchanging prisoners. The Communists demanded the forced repatriation (return) of all prisoners held by the UN side. The UN insisted on voluntary repatriation—allowing prisoners to decide for themselves whether they wished to go back to their homelands. After two years of seemingly endless negotiations, the Communists finally accepted the principle of voluntary repatriation.

A cease-fire agreement was signed in July 1953. Each side withdrew $1\frac{1}{4}$ miles from the final battle line, thus forming a $2\frac{1}{2}$-mile demilitarized zone between them. U.S. troops remained in South Korea to help maintain the uneasy truce.

Total casualties in the Korean War amounted to 1.5 million for the Communist side and 580,000 for the UN forces. UN losses included 54,000 U.S. troops killed and 103,000 wounded.

FURTHER CHALLENGES TO PEACE

Six months before the signing of the Korean cease-fire, Truman's term ended, and Dwight D. Eisenhower, the victorious Republican candidate in the 1952 election, assumed the presidency. To carry out his foreign policy, Eisenhower chose John Foster Dulles as his secretary of state. Dulles argued that containment was not a bold enough response to the Communists because it allowed them to keep what they already had. He wanted a "rollback" of Communist power and "massive retaliation" in case of further aggression.

The Dulles Eisenhower change in policy turned out to be more talk than action. This became clear from developments in Indochina. When the French returned to reclaim their Southeast Asian possessions after World War II, they met resistance from nationalists who wanted independence. Opposition to the French was particularly strong in Vietnam. Nationalists there were led by a Soviet-trained Communist, Ho Chi Minh. The United States aided France with money and supplies, but by 1954, the French cause seemed doomed. Direct intervention by U.S. troops might have saved the French. But Eisenhower refused to go this far, and the French were defeated. Vietnam was then divided in much the same way as Korea, with a Communist north and a non-Communist south.

The United States also chose not to intervene in Hungary. When a popular uprising in 1956 threatened Soviet control there, the Russians sent in tanks and brutally put down the rebellion. The United States made no military response, although it did take in thousands of Hungarian refugees.

The Middle East

An area of special concern to the United States after World War II was the Middle East (northeastern Africa and southwestern Asia). It is economically important because of its vast oil fields. It is strategically important because of its location and because it contains the Suez Canal, one of the world's main arteries of sea commerce. The Middle East is also the home of the Jewish state of Israel, re-established in 1948. From the beginning, the United States and Israel had a friendly relationship. For one thing, Israel is the only democracy in the region. There are also close ties between Israelis and American Jews.

THE SUEZ CRISIS   In 1956, Gamal Abdel Nasser, the president of Egypt, received a promise of financial help from the United States and Britain. Egypt wanted to build a huge dam at Aswan, on the upper Nile River, to supply irrigation and hydroelectric power. When Nasser strengthened his ties with the Soviet Union, however, Britain and the United States withdrew their offer. Nasser retaliated by seizing control of the Suez Canal. This vital link between the Mediterranean and Red seas had been owned and operated by a private company whose shareholders were mostly British and French. The canal's status as an international waterway, open to ships of all nations, had been guaranteed by an 1888 treaty. Nasser announced that Egypt would operate the canal and use the toll money to pay for the Aswan Dam.

Israel, meanwhile, had been troubled by border raids from Egypt. (The Egyptians and other Arabs in the region had sworn to destroy the Jewish state.) In October 1956, the Israelis invaded Egypt, quickly overran the Sinai Peninsula, and advanced to within a few miles of the Suez Canal. A British-French force then invaded Egypt and seized the northern part of the canal. In response, the Egyptians scuttled a number of their own ships in the waterway, making it unusable.

The United Nations, with U.S. and Soviet support, severely criticized the actions of Israel, Britain, and France. The three countries agreed to a cease-fire, and a UN emergency force went to Egypt to supervise the truce. UN engineering teams then cleared the Suez Canal, which was reopened to shipping in 1957.

THE EISENHOWER DOCTRINE   After the Suez crisis, President Eisenhower authorized economic and military aid to any Middle Eastern nation requesting help against Communist aggression. This policy became known as the *Eisenhower Doctrine*. It was the basis for U.S. intervention in the Middle East in 1958, when Lebanon's president asked for help in putting down a civil war.

Soviet-U.S. Relations

Relations between the United States and the Soviet Union shifted several times in the 1950s. The first modification grew out of the death of Stalin in 1953. After a long power struggle, Nikita Khrushchev became the new Soviet leader. In the "thaw" that followed, there was some increase in freedom within the Soviet Union and a spirit of greater cooperation abroad.

In 1955, the leaders of the United States, Britain, France, and the Soviet Union met at Geneva, Switzerland. Their purpose was to discuss nuclear arms control. (The U.S. monopoly on atomic weapons had been brief. The Soviet Union successfully tested an atomic bomb in 1949. And early in the 1950s, both the Russians and the Americans developed even more powerful hydrogen bombs.) The main result of the Geneva summit

"Don't Mind Me–Just Go Right On Talking" (From *The Herblock Book*, Beacon Press, 1952)

conference was an increase in cultural exchange between East and West. Improved relations led to a visit by Khrushchev to the United States in the summer of 1959.

Eisenhower planned to visit the Soviet Union the following year, after another summit conference in Paris. Just before this meeting, however, Khrushchev announced that an American spy plane had been shot down over the Soviet Union. The United States admitted that it had been flying such planes, called U-2s, over the Soviet Union for several years. Because of the U-2 incident, Khrushchev broke up the Paris meeting and canceled the invitation to Eisenhower to visit the Soviet Union.

Latin America

During World War II, all but one of the nations of Latin America actively supported the Allied cause. (Argentina did not declare war on the Axis powers until March 1945.) After the war, they all joined the United Nations. They also allied themselves with the United States in the *Organization of American States (OAS)*, founded in 1948. The goal of the OAS was to promote cooperation and prevent disputes.

These alliances, however, left many problems still unsolved. Relations between the United States and Latin America during the Cold War period were not always friendly. For many Latin Americans, the United States was not a good neighbor, but rather the "colossus of the north"— powerful and overbearing. Americans controlled much of the wealth in Latin America. They cooperated with wealthy landowners and with local rulers, who were often dictators. The majority of Latin Americans were poor. But most U.S. government aid was going to Europe and Asia, not to Latin America.

Revolts and military takeovers were common. The most important one during the postwar period occurred in Cuba. In 1959, Fidel Castro overthrew the Cuban dictator Fulgencio Batista. At first, most Americans were sympathetic to Castro. But they changed their minds when he seized U.S. property, executed hundreds of his opponents, and announced that he was a Communist. Soon, Khrushchev pledged that the Soviet Union would give military aid to Cuba. The United States then broke off diplomatic relations with Cuba (1961), and the OAS voted to exclude Cuba from participation in inter-American activities (1962).

True-False Test

1. The Atlantic Charter included the constitution of the United Nations.
2. At the Teheran conference, the United States was represented by President Harry Truman.

3. The Nuremberg trials were held to try leaders of Nazi Germany who were accused of war crimes.
4. The satellites of the Soviet Union are Communist nations located between the Soviet Union and Western Europe.
5. The Truman Doctrine was developed in order to prevent a Communist takeover of China and Southeast Asia.
6. Although Communist countries were eligible to participate in the Marshall Plan, they did not do so.
7. During the Berlin blockade of 1948–1949, Western powers supplied West Berliners by plane.
8. The Korean War began when Chinese troops invaded South Korea in 1950.
9. Both the Soviet Union and the United States opposed the 1956 attacks on Egypt by Israel, Britain, and France.
10. The victorious Cuban revolution of 1959 was led by Fulgencio Batista.

Matching Test

COLUMN A	COLUMN B
1. Big Three	a. military alliance of Western nations
2. denazification	b. plan aimed at preventing spread of communism in Middle East
3. George Kennan	c. secretary of state under President Truman
4. George C. Marshall	d. secretary of state under President Eisenhower
5. NATO	e. military alliance of Communist nations
6. Warsaw Pact	f. shooting down of American spy plane over Soviet Union
7. Douglas MacArthur	g. group that convened several times during World War II to discuss military strategy and peace plans
8. John Foster Dulles	h. leader of UN forces during Korean War
9. Eisenhower Doctrine	i. advocate of policy of containment
10. U-2 incident	j. program aimed at removing Hitler's followers from important posts in Germany

Map Test

Answer the following questions by studying the maps on pages 442 and 446, and the text.

1. Name the Asian countries that are separated by the Yalu River.
2. Which two Communist governments in postwar Eastern Europe were not members of the Warsaw Pact?
3. Which countries joined NATO in 1952? in 1955? in 1982?
4. Name the capitals of North and South Korea.
5. What is the significance of the 38th parallel?

Essay Questions

1. What was the Cold War? When, how, and why did it come about?
2. What was containment? Why did Dulles criticize it? Explain how his policy differed.
3. One historian has written: "The Marshall Plan was a superb blend of ideals and self-interest in diplomacy." Explain.
4. What were some achievements of the United Nations?
5. Describe the main events of the Korean War.

CHAPTER 29

Prosperity at Home

T HE UNITED STATES experienced some readjustment problems after World War II, as it had after World War I. It soon overcame them, however, and entered an era of prosperity—the greatest it had ever known.

TRUMAN'S PRESIDENCY

When Truman unexpectedly became president in April 1945, he said that he felt as if "the moon, the stars, and all the planets" had fallen on him. This down-to-earth Missourian had definite ideas about what he wanted to achieve as president. But he encountered stiff opposition to many of his proposals.

Return to a Peacetime Economy

As soon as the war was over, the government released millions of people from military service. Their return to civilian life was made easier by the *Servicemen's Readjustment Act* of 1944 (often called the "GI Bill of Rights"). It provided them with cash payments; education at government expense; unemployment benefits; and loans to buy homes, farms, and businesses.

Industry began to switch over from producing war materials to making peacetime goods. The removal of price controls and the great demand for consumer goods caused a sharp rise in prices. Workers,

Rock Star, Elvis Presley

demanding pay increases to keep up with the rising cost of living, went on strike in several major industries. The higher prices and strikes, together with mounting production costs, led to inflation. It became a serious problem and remained one throughout much of the Cold War period.

A Mixed Record

Unlike Roosevelt, Truman did not start out with solid Democratic support in Congress. His influence on lawmaking was further weakened after the Republicans won majorities in both houses of Congress in 1946. Congress was able to pass (and repass over Truman's veto) a bill strongly opposed by the president and by organized labor. This was the *Taft-Hartley Act* of 1947. It aimed to curb the power of big labor and to correct certain labor abuses, such as misuse of union funds. Among other things, it prohibited (1) the closed shop (a plant where only union members may be hired), (2) union contributions to political campaigns, and (3) jurisdictional strikes (strikes called when two unions dispute the right to represent workers). It compelled unions to file annual financial reports. It also required union leaders to take an oath that they were not members of the Communist party. In addition, the law provided for a "cooling-off" period of 60 days before a strike could be called.

The Taft-Hartley Act did not eliminate labor abuses, as its backers had hoped. Nor did it decrease union membership, as its opponents had feared.

Some members of Congress had vowed to repeal the New Deal, but they could not gain majority support. The legislature did show its disapproval of Roosevelt's length of service, which broke the two-term tradition established by Washington. It introduced the Twenty-second Amendment, limiting future presidents (after Truman) to two terms in office. The amendment became part of the Constitution in 1951.

CIVIL RIGHTS AND THE ELECTION OF 1948   Truman wanted to improve conditions for black Americans. He asked Congress to enact laws against lynching and poll taxes, and to set up a commission to combat discriminatory hiring practices. Southern senators blocked these proposals by threatening to filibuster. So Truman acted on his own. He appointed the first black federal judge, named blacks to other federal offices, and began to desegregate the armed forces.

Truman's stand on civil rights cost him votes in the South. When he ran for election in his own right in 1948, a group of Southern Democrats formed the *States' Rights* ("Dixiecrat") *party*. Its presidential candidate, Strom Thurmond, was extremely conservative. The Democratic party was further split by leftists who found Truman too conservative. They favored Henry Wallace, candidate of a new *Progressive party*. The Republicans nominated Thomas E. Dewey, governor of New York.

Few people expected Truman to win the election. But the president was an aggressive campaigner. He traveled thousands of miles, attacking the "do-nothing" 80th Congress in peppery speeches. He won a surprise victory, and the Democrats regained control of Congress.

THE FAIR DEAL   From the beginning, Truman had supported a program of domestic reforms. After winning the 1948 election, he launched a program that he called the Fair Deal. A Democratic majority in Congress, Truman thought, gave his proposals a good chance of being passed. He recommended an increase in the minimum wage, an expansion of social security, increased public housing and slum clearance, federal aid to education, and national health insurance. But Congress enacted only the first three proposals. Federal aid to education was controversial because of differing views about whether to help parochial schools (those run by religious organizations). And national health insurance was strongly attacked by the American Medical Association as "socialistic."

THE HUNT FOR SUBVERSIVES

The lack of response to Fair Deal proposals had several causes. One of them was the nation's pressing concern with foreign affairs—aid to Europe and, after 1950, the Korean War. Another factor was the public's preoccupation with questions of loyalty and security.

The Cold War made Americans extremely concerned about subversives in their midst. (Subversives are people who try to weaken or overthrow a government.) As early as 1947, Truman set up loyalty boards to investigate federal employees. Workers could be fired if there were "reasonable grounds" to believe that they were disloyal. By 1951, more than 3 million employees had been cleared, about 2000 had resigned, and some 200 had been fired.

Important Trials

Concern over Communist subversion increased after a series of well-publicized trials in the late 1940s and early 1950s. One of the most sensational cases involved Alger Hiss, a former high-ranking State Department employee. Hiss, a New Deal Democrat, was accused by journalist Whittaker Chambers of having been a Communist spy in the 1930s. After Hiss denied the charge, he was tried for perjury (lying under oath.) He could not be tried on the charge of spying because too much time had passed since the alleged crime had occurred.

Hiss was eventually convicted, and served almost four years in prison. He continued to insist on his innocence. But there were inconsistencies in his story—as there were in that of Chambers. Truman insisted that the case was invented to make the Democrats appear "soft on communism." The Hiss-Chambers affair certainly cast doubts on the Democratic administration. It also brought nationwide attention to a young California congressman, Richard Nixon, who played a key role in presenting the case against Hiss.

Even more sensational was the trial of Ethel and Julius Rosenberg. They were accused of passing atomic secrets to the Soviet Union. The Rosenbergs had been involved with left-wing politics for years. In their trial, they refused to discuss whether they were Communists but vigorously denied that they had been spies. Nevertheless, they were found guilty of treason in 1951. After many appeals and delays, they were executed two years later.

McCarthyism

Widespread fear of Communist subversion prompted Congress to pass the *Internal Security Act (McCarran Act)* of 1950. (It was enacted over Truman's veto.) The law required Communist organizations to register with the Justice Department, and barred Communists from employment in defense plants. It also permitted the deportation of any alien who was a member of a totalitarian (Communist, Nazi, or Fascist) organization, and forbade the entry of such persons into the United States. Most of the act's provisions were later declared unconstitutional.

In 1950, the American public seemed willing to accept almost any means of ferreting out subversives. This was why Joseph R. McCarthy, a relatively unknown Wisconsin senator, was able to go so far with so little. Early that year, he charged that there were 205 Communists in the

"I have here in my hand—" (From *Herblock's Here and Now*, Simon & Schuster, 1968)

State Department. (He later reduced the total to 57.) A special Senate subcommittee conducted an investigation and declared his charges false, but by then, he had moved on to other targets.

For some four years, McCarthy was constantly in the public eye. He made sweeping attacks on various branches of the government, the Protestant clergy, higher education, and the media. Many organizations, fearful of being accused of employing subversives, carried out "witch hunts" of their own. They fired the innocent, along with the guilty. "McCarthyism" came to mean hysterical anticommunism.

McCarthy, a Republican, had little use for the Democrats. But even after the Republicans came into office with Eisenhower's victory in 1952, McCarthy's attacks continued. The Wisconsin senator eventually went too far. He accused the army of harboring Communists. Televised hearings before a Senate committee convinced many viewers that McCarthy was a bully and a liar. His influence waned in 1954, when the Senate finally censured (officially reprimanded) him for his conduct.

By this time, the worst of the hysteria had died down. But it had damaged or destroyed the reputations and careers of many Americans. It did harm, too, by weakening the influence of moderate anti-Communists trying to alert the public to real threats from the Soviet Union.

EISENHOWER IN THE WHITE HOUSE

When Truman decided, in 1952, not to run again, the Democrats nominated Governor Adlai Stevenson of Illinois as their candidate for president. The Republicans chose Dwight D. Eisenhower, the nation's most popular hero of World War II. Republicans campaigned on the theme that it was "time for a change" (and time to end the war in Korea). "Ike" Eisenhower scored an overwhelming victory, receiving 442 electoral votes to Stevenson's 89.

Four years later, Eisenhower ran against Stevenson a second time. The president won re-election by an even greater margin than before, receiving 457 electoral votes to his opponent's 73.

The Middle of the Road

Eisenhower was a cautious man who tried to steer a course between extremes. He disliked McCarthyism but did not take a public stand against McCarthy until late in the senator's career. He wanted to keep the Russians in check without going to war. As noted in Chapter 28, the aggressive language of Secretary of State John Foster Dulles rarely led to the actual use of U.S. troops abroad.

Eisenhower's attitude toward the role of the federal government was somewhat contradictory. He attacked the Tennessee Valley Authority as an example of "creeping socialism." In his view, state and local ownership of natural resources was preferable to national ownership. (During his term, rights to offshore oil along the Gulf of Mexico and the Pacific coast were awarded to the states, rather than to the federal government.) And yet, the Eisenhower administration was responsible for two giant federal projects. One was a program for interstate

In the councils of Government, we must guard against the acquisition of unwarranted influence, whether sought or unsought, by the military-industrial complex. The potential for the dangerous rise of misplaced power exists and will persist.

—*Dwight D. Eisenhower's Farewell Address, January 1961*

highways. A 41,000-mile network of new roads eventually linked most of the nation's cities, at a cost of more than $100 billion. The other was the St. Lawrence Seaway, a huge transportation and hydroelectric project undertaken jointly with Canada. Completed in 1959, it enabled ocean-going vessels to travel from the Atlantic to ports on the Great Lakes.

The Warren Court

Probably the most important appointment of Eisenhower's presidency was that of Earl Warren, former governor of California, as chief justice of the United States. The Warren Court, which lasted from 1953 until 1969, handed down a number of decisions that vitally affected American society. Decades later, these rulings were still causing controversy.

SCHOOL DESEGREGATION   The first major case to be decided under Warren involved racial segregation. (Actually, the Court ruled on several separate cases, but the decision is known by the name of the first one on the list, Brown.) A black girl, Linda Carol Brown, had been turned away from a public school in Topeka, Kansas, because it was reserved for whites. With backing from the NAACP, her father sued on the grounds that she was being denied equal protection of the laws. In *Plessy* v. *Ferguson* (1896), the Supreme Court had ruled that "separate but equal" accommodations for blacks and whites were constitutional. In *Brown* v. *Board of Education of Topeka* (1954), the Court reversed the earlier decision. The justices ruled unanimously that "in the field of public education the doctrine of 'separate but equal' has no place. Separate educational facilities are inherently unequal."

The *Brown* decision aroused a storm of protest, especially in the South, where separate school systems were common. The Court set no procedures for desegregating schools, although it recommended, in 1955, that local school districts carry out its decision "with all deliberate speed." Many Southerners, including 100 members of Congress, vowed to resist desegregation. Every September brought tension, and often violence, as black children tried to enroll in white schools. Eisenhower remained silent on the issue until the fall of 1957. At that time, rioting broke out in Little Rock, Arkansas. The president was then forced to send in federal troops to maintain order. Desegregation in schools and in other public institutions came about slowly and with much opposition.

OTHER DECISIONS   Civil rights was only one field in which the Warren Court made far-reaching decisions. Another involved criminal justice. In *Gideon* v. *Wainwright* (1963), the Court ruled that persons accused of a felony have a right to free legal service if they are too poor

LANDMARK SUPREME COURT DECISIONS UNDER WARREN

Case	Background	Decision	Significance
Brown v. Board of Education of Topeka (1954)	Parents of black child, excluded from local school on grounds of race, sued to have her admitted.	Court held that racially segregated public schools are, by their nature, unequal and, thus, unconstitutional.	Set precedent for ending all forms of racial segregation.
Watkins v. U.S. (1957)	Labor organizer John Watkins, who refused to answer questions about Communist affiliation of others, was convicted of contempt of Congress.	Court reversed Watkins's conviction on grounds that Congress had overstepped its authority.	Limited power of congressional investigating committees.
Mapp v. Ohio (1961)	Dollree Mapp was convicted of possessing "lewd . . . . books" after police had searched her house without warrant to do so.	Court reversed Mapp's conviction on grounds that evidence against her had been obtained illegally.	Limited police power of search and seizure.
Baker v. Carr (1962)	Charles Baker and other Tennesseeans charged that state legislature discriminated against urban voters by over-representing rural voters.	Court ruled that state legislative districts should be based "substantially" on population.	Established principle of "one man, one vote," which led to widespread reapportionment of legislative districts.

Case	Background	Ruling
Engel v. Vitale (1962)	Parents of several school-children in New York sought ban on state-mandated school prayer.	Court held that school prayer is unconstitutional attempt to "establish" religion.	Banned organized prayer in public schools.

Case	Background	Decision	Effect
Engel v. Vitale (1962)	Parents of several school-children in New York sought ban on state-mandated school prayer.	Court held that school prayer is unconstitutional attempt to "establish" religion.	Banned organized prayer in public schools.
Abingdon School District v. Schempp (1963)	Edward Schempp family protested against Bible reading in Pennsylvania schools.	Court ruled that Bible reading is religious exercise and, thus, violates First Amendment.	Banned devotional Bible reading in public schools.
Gideon v. Wainwright (1963)	Clarence Gideon, accused of robbery and denied court-appointed lawyer, defended himself and was convicted.	Court overturned Gideon's conviction on grounds that he had right to counsel.	Required legal representation for accused in all state cases of criminal prosecution.
Escobedo v. Illinois (1964)	After confessing to murder, Danny Escobedo was convicted of the crime.	Court reversed Escobedo's conviction because he had been denied lawyer during questioning.	Established right of accused to have lawyer present during questioning.
Miranda v. Arizona (1966)	After signing confession, Ernesto Miranda was accused of kidnapping and attacking 18-year-old girl.	Court reversed Miranda's conviction since he had not been informed of his rights at time of arrest.	Required police to inform suspects of rights to silence and to counsel before being questioned.

to pay for a lawyer. In *Escobedo* v. *Illinois* (1964), the justices declared that a criminal suspect cannot be denied a lawyer during questioning. The *Miranda* v. *Arizona* decision of 1966 held that suspects must be warned of their rights to be silent or to have a lawyer before they are questioned.

Many Americans opposed these rulings, arguing that they "coddled" criminals and made law enforcement too difficult. Widespread opposition was also touched off by Supreme Court decisions that forbade organized prayer and Bible reading in public schools. Conservative groups even demanded Warren's impeachment.

Progress Against Discrimination

The *Brown* decision was one sign of increased concern for the rights of black Americans. There were other signs as well. Eisenhower completed the desegregation of the armed forces, begun under Truman. In 1957, Congress passed a civil rights law, the first since reconstruction. It removed some of the obstacles that prevented blacks from voting. It also set up a special division in the Justice Department to protect the rights of blacks.

But the efforts of black Americans working on their own behalf made the greatest difference. Pressure from the NAACP and similar groups spurred the integration of schools and other institutions.

One local movement did much to encourage black Americans in their crusade for equal rights. It took place in Montgomery, Alabama, in 1955 and 1956. After a black woman named Rosa Parks refused to give her bus seat to a white man, she was arrested. Blacks then organized a boycott of the local bus system that eventually led to its desegregation. The boycott's leader, the Reverend Martin Luther King, Jr., gained national prominence as a civil rights activist.

A VARIETY OF ACHIEVEMENTS

By the mid-20th century, Americans were excelling in almost every field of human endeavor. The products of their ingenuity and creativity, ranging from soft drinks and movies to automobiles and computers, were in demand all over the world.

The "Affluent Society"

Beginning in the late 1940s, the United States entered a 20-year period of unmatched prosperity. The GNP rose to levels undreamed of

POPULATION GROWTH (1910–1990)

Year	Total	Urban*		Rural	
		Number	Percent	Number	Percent
1910	91,972,000	41,999,000	46%	49,973,000	54%
1920	105,711,000	54,158,000	51%	51,553,000	49%
1930	122,775,000	68,955,000	56%	53,820,000	44%
1940	131,670,000	74,424,000	57%	57,246,000	43%
1950	150,698,000	96,468,000	64%	54,230,000	36%
1960	179,323,000	125,269,000	70%	54,054,000	30%
1970	203,212,000	149,325,000	73%	53,887,000	27%
1980	226,546,000	167,051,000	74%	59,495,000	26%
1990	248,710,000	187,054,000	75%	61,656,000	25%

*Urban population is defined as all persons living in places of 2500 inhabitants or more.

earlier. Americans in the postwar era attained one of the highest standards of living the world had ever known. Employment was up and so were wages. Consumer goods had been in short supply during the war. Now, demand and sales soared. By the mid-1950s, nine out of ten American families owned a refrigerator, three out of four owned at least one car, and three out of five owned a house.

Another postwar phenomenon was a "baby boom." The soaring birthrate caused the nation's population to grow almost 20 percent between 1950 and 1960. Many young American families moved to suburbs, attracted by government housing aid, new highways, cheap gasoline, and open spaces.

John Kenneth Galbraith, an economist, called the United States in the 1950s an "affluent society." (His 1958 book *The Affluent Society* made the term popular.) But Galbraith was very critical of this wealth. Many Americans lived well in private, he said, but skimped on public services. Schools, hospitals, parks, and transportation systems were consistently rundown and badly maintained. Furthermore, Galbraith wrote, the affluence was far from universal. In 1957, according to one estimate, over 32 million people had incomes below the poverty level. This represented nearly one-fifth of the total population.

Science and Technology

Americans made scientific and technological breakthroughs in several areas. Many of these achievements came about because of a new partnership that began during World War II. It linked the government, large corporations, and universities.

The most notable advance was probably the development of

atomic energy, in which refugees from Fascist Europe played a key role. They included Albert Einstein (from Germany), Enrico Fermi (from Italy), and Leo Szilard and Edward Teller (both from Hungary). In the early years after the war, atomic energy seemed to offer unlimited possibilities for future growth. One milestone of this period was the launching of the first nuclear-powered submarine, the *Nautilus,* in 1954. It sailed across the North Pole, under the polar icecap, in 1958. Another milestone that same year was the opening of the first American nuclear power plant, at Shippingport, Pennsylvania.

MEDICINE   Advances in medicine helped relieve suffering and bring hope to millions. None was more welcome than an antipolio

TECHNOLOGICAL DEVELOPMENTS (1930–1960)

Date	Inventor	Invention
1930	Richard Drew	Made first cellophane adhesive tape
1934	Wallace H. Carothers	Developed nylon
1936	Fred Waring	Invented food and beverage blender
1938	Games Slayter	Patented fiberglass
1939	Edwin H. Armstrong	Perfected frequency modulation (FM)
1940	Chester F. Carlson	Patented first dry copying machine (xerography)
1945	International team of scientists	Exploded first atomic bomb
1945	Percy L. Spencer	Marketed first commercial microwave oven
1945	John Mauchly and J. Presper Eckert, Jr.	Completed first large electronic digital computer (Eniac)
1947	Edwin H. Land	Invented Polaroid (self-developing) camera
1948	Peter Goldmark	Invented long-playing record
1948	Kevin Tuohy	Introduced first corneal contact lenses
1948	Walter Brattain, John Bardeen, William Shockley	Invented transistor
1954	Bell Telephone Laboratories	Developed solar battery
1960	Theodore H. Maiman	Demonstrated first practical laser

vaccine, developed by Jonas Salk in the early 1950s. Beginning in 1955, millions of Americans were given the vaccine. Incidence of the disease dropped 80 percent. It was further reduced after the introduction, in 1961, of an oral vaccine, developed by Albert Sabin.

Measles became much less common after 1962, when John Enders discovered a vaccine to combat it. Antibiotic drugs developed by Selman Waksman proved useful in treating serious bacterial infections. Antihistamines eased the discomfort of allergy sufferers, while cortisone helped combat such crippling diseases as rheumatoid arthritis.

SPACE A brand new application of science and technology was the conquest of space. Americans were shocked in 1957, when the Soviet Union launched the first artificial satellite, *Sputnik*, and sent it into orbit around the earth. The United States then stepped up its own space program. The National Aeronautics and Space Administration (NASA) was created in 1958. That year, the first U.S. satellite, *Explorer I*, was launched.

A number of "firsts" in space were achievements of the Soviet Union. It sent a cosmonaut into orbit in 1961, and three cosmonauts in one vehicle in 1964. A Russian made the first "space walk" in 1965.

The United States was not far behind in matching these feats. In 1962, John Glenn became the first American to orbit the earth. Three years later, the first American space walk was carried out, and two

What great discoveries lie ahead? (Palmer in *The Springfield* (Mo.) *Leader & Press*)

American spaceships completed the world's first meeting in space, a technique known as rendezvous and docking.

Beginning in the mid-1960s, NASA concentrated much of its effort on Project Apollo, designed to land astronauts on the moon. It attained its objective in July 1969, when Neil Armstrong and Edwin Aldrin became the first humans to set foot on the moon's surface. Said Armstrong: "That's one small step for a man, one giant leap for mankind."

After Project Apollo, NASA focused on a space shuttle program. Unlike earlier projects, this one featured reusable launch vehicles, promising greater economy and, thus, more frequent voyages. American astronauts piloted the world's first reusable space shuttle in 1981.

In 1995, astronaut Norman Thagard joined the crew of an orbiting Russian space station. From this cooperative venture, NASA hoped to learn at first hand how humans fare during extended periods in space.

The many space probes—with and without astronauts—have yielded much new data about weather, the sun's rays, and the other planets in our solar system. Orbiting communications satellites now aid in relaying international radio, telephone, and television signals.

ELECTRONICS Space travel would never have been possible without new developments in electronics. Several earlier innovations, such as X-ray tubes and radio, grew out of this branch of electrical engineering. But electronics came into its own only with miniaturization—the replacement of bulky vacuum tubes by tiny transistors.

One electronic device that took firm hold in the United States after World War II was television. The first sets for home use were sold in the 1930s, but output was held down by World War II. In 1947, fewer than 15,000 American families owned television sets. Just ten years later, however, there were 40 million sets in use. President Roosevelt had appeared on TV as early as 1939 (at the New York World's Fair). But the first presidential inauguration to be televised was Truman's in 1949. The political conventions of 1952 were the first to be televised nationally. The new medium demonstrated its power when televised hearings by a Senate committee helped end Senator McCarthy's career in 1954.

Even more revolutionary in its impact on American society was the computer. This electronic device could store huge quantities of data and process it in seconds. The first mass-produced computer went on the market in 1951. Within 20 years, computers were being used to direct space flights; set type; book airline seats; keep inventories; and prepare payrolls, bills, and bank statements. In industry, computers took over many complex operations, from making aspirin to pouring steel. This industrial development, known as automation, had a serious drawback—a decrease in the demand for unskilled labor. Computer applications, however, opened up many new jobs for skilled technicians.

Entertainment

Before and during World War II, radio had been the nation's favorite home entertainment. After the war, television took its place. Night after night, whole families sat watching comedy shows, variety programs, and old movies. Television excelled in drama, sports, and news. An estimated 600 million people in 49 countries watched Neil Armstrong step out onto the moon. But TV's prime purpose was to sell products, and the general level of programming was low. The chairman of the FCC once called television a "vast wasteland."

Television made spectator sports a bigger business than ever. Millions of fans watched football, baseball, and basketball games. One of the most important sports milestones of the immediate postwar era had little to do with television, however. This was the end of segregation in professional sports. In 1947, Jackie Robinson, hired by the Dodgers (then of Brooklyn), became the first black player in major league baseball. In succeeding years, black and Hispanic athletes won fame in nearly all sports—from track and basketball to golf and tennis.

Musical entertainment also flourished during and after the war. Outstanding Broadway shows of the period included *Oklahoma!* (1943), *Carousel* (1945), *Kiss Me, Kate* (1948), *South Pacific* (1949), *The King and I,* (1951), *My Fair Lady* (1956), and *West Side Story* (1957). These and many similar shows were later produced as movies. A new kind of music, rock and roll, became popular in the 1950s. It combined elements of white "country" music and black rhythm-and-blues, always with an insistent beat. In the 1960s, as rock, this music became more sophisticated, louder (with electronic help), and more elaborately performed.

The Arts

American creative artists in every medium represented a wide range of outlooks. Many of them were concerned about the role of the individual in the complex world of modern mass society.

FICTION AND DRAMA   Several novels published after World War II dealt with the war itself. They included Norman Mailer's *The Naked and the Dead* (1948) and James Jones's *From Here to Eternity* (1951). An American war novel noted for its grim humor was Joseph Heller's *Catch 22*, which appeared in 1961.

Both Mailer and Heller were Jews, as were several other talented American novelists of the period. Some dealt specifically with the Jewish experience in their works, while others, like Mailer and Heller, typically did not. Notable works were J. D. Salinger's *The Catcher in the Rye* (1951), Saul Bellow's *The Adventures of Augie March* (1953),

Bernard Malamud's *The Assistant* (1957), and Philip Roth's *Goodbye, Columbus* (1959).

A number of gifted writers used the middle-class suburbs of the nation as background. The somber novels of James Gould Cozzens centered on difficult moral choices. His works included *Guard of Honor* (1948) and *By Love Possessed* (1957). Morality was also a concern of John Cheever, a master of the witty and sophisticated short story. Another talented short story writer was John Updike. He conveyed a sense of the magic in ordinary people and settings in his novel *Rabbit, Run* (1960).

Black Americans contributed outstanding work in the postwar years. Ralph Ellison, in *Invisible Man* (1952), wrote of a young black's search for identity. Other widely read black writers included essayist and novelist James Baldwin and poet Gwendolyn Brooks. Lorraine Hansberry's award-winning play *A Raisin in the Sun* (1959) was later made into a film.

Southern experience was the common bond of another group of writers. William Faulkner created mythical Yoknapatawpha County in a series of novels published from the 1920s through the 1950s. Robert Penn Warren is best known for his powerful novel about Southern politics, *All the King's Men* (1946). Three women, Flannery O'Connor, Eudora Welty, and Carson McCullers, portrayed in their novels and short stories a variety of memorable Southern characters.

Playwright Tennessee Williams, also a Southerner, wrote of doomed romantic dreams in *The Glass Menagerie* (1945) and *A Streetcar Named Desire* (1947). Arthur Miller spoke out against conformity in *Death of a Salesman* (1949) and *The Crucible* (1953). The latter play deals with the Salem witchcraft trials of 1692. Audiences in the early 1950s saw parallels with the "witch hunts" of the McCarthy era.

THE VISUAL ARTS   In the 1950s, New York became the world center for modern art, as Paris had been earlier in the century. The painters who worked in New York created a new style called abstract expressionism. It was characterized by big canvases, swirling with color. Jackson Pollock was a leading abstract expressionist and one of the most controversial and imitated American painters of the time. To create rhythmic designs, he tacked his canvases to the floor and dripped paint on them in successive layers. The paint was often mixed with sand to create unusual textures.

Another postwar movement in which Americans played a leading role was pop art. Its name came from its interest in images from the mass (popular) media. Robert Rauschenberg created collages that included rags, tin cans, and newspaper photos. Claes Oldenburg specialized in oversized sculptures of such everyday objects as ice-cream cones, clothespins, and hamburgers. In a class by himself was the sculptor

Alexander Calder. He used sheet metal and wire to create mobiles (moving sculptures) and stabiles (stationary sculptures). His carefully balanced works are graceful and often humorous.

In the midst of all this experimentation, the tradition of realism continued to flourish. One of the most popular of all 20th-century American artists was Edward Hopper. He was noted for his Cape Cod landscapes and lonely urban scenes. Georgia O'Keeffe painted Southwestern landscapes and still lifes with precision. Rural Northeastern scenes were the subjects of many paintings by Andrew Wyeth.

MUSIC   Serious music reached a wider audience in the mid-20th century than ever before. Almost every city of any size had a symphony orchestra, and summer festivals of classical music and opera drew large crowds. Standard European works were the favorites, but American composers were represented, too. Charles Ives often used bits of hymn tunes and patriotic songs in his vocal and orchestral music. Folk melodies appeared in such works of Aaron Copland as his *Lincoln Portrait* (1942) and *Appalachian Spring* (1944).

TEN NOTABLE AMERICANS OF MODERN TIMES

LEONARD BERNSTEIN (1918–1990)   He was the first conductor born and trained in the United States to have a substantial career abroad. Associated most closely with the New York Philharmonic, he toured widely with it and other orchestras. His own compositions included both musical comedy, such as *West Side Story* (1957), and serious music, such as *Mass*, which opened Washington's John F. Kennedy Center in 1971.

MARY McLEOD BETHUNE (1875–1955)   This energetic South Carolinian founded a school for black children at Daytona Beach, Florida, which later become Bethune-Cookman College. She is best known as a member of the so-called "Black Cabinet" of President Franklin Roosevelt. This group often met informally with FDR to urge an end to segregation and the expansion of opportunites for black Americans.

AMELIA EARHART (1898?–1937)   She was already an experienced pilot when, in 1928, she became the first woman to fly the Atlantic (as a passenger). She was soon setting speed and distance records of her own. In 1935, she became the first pilot to fly alone from Hawaii to the U.S. mainland. Two-years later, on a flight over the Pacific, her plane disappeared, never to be found.

ALBERT EINSTEIN (1879–1955)   Born in Germany, this Nobel prize-winning physicist first attracted worldwide attention with several papers published in 1905. One, outlining the special theory of relativity, proposed a new relationship between matter and energy. It drastically changed the laws of physics, and laid the basis for the release of atomic energy. Einstein, a Jew, settled in the United States when Hitler came to power, joined the Institute for Advanced Study at Princeton, and became an American citizen.

MARTHA GRAHAM (1894?–1991)   One of the greatest modern dancers, she was born in Pittsburgh and founded her own school and dance company in New York City. The dances she choreographed—more than 145—were intense expressions of human emotion. Among the American composers who wrote music for her were Aaron Copland (*Appalachian Spring*) and William Schuman (*Judith*).

HELEN KELLER (1880–1968)   Her life was a triumph over difficulties. When she was less than two years old, an illness left her deaf, blind, and mute. A devoted teacher, Annie Sullivan, taught her how to communicate. An early work of Keller's, *The Story of My Life* (1902), attracted nationwide attention. After graduating from Radcliffe College in 1904, she wrote several more books and gave lectures. She worked on behalf of the blind, pacifism, and women's rights, and in opposition to child labor and capital punishment.

MARGARET MEAD (1901–1978)   This world-famous anthropologist was one of the first women to make a name for herself in what had been a man's field. Her work in the Pacific led to one of her best-known books, *Coming of Age in Samoa* (1928). In her long career as a writer and teacher, she emphasized the influence of culture on personality. She also did much to make photography an important tool of her profession.

ERNEST PYLE (1900–1945)   A farm boy from Indiana, he first gained popularity as a newspaper columnist with pieces written while traveling around the United States. "Ernie" Pyle became the best known of all World War II correspondents, writing in a down-to-earth style that reflected his deep affection for the ordinary "G.I. Joe." After covering the invasion of Italy and the liberation of Paris, he traveled to the Pacific, where he was killed during the Battle of Okinawa.

B. F. SKINNER (1904–1990)   In the field of psychology, he emphasized behaviorism. This is the idea that human behavior is best explained as a series of responses to outside stimuli. His controversial ideas about behavior modification influenced the administration of schools, prisons, and mental institutions. *Walden Two* (1948) depicts a utopian community operated on behaviorist principles.

ALFRED STIEGLITZ (1864–1946)   This photographer convinced Americans that photography is an art form. He opened a photographic and art gallery in New York City in 1905, where he exhibited the works of new and innovative artists. Many of his own photographs depict the skyscrapers and people of New York. He pioneered in rain, snow, and night scenes, and in color photography.

Matching Test

Column A	Column B
1. Thomas E. Dewey	**a.** person responsible for famous bus boycott in 1955
2. Whittaker Chambers	
3. Adlai Stevenson	**b.** first black player in major league baseball
4. Earl Warren	
5. Rosa Parks	**c.** Truman's opponent in 1948 election
6. *Nautilus*	
7. Jonas Salk	**d.** author of *Death of a Salesman*
8. Apollo	**e.** witness who accused Alger Hiss of being a spy
9. Jackie Robinson	
10. Arthur Miller	**f.** Democratic candidate for president in 1952
	g. developer of successful polio vaccine
	h. project to land astronauts on moon
	i. first nuclear-powered submarine
	j. chief justice of United States from 1953 to 1969

Multiple-Choice Test

1. The Taft-Hartley Act was an attempt to (a) legalize the closed shop (b) curb the power of big labor (c) prohibit collective bargaining (d) prevent the growth of craft unions.
2. The Twenty-second Amendment (a) abolished prohibition (b) changed the date of presidential inaugurations (c) limited presidents to two terms (d) lowered the voting age.
3. Truman's Fair Deal proposals included all of the following *except* (a) school desegregation (b) increased public housing (c) national health insurance (d) federal aid to education.
4. The conviction of Alger Hiss focused nationwide attention on a young congressman named (a) Strom Thurmond (b) Joseph McCarthy (c) Richard Nixon (d) John Foster Dulles.
5. All of the following took place during Eisenhower's administration *except* (a) the beginning of an interstate highway program (b) construction of the St. Lawrence Seaway (c) the *Brown v. Topeka* decision (d) the Rosenberg trial.

6. In the case of *Miranda* v. *Arizona,* the Supreme Court ruled that (a) legislative districts should be reapportioned (b) organized school prayer is unconstitutional (c) criminal suspects have to be told of their rights before they are questioned (d) everyone being tried for a felony is entitled to a lawyer.
7. Martin Luther King, Jr., first gained national prominence because of a bus boycott in (a) Montgomery, Alabama (b) Washington, D.C. (c) Little Rock, Arkansas (d) Topeka, Kansas.
8. U.S. astronauts first set foot on the moon in (a) 1957 (b) 1958 (c) 1964 (d) 1969.
9. The use of computers to direct industrial operations is known as (a) miniaturization (b) electronics (c) automation (d) space technology.
10. All of the following are noted for their novels about World War II *except* (a) Norman Mailer (b) Ralph Ellison (c) James Jones (d) Joseph Heller.

Essay Questions

1. Name five of the domestic reforms that President Truman sought to introduce during his administration.
2. What was McCarthyism? When and why did it flourish? What were its main results?
3. Describe the background of the *Brown* v. *Topeka* decision. What did the Supreme Court rule? Why was its decision important?
4. Describe three of the other major decisions of the Supreme Court under Chief Justice Warren. Why were they controversial?
5. How did electronics change American life after World War II?

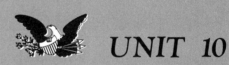

UNIT 10

Challenges of
the Modern
Era

CHAPTER 30

Idealism and Commitment

MANY AMERICANS, by 1960, were beginning to feel that their country was drifting. The United States, they believed, should be more active in promoting the well-being of its citizens and supporting democracy overseas. The early years of the Sixties were marked by a heightened sense of idealism, as the nation tried to carry out ambitious commitments, both at home and abroad. The second half of the decade was dominated by the Vietnam War, a foreign involvement that led to much turmoil and dissension.

THE KENNEDY YEARS

Since Eisenhower could not run for a third term in 1960, the Republicans nominated his vice president, Richard M. Nixon. The Democratic candidate for president was a wealthy young senator from Massachusetts, John Fitzgerald Kennedy.

A new element was introduced into presidential campaigning when the two candidates held a series of televised debates. Millions of Americans watched them argue the issues of the day. Many observers felt that the debates played a decisive role in the election. Kennedy projected an image of youth and vigor. Nixon, on the other hand, looked awkward and insecure. Another factor in the presidential campaign was Kennedy's Roman Catholicism. People wondered whether his religion would cause him to lose votes among the Protestant majority. In the end, however, this issue was probably less damaging to Kennedy's chances than it had been to Al Smith's in 1928.

In the election, the popular vote was very close. Kennedy received 34,227,000 votes to Nixon's 34,109,000. But Kennedy carried most of the larger states, winning 303 electoral votes to Nixon's 219. "JFK," as Kennedy was often called, was the youngest man ever elected president. (Theodore Roosevelt was younger when he took office in 1901, but he had succeeded to the presidency as a result of McKinley's assassination.)

Foreign Affairs

Soon after his inauguration, Kennedy proposed two new foreign aid programs. Both went into effect in 1961.

One innovation, the Peace Corps, was designed to promote world friendship. Under this program, American volunteers go to developing countries, live among the people, and contribute knowledge and technical help. Since its founding, the Peace Corps has sent more than 75,000 volunteers abroad. They teach school, train workers to operate modern machinery, and demonstrate improved methods of farming and sanitation.

The second program aimed to help Latin America. Much of the region suffered from economic distress and political instability. Kennedy was determined to improve this situation. He asked the countries of the Western Hemisphere "to join a new *Alliance for Progress*—a vast effort to satisfy the basic needs of the American people for homes, work and land, health and schools." As planned, the project was to use U.S. capital and

Rocky soil. (Hesse in the *St. Louis Globe-Democrat*)

technical skill to foster Latin American domestic reform and self-help. To carry it out, Kennedy called for a minimum of $20 billion in loans and grants from the United States over the next decade. Unfortunately, the alliance did not accomplish much. Funds from the United States were limited, and Latin American countries were slow to enact reforms.

THE BAY OF PIGS   Kennedy ran into trouble in Latin America early in his administration. After the 1959 revolution in Cuba, many Cubans fled to the United States to escape Castro's oppressive rule. Some of these exiles wanted to overthrow the Castro regime. The U.S. Central Intelligence Agency (CIA) began to train a small army of them for that purpose. When Kennedy became president, he was advised that the force was ready. Despite his personal doubts about its chances of success, he authorized an invasion.

In April 1961, some 1500 troops were landed at the Bay of Pigs, on the southern coast of Cuba. The invaders expected U.S. air support, which Kennedy called off at the last minute. They also hoped for an uprising by anti-Castro Cubans, but it did not take place. Within three days, the vastly outnumbered invaders were crushed by Castro's army.

TENSIONS IN GERMANY   The east-west division of Germany continued to be a sore spot in international relations. Ever since 1948, when the Soviet Union first attempted to cut off Berlin from the West, the Russians had made periodic efforts to force the United States, Britain, and France to withdraw their troops from the western part of the city. In 1961, the Russians once again demanded that the Western Allies leave West Berlin. The Russians also insisted that, before the end of the year, the Allies sign a peace treaty confirming the existing division of Germany. The Allies rejected these demands. Kennedy then called for an increase in NATO forces and a buildup of U.S. military strength. Suddenly, the East Germans put up a fortified wall between East and West Berlin, effectively separating the two parts of the city. The Berlin Wall closed off an escape route that some 3 million East Germans had used since 1949 to flee to the West.

In response to the building of the wall, Kennedy ordered additional U.S. troops to Berlin. He also sent Vice President Lyndon Johnson to the city to assure the West Berliners that the United States would not abandon them. Faced with this display of American force and determination, the Soviets backed down on their demands.

THE CUBAN MISSILE CRISIS   The most dangerous U.S.-Soviet confrontation of the Kennedy years involved Cuba. In the fall of 1962, the United States discovered that the Soviet Union was constructing offensive military bases in Cuba. Photographs taken by U.S. planes showed that

"I have a dream...."

"Ask what you can do for your country."

Martin Luther King, Jr.

John F. Kennedy

Soviet technicians were building launching sites for missiles, as well as airfields for long-range jet bombers. Medium-range missiles were already in place, and installations for intermediate-range missiles were nearing completion. These would be capable of delivering nuclear warheads to most targets in North America.

Kennedy acted quickly. He set up a blockade of Cuba by ordering U.S. armed forces to turn back any ship carrying offensive military equipment to the island. He also demanded that existing missiles be dismantled and removed immediately. The Soviet leaders backed away from a showdown. They called back ships that were carrying offensive weapons to Cuba. They also agreed to stop building missile bases, to destroy completed sites, and to dismantle and remove their missiles. Kennedy, in turn, promised to lift the blockade and assured the Soviets that the United States would not invade Cuba. Each side carried out its part of the agreement, and the world breathed easier.

After the Cuban crisis subsided, the two superpowers agreed to set up a telephone "hot line" between Moscow and Washington, D.C. Its purpose was to provide for instant communication between the two capitals. The two nations also worked out a nuclear test ban treaty. It prohibited the testing of nuclear weapons in the atmosphere, in outer space, and underwater (but not underground). Signed by the United States, the Soviet Union, and Great Britain, the treaty went into effect in the fall of 1963.

The New Frontier

The Kennedy administration's domestic program was called the New Frontier. The term came from a campaign speech in which Kennedy had said that "we stand today on the edge of a new

My fellow Americans: ask not what your country can do for you—ask what you can do for your country.

My fellow citizens of the world: ask not what America will do for you, but what together we can do for the freedom of man.

—*John F. Kennedy's Inaugural Address, January 1961*

frontier—the frontier of the Sixties."

Kennedy's program was ambitious. His proposals included aid to education, medical care for the aged, and tax reforms to encourage economic growth. Although Congress was controlled by the Democrats, leading members were conservatives, who exhibited little interest in reform. As a result, most of Kennedy's recommendations received only lukewarm support and bogged down in the legislature.

CIVIL RIGHTS   Kennedy tried to achieve progress in civil rights without confronting Congress. For instance, when the University of Mississippi refused to admit a black student, the president sent in troops to protect the student's right to enroll. The government also brought suit in several state courts to secure voting rights for blacks deprived of the franchise. Using his executive powers, Kennedy issued an order barring racial and religious discrimination in federally aided housing. When he did finally submit proposals to Congress to strengthen civil rights laws,

I have a dream that one day this nation will rise up and live out the true meaning of its creed: "We hold these truths to be self-evident: that all men are created equal." . . .

I have a dream that my four little children will one day live in a nation where they will not be judged by the color of their skin but by the content of their character. . . .

. . . And if America is to be a great nation, this must become true. So let freedom ring . . . .

. . . when we allow freedom to ring—when we let it ring from every village and every hamlet, from every state and every city, we will be able to speed up that day when all of God's children, black men and white men, Jews and Gentiles, Protestants and Catholics, will be able to join hands and sing in the words of the old Negro spiritual, "Free at last! Free at last! Thank God Almighty, we are free at last!"

—*Martin Luther King, Jr., speaking at the March on Washington, August 28, 1963* they made no more headway than other parts of his legislative program.

Civil rights groups continued to fight discrimination. Inspired by the leadership of Martin Luther King, Jr., they followed a policy of nonviolent civil disobedience—refusal to obey laws regarded as unjust. They held "sit-ins" at segregated public eating places and transportation facilities, forcing them to abandon discriminatory practices. In August 1963, peaceful protesters staged a vast March on Washington.

ASSASSINATION   Kennedy's administration came to a tragic end in Dallas, Texas, on November 22, 1963. While riding in an open car to address a luncheon gathering, the president was shot by a sniper and killed. Lee Harvey Oswald was charged with the slaying, but he himself was murdered before he could be brought to trial.

Vice President Johnson was immediately sworn in as president. He pledged to support Kennedy's ideas and ideals and to make every effort to translate them into action. The new president's confidence and firmness reassured the nation and helped ease the shock of the sudden change in leadership.

JOHNSON AND THE GREAT SOCIETY

Lyndon Baines Johnson was a very different personality from the polished, sophisticated Kennedy. A rough-hewn Texan, Johnson had served in Congress since the 1930s—first as a representative and then as a senator. Before his election as vice president, he had been majority leader of the Senate. Although his background differed from Kennedy's, Johnson shared the same liberal aims.

The new president declared his intention to build a "Great Society." His goals included peace and freedom throughout the world, improved living conditions for Americans, and encouragement and support of the arts and sciences. In the first few years of his administration, Johnson maintained a close working relationship with Congress. He won congressional approval for several key Kennedy proposals and for a number of his own Great Society recommendations.

One of the first Great Society measures to be passed had been drawn up by the Kennedy administration. This *Civil Rights Act of 1964* contained some of the broadest guarantees of equal rights for blacks ever passed by Congress. The federal government was granted additional authority to speed school desegregation, curb violations of voting rights of blacks, and end racial discrimination by employers and unions. The act also outlawed segregation in such public places as hotels, restaurants, stores, and theaters.

GREAT SOCIETY LEGISLATION (1964–1968)

Act	Purpose	Provisions
Civil Rights Act (July 1964)	To speed integration of blacks into American society	Outlawed segregation in public places and discrimination in employment; expanded voting rights
Economic Opportunity Act (August 1964)	To eliminate poverty	Established Office of Economic Opportunity (OEO) to coordinate program in job training, education, and employment
Elementary and Secondary School Act (April 1965)	To upgrade American education	Granted first large-scale federal aid to public schools
Social Security Amendments (July 1965)	To provide federal health insurance	Set up Medicare and Medicaid systems
Voting Rights Act (August 1965)	To end limitations to black suffrage	Suspended literacy tests and authorized federal registration of voters in some areas
Immigration Act (October 1965)	To change immigration policy	Provided that former system of national quotas be eliminated by July 1968; set up new quota system, particularly for peoples of Western Hemisphere

Act	Purpose	Description
Higher Education Act (November 1965)	To aid college students in financial need	Provided first federal scholarships for college undergraduates
Clean Waters Restoration Act (November 1966)	To control water pollution	Granted federal funds for community sewage-treatment plants and for research to control pollution
Fair Packaging and Labeling Act (November 1966)	To help consumers	Set quantity and contents standards for labeling of many common supermarket and drugstore items
Air Quality Act (November 1967)	To control air pollution	Provided funds for research; also empowered federal government to assist states in setting clean air standards and reducing air pollution
Open Housing Act (April 1968)	To broaden rights of black Americans	Extended protection for civil rights workers; banned discrimination in most housing
Consumer Credit Protection Act (Truth-in-Lending Act) (May 1968)	To help installment buyers	Required lenders to provide consumers with written information on interest and other charges
Housing and Urban Development Act (August 1968)	To provide living quarters for low- and moderate-income families	Provided federal subsidies for building, renting, and buying housing

Democratic Victory in 1964

Johnson was the natural Democratic choice for president in 1964. Senator Hubert H. Humphrey of Minnesota was picked as his running mate. The Republicans, dominated by their party's conservative wing, chose Senator Barry M. Goldwater of Arizona as their presidential candidate.

Goldwater called for a more aggressive policy toward communism abroad. At home, he argued, the expanding powers of the federal government were destroying American self-reliance and freedom. He was particularly critical of social welfare programs. Goldwater also condemned federal action in behalf of civil rights as unconstitutional. The problem of segregation, he insisted, should be handled by the states and local communities.

Johnson emphasized the need for restraint in foreign policy in order to prevent the outbreak of nuclear war. He also defended the welfare state. Prosperity and progress at home, he said, were founded on the federal programs already in effect. He pledged to expand them.

Johnson won by a landslide. He received a record-breaking popular vote of 43 million to Goldwater's 27 million, and 486 electoral votes to his opponent's 52. The Democrats also strengthened their hold on Congress.

New Programs

Even before his sweeping victory in 1964, Johnson had been able to get several new programs through Congress. He had declared a "War on Poverty" and set up an Office of Economic Opportunity to coordinate this many-sided effort. A Job Corps aimed to train unemployed youths. A domestic peace corps, called VISTA, sent volunteers into poor regions of the United States. After the election, Johnson persuaded Congress to pass other liberal measures. Project Head Start offered preschool learning programs for poor children. A Community Action Program was designed to help city neighborhoods.

Johnson focused his attention on other problems as well—securing laws to broaden civil rights, provide medical care for the aged, improve education, reduce environmental pollution, and revitalize inner cities. Not since the early New Deal had so much reform legislation been enacted.

Critics complained that too many changes were being made in too short a time. Conservatives opposed the growth in federal programs. Even Americans who favored Johnson's aims felt that many of the projects were poorly planned and administered. And when ambitious schemes did not succeed, people became disappointed and angry. Beginning in 1964, for example, urban riots destroyed buildings and took lives summer after summer, particularly in black ghettos.

WAR IN VIETNAM

The main reason for Johnson's limited success with his Great Society programs was his increasing involvement with a war in Vietnam. It eventually forced him out of office.

Background

In 1954, France, defeated by nationalist troops in Vietnam, gave up its hold on this former colony in Southeast Asia. The country had then been divided into two states—a Communist one in the north and an anti-Communist one in the south. In North Vietnam, Ho Chi Minh led the Vietminh party, which ruled with Soviet and Chinese support. In South Vietnam, the pro-Western government's opposition to Vietminh sympathizers there (known as the Vietcong) was strongly encouraged by the United States. U.S. leaders at this time feared a "domino effect" in Southeast Asia. They believed that if one non-Communist country, such as South Vietnam, became Communist, nearby countries would also topple until the whole region was in the Communist camp.

A national election was scheduled for 1956, when all Vietnamese would choose the leaders who would reunite their country. When it appeared that the Communists might win, South Vietnam, with U.S. backing, refused to permit the election to take place. South Vietnamese officials became increasingly dictatorial in their efforts to suppress the Vietcong.

In 1959, North Vietnam adopted a policy aimed at overthrowing the South Vietnamese government, especially by arming and training the Vietcong. As these guerrillas grew stronger, U.S. aid to South Vietnam increased. Economic assistance had begun under Eisenhower. The Kennedy administration increased this aid, stepped up shipments of military equipment, and sent technicians to advise the South Vietnamese army. In spite of American help, South Vietnam was unable to curb the Vietcong.

Increased U.S. Involvement

When Lyndon Johnson became president, he was determined that South Vietnam would not fall to communism, even if direct American intervention was necessary. He won the congressional approval he needed with the *Tonkin Gulf Resolution* of 1964. Two U.S. destroyers reported that they had been fired on by North Vietnamese gunboats in the Gulf of Tonkin. Johnson then asked Congress to pass a resolution authorizing the president to "take all necessary measures to repel any armed attack against forces of the United States and to prevent further aggression." Congress passed the resolution with only two dissenting votes.

"When I started, he was just about so big." (Canfield in *The Newark Evening News*)

Armed with the resolution and encouraged by his landslide victory in the 1964 election, Johnson poured troops into Vietnam. The total of Americans there jumped from 23,000 in 1964 to 184,000 a year later. North Vietnam countered by sending its troops into the south. The United States in turn bombed strategic targets in North Vietnam.

By mid-1968, there were more than half a million U.S. troops in South Vietnam. Thousands more were stationed on ships offshore and at nearby bases. Ground forces fought hundreds of bloody battles with the enemy in the highlands, rain forests, and rice paddies of South Vietnam. In the air, U.S. bombers and fighters struck at the routes used by the North Vietnamese to move southward. Military and industrial targets within North Vietnam were bombed as well. U.S. war costs rose sharply—from $6 billion in 1966 to $29 billion in 1969.

Opposition to the War

By 1967, there was widespread opposition in the United States to the increasing escalation (stepping up) of the war and the rising cost in lives and money. U.S. "search-and-destroy" missions were causing Vietnamese civilians great suffering—as nightly television newscasts made clear. A growing number of Americans felt that the conflict was a civil war in which the United States should not interfere. Others criticized the South Vietnamese government—which the United States was pledged to support—as corrupt and undemocratic. Opponents of the war held peace demonstrations, protested against the draft, and signed petitions demanding a halt to the bombing of North Vietnam.

Political leaders of both parties voiced their concern, too. Johnson's popularity declined, and antiwar Democrats challenged him for the party's nomination in the presidential campaign of 1968. In March of that year, Johnson took the first step to de-escalate the war. He ordered a halt to the bombing of most of North Vietnam. He also stated that he would neither seek nor accept nomination for another term.

The presidential campaign of 1968 centered largely on the war in Vietnam. The Democrats nominated Johnson's vice president, Hubert Humphrey, who defended the administration's record. The Republicans chose Richard Nixon. Although he pledged to end the war, he offered few concrete suggestions for doing so. But he was aided by a Democratic split. Antiwar Democrats gave Humphrey only lukewarm support. And many conservative Democrats favored George Wallace's *American Independent party*. In the election, Nixon's popular margin was not large, but his electoral votes were substantial—302 to Humphrey's 191. Wallace won nearly 10 million votes, the largest total in history for a third-party candidate. (One elector, pledged to Nixon, later voted for Wallace, a switch that reduced Nixon's electoral total to 301.)

Four years later, Nixon ran for a second term. His Democratic opponent was Senator George McGovern of South Dakota. Nixon scored an overwhelming victory, carrying 49 states. His only losses were Massachusetts and the District of Columbia.

Continuing Conflict

Nixon called for "peace with honor" in Vietnam. He continued cease-fire talks that had begun late in Johnson's term. And he urged "Vietnamization" of the war, by which he meant that the South Vietnamese should begin to assume a larger share of the fighting. Between 1969 and 1972, almost half a million U.S. soldiers were pulled out of Vietnam, leaving only about 60,000.

Protests against the war died down. Then, in the spring of 1970, Nixon sent thousands of U.S. troops into Cambodia to destroy North Vietnamese supply sites there. American protestors took to the streets again. Massive antiwar demonstrations were held in Washington, D.C., in other cities, and on hundreds of college campuses. The country became more and more divided as opponents of the administration's war policy, the "doves," clashed with its supporters, the "hawks." At Kent State University in Ohio, four students taking part in an antiwar

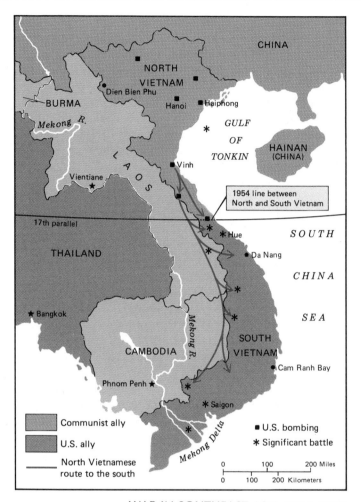

WAR IN SOUTHEAST ASIA (1964–1976)

demonstration were killed by members of the National Guard. Two more students were shot to death by police at Jackson State University in Mississippi. Later in the year, Congress repealed the Gulf of Tonkin Resolution. Nixon, however, ignored this move.

In the spring of 1972, the North Vietnamese launched an all-out drive against key South Vietnamese positions. Nixon then resumed the bombing of strategic targets in North Vietnam. He also authorized the mining of North Vietnamese ports and the bombing of rail and highway links with China. The heaviest U.S. bombings of the war occurred in December 1972. In that month, round-the-clock raids were carried out for 12 days in the Hanoi-Haiphong area.

Cease-Fire and Final Withdrawal

Formal peace talks had been going on in Paris ever since 1968. Finally, in January 1973, the delegates hammered out an agreement that was acceptable to the four main parties—the United States, North Vietnam, South Vietnam, and the Vietcong. All fighting throughout North and South Vietnam was to end immediately. The United States was to withdraw all its military personnel from Vietnam within 60 days. North Vietnamese troops in the south were allowed to remain, but reinforcements were not permitted. The existing South Vietnamese government was to remain in power, pending an election, for which no date was set. The United States accepted the principle that "Vietnam is one country temporarily divided into two zones."

Despite the cease-fire, fighting soon erupted again throughout South Vietnam. Each side blamed the other for the outbreaks. Early in 1975, the North Vietnamese launched a major offensive against government outposts in the central part of the country. The South Vietnamese army retreated, panic swept the country, and resistance collapsed. At the end of April, South Vietnam surrendered. In the final days of the war, large numbers of South Vietnamese, fearing Communist control, fled the country. The United States took in more than half a million of these refugees.

In 1976, North and South Vietnam were officially reunited as the Socialist Republic of Vietnam. Hanoi was made its capital. Saigon, the former capital of South Vietnam, was renamed Ho Chi Minh City. Native Communist groups, aided by North Vietnam, also gained control of two neighboring countries—Laos and Cambodia.

By war's end, U.S. casualties totaled more than 57,000 dead and 150,000 wounded. U.S. war costs were in excess of $100 billion. At least a million Vietnamese, both southerners and northerners, died as a result of the war. Countless others were wounded or made homeless.

The Vietnam War was the longest war in American history. It was also the most divisive conflict since the Civil War.

True-False Test

1. A decisive feature of the 1960 presidential campaign was a series of TV debates between the two main candidates.
2. One of Kennedy's innovations was a domestic program known as VISTA.
3. The Alliance for Progress was aimed at ending economic hardship in Southeast Asia.

4. The Berlin Wall, dividing East and West Berlin, was built in 1961.
5. One outcome of the Cuban missile crisis was the establishment of a telephone "hot line" between Washington, D.C., and Moscow.
6. The 1963 March on Washington featured a stirring speech by Martin Luther King, Jr.
7. Johnson's Great Society program was rejected by Congress.
8. The Office of Economic Opportunity was set up to coordinate the various programs of Johnson's War on Poverty.
9. U.S. economic assistance to South Vietnam began under President Johnson.
10. When President Nixon came into office, he increased the number of American troops in South Vietnam.

Matching Test

Column A	Column B
1. Peace Corps	a. far-reaching law to aid black Americans
2. Bay of Pigs	b. site of student casualties during protest against U.S. invasion of Cambodia
3. sit-in	c. leader of Vietminh in Vietnam War
4. Civil Rights Act of 1964	d. learning program for preschool children
5. Barry Goldwater	e. authorization for president to take measures necessary to repel armed attacks
6. Project Head Start	f. Democratic opponent of Richard Nixon in 1968 presidential campaign
7. Ho Chi Minh	g. program that sends U.S. volunteers abroad to help people in developing countries
8. Gulf of Tonkin Resolution	h. protest against segregated public facilities
9. Hubert Humphrey	i. Republican opponent of Lyndon Johnson in 1964 presidential campaign
10. Kent State University	j. site of U.S.-backed invasion of Cuba in 1961

Map Test

Answer the following questions by studying the map on page 486 and the text.

1. Name three Southeast Asian countries that were officially neutral at the outbreak of the Vietnam War.
2. What river flows past the capital cities of two of these countries?
3. Which location would more likely have been the site of a large American military base in the 1960s, Haiphong or Cam Ranh Bay?
4. Through which countries did the Vietminh secretly send soldiers and supplies to South Vietnam?
5. What city became the joint capital of the two sections of Vietnam after they were reunited in 1976? What city was renamed after the reunification? Explain how these changes reflect the outcome of the war.

Essay Questions

1. What were the aims of the Peace Corps and the Alliance for Progress? How successful was each of these programs?
2. What led to the Cuban missile crisis of 1962? How was it resolved?
3. Describe four domestic programs begun during President Johnson's administration. What problems at home and abroad limited their effectiveness?
4. What was the argument in support of U.S. involvement in Vietnam? against U.S. involvement? What forms did antiwar protest take?
5. How did the Vietnam War end? What happened to North and South Vietnam?

CHAPTER 31

Political Concerns in a Troubled Period

T HE UNITED STATES observed its bicentennial in 1976. The 200th anniversary of the nation's independence was celebrated with historic recreations, exhibits, and a great parade of sailing ships—called "Opsail"—in New York Harbor. But the occasion also led to serious discussions about the national purpose. The American mood was less optimistic than it had been a decade earlier. As one historian put it: "Americans seemed to be discovering limits for the first time—the limits of their own national virtue and the limits of their world power."

One sign of change was a shift in the balance of power in the United Nations. By 1970, the UN had over 120 members. In earlier years, the majority of members had belonged to one of two groups. One was the Western bloc (sometimes called the Free World). It consisted of the United States and most of the countries of the Western Hemisphere and Western Europe. The other group, the Communist bloc, was made up of the Soviet Union and its satellites. As more and more nations joined the UN—the majority of them Third World states—a third, nonaligned, group emerged. Its members tried to pursue a course independent of either of the superpowers. By the 1970s, this Afro-Asian bloc had the largest membership and held the balance of power. (There was also a shift of influence away from the Security Council and in favor of the General Assembly.) Neither the United States nor the Soviet Union could count on the almost automatic support they had formerly received.

THE NIXON YEARS

As the United States entered the Seventies, the occupant of the White House was Richard Nixon. A Californian, Nixon came to the presidency

The Third World makes its weight felt at the UN. (Bastian in the *San Francisco Chronicle*)

after many years of experience in politics. He had served in Congress as a representative and senator, and then as vice president under Eisenhower. He had traveled widely and was especially interested in foreign affairs. In this field, he worked closely with his national security adviser (later secretary of state), Henry Kissinger. Among other things, Kissinger negotiated the Vietnam cease-fire in 1973.

Nixon and Kissinger wanted to downplay Cold War divisions and tensions. They concentrated their efforts on the two most powerful Communist nations, the Soviet Union and China.

Détente With the Soviet Union

During Nixon's administration, relations between the United States and the Soviet Union entered a phase referred to as *détente*. (This French word means "easing of tension.") One sign of détente was an attempt to reduce armaments.

Since the 1950s, the United States and the Soviet Union had been developing ever more powerful nuclear weapons. Some, known as intercontinental ballistic missiles, or ICBMs, were offensive weapons, capable of reaching targets thousands of miles away. Others, intended for defense, were antiballistic missiles, or ABMs. Because each superpower was capable of completely destroying the other, the danger of nuclear holocaust loomed larger and larger. People also worried about the enormous cost of the arms race. Nuclear weapons required huge sums

Hostages in Iran, 1979   *Nixon in China, 1972*

that were sorely needed for other purposes.

In 1969, the United States and the Soviet Union agreed to begin *Strategic Arms Limitation Talks* (*SALT*). The first result was an agreement signed in 1972. Both the Russians and the Americans pledged to keep ICBMs at current levels and to limit the construction and installation of ABMs. But the SALT agreement did not put an end to the arms race. Only existing strategic (long-range) missiles were dealt with. Nothing was said about other types of weapons that already existed or that might be developed.

In 1972, President Nixon visited the Soviet Union. (He was the first U.S. president to do so since World War II.) Nixon and the Soviet premier, Leonid Brezhnev, officially signed the SALT agreement. The two leaders also planned joint space efforts, further arms reductions, and cultural and scientific exchanges. In addition, Nixon agreed to end the U.S. trade ban that had been in effect since 1949. The first major result was a U.S.-Soviet grain agreement. Faced with a serious food shortage because of crop failure, Russia ordered $750 million worth of wheat from the United States, to be delivered over a three-year period. This was the largest grain transaction ever negotiated between two countries. The Russians also arranged to buy industrial products and equipment from several American companies.

Recognizing China

Ever since 1949, the United States had regarded the Nationalist regime on Taiwan as the legitimate government of China, and, unlike a number of other Western nations, had ignored the existence of the People's Republic on the mainland. As time went by, however, this policy seemed to make less and less sense. The People's Republic ranked first in world population and third in size.

In 1971, Nixon sent Kissinger on a secret mission to Beijing, capital of the People's Republic. When Kissinger returned, the president announced to a startled world that he himself would visit China the following year. Nixon's trip was a great personal success. It began a long process of normalizing relations between the United States and the People's Republic. Trade and travel restrictions were eased, and a brisk exchange of people and goods developed. In 1979, during President Carter's administration, the United States cut its formal ties with Nationalist China and established full diplomatic relations with the People's Republic. (In the United Nations, the People's Republic had been installed, and the Nationalists expelled, in 1971.)

Domestic Strategies

Although Nixon was responsible for unusual breakthroughs in foreign affairs, his domestic policy was more conservative. He believed that the pace of reform had been too fast in the 1960s. Government, he said, was interfering too much in people's lives. He appealed to what he called "Middle America" or the "silent majority"—people who were, as one observer put it, "unyoung, unblack, and unpoor."

THE SUPREME COURT   One of Nixon's main concerns was the Supreme Court. He thought that the justices had become "super-legislators with a free hand to impose their social and political viewpoints upon the American people." When Earl Warren retired in 1969, Nixon appointed a new chief justice, Warren Burger—a critic of the Warren Court.

Before Nixon's administration ended, the president had a chance to name three additional Supreme Court justices. He hoped that his appointees would make the Court a less reform-minded body. The Court's record in this regard was mixed, however. Some of its decisions, like those of the Warren Court, were also attacked by conservatives. One of the most controversial was *Roe* v. *Wade*, handed down in 1973. It stated that women had a constitutional right to an abortion during the first three months of pregnancy.

ECONOMIC PROBLEMS   By the time of Nixon's administration, the American economy was not so stable as it had been in the 1950s and early 1960s. Inflation was at a record high, mainly because Johnson had spent a great deal on war and social reforms without increasing taxes. Economic growth was slow, and unemployment rising. This combination of stagnation and inflation is known as stagflation.

An additional problem had to do with oil. In 1973, the *Organization of Petroleum Exporting Countries (OPEC)*—a group of Middle Eastern and other major oil-producing nations—suddenly decided to limit their exports of oil. They also boosted the price higher than it had ever been. In the 20th century, industrial nations depended as much on oil and its by-products as they had on coal in the 19th century. Higher oil prices led to higher costs for many basic necessities, including gasoline, heating oil, electricity, plastics, and synthetic fibers.

ATTEMPTED SOLUTIONS   To halt the rise in inflation, Nixon tried a system of wage and price controls. The first ones, which went into effect in August 1971, were mandatory. Later ones were voluntary, and the whole program ended in April 1974. The inflation rate did fall, only to rise again when controls were lifted. Americans in the late 1970s experienced double-digit inflation, meaning that the cost of living rose 10 percent or more a year.

Nixon also tried to lower federal spending by cutting social welfare programs. He abolished the Office of Economic Opportunity and reduced funds for job training, urban renewal, and educational assistance.

A key Nixon idea was what he called the New Federalism. States and localities were to assume a greater responsibility for social services. To help them do so, the administration proposed a system of revenue sharing. Under this program, the federal government returned to states, counties, and cities some of the taxes it had collected. This money could be used for ordinary operating expenses, as well as for needed improvements. Many localities found, however, that they did not receive enough money to pay for all the services they were now expected to provide.

The Watergate Crisis

Nixon's presidency had many accomplishments to its credit. But it is remembered chiefly for a domestic scandal that brought the administration to an early end. The crisis started during Nixon's first term.

THE BEGINNINGS   In June 1972, during Nixon's campaign for re-election, five men were arrested for breaking into the headquarters of the Democratic National Committee. It was located in the Watergate apartment and office complex in Washington, D.C. The intruders, equipped with cameras and electronic "bugging" devices, were led by James McCord, the security coordinator of the Republican Committee for the Re-election of the President (CRP). The White House dismissed the break-in as a "third-rate burglary attempt," and the incident seemed to be forgotten.

In January 1973, the five Watergate burglars and two higher-ups accused of directing the break-in were convicted of conspiracy, burglary, and wiretapping. But the affair did not end there. Two months later, the trial judge, John Sirica, disclosed a letter from McCord. It charged that pressure had been applied to McCord and the other defendants to plead guilty and remain silent. It also stated that "others" were involved in the spying, and that government witnesses had committed perjury during the trial.

To what extent were members of the Nixon administration involved in the Watergate conspiracy? Answers to this question were sought by many. They included a new federal jury; newspaper reporters conducting inquiries of their own; a special Senate committee chaired by Sam Ervin of North Carolina; and a special federal prosecutor, Archibald Cox, brought in by the Justice Department to investigate the affair.

UNFOLDING SCANDAL   The various investigations revealed that members of the White House staff and officials of CRP had planned the Watergate break-in and, after the arrests, had covered up their part in it. Money raised by CRP for the election campaign had been used illegally— to pay for the Watergate operation, to fund sabotage activities against Democratic candidates, and to buy the silence of the Watergate defendants during the trial. It appeared, too, that the administration had been involved in other illegal operations designed to collect damaging evidence about its opponents. A number of high-ranking administration officials were either fired by the president or forced to resign. Many of them were later brought to trial, found guilty, and sent to jail.

THE WHITE HOUSE TAPES   During the Senate committee hearings in the summer of 1973, one witness revealed, almost by chance, that Nixon had secretly tape-recorded many conversations at the White House and elsewhere. Both the Senate committee and Special Prosecutor Cox then asked to hear certain tapes. Nixon refused. He argued that he would seriously injure national security, the doctrine of separation of powers, and the integrity of the presidency by surrendering such confidential material.

In October 1973, a court ruled that Nixon had to turn over some key tapes requested by Cox. The president offered him written summaries instead. When Cox declined the offer, Nixon ordered that he be fired. The attorney general resigned rather than dismiss Cox. The deputy attorney general also refused, and was fired. This "Saturday Night Massacre" raised a storm of criticism. Impeachment resolutions were introduced in the House of Representatives. Nixon then agreed to surrender the disputed tapes.

AGNEW'S RESIGNATION   While the Watergate scandal was unfolding, it was revealed that Vice President Spiro Agnew was under investigation by the Justice Department. He was suspected of extortion, bribery, and tax fraud. According to reports, he had accepted bribes while serving both as governor of Maryland and as vice president. Faced with indictment and trial, Agnew resigned in October 1973. He pleaded "no contest" to a charge of federal income tax evasion, and was sentenced to three years probation and fined $10,000. Nixon nominated Representative Gerald R. Ford of Michigan to succeed Agnew. This was the first time that the Twenty-fifth Amendment, ratified in 1967, was used to fill a vice presidential vacancy.

NIXON'S RESIGNATION   Controversy over Nixon's tapes preoccupied the nation for months. There were demands for additional tapes, which Nixon resisted. Instead, he supplied transcripts (written versions), with many portions deleted. Finally, in July 1974, the Supreme Court ruled that the president had to surrender the requested tapes. Both transcripts and tapes revealed that Nixon had been involved in the sordid events of the Watergate affair almost from the beginning.

Meanwhile, early in 1974, the House of Representatives had begun an impeachment inquiry. For six months, its Judiciary Committee examined evidence and conducted investigations. It then recommended that the House vote to impeach the president on the grounds that he had misused the powers of his office, violated the constitutional rights of citizens, and refused to cooperate with the committee.

Nixon realized that he had lost the support of the public, the press, and his own party. Impeachment by the House and conviction by the Senate seemed likely. Therefore, on August 9, 1974, Nixon resigned. He was the first president in the nation's history to resign from office.

FORD'S PRESIDENCY

Gerald Ford became president immediately after Nixon's resignation. During his 29 months in office, he continued Nixon's basic foreign and domestic policies. (Ford presided over the final U.S. withdrawal from Vietnam.) The new president named Nelson A. Rockefeller, former governor of New York, as his vice president. For the first time in American history, the two chief executives of the United States were in office by appointment, rather than election.

When Ford took office, his basic decency pleased the American people. Public opinion, however, soon became more divided. In September, the new president granted Nixon "a full, free, and absolute pardon" for all federal crimes that he "committed or may have committed or taken part in" while in office. Ford took this step, he said, to avoid the "prolonged and divisive debate" that would have resulted from the possible indictment and trial of the former president. He also wanted to spare Nixon further punishment. Some Americans hailed the pardon as an act of mercy.

Others thought that it violated the constitutional principle of equal justice for all. Why should the main figure in the Watergate affair be free from prosecution, they asked, when many of his subordinates had gone to prison?

Our long national nightmare is over. Our Constitution works. Our great republic is a government of laws and not of men.

—*Gerald R. Ford, on being sworn in as president,*
August 1974

In foreign affairs, one of the main accomplishments of the Ford administration was the *Helsinki Agreement.* In 1975, after three years of talks, representatives of the United States, Canada, and 33 European nations, including the Soviet Union, met in Helsinki, Finland. There, they signed a document called the "final act of the conference on security and cooperation in Europe." It provided for (1) greater East-West economic cooperation, (2) respect for human rights, (3) the freer movement of people and ideas from one country to another, and (4) acceptance by the signers of the changes that had taken place in European boundaries since World War II.

Despite the Helsinki Agreement, the Soviet Union continued to suppress free speech by exiling or imprisoning Soviet dissidents who publicly criticized the government. It also denied exit visas to Soviet Jews who wanted to emigrate to Israel. And it harassed foreign correspondents whose reports displeased the authorities.

CARTER IN THE WHITE HOUSE

Gerald Ford ran for election as president in his own right in 1976. The Democrats nominated James Earl ("Jimmy") Carter, a former governor of Georgia, who was relatively unknown outside his state. In his campaign speeches, Carter stressed the need for openness, honesty, trust, and morality. Such themes drew the attention of a public that had grown cynical toward officials in Washington and weary of politics in general, because of Vietnam and Watergate. Carter's promise to make government "as good and decent as are the American people" struck a responsive chord. He won by a very slim margin, capturing 297 electoral votes to his opponent's 240. His running mate, Senator Walter Mondale of Minnesota, became vice president.

An Outsider in Washington

During his campaign, Carter had stressed that he was an outsider in Washington—unspoiled by "politics as usual." Once elected, however, he realized that he would have to deal with the existing institutions of government to accomplish anything. His sincerity was genuine, but he seemed unable to transform good intentions into a workable program. For example, he could not win Congress's support for his proposals to reform the welfare system and the tax structure.

One of Carter's major domestic interests was energy conservation. Early in his administration, he presented Congress with a national energy bill designed to conserve domestic supplies of oil and reduce dependence on imports. But disagreement over various parts of the plan prevented its passage.

By 1979, the nation's energy situation had reached crisis proportions. The cost of foreign oil continued to rise, and a political upheaval in Iran cut off imports from that country. Carter held a ten-day "domestic summit," consulting with experts in many fields. In a televised speech, he lamented the country's "crisis of confidence" and proposed an ambitious energy program that would take ten years and cost $142 billion. Included were proposals to develop synthetic fuels and solar energy. The public reacted unfavorably to Carter's gloomy outlook, and Congress passed only a scaled-down version of his proposals.

Carter's most serious domestic problem was the economy. By the end of his term, inflation had reached almost 12 percent a year. To bring it down, banks raised interest rates to high levels. The high rates were especially damaging to the construction business and the automobile industry (already suffering from Japanese competition).

Foreign Affairs

In his inaugural address, Carter declared that "we can never be indifferent to the fate of freedom elsewhere. Our moral sense dictates a clear-cut preference for those societies which share with us an abiding respect for individual human rights." The theme of human rights became a key element of the administration's foreign policy. The United States warned South Africa that it could no longer rely on American support if it continued to deny equal rights to its black majority. The administration reduced foreign aid to Argentina, Uruguay, and Ethiopia because of human rights violations in these countries. It barred export of advanced computers and specialized oil equipment to the Soviet Union because that country suppressed free speech and restricted its citizens' right to emigrate. When the Soviets suddenly invaded Afghanistan in 1979, Carter cut off sales of grain and high-technology equipment.

THE PANAMA CANAL TREATIES   For years, the people of Panama, and other Latin Americans as well, had resented U.S. control over the Panama Canal. In 1964, violent anti-American riots led to negotiations on a new treaty that would satisfy Panama's demands and also safeguard U.S. interests. Thirteen years later, an agreement was reached. The two Panama Canal treaties provided for the transfer of control of the waterway by the year 2000, and guaranteed its permanent neutrality. Until the turn of the century, the United States would continue to operate the canal. It would also retain the right to use about a third of the former Canal Zone for military bases, canal operations, and employee housing. The Senate ratified the treaties in 1978.

THE CAMP DAVID AGREEMENT   The tense relations between Israel and its Arab neighbors were a continuing concern throughout the world. After the Suez crisis of 1956, there was an uneasy peace until 1967, when Israel was threatened by a joint Arab invasion. In the so-called "Six-Day War," Israel defeated Egypt, Jordan, and Syria. The Israelis gained control of all of Jerusalem, which had formerly been split between Israel and Jordan. They also took the Sinai peninsula and the Gaza Strip from Egypt, the Golan Heights from Syria, and land along the west bank of the Jordan River from Jordan. War broke out again in 1973, when Egypt and Syria launched a surprise attack on the Israelis in the Sinai and on the Golan Heights. The Soviet Union rushed military equipment to the Arab side, and the United States airlifted supplies to the Israelis. A major confrontation between the two superpowers was narrowly averted by a cease-fire, supervised by a UN emergency force.

In 1977, President Anwar Sadat of Egypt startled the world by declaring his willingness to discuss a peace settlement with Israel—the first to be negotiated by an Arab state. His dramatic announcement led to an exchange of visits between him and Menachem Begin, Israel's prime minister. When their talks faltered in 1978, President Carter invited the two leaders to meet privately at Camp David, the presidential retreat in Maryland. There, they agreed on a tentative plan, which was refined during the next six months. The 30-year state of war between Egypt and Israel was ended in March 1979, when Sadat and Begin signed a formal treaty in Washington, D.C.

THE HOSTAGE CRISIS   A severe blow to Carter's prestige—and that of the entire United States—occurred in Iran. This strategic Middle Eastern country deposed its ruler, the Shah, early in 1979. It then came under the control of Islamic fundamentalists led by the Ayatollah Ruhollah Khomeini. The United States had been closely allied with the Shah. Because of this, the Iranian revolutionists attacked the United States as the "great Satan."

In October 1979, the exiled Shah entered the United States for medical treatment. Shortly afterward, Iranian militants stormed the U.S. embassy in the capital city of Teheran. They took more than 60 hostages and vowed not to release them until the Shah was returned to Iran to stand trial.

Months passed while Carter and his aides tried to obtain the release of the hostages through diplomatic means. When diplomacy failed, a rescue by helicopter was attempted. It failed, too. Even after the Shah's death in July 1980, the captivity continued.

Only after the election of a new American president in November 1980 did the United States and Iran begin to reach an agreement. The hostages were finally returned to the United States in January 1981. Their ordeal had lasted 444 days. The prolonged crisis in Iran left the American people feeling angry and frustrated.

REAGAN: A SHIFT TO THE RIGHT

In the presidential campaign of 1980, the Republican candidate was a former movie actor and governor of California, Ronald Reagan. Like Carter, Reagan was an outsider in Washington. His amiable personality and appeal to conservative interests found a wide response. Carter, on the other hand, had been damaged by the long hostage crisis, the lagging economy, and continuing high inflation. He fared poorly. Reagan won an overwhelming victory in the electoral vote—489 to 49. Four years later, running against Democratic candidate Walter Mondale, Reagan won reelection by an even greater landslide—525 to 13.

Reagan's victories marked the end of the New Deal coalition that had held together for nearly 50 years. Many who voted for him had formerly thought of themselves as traditional Democrats—working people, liberals, and members of minority groups. Only black voters, as a bloc, remained firmly in the Democratic camp.

As a conservative, Reagan aimed to reverse trends that he and his supporters felt had harmed the nation in recent years. Above all, he wanted to cure the nation's economic ills and strengthen its position in world affairs.

Dealing With the Nation's Economy

As a cure for the country's economic woes, Reagan and his advisers proposed a policy known as "supply-side" economics. It was based on the idea that financial incentives and benefits should be provided to producers and investors—the suppliers of goods and services. If this were done, corporations and wealthy individuals would have more funds at their disposal for investment. The economy would then expand, new jobs would open up, and prosperity would "trickle down" to the population at large.

THE PLAN IN ACTION   One important part of Reagan's economic program was a reduction in taxes. Congress provided for several cuts to go into effect in the early 1980s. In 1986, after Reagan's re-election, it passed a sweeping new income tax law that lowered rates, closed loopholes that had benefited the wealthy, and removed millions of low-income Americans from the tax rolls.

Since the tax cuts reduced federal income, supply-side economics also called for a second move—reducing government expenses. This reduction was accomplished by trimming social programs, especially in the field of welfare. Some programs were kept from expanding, while others were cut back. Another aspect of "Reaganomics" was deregulation. This meant eliminating or not enforcing government regulations by bodies such as the Environmental Protection Agency and the Food and Drug Administration. Many of their rules, it was felt, not only cost too much but burdened consumers and hampered business growth. The Reagan administration also cut back on financial aid to states and cities.

Reagan's plan was a significant change in government policy. Since the New Deal, the federal government had assumed more and more responsibility for the well-being of citizens. Welfare-state measures were traditionally associated with the Democrats, but previous Republican presidents had retained them almost unchanged. President Nixon boasted that his administration had greatly increased spending on food assistance to the needy. Now the trend was reversed.

MIXED RESULTS   One hopeful change during the Reagan administration was a fall in the rate of inflation. In 1980, it had soared to 16 percent. By 1988, it stood at 4 percent. Unemployment generally remained low, too. When Reagan took office, the rate was 7.1 percent; when he left, it was down to 5.5.

But Reaganomics had unfortunate effects, as well. Deregulation led to a relaxation of antitrust prosecutions, which in turn caused a rash of business mergers. Many companies were swallowed up or wiped out. Savings and loan institutions (S&Ls), allowed to broaden their investments, made many unwise loans. Numerous S&Ls failed, and bailing out the industry—that is, paying off insured depositors—promised to cost taxpayers billions of dollars.

Another problem was the huge deficit. When Reagan took office, he promised a balanced budget by 1984. But slashes in government spending did not compensate for the money lost by cutting taxes. The result was a growing gap between government income and expenses. During his administration, the national debt rose from $908 billion to $2.6 trillion.

Foreign Problems

Reagan and his supporters believed that Carter's foreign policy was one of drift and uncertainty that had endangered the nation. One remedy, they believed, was increased military spending. Reagan proposed the Strategic Defense Initiative (nicknamed "Star Wars"), a defensive shield of laser weapons and space stations to intercept enemy missiles. Because of its huge projected costs and uncertain reliability, SDI had many critics, but work on it continued.

CENTRAL AMERICA AND THE CARIBBEAN   Latin America was one area where Reagan tried to reassert U.S. authority. In El Salvador, open revolt against the military regime began in 1980. Both sides resorted to murder and other violence. The United States supported the Salvadoran government with money, military advisers, and intelligence.

In Nicaragua, Marxist rebels (called Sandinistas) overthrew the country's dictator in 1979. When a counter-revolutionary force (the contras) took up arms against the government, it received American aid.

In 1983, the United States invaded the tiny Caribbean island of Grenada, claiming that it was falling under Cuban Communist control. U.S. forces deported hundreds of Cuban workers and advisers, and Grenada installed a new government more favorable to American interests.

THE MIDDLE EAST   Another region of U.S. involvement was the Middle East. In Lebanon, a civil war had broken out between Muslims and Christians in the 1970s. In 1982, Israeli forces invaded Lebanon to counter attacks on Israel by Palestinian guerrillas based on Lebanese soil. Israel pushed as far north as Beirut, the capital, and forced the evacuation of several thousand guerrillas. U.S. marines participated in a multinational effort to restore peace to the war-torn country. Unfortunately, their vulnerable location exposed them to attacks from snipers and artillery. Most devastating of all was a suicide assault by a terrorist, who drove an explosive-laden truck into their barracks. More than 250 marines lost their lives before Reagan ordered the force withdrawn.

A complex series of events linking the Middle East with Central America—specifically, Iran and Nicaragua—came to light in 1986. Some American hostages were still being held in Lebanon, and it was widely believed that Iran supported the terrorists who held them. In an effort to obtain their release, U.S. representatives secretly sold weapons to Iran. (Iran had been at war with Iraq since 1980.) Profits from the sales were then used to buy arms for the Nicaraguan contras. U.S. laws prohibited both arms sales to Iran and military aid to the contras.

Government investigations of the Iran-contra scandal implicated members of Reagan's National Security Council, some of whom were convicted of acting illegally. The president denied knowledge of the arms deal, and no evidence proved his involvement.

RELATIONS WITH THE SOVIET UNION   When he first became president, Reagan was an outspoken Cold Warrior. In sharp criticisms of the Soviet Union, he said that it displayed "the aggressive impulses of an evil empire." Over the years, however, he softened his stance.

Reagan's changed attitude owed much to a new Soviet leader, Mikhail Gorbachev, who came to power in 1985. Although a committed Communist, Gorbachev wanted sweeping changes in the Soviet Union. He advocated *glasnost* (openness), which meant, among other things, relaxing censorship, allowing dissidents and others to emigrate, and candidly discussing the grave economic and social problems of the nation. These could be remedied, Gorbachev believed, by *perestroika* (restructuring)—mainly reforms to lessen central control of the economy.

Gorbachev and Reagan met several times and established a friendly working relationship. A major result was a treaty, signed in 1987, that limited nuclear weapons in Europe.

BUSH TAKES OVER

George Bush, who had served Reagan loyally as vice president throughout his administration, was a logical choice for the Republican presidential nomination in 1988. To oppose him, the Democrats nominated Michael Dukakis, the governor of Massachusetts.

The campaign relied heavily on negative television advertising that stressed symbolism over substance. For instance, Bush appeared at a flag factory to accuse Dukakis of a lack of patriotism. (He had vetoed a state bill requiring students to recite the Pledge of Allegiance because he believed the requirement to be unconstitutional.) Bush won a solid victory, with 54 percent of the popular vote and an electoral margin of 426 to 112. He became the first vice president since Martin Van Buren to be elected president.

Domestic Issues

Bush shared most of Reagan's conservative aims but indicated that he might be more moderate in pursuing them. His inaugural address urged Americans to rise above material concerns and "make kinder the face of the nation and gentler the face of the world."

One of the most difficult domestic issues facing Bush was a sluggish economy. Although it continued to grow, it did so more slowly than it had at any time in the previous 45 years. Unemployment rose, especially in the automobile and construction industries. In many fields, including cars and electronics, American businesses had trouble competing with Asian rivals, particularly Japan. A recession that began in 1990 weakened confidence as well as incomes.

Recession meant that funds were lacking to cope with other troublesome problems, including urban decay, crime, drugs, and inadequate education and health care systems. Bush had made a campaign pledge of "no new taxes." Although he went back on his pledge by agreeing to some increases (in income taxes on the wealthiest and on such items as gasoline, cigarettes, and liquor), the gap between government income and expenses continued. In 1991, the budget deficit climbed to $268 billion, the highest in U.S. history.

Foreign Concerns

In several regions of the world, easing tensions seemed to point to a more peaceful future. While the United States did not play a prominent role in all instances, its careful diplomacy enabled Americans to steer a moderate course in difficult times. In Central America, the end of civil war in both Nicaragua and El Salvador provided a hopeful sign for this troubled region. In South Africa, white and black leaders negotiated to create a less racist, more democratic regime.

THE MIDDLE EAST   The early 1990s saw an apparent end to the bloody civil war in Lebanon, after 16 years and 150,000 deaths. Peace brought the release of the last American hostages there. Another hopeful sign was the beginning of Israeli-Palestinian negotiations, aimed at settling long-standing differences between the two peoples.

A serious menace to security in the region was Iraq. Although its war with Iran had depleted its military forces, the Iraqi dictator, Saddam Hussein, quickly rebuilt them (with American and other Western aid). In the summer of 1990, he suddenly invaded Iraq's oil-rich neighbor, Kuwait.

With UN approval, the United States organized an army of over 400,000 Americans and some 265,000 others, including Egyptians, Saudi Arabians, British, and French. When the Iraqis ignored a UN deadline to withdraw from Kuwait by January 15, 1991, the American-led forces launched a massive air and missile attack, followed by a 100-hour ground war, which led to Iraq's surrender. The six-week Gulf War cost the allies fewer than 250 combat deaths. Iraqi casualties totaled at least 100,000. Despite his defeat, Hussein remained in power.

END OF THE COLD WAR   Probably the most dramatic foreign development during the Bush administration was the end of the Cold War, which had dominated international relations since the 1940s. The change began in 1980 with developments in Poland. There, an independent trade union called Solidarity won wide popular support. Its activities led to free elections in 1989 that forced out the Communist dictatorship and initiated a return to a free-market economy.

The Soviet Union let its former satellite go its own way. It continued its hands-off policy during a stunning series of events that transformed eastern Europe beginning in late 1989. In East Germany, widespread demands for reform and free access to the West led to the downfall of the hard-line Communist regime and the opening of the Berlin Wall. The two Germanys reunited as a single nation in 1990.

Meanwhile, revolutionary forces were at work in other Soviet satellites. In a few months, Hungary, Bulgaria, Czechoslovakia, and Romania overturned their dictatorship and set up more democratic regimes. The Warsaw Pact disbanded in July 1991. Yugoslavia came to an end as a unified country after ethnic violence split it apart into separate units similiar to those that had existed before 1918.

Turmoil swept the Soviet Union itself. In the Baltic region, Lithuania, Latvia, and Estonia declared their independence. Other republics began to break away, as well. In late 1991, the Soviet Union officially disbanded. Gorbachev resigned, stating that "An end has been put to the cold war and to the arms race, as well as to the mad militarization of the country, which has crippled our economy."

Several former Soviet republics formed a loose union, the *Commonwealth of Independent States*. Russia, the largest republic in the C.I.S., assumed the Soviet Union's seat on the UN Security Council. The Russian president, Boris Yeltsin, became the dominant leader of the region after Gorbachev's resignation. Early in 1993, he and Bush signed a far-reaching disarmament pact providing for big cuts in long-range nuclear missiles.

CLINTON, A "NEW DEMOCRAT"

The 1992 presidential election restored the Democrats to the White House. But the winner, Bill Clinton, aimed to distance himself from the image many Americans had of traditional Democrats: liberal, "tax and spend" politicians devoted to big government. As a "New Democrat," he said, he favored a balanced budget and smaller government.

A Three-Man Race

In 1992 President Bush ran for a second term as the Republican candidate. The Democrats nominated Bill Clinton, governor of Arkansas. Clinton, who had grown up in a troubled family, spent a year at Oxford University as a Rhodes scholar and earned a law degree from Yale University. His drive and outgoing personality helped him overcome allegations about his past, especially his conduct and draft status during the Vietnam War (in which he did not serve). The third candidate was H. Ross Perot, a billionaire Texas businessman. Perot, who ran as an independent opposed to the way in which national politics was conducted, relied on a corps of volunteers to get his name on all 50 state ballots. He spent millions of his own money in the process.

The main concern in the campaign was the economy. The national debt was almost $4 trillion, and the deficit continued to mount. As the recession lengthened, unemployment remained high. Bush's failure to respond effectively to the nation's economic problems caused his popularity to drop steadily. (It had been high as the campaign began because of his successful handling of the Gulf War.) Clinton emphasized change, portraying the "New Democrats" as a moderate part dedicated to helping people "who work hard and play by the rules." Perot won support from many who distrusted professional politicians. But his erratic behavior—he dropped out of the race and later reentered—cost him followers.

The 1992 election embraced a new style of campaigning. Instead of relying on convention coverage, television commercials, and interviews with journalists, all three major candidates made extensive use of call-in shows, televised town meetings, and rallies relayed by satellite. In-depth polls of voters reported likely election results almost daily. The biggest election turnout in 30 years brought victory for Clinton. He achieved a sizable electoral margin of 370 to 168 (with no electoral votes for Perot). But, while Clinton won 43 percent of the popular vote and Bush 38, Perot tallied a surprising 19 percent. This meant that he did better than any third-party candidate since Theordore Roosevelt in 1912. It also meant that Clinton—like Woodrow Wilson, among others—won with a plurality rather than a majority of the popular vote.

Change at Home

Clinton's victory brought generational change. Both Clinton and his running mate, Senator Al Gore of Tennessee, were "baby boomers" (born after World War II). The 1992 election resulted in congressional change, too. Democrats remained in a majority, but there was substantial turnover, with more new members than there had been since 1948. The number of women, blacks, and Hispanics in Congress almost doubled. Among the six women elected to the Senate was the first African American woman, Carol Moseley-Braun of Illinois. Winners also included the first representative of Korean descent and the first Native American senator in 60 years.

Although voters re-elected most incumbents, they indicated their dissatisfaction with professional politicians by voting not only for Perot but also for term limits. Initiatives in 14 states set limits of varying lengths on the terms of senators and representatives, and, in most cases, for state legislators as well. (In 1995, the Supreme Court declared such restrictions unconstitutional.)

EARLY INITIATIVES   Clinton, more liberal on social issues than his Republican predecessors, was able to use executive orders to make some early changes. For instance, he lifted a "gag rule" that had prevented abortion counseling by clinics that received federal aid. The president also gained congressional approval for some measures. One was a family leave bill that required companies with 50 or more employees to give unpaid leave to workers facing family or medical emergencies.

In other cases, however, Clinton faced stiff opposition to his agenda. He wanted to overturn the armed forces' ban on homosexuals serving in the military but failed to get congressional consent. Instead, new rules provided for a "don't ask, don't tell" policy: questions on sexual orientation were omitted from enlistment forms, but avowed gays could not serve.

Clinton's 1993 budget, designed to reduce the deficit by almost $500 billion through 1998, curbed Medicare and Medicaid funding and raised taxes for the wealthy. Congress passed it (without a single Republican vote). Another presidential initiative, stricter gun control, was signed into law in the so-called Brady Bill, which set a five-day waiting period for handgun purchases.

The biggest single setback of Clinton's early months in office involved health-care reform. By the early 1990s, medical costs were soaring and more than 35 million Americans lacked health insurance. A task force headed by the president's wife, Hillary Rodham Clinton, worked several months to draft a plan that would contain expenses and broaden coverage. A complex proposal, announced by Clinton in September 1993, aroused strong objections from private health insurers, the American Medical Association, and many employers. Congress reflected much of this opposition, and the proposal was finally abandoned a year later.

There was more agreement between the White House and the legislative branch on the issue of crime, a continuing concern among Americans of all political leanings. In 1994 Congress passed, and the president signed, a tough new crime control law. It provided for the hiring of 100,000 additional police officers over the next six years; expanded the number of federal crimes that are punishable by death; and required life sentences for people convicted of three serious felonies (the "three-strikes-you're-out" mandate).

CONFLICT AND COMPROMISE   As the time for congressional elections approached, late in 1994, Republicans sensed victory. Clinton's standing was low, partly because of such rebuffs as the health-care defeat. Also plaguing the president were problems dating back to his Arkansas days: allegations of sexual misconduct and financial illegalities centering on a land deal and a failed savings and loan company (the "Whitewater affair").

Led by a Georgia congressman, Newt Gingrich, the Republicans did indeed capture both houses of Congress for the first time since 1954. Most of them pledged to carry out the so-called Contract With America, which called for tax cuts, congressional term limits, a stronger military, and, most important, a constitutional amendment requiring a balanced budget. Although some Contract provisions were enacted into law, the balanced-budget amendment was defeated.

Budget issues divided the president and Congress throughout 1995. The president agreed on the need to balance the budget, but argued that the cuts in entitlements (government benefits) proposed by Republicans were too drastic. Matters reached a crisis stage late in the year, when the government had to shut down nonessential services after Congress refused to pass funding bills.

Clinton's legislative strategy in the election year of 1996 was to avoid head-on collisions with his Republican opposition. Instead, he aimed for similar goals but not necessarily for their implementation. One of his most important compromises was a welfare reform bill that replaced federal payments to the poor with block grants (unrestricted federal aid) to be administered by the states. The law also set time limits on most welfare payments and barred aid to legal immigrants (a provision that Clinton vowed to overturn). In essence, the law ended federal assistance to poor families, a program that dated back to the New Deal.

Clinton, with no primary opposition, was renominated for the presidency by the Democrats. For their presidential candidate, the Republicans chose Senator Robert Dole of Kansas, a longtime Washington insider. He ran on the Republican platform, a conservative agenda that, among other things, called for the denial of citizenship to children of illegal immigrants and an amendment outlawing abortion.

Clinton was helped by a good economy (unemployment was lower than it had been in years) and by the fact that many Americans blamed the Republicans for the government shutdowns. Clinton took an early lead against Dole and never lost it. His victory, with 379 to 159 electoral votes, made him the first Democrat to be re-elected since Franklin Roosevelt. Still, he failed again to win a majority of the popular vote, and the Republicans retained their hold on Congress.

Relations With Other Countries

Early in his first term, Clinton committed his administration to gaining approval for the North American Free Trade Agreement (NAFTA), which had originated during the Bush administration. This pact called for the establishment of a huge free-trade zone comprising the United States, Mexico, and Canada. Many Democrats voted against NAFTA, fearing a loss of jobs to Mexico. When Congress passed the legislation in 1993, it did so only because of widespread Republican support.

In the Caribbean region, the United States acted to restore order to Haiti. In 1990 Jean-Bertrand Aristide had been elected president of the country, but he was later expelled by a military coup and took refuge in the United States. Intervention by the UN and the United States restored Aristide to power in 1994.

Another trouble spot was the former Yugoslavia. Beginning in the early 1990s, clashes among Serbs, Croats, and Bosnian Muslims led to widespread death and devastation. After months of inaction on the part of the Western allies, the United States sponsored cease-fire negotiations among the warring factions at Dayton, Ohio, in 1995. Americans then formed part of a NATO multinational force stationed in the Balkans to supervise a return to peacetime relations.

The Clinton administration also worked to advance the cause of peace in Asia. It sponsored an important agreement between the Israeli prime minister and the head of the Palestine Liberation Organization (PLO), preparing the way for Palestinian self-rule. It negotiated with North Korea to limit the latter's nuclear capability. And, years after the end of a tragic war, it resumed diplomatic relations with Vietnam.

CLINTON'S SECOND TERM

With a Democrat in the White House and Republicans in control of Congress, the partisan rhetoric persisted on the national scene. The continued economic prosperity meant that many of the budget discussions centered on how best to use the surplus. Other major legislation, however, remained stalled. Not all of the deadlock came from partisan bickering. There were real divisions among the Congressional Republicans themselves, particularly between the more conservative Republicans in the House and the less dogmatic Senate Republicans.

Impeachment and Acquittal

The major event of Clinton's second term, however, involved the many scandals which dogged his presidency. During his first term Clinton and his wife, Hillary Rodham Clinton, were the subjects of a federal investigation into questionable financial dealings while Clinton was governor of Arkansas. In addition, a former Arkansas state employee, Paula Jones, brought charges against Clinton claiming that he had sexually harassed her while he was governor.

Clinton had hoped to avoid going to trial on the Paula Jones sexual harassment suit until after he left office. In 1997, however, the Supreme Court rejected his claim of presidential immunity. As the lawsuit proceeded, a young former White House intern, Monica Lewinsky, was called to testify about an alleged affair with Clinton. Clinton himself was also questioned about the affair. Both denied it. But having received evidence to the contrary, Kenneth Starr, the special prosecutor appointed to look into the Clinton's financial dealings in Arkansas, launched a probe into the Lewinsky matter. Mounting evidence eventually forced both Monica Lewinsky and Bill Clinton to admit that they had had an "inappropriate relationship."

Jones' lawsuit was eventually dismissed. The judge ruled that there was no evidence that Jones' career had suffered as a result of turning down Cinton's alleged advances. But Kenneth Starr concluded that Clinton had abused his power as president and obstructed justice in an attempt to keep his affair with Ms. Lewinsky secret. Starr, therefore, turned over his evidence to the House or Representatives for possible impeachment proceedings.

In the midst of the scandal, Clinton paradoxically retained a high degree of public support. The American public apparently saw the investigation by Starr, a Republican, and the attempt to impeach Clinton by the Republican-dominated House as a partisan move. In addition, while disapproving of the affair with Lewinsky, the public also apparently felt the political rhetoric to be somewhat hypocritical as several members of Congress themselves admitted to having had extramarital affairs. In the Congressional elections in November of 1998 the Republicans suffered substantial losses.

Despite the election results, in December the House voted along almost straight-party lines to impeach the President. This was only the second time in United States history that a president was impeached, the other being the impeachment of Andrew Johnson after the Civil War.

The Senate then had the Constitutional responsibility of trying the President and actually deciding whether he should be removed from office. The issue before the Senators was not only whether there was substantive evidence that Clinton had broken the law, but even if he were guilty, whether his actions were of a sufficiently serious nature to warrant his removal from office. While they held widely differing views on these issues, the Senators managed to obtain consensus on how to avoid sensationalism in the trial proceedings. This included videotaped questioning of a limited number of witnesses and no live testimony. In the end the Senate voted down the articles of impeachment and Clinton remained in office.

Foreign Affairs

In the midst of the mounting impeachment crisis and its aftermath, Clinton still managed to conduct a very active foreign policy. During his second term the major focus was on Eastern Europe and the Middle East, but there were significant developments in other areas as well.

RUSSIA AND CHINA   The Clinton administration maintained somewhat strained relations with Russia and China. Under Yeltsin's successor, Vladimir Putin, Russia continued to struggle with the introduction of democratic rule and a capitalist economy. The task was compounded by the prolonged war for independence waged in Chechnya, a small, mostly Muslim region of Russia to the west of the Caspian Sea. The United States supported a multi-billion dollar loan bailout plan proposed by the international financial community to keep the government and the economy afloat. At times, however, Putin's efforts to reassert Russia's former political and military influence abroad placed Russia and the United States on opposite sides of an issue.

Bill Clinton visited China in 1998, but relations between China and the United States also remained uneasy. The United States continued to be sharply critical of human rights abuses in China and concerned about China's intentions towards the tiny island country of Taiwan. China regards Taiwan as a "renegade province" and rightfully part of mainland China. Certain business practices also drew American ire. For example, Clinton used the threat of harsh sanctions to force a crackdown on the blackmarket sale of American computer programs and music recordings within China. A series of incidents also helped to continue the strained relations, including the inadvertent bombing of the Chinese embassy by NATO warplanes during the Kosovo crisis (described below) and revelations of possible spying activities at an American nuclear research center.

AFRICA   In 1998 Clinton made an unprecedented tour of Africa in an effort to shore up relations with that continent, particularly after the failed legacy of U.S. involvement from his first term. In 1994, after efforts at peacekeeping in the East African nation of Somalia resulted in the deaths of 26 American soldiers, Clinton had pulled out all U.S. forces in that country. In this same year a civil war in Rwanda between the two ethnic groups of Hutus and Tutsis had resulted in the genocide of over half a million Tutsis and forced millions to flee the country as refugees. The failure of the Somalian mission haunted U.S. policy. The United States hesitated and then abandoned any plans to lead international intervention to help humanitarian efforts to aid the refugees.

NATO AND KOSOVO   During Clinton's second administration, NATO, which had not disbanded with the end of the Cold War, continued to play an important role in American foreign policy. Despite Russian opposition, NATO expanded its membership to include the newly independent Eastern European countries of the Czech Republic, Hungary, and

Poland. Not surprisingly, therefore, NATO served as the main vehicle for United States and European intervention in the trouble spots of Eastern Europe. There for the first time in its history NATO actually used military force.

While a cease-fire agreement was reached in Dayton, Ohio, among the ethnic groups in Bosnia-Herzegovina (see page 509), ethnic tensions built up in neighboring Serbia. Serbian president Slobodan Milosevic launched major offensives against the ethnic Albanian population in the province of Kosovo. Attempts to draw Milosevic to the peace table failed and in 1999 NATO launched an air offensive which resulted in Serbia's withdrawing its forces from Kosovo. Milosevic was eventually defeated in the 2000 election and turned over to stand trial before the United Nations war crimes tribunal for his role in the atrocities committed during the conflict.

NORTHERN IRELAND: RENEWED HOPE   For many years Northern Ireland has been the scene of violence between the mostly Catholic Nationalists, who want to merge with the Republic of Ireland, and the mostly Protestant Unionists, who want to remain part of Great Britain. The British government and army have attempted, with little success, to maintain peace.

President Clinton gave strong support to peace efforts in Northern Ireland, particularly through his special envoy to Northern Ireland, former Senator George Mitchell. Their personal efforts helped to bring about the 1998 Good Friday Peace Accord involving the leaders of most of the political factions in Northern Ireland and the British and Irish governments. While the promise of the Accord has not yet been fulfilled, it may well provide the basis for a final peace settlement in Northern Ireland.

MIDDLE EAST: DASHED HOPES   Clinton continued personally to play a role in trying to arrange a diplomatic solution to the conflict in the Middle East. In 1998 he mediated a preliminary agreement between the Israeli prime minister and the head of the Palestine Liberation Organization. This agreement was designed to reduce tensions and pave the way for more substantive talks on a permanent solution. Subsequently, in 2000 he sponsored a Middle East summit between the two sides at the presidential retreat in Camp David, Maryland. The talks were prolonged and intense, but in the end they collapsed. Subsequently both sides moved further away from any compromise and their relationship hardened into a series of Palestinian suicide bombing attacks and harsh Israeli reprisals.

Meanwhile the United States experienced terrorist attacks overseas by Moslem fundamentalist groups. The first occurred in 1998 on the U.S. embassies in the African nations of Kenya and Tanzania. The attack was believed to have been ordered by the Saudi Arabian religious extremist Osama bin Laden. He operated out of Afghanistan, where a fundamentalist

Islamic group called the Taliban had managed to gain control. The second attack took place in 2000 on the *USS Cole* off the coast of Yemen in the Persian Gulf.

In Iraq Clinton was confronted with the legacy of the Persian Gulf War. Following this war Iraq's leader Saddam Hussein had been forced to allow the inspection and destruction of Iraq's chemical, biological, and nuclear weapon capabilities. The U.N. inspection process dragged on for years, however, with Hussein alternating between being defiant and agreeing to cooperate. Finally, in 1998 matters came to a head when Iraq refused to turn over to U.N. inspectors documents related to its weapons holdings. Clinton launched four days of air strikes on Iraq in an effort to force compliance. This hard line approach, however, had little international support and was further eroded when it was revealed that the United States had used the U.N. weapons inspection team for spy activities.

THE 2000 ELECTION

Following his eight-year stint as Vice President, Al Gore was the consensus pick to lead the Democratic Party into the new millennium. The Republican race was much more wide open. George W. Bush, son of former President Bush, eventually captured the Republican nomination.

The major policy issues of the 2000 campaign centered around two major concerns for the nation's elderly: Social Security and prescription drug coverage. Issues of personality and personal integrity, however, played a major role in the campaign. Bush, whose only prior political experience was as governor of Texas, highlighted his "outsider" status, while attempting to link Gore to the numerous scandals of the Clinton presidency. Gore, on the other hand, stressed his long political history and vast knowledge of public policy issues, while criticizing Bush for his lack of experience. Bush's friendly, "every man" personality played well with certain voters, especially when contrasted with Gore's rather stiff and impersonal demeanor.

On November 7th, 2000, just over half of all eligible voters cast their votes for president and went home to watch the election returns on television. Exit polls by the major TV networks showed the two candidates running neck and neck. Around mid-evening, the major networks announced that the state of Florida was won by Gore, thereby giving him enough votes in the Electoral College to win the presidency. The nation was stunned, however, when the networks retracted their prediction in Florida and instead predicted a Bush victory.

America awoke the next morning still not knowing who their next president was going to be. To the nation's continued amazement, the electoral process had still not yielded a definitive answer after several weeks. The final result hinged on the extremely close count in the state of Florida.

Recounts and legal challenges right up to the Supreme Court were mounted by both candidates, and it was not until mid-December that George W. Bush was officially declared the winner in Florida. This gave him enough votes in the Electoral College to win the election, although he had a smaller share of the popular vote than Gore. The 2000 contest for the presidency between Gore and Bush produced one of the closest races ever in our nation's history.

THE NEW MILLENNIUM

With the new millennium we reach a point in United States history where developments are so recent that it is difficult to fully assess their impact or to know their ultimate outcome. They are part of "history in the making" and we hope that you will follow current events in newspapers and news broadcasts.

From our present vantage point, however, we can identify several challenges at home and abroad that will most likely present themselves to the American people. At home are the issues of maintaining a robust economy and of dealing with the changes that an aging population will bring. The scourge of the AIDS (Acquired Immune Deficiency Syndrome) epidemic remains a worldwide problem. The threat of nuclear conflict in particularly tense regions of the world such as Korea and between India and Pakistan demands attention. In addition, the threat of terrorist attacks within U.S. borders as well as overseas has become a grim reality. This has prompted military action on the part of the United States in Afghanistan and Iraq, which may have far-reaching consequences.

THE TRAGEDY OF SEPTEMBER 11, 2001   In 1993 the World Trade Center in New York City had been bombed by followers of radical Sheik Omar Abedel Rahman, whose goal was to force the United States to end its support of Israel and Egypt. But on September 11, 2001, a tragedy of even greater proportions occurred. On that day terrorists belonging to the al-Qaida network established by Osama bin Laden hijacked four jetliners, driving two into the Twin Towers of the World Trade Center and one into the Pentagon in Washington, D.C. The fourth crashed in a field in Pennsylvania. Over 3,000 people lost their lives, including rescue workers on the scene when the Twin Towers collapsed.

AFGHANISTAN   The Bush administration almost immediately demanded that the Taliban in Afghanistan turn over Osama bin Laden. The Taliban's subsequent refusal to turn over bin Laden resulted in their downfall as anti-Taliban Afghan forces supported by American troops and air power launched attacks. Bin Laden, however, managed to elude capture.

Internal divisions in Afghanistan have so far hampered efforts to form an effective and stable Afghan government.

IRAQ   The September 11, 2001, attacks also prompted the United States to refocus its attention on Iraq. Diplomatic efforts succeeded in obtaining a resumption of U.N. inspections for weapons of mass destruction. Iraqi officials, however, dragged their feet and were often uncooperative with U.N. weapons inspectors. Despite opposition from a number of countries, including France, Germany and Russia, the United States and other allies launched an attack on Iraq in March of 2003, which succeeded in capturing the major Iraq cities within a matter of weeks. The Bush administration then began the task of trying to replace the totalitarian regime of Saddam Hussein and to secure an Israeli-Palestinian peace agreement. Saddam Hussein was captured in December of 2003 and would most likely face a trial in 2004. The United States hoped to turn over governance of Iraq to the Iraquis by June of 2004.

True-False Test

1. By 1980, the Western bloc of countries formed the largest membership group in the UN.
2. A notable achievement of President Nixon was normalizing relations with Communist China.
3. A special presidential election was held in 1974 after Nixon resigned.
4. President Gerald Ford pardoned former President Nixon.
5. During Carter's presidency, American industries and consumers benefited from a decline in oil prices.
6. The Panama Canal treaties provided that control of the canal would be transferred to the UN by the year 2000.
7. The 30-year state of war between Egypt and Israel was ended by the Camp David agreement of 1979.
8. The Reagan administration aided government forces in El Salvador and antigovernment forces in Nicaragua.
9. The main issue in the election campaign of 1992 was welfare reform.
10. An important achievement of Clinton's first term was the expansion of health insurance to all Americans.

Matching Test

COLUMN A	COLUMN B
1. Henry Kissinger	a. Soviet leader who came to power in 1985
2. détente	b. dictator of Iraq
3. Mikhail Gorbachev	c. association of oil-producing nations
4. Saddam Hussein	d. presiding judge at trial of Watergate burglars
5. NAFTA	e. secretary of state under Nixon
6. Solidarity	f. relaxation of tensions between United States and USSR
7. OPEC	g. union that initiated democratic reforms in Poland
8. John Sirica	h. vice president under Nixon
9. Spiro Agnew	i. Western Hemisphere trade agreement
10. SDI	j. defensive space shield using laser weapons

Essay Questions

1. Summarize the Watergate crisis of 1972–1974, citing the White House tapes, the "Saturday Night Massacre," and the Supreme Court.
2. How did the hostage crisis in Iran come about? How did it end?
3. Outline the causes and effects of the Gulf War of 1990.
4. How and when did the Cold War come to and end?
5. What were the main accomplishments of Clinton's two terms in office?
6. Summarize the events that led to Clinton's impeachment.
7. Why did the United States become involved in hostilities in Afghanistan and Iraq during George W. Bush's presidency?

CHAPTER 32

Recent Changes in American Society

AMERICANS HAVE ALWAYS thought of change as progress. As the 21st century neared, however, many people were not so sure that the two were synonymous. Both the pace and direction of change were causing bewilderment and arousing opposition.

THE POLITICAL SCENE

The American Constitution has proved to be one of the most lasting frameworks of government in the world. Although it was adopted about 200 years ago, it still works well. But its operation has been significantly affected by several developments in the later 20th century.

Voters and Voting

Between 1961 and 1971, three constitutional amendments expanded American voting rights. The Twenty-third Amendment, ratified in 1961, granted residents of the District of Columbia the right to vote for president. They had previously been excluded from national elections because the Constitution provides that presidential electors are to be chosen by the states.

The Twenty-fourth Amendment, ratified in 1964, provided that failure to pay a poll tax could not keep a citizen from voting in any federal election. Five Southern states still levied poll taxes when the amendment was passed.

**VOTER PARTICIPATION
IN PRESIDENTIAL ELECTIONS**
(percentage of eligible voters
casting ballots)

Year	Percent	Year	Percent
1824	26.9	1912	58.8
1828	57.6	1916	61.6
1832	55.4	1920	49.2
1836	57.8	1924	48.9
1840	80.2	1928	56.9
1844	78.9	1932	52.5
1848	72.7	1936	56.9
1852	69.6	1940	58.9
1856	78.9	1944	56.0
1860	81.2	1948	51.1
1864*	73.8	1952	61.6
1868	78.1	1956	59.3
1872†	71.3	1960	62.8
1876	81.8	1964	61.9
1880	79.4	1968	60.9
1884	77.5	1972	55.2
1888	79.3	1976	53.5
1892	74.7	1980	52.6
1896	79.3	1984	53.1
1900	73.2	1988	50.1
1904	65.2	1992	55.0
1908	65.4	1996	49.0

*without Confederate states
†without Mississippi, Texas, and Virginia

The Twenty-sixth Amendment, ratified in 1971, granted 18-year-olds the right to vote in state and local (as well as federal) elections. In 1970, Congress had lowered the voting age from 21 to 18 in all elections. The Supreme Court then upheld the right of Congress to act in federal elections, but not in state and local contests. The amendment was designed to overcome this objection.

Ironically, these moves to expand the electorate did not increase voter participation, as had been anticipated. In the present century, the proportion of eligible American voters casting ballots in a presidential election averaged less than 60 percent. (By contrast, the average voter turnout in Great Britain was 85 percent, and in Denmark, 90 percent.) In 1988, about 50 percent of eligible voters took part. George Bush, the winning candidate, received about 53 percent of all votes cast. Thus, he was elected by scarcely more than a fourth of the nation's eligible voters. Although turnout rose in the 1992 election, it fell again in 1996 to the lowest level since 1924.

Political Campaigns

Reduced voter involvement in presidential elections may have resulted in part from a decline in the traditional power and influence of political parties. Beginning in the 1960s, their role in national campaigns grew increasingly less important. Instead of working through party organizations, prospective candidates competing for the presidential nomination sought support directly from voters in state primaries or caucuses. In addition, party loyalty exerted less pull on voters. On election day, more and more people disregarded party affiliation and voted for the candidate with the greater appeal.

THE MASS MEDIA   A key factor in political campaigning was the ever-growing power of the mass media, especially television. In 1948, Truman had had to travel across the United States, making speeches to a few hundred people at a time along the way. By 1960, when Kennedy and Nixon ran for the presidency, millions of people were in the viewing audience for a single televised debate.

Many people were worried about the new style of campaigning. They felt that it emphasized image more than content. How could voters learn anything about a candidate by watching a 7-second "sound bite." News coverage and interviews suffered from the same flaw, critics said. Politicians who gained reputations as effective "communicators" were admired less for their ideas than for their ease in front of the television cameras.

Critics of television campaigning also complained about its high cost. Because commercial air time was so expensive, candidates with ample campaign funds had a decided advantage over their less affluent opponents.

SINGLE-ISSUE POLITICS   Another political development receiving increased attention was single-issue politics. This type of political activity focused on a specific objective—gun control, busing, nuclear power, and women's rights, among others. Single-issue pressure groups worked to elect or defeat candidates on the basis of their position on a particular cause. For example, was a candidate for or against abortion? Advanced computer techniques helped organizations identify sympathetic voters and solicit financial and political support from them.

CAMPAIGN SPENDING   Few political issues raised more concern than the exorbitant cost of political campaigning. Presidential candidates in 1996 spent in excess of $1 billion, as did congressional candidates, bringing the combined total of campaign expenditures for the national election to more than $2 billion.

Congress had tried some 20 years earlier to restrain political spending. In 1971, it passed the *Federal Election Campaign Act.* This law set limits on how much money candidates for federal office could spend on political advertising. Limits were also put on the amount that candidates or their families could give toward their own campaigns. (The latter restriction was struck down by the Supreme Court in 1976 as a violation of the First Amendment.) The *Campaign Finance Act,* passed in 1974, had four important provisions:

1. It set a $1000 limit on individual campaign contributions.
2. It provided for public financing of presidential election campaigns through a voluntary income tax checkoff.
3. It allotted a spending budget for each candidate in a presidential election.
4. It created a Federal Election Commission to enforce the act.

Both laws required that all election campaign contributions and expenditures be made public.

Although these acts limited the amount that individuals could spend, they did not restrict group contributions. The result was a dramatic increase in the number of political action committees (PACs) sponsored by various special-interest groups. PACs were set up by unions, professional organizations, and business and industrial associations. They raised large sums to help elect the presidential and congressional candidates who favored their interests.

Between the early Seventies and late Eighties, PAC contributions to congressional candidates increased from $8 million to more than $100 million. Some critics were becoming concerned that such special-interest groups were exerting far too much influence on government. A leading senator observed that "when these political action committees give money, they expect something in return other than good government." Observers also criticized PACs for giving a large portion of their contributions to incumbent officeholders, which made it more difficult for challengers to win elections.

Another loophole utilized in political campaigns was so-called "soft money"—funds contributed not to candidates but to party organizations and thus not subject to spending limits. Party organizations were supposed to use the money for general party-building activities, but they found ways to aid individual candidates—for instance, by paying the salaries of a candidate's campaign workers. One representative complained that Congress had become a "coin-operated legislative machine." During the 1996 election campaign, critics charged that large sums of "soft money" had been contributed by companies that stood to profit from federal policy-making and by foreign donors who sought favorable treatment for their business interests. Despite public clamor for an end to such practices, it seemed

Personal computer

Skyscraper

Astrodome, Houston

unlikely that significant campaign-finance reform would be forthcoming, given the fact that it had to come from the very people who profited most from keeping the system as it was.

The Expansion of Government

"The era of big government is over," announced President Bill Clinton approvingly in his State of the Union address in 1995. In taking this position, he reflected the feelings of many Americans in the late 1900s. Government was increasingly seen—even by politicians running for office—as too big, too expensive, and too meddlesome in the daily life of the nation's citizens.

Government had indeed expanded tremendously after World War II. The number of civilians employed at the federal level grew from slightly over 2 million in 1950 to more than 3 million in 1990. But the greatest increase during this period was at the state and local levels. While the number of federal employees rose by about 50 percent, the total working for state and local governments jumped over 200 percent.

Government expenditures also grew, and so did the debt. At all levels, governments were spending more than they were taking in. By the 1990s, interest on the federal debt amounted to a fifth of national expenses yearly. More and more people demanded restraint in spending and a balanced budget.

Government, especially on the federal level, played a huge role in American life. It regulated a host of products and services, from electric hair dryers to air traffic. It subsidized farmers and loaned money to industry. It provided funds to the elderly and to the victims and communities affected by natural disasters.

Although the scope and cost of government programs alarmed many Americans, they could not agree on reductions. Few people were willing

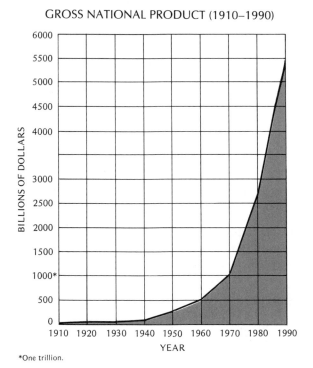

GROSS NATIONAL PRODUCT (1910–1990)

*One trillion.

to give up government benefits to which they felt entitled. Politicians, loath to antagonize any large voting bloc, ducked the hard choices that many economists felt were necessary in order to reduce the deficit.

THE AMERICAN ECONOMY

Americans in the late 20th century continued to have a high standard of living. In the 1970s, the GNP passed the trillion-dollar mark and continued to rise dramatically. The Gross Domestic Product (GDP), which replaced the GNP as the official measure of the size of the U.S. economy in 1991, rose to nearly $5.5 trillion in the early 1990s. But this growth was far from even, and it did not benefit everyone.

Trends in Growth

Two trends of the period concerned the nature of employment in the United States. One trend was a decline in the number of workers who produced goods. A 1982 survey revealed that, for the first time, more Americans worked in finance, real estate, insurance, and service industries than in manufacturing, mining, and construction. The percentage of the work force employed in the service sector continued to rise, while the percentage in manufacturing steadily declined. McDonald's, the fast-food chain, employed more people than U.S. Steel.

Many economists were concerned about the change from a manufacturing to a service economy. For one thing, service jobs pay poorly. For another, they have less "ripple effect" on the economy than do manufacturing jobs. Automobile production, for example, spurs employment in steel, tires, glass, plastics, and other industries. But a haircut is an end in itself. Economists also argued that the United States needs a solid manufacturing base to remain financially sound, industrially self-sufficient, and militarily strong.

The other trend affecting employment was technological change. Computer operations were replacing manual work in industries as varied as steel manufacture, coal mining, and printing. High technology was expected to have a significant impact on American workers, although the experts were not sure how. Pessimists feared that automation would reduce the total number of jobs. Optimists predicted that expansion in technology—in such fields as computers, telecommunications, and robotics, for example—would create many new jobs.

Another feature of American economic life in the late 20th century was continued business consolidation. Certain earlier forms of merger, such as trusts, were no longer common or even legal. But others had taken their place. One type was the conglomerate—a combination of two or more unrelated businesses. Thus, a communications enterprise might own a corporation making baking goods, a hotel chain, and an insurance company.

Another important form of business organization was the multinational corporation—a company doing business in more than one country. One American giant, General Electric, had plants in more than 25 foreign locations. Many multinationals had tremendous economic power. The annual budgets of some, such as Exxon, Mobil, or General Motors, far exceeded the budgets of entire small nations.

As businesses consolidated in an atmosphere of intense competition, they often resorted to "downsizing"—streamlining their organizations by laying off hundreds of employees. Many companies shut down entire operations or moved them from the United States to developing countries where wages were low. Skilled, experienced workers, no longer certain of steady employment, lost the sense of security that had undergirded their lives.

Challenges for the Future

In spite of its wealth, the United States faced serious economic problems in the late 1900s. Its economic growth was slow compared to what it had been after World War II. In the period from the mid-1980s to the mid-1990s, the growth rate of the U.S. economy averaged 1.2 percent a year, while that of Japan was 3.6, China's was 6.5, and South Korea's stood at 8.1.

Many U.S. industries were losing their competitive edge, especially in relation to the Pacific Rim nations. Japanese steel, automobiles, cameras, television sets, and electronic equipment captured a large share of the American market. Not only were these products priced lower than their American-made equivalents, they were often of better quality. Japanese industries benefited from a highly disciplined work force, government subsidies, and a national industrial policy that stressed long-term planning rather than short-term profits.

Because Americans were buying so much abroad, the United States experienced an ever-increasing trade deficit. In other words, it consistently spent more on foreign imports than it earned by selling exports. This imbalance increased fivefold between 1980 and 1990.

No single problem seemed as difficult to cope with as poverty. Efforts such as President Johnson's War on Poverty did make some difference. The percentage of poor people declined from 22 percent in 1960 to a low of 11 percent in 1973. But then it started to climb again; by 1990, it was 13.5 percent.

The gap between rich and poor, instead of narrowing, was actually getting wider. In 1970, the 20 percent of Americans with the highest income received about 41 percent of total U.S. family income, while the lowest fifth received 5.5 percent. By 1990, the top fifth was getting over 44 percent, while the lowest fifth got only 4.6 percent. To put it simply, the rich were getting richer and the poor poorer.

One very visible indication of poverty was the number of homeless people living on the streets of many American cities. The 1990 census, trying to reach as many as possible in one single overnight sweep, counted almost 230,000. Advocates of the homeless estimated a total of between 1 and 3 million.

Many experts were concerned about a group they called the "underclass"—a solid core of poor people who were mostly minority inhabitants of urban slums. From one generation to the next, they seemed unable to rise from the bottom of the economic ladder. This group provided a disproportionate number of the nation's unemployed, school dropouts, drug addicts, and criminals.

PEOPLE AND PROTEST

Whatever their nation's problems, the American people remained enterprising and hopeful. As always, they were on the move. Their energy was apparent, too, in their ceaseless efforts to improve society, especially through organized protest movements.

Population Shifts

Two important movements of population characterized the late 20th century. One population shift had been gaining momentum since the 1950s. This was a flow from cities to outlying areas. By 1970, more Americans lived in suburbs than in either cities or rural communities. Another shift carried population away from the Northeast and Midwest (sometimes called the Frostbelt or Snowbelt) into the South and Southwest (the Sunbelt). The mild climate of this southern region attracted many people, especially after air conditioning became common in the 1960s. The Sunbelt also drew corporations—textile manufacturers, for example—because unions there were weak, and labor costs lower. Between 1970 and 1990, population in the Frostbelt increased by only about 4 percent. In the Sunbelt, however, population increases ranged from a low of 15 percent in Louisiana to a high of 49 percent in California. Among the fastest-growing metropolitan areas in the country, all in the Sunbelt, were Orlando, Florida; Phoenix, Arizona; San Diego, California; and Dallas, Texas.

The movement of large segments of the population to the suburbs and the Sunbelt brought hard times to aging cities in the North. As businesses and middle-class residents moved out, tax revenues fell. The older sections of these urban centers (the inner cities) were increasingly inhabited by poor and minority families. These were the very people most in need of such public services as transportation and medical care, for which there was no longer enough money.

While millions of Americans moved about within the country, the nation continued to attract other people from all over the world. After the quota system ended in the 1960s, proportionately fewer newcomers came from Europe, and more from Asia. The total yearly limit on immigrations was set at 290,000, but the president had discretion to add to this number "for humanitarian concerns." Thus, in the 1970s thousands of refugees were admitted from Southeast Asia. In 1980, over 125,000 Cubans fled by boat from the Castro regime. Other "boat people" included thousands of Haitians. Special provision was made for Soviet Jews in 1989 and for Kuwaitis and Lebanese in 1991. In 1990, a new law raised the total yearly limit to 700,000 until 1995 and 675,000 thereafter.

A special problem was the vast number of illegal immigrants, most of whom had crossed the border from Mexico. In 1980, an estimated 7 million Hispanics were in the United States illegally. These so-called "undocumented aliens" lived in the shadows, forced to accept low wages and often deprived of adequate education and health care. In 1986, Congress passed a law granting amnesty (pardon) to illegals living in the country since 1982. More than 3 million applied for and received legal status. Without doubt, however, the nation still harbored many illegal immigrants, and thousands more were arriving every day.

The Women's Movement

Population shifts were not the only changes affecting the United States in the late 1900s. Another was a revival of feminism, sometimes called the women's liberation movement. Its goal was to gain full equality for American women.

After World War II, the ideal career for American women was widely thought to be that of full-time homemaker. Millions of women did work outside the home. But they usually did so only until they got married, or during emergencies.

A significant change began to take place in the 1960s, sparked by the publication, in 1963, of Betty Friedan's book *The Feminine Mystique*. Friedan argued that women were being stifled and should lead fuller lives. Her message found a wide audience. Many people joined the *National Organization for Women (NOW)*, which Friedan helped found in 1966.

NOW and other feminist organizations worked to broaden opportunities for women. The feminists were aided by the Civil Rights Act of 1964, which banned job discrimination on the basis of sex as well as race. More women went to college and graduate school than ever before. More of them entered traditionally male professions—law, medicine, engineering, and police work. A notable breakthrough was President Reagan's 1981 appointment of Sandra Day O'Connor as the first woman justice of the Supreme Court. (Ruth Bader Ginsburg, appointed by Clinton in 1993, became the second woman on the Court.) Another was the 1983 flight of Sally K. Ride, America's first woman astronaut to journey into space. Still another was the nomination of Geraldine Ferraro as the Democratic candidate for vice president in 1984. Other landmarks were President Clinton's appointment of Janet Reno as the first woman attorney general (1993) and Madeleine Albright as the first woman secretary of state (1997).

Woman's place is in the House and in the Senate.

—*Connecticut politician Gloria Schaffer, 1976*

More and more women joined the work force, especially when the nation's prosperity was threatened by economic ills. In 1950, 34 percent of women over 16 held jobs. By 1990, this total had reached almost 60 percent. By this date, too, over half of all married women worked full time at jobs outside the home.

Women still had important goals to attain, however. Most of them continued to hold low-paying jobs as clerks, waitresses, and the like. They earned less than men, even for the same type of work. For example, in 1990 the median yearly salary for a woman psychologist was $22,000; a male psychologist earned $31,000. Women were also still underrepresented in politics, higher education, and corporate decision making.

Ethnic Struggles

In earlier times, Americans thought of their country as a "melting pot." Foreign newcomers were expected to discard their differences in culture and become part of a single American nationality. In the 1960s, a different ideal, cultural pluralism, gained favor. Its advocates believed that ethnic groups should be proud of their distinctive customs and retain at least some of them. Out of this belief grew multiculturalism—an emphasis in schools and other institutions on teaching about all the cultures that built America.

Not all ethnic groups found American society to be a truly open one. Black Americans had long been working to gain greater acceptance, as well as to end discrimination. Similar movements were organized by Hispanics and Native Americans.

AFRICAN AMERICANS   The civil rights movement of the early 1960s had a number of achievements to its credit. Most important, it had succeeded in putting an end to legal segregation. The goals of leaders like Martin Luther King, Jr., became part of President Johnson's Great Society aims. They were embodied in such laws as the civil rights acts of 1964 and 1968. (Johnson also took an important step when he appointed Thurgood Marshall the first black Supreme Court justice.)

Some blacks opposed integration. Leaders like Stokely Carmichael wanted black people to remain separate from mainstream American society. Such militants stressed the concept of "black power," which would organize African Americans into strong political and economic power blocs. These did not materialize, however, and blacks' impatience with their slow progress was one factor in the ghetto riots that disrupted many inner cities in the late 1960s. The worst broke out in the spring of 1968, after Martin Luther King, Jr., was assassinated.

Efforts to integrate public schools continued. The stress was no longer on de jure segregation—segregation required by law. Instead, efforts were made to end de facto segregation. It existed without legal authority, usually because of traditional housing patterns that separated blacks from whites. One way of achieving school integration was to bus black children to white neighborhoods and white children to black ones. Although the Supreme Court upheld the legality of busing, it also ruled that courts could not force busing between a city and its suburbs. In the early 1990s, de facto segregation was the norm in many schools, especially in the North.

Some blacks (as well as other minority groups and women) favored a policy known as affirmative action. This meant the active recruitment, in jobs and education, of people from groups that had experienced discrimination. Many people opposed affirmative action because they considered it an unfair quota system. In 1978, the Supreme Court, in *Regents of University of California* v. *Bakke*, ruled against specific numerical quotas. But it did not outlaw affirmative action as such.

There were some signs of progress for black Americans, who numbered about 34.6 million in 2000. Black enrollment in colleges and universities reached a record high. There were personal milestones, as well. One was the first space flight of a black astronaut, Guion S. Bluford, Jr., in 1983. Another was the strong showing of Jesse Jackson as a black contender for the Democratic presidential nomination in 1988. Two others occurred in 1989. L. Douglas Wilder became the first black to be elected governor of a state (Virginia). And Colin Powell became the first black to serve as chairman of the Joint Chiefs of Staff and later Secretary of State.

But racism was still widespread in American society. An inequality still plagued African Americans. The rate of unemployment was more than twice as high for blacks as for whites. And the median income for a black family was only 60 percent that of a white family.

HISPANIC AMERICANS   The largest ethnic group in the United States was made up of Spanish-speaking Americans, known as Hispanics or Latinos. They numbered about 35.3 million in 2000. (Added to this total was a large number of illegal aliens.) Spanish-speaking Americans came chiefly from Puerto Rico, Cuba, and Mexico. Puerto Ricans were concentrated in New York City and other cities of the Northeast, Cubans in Florida, and Mexicans in California and the Southwest.

Puerto Ricans and Cubans faced various problems. Some met discrimination simply because they were newcomers who spoke Spanish. Many Puerto Ricans were poor and uneducated, but they had the advantage of being U.S. citizens. Although Cubans did not arrive as citizens, they tended to be from the middle class and thus had an easier time finding work.

Mexican-Americans formed the largest group of Hispanics in the United States. Some were descended from Californios and from Mexicans living in the Southwest before 1848. Most, however, had moved north more recently—either as legal immigrants or as illegal aliens. Many were poor and illiterate. Lacking opportunities at home, they hoped to find jobs and improve their living conditions in the United States.

Thousands of Mexicans worked as migrant field laborers. They were often exploited by growers, who took advantage of the fact that unofficial immigrants had no legal rights. In the 1960s, a Mexican-American, Cesar Chavez, organized migrant workers into a union called the *United Farm Workers (UFW)*. To gain support, Chavez urged American consumers to boycott the produce of growers who refused to recognize the UFW. The UFW also organized strikes against uncooperative producers. The union won recognition from the growers in 1970.

Activists in the UFW called themselves "Chicanos" (from the Mexican word *chico*, meaning "fellow"). Chicanos organized in cities as well as rural areas. One party, *La Raza Unida*, concentrated on political action, such as registering voters. Other Chicano aims were bilingual education (education in both Spanish and English) and improved public services in Mexican-American neighborhoods.

NATIVE AMERICANS   A small but distinctive minority, Native Americans had been involved in a struggle for ethnic survival for many centuries. During the New Deal period, they had been encouraged to preserve their culture and run their own affairs. But this policy was not very realistic. Most reservations were so poor that Native Americans who lived on them could not support themselves. Many had to depend on welfare, and a sizable number suffered from alcoholism and other diseases.

In the 1950s, a change in policy called for termination (doing away with reservations) and relocation (moving the Native Americans elsewhere). Most Native Americans resisted termination. And those who were relocated did not like urban life. Some 90 percent returned to their former homes. In 1970, President Nixon announced yet another policy—"self-determination without termination." It permitted Native Americans to supervise the various federal programs carried out on their reservations and to control their own educational facilities.

Native Americans became more militant and staged several demonstrations to call attention to their plight. In 1969, one group occupied Alcatraz Island, in San Francisco's harbor. In 1972, members of the *American Indian Movement* marched on the Bureau of Indian Affairs in Washington, D.C. The following year, they seized the town of Wounded Knee, South Dakota, and demanded that the Senate hold hearings on Indian treaties.

Relatively little was gained by these events. More lasting results were achieved by another organization, the *Native American Rights Fund*. It sponsored lawsuits to fight for Native American rights to land, water, minerals, and fishing. Some of these suits resulted in sizable financial settlements. Many tribal groups also profited from the operation of tax-free gambling casinos on their reservations.

The Environment

In the 1960s, Americans became aware as never before of the pressing need to protect their environment. A key event in arousing this concern was the publication in 1962 of *Silent Spring* by Rachel Carson. The author, a marine biologist, was most concerned about the harmful effects of DDT and other pesticides. The "silent spring" she wrote about was a season in the future when migrating birds, their numbers sharply reduced, would fail to return.

As crude a weapon as the cave man's club, the chemical barrage has been hurled against the fabric of life.

—*Rachel Carson,* Silent Spring

Spurred by Carson and others, Americans learned that many of their rivers and lakes had been fouled by chemical and human wastes. They realized that industrial and automobile fumes contributed to the smog that often made city air almost unbreathable. Beautiful countryside had been stripped bare by mining and logging companies, and littered with garbage and junked vehicles.

Beginning in the 1960s, the federal government passed many laws to protect the environment. Some of them set standards for cleaner air and water. Others provided state and local governments with funds to make improvements. The amount of harmful emissions from new autos was severely limited by law. DDT was banned. The *Endangered Species Act* of 1973 was aimed at protecting animal and plant species whose existence was threatened by modern technology. Federal efforts were coordinated by the Environmental Protection Agency (EPA), established in 1970.

A special environmental concern was waste disposal. Americans threw away mountains of refuse every day. Many communities instituted programs aimed at recycling as much of this refuse as possible. A more troublesome aspect of the problem was toxic, or hazardous, waste. The government created a "superfund" to clean up harmful substances. It also made plans for disposal sites for radioactive waste.

International environmental concerns posed special problems. One concern was acid rain—moisture-borne sulfur dioxide pollutants caused mainly by auto and factory emissions. Originating in the midwestern United States, it drifts eastward to damage vegetation and lakes in Canada as well as New England. Only after years of pressure by environmentalists did the U.S. government mandate tough new emission standards in the *Clean Air Act* of 1990. Another concern was depletion of the ozone layer, which results from an excess of chlorofluorocarbons (CFCs)—chemicals emitted by refrigerants and aerosols. By the 1990s, a reduction in the use of CFCs seemed to be slowing the damage. A third problem, the greenhouse effect, results from a buildup of carbon dioxide and other gases that allow the sun's heat to enter but not leave the atmosphere. Experts feared such long-range effects as melting of the polar ice caps and the spread of deserts.

Consumer Protection

Closely related to environmental concerns was a movement to protect consumers. Like the crusade for a healthier environment, the consumer movement had its founder and its bible—in this case, Ralph Nader and his book *Unsafe at Any Speed* (1965). Nader charged that the automobile industry was endangering human lives by stressing style, horsepower, and comfort, rather than safety, in its cars. After holding an investigation, Congress passed laws to improve car and highway safety.

Interest in other consumer issues grew as well. The federal government began to require safety standards for a wide range of products, such as electrical appliances and children's toys. It limited or banned the use of various food additives. After the Surgeon General issued a report linking smoking and lung cancer, cigarette advertising was banned from radio and television, and smoking was prohibited in many offices, restaurants, and other areas of public accommodation. A number of other consumer laws promoted truth in labeling and protected the rights of people who bought on credit.

Social Concerns

For many people, questions of ethnic rights or environmental protection were not the main issues. They worried about other threats, about danger signals that seemed to indicate a fundamental crisis in American society. A major concern was crime, especially violent crime. The murder rate per 100,000 persons doubled between 1960 and 1990. In the same period, the rate for aggravated assault quadrupled. Although the crime rate declined in the 1990s, public concern did not lessen very much. As one government report stated, "The existence of crime, the talk about crime, the reports of crime, and the fear of crime have eroded the basic quality of life of many Americans."

One factor in the perception of crime was the incidence of highly publicized acts of violence and terrorism. A bomb explosion at New York City's World Trade Center in 1993, which killed six people, was blamed on Islamic fundamentalists. In Waco, Texas, meanwhile, federal authorities accused members of a religious cult, the Branch Davidians, of stockpiling weapons. In April, armed troops of the Bureau of Alcohol, Tobacco and Firearms stormed the Branch Davidian complex, a fire broke out, and 80 Branch Davidians died. Two years to the day after the Waco disaster, a huge explosion destroyed a federal government building in Oklahoma City, resulting in 168 deaths. The men accused were linked to the so-called militias—a movement of right-wing extremists who held that the federal government was determined to deprive citizens of their liberty (especially their liberty to own weapons).

In general, American society was violent. The homicide rate was much higher than in other industrialized nations, such as Britain and Japan. According to one estimate, half the homes in the United States contained at least one gun. Television and movies offered a constant diet of mayhem and murder. The shocking assassination of President Kennedy was followed by two attempts on Ford's life and one on Reagan's.

The surge in crime and violence was linked to an increase in drug abuse. Millions of Americans suffered from alcoholism. (It was estimated that half the fatalities on the nation's highways were caused by drunk drivers.) Huge quantities of stimulants and tranquilizers ("uppers" and "downers") were bought and sold, legally and illegally. Marijuana, cocaine, and heroin circulated freely—among rebellious young people, show business celebrities, and wealthy professionals.

Many Americans worried about changes in their society that seemed to threaten its most basic institutions. A so-called "sexual revolution" that began in the Sixties resulted in, among other things, a relaxation of censorship in movies and a campaign to guarantee the rights of homosexuals. Thousands of couples lived together without getting married, and the number of children born to single mothers rose sharply. The divorce rate was five times higher in 1990 than it had been in 1940.

An especially troublesome issue was abortion. After it was legalized by the 1973 decision in *Roe* v. *Wade*, two sharply opposing factions took shape. Antiabortion forces (calling themselves "pro-life") wanted to outlaw the procedure entirely, while advocates of abortion (calling themselves "pro-choice") wanted to retain it. Polls revealed that the majority of Americans favored legal abortion, but with restrictions that would limit its availability.

Another grave problem was the disease known as Acquired Immune Deficiency Syndrome (AIDS), first reported in the United States in 1981. Transmitted mainly by sexual contact or infected needles, it is caused by a virus that destroys a person's immune system. AIDS is invariably fatal, and there is no immunization against it. By the mid-1990s, it had caused more than 200,000 deaths.

Yet another concern was education. In spite of its high standard of living, the United States lagged behind many other industrialized nations in preparing its young people for the future. According to surveys conducted in the mid-1990s, 44 percent of American fourth-graders read below grade level. And fewer than half of high-school students demonstrated even a rudimentary knowledge of U.S. history.

There was no consensus on solutions to social problems. Conservatives stressed individual and family values that they felt had been seriously weakened. An especially powerful voice for this point of view was that of the Christian Coalition, a religious-right group led by television evangelist Pat Robertson. Among its goals was a constitutional amendment to restore prayer in public schools, together with a redirection of American life away from "permissiveness," affirmative action, and welfare dependency.

Other Americans placed more emphasis on such societal factors as racial discrimination, structural unemployment, and inadequate education. Although they agreed that government needed streamlining, they saw a continuing need to provide a safety net for the disadvantaged.

Whatever the disagreements over policy, confidence in the nation's ability to overcome its problems remained strong. There was every reason to believe that, as in the past, the inventiveness, democratic values, and fundamental decency of the American people would continue to prevail.

Matching Test

COLUMN A	COLUMN B
1. conglomerate	a. corporation with operations in more than one country
2. multinational	
3. Betty Friedan	b. active recruitment of women and minorities in jobs and education
4. Sandra Day O'Connor	
5. Colin Powell	
6. Janet Reno	c. first woman justice of Supreme Court
7. acid rain	
8. affirmative action	d. author of *Silent Spring*
9. Cesar Chavez	e. organizer of Mexican migrant laborers into United Farm Workers
10. Rachel Carson	
	f. first black chairman of Joint Chiefs of Staff
	g. pollutant caused by sulfur dioxide emissions
	h. feminist who helped found National Organization for Women
	i. combination of two or more different kinds of businesses
	j. first woman attorney general

Multiple-Choice Test

1. The Twenty-fourth Amendment to the Constitution   (a) gave residents of the District of Columbia the right to vote for president   (b) outlawed poll taxes   (c) gave 18-year-olds the right to vote   (d) guaranteed women equal rights.

2. Between 1960 and 1990, the percentage of eligible American voters casting ballots in presidential elections **(a)** increased **(b)** decreased **(c)** stayed about the same **(d)** was higher than it had ever been before.

3. A major trend in American political life in the late 20th century was **(a)** the growing importance of political parties **(b)** the decline of state primaries **(c)** the end of limits on campaign financing **(d)** the increased use of television in campaigning.

4. The Federal Election Campaign Act of 1971 **(a)** effectively reduced election campaign spending **(b)** set a limit on individual campaign contributions **(c)** outlawed PACs **(d)** forbade "soft money" contributions.

5. In the late 20th century, the United States was becoming **(a)** a service economy **(b)** a manufacturing economy **(c)** an agricultural economy **(d)** a trading economy.

6. The United States experienced a trade deficit in the late 1990s because it **(a)** exported more products than it imported **(b)** spent more on imports than it earned on exports **(c)** used high protective tariffs to keep out foreign goods **(d)** did not buy enough goods overseas.

7. Between 1950 and 1990, the number of women over 16 in the work force **(a)** decreased by half **(b)** decreased by 27 percent **(c)** increased slightly **(d)** almost doubled.

8. The idea of cultural pluralism emphasized **(a)** pride in ethnic customs **(b)** the need to give up cultural differences **(c)** a limit on all foreign immigration **(d)** a reduction in illegal immigration.

9. The environmentalist movement was greatly stimulated by the publication of **(a)** *The Feminine Mystique* **(b)** the Surgeon General's report on smoking **(c)** *Silent Spring* **(d)** *Unsafe at Any Speed.*

10. Between 1940 and 1990, the divorce rate in the United States **(a)** doubled **(b)** tripled **(c)** decreased sharply **(d)** increased fivefold.

Essay Questions

1. What effect has television had on politics since the 1950s?
2. In what ways has government expanded in the past few decades?
3. What were the main economic problems of the United States in the late 20th century?
4. What two shifts in United States population characterized the late 1990s? How did these changes affect cities in the Northeast and Midwest?
5. What remedies did conservative Americans stress as solutions for the social problems of the late 20th century?

UNIT 11

The Federal Government and Civic Responsibility

CHAPTER 33

The Federal Government

THE FEDERAL GOVERNMENT is the national government of the entire United States. It was established by the Constitution, ratified in 1789. As you read this chapter, you will find it helpful to refer to the Constitution, which begins on page 567.

The document begins with the Preamble, or introduction, which states the purposes and aims of the Constitution. Its opening phrase, "We the people," makes clear the American commitment to self-government. The Preamble is followed by a series of seven articles. The first three, subdivided into sections, describe the structure and functions of the three main branches of the government—the legislative, executive, and judicial departments.

THE LEGISLATIVE DEPARTMENT

The legislative branch of any government is the one that makes its laws. In the United States, this branch is called Congress. It consists of the House of Representatives (often called simply the House) and the Senate.

The House of Representatives

The House has a total of 435 members, a limit set by Congress in 1929. Each member, elected for a two-year term, represents a district

APPORTIONMENT OF HOUSE SEATS BY STATE*
(2000 census)

State	Number of Seats	State	Number of Seats
Alabama	7	Montana	1
Alaska	1	Nebraska	3
Arizona	8	Nevada	3
Arkansas	4	New Hampshire	2
California	53	New Jersey	13
Colorado	7	New Mexico	3
Connecticut	5	New York	29
Delaware	1	North Carolina	13
Florida	25	North Dakota	1
Georgia	13	Ohio	18
Hawaii	2	Oklahoma	5
Idaho	2	Oregon	5
Illinois	19	Pennsylvania	19
Indiana	9	Rhode Island	2
Iowa	5	South Carolina	6
Kansas	4	South Dakota	1
Kentucky	6	Tennessee	9
Louisiana	7	Texas	32
Maine	2	Utah	3
Maryland	8	Vermont	1
Massachusetts	10	Virginia	11
Michigan	15	Washington	9
Minnesota	8	West Virginia	3
Mississippi	4	Wisconsin	8
Missouri	9	Wyoming	1

*The above apportionment went into effect January 3, 2003.

within a state. The number of representatives from a state is proportionate to the state's popluation, based on the latest official federal census. Each state, no matter how small, is entitled to at least one representative. To qualify for election to the House of Representatives, a person must be at least 25 years old, a citizen of the United States for at least seven years, and a resident of the state in which he or she is a candidate.

The presiding officer, called the Speaker of the House, is elected by the representatives from among their own members. The Speaker has the same voting privileges as any other member of the House.

The House of Representatives has three powers that it alone can exercise:

1. It originates revenue (tax) bills.
2. It brings charges of impeachment against government officials.
3. It elects a president if no candidate receives a majority of the electoral votes.

The Senate

Each state, regardless of size or population, has two senators. Since there are 50 states at the present time, the Senate has 100 members. Senators are elected for six-year terms. The terms are so arranged that a third of them expire every two years. To qualify for election to the Senate, a person must be at least 30 years old, a citizen of the United States for at least nine years, and a resident of the state that she or he seeks to represent.

The presiding officer, called the president of the Senate, is the vice president of the United States. This official casts no vote, except when there is a tie. To serve in the vice president's absence, the senators elect a president *pro tempore* (a temporary chair) from among their own members.

The Senate has four powers that it alone can exercise:

1. It tries impeached officials.
2. It confirms appointments made by the president.
3. It ratifies treaties.
4. It elects a vice president if no candidate receives a majority of the electoral votes.

Payment and Privileges

Each representative and senator receives an annual salary of $129,500. Some of this income is tax-exempt because most members of Congress must maintain two residences—one in Washington, D.C., and another in the home state. They also receive an allowance toward one round trip home per session. In addition, each member is entitled to an office in Washington and in the home district; funds to employ assistants and clerical help; an allowance for stationery, telephone service, and telegrams; and free postage for official letters—called the franking privilege. Representatives and senators who have served at least five years become eligible for a pension at age 62.

The Constitution provides that members of Congress may not be arrested while traveling to, attending, or returning from sessions of Congress, except in cases of treason, felony, or breach of the peace. Nor are they legally liable for any speeches or statements made on the floor of Congress. This privilege is known as congressional immunity.

When and How Congress Meets

In November of each even-numbered year, elections are held for all representatives and a third of the senators. The legislative body that

Supreme Court Building   U.S. Capitol

results is called a new Congress (even though two-thirds of the senators have already served two or four years). Each Congress holds two regular sessions. The first begins on January 3 of the odd-numbered year after the election. The second session begins on January 3 of the next year. Each session lasts as long as Congress thinks necessary. Special sessions of Congress, or of either house, may be called by the president. Since the First Congress, which began its term in 1789, congresses have been numbered consecutively. Thus, the Fiftieth Congress began in 1887, and the Hundredth convened in 1987.

Congressional sessions are held in the Capitol, in Washington, D.C. The south wing of this huge building is occupied by the House of Representatives, and the north wing by the Senate. In both chambers, members sit in semicircular rows facing the presiding officer. Democrats sit on one side of the hall, and Republicans on the other. From a public gallery in each chamber, visitors may observe Congress in action.

Congressional Leaders and Employees

When a new Congress begins, the members of each political party, in the House and in the Senate, hold informal conferences called caucuses. At these meetings, the various officials of the two chambers are chosen. The caucus of the majority party in the Senate selects a president *pro tempore* to preside over the Senate when the vice president is absent. The caucus of the majority party in the House selects a Speaker to preside over the House.

In addition, each party selects (1) a floor leader (known either as the majority leader or the minority leader) to direct the legislative program of the party and maintain party unity on pending legislation; and (2) a party whip to keep track of legislation and notify members to be on hand when important matters come up for a vote.

The legislative branch consists of many people besides the 435 representatives and 100 senators. Thousands of employees staff the offices of the elected members of both houses, serve as assistants to congressional committees, and carry out routine duties.

The following is a list of the important employees of Congress, along with their duties:

1. The clerk of the House serves as the executive secretary of the chamber. He or she presides at the start of a new Congress until a Speaker is elected. The clerk also maintains the record of proceedings and keeps track of the progress of bills and resolutions. The official who carries out similar duties in the Senate is called the secretary of the Senate.
2. The parliamentarian in each house advises the presiding officer on questions of procedure.
3. The sergeant at arms in the House maintains order, summons witnesses to appear before congressional committees, and disburses the salaries of members of Congress. In the Senate, the sergeant at arms also has charge of the public galleries, supervises the doorkeepers and Capitol police, and rounds up a quorum if directed to do so. (A quorum is the number of members who must be present in order for business to be transacted legally.)
4. The doorkeeper in the House controls admission to the floor of the chamber, has charge of the document room, and supervises the pages (messengers).
5. The chaplain in each house opens the daily sessions with prayer.
6. The postmaster in each house handles the large quantity of mail received by members of Congress.

Congressional Committees

Thousands of new legislative proposals are introduced at each session of Congress. It would be impossible for the entire Senate or House to consider each bill carefully or debate its wording. Each house, therefore, works through committees.

The most important type of congressional committee is the standing committee. There are 38 of these, 16 in the Senate and 22 in the House. Each deals with a broad area of legislation. When a bill is introduced in Congress, the Speaker of the House or the presiding officer of the Senate refers it to the proper standing committee for consideration. It is then passed along to a subcommittee that specializes in handling such issues.

Standing committees discuss proposed legislation, and frequently change it. They may hold public hearings at which people answer

SOME IMPORTANT STANDING COMMITTEES OF CONGRESS

House of Representatives	Senate
Agriculture	Appropriations
Appropriations	Banking, Housing, and Urban Affairs
Armed Services	Energy and Natural Resources
Foreign Affairs	Finance
Rules	Foreign Relations
Ways and Means	Judiciary

questions and present arguments for or against a bill. If the committee, by a majority vote, approves a bill, it is brought before either house for a vote. If the committee rejects a bill, no further action is taken on the proposal.

The party in power has majority representation on each standing committee. Members usually continue on the same committee term after term. The member of the majority party who has served longest on the committee is usually its chair, or head. This custom is known as seniority.

There are two other types of congressional committees. One, the select committee, deals with a specific issue that does not fall within the scope of a standing committee. For example, a select committee of the Senate investigated the Watergate scandal of the 1970s. The other type is a joint committee, made up of members of both houses. The commonest joint committee is a conference committee. It considers a bill that has passed both houses of Congress in different form, and then works out a single bill on which the Senate and the House can agree.

The standing committees and select committees exercise broad investigative powers. They may hold inquiries to determine whether existing laws are working properly or whether new laws are needed. Committees may also investigate programs authorized by Congress to determine whether they are being administered properly.

How a Bill Becomes a Law

If a bill is reported out of committee, it goes to the floor of the House or the Senate to be debated and voted upon. If a bill passes both houses by a majority vote and is signed by the president, it becomes a law.

If the president vetoes a bill, it goes back to the house where it originated. If the bill is repassed by a two-thirds vote of both houses, the president's veto is overridden, and the bill becomes a law.

If the president takes no action on a bill within ten days, it becomes a law without his signature, provided Congress is in session. If Congress is not in session or adjourns before the ten-day period is up, the bill is automatically vetoed. This procedure is known as a pocket veto.

Other Activities of Congress

Congress has other duties besides legislating for the nation. It governs the District of Columbia, where Washington is located. It supervises the operations of the Government Printing Office, which handles government publications. It maintains the Library of Congress, which houses the world's largest collection of books, manuscripts, papers, and pamphlets. The library's Legislative Reference Service supplies information and special studies to help members of Congress in their legislative work.

Congress is also responsible for the General Accounting Office, which audits (examines) the government's financial records. In addition, Congress controls the Congressional Budget Office, which analyzes the cost of federal programs.

THE EXECUTIVE DEPARTMENT

The executive branch of the federal government carries out (executes) the laws of the United States. It is headed by the president. It also includes presidential assistants, the executive departments, and numerous independent agencies.

The President

The president is also known as the chief executive of the nation. To be eligible for election to this office, a person must be a native-born citizen, at least 35 years old, and a resident of the United States for at least 14 years. (There is no legal barrier to a woman serving as president, but none ever has. For the sake of convenience, this discussion will use masculine pronouns in referring to the chief executive.)

The president is elected for a term of four years. He is limited to two elected terms, or to only one elected term if he has served more than two years of another president's term. In case a president dies, resigns, or is removed by impeachment, the vice president succeeds him. If there is no vice president, the Speaker of the House and then the president *pro tempore* of the Senate are next in line. They are followed by the members of the cabinet in the order of the creation of their departments.

The president receives an annual salary of $200,000 and an allowance of $50,000 for official expenses (both taxable). He may spend an additional $100,000 (nontaxable) for travel and official entertainment. He also receives the use of the White House as a residence and office, a large staff, and personal transportation facilities. When he retires, he is provided with a lifetime pension of $143,800 a year, as well as free mailing privileges, free office space, and up to $96,000 a year for office help.

Widows of former presidents are granted lifetime pensions of $20,000 a year.

ELECTING A PRESIDENT   Theoretically, the president is elected by a specially chosen group called the electoral college. But the system originally outlined in the Constitution (see Article II, Section 1) has been greatly modified. For all practical purposes, it can be said that the president is elected by the people.

During the summer of the presidential election year, each political party holds a national convention. Delegates nominate candidates for president and vice president. In every state, each party selects a slate of electors pledged to the party's candidates for national office.

Presidential election day is the first Tuesday after the first Monday in November. At that time, voters in each state go to the polls and choose the slate of electors they prefer. (In most states, the names of the candidates for president and vice president appear on the ballot, but they are used merely to identify the electors pledged to them.) The party that receives the most popular votes for its electors in any state captures all the electoral votes of the state.

About six weeks after the election (the first Monday after the second Wednesday in December), the electors assemble at their respective state capitals and cast two votes—one for president and one for vice president. These are sent to Washington, D.C. Early in January, the ballots are opened and counted before a joint session of Congress. The announcement that follows merely serves to confirm officially the names of the winners, which the public has known ever since the popular votes were tallied on election day.

At present, the electoral college consists of 538 members. There is one member for each seat in Congress, plus three for the District of Columbia. A total of 270 electoral votes are needed to elect a president and a vice president.

The president is inaugurated on January 20 following the November election. He takes the following oath: "I do solemnly swear (or affirm) that I will faithfully execute the office of president of the United States, and will, to the best of my ability, preserve, protect, and defend the Constitution of the United States."

POWERS OF THE PRESIDENT   As the person chiefly responsible for carrying out the nation's laws, the president interacts with Congress in a number of ways. He delivers annual messages in which he reports on the state of the Union, proposes a legislative program, and presents a budget. He signs or vetoes laws. He can also call either house or the whole Congress into special session if he deems it necessary.

The Constitution also designates the president as the commander in chief of the nation's armed forces. Military officers owe their primary

Top Hat. (By permission of Bill Mauldin and Wil-Jo Associates, Inc.)

loyalty to him. He has a voice in overall military strategy. And, although Congress alone has the power to declare war, the president may send troops abroad if there is a threat of danger.

The president plays a key role in foreign affairs. He makes treaties with other nations (with the consent of two-thirds of the Senate). He appoints diplomatic officials, also with the consent of the Senate. He himself is the nation's chief diplomat, meeting with heads of state and directing negotiations in such matters as peace settlements and arms agreements.

The president also has some judicial powers. He appoints Supreme Court justices and other federal judges (with the consent of the Senate). And he can affect the sentences of persons convicted of federal crimes. He may grant a reprieve, which postpones a sentence (such as execution). Or he may issue a pardon, freeing a person from serving a full sentence.

The president plays other roles that are not mentioned in the Constitution. He is the leader of his political party. As such, he may work to raise funds or to help elect other party members. He may also aid party members through appointments to federal office and grants of federal funds in key areas.

Another presidential role is that of chief of state. He carries out a wide range of ceremonial duties, from proclaiming Mother's Day to greeting astronauts and attending state funerals.

The Vice President

The qualifications for the office of vice president are the same as those for president. He is elected along with the president for a term of four years. His only constitutional duty (unless he succeeds to the presidency or serves temporarily as acting president) is to preside over the Senate. The president, with the consent of the Senate, has the power to appoint a new vice president whenever the office becomes vacant.

A president may ask his vice president to head a commission or undertake various missions abroad. In general, however, a vice president has few official duties and practically no power.

The Executive Office of the President

The presidency has often been called the hardest job in the world. Among those who help make it easier are some 1500 special assistants, advisers, aides, and other support personnel in the Executive Office of the President. Their titles and functions may differ somewhat from one administration to the next, since much depends on an individual president's style of leadership. The Executive Office includes a number of agencies with special duties, as follows:

1. The White House Office comprises the president's personal staff, administrative assistants, special counsel, press secretary, legislative counsel, military aides, and various special assistants. There are also numerous clerks, stenographers, and other office personnel.
2. The Office of Management and Budget prepares the annual budget that the president submits to Congress. It also oversees the performance of the entire executive branch.
3. The National Security Council advises the president on military and foreign policy. It also supervises the Central Intelligence Agency (CIA), which keeps watch over military developments in other countries and gathers information relating to national security.
4. The Council of Economic Advisers advises the president on the nation's economic health and helps him prepare his economic reports to Congress.
5. Other agencies within the Executive Office advise the president on domestic policies and programs, on scientific and technological developments, on environmental problems, and on foreign trade.

Executive Departments

George Washington, the first president, had three executive departments. Today there are 15. The heads of these departments (plus the American ambassador to the United Nations) make up the cabinet. It meets with the president periodically to discuss government policy.

The 15 executive departments and the independent agencies employ more than 3 million civilian employees. It is these workers whom most people think of when they speak of the federal bureaucracy. (A bureaucracy consists of the nonelected personnel who perform the functions of a large organization.)

The departments will be discussed in the order of their creation. The head of each is known as the secretary. The only exception is the Department of Justice, whose head is called the attorney general.

1. The Department of State (created in 1789) handles all matters relating to foreign affairs. It carries on diplomatic correspondence with other nations and maintains the Foreign Service. The State Department also negotiates treaties and issues passports.
2. The Treasury Department (created in 1789) collects federal taxes and other revenue, from which it pays the government's bills. It coins and prints money, and borrows funds through the sale of bonds. The Treasury Department operates the Secret Service, the Bureau of Narcotics, and the Internal Revenue Service (IRS).
3. The Department of Defense (created in 1789 as the War Department and renamed in 1947) directs and coordinates the operations of the American armed forces. The three branches—the army, the navy, and the air force—exist as equal and separate departments within the Defense Department. Each is headed by a secretary. Only the secretary of defense, however, is a member of the cabinet.
4. The Department of Justice was not created as such until 1870, although the office of attorney general goes back to 1789. The Justice Department prosecutes violators of federal laws and administers the federal court system and federal prisons. Two of its important agencies are the Antitrust Division and the Civil Rights Division. Also within the department are the Federal Bureau of Investigation (FBI) and the Immigration and Naturalization Service.
5. The Department of the Interior (created in 1849) contains a number of bureaus. One has charge of the management and disposition of public lands. Another develops and conserves natural resources. Still others supervise Indian affairs, national parks, and American overseas possessions.
6. The Department of Agriculture was created in 1862, although the secretary did not become a cabinet member until 1889. This department conducts research on animal and plant diseases, and works to improve seeds, develop hardier plants, and increase production. The Agriculture Department also supervises meat inspection, manages the national forest reserves, and administers federal farm laws.
7. The Department of Commerce (created in 1903) supervises shipping and navigation, regulates weights and measures, issues patents, and

registers trademarks. In addition, it directs the federal census and operates the National Weather Service.

8. The Department of Labor (created in 1913) enforces the Fair Labor Standards Act and collects and publishes labor statistics. It also administers the federal government's share of the unemployment insurance and employment service programs. Another function is the monitoring of occupational health and safety.

9. The Department of Health and Human Services (created as the Department of Health, Education, and Welfare in 1953) was reorganized under its present name in 1979. Its chief bureaus are the Social Security Administration, the Public Health Service, and the Food and Drug Administration.

10. The Department of Housing and Urban Development (created in 1965) is responsible for such federal programs as public housing, urban renewal, community planning, and mass transportation.

11. The Department of Transportation (created in 1966) administers the federal highway program and the coast guard. It also promotes highway, railroad, and air safety. Major bureaus include the Federal Aviation Agency and the St. Lawrence Seaway Development Corporation.

12. The Department of Energy (created in 1977) regulates hydroelectric power, controls the use of nuclear energy, formulates the nuclear weapons program, and coordinates energy research and development.

13. The Department of Education (created in 1979) administers federal education programs.

14. The Department of Veterans Affairs (created in 1989) operates programs to benefit veterans and their families, including education, disability compensation, and pensions.

15. The Department of Homeland Security (created in 2002 in the aftermath of the tragic terrorist attacks on September 11, 2001) is responsible for coordinating efforts to prevent terrorist attacks within the United States.

Independent Agencies

The executive branch of the federal government includes about 50 independent agencies. Their activities cover a broad range, from operating the Tennessee Valley Authority (TVA) to administering the many scientific, educational, and cultural establishments that make up the Smithsonian Institution.

A number of executive agencies are important for their regulatory function. They have the power to make (and enforce) rules. For example, the Federal Communications Commission (FCC) regulates radio and television broadcasting. The nation's oldest regulatory agency, the Interstate Commerce Commission (ICC), which regulated interstate railroads, buses, trucks, pipelines, and water carriers, was disbanded in 1995.

SOME IMPORTANT INDEPENDENT AGENCIES

Agency	Function
Civil Service Commission	Administers federal merit system
Environmental Protection Agency (EPA)	Coordinates federal antipollution activities
Equal Employment Opportunity Commission (EEOC)	Enforces laws against job discrimination by race, color, religion, sex, national origin, age, or disability
Federal Communications Commission (FCC)	Regulates radio and television communications
Federal Reserve Board	Controls the money supply
Federal Trade Commission (FTC)	Enforces antitrust laws and takes action against false and misleading advertising
National Aeronautics and Space Administration (NASA)	Directs space research and development
National Labor Relations Board (NLRB)	Conducts union elections and investigates unfair labor practices
Nuclear Regulatory Commission (NRC)	Regulates atomic energy
Securities and Exchange Commission (SEC)	Regulates the purchase and sale of stocks and bonds
Selective Service System	Maintains a registry of young men who can be drafted into the armed services
United States Postal Service	Operates the postal system

THE JUDICIAL DEPARTMENT

The judicial branch of the federal government (or judiciary, as it is sometimes called) interprets the laws passed by Congress and enforced by the executive branch. It consists mainly of three levels of courts: district courts, circuit courts of appeals, and the Supreme Court. There are also several special courts that deal with particular types of cases.

Federal judges are appointed for life by the president, with the consent of the Senate. They can be removed only by impeachment.

The Constitution grants the federal courts jurisdiction over the following categories of cases:

1. Cases arising under the Constitution, laws, or treaties of the United States.
2. Cases involving ambassadors, consuls, or other American diplomatic representatives abroad.
3. Cases of admiralty or maritime jurisdiction—that is, legal disputes arising on board ship or relating to shipping.
4. Controversies in which the United States itself is a party.
5. Controversies between two or more states, between citizens of different states, or between a state and a citizen of another state.

District Courts

The district courts are the lowest courts in the federal judicial system. It is here that most federal cases are first brought to trial. There are 94 of these courts—90 in the United States and one each in Puerto Rico, Guam, the Virgin Islands, and the Northern Mariana Islands. Each has from 2 to 27 judges, depending on the amount of judicial work in the district.

Circuit Courts of Appeals

The circuit courts of appeals have appellate jurisdiction only. That is, a circuit court tries only cases that are appealed (brought to it for reexamination). Many of these come from the district courts. Other cases involve the rulings of federal regulatory agencies, such as the EPA or SEC. There are 12 judicial circuits in the United States and its territories, each with a circuit court of appeals. In addition, there is a Court of Appeals for the Federal Circuit, which has nationwide jurisdiction and hears appeals in cases involving patents, trademarks, contracts, and international trade. Each court has from 6 to 28 judges, depending on its caseload.

The Supreme Court

The only court specified by name in the Constitution is the Supreme Court. It is the highest court in the land. It consists of a chief justice and eight associate justices.

The Supreme Court has both original and appellate jurisdiction. Original jurisdiction involves cases that are brought directly before it without first being heard in a lower court. Appellate jurisdiction involves cases that are appealed to it from lower courts, state and federal.

The Supreme Court has the power of judicial review. It may declare acts of Congress, presidential actions, or acts of state governments unconstitutional and, therefore, invalid. The nine justices vote on a case, and a simple majority decides the matter. Decisions are final.

Special Courts

1. The Claims Court hears claims brought against the U.S. government.
2. The Court of International Trade rules on civil actions against the U.S. government arising from federal import laws.
3. The Court of Military Appeals reviews court-martial convictions of military personnel.
4. The Tax Court tries cases involving tax disputes between individuals and the government.
5. The Temporary Emergency Court of Appeals has jurisdiction over appeals from district courts relating to economic stabilization and energy conservation laws.
6. The Court of Veterans Appeals reviews decisions of the Board of Veterans Appeals.

Multiple-Choice Test

1. The House of Representatives has the sole power to   (a) approve presidential appointments   (b) impeach federal officials   (c) override presidential vetoes   (d) hold party caucuses.
2. The Senate differs from the House of Representatives in that   (a) it is in session continuously   (b) a two-thirds vote is required to pass bills   (c) senators must be native-born Americans   (d) its members serve six-year terms.
3. A new Congress comes into existence   (a) every year   (b) every two years   (c) every six years   (d) whenever a new president takes office.
4. Usually, after a bill has been introduced into either house of Congress, it is first   (a) signed by the presiding officer of that house   (b) debated by members of that house   (c) referred to a committee of that house   (d) considered by a joint committee representing both houses.
5. The number of electoral votes needed to elect a president is   (a) 538   (b) 270   (c) 435   (d) 100.
6. In his inaugural oath, the president swears to preserve, protect, and defend   (a) democracy   (b) the nation   (c) the states   (d) the Constitution.
7. The Constitution gives the president the power to   (a) declare war   (b) regulate commerce   (c) command the armed forces   (d) remove Supreme Court justices.
8. Which of the following is an employee of the executive branch of the federal government?   (a) a page in the Senate   (b) a secretary of a member of the House of Representatives   (c) an associate justice of the Supreme Court   (d) the American ambassador to France.

9. A decision of the Supreme Court declaring a law unconstitutional requires (a) a simple majority vote (b) a two-thirds vote (c) a three-fourths vote (d) a unanimous vote.
10. All of the following courts belong to the federal court system *except* (a) a circuit court of appeals (b) a district court (c) a magistrate's court (d) the Claims Court.

Matching Test

COLUMN A

1. National Aeronautics and Space Administration
2. Civil Service Commission
3. Environmental Protection Agency
4. Federal Communications Commission
5. Federal Reserve Board
6. Federal Trade Commission
7. Interstate Commerce Commission
8. National Labor Relations Board
9. Securities and Exchange Commission
10. Selective Service System

COLUMN B

a. licenses TV stations
b. coordinates civilian space programs
c. protects stock market investors
d. controls the money supply
e. regulates railroads operating interstate
f. supervises federal hiring and firing
g. seeks to prevent false advertising
h. works to eliminate air pollution
i. administers the draft
j. supervises union elections

Essay Questions

1. Read Article I, Section 2, of the Constitution and indicate how many members the first House of Representatives had. What provision did Congress make about membership in 1929? What role does the census play in House membership?
2. Why did the congressional committee system come into being? Describe how it works.
3. Discuss briefly five major responsibilities of the president.
4. List three agencies that are included in the Executive Office of the President, and describe how each helps the chief executive carry out his duties.
5. List any five executive departments, and describe the chief functions of each.

CHAPTER 34

Civic Responsibility

Since the constitution was adopted, in 1789, the federal government has developed and changed greatly (as described in Chapter 33). It has become extremely complex, with hundreds of different parts and millions of employees. None of this complicated system would work without the participation of the American people. A basic principle that has shaped the development of the United States is civic responsibility—the idea that people can, and should, play a part in governing themselves. Ideally, civic responsibility means more than political involvement. At its broadest, it means tolerance, courtesy, and mutual respect in human relationships, from the close family circle outward.

AMERICAN IDEALS

Civic responsibility in America is based on certain widely held ideals—goals toward which people strive. Few Americans would claim that the United States has realized every one of these goals. But most citizens would agree that the country has made great progress toward attaining its ideals.

One of the most important American ideals is freedom. The United States is celebrated in the national anthem as "the land of the free." Among the first European settlers were English Separatists and Puritans seeking freedom to worship as they pleased. Ironically, they did not grant such freedom to others, such as Baptists and Quakers, whose form of worship differed from theirs. But religious toleration grew as America grew. One of many landmarks was the *Virginia Statute of Religious Freedom*, adopted in 1785. It stated that " all men shall be free to profess, and by argument to maintain, their opinion in matters of religion." Thomas Jefferson, who drafted the law, regarded this milestone as so important that he requested his authorship to be noted on his gravestone.

Closely related to the American belief in freedom is the value placed on equality. The Declaration of Independence proclaims that "all men are created equal." Even at the time the Declaration was adopted, in 1776, many Americans were aware of the contradiction between this noble statement and the existence of slavery. Freedom for enslaved blacks finally came after the bloody conflict of the Civil War, in the 1860s. But many more decades passed before black Americans began to achieve true equality.

Women in America also had a long struggle to lift themselves out of second-class citizenship. The black abolitionist and feminist Sojourner Truth put it simply: "We do as much, we eat as much, we want as much." Only in the 20th century did American women begin to gain an equal place in political life, in education, and at work.

The American ideal of democracy is embodied in the political system by which the nation tries to realize its goals of freedom and equality. Democracy was *not* a goal of the Founders. They were afraid of mob rule and did not want to give the people too much power. Therefore, only one part of the federal government—the House of Representatives— was to be elected directly by the voters. In time, however, both the president and the Senate came to be chosen by popular vote. Thus, the nation began to realize Lincoln's ideal of "government of the people, by the people, and for the people."

Americans also value achievement, work, and success. These ideals may be summed up in the single word "opportunity." From the beginning, immigrants came with the hope of improving their lot. In fact, America's very first settlers, the Indians, were looking for a better life (in the form of plentiful game) when they walked the land bridge from Asia to America. Obstacles growing out of prejudice and discrimination often made life hard for newcomers. But work and striving turned the "American Dream" into a reality for millions. Its promise beckons as strongly today as it did generations ago.

Along with opportunity goes the ideal of progress. In the dark days of Europe's early Middle Ages, the human condition was regarded as more or less fixed. Sons expected to live like their fathers, daughters like their mothers. But America did not accept old patterns as inevitable. The future could be better than the past. Out of confidence came progress. Did ocean travel take too long? Americans dug the Panama Canal to shorten voyages. Were cities running out of space? Architects built upward to "scrape" the sky. Was polio crippling thousands? Scientists

Liberty Bell

Statue of Liberty

Bald Eagle

American Flag

found a way to prevent it. A typically American slogan (that of the United States Air Force) puts it this way: "The difficult we do immediately. The impossible takes a little longer."

RIGHTS AND RESPONSIBILITIES OF CITIZENS

The body of the American Constitution outlines the basic framework of the federal government. The first ten amendments, the Bill of Rights, guarantee the fundamental rights of American citizens. (The privileges protected by the Bill of Rights are often known as civil rights or civil liberties.) Just as the federal government has been adapted to serve a large, complex nation, so have citizen rights been expanded and developed to protect a changing population. Tradition, laws, later constitutional amendments, court decisions—all have played a part in this process.

Rights

There is no simple list of all the rights that American citizens enjoy. The following eight rights, however, are among the most important:

1. **The vote.** Virtually all American citizens 18 years old and older have the right to vote. (An exception in some states is made for persons serving prison terms for felonies.) Voting rights are protected by several constitutional amendments: the Fifteenth, Nineteenth, Twenty-third, Twenty-fourth, and Twenty-sixth. In order to vote, a person must register. Individual states determine registration procedures.

Federal law, however, affects state practices. It says, for example, that states cannot have a residency requirement longer than 30 days. In addition, it requires areas with significant numbers of residents who do not speak English to provide ballots written in the residents' own language.

2. **Freedom of religion.**   Freedom of religion is guaranteed by the First Amendment, which says that "Congress shall make no law respecting an establishment of religion, or prohibiting the free exercise thereof." There has been a great deal of dispute over just what is meant by "an establishment of religion" and "the free exercise thereof." For instance, the Supreme Court ruled that school prayers violate the "no establishment" clause. But it also held that it is constitutional for the House and Senate to employ chaplains, who open legislative sessions with prayer. The Court ruled that "free exercise" did not allow a Mormon to have several wives, even though he argued that his religion required him to do so. On the other hand, courts held that California Navajos could use peyote—a drug prohibited by state law—because their religion called for it.

3. **Free speech and press.**   These rights, guaranteed by the First Amendment, are grouped together because they jointly affect many forms of communication. Over the years, they have been interpreted as protecting not only public speech and newspapers but also periodicals, radio and television, and motion pictures. The Supreme Court even held that clothing can be a form of "speech." It ruled against Iowa school authorities who had prohibited students from wearing black armbands as a form of protest against the Vietnam War.

   The First Amendment does not protect absolute freedom of expression. In 1919, Supreme Court Justice Oliver Wendell Holmes, Jr., laid down an important principle. Speech can be controlled, he said, if it creates "a clear and present danger." For example, the guarantee of free speech should never "protect a man in falsely shouting fire in a theater and causing a panic." The Court also ruled that freedom of expression does not protect those who libel others or advertise falsely.

4. **Assembly and petition.**   The First Amendment declares that people have the right "peaceably to assemble, and to petition the government for a redress of grievances." In other words, they are free to meet together and to ask the authorities to correct wrongs. This protection covers such actions as picketing, demonstrations, rallies, and parades. Localities may, however, regulate such activities by requiring permits. But such authorizations can be used only to regulate traffic and protect persons and property, not to stifle free speech.

5. **Security of property.**   The Fourth Amendment guarantees that "unreasonable searches and seizures" will not be used against Americans "in their persons, houses, papers, and effects." This right is further

protected by the Fourteenth Amendment, which holds that no one can be deprived of "life, liberty, or property without due process of law." These guarantees are designed to prohibit abuses by police and other authorities. This does not mean that homes and property are completely off limits. The courts ruled that the police may search a person in connection with a lawful arrest. And they may search an automobile if they have good reason to believe that its driver has committed a crime.

6. **Rights of the accused.**   People accused of wrongdoing have a number of rights, protected by the Fifth, Sixth, Eighth, and Fourteenth amendments. The Constitution lists, among other things, the right to a grand jury indictment, to a fair trial, and to trial by jury. It also states that no one can be tried twice for the same crime or be compelled to testify against himself or herself. In recent years, the Supreme Court has expanded the rights of the accused. For example, it ruled that defendants should be provided with legal counsel (the services of a lawyer), and that persons under arrest must be informed of their rights.

7. **Free public education.**   Education at public expense is not guaranteed by the Constitution. It did not become generally available, in fact, until the 19th century. But education is now regarded as so important that young people are required to attend school. The right to education is so fundamental that black civil rights leaders made it the key issue in their struggle for equality in the mid-20th century. In the landmark case of *Brown* v. *Board of Education of Topeka* (1954), the Supreme Court ruled that separate schools for black children violated the Fourteenth Amendment's "equal protection" clause.

8. **Livelihood.**   Americans have the right to choose the kind of work they want to do and to try to find it wherever they can. If they have no job or cannot work, they may receive money or other aid from the government. The Constitution contains no specific guarantees that apply to livelihood. But many government laws protect workers. Other laws authorize wide-ranging programs to aid the retired, the disabled, and the unemployed.

Responsibilities

Members of any community, from the smallest family to the largest nation, learn that membership involves responsibilities as well as rights. Citizens have the right to governmental protection against enemies from outside and lawlessness from within. In return, they are expected to defend their country if called upon, and to obey the law. Obedience to the law is a duty that citizens must fulfill. Duties also include paying taxes and serving on juries when summoned.

Other contributions of citizens—the "shoulds," rather than the "musts"—are responsibilities that enable the government to function properly. As with rights, there is no definite list of citizen responsibilities in the United States. The eight that follow are closely associated with the rights discussed earlier in this chapter:

1. **Political participation.**   Unlike the citizens of many other countries, Americans are not required to vote. Many, in fact, do not. When a large percentage of eligible voters fail to go to the polls, as has happened often in the 20th century, presidents and other government officials may actually be elected by a minority of the people. Democracy depends on citizen participation. This means that people have a responsibility not only to vote but also to know something about public issues.
2. **Understanding differences.**   The United States is a pluralist society. Its people come from every country in the world. Americans need to be tolerant of their fellow citizens' differences—in appearance, in language, in religion, and in everyday customs. These differences make for strength, not weakness.
3. **Consideration for others' opinions.**   Because there is freedom of expression in the United States, the range of opinions is vast. Inevitably, some people will speak and write in favor of causes that others find objectionable. Some want gun control; others want total freedom to own firearms. Some urge a wider use of capital punishment; others advocate a complete end to the death penalty. Some want marijuana to be legalized; others want stricter laws against it. Although no one can be expected to accept beliefs that he or she opposes, good citizenship requires that the expression of such beliefs be tolerated.
4. **Speaking up.**   Citizens in a democracy have a responsibility to let their voices be heard. Supreme Court Justice Robert Jackson wrote: "It is not the function of our Government to keep the citizen from falling into error; it is the function of the citizen to keep the Government from falling into error." Many political issues confront citizens in their everyday lives: raising local taxes; building a nuclear power plant; increasing police patrols; moving a health facility. Public meetings, petitions, letters to members of Congress—all of these methods register public opinion and shape the decisions made by governments.
5. **Respect for property.**   According to an old English saying, "A man's house is his castle." Respect for property, however, goes beyond consideration for people's homes and personal possessions. It extends to public property as well, for this property belongs to everyone. Littering, vandalism, and destruction make the environment ugly and even harmful.
6. **Cooperating with law enforcement.**   In a democracy, the police are servants of the people. But without public help, their task is almost

First lesson. (Engelhardt in
the *St. Louis Post-Dispatch*)

impossible. Those who know of wrongdoing should report it. And witnesses must be prepared to testify if called upon. No one wants to live in the midst of crime. But it flourishes where people remain silent.

7. **Education.**   The right to free public education is meaningless if people do not take advantage of it. Schooling is available to all. So are free libraries and museums. Through these institutions, Americans of all ages can explore the riches of the past, discover the workings of the world around them, and make intelligent plans for the future.

8. **Work.**   The United States was built on hard work, from earliest times onward. Responsible citizens prepare for vocations that will support them and their families. On his 90th birthday, W. E. B. Du Bois wrote to his newborn great-grandson: "The return from your work must be the satisfaction which that work brings you and the world's need of that work."

BECOMING A CITIZEN

Most Americans are citizens by birth. That is, they have been born in the United States, and their parents are either Americans or foreign-born residents of the United States. Children born to American citizens living abroad are also considered to be native-born citizens.

Aliens

There are several million people living in the United States who are aliens—citizens not of the United States but of some other country. Those who have come openly to study, work, and, perhaps, stay permanently are legal aliens. They are protected by the laws and have most of the rights of citizens, except voting and holding public office. Every January, they must register with the Immigration and Naturalization Service, a branch of the Justice Department.

There are also millions of illegal aliens in the United States. They have entered the country secretly and have no legal standing. Although many hold jobs, they are not entitled to benefits such as workmen's compensation and unemployment insurance. If caught, they risk being deported to their own countries.

Naturalized Citizens

Legal aliens who wish to become naturalized citizens of the United States may do so under certain conditions. Such persons must be at least 18 years old. They must have been lawful residents of the United States continuously for five years, and physically present in the country for at least half this period. For spouses of U.S. citizens, the period of residence is usually three years. Special provisions are also made for veterans of the armed forces.

An applicant for naturalization must also fulfill the following three conditions:

1. He or she must demonstrate an understanding of the English language, including an ability to read, write, and speak words in ordinary usage. Exceptions are (a) persons physically unable to do so and (b) those who are over 50 and have been lawful permanent residents for at least 20 years.
2. He or she must be a person of good moral character, "attached to the principles and form of government of the United States."
3. He or she must demonstrate a knowledge and understanding of the fundamentals of United States history and the principles and form of the American government.

An alien who meets these conditions and wants to be naturalized first files a petition and pays a fee. The applicant must then appear at a preliminary hearing, with two witnesses who know him or her personally. At this hearing, the judge may ask questions to test the applicant's knowledge of American history and government. The applicant may be accompanied by a lawyer or a representative of a social service agency.

A 30-day waiting period follows the preliminary hearing. If no problems arise, the applicant then appears in court. There, he or she takes an oath, renouncing allegiance to the former country and swearing loyalty to the United States. Foreign-born children under 16 automatically become citizens when both parents are naturalized. Naturalized American citizens are entitled to all the rights of native-born citizens, except that they cannot become president or vice-president.

I hereby declare, on oath, that I absolutely and entirely renounce and abjure all allegiance and fidelity to any foreign prince, potentate, state or sovereignty, to whom or which I have heretofore been a subject or citizen; that I will support and defend the Constitution and laws of the United States of America against all enemies, foreign and domestic; that I will bear arms on behalf of the United States when required by the law; that I will perform noncombatant service in the armed forces of the United States when required by the law; that I will perform work of national importance under civilian direction when required by the law; and that I take this obligation freely without any mental reservation or purpose of evasion; so help me God.

—The Oath of Allegiance

AMERICANS' PATRIOTIC HERITAGE

Patriotism means love for one's country. This feeling is often aroused by symbols, such as flags and other objects designed to represent a nation's traditions and ideals. In addition, verbal expressions of patriotism—mottoes, poems, slogans, and such—help people reaffirm national loyalty. Many American symbols are known and recognized the world over.

The American Flag

The flag of the United States has 13 horizontal stripes, 7 red and 6 white. They represent the 13 original states. In the upper left corner is a rectangle called the union. It consists of 50 five-pointed stars against a blue background. There are 5 rows of 6 stars each, alternating with 4 rows of 5 stars each. The stars represent the states of today. The red in the flag stands for courage; the white, purity; the blue, loyalty.

The American flag is often called the Stars and Stripes. It is also known as Old Glory. This name comes from a specific large flag given to a Massachusetts ship captain, William Driver, in 1831.

ORIGIN AND CHANGES During the colonial period, many different flags were in use in Britain's North American colonies. Several of them combined red and white stripes with a union consisting of the British flag.

During the Revolution, on June 14, 1777, the Continental Congress passed this resolution: "Resolved, that the Flag of the United States be thirteen stripes alternate red and white, that the union be thirteen stars white in a blue field representing a new constellation."

Some people believe that Betsy Ross of Philadelphia designed the first Stars and Stripes in 1776. This claim, however, was not made until almost 100 years later, by her grandson. There is no firm evidence to prove it (or disprove it).

When Vermont and Kentucky joined the Union in the 1790s, two new stars and stripes were added to the flag. When additional states were soon created, it was clear that the flag might become cluttered and unwieldy. In 1818, Congress set the number of stripes at 13 and provided that a new star should be added for each new state.

DISPLAYING THE FLAG   A weather-resistant flag may be flown outdoors in any weather, and around the clock if it is properly illuminated. A code adopted by Congress in 1976 (and later expanded) lists the following special days when the flag ought to be displayed:

New Year's Day, January 1
Inauguration Day, January 20
Martin Luther King Day, third Monday in January
Lincoln's Birthday, February 12
Washington's Birthday, third Monday in February
Easter Sunday (date varies)
Mother's Day, second Sunday in May
Armed Forces Day, third Saturday in May
Memorial Day, last Monday in May (half-staff until noon)
Flag Day, June 14
Independence Day, July 4
Labor Day, first Monday in September
Citizenship Day, September 17
Columbus Day, second Monday in October
Veterans Day, November 11
Thanksgiving Day, fourth Thursday in November
Christmas Day, December 25

In addition, the flag should be displayed on state holidays and in or near every polling place on election days. When schools are in session, the flag should be displayed on, or in front of, the school.

Several rules govern how the flag is to be displayed. When it is raised or lowered, it should not touch the ground. It should be hoisted briskly and lowered slowly and ceremoniously. When used on a speaker's platform, the flag, if displayed flat, should be placed above and behind the speaker, with the union at the top and to the audience's left. If hung from a staff, the flag should be at the speaker's right. In a parade, the flag should be on the marchers' right or in front at the center.

When a flag is in such condition that it is no longer a fitting emblem for display, it should be destroyed in a dignified way. The preferred method is by burning.

SALUTING THE FLAG   The flag receives special attention when it is being raised or lowered, when it is passing in a parade, or during recitation of the Pledge of Allegiance (see page 560). At that time, everyone present should face the flag and stand at attention.

Men and women in uniform should give the military salute. Men with hats should remove them with the right hand, holding them at the left shoulder so that the hand is over the heart. Men without hats should place the right hand over the heart. Women should stand at attention.

The Great Seal, Emblem, and Motto

The Great Seal of the United States was adopted in 1782. The face of the seal is affixed to official documents.

Both the face and the reverse of the Great Seal appear on the back of the $1 bill. If you look at one, you will see the reverse of the seal at the left. The pyramid has 13 layers of stone, representing the original states. The bottom layer bears a date in Roman numerals, MDCCLXXVI (1776), the year of the Declaration of Independence. Below the pyramid are the Latin words *Novus Ordo Seclorum*—"a new order of the ages." Above the pyramid is the eye of Providence and another Latin motto, *Annuit Coeptis*—"He [God] has favored our undertaking."

On the right of the dollar bill is the face of the seal. It bears a prominent image of the bald eagle, the official emblem of the United States, adopted in 1782. (The bird is not actually bald, but its pure white head may appear so.) The eagle's beak holds a ribbon with the Latin words *E Pluribus Unum*—"Out of many, one" (one nation created out of a union of states). This phrase, chosen in 1776 by Benjamin Franklin, Thomas Jefferson, and John Adams, was the motto of the United States before 1956. In that year, a new official motto, "In God We Trust," was adopted. It appears on all U.S. currency.

The eagle on the face of the seal wears a shield with 13 stripes (the original states). In its right claw, it holds an olive branch with 13 leaves and 13 olives. In its left claw are 13 arrows. (The symbolism indicates that the nation desires peace but is prepared for war.) Above the eagle's head are 13 stars, surrounded by rays of light breaking through clouds.

The Liberty Bell

This large bronze bell, now housed in a special building in Philadelphia, was originally a symbol of religious freedom. The Pennsylvania

Assembly ordered it from London in 1752 to commemorate the colony's 50th anniversary of religious freedom under Penn's Charter of Liberties and Privileges. The bell was inscribed with a biblical quotation, "Proclaim Liberty throughout the land unto all the inhabitants thereof" (Leviticus 25 : 10).

The bell, which hung in the State House (now Independence Hall), rang out on several occasions during the Revolutionary period. It rang to protest against the Stamp Act and tea tax, to announce the battles of Lexington and Concord, and to announce the reading of the Declaration of Independence on July 8, 1776. Thus, it acquired the name Liberty Bell.

The bell cracked several times—soon after its arrival in 1752, when tolling the death of Chief Justice Marshall in 1835, and when tolling on Washington's Birthday in 1846. This third time, it was so badly damaged that it could not be tolled again.

The Statue of Liberty

The largest statue ever made stands at the entrance of New York Harbor, on its own small island. It is 151 feet tall and is made of copper sheets over an iron framework. The idea of the monument was suggested in France, as a commemoration of the American and French revolutions. France raised the funds for the statue, while money for the pedestal came from the United States. The figure was designed by Frédéric Auguste Bartholdi, and the framework was built by Alexandre Gustave Eiffel, who designed Paris's Eiffel Tower. The statue, shipped to the United States in more than 200 separate cases, was installed in 1885 and dedicated by President Cleveland on October 28, 1886.

The statue's proper name is *Liberty Enlightening the World*. She

---

Not like the brazen giant of Greek fame,
   With conquering limbs astride from land to land;
   Here at our sea-washed, sunset gates shall stand
A mighty woman with a torch, whose flame
Is the imprisoned lightning, and her name
   Mother of Exiles. From her beacon-hand
   Glows world-wide welcome; her mild eyes command
The air-bridged harbor that twin cities frame.
"Keep ancient lands, your storied pomp!" cries she
   With silent lips. "Give me your tired, your poor,
Your huddled masses yearning to breathe free,
   The wretched refuse of your teeming shore.
Send these, the homeless, tempest-tost to me,
   I lift my lamp beside the golden door!"

                 —The New Colossus, *Emma Lazarus*

wears a classical robe and a seven-spiked crown. At her feet are the broken chains of tyranny. In her upraised right arm, she holds the torch of freedom. In her left, she carries a book bearing the date of the Declaration of Independence. Below the statue is a poem by Emma Lazarus, placed there in 1908. Called "The New Colossus," the poem compares the Statue of Liberty with the ancient Colossus of Rhodes. (Long ago, this giant figure of a man stood straddling the harbor of the Mediterranean island of Rhodes.)

Uncle Sam

This lanky old gentleman in old fashioned clothes has personified the United States since the War of 1812. During the war, a slaughterhouse in Troy, New York, stamped cases of provisions with the initials "U.S." ("United States"), but employees joked that they really stood for the inspecting superintendent, Samuel ("Uncle Sam") Wilson.

Uncle Sam took on the form that we recognize today in the 1860s. It was then that Thomas Nast, the greatest American cartoonist of the day, sketched a tall figure with long hair and a goatee, wearing striped pants and carrying a top hat.

The Pledge of Allegiance

The Pledge of Allegiance dates back to 1892, when the nation was celebrating the 400th anniversary of Columbus's discovery of America. The pledge was written by Francis Bellamy, a Massachusetts Baptist minister, for presentation at the World's Columbian Exposition at Chicago. The pledge first appeared in a Boston weekly, *Youth's Companion*, on September 8, 1892. The words "under God" were added in 1954.

I pledge allegiance to the flag of the United States of America and to the Republic for which it stands, one Nation under God, indivisible, with liberty and justice for all.

—The Pledge of Allegiance

The National Anthem

"The Star-Spangled Banner" was written by a Baltimore lawyer, Francis Scott Key, during the War of 1812. Through the night of September 13–14, 1814, Key watched as the British bombarded Fort McHenry, in Baltimore Harbor. After 25 hours of shelling, the flag still flew the next morning, inspiring Key to write a poem (which was first

Oh! say, can you see, by the dawn's early light,
What so proudly we hailed at the twilight's last gleaming?
Whose broad stripes and bright stars, thro' the perilous fight,
O'er the ramparts we watched were so gallantly streaming?
And the rockets' red glare, the bombs bursting in air,
Gave proof thro' the night that our flag was still there.
Oh! say, does that star-spangled banner yet wave
O'er the land of the free and the home of the brave?

On the shore, dimly seen thro' the mist of the deep,
Where the foe's haughty host in dread silence reposes,
What is that which the breeze, o'er the towering steep,
As it fitfully blows, half conceals, half discloses?
Now it catches the gleam of the morning's first beam,
In full glory reflected, now shines on the stream.
'Tis the star-spangled banner. Oh! long may it wave
O'er the land of the free and the home of the brave!

And where is that band who so vauntingly swore
That the havoc of war and the battle's confusion
A home and a country should leave us no more?
Their blood has washed out their foul footstep's pollution.
No refuge could save the hireling and slave
From the terror of flight or the gloom of the grave,
And the star-spangled banner in triumph doth wave
O'er the land of the free and the home of the brave.

Oh! thus be it ever when freemen shall stand
Between their loved home and the war's desolation,
Blest with vict'ry and peace, may the Heav'n-rescued land
Praise the Pow'r that hath made and preserved us a nation.
Then conquer we must, when our cause it is just,
And this be our motto, "In God is our trust."
And the star-spangled banner in triumph shall wave
O'er the land of the free and the home of the brave.

—The Star-Spangled Banner

called "Defence of Fort M'Henry"). It was soon being sung to the melody of an English song, "To Anacreon [a Greek god] in Heaven," written by John Stafford Smith. Not until 1931, however, did "The Star-Spangled Banner" become the official national anthem of the United States.

True-False Test

1. Freedom of religion is guaranteed by the Fourth Amendment.
2. The Bill of Rights says that persons accused of crimes are entitled to a jury trial.

3. Naturalized citizens of the United States are required to vote in presidential elections.
4. Legal aliens must register with the Immigration and Naturalization Service once a year.
5. In the oath of allegiance, applicants for citizenship swear to defend the president of the United States.
6. The design of the first official flag of the newly independent United States was specified by a congressional resolution of 1777.
7. The American flag should never be flown at night.
8. The Pledge of Allegiance was written by Thomas Jefferson.
9. The Liberty Bell is inscribed with a quotation from the Bible.
10. American schoolchildren raised funds to pay for the Statue of Liberty.

Matching Test

COLUMN A

1. First Amendment
2. Fourth Amendment
3. Thomas Nast
4. Oliver Wendell Holmes, Jr.
5. Francis Bellamy
6. Francis Scott Key
7. "In God We Trust"
8. *E Pluribus Unum*
9. Frédéric Bartholdi
10. Emma Lazarus

COLUMN B

a. wrote the Pledge of Allegiance
b. wrote the national anthem
c. protects freedom of the press
d. popularized the figure of Uncle Sam
e. wrote the poem at the base of the Statue of Liberty
f. protects against "unreasonable searches and seizures"
g. first motto of the United States
h. designed the Statue of Liberty
i. stated the "clear and present danger" principle
j. present motto of the United States

Essay Questions

1. Which of the American ideals discussed in this chapter is most important to you? Why?
2. What is the Bill of Rights? Read through one of its amendments on pages 581–583, and explain what it means.
3. What are the main duties of an American citizen?
4. How does a person become a naturalized citizen of the United States?
5. Explain the symbolism of the American flag.

Appendix

THE DECLARATION OF INDEPENDENCE

[*Note:* Capitalization, spelling, punctuation, and paragraphing have been modernized. In addition, the signers' names have been rearranged and grouped alphabetically by state.]

In Congress, July 4, 1776

The Unanimous Declaration of the Thirteen
United States of America

W HEN, IN THE COURSE of human events, it becomes necessary for one people to dissolve the political bands which have connected them with another, and to assume, among the powers of the earth, the separate and equal station to which the laws of nature and of nature's God entitle them, a decent respect to the opinions of mankind requires that they should declare the causes which impel them to the separation.

We hold these truths to be self-evident: that all men are created equal; that they are endowed by their Creator with certain unalienable rights; that among these are life, liberty, and the pursuit of happiness.

That to secure these rights, governments are instituted among men, deriving their just powers from the consent of the governed. That, whenever any form of government becomes destructive of these ends, it is the right of the people to alter or to abolish it, and to institute new government, laying its foundation on such principles, and organizing its powers in such form, as to them shall seem most likely to effect their safety and happiness. Prudence, indeed, will dictate that governments long established should not be changed for light and transient causes; and, accordingly, all experience hath shown that mankind are more disposed to suffer, while evils are sufferable, than to right themselves by abolishing the forms to which they are accustomed. But when a long train of abuses and usurpations, pursuing invariably the same object, evinces a design to reduce them under absolute despotism, it is their right, it is their duty, to throw off such government, and to provide new guards for their future security.

Such has been the patient sufferance of these colonies; and such is now the necessity which constrains them to alter their former systems of government. The history of the present King of Great Britain is a history of repeated injuries and usurpations, all having in direct object the establishment of an absolute tyranny over these states. To prove this, let facts be submitted to a candid world.

He has refused his assent to laws the most wholesome and necessary for the public good.

He has forbidden his governors to pass laws of immediate and pressing importance, unless suspended in their operation till his assent should be obtained; and, when so suspended, he has utterly neglected to attend to them.

He has refused to pass other laws for the accommodation of large districts of people, unless those people would relinquish the right of representation in the legislature—a right inestimable to them and formidable to tyrants only.

He has called together legislative bodies at places unusual, uncomfortable, and distant from the depository of their public records, for the sole purpose of fatiguing them into compliance with his measures.

He has dissolved representative houses repeatedly, for opposing, with manly firmness, his invasions on the rights of the people.

He has refused, for a long time after such dissolutions, to cause others to be elected; whereby the legislative powers, incapable of annihilation, have returned to the people at large for their exercise; the state remaining, in the meantime, exposed to all the dangers of invasion from without and convulsions within.

He has endeavored to prevent the population of these states; for that purpose obstructing the laws for naturalization of foreigners, refusing to pass others to encourage their migration hither, and raising the conditions of new appropriations of lands.

He has obstructed the administration of justice by refusing his assent to laws for establishing judiciary powers.

He has made judges dependent on his will alone for the tenure of their offices and the amount and payment of their salaries.

He has erected a multitude of new offices and sent hither swarms of officers to harass our people and eat out their substance.

He has kept among us, in times of peace, standing armies, without the consent of our legislatures.

He has affected to render the military independent of, and superior to, the civil power.

He has combined with others to subject us to a jurisdiction foreign to our constitution and unacknowledged by our laws, giving his assent to their acts of pretended legislation:

For quartering large bodies of armed troops among us;

For protecting them, by a mock trial, from punishment for any murders which they should commit on the inhabitants of these states;

For cutting off our trade with all parts of the world;

For imposing taxes on us without our consent;

For depriving us, in many cases, of the benefits of trial by jury;

For transporting us beyond seas to be tried for pretended offenses;

For abolishing the free system of English laws in a neighboring province, establishing therein an arbitrary government and enlarging its boundaries, so as to render it at once an example and fit instrument for introducing the same absolute rule into these colonies;

For taking away our charters, abolishing our most valuable laws, and altering fundamentally the forms of our governments;

For suspending our own legislatures, and declaring themselves invested with power to legislate for us in all cases whatsoever.

He has abdicated government here by declaring us out of his protection and waging war against us.

He has plundered our seas, ravaged our coasts, burned our towns, and destroyed the lives of our people.

He is, at this time, transporting large armies of foreign mercenaries to complete the works of death, desolation, and tyranny already begun with circumstances of cruelty and perfidy scarcely paralleled in the most barbarous ages, and totally unworthy the head of a civilized nation.

He has constrained our fellow citizens taken captive on the high seas to bear arms against their country, to become the executioners of their friends and brethren, or to fall themselves by their hands.

He has excited domestic insurrections among us, and has endeavored to bring on the inhabitants of our frontiers the merciless Indian savages, whose known rule of warfare is an undistinguished destruction of all ages, sexes, and conditions.

In every stage of these oppressions we have petitioned for redress in the most humble terms. Our repeated petitions have been answered only by repeated injury. A prince whose character is thus marked by every act which may define a tyrant is unfit to be the ruler of a free people.

Nor have we been wanting in attentions to our British brethren. We have warned them, from time to time, of attempts by their legislature to extend an unwarrantable jurisdiction over us. We have reminded them of the circumstances of our emigration and settlement here. We have appealed to their native justice and magnanimity; and we have conjured them, by the ties of our common kindred, to disavow these usurpations, which would inevitably interrupt our connections and correspondence. They, too, have been deaf to the voice of justice and consanguinity. We must, therefore, acquiesce in the necessity which denounces our separation, and hold them, as we hold the rest of mankind, enemies in war, in peace friends.

We, therefore, the representatives of the United States of America, in General Congress assembled, appealing to the Supreme Judge of the world for the rectitude of our intentions, do, in the name and by authority of the good people of these colonies, solemnly publish and declare: that these united colonies are, and of right ought to be, free and independent states; that they are absolved from all allegiance to the British crown, and that all political connection between them and the state of Great Britain is, and ought to be, totally dissolved; and that, as free and independent states, they have full power to levy war, conclude peace, contract alliances, establish commerce, and to do all other acts and things which independent states may of right do. And for the support of this declaration, with a firm reliance on the protection of Divine Providence, we mutually pledge to each other our lives, our fortunes, and our sacred honor.

[Signed by]   **John Hancock**
[Massachusetts]

[Connecticut]
Samuel Huntington
Roger Sherman
William Williams
Oliver Wolcott

[Delaware]
Thomas McKean
George Read
Caesar Rodney

[Georgia]
Button Gwinnett
Lyman Hall
George Walton

[Maryland]
Charles Carroll
    of Carrollton
Samuel Chase
William Paca
Thomas Stone

[Massachusetts]
John Adams
Samuel Adams
Elbridge Gerry
Robert Treat Paine

[New Hampshire]
Josiah Bartlett
Matthew Thornton
William Whipple

[New Jersey]
Abraham Clark
John Hart
Francis Hopkinson
Richard Stockton
John Witherspoon

[New York]
William Floyd
Francis Lewis
Philip Livingston
Lewis Morris

[North Carolina]
Joseph Hewes
William Hooper
John Penn

[Pennsylvania]
George Clymer
Benjamin Franklin
Robert Morris
John Morton
George Ross
Benjamin Rush
James Smith
George Taylor
James Wilson

[Rhode Island]
William Ellery
Stephen Hopkins

[South Carolina]
Thomas Heyward, Jr.
Thomas Lynch, Jr.
Arthur Middleton
Edward Rutledge

[Virginia]
Carter Braxton
Benjamin Harrison
Thomas Jefferson
Francis Lightfoot Lee
Richard Henry Lee
Thomas Nelson, Jr.
George Wythe

THE CONSTITUTION
OF THE UNITED
STATES
OF AMERICA

[*Note:* Footnotes, headings, and explanations have been added to aid the reader. The explanations within the body of the text are enclosed in brackets []. The parts of the Constitution that are no longer in effect are printed in *italic* type. Capitalization, spelling, and punctuation have been modernized. In addition, the signers' names have been rearranged and grouped alphabetically by state.]

PREAMBLE[1]

We the people of the United States, in order to form a more perfect Union, establish justice, insure domestic tranquility,[2] provide for the common defense, promote the general welfare, and secure the blessings of liberty to ourselves and our posterity [descendants], do ordain [issue] and establish this Constitution for the United States of America.

ARTICLE I. Legislative Department

Section 1. Congress

All legislative powers herein granted shall be vested in a Congress of the United States, which shall consist of a Senate and House of Representatives.

---

[1]Introduction.

[2]"Insure domestic tranquility" means *assure peace within the nation.*

Section 2.   House of Representatives

[1] The House of Representatives shall be composed of members chosen every second year by the people of the several states, and the electors [voters] in each state shall have the qualifications requisite [required] for electors of the most numerous branch of the state legislature.

[2] No person shall be a representative who shall not have attained to [reached] the age of twenty-five years and been seven years a citizen of the United States, and who shall not, when elected, be an inhabitant of that state in which he shall be chosen.

[3] Representatives and direct taxes[1] shall be apportioned [divided] among the several states which may be included within this Union according to their respective numbers [population], *which shall be determined by adding to the whole number of free persons, including those bound to service for a term of years* [indentured servants], *and excluding Indians not taxed, three-fifths of all other persons.*[2] The actual enumeration [census] shall be made within three years after the first meeting of the Congress of the United States, and within every subsequent term of ten years, in such manner as they shall by law direct. The number of representatives shall not exceed one for every thirty thousand, but each state shall have at least one representative; *and until such enumeration shall be made, the State of New Hampshire shall be entitled to choose three, Massachusetts eight, Rhode Island and Providence Plantations one, Connecticut five, New York six, New Jersey four, Pennsylvania eight, Delaware one, Maryland six, Virginia ten, North Carolina five, South Carolina five, and Georgia three.*[3]

[4] When vacancies happen in the representation from any state, the executive authority [governor] thereof shall issue writs of election[4] to fill such vacancies.

[5] The House of Representatives shall choose their Speaker and other officers; and shall have the sole power of impeachment.[5]

Section 3.   Senate

[1] The Senate of the United States shall be composed of two senators from each state, *chosen by the legislature thereof,*[6] for six years; and each senator shall have one vote.

---

[1]Modified by Amendment XVI, which granted Congress the power to levy a direct tax on individual incomes rather than on the basis of state populations.

[2]"Other persons" refer to slaves. Amendment XIII abolished slavery; Amendment XIV specifically eliminated the three-fifths formula.

[3]Temporary provision.

[4]"Issue writs of election" means *call a special election.*

[5]"Power of impeachment" means *right to charge federal officials with misconduct.*

[6]Replaced by Amendment XVII, which provided for popular election of senators.

[2] *Immediately after they shall be assembled in consequence of the first election, they shall be divided as equally as may be into three classes. The seats of the senators of the first class shall be vacated at the expiration of the second year, of the second class at the expiration of the fourth year, and of the third class at the expiration of the sixth year,*[1] so that one-third may be chosen every second year; *and if vacancies happen by resignation, or otherwise, during the recess of the legislature of any state, the executive* [governor] *thereof may make temporary appointments until the next meeting of the legislature, which shall then fill such vacancies.*[2]

[3] No person shall be a senator who shall not have attained to the age of thirty years and been nine years a citizen of the United States, and who shall not, when elected, be an inhabitant of that state for which he shall be chosen.

[4] The vice president of the United States shall be president of the Senate, but shall have no vote, unless they be equally divided [tied].

[5] The Senate shall choose their other officers, and also a president pro tempore [temporary presiding officer], in the absence of the vice president, or when he shall exercise the office of president of the United States.

[6] The Senate shall have sole power to try all impeachments.[3] When sitting for that purpose, they shall be on oath or affirmation.[4] When the president of the United States is tried, the chief justice [of the United States] shall preside; and no person shall be convicted without the concurrence [agreement] of two-thirds of the members present.

[7] Judgment in cases of impeachment shall not extend further than to removal from office, and disqualification to hold and enjoy any office of honor, trust, or profit under the United States; but the party convicted shall nevertheless be liable and subject to indictment, trial, judgment, and punishment, according to law.

Section 4. Elections and Meetings of Congress

[1] The times, places, and manner of holding elections for senators and representatives shall be prescribed [designated] in each state by the legislature thereof; but the Congress may at any time by law make or alter such regulations, except as to the places of choosing senators.

---

[1]Temporary provision, designed to organize the first Senate in such a way that, thereafter, only one-third of its members would be subject to replacement at each successive election.

[2]Modified by Amendment XVII, which permits a governor to select a temporary replacement to fill the vacancy until the next election.

[3]"To try all impeachments" means *to conduct the trials of officials impeached by the House of Representatives.* When trying such cases, the Senate serves as a court.

[4]If taking an oath violates a member's religious principles, that person may "affirm" rather than "swear."

[2] The Congress shall assemble at least once in every year, *and such meeting shall be on the first Monday in December,*[1] unless they shall by law appoint a different day.

Section 5.   Rules and Procedures of the Two Houses

[1] Each house shall be the judge of the elections, returns, and qualifications of its own members,[2] and a majority of each shall constitute a quorum[3] to do business; but a smaller number may adjourn from day to day, and may be authorized to compel the attendance of absent members, in such manner, and under such penalties, as each house may provide.

[2] Each house may determine the rules of its proceedings, punish its members for disorderly behavior, and with the concurrence of two-thirds, expel a member.

[3] Each house shall keep a journal [record] of its proceedings, and from time to time publish the same, excepting such parts as may in their judgment require secrecy; and the yeas [affirmative votes] and nays [negative votes] of the members of either house on any question shall, at the desire of one-fifth of those present, be entered on the journal.

[4] Neither house, during the session of Congress, shall, without the consent of the other, adjourn for more than three days, nor to any other place than that in which the two houses shall be sitting.

Section 6.   Members' Privileges and Restrictions

[1] The senators and representatives shall receive a compensation [salary] for their services, to be ascertained [fixed] by law and paid out of the treasury of the United States. They shall in all cases except treason, felony [serious crime], and breach of the peace [disorderly conduct], be privileged [immune] from arrest during their attendance at the session of their respective houses, and in going to and returning from the same; and for any speech or debate in either house, they shall not be questioned in any other place.[4]

[2] No senator or representative shall, during the time for which he was elected, be appointed to any civil office under the authority of the

---

[1]Amendment XX changed this date to January 3.

[2]This provision empowers either house, by a majority vote, to refuse to seat a newly elected member.

[3]A "quorum" is the *number of members that must be present in order to conduct business.*

[4]"They shall not be questioned in any other place" means that *they may not be sued for slander or libel.* Freedom from arrest during congressional sessions and freedom of speech within the halls of Congress—two privileges granted to members of Congress—are known as *congressional immunity.*

United States, which shall have been created, or the emoluments [salary] whereof shall have been increased, during such time; and no person holding any office under the United States shall be a member of either house during his continuance in office.

Section 7. Lawmaking Procedures

[1] All bills for raising revenue shall originate [be introduced] in the House of Representatives; but the Senate may propose or concur with [approve] amendments as on other bills.

[2] Every bill which shall have passed the House of Representatives and the Senate shall, before it becomes a law, be presented to the president of the United States; if he approve, he shall sign it, but if not, he shall return it, with his objections, to that house in which it shall have originated, who shall enter the objections at large on their journal, and proceed to reconsider it. If after such reconsideration two-thirds of that house shall agree to pass the bill, it shall be sent, together with the objections, to the other house, by which it shall likewise be reconsidered, and, if approved by two-thirds of that house, it shall become a law. But in all such cases the votes of both houses shall be determined by yeas and nays, and the names of the persons voting for and against the bill shall be entered on the journal of each house respectively. If any bill shall not be returned by the president within ten days (Sundays excepted) after it shall have been presented to him, the same shall be a law, in like manner as if he had signed it, unless the Congress by their adjournment prevent its return, in which case it shall not be a law.[1]

[3] Every order, resolution, or vote to which the concurrence of the Senate and House of Representatives may be necessary (except on a question of adjournment) shall be presented to the president of the United States; and before the same shall take effect, shall be approved by him, or, being disapproved by him, shall be repassed by two-thirds of the Senate and House of Representatives, according to the rules and limitations prescribed in the case of a bill.

Section 8. Powers of Congress

The Congress shall have power:

[1] To lay and collect taxes, duties, imposts, and excises,[2] to pay the

---

[1] If Congress adjourns before the ten-day period is up, the president can kill a bill by ignoring it ("putting it in his pocket"). Therefore, this type of presidential rejection is called a *pocket veto*.

[2] "Duties, imposts, and excises" are forms of taxation. Duties and imposts are taxes on imports. Excises are taxes on goods produced or services performed within a country.

debts and provide for the common defense and general welfare of the United States; but all duties, imposts, and excises shall be uniform [the same] throughout the United States;

[2] To borrow money on the credit of the United States;

[3] To regulate commerce with foreign nations, and among the several states, and with the Indian tribes;

[4] To establish a uniform rule of naturalization, and uniform laws on the subject of bankruptcies throughout the United States;

[5] To coin money, regulate the value thereof, and of foreign coin, and fix [set] the standard of weights and measures;

[6] To provide for the punishment of counterfeiting[1] the securities and current coin of the United States;

[7] To establish post offices and post roads;

[8] To promote the progress of science and useful arts by securing for limited times to authors and inventors the exclusive right to their respective writings and discoveries;[2]

[9] To constitute tribunals [establish courts] inferior to [lower than] the Supreme Court;

[10] To define and punish piracies and felonies committed on the high seas[3] and offenses against the law of nations [international law];

[11] To declare war, grant letters of marque and reprisal,[4] and make rules concerning captures on land and water;

[12] To raise and support armies, but no appropriation of money to that use shall be for a longer term than two years;

[13] To provide and maintain a navy;

[14] To make rules for the government and regulation of the land and naval forces;

[15] To provide for calling forth the militia[5] to execute [carry out] the laws of the Union, suppress [put down] insurrections [rebellions], and repel [drive back] invasions;

[16] To provide for organizing, arming, and disciplining [training] the militia, and for governing such part of them as may be employed in the service of the United States, reserving to the states respectively the appointment of the officers, and the authority of training the militia according to the discipline [regulations] prescribed by Congress;

---

[1]Making an imitation with the intent of passing it as the genuine article.

[2]Copyright and patent laws, passed by Congress on the basis of this clause, protect the rights of authors and inventors.

[3]Open ocean; waters outside the territorial limits of a country.

[4]Letters of marque and reprisal are government licenses issued to private citizens in time of war authorizing them to fit out armed vessels (called *privateers*) for the purpose of capturing or destroying enemy ships.

[5]Citizen soldiers who are not in the regular armed forces but are subject to military duty in times of emergency; for example, the National Guard.

[17] To exercise exclusive legislation[1] in all cases whatsoever, over such district (not exceeding ten miles square) as may, by cession of particular states, and the acceptance of Congress, become the seat of government of the United States, and to exercise like authority over all places purchased by the consent of the legislature of the state in which the same shall be, for the erection of forts, magazines, arsenals, dockyards, and other needful buildings; and

[18] To make all laws which shall be necessary and proper for carrying into execution the foregoing powers and all other powers vested by this Constitution in the government of the United States, or in any department or officer thereof.[2]

Section 9.   Powers Denied to the Federal Government

[1] *The migration or importation of such persons as any of the states now existing shall think proper to admit shall not be prohibited by the Congress prior to the year 1808; but a tax or duty may be imposed on such importation, not exceeding ten dollars for each person.*[3]

[2] The privilege of the writ of habeas corpus[4] shall not be suspended, unless when in cases of rebellion or invasion the public safety may require it.

[3] No bill of attainder[5] or ex post facto law[6] shall be passed.

[4] No capitation [head] or other direct tax shall be laid, unless in proportion to the census or enumeration herein before directed to be taken.[7]

[5] No tax or duty shall be laid on articles exported from any state.

[6] No preference shall be given by any regulation of commerce or revenue to the ports of one state over those of another; nor shall vessels bound to, or from, one state be obliged to enter, clear, or pay duties in another.

---

[1]"To exercise exclusive legislation . . . over such district" means *to be solely responsible for making the laws for a designated area.*

[2]This is the so-called "elastic clause" of the Constitution, which allows Congress to carry out many actions not specifically listed.

[3]This temporary provision prohibited Congress from interfering with the importation of slaves ("such persons") before 1808.

[4]A "writ of habeas corpus" is a court order obtained by a person taken into custody, demanding to know the reasons for imprisonment. If the court rules that the reasons are insufficient, the prisoner is released.

[5]A law that deprives a person of civil rights without a trial.

[6]A law that punishes a person for a past action that was not unlawful at the time it was committed.

[7]Modified by Amendment XVI.

[7] No money shall be drawn from the treasury, but in consequence of appropriations made by law; and a regular statement and account of the receipts and expenditures of all public money shall be published from time to time.

[8] No title of nobility shall be granted by the United States; and no person holding any office of profit or trust under them shall, without the consent of the Congress, accept of any present, emolument, office, or title, of any kind whatever, from any king, prince, or foreign state.

Section 10. Powers Denied to the States

[1] No state shall enter into any treaty, alliance, or confederation; grant letters of marque and reprisal; coin money; emit bills of credit;[1] make anything but gold and silver coin a tender [legal money] in payment of debts; pass any bill of attainder, ex post facto law, or law impairing the obligation of contracts,[2] or grant any title of nobility.

[2] No state shall, without the consent of the Congress, lay any imposts or duties on imports or exports, except what may be absolutely necessary for executing its inspection laws; and the net produce [income] of all duties and imposts, laid by any state on imports or exports, shall be for the use of the treasury of the United States; and all such laws shall be subject to the revision and control of the Congress.

[3] No state shall, without the consent of Congress, lay any duty of tonnage,[3] keep troops[4] or ships of war in time of peace, enter into any agreement or compact with another state or with a foreign power, or engage in war unless actually invaded or in such imminent [threatening] danger as will not admit of delay.

ARTICLE II. Executive Department

Section 1. President and Vice President

[1] The executive power shall be vested in a president of the United States of America. He shall hold his office during the term of four years,[5] and, together with the vice president, chosen for the same term, be elected as follows:

[2] Each state shall appoint, in such manner as the legislature thereof may direct, a number of electors, equal to the whole number of senators

---

[1]"Emit bills of credit" means *issue paper money.*

[2]"Impairing the obligation of contracts" means *weakening the obligations persons assume when they enter into legal agreements.*

[3]"Duty of tonnage" means a *tax based upon a vessel's cargo-carrying capacity.*

[4]Other than militia.

[5]Amendment XXII limits a president to two terms.

and representatives to which the state may be entitled in the Congress; but no senator or representative, or person holding an office of trust or profit under the United States, shall be appointed an elector.

[3] *The electors shall meet in their respective states, and vote by ballot for two persons, of whom one at least shall not be an inhabitant of the same state with themselves. And they shall make a list of all the persons voted for, and of the number of votes for each; which list they shall sign and certify, and transmit sealed to the seat of the government of the United States, directed to the president of the Senate. The president of the Senate shall, in the presence of the Senate and House of Representatives, open all the certificates, and the votes shall then be counted. The person having the greatest number of votes shall be the president, if such number be a majority of the whole number of electors appointed; and if there be more than one who have such majority, and have an equal number of votes, then the House of Representatives shall immediately choose by ballot one of them for president; and if no person have a majority, then from the five highest on the list the said House shall in like manner choose the president. But in choosing the president, the votes shall be taken by states, the representation from each state having one vote; a quorum for this purpose shall consist of a member or members from two-thirds of the states, and a majority of all the states shall be necessary to a choice. In every case, after the choice of the president, the person having the greatest number of votes of the electors shall be the vice president. But if there should remain two or more who have equal votes, the Senate shall choose from them by ballot the vice president.*[1]

[4] The Congress may determine the time of choosing the electors, and the day on which they shall give their votes; which day shall be the same throughout the United States.

[5] No person except a natural-born citizen, *or a citizen of the United States at the time of the adoption of this Constitution,*[2] shall be eligible to the office of president; neither shall any person be eligible to that office who shall not have attained to the age of thirty-five years and been fourteen years a resident within the United States.

[6] In case of the removal of the president from office, or of his death, resignation, or inability to discharge the powers and duties of the said office, the same shall devolve on the vice president, and the Congress may by law provide for the case of removal, death, resignation, or inability, both of the president and vice president, declaring what officer shall then act as president, and such officer shall act accordingly, until the disability be removed, or a president shall be elected.[3]

---

[1] Replaced by Amendment XII.

[2] Temporary provision.

[3] Modified by Amendments XX and XXV.

[7] The president shall, at stated times, receive for his services a compensation, which shall neither be increased nor diminished [decreased] during the period for which he shall have been elected, and he shall not receive within that period any other emolument from the United States, or any of them.

[8] Before he enter on the execution of his office, he shall take the following oath or affirmation:

"I do solemnly swear (or affirm) that I will faithfully execute the office of President of the United States, and will, to the best of my ability, preserve, protect, and defend the Constitution of the United States."

Section 2. Powers of the President

[1] The president shall be commander in chief of the army and navy [all the armed forces] of the United States, and of the militia of the several states, when called into the actual service of the United States; he may require the opinion in writing of the principal officer in each of the executive departments upon any subject relating to the duties of their respective offices; and he shall have power to grant reprieves[1] and pardons[2] for offenses against the United States except in cases of impeachment.

[2] He shall have power, by and with the advice and consent of the Senate, to make treaties, provided two-thirds of the senators present concur; and he shall nominate, and, by and with the advice and consent of the Senate, shall appoint ambassadors, other public ministers and consuls, judges of the Supreme Court, and all other officers of the United States whose appointments are not herein otherwise provided for and which shall be established by law; but the Congress may by law vest the appointment of such inferior officers as they think proper in the president alone, in the courts of law, or in the heads of departments.

[3] The president shall have power to fill up all vacancies that may happen during the recess of the Senate, by granting commissions which shall expire at the end of their next session.

Section 3. Duties and Responsibilities of the President

He shall, from time to time, give to the Congress information of the state of the Union, and recommend to their consideration such measures as he shall judge necessary and expedient [advisable]; he may, on extraordinary [special] occasions, convene both houses, or either of them, and in case of disagreement between them with respect to the time of adjourn-

---

[1]A "reprieve" is a postponement of the execution of a sentence.

[2]A "pardon" is a release from penalty.

ment, he may adjourn them to such time as he shall think proper; he shall receive ambassadors and other public ministers; he shall take care that the laws be faithfully executed, and shall commission [appoint] all the officers of the United States.

Section 4.   Impeachment

The president, vice president, and all civil officers[1] of the United States, shall be removed from office on impeachment for, and conviction of, treason, bribery, or other high crimes and misdemeanors [offenses].

ARTICLE III. Judicial Department

Section 1.   Federal Courts

The judicial power of the United States shall be vested in one Supreme Court, and in such inferior [lower] courts as the Congress may from time to time ordain and establish. The judges, both of the Supreme and inferior courts, shall hold their offices during good behavior, and shall, at stated times, receive for their services a compensation, which shall not be diminished during their continuance in office.

Section 2.   Jurisdiction of Federal Courts

[1] The judicial power shall extend to all cases in law and equity[2] arising under this Constitution, the laws of the United States, and treaties made, or which shall be made, under their authority; to all cases affecting ambassadors, other public ministers, and consuls; to all cases of admiralty and maritime jurisdiction;[3] to controversies [disputes] to which the United States shall be a party; to controversies between two or more states, between a state and citizens of another state,[4] between citizens of different

---

[1]"Civil officers" include executive and judicial officials, but not members of Congress or officers in the armed forces.

[2]"Cases in law" refers mainly to disputes that arise from the violation of, or the interpretation of, federal laws, treaties, or the Constitution. "Equity" is a branch of the law that deals more generally with the prevention of injustice.

[3]Legal disputes involving ships and shipping on the high seas, in territorial waters, and on the navigable waterways within the country.

[4]Modified by Amendment XI, which provides that a state may not be sued in the federal courts by a citizen of another state (or by a citizen of a foreign country). A state, however, retains the right to sue a citizen of another state (or a citizen of a foreign country) in the federal courts.

states, between citizens of the same state claiming lands under grants of different states, and between a state, or the citizens thereof, and foreign states, citizens, or subjects.[1]

[2] In all cases affecting ambassadors, other public ministers, and consuls, and those in which a state shall be a party, the Supreme Court shall have original jurisdiction.[2] In all the other cases before mentioned, the Supreme Court shall have appellate jurisdiction,[3] both as to law and fact, with such exceptions and under such regulations as the Congress shall make.

[3] The trial of all crimes, except in cases of impeachment, shall be by jury; and such trial shall be held in the state where the said crimes shall have been committed; but when not committed within any state, the trial shall be at such place or places as the Congress may by law have directed.

Section 3.   Treason

[1] Treason against the United States shall consist only in levying [carrying on] war against them, or in adhering to [assisting] their enemies, giving them aid and comfort. No person shall be convicted of treason unless on the testimony of two witnesses to the same overt [open; public] act, or on confession in open court.

[2] The Congress shall have power to declare the punishment of treason, but no attainder of treason shall work corruption of blood or forfeiture except during the life of the person attainted.[4]

ARTICLE IV.   Interstate Relations

Section 1.   Official Acts and Records

Full faith and credit shall be given in each state to the public acts, records, and judicial proceedings of every other state.[5] And the Congress

---

[1]Modified by Amendment XI (see footnote 4, page 577).

[2]"Original jurisdiction" means the authority of a court to hear cases that have not previously been tried by lower courts.

[3]"Appellate jurisdiction" means the authority of a court to review cases that have previously been tried by lower courts.

[4]Punishment imposed on someone for treason may not be extended to that person's children or heirs.

[5]The official acts of each state must be accepted by the other states. The "full faith and credit" clause applies to court judgments, contracts, marriages, corporation charters, etc.

may, by general laws, prescribe the manner in which such acts, records, and proceedings shall be proved, and the effect thereof.

Section 2.   Mutual Obligations of States

[1] The citizens of each state shall be entitled to all privileges and immunities of citizens in the several states.

[2] A person charged in any state with treason, felony, or other crime, who shall flee from justice and be found in another state, shall, on demand of the executive authority of the state from which he fled, be delivered up, to be removed to the state having jurisdiction of the crime.[1]

[3] *No person held to service or labor in one state, under the laws thereof, escaping into another, shall, in consequence of any law or regulation therein, be discharged from such service or labor, but shall be delivered up on claim of the party to whom such service or labor may be due.*[2]

Section 3.   New States and Territories

[1] New states may be admitted by the Congress into this Union; but no new state shall be formed or erected within the jurisdiction of any other state; nor any state be formed by the junction [joining] of two or more states, or parts of states, without the consent of the legislatures of the states concerned as well as of the Congress.

[2] The Congress shall have power to dispose of and make all needful rules and regulations respecting the territory or other property belonging to the United States; and nothing in this Constitution shall be so construed [interpreted] as to prejudice [damage] any claims of the United States, or of any particular state.

Section 4.   Federal Guarantees to the States

The United States shall guarantee to every state in this Union a republican form of government, and shall protect each of them against invasion; and on application of the legislature, or of the executive (when the legislature cannot be convened), against domestic violence [riots].

---

[1]The delivery by one state or government to another of fugitives from justice is called *extradition*.

[2]Since the phrase "person held to service or labor" refers to a slave, this clause was nullified by Amendment XIII.

ARTICLE V. Amending the Constitution

The Congress, whenever two-thirds of both houses shall deem [think] it necessary, shall propose amendments to this Constitution, or, on the application of the legislatures of two-thirds of the several states, shall call a convention for proposing amendments, which, in either case, shall be valid, to all intents and purposes, as part of this Constitution when ratified by the legislatures of three-fourths of the several states, or by conventions in three-fourths thereof, as the one or the other mode [method] of ratification may be proposed by the Congress; provided *that no amendment which may be made prior to the year 1808 shall in any manner affect the first and fourth clauses in the ninth section of the first article; and*[1] that no state, without its consent, shall be deprived of its equal suffrage in the Senate.

ARTICLE VI. Public Debts; Federal Supremacy; Oaths of Office

[1] All debts contracted and engagements [agreements] entered into before the adoption of this Constitution shall be as valid [binding] against the United States under this Constitution as under the Confederation.

[2] This Constitution, and the laws of the United States which shall be made in pursuance thereof, and all treaties made, or which shall be made, under the authority of the United States, shall be the supreme law of the land; and the judges in every state shall be bound thereby, anything in the constitution or laws of any state to the contrary notwithstanding.[2]

[3] The senators and representatives before mentioned, and the members of the several state legislatures, and all executive and judicial officers, both of the United States and of the several states, shall be bound by oath or affirmation to support this Constitution; but no religious test shall ever be required as a qualification to any office or public trust under the United States.

ARTICLE VII. Ratification

The ratification of the conventions of nine states shall be sufficient for the establishment of this Constitution between the states so ratifying the same.

---

[1]Temporary provision.

[2]This "supremacy clause" means that federal laws always override state legislation in cases of conflict.

Done in convention, by the unanimous consent of the states present, the 17th day of September, in the year of our Lord 1787, and of the independence of the United States of America the twelfth. In witness whereof we have hereunto subscribed our names.

[Signed by]   **George Washington**
[President and Deputy from Virginia]

[Connecticut]
William Samuel Johnson
Roger Sherman

[Delaware]
George Read
Gunning Bedford, Jr.
John Dickinson
Richard Bassett
Jacob Broom

[Georgia]
William Few
Abraham Baldwin

[Maryland]
James McHenry
Dan of St. Thomas
   Jenifer
Daniel Carroll

[Massachusetts]
Nathaniel Gorham
Rufus King

[New Hampshire]
John Langdon
Nicholas Gilman

[New Jersey]
William Livingston
David Brearley
William Paterson
Jonathan Dayton

[New York]
Alexander Hamilton

[North Carolina]
William Blount
Richard Dobbs Spaight
Hugh Williamson

[Pennsylvania]
Benjamin Franklin
Thomas Mifflin
Robert Morris
George Clymer
Thomas Fitzsimons
Jared Ingersoll
James Wilson
Gouverneur Morris

[South Carolina]
John Rutledge
Charles Cotesworth
   Pinckney
Charles Pinckney
Pierce Butler

[Virginia]
John Blair
James Madison, Jr.

AMENDMENTS TO THE CONSTITUTION

[*Note:* The first ten amendments to the Constitution make up the Bill of Rights. The date in parentheses after each amendment is the year in which it was adopted.]

AMENDMENT I. Freedom of Religion, Speech, Press, Assembly, and Petition (1791)

Congress shall make no law respecting an establishment of religion, or prohibiting the free exercise thereof;[1] or abridging [reducing] the freedom of speech or of the press; or the right of the people peaceably to assemble, and to petition the government for a redress [correction] of grievances.

AMENDMENT II. Right to Bear Arms (1791)

A well-regulated militia being necessary to the security of a free state, the right of the people to keep and bear arms shall not be infringed [weakened].

AMENDMENT III. Quartering of Troops (1791)

No soldier shall, in time of peace, be quartered [assigned to live] in any house without the consent of the owner, nor in time of war, but in a manner to be prescribed by law.

---

[1]"The free exercise thereof" refers to freedom of worship.

AMENDMENT IV. Searches and Seizures (1791)

The right of the people to be secure [safe] in their persons, houses, papers, and effects [belongings] against unreasonable searches and seizures shall not be violated; and no [search] warrants shall issue but upon probable cause,[1] supported by oath or affirmation, and particularly describing the place to be searched, and the persons or things to be seized.

AMENDMENT V. Rights of the Accused; Property Rights (1791)

No person shall be held to answer for a capital or otherwise infamous crime unless on a presentment or indictment of a grand jury,[2] except in cases arising in the land or naval forces, or in the militia, when in actual service in time of war or public danger; nor shall any person be subject for the same offense to be twice put in jeopardy of life or limb;[3] nor shall be compelled in any criminal case to be a witness against himself; nor be deprived of life, liberty, or property without due process of law;[4] nor shall private property be taken for public use without just compensation.[5]

AMENDMENT VI. Additional Rights of the Accused (1791)

In all criminal prosecutions [trials], the accused shall enjoy the right to a speedy and public trial by an impartial [fair] jury of the state and district wherein the crime shall have been committed, which district shall have been previously ascertained by law; and to be informed of the nature and cause of the accusation; to be confronted with the witnesses against him; to have compulsory process for obtaining witnesses in his favor;[6] and to have the assistance of counsel for his defense.

---

[1] "Probable cause" means *a reasonable ground of suspicion.*

[2] "A capital or otherwise infamous crime" refers to serious offenses punishable by death or by imprisonment. Before someone may be tried for such a crime, a grand jury must decide that sufficient evidence exists to bring that person to trial.

[3] A person may not be tried twice for the same offense (double jeopardy).

[4] "Due process of law" means *proper legal procedure.*

[5] The government has the power of *eminent domain,* or the right to take private property for public use. This provision requires the government to pay the owner a fair price for such property.

[6] The accused person has the right to request the court to issue an order, or subpoena, compelling a witness to appear in court.

AMENDMENT VII. Civil Suits (1791)

In suits at common law[1] where the value in controversy shall exceed twenty dollars, the right of trial by jury shall be preserved, and no fact tried by a jury shall be otherwise re-examined in any court of the United States, than according to the rules of the common law.

AMENDMENT VIII. Bails, Fines, and Punishments (1791)

Excessive bail shall not be required, nor excessive fines imposed, nor cruel and unusual punishments inflicted.

AMENDMENT IX. Rights Not Listed (1791)

The enumeration [listing] in the Constitution of certain rights shall not be construed to deny or disparage [weaken] others retained by the people.

AMENDMENT X. Powers Reserved to the States and People (1791)

The powers not delegated to the United States by the Constitution, nor prohibited by it to the states, are reserved to the states respectively, or to the people.

AMENDMENT XI. Suits Against States (1798)

The judicial power of the United States shall not be construed to extend to any suit in law or equity, commenced or prosecuted against one of the United States by citizens of another state, or by citizens or subjects of any foreign state.

AMENDMENT XII. Election of President and Vice President (1804)

[1] The electors shall meet in their respective states, and vote by ballot for president and vice president, one of whom at least shall not be an

---

[1]"Common law" is law based on custom and precedent (past decisions made in similar cases). Originating in England, it was brought to the English colonies by the early settlers and became the foundation of the American legal system.

inhabitant of the same state with themselves; they shall name in their ballots the person voted for as president, and in distinct [separate] ballots the person voted for as vice president; and they shall make distinct lists of all persons voted for as president, and of all persons voted for as vice president, and of the number of votes for each, which lists they shall sign and certify, and transmit sealed to the seat of the government of the United States, directed to the president of the Senate.

[2] The president of the Senate shall, in the presence of the Senate and House of Representatives, open all the certificates, and the votes shall then be counted; the person having the greatest number of votes for president shall be the president, if such number be a majority of the whole number of electors appointed; and if no person have such majority, then from the persons having the highest numbers not exceeding three on the list of those voted for as president, the House of Representatives shall choose immediately, by ballot, the president. But in choosing the president, the votes shall be taken by states, the representation from each state having one vote; a quorum for this purpose shall consist of a member or members from two-thirds of the states, and a majority of all the states shall be necessary to a choice. And if the House of Representatives shall not choose a president whenever the right of choice shall devolve upon them, *before the fourth day of March next following*,[1] then the vice president shall act as president, as in the case of the death or other constitutional disability of the president.

[3] The person having the greatest number of votes as vice president shall be the vice president, if such number be a majority of the whole number of electors appointed; and if no person have a majority, then, from the two highest numbers on the list, the Senate shall choose the vice president; a quorum for the purpose shall consist of two-thirds of the whole number of senators, and a majority of the whole number shall be necessary to a choice. But no person constitutionally ineligible to the office of president shall be eligible to that of vice president of the United States.

AMENDMENT XIII.   Abolition of Slavery (1865)

Section 1. Slavery Forbidden

Neither slavery nor involuntary servitude [compulsory service], except as a punishment for crime whereof the party shall have been duly convicted, shall exist within the United States, or any place subject to their jurisdiction.

---

[1]Changed to January 20 by Amendment XX.

Section 2. Enforcement Power

Congress shall have power to enforce this article [amendment] by appropriate [suitable] legislation.

AMENDMENT XIV. Citizenship and Civil Rights (1868)

Section 1. Rights of Citizens

All persons born or naturalized in the United States, and subject to the jurisdiction thereof, are citizens of the United States and of the state wherein they reside.[1] No state shall make or enforce any law which shall abridge the privileges or immunities of citizens of the United States; nor shall any state deprive any person of life, liberty, or property, without due process of law;[2] nor deny to any person within its jurisdiction the equal protection of the laws.[3]

Section 2. Apportionment of Representatives in Congress

Representatives shall be apportioned among the several states according to their respective numbers, counting the whole number of persons in each state, excluding Indians not taxed.[4] But when the right to vote at any election for the choice of electors for president and vice president of the United States, representatives in Congress, the executive and judicial officers of a state, or the members of the legislature thereof, is denied to any of the *male* inhabitants of such state, being *twenty-one* years of age and citizens of the United States, or in any way abridged, except for participation in rebellion or other crime, the basis of representation therein shall be reduced in the proportion which the number of such *male* citizens shall bear to the whole number of *male* citizens *twenty-one* years of age in such state.[5]

---

[1]This clause made the former slaves citizens.

[2]The primary purpose of this clause was to protect the civil rights of the former slaves. However, after the Supreme Court broadened the meaning of the word "person" to include "corporation," the clause began to be used to protect business interests as well.

[3]The "equal protection" clause has served as the legal basis for many civil rights cases.

[4]This clause nullifies the three-fifths formula of Article I, Section 2.

[5]Italicized words in this section were invalidated by Amendments XIX and XXVI.

Section 3.   Persons Disqualified From Public Office

No person shall be a senator or representative in Congress, or elector of president and vice president, or hold any office, civil or military, under the United States, or under any state, who, having previously taken an oath, as a member of Congress, or as an officer of the United States, or as a member of any state legislature, or as an executive or judicial officer of any state, to support the Constitution of the United States, shall have engaged in insurrection or rebellion against the same, or given aid or comfort to the enemies thereof. But Congress may, by a vote of two-thirds of each house, remove such disability.

Section 4.   Valid Public Debt Defined

The validity [legality] of the public debt of the United States, authorized by law, including debts incurred for payment of pensions and bounties [extra allowances] for services in suppressing insurrection or rebellion, shall not be questioned. But neither the United States nor any state shall assume or pay any debt or obligation incurred in aid of insurrection or rebellion against the United States, or any claim for the loss or emancipation [liberation] of any slave; but all such debts, obligations, and claims shall be held illegal and void.

Section 5.   Enforcement Power

The Congress shall have power to enforce, by appropriate legislation, the provisions of this article.

AMENDMENT XV.   Right of Suffrage (1870)

Section 1.   Blacks Guaranteed the Vote

The right of citizens of the United States to vote shall not be denied or abridged by the United States or by any state on account of race, color, or previous condition of servitude [slavery].

Section 2.   Enforcement Power

The Congress shall have power to enforce this article by appropriate legislation.

AMENDMENT XVI.   Income Taxes (1913)

The Congress shall have power to lay and collect taxes on incomes, from whatever source derived, without apportionment among the several states, and without regard to any census or enumeration.

AMENDMENT XVII.   Popular Election of Senators (1913)

[1] The Senate of the United States shall be composed of two senators from each state, elected by the people thereof, for six years; and each senator shall have one vote. The electors [voters] in each state shall have the qualifications requisite for electors of the most numerous branch of the state legislatures.[1]

[2] When vacancies happen in the representation of any state in the Senate, the executive authority of such state shall issue writs of election to fill such vacancies: Provided, that the legislature of any state may empower [authorize] the executive thereof to make temporary appointments until the people fill the vacancies by election as the legislature may direct.

[3] *This amendment shall not be so construed as to affect the election or term of any senator chosen before it becomes valid as part of the Constitution.*[2]

AMENDMENT XVIII.   Prohibition (1919)[3]

Section 1.   Intoxicating Liquors Prohibited

After one year from the ratification of this article, the manufacture, sale, or transportation of intoxicating liquors within, the importation thereof into, or the exportation thereof from the United States and all territory subject to the jurisdiction thereof, for beverage purposes, is hereby prohibited.

---

[1]This amendment changed the method of electing senators as given in Article I, Section 3.

[2]Temporary provision designed to protect those elected under the system previously in effect.

[3]This entire amendment was repealed in 1933 by Amendent XXI.

Section 2.   Enforcement Power

The Congress and the several states shall have concurrent power to enforce this article by appropriate legislation.

Section 3.   Conditions of Ratification

This article shall be inoperative unless it shall have been ratified as an amendment to the Constitution by the legislatures of the several states, as provided in the Constitution, within seven years from the date of the submission hereof to the states by the Congress.

AMENDMENT XIX.   Women's Suffrage (1920)

[1] The right of citizens of the United States to vote shall not be denied or abridged by the United States or by any state on account of sex.

[2] Congress shall have power to enforce this article by appropriate legislation.

AMENDMENT XX.   Presidential and Congressional Terms[1] (1933)

Section 1.   Terms of Office

The terms of the president and vice president shall end at noon on the 20th day of January, and the terms of senators and representatives at noon on the 3d day of January, of the years in which such terms would have ended if this article had not been ratified; and the terms of their successors[2] shall then begin.

Section 2.   Convening Congress

The Congress shall assemble at least once in every year, and such meeting shall begin at noon on the 3d day of January, unless they shall by law appoint a different day.[3]

---

[1]This amendment is often called the "Lame Duck" Amendment because it shortened the period (from four months to two) between the elections in November and the time when defeated officeholders or officeholders who do not run again (known as "lame ducks") leave office.

[2]A "successor" is a person who is elected or appointed to replace another in a public office.

[3]This section changed the date given in Article I, Section 4.

Section 3.   Presidential Succession

If, at the time fixed for the beginning of the term of the president, the president-elect[1] shall have died, the vice president-elect shall become president. If a president shall not have been chosen before the time fixed for the beginning of his term, or if the president-elect shall have failed to qualify, then the vice president-elect shall act as president until a president shall have qualified; and the Congress may by law provide for the case wherein neither a president-elect nor a vice president-elect shall have qualified, declaring who shall then act as president, or the manner in which one who is to act shall be selected, and such person shall act accordingly until a president or vice president shall have qualified.

Section 4.   Selection of President and Vice President

The Congress may by law provide for the case of the death of any of the persons from whom the House of Representatives may choose a president whenever the right of choice shall have devolved upon them, and for the case of the death of any of the persons from whom the Senate may choose a vice president whenever the right of choice shall have devolved upon them.

Section 5.   Effective Date

Sections 1 and 2 shall take effect on the 15th day of October following the ratification of this article.[2]

Section 6.   Conditions of Ratification

This article shall be inoperative unless it shall have been ratified as an amendment to the Constitution by the legislatures of three-fourths of the several states within seven years from the date of its submission.[3]

AMENDMENT XXI.   Repeal of Prohibition (1933)

Section 1.   Amendment XVIII Repealed

The Eighteenth Article of amendment to the Constitution of the United States is hereby repealed.

---

[1] A "president-elect" is a person who has been elected to the presidency but has not yet assumed office.

[2] Temporary provision.

[3] Temporary provision.

Section 2. Shipment of Liquor Into "Dry" Areas

The transportation or importation into any state, territory, or possession of the United States for delivery or use therein of intoxicating liquors in violation of the laws thereof is hereby prohibited.[1]

Section 3. Conditions of Ratification

This article shall be inoperative unless it shall have been ratified as an amendment to the Constitution by conventions in the several states,[2] as provided in the Constitution, within seven years from the date of the submission hereof to the states by the Congress.[3]

AMENDMENT XXII. Limiting Presidential Terms (1951)

Section 1. Limit Placed on Tenure

No person shall be elected to the office of the president more than twice, and no person who has held the office of president, or acted as president, for more than two years of a term to which some other person was elected president shall be elected to the office of the president more than once. *But this article shall not apply to any person holding the office of president when this article was proposed by the Congress, and shall not prevent any person who may be holding the office of president, or acting as president, during the term within which this article becomes operative from holding the office of president or acting as president during the remainder of such term.[4]*

Section 2. Conditions of Ratification

This article shall be inoperative unless it shall have been ratified as an amendment to the Constitution by the legislatures of three-fourths of the several states within seven years from the date of its submission to the states by the Congress.[5]

---

[1]This section allowed individual states to prohibit the use of intoxicating liquors if they wished to.

[2]This was the first amendment to be submitted by Congress for ratification by state conventions rather than state legislatures.

[3]Temporary provision.

[4]Temporary provision.

[5]Temporary provision.

AMENDMENT XXIII.   Suffrage for Washington, D.C. (1961)

Section 1.   D.C. Presidential Electors

The district constituting [making up] the seat of government of the United States shall appoint in such manner as the Congress may direct:

A number of electors of president and vice president equal to the whole number of senators and representatives in Congress to which the district would be entitled if it were a state, but in no event more than the least populous state;[1] they shall be in addition to those appointed by the states, but they shall be considered, for the purposes of the election of president and vice president, to be electors appointed by a state; and they shall meet in the district and perform such duties as provided by the Twelfth Article of amendent.[2]

Section 2.   Enforcement Power

The Congress shall have power to enforce this article by appropriate legislation.

AMENDMENT XXIV.   Poll Taxes (1964)

Section 1.   Poll Tax Barred

The right of citizens of the United States to vote in any primary or other election for president or vice president, for electors for president or vice president, or for senator or representative in Congress, shall not be denied or abridged by the United States or any state by reason of failure to pay any poll tax or other tax.

Section 2.   Enforcement Power

The Congress shall have the power to enforce this article by appropriate legislation.

---

[1]At the present time, the District of Columbia is entitled to three electors.

[2]By providing for electors, this amendment gave residents of Washington, D.C., the right to vote for president and vice president.

AMENDMENT XXV. Presidential Succession and Disability (1967)

Section 1. Elevation of Vice President

In case of the removal of the president from office or his death or resignation, the vice president shall become president.

Section 2. Vice Presidential Vacancy

Whenever there is a vacancy in the office of the vice president, the president shall nominate a vice president who shall take the office upon confirmation by a majority vote of both houses of Congress.

Section 3. Temporary Disability

Whenever the president transmits to the president pro tempore of the Senate and the Speaker of the House of Representatives his written declaration that he is unable to discharge the powers and duties of his office, and until he transmits to them a written declaration to the contrary, such powers and duties shall be discharged by the vice president as acting president.

Section 4. Other Provisions for Presidential Disability

[1] Whenever the vice president and a majority of either the principal officers of the executive departments, or of such other body as Congress may by law provide, transmit to the president pro tempore of the Senate and the Speaker of the House of Representatives their written declaration that the president is unable to discharge the powers and duties of his office, the vice president shall immediately assume the powers and duties of the office as acting president.

[2] Thereafter, when the president transmits to the president pro tempore of the Senate and the Speaker of the House of Representatives his written declaration that no inability exists, he shall resume the powers and duties of his office unless the vice president and a majority of either the principal officers of the executive department, or of such other body as Congress may by law provide, transmit within four days to the president pro tempore of the Senate and the Speaker of the House of Representatives their written declaration that the president is unable to discharge the powers and duties of his office. Thereupon Congress shall decide the issue, assembling within 48 hours for that purpose if not in session. If the Congress, within 21 days after receipt of the latter written declaration, or, if

Congress is not in session, within 21 days after Congress is required to assemble, determines by two-thirds vote of both houses that the president is unable to discharge the powers and duties of his office, the vice president shall continue to discharge the same as acting president; otherwise, the president shall resume the powers and duties of his office.

AMENDMENT XXVI.   The Vote for 18-Year-Olds (1971)

Section 1.   Lowering the Voting Age

The right of citizens of the United States, who are 18 years of age or older, to vote shall not be denied or abridged by the United States or by any state on account of age.

Section 2.   Enforcement Power

The Congress shall have power to enforce this article by appropriate legislation.

AMENDMENT XXVII.   Congressional Pay Raises (1992)

No law varying the compensation for the services of the Senators and Representatives shall take effect until an election of Representatives shall have intervened.[1]

---

[1]This amendment bars Congress from voting itself immediate pay raises. It was first proposed by James Madison in 1789, and the ratification process took more than 200 years. The amendment became part of the Constitution only after the 38th state (Michigan) ratified it in 1992. Most amendments are ratified more quickly. In recent years, Congress has set a seven-year time limit for ratification of newly proposed amendments. Thus, if the necessary three-fourths (38) of the states have not ratified the amendment in that period, it becomes invalid.

PRESIDENTS AND VICE PRESIDENTS OF THE UNITED STATES

No.	President	Years in Office	Political Party	State (when elected)	Vice President	State (when elected)
1	George Washington (b. 1732–d. 1799)	1789–1797	None	Virginia	John Adams	Massachusetts
2	John Adams (b. 1735–d. 1826)	1797–1801	Federalist	Massachusetts	Thomas Jefferson	Virginia
3	Thomas Jefferson (b. 1743–d. 1826)	1801–1809	Democratic-Republican	Virginia	Aaron Burr George Clinton	New York New York
4	James Madison (b. 1751–d. 1836)	1809–1817	Democratic-Republican	Virginia	George Clinton Elbridge Gerry	New York Massachusetts
5	James Monroe (b. 1758–d. 1831)	1817–1825	Democratic-Republican	Virginia	Daniel D. Tompkins	New York
6	John Quincy Adams (b. 1767–d. 1848)	1825–1829	National Republican	Massachusetts	John C. Calhoun	South Carolina
7	Andrew Jackson (b. 1767–d. 1845)	1829–1837	Democratic	Tennessee	John C. Calhoun Martin Van Buren	South Carolina New York
8	Martin Van Buren (b. 1782–d. 1862)	1837–1841	Democratic	New York	Richard M. Johnson	Kentucky
9	William H. Harrison (b. 1773–d. 1841)	1841 (died in office)	Whig	Ohio	John Tyler	Virginia
10	John Tyler (b. 1790–d. 1862)	1841–1845	Whig	Virginia	(vacant)	
11	James K. Polk (b. 1795–d. 1849)	1845–1849	Democratic	Tennessee	George M. Dallas	Pennsylvania

PRESIDENTS AND VICE PRESIDENTS OF THE UNITED STATES (cont.)

No.	President	Years in Office	Political Party	State (when elected)	Vice President	State (when elected)
12	Zachary Taylor (b. 1784–d. 1850)	1849–1850 (died in office)	Whig	Louisiana	Millard Fillmore	New York
13	Millard Fillmore (b. 1800–d. 1874)	1850–1853	Whig	New York	(vacant)	
14	Franklin Pierce (b. 1804–d. 1869)	1853–1857	Democratic	New Hampshire	William R. King	Alabama
15	James Buchanan (b. 1791–d. 1868)	1857–1861	Democratic	Pennsylvania	John C. Breckinridge	Kentucky
16	Abraham Lincoln (b. 1809–d. 1865)	1861–1865 (died in office)	Republican	Illinois	Hannibal Hamlin Andrew Johnson	Maine Tennessee
17	Andrew Johnson (b. 1808–d. 1875)	1865–1869	Republican	Tennessee	(vacant)	
18	Ulysses S. Grant (b. 1822–d. 1885)	1869–1877	Republican	Illinois	Schuyler Colfax Henry Wilson	Indiana Massachusetts
19	Rutherford B. Hayes (b. 1822–d. 1893)	1877–1881	Republican	Ohio	William A. Wheeler	New York
20	James A. Garfield (b. 1831–d. 1881)	1881 (died in office)	Republican	Ohio	Chester A. Arthur	New York
21	Chester A. Arthur (b. 1829–d. 1886)	1881–1885	Republican	New York	(vacant)	
22	Grover Cleveland (b. 1837–d. 1908)	1885–1889	Democratic	New York	Thomas A. Hendricks	Indiana

No.	President	Term	Party	State	Vice President	State
23	Benjamin Harrison (b. 1833–d. 1901)	1889–1893	Republican	Indiana	Levi P. Morton	New York
24	Grover Cleveland (b. 1837–d. 1908)	1893–1897	Democratic	New York	Adlai E. Stevenson	Illinois
25	William McKinley (b. 1843–d. 1901)	1897–1901 (died in office)	Republican	Ohio	Garret A. Hobart Theodore Roosevelt	New Jersey New York
26	Theodore Roosevelt (b. 1858–d. 1919)	1901–1909	Republican	New York	(vacant 1901–1905) Charles W. Fairbanks	Indiana
27	William H. Taft (b. 1857–d. 1930)	1909–1913	Republican	Ohio	James S. Sherman	New York
28	Woodrow Wilson (b. 1856–d. 1924)	1913–1921	Democratic	New Jersey	Thomas R. Marshall	Indiana
29	Warren G. Harding (b. 1865–d. 1923)	1921–1923 (died in office)	Republican	Ohio	Calvin Coolidge	Massachusetts
30	Calvin Coolidge (b. 1872–d. 1933)	1923–1929	Republican	Massachusetts	(vacant 1923–1925) Charles G. Dawes	Illinois
31	Herbert C. Hoover (b. 1874–d. 1964)	1929–1933	Republican	California	Charles Curtis	Kansas
32	Franklin D. Roosevelt (b. 1882–d. 1945)	1933–1945 (died in office)	Democratic	New York	John N. Garner Henry A. Wallace Harry S. Truman	Texas Iowa Missouri
33	Harry S. Truman (b. 1884–d. 1972)	1945–1953	Democratic	Missouri	(vacant 1945–1949) Alben W. Barkley	Kentucky
34	Dwight D. Eisenhower (b. 1890–d. 1969)	1953–1961	Republican	New York	Richard M. Nixon	California

PRESIDENTS AND VICE PRESIDENTS OF THE UNITED STATES (cont.)

No.	President	Years in Office	Political Party	State (when elected)	Vice President	State (when elected)
35	John F. Kennedy (b. 1917–d. 1963)	1961–1963 (died in office)	Democratic	Massachusetts	Lyndon B. Johnson	Texas
36	Lyndon B. Johnson (b. 1908–d. 1973)	1963–1969	Democratic	Texas	(vacant 1963–1965) Hubert H. Humphrey	Minnesota
37	Richard M. Nixon (b. 1913–d. 1994)	1969–1974 (resigned)	Republican	New York	Spiro T. Agnew Gerald R. Ford	Maryland Michigan
38	Gerald R. Ford (b. 1913–)	1974–1977	Republican	Michigan	Nelson A. Rockefeller	New York
39	Jimmy Carter (b. 1924–)	1977–1981	Democratic	Georgia	Walter F. Mondale	Minnesota
40	Ronald W. Reagan (b. 1911–)	1981–1989	Republican	California	George H. W. Bush	Texas
41	George H. W. Bush (b. 1924–)	1989–1993	Republican	Texas	J. Danforth "Dan" Quayle	Indiana
42	William Jefferson Blythe Clinton (b. 1946–)	1993–2001	Democratic	Arkansas	Albert Arnold Gore, Jr.	Tennessee
43	George W. Bush (b. 1946–)	2001–	Republican	Texas	Richard Cheney	Wyoming

GLOSSARY

abolition   before Civil War, reformers' goal of ending slavery

affirmative action   active recruitment, in jobs and education, of people formerly discriminated against (women and members of minority groups)

alien   one who is not a citizen of country in which he or she resides

amendment   change in bill, law, or constitution

Americanization   teaching of American culture to immigrants

anarchism   belief in abolition of all government

anti-Semitism   hostility to Jews and discrimination against them

appeal   taking of case of law to higher court for rehearing

appeasement   policy of making concessions to aggressors in order to maintain peace

appellate jurisdiction   authority of court to review decisions of lower court

armistice   temporary halt to fighting by agreement between opposing sides

assembly line   arrangement of workers, machines, and equipment in which product being manufactured passes along moving belt from one operation to the next until it is completed

assumption   accepting (assuming) responsibility for someone else's debts or other obligations

automation   automatic control of manufacturing processes by mechanical or electronic devices (such as computers) that replace human effort and decision making

bank run   rush of depositors to withdraw money from bank

bill   written proposal for new law

bill of attainder   law that deprives person of civil rights without trial

bipartisan   supported by two political parties; in U.S., having both Democratic and Republican backing

blockade   to cut off access to or from port, coastline, or any vital area, by means of naval patrol or other armed force

block grant   federal financial aid to states, given with few guidelines on use

"blue laws"   laws forbidding certain practices regarded as sinful, especially violations of the Sabbath

boss   in politics, party head who controls political machine

boycott   to refrain from buying or selling in order to force change in policy

buffer state   neutral territory between rival powers

bureaucracy   large, complex governmental organization staffed chiefly by non-elective personnel

cabinet   in U.S., presidential advisory group composed of heads of executive departments

capital   money used for investment purposes

capitalism   economic system based on private ownership of resources and means of production, and free competition among producers; also known as free enterprise

cash crop   crop grown for sale rather than for farmer's private use

caucus   political meeting to select candidates for nomination or to decide on policy

cease-fire   temporary suspension of hostilities

censure   in U.S. Congress, official reprimand of member

census   official count of population; in U.S., taken every ten years

checks and balances   system of limiting power of each branch of government through controls exercised by other branches

circumnavigate   to go completely around

city-manager plan   form of city government in which voter-elected commissioners hire professional manager

civil disobedience   *see* nonviolent civil disobedience

civil rights (civil liberties)   guarantees against abuse of government power; also, protection against such discriminatory acts as limiting equal access to public facilities

civil service   system of hiring governmental employees by means of competitive examinations; also known as merit system

closed shop   workplace that hires only union members

coalition   alliance, often temporary, of people or groups with different views

collective bargaining   negotiations between labor and management

combination   alliance of businesses to increase their assets and power

commission plan   form of city government in which voters elect heads of various city departments; acting together, department heads also serve as city's legislature

common law   law based on court decisions rather than legislative code; basis of legal system in England and most English-speaking nations

communism   system in which government controls all economic activity; Communist groups frequently resort to revolution as means of gaining control

concurrent powers   under U.S. Constitution, powers shared by national and state governments

conglomerate   combination of two or more businesses in unrelated fields

congressional immunity   exemption of members of Congress from various legal penalties (such as arrest) while on legislative business

conscription   *see* draft

conservation   protection of natural resources, especially against commercial exploitation

containment   policy of restricting Soviet influence and territorial expansion

convention   *see* national nominating convention

convoy system   use of warship escort to protect merchant ships against attack

cooperative (co-op)   business owned and operated by those who buy its goods and services

corporation   business organization owned by investors who purchase shares of stock in the enterprise

craft union   labor union with membership limited to skilled workers practicing the same craft

cultural pluralism   belief that various ethnic groups should preserve their distinctive customs and values

culture   way of life of given group of people; includes both objects (material culture) and values and beliefs (nonmaterial culture)

culture area   geographic region inhabited by peoples with similar way of life

"dark horse"   in U.S. politics, relatively unknown candidate for office

de facto **segregation**   separation of races that actually exists, though not by law

deficit spending   expending more than one receives as income; when practiced by government, resulting deficits are covered by borrowing money from public through sale of bonds

deflation   constantly falling prices

de jure **segregation**   separation of races authorized or required by law

delegated powers   powers given to federal government by U.S. Constitution

demilitarized zone   area kept free from all military forces

depression   period of slow business activity and high unemployment

desegregation   removal of barriers that cause separation of races, as in education or housing

détente   relaxation of tensions, especially between United States and Soviet Union

dictatorship   government in which all power is concentrated in single individual or small group

direct democracy   form of government in which people rule themselves directly rather than being governed by elected representatives

direct primary   election in which voters select party candidates to run in general election

discrimination   practice of treating minority group less favorably than the majority

disfranchise   to deprive of the right to vote

dividend   part of corporation profits paid to shareholder

domesticate   to cultivate plants and tame animals for human use and benefit

double jeopardy   trial for same offense twice

draft (conscription)   compulsory enrollment for military service

dry farming   type of agriculture using special methods of plowing and planting to conserve moisture in soil

duty   tax on imports

"elastic clause"   Article I, Section 8, Clause 18 of U.S. Constitution; gives Congress authority to pass laws in addition to those specified in preceding clauses

emancipate   to free from bondage, slavery, or oppression

embargo   official prohibition of trade

eminent domain   right of government to take private property for public use (Fifth Amendment requires government to pay owner a fair price for such property)

entitlement   government benefit

established church (established religion)   official church (or religion) of state or nation, recognized by law; religious institution supported by public taxes

ethnic group   people who share distinct cultural heritage

excise tax   tax levied on manufacture, sale, or use of certain products within a country

ex post facto law   law that punishes person for action that was not unlawful when committed

extradition   delivery of fugitive from one authority (such as state or country) to another for purposes of trial or punishment

fascism   political system that glorifies all-powerful state at expense of individual

federalism   system whereby power is shared by central (national) government and regional (state) governments

felony   major criminal offense, such as burglary, arson, kidnapping, or murder

feminism   movement aimed at achieving equality for women

filibuster   in U.S. Senate, attempt to prevent passage of bill by talking indefinitely

foreclosure   seizure of property when owner fails to make mortage payments

franchise   right to vote

franking privilege   right of free postage granted to members of Congress for official mailings

free enterprise   *see* capitalism

free silver   demand that unlimited amounts of silver be purchased by government for coinage

frontier   edge of settled area, bordering wilderness

funding   paying off debts in full

genocide   mass killing of national, racial, or religious group

gold standard   use of gold as only backing for paper money

graduated income tax   income tax that takes proportionately more from higher incomes

"grandfather clause"   means by which several Southern states disfranchised most blacks; by terms of clause, anyone could vote without restriction whose ancestors (grandfathers or fathers) had been qualified to vote in 1867 (before blacks acquired citizenship and voting rights)

Gross Domestic Product (GDP)   as of 1991, total annual value of U.S. goods and services

Gross National Product (GNP)   total value of goods and services produced by a country annually

guerrilla warfare   surprise attacks carried out by small bands of raiders

habeas corpus   legal document by which arrested person can find out reasons for imprisonment

holding company   business combination in which central organization controls several member companies through stock ownership

home rule   local government free from outside control

humanitarian   person dedicated to improving human welfare and promoting social reform

immigration   population movement into a country for purposes of settlement

impeach   to bring charges of wrongdoing against government official

imperialism   policy of expanding nation's power by acquiring foreign territories or assuming political or economic control over them

impressment   practice of forcing people into service, especially seamen of one country into navy of another

indemnity   fine paid as compensation for loss or damage

indentured servant   person who agreed (through document called indenture) to work for certain number of years in exchange for passage to America

industrial union   union made up of all workers, skilled and unskilled, in given industry, such as steel manufacture

industrialization   change from manufacture by hand to large-scale machine production in factories

inflation   constantly rising prices

initiative   procedure by which voters ask legislature to consider proposed law

injunction   court order directing that an action be carried out or stopped

installment buying   buying of goods and services without making full payment at time of purchase but promising to make partial payments periodically

integration   process of bringing together groups that had been kept apart

interchangeable parts   separate elements of manufactured product that are made exactly alike to facilitate assembly and repair

internal improvements   transportation facilities such as roads and canals, especially those financed by government

interstate commerce   commerce involving two or more states

intrastate commerce   commerce within state borders

isolationism   policy that favors keeping nation aloof from foreign entanglements

"Jim Crow"   laws and customs segregating blacks from whites; term derived from black character in popular minstrel show

joint-stock company   business organization established and owned by group of shareholders (stockholders) who pool their money to finance new venture (such as founding of overseas colony)

judicial review   power of Supreme Court to declare laws and presidential actions unconstitutional

jurisdiction   authority of court to judge

jurisdictional strike   strike called when two unions dispute each other's right to represent workers

laissez faire   policy advocating little or no government interference in economy; French phrase means "let do" or "let alone"

"lame duck"   in U.S. politics, officeholder whose term continues after election of successor

language family   group of related languages

latitude   distance north or south of equator

lobby   special-interest group that tries to influence public officials to make favorable policy decisions, or exerts pressure on lawmakers to pass legislation the group supports

longitude   distance east or west of prime meridian (at Greenwich, England)

loose construction   belief that government may exercise powers beyond those specifically listed in Constitution in order to carry out authorized functions

marque and reprisal, letters of   wartime licenses enabling private citizens to fit out civilian vessels as warships. *See* privateer

mass media   means of communication, such as radio and television, that reach very large audiences

mass production   manufacture of goods in large quantities by machine

materialism   emphasis on acquiring goods rather than seeking spiritual, intellectual, or cultural fulfillment

mercantilism   economic theory advocating national self-sufficiency and accumulation of gold and silver

mercenary   soldier who fights (usually in foreign army) solely for pay

merger   business combination in which two or more companies are combined

merit system   *see* civil service

migration   large-scale population movement

militarism   policy that glorifies nation's armed forces and aggressive spirit

militia   armed force made up of civilians who serve only in emergency

misdemeanor   criminal offense less serious than felony

monopoly   exclusive control over supply of product or service "muckraker"   writer, especially in Progressive era, who exposed conditions needing reform

multiculturalism   movement to encourage education about all cultures that have contributed to life in the United States

multinational corporation   company operating plants and offices in more than one country

national nominating convention   meeting of political party delegates from every state to choose candidates for president and vice president

nationalism   loyalty to one's nation and support of its interests

nativism   movement to "protect" jobs and living standards of citizens by such means as limiting immigration

naturalization   process by which foreign-born person becomes citizen

naval stores   items used in building wooden ships, such as pitch and tar

neutrality   policy of not taking sides, as in war

nomad   member of group that moves from place to place in search of food

nonviolent civil disobedience   peaceful refusal to obey laws regarded as unjust

northwest passage   route through or around North America to Orient

nullification   doctrine that state can declare invalid (nullify) federal action it considers unconstitutional

open range   unfenced, unsettled land in West owned by federal government

original jurisdiction   authority of court to conduct first hearing of case

pacifism   opposition to war as means of settling disputes or achieving national policy

panic   widespread fear of business collapse that leads to hasty financial transactions and sharp drop in value of stocks, bonds, and other property

parity   price for farm products based on price in earlier base period

parochial school   school run by religious organization

partnership   business organization owned by two or more individuals

patronage   jobs or contracts rewarded by political leaders to their supporters

perjury   lying in court of law while under oath to tell the truth

pioneer   person who is among the first to enter into or settle in a region

planned community   cooperative endeavor whose members try to live in harmony and set an example for society at large

pocket veto   automatic veto of bill after adjournment by Congress; if president does not sign bill within ten days ("pockets" it), it is considered vetoed

political action committee (PAC)   group sponsored and funded by organization in order to financially support political candidates favoring its interests

political machine   party organization devoted to getting members to vote and rewarding loyal supporters with jobs

poll tax   tax required in order to vote

pool   informal agreement among competing companies to fix prices, share profits, or divide markets

popular (squatter) sovereignty   rule by the people; in pre–Civil War period, idea that voters in a territory could decide for or against slavery there

post road   road over which mail (post) is transported

privateer   privately owned merchant or fishing vessel authorized to attack or capture enemy ships in wartime

prohibition   ban against manufacturing and selling alcoholic beverages

propaganda   ideas, facts, or rumors spread for purpose of helping or harming a cause

proprietary colony   in U.S. colonial period, colony sponsored by one or more individuals who had obtained grant of land from British monarch for purpose of establishing and governing settlements

protectionism   policy of maintaining high protective tariffs

protective tariff   high tax placed on imports in order to protect domestic producers from foreign competition

protectorate   nation partially controlled by another

public works   roads, bridges, schools, and other structures built for public use and paid for by government

quorum   number of members of organization, such as U.S. Senate, that must be present in order for business to be transacted legally

racism   belief that certain races are superior to others; prejudice and discrimination based on this belief

ratify   to approve amendment proposed by Congress or treaty proposed by executive branch

realism   in literature, attempt to describe life as it is; in art, attempt to portray accurately and realistically

recall   procedure by which voters can remove elected official before expiration of term

recession   period of moderate business decline

reconstruction   restoration of Confederate states to Union after Civil War

referendum   practice of allowing voters to approve or disapprove proposed law

regionalism   in literature, stress on particular geographic area

religious toleration   attitude that allows people of different faiths to worship as they please

reparations   payments imposed on defeated nation for war damages

repeal   to revoke law or tax by legislative action or judicial ruling

representative assembly   lawmaking body whose members are chosen by the voters

reprieve   postponement of sentence or punishment

reserved powers   under U.S. Constitution, powers retained by states

rotation in office   periodic replacement of employees in government jobs

royal colony   in U.S. colonial period, colony supervised by British monarch through appointed governor and council

rural   relating to countryside, country life, or farming

sanction   action, such as trade restriction, taken by one or more nations to enforce adherence to international law by another nation

satellite   in post–World War II era, country dominated by Soviet Union

secession   formal withdrawal from membership in organization, as a state from the Union

securities   stocks and bonds

sedition   treasonable behavior, especially incitement to disorder or rebellion

segregation   separation of peoples, especially along racial lines

self-governing colony   in U.S. colonial period, colony in which voters elected governor and members of both assembly and council

separation of church and state   principle whereby government cannot interfere with religious beliefs or practices, and religious groups cannot impose their views on government

separation of powers   division of governmental authority and duties among legislative, executive, and judicial branches

settlement house   community center to aid city dwellers, especially poor immigrants

slash-and-burn agriculture   type of farming that clears land by cutting and then burning shrubs, bushes, vines, and trees

socialism   economic system based on public, rather than private, ownership of means of production

specie   gold or silver (rather than paper) money

speculator   person who makes risky investments in hope of gaining big profits

sphere of influence   area dominated by foreign power

spoils system   practice of rewarding party workers with government jobs

squatter sovereignty   *see* popular sovereignty

stagflation   combination of slow economic growth and inflation

states' rights   doctrine favoring state over national authority

stock market   exchange where stocks and bonds are traded

strict construction   belief that government is limited by Constitution to exercise only powers specifically granted

subversive   person who tries to weaken or overthrow government

suffrage   right to vote

suffragist   one who worked to gain the vote for women

supply-side economics   policy of favoring producers and investors, rather than consumers, in order to stimulate economic growth

tariff   tax on imported goods

technology   methods, tools, and machinery employed to satisfy needs of everyday life

temperance moderation in, or total abstinence from, drinking alcoholic beverages

terrorism use of violence to intimidate or instill fear

Third World developing nations of Asia, Africa, and Latin America

totalitarian state dictatorial political regime that attempts to control every aspect of citizens' lives

town meeting general meeting of town's inhabitants for purpose of self-government, especially in New England

treason betrayal of one's country, especially in wartime

truce suspension of fighting, often for fixed period

trust large business combination consisting of several corporations in same field; especially combination formed for purpose of reducing competition or creating monopoly

ultimatum final demand not subject to negotiation

urban relating to cities

vertical integration business practice of acquiring control over all stages of production, from raw materials to finished products

veto to reject or declare invalid

welfare state nation in which government assumes prime responsibility for citizens' well-being

writs of assistance in colonial America, legal documents that served as general search warrants

"yellow journalism" policy of newspaper or popular magazine to emphasize sensational news events

INDEX

The italic letters *b, c, m,* or *n* following a page number indicate that the reference is to biography feature (*b*), a chart or table (*c*), a map (*m*), or a footnote (*n*).